# CONTENTS & ACKNOWLEDGEMENTS

The Scottish Football League,
Hampden Park, Glasgow G42 9EB.
Secretary: Peter Donald
Telephone Number: (0141) 620 4160
Telefax Number: (0141) 620 4161
e-mail: info@scottishfootballleague.com
website: www.scottishfootballleague.com

Published, Produced & Printed on behalf of
The Scottish Football League by:

# ˙CRE8

CRE8, The Kiln, The Old Brewery,
Priory Lane, Burford, Oxfordshire, OX18 4SG.
Telephone Number: (01993) 822811
Telefax Number: (01993) 822887
ISDN: (01993) 822899
e-mail: studio@cre8ing.com
website: www.cre8ing.com

ISBN 0-9548556-1-2

The Scottish Premier League,
Hampden Park, Glasgow, G42 9DE.
Secretary: Iain J. Blair
Telephone Number: (0141) 620 4140
Telefax Number: (0141) 620 4141
Website: www.scotprem.com

# ACKNOWLEDGEMENTS

**Editorial contributions by:** Stephen Halliday (The Scotsman), Roddy Forsyth (The Daily Telegraph & Radio 5 Live), John Litster (Programme Monthly & Football Collectable Magazine), Darryl Broadfoot (The Herald), Jim Black (President, SFWA) David Ross (Freelance) Richard McBrearty (Scottish Football Museum) & Forrest H.C. Robertson

**Photographs by:** SNS Group, Brian Stewart, Action Images, Frank Tocher, Richard McBrearty, St. Mirren F.C., Alan Rhodes, The Scottish Professional Footballers' Association & Connect Communications.

The Scottish Football League would like to express appreciation to the following individuals and organisations:-

David C. Thomson (Editor); all of the staff at The Scottish Football League and in particular, Jan Murdoch, Anton Fagan, Brian Jamieson, Maureen Cooper and Geraldine Walsh; Greig Mailer and Gavin McCann of The Scottish Premier League; all SFL and SPL clubs; Jim Jeffrey; our contributors; the various sectors of the media for their co-operation and everyone at CRE8 and in particular, Bob Magill, Roisin McClory, Mark Rogers, Ben Goddard, Will Burroughs, Mark Scarrott & Michael Saunders.

Sincere thanks to Alan and Heather Elliott for their time and effort in providing statistical information for this publication.

I am once again privileged to have this opportunity in extending to all fans, a very warm welcome to the 2005/06 edition of The Scottish Football Review.

As you will have already noticed, this season's edition is sponsored by Bell's, whom of course, The Scottish Football League have enjoyed a close working relationship with in recent years, and I would like to thank them for once again having agreed to sponsor this prestigious title. As you will probably be aware, Bell's parent company, Diageo, announced at the start of this season that the Bell's sponsorship of The Scottish Football League Championship and Bell's Cup competitions would not be renewed when the current deal ends in May, 2006. On behalf of The Scottish Football League, I would like to thank Lord Macfarlane and his colleagues for the tremendous support football has received from Bell's over the years. Although we are disappointed that the current sponsorship deal with Bell's will not be renewed, having enjoyed an extremely close working relationship with them since they first sponsored The Scottish Football League Championship back in season 1994/95, we respect their decision and I am confident that the final season of their sponsorship will be both exciting and memorable.

Season 2004/05 once again proved intriguing and eventful both on and off the park and I would take this opportunity in congratulating Falkirk in winning the Bell's First Division and, at long last, gaining promotion to The Scottish Premier League, to Brechin City for winning the Bell's Second Division and promotion to the First Division along with Stranraer, who were promoted for the second consecutive season, and to two of our newest member clubs, Gretna, who won The Bell's Third Division in convincing fashion and scored 130 League goals in the process, together with Peterhead, who gained promotion as runners-up. The CIS Insurance Cup was won by Rangers, who defeated Motherwell 5-1 at Hampden Park, while Falkirk recorded a League and Cup double by defeating Ross County 2-1 in The Bell's Cup Final at McDiarmid Park.

As we actively pursue a new sponsor for both our League Championship and League Challenge Cup competition, it is encouraging to report that overall last season, attendance figures in the three divisions of the League Championship increased by 2.2%, which is the fifth consecutive season that attendances have risen, resulting in a 10% increase during this period. Although our three divisions have been extremely competitive over the past few years with most championship, promotion and relegation issues not being settled until the final couple of weeks or so of the season, member clubs at the League's Annual General Meeting in May, 2005 agreed to introduce Play-Offs at the end of this season. This is not the first time that we have had Play-Offs, having proved extremely successful and popular with supporters during the mid nineties. I have no doubt that the Play-Offs will increase further, the competitive nature of our three divisions during the course of this season and I am equally certain that the series of Play-Off matches will be dramatic as well as enjoying a high level of spectator and media interest.

Despite some ill informed and misguided comment in certain sectors of the media in recent times, the League Cup continues to provide spectators with a number of epic encounters each season. Our sponsors, CIS Insurance, have given wonderful backing to this competition during the past few years and although the current deal ends this season, we are currently in discussions with them regarding extending the sponsorship of the competition for a further term. The current sponsorship deal with CIS Insurance combined with our television deal with BBC Television Scotland is worth in excess of £2 million per annum to the 42 SFL and SPL clubs. Indeed, I have already placed on record my views that it was wrong to remove the European place for the team winning the League Cup a few years ago and I wish to re-emphasise my personal belief that an automatic place in the UEFA Cup should be reinstated. Hopefully, we can engage in a positive exchange of dialogue with all of the interested parties concerned.

Finally, I do hope that you have an exciting and enjoyable season and that the 26th edition of the Review keeps you up-to-date with the Scottish football scene.

**JOHN SMITH**
President,
The Scottish Football League

# WELCOME MESSAGE FROM **THE SCOTTISH PREMIER LEAGUE**

**Welcome to this season's edition of The Scottish Football Review. Last season had to be the most thrilling finale to the competition in the SPL's short history.**

We had a remarkable end to the season with Rangers being crowned Bank of Scotland Premierleague Champions by a single point on a dramatic final day. A weekend in which, perhaps uniquely in Europe, every game mattered in relation to the title, relegation or the European place. The very fact that I was hovering in a heli-copter somewhere over Linlithgow, with our trophy and our colleagues at the Bank of Scotland, as the final whistle went tells its own story. Few of those involved will forget the final moments of last season whether they were at Fir Park, Easter Road or glued to the coverage on Setanta Sports or BBC Radio Scotland.

The other domestic honours, the Tennent's Scottish Cup and The CIS Insurance Cup, were scooped by Celtic and Rangers respectively to the disappointment of the supporters, players and management of Dundee United and Motherwell. We were also delighted to welcome Falkirk, the Bell's SFL First Division Champions, to the SPL.

Our clubs have introduced a number of initiatives for season 2005/06. An SPL Match Delegate will attend every League match to report on a range of issues from the quality of refereeing, fair play and the condition of the pitches. The aim is to ensure standards are maintained and raised. We have re-launched our website, www.scotprem.com, to improve communications and give the supporters an insight into how the league is run. In partnership with our title sponsors, we have also implemented the Bank of Scotland Premierleague Passport for primary school kids who are season ticket holders at our clubs. Over 6,000 children have the opportunity now to attend away matches free of charge.

A record number of fans are attending our games each weekend. Year-on-year growth of 3% was achieved last season which

meant that over 3.5 million supporters attended our matches. Out of the five highest aggregate totals for the number of people attending the top flight in Scotland since the 1960s, four have occurred since the inception of the SPL. But we are not complacent and are working to attract more fans to our grounds.

The new live television broadcasting contract with Setanta Sports has received widespread industry and consumer praise. Their coverage of the excitement generated on the final day of the season provided an excellent conclusion to the first year of their four year contract.

Through our partnership with TWI, our matches can be seen via a combination of live, delayed, highlight and news access packages by 150 million people in over 100 countries across the world.

As a nation, we can be guilty of focussing too much on what is not going right as opposed to what is working. As our European standing shows, as a League, we are punching above our weight. But investment in youth development remains a priority. Over £7 million was invested by our clubs last year which in a number of cases equated to over 10% of their annual turnover. Compared to our first season in 1998/99, we now have three times the number of young Scots playing regular first team football. The percentage of foreigners across our clubs' squads has also reduced which bodes well for the national side.

Our clubs are also aware of the positive influ-ence that they can have on their communities. They have a variety of initiatives, often linked with their coaching schemes, that tackle social issues such as drug use, unemployment, health, racism, sectarianism and crime.

Season 2005/06 looks like being one of the best. May you enjoy it whoever you support.

**LEX GOLD**
Chairman,
The Scottish Premier League

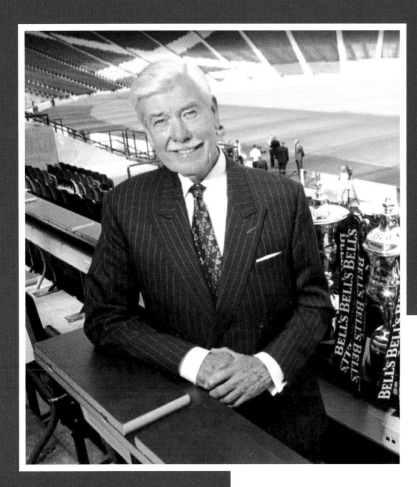

## WELCOME MESSAGE FROM THE SPONSORS BELL'S

**A very warm welcome from everyone at BELL'S to all reading this prestigious publication.**

BELL'S have always been proud to support Scottish football. We were the first sponsors of the League Cup in the late 70's and the early 80's, the **BELL'S** League Championship in the mid 90's and are the current sponsors of The Scottish Football League until the end of this season.

Our role may have changed over the years but we have always been a passionate supporter of Scottish football and are privileged to be part of the sports' success story.

As sponsors of The Scottish Football League, it is appropriate for **BELL'S** to support the SFL Year Book for season 2005/06. This 'Bible' of Scottish football gives fans all the information they need to follow their team, home and away, and as the 'spirit of Scottish football', **BELL'S** has enjoyed being with you on those travels.

We look forward to a memorable season and on behalf of my colleagues at **BELL'S**, I would like to thank you all for your support over the last seven years.

**Lord Macfarlane of Bearsden KT,**
Honorary Life President of BELL'S

# LOOKING BACK TO THE **FUTURE**

**Distance invariably lends enchantment to a cherished memory. But this nostalgia junkie offers no apology for expressing the belief that it really was a better game in the good old days.**

Then along came the purveyors of 'double speak', the tactical con men and the television pundits to educate us mere mortals about how football should really be played. Don't worry so much about being entertained. Concern yourself more about tactical awareness and closing down the opposition.

Oh, really? Say what you like, football is basically a simple game too often complicated by certain prominent individuals who 'talk a good game'. Those who have constantly bemoaned dwindling attendances and the growing apathy of fans from John O'Groats to Berwick might like to reflect on the irrefutable fact that football is part of the entertainment industry.

Go watch a low budget movie that fails to capture the imagination and it's a case of exit stage left. Hollywood's answer has often been to film the sequel and fill it full of big names. Same rubbish - star appeal.

Scottish football, it might be said, chose to follow a similar route. Never mind the quality, feel the width of an influx of foreign players whose reputations have often not justified the price tag or their inflated salaries. If he's Italian, Spanish, Danish, Swedish or French, he must be good and in certain instances that has been the case. Laudrup and Larsson, for example, did for our game what an

army of public relations personnel could not have achieved in a decade.

But the so-called 'revolution' had a downside. It was no coincidence that the influx of Continentals coincided with a period of sustained neglect of our own youngsters. In some instances, the development of home grown talent all but ceased, impacting significantly on the national team.

Yet, Scottish football existed for more than 100 years through the talents of Scots. There was a time when a top English team who didn't boast at least one Scot in its line-up was the exception rather than the rule.

Answer me this. What have the following got in common?

Conn, Bauld, Wardhaugh. Smith, Johnstone, Reilly, Turnbull and Ormond. Smith, Penman, Cousin, Gilzean and Robertson. Ritchie, Shearer, Caldow, Greig, McKinnon and Baxter. Johnstone, Wallace, Chalmers, Auld and Lennox.

Every one a Scot and integral parts of the great Heart of Midlothian, Hibernian, Dundee, Rangers and Celtic teams of the 1950s and 60s.

Fast forward two or three decades on from the 'Terrible Trio' and the 'Famous Five' to the hugely successful Dundee United and Aberdeen teams of the 1980s. The story's the same one.

The Old Firm were the economic powers in the land but the alarming

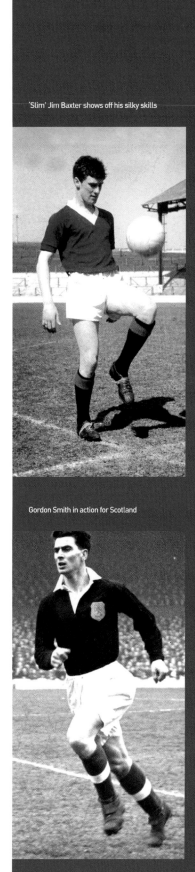

'Slim' Jim Baxter shows off his silky skills

Gordon Smith in action for Scotland

**DUNDEE** Scottish League Champions season 1961.62

Celtic's Bobby Lennox in action

Dundee's Ian Ure (left) and Alex Harley of
Third Lanark in action during season 1961.62

Aberdeen captain Willie Miller holds aloft the
European Cup Winners' Cup after their
victory over Real Madrid in season 1982.83

gulf that has developed since the early to mid 1990s was nowhere near as great.

Interestingly, in season 1990/91, Aberdeen lost out to Rangers on the final day of the League campaign when a draw at Ibrox would have been sufficient for the Dons to clinch the Championship. It should also be noted that as recently as season 1993/94, the final Premier Division Championship table read Rangers 58 points, Aberdeen 55 and Motherwell 54. But in subsequent seasons, it has been a two-horse race, with the only question being, which half of the Old Firm would be crowned League Champions?

To blame all of the game's ills on the influx of players from abroad and the desire of clubs to live far beyond their means would be grossly unfair. Other factors, such as the reluctance of school teachers to encourage extra curricular activities coupled to a more affluent society with a much greater range of recreational pursuits, have also had a significant impact.

But, mercifully, there are encouraging signs that the times they are a changing. The Old Firm's dominance is once again being challenged. Hibs are enjoying a resurgence, interestingly mainly as a consequence of a youth policy that has unearthed several talented and highly promising players such as Scott Brown, Garry O'Connor and Derek Riordan, among others. Hearts, too, have re-emerged as a force, albeit there is a strong Eastern European influence at Tynecastle.

However, while Edinburgh's Big Two are flexing their collective muscles in such an encouraging manner, there is no short term fix. The patient has survived the surgery but will spend a while longer in the recovery room before being given a clean bill of health.

The emergence of Zander Diamond at Aberdeen, Ross McCormack at Rangers, Craig Beattie and Aiden McGeady at Celtic, Dundee United's Mark Wilson, Kilmarnock's Stephen Naismith and David Clarkson at Motherwell is a welcome indicator that the game north of the border is far from being in a state of terminal decline.

But the future wellbeing of Scottish football is dependent on the continuing development of the game at grassroots level and it is heartening to observe that much is being done - largely behind the scenes - to encourage youngsters to further their skills and talents.

The Scottish Football League led the way a number of years ago with the introduction of a detailed Youth Development Programme which was subsequently handed over to The Scottish Football Association.

Basically, the programme comprises a two-tier structure, namely, Performance and Initiative levels, and the SFA's Football Development Department monitors, assesses and controls various age groups from the tender age of 3 through to 17.

Tommy McIntyre is the SFA's Head of Youth Development and is naturally anxious to stress the need for patience while, at the same time, keen to emphasise the positive results that are being achieved. The former Hibernian defender's principal role is to observe and oversee grassroots provision and performance, including young players at senior clubs, through a programme of coaching and education. Assistance and support is given to volunteers as well as the professionals. The youth action plan is being driven by six Regional Managers, who are employed by the SFA.

"That effectively means that the country is split into six regions," explained McIntyre. "It is a hands on approach with these Regional Managers identifying coaches and supporting volunteers."

There is also a heavy emphasis placed on youngsters having fun as part of what McIntyre stresses is a long term development.

"I very much back the idea of fun fours for kids and seven-a-side games to prepare youngsters for the adult game," says McIntyre.

"The senior clubs play soccer sevens as part of the Initiative Programme and nothing is done in isolation.

"We are looking to keep people interested from start to finish and I am pleased with the way things have gone so far. There is a lot of talent out there.

"There is not a lot of money in football right now and clubs are being forced to bring on young players because of the financial constraints. But I am excited by what the clubs hope to achieve because everyone is trying to raise the bar.

"There are a lot of good young players at all the clubs and that is testimony to the work that has already been done in that area. Eventually, through the continuation of the development programme, the country as a whole will benefit."

McIntyre is reluctant to say when the spin-off will become evident. But he claims that the game is starting to reap the benefits at national level, highlighting the parts played by such as Craig Gordon, James McFadden and Craig Beattie in Scotland's resurgence under Walter Smith.

"In an ideal world, we will eventually have a conveyor belt of talent," added McIntyre. "It is never too late. First and foremost people recognised the need for change because what was good enough 10 to 15 years ago is not acceptable today."

In a lifetime of watching football - I saw my first game at Dens Park, home of my beloved Dundee, in 1957 while still wearing short pants - I have often fretted over the state of the game.

But in more recent years, what had simply been concerns developed into genuine fears for the future of football in this country. It appeared that the game was moving inexorably towards self destruction.

It seemed to me at any rate that greed would inevitably destroy the game and lead to the eventual collapse of football's infrastructure. I believe I was very nearly proved correct in that thinking. However, the wake-up call in the form of several clubs being forced into administration came just in time. Some may yet perish but the general prognosis is far more encouraging.

The money-grabbers have been forced to indulge in a reality check.

The gravy train came hurtling off the rails and has been replaced by a more streamlined model. Players' pay-packets are smaller. Overly ambitious Chairmen have had their wings clipped and the real money men - the bankers - have taken a stance, not before time. And, with the problems of youth development being tackled with renewed vigour at grassroots level, there are further encouraging signs of a regeneration that offers genuine hope for the future.

Perhaps it will be a while yet before we again witness the sight of Aberdeen, Celtic and Rangers winning European trophies or the new generation of Scotland players emulating the feats of their predecessors who competed at the Finals of six World Cup tournaments between 1974 and 1998 and the European Championships of 1992 and 1996.

But I sense that a new dawn is breaking over Scottish football, thanks largely to the actions of those who refused to simply stand back and watch the game continue on its lemming-like descent into oblivion.

But one thing continues to puzzle me. How come, with such talents at the national team's disposal as Denis Law, Jim Baxter, John White, Dave Mackay, Jimmy Johnstone, Alan Gilzean, Ian St. John, Billy McNeill and John Greig, did we fail to win the World Cup in 1962, 1966 and 1970?

Maybe it was just an illusion. Perhaps the game wasn't so much better after all.

But a slice of nostalgia never did anyone any harm.

Linney, Hamilton, Cox, Seith, Ure and Wishart, Smith, Penman, Cousin, Gilzean and Robertson. 28th April, 1962 at Muirton Park, Perth and Dundee have just beaten St. Johnstone 3-0, to be crowned Scottish League Champions.

Trust me, it doesn't get any better than that!

**JIM BLACK**
(President of The Scottish Football Writers' Association)

Gothenburg goalkeeper Thomas Wernersson (left) does enough to deny Billy Kirkwood in the 1986.87 UEFA Cup Final Second Leg at Tannadice

Hearts' and Scotland goalkeeper Craig Gordon

Dundee United's Mark Wilson

Celtic and Scotland forward Craig Beattie

Tennent's Scottish Cup

Internationals

UEFA Champions League & UEFA Cup

# DATES FOR YOUR DIARY 2005.06

## TENNENT'S SCOTTISH CUP 2005.06
**First Round** Saturday, 19th November, 2005
**Second Round** Saturday, 10th December, 2005
**Third Round** Saturday, 7th January, 2006
**Fourth Round** Saturday, 4th February, 2006
**Fifth Round** Saturday, 25th February, 2006
**Semi-Finals** Saturday, 1st & Sunday, 2nd April, 2006
**Final** Saturday, 13th May, 2006

## TENNENT'S SCOTTISH QUALIFYING CUPS 2005.06
North
**First Round** Saturday, 27th August, 2005
**Second Round** Saturday, 17th September, 2005
**Semi-Finals** Saturday, 15th October, 2005
**Final** Saturday, 5th November, 2005

South
**Preliminary Round** Saturday, 27th August, 2005
**First Round** Saturday, 17th September, 2005
**Second Round** Saturday, 15th October, 2005
**Semi-Finals** Saturday, 11th March, 2006
**Final** Saturday, 29th April, 2006

## FIFA WORLD CUP 2006 -
## QUALIFYING COMPETITION GROUP 5
**Scotland –v- Italy** Saturday, 3rd September, 2005
**Norway –v- Scotland** Wednesday, 7th September, 2005
**Scotland –v- Belarus** Saturday, 8th October, 2005
**Slovenia –v- Scotland** Wednesday, 12th October, 2005
Play-Offs (Provisional)
**First Leg** Saturday, 12th November, 2005
**Second Leg** Wednesday, 16th November, 2005

## INTERNATIONAL CHALLENGE MATCH
**Austria –v- Scotland** Wednesday, 17th August, 2005

## EUROPEAN "UNDER-21" CHAMPIONSHIP, 2004.06
## QUALIFYING MATCHES GROUP 5
**Scotland –v- Italy** Friday, 2nd September, 2005
**Norway –v- Scotland** Tuesday, 6th September, 2005
**Scotland –v- Belarus** Friday, 7th October, 2005
**Slovenia –v- Scotland** Tuesday, 11th October, 2005

## "UNDER-21" INTERNATIONAL CHALLENGE MATCH
**Austria –v- Scotland** Tuesday, 16th August, 2005

## SCOTLAND FUTURE TEAM
Future Cup
**Scotland –v- Poland** Tuesday, 6th December, 2005
**Scotland –v- Turkey** Date still to be confirmed. Spring, 2006

## UEFA "UNDER-19" CHAMPIONSHIP 2005/06
First Round, Qualifying Group, Hosted by
Switzerland, 7th-14th October, 2005
**Scotland, Switzerland, Finland and Andorra**
The winners and runners-up of the First Qualifying
Round groups, as well as the best third place team,
will qualify for the Second Qualifying Round.

## "UNDER-19" INTERNATIONAL CHALLENGE MATCHES
**Scotland –v- Denmark** Tuesday, 6th September, 2005
**Scotland –v- Denmark** Thursday, 8th September, 2005
**Portugal –v- Scotland** Monday, 5th December, 2005
**Portugal –v- Scotland** Wednesday, 7th December, 2005

## UEFA "UNDER-17" CHAMPIONSHIP 2005.06
First Round, Qualifying Group, Hosted by Hungary
26th-30th September, 2005
**Scotland, Hungary, Albania and Cyprus**
The winners and runners-up of the First Qualifying
Round groups, as well as the best third place team,
will qualify for the Second Qualifying Rounds

## WOMEN'S FIFA WORLD CUP 2007 –
## QUALIFYING COMPETITION
**Russia –v- Scotland** Sunday, 28th August, 2005
**Scotland –v- Rep. of Ireland** Sunday, 25th September, 2005
**Germany –v- Scotland** Thursday, 13th October, 2005
**Scotland –v- Switzerland** Wednesday, 26th April, 2006
**Rep. of Ireland –v- Scotland** Saturday, 6th May, 2006
**Scotland –v- Russia** Wednesday, 24th May, 2006

## UEFA WOMEN'S "UNDER-19" CHAMPIONSHIP 2005.06
First Round, Qualifying Group, Hosted by England
27th September to 1st October, 2005
**Scotland, England, Croatia and Faroe Islands**
The winners and runners-up of the First Qualifying Round
groups will qualify for the Second Qualifying Round.

## WOMEN'S "UNDER-19" INTERNATIONAL
## CHALLENGE MATCH
**Northern Ireland –v- Scotland**
Saturday, 10th September, 2005

## UEFA CHAMPIONS LEAGUE
Qualifying Round 1
**First-Leg matches:**
Tuesday, 12th & Wednesday, 13th July, 2005
**Second-Leg matches:**
Tuesday 19th & Wednesday, 20th July, 2005
Qualifying Round 2
**First-Leg matches:**
Tuesday 26th & Wednesday, 27th July, 2005
**Second-Leg matches:**
Tuesday 2nd & Wednesday, 3rd August, 2005
Qualifying Round 3
**First-Leg matches:**
Tuesday 9th & Wednesday 10th August, 2005
**Second-Leg matches:**
Tuesday 23rd & Wednesday 24th August, 2005
Group Stage:
**1st Match Days:** Tuesday, 13th September &
Wednesday, 14th September, 2005
**2nd Match Days:** Tuesday, 27th September &
Wednesday, 28th September, 2005

**3rd Match Days:** Tuesday, 18th October &
Wednesday, 19th October, 2005
**4th Match Days:** Tuesday, 1st November &
Wednesday, 2nd November, 2005
**5th Match Days:** Tuesday, 22nd November &
Wednesday, 23rd November, 2005
**6th Match Days:** Tuesday, 6th December &
Wednesday, 7th December, 2005
First Knock-Out Round:
**First-Leg matches:**
Tuesday, 21st & Wednesday, 22nd February, 2006
**Second-Leg matches:**
Tuesday, 7th & Wednesday, 8th March, 2006
Quarter Finals:
**First-Leg matches:**
Tuesday, 28th & Wednesday, 29th March, 2006
**Second-Leg matches:**
Tuesday, 4th & Wednesday, 5th April, 2006
Semi Finals:
**First-Leg matches:**
Tuesday, 18th & Wednesday, 19th April, 2006
**Second-Leg matches:**
Tuesday, 25th & Wednesday, 26th April, 2006
**Final:** Wednesday, 17th May, 2006

## U.E.F.A. CUP
First Qualifying Round:
**First-Leg matches:** Thursday, 14th July, 2005
**Second-Leg matches:** Thursday, 28th July, 2005
Second Qualifying Round:
**First-Leg matches:** Thursday, 11th August, 2005
**Second-Leg matches:** Thursday, 25th August, 2005
First Round:
**First-Leg matches:** Thursday, 15th September, 2005
**Second-Leg matches:** Thursday, 29th September, 2005
Group Stage:
**1st Match Day:** Thursday, 20th October, 2005
**2nd Match Day:** Thursday, 3rd November, 2005
**3rd Match Day:** Thursday, 24th November, 2005
**4th Match Days:** Wednesday, 30th November &
Thursday, 1st December, 2005
**5th Match Days:** Wednesday, 14th December &
Thursday, 15th December, 2005
First Knock-Out Round:
**First-Leg matches:**
Wednesday, 15th & Thursday, 16th February, 2006
**Second-Leg matches:** Thursday, 23rd February, 2006
Second Knock-Out Round:
**First-Leg matches:** Thursday, 9th March, 2006
**Second-Leg matches:**
Wednesday, 15th & Thursday, 16th March, 2006
Quarter Finals:
**First-Leg matches:** Thursday, 30th March, 2006
**Second-Leg matches:** Thursday, 6th April, 2006
Semi-Finals:
**First-Leg matches:** Thursday, 20th April, 2006
**Second-Leg matches:** Thursday, 27th April, 2006
**Final:** Wednesday, 10th May, 2006

# BANK OF SCOTLAND PREMIERLEAGUE FIXTURES **SEASON 2005.06**

**SATURDAY, JULY 30TH, 2005**
Dundee United v. Aberdeen
Falkirk v. Inverness CT
Hibernian v. Dunfermline Athletic
Kilmarnock v. Hearts
Motherwell v. Celtic (12.30pm)
**SUNDAY, JULY 31ST, 2005**
Rangers v. Livingston (2.00pm)
**SATURDAY, AUGUST 6TH, 2005**
Aberdeen v. Kilmarnock
Celtic v. Dundee United
Inverness CT v. Rangers
Livingston v. Falkirk
Motherwell v. Dunfermline Athletic
**SUNDAY, AUGUST 7TH, 2005**
Hearts v. Hibernian (2.00pm)
**SATURDAY, AUGUST 13TH, 2005**
Celtic v. Falkirk
Dunfermline Athletic v. Inverness CT
Hibernian v. Livingston
Kilmarnock v. Motherwell
**SUNDAY, AUGUST 14TH, 2005**
Aberdeen v. Rangers (2.00pm)
Dundee United v. Hearts
**SATURDAY, AUGUST 20TH, 2005**
Falkirk v. Hibernian
Hearts v. Aberdeen
Inverness CT v. Kilmarnock
Livingston v. Dunfermline Athletic
Motherwell v. Dundee United
Rangers v. Celtic (12.30pm)
**SATURDAY, AUGUST 27TH, 2005**
Aberdeen v. Falkirk
Hearts v. Motherwell
Kilmarnock v. Livingston
Rangers v. Hibernian
**SUNDAY, AUGUST 28TH, 2005**
Dundee United v. Inverness CT
Dunfermline Athletic v. Celtic (2.00pm)
**SATURDAY, SEPTEMBER 10TH, 2005**
Celtic v. Aberdeen
Falkirk v. Rangers
Hibernian v. Dundee United
Inverness CT v. Motherwell
Kilmarnock v. Dunfermline Athletic
**SUNDAY, SEPTEMBER 11TH, 2005**
Livingston v. Hearts (2.00pm)
**SATURDAY, SEPTEMBER 17TH, 2005**
Dundee United v. Livingston
Dunfermline Athletic v. Aberdeen
Inverness CT v. Hearts
Motherwell v. Falkirk
Rangers v. Kilmarnock
**SUNDAY, SEPTEMBER 18TH, 2005**
Hibernian v. Celtic (2.00pm)
**SATURDAY, SEPTEMBER 24TH, 2005**
Aberdeen v. Livingston
Celtic v. Inverness CT
Dunfermline Athletic v. Dundee United
Hearts v. Rangers (12.30pm)
Kilmarnock v. Falkirk
Motherwell v. Hibernian
**SATURDAY, OCTOBER 1ST, 2005**
Aberdeen v. Motherwell
Dundee United v. Kilmarnock
Livingston v. Celtic
Rangers v. Dunfermline Athletic

**SUNDAY, OCTOBER 2ND, 2005**
Falkirk v. Hearts (2.00pm)
Hibernian v. Inverness CT
**SATURDAY, OCTOBER 15TH, 2005**
Celtic v. Hearts
Dunfermline Athletic v. Falkirk
Hibernian v. Kilmarnock
Inverness CT v. Aberdeen
Motherwell v. Livingston
**SUNDAY, OCTOBER 16TH, 2005**
Dundee United v. Rangers (2.00pm)
**SATURDAY, OCTOBER 22ND, 2005**
Aberdeen v. Hibernian
Falkirk v. Dundee United
Hearts v. Dunfermline Athletic
Livingston v. Inverness CT
Rangers v. Motherwell
**SUNDAY, OCTOBER 23RD, 2005**
Kilmarnock v. Celtic (2.00pm)
**WEDNESDAY, OCTOBER 26TH, 2005**
Aberdeen v. Dundee United (7.45pm)
Celtic v. Motherwell (7.45pm)
Dunfermline Athletic v. Hibernian (7.45pm)
Hearts v. Kilmarnock (7.45pm)
Inverness CT v. Falkirk (7.45pm)
Livingston v. Rangers (7.45pm)
**SATURDAY, OCTOBER 29TH, 2005**
Dunfermline Athletic v. Motherwell
Falkirk v. Livingston
Hibernian v. Hearts
Kilmarnock v. Aberdeen
Rangers v. Inverness CT
**SUNDAY, OCTOBER 30TH, 2005**
Dundee United v. Celtic (2.00pm)
**SATURDAY, NOVEMBER 5TH, 2005**
Hearts v. Dundee United
Inverness CT v. Dunfermline Athletic
Livingston v. Hibernian
Motherwell v. Kilmarnock
Rangers v. Aberdeen
**SUNDAY, NOVEMBER 6TH, 2005**
Falkirk v. Celtic (2.00pm)
**SATURDAY, NOVEMBER 19TH, 2005**
Celtic v. Rangers (12.30pm)
Dundee United v. Motherwell
Dunfermline Athletic v. Livingston
Hibernian v. Falkirk
Kilmarnock v. Inverness CT
**SUNDAY, NOVEMBER 20TH, 2005**
Aberdeen v. Hearts (2.00pm)
**SATURDAY, NOVEMBER 26TH, 2005**
Celtic v. Dunfermline Athletic
Falkirk v. Aberdeen
Inverness CT v. Dundee United
Livingston v. Kilmarnock
Motherwell v. Hearts
**SUNDAY, NOVEMBER 27TH, 2005**
Hibernian v. Rangers (2.00pm)
**SATURDAY, DECEMBER 3RD, 2005**
Dundee United v. Hibernian
Dunfermline Athletic v. Kilmarnock
Hearts v. Livingston
Motherwell v. Inverness CT
Rangers v. Falkirk
**SUNDAY, DECEMBER 4TH, 2005**
Aberdeen v. Celtic (2.00pm)

**SATURDAY, DECEMBER 10TH, 2005**
Aberdeen v. Dunfermline Athletic
Celtic v. Hibernian
Falkirk v. Motherwell
Hearts v. Inverness CT
Livingston v. Dundee United
**SUNDAY, DECEMBER 11TH, 2005**
Kilmarnock v. Rangers (2.00pm)
**SATURDAY, DECEMBER 17TH, 2005**
Dundee United v. Dunfermline Athletic
Falkirk v. Kilmarnock
Hibernian v. Motherwell
Livingston v. Aberdeen
Rangers v. Hearts
**SUNDAY, DECEMBER 18TH, 2005**
Inverness CT v. Celtic (2.00pm)
**MONDAY, DECEMBER 26TH, 2005**
Celtic v Livingston
Dunfermline Athletic v. Rangers
Hearts v. Falkirk
Inverness CT v. Hibernian
Kilmarnock v. Dundee United
Motherwell v. Aberdeen
**SATURDAY, DECEMBER 31ST, 2005**
Aberdeen v. Inverness CT
Falkirk v. Dunfermline Athletic
Kilmarnock v. Hibernian
Livingston v. Motherwell
Rangers v. Dundee United
**SUNDAY, JANUARY 1ST, 2006**
Hearts v. Celtic (2.00pm)
**SATURDAY, JANUARY 14TH, 2006**
Celtic v. Kilmarnock
Dundee United v. Falkirk
Dunfermline Athletic v. Hearts
Hibernian v. Aberdeen
Inverness CT v. Livingston
Motherwell v. Rangers
**SATURDAY, JANUARY 21ST, 2006**
Dundee United v. Aberdeen
Falkirk v. Inverness CT
Hibernian v. Dunfermline Athletic
Kilmarnock v. Hearts
Motherwell v. Celtic
Rangers v. Livingston
**SATURDAY, JANUARY 28TH, 2006**
Aberdeen v. Kilmarnock
Celtic v. Dundee United
Dunfermline Athletic v. Motherwell
Hearts v. Hibernian
Inverness CT v. Rangers
Livingston v. Falkirk
**TUESDAY, FEBRUARY 7TH, 2006**
Dundee United v. Hearts (7.45pm)
**WEDNESDAY, FEBRUARY 8TH, 2006**
Aberdeen v. Rangers (7.45pm)
Celtic v. Falkirk (7.45pm)
Dunfermline Athletic v Inverness CT (7.45pm)
Hibernian v. Livingston (7.45pm)
Kilmarnock v. Motherwell (7.45pm)
**SATURDAY, FEBRUARY 11TH, 2006**
Falkirk v. Hibernian
Hearts v. Aberdeen
Inverness CT v. Kilmarnock
Livingston v. Dunfermline Athletic
Motherwell v. Dundee United
Rangers v. Celtic

**SATURDAY, FEBRUARY 18TH, 2006**
Aberdeen v. Falkirk
Dundee United v. Inverness CT
Dunfermline Athletic v. Celtic
Hearts v. Motherwell
Kilmarnock v. Livingston
Rangers v. Hibernian
**SATURDAY, MARCH 4TH, 2006**
Celtic v. Aberdeen
Falkirk v. Rangers
Hibernian v. Dundee United
Inverness CT v. Motherwell
Kilmarnock v. Dunfermline Athletic
Livingston v. Hearts
**SATURDAY, MARCH 11TH, 2006**
Dundee United v. Livingston
Dunfermline Athletic v. Aberdeen
Hibernian v. Celtic
Inverness CT v. Hearts
Motherwell v. Falkirk
Rangers v. Kilmarnock
**SATURDAY, MARCH 18TH, 2006**
Aberdeen v. Livingston
Celtic v. Inverness CT
Dunfermline Athletic v. Dundee United
Hearts v. Rangers
Kilmarnock v. Falkirk
Motherwell v. Hibernian
**SATURDAY, MARCH 25TH, 2006**
Aberdeen v. Motherwell
Dundee United v. Kilmarnock
Falkirk v. Hearts
Hibernian v. Inverness CT
Livingston v. Celtic
Rangers v. Dunfermline Athletic
**SATURDAY, APRIL 1ST, 2006**
Celtic v. Hearts
Dundee United v. Rangers
Dunfermline Athletic v. Falkirk
Hibernian v. Kilmarnock
Inverness CT v. Aberdeen
Motherwell v. Livingston
**SATURDAY, APRIL 8TH, 2006**
Aberdeen v. Hibernian
Falkirk v. Dundee United
Hearts v. Dunfermline Athletic
Kilmarnock v. Celtic
Livingston v. Inverness CT
Rangers v. Motherwell

**FALKIRK:**
BELL'S FIRST DIVISION CHAMPIONS

**BRECHIN CITY:**
BELL'S SECOND DIVISION CHAMPIONS

**GRETNA:**
BELL'S THIRD DIVISION CHAMPIONS

**BELL'S**
SCOTTISH FOOTBALL LEAGUE

# BELL'S SCOTTISH
# FOOTBALL LEAGUE FIXTURES **SEASON 2005.06**

**SATURDAY, AUGUST 6TH, 2005**
**FIRST DIVISION**
Brechin City v. Hamilton Academical
Dundee v. St. Mirren
Ross County v. Clyde
St. Johnstone v. Queen of the South
Stranraer v. Airdrie United
**SECOND DIVISION**
Alloa Athletic v. Peterhead
Ayr United v. Dumbarton
Gretna v. Forfar Athletic
Morton v. Raith Rovers
Partick Thistle v. Stirling Albion
**THIRD DIVISION**
Albion Rovers v. Arbroath
East Fife v. Berwick Rangers
East Stirlingshire v. Cowdenbeath
Elgin City v. Montrose
Queen's Park v. Stenhousemuir
**SATURDAY, AUGUST 13TH, 2005**
**FIRST DIVISION**
Airdrie United v. Ross County
Clyde v. Dundee
Hamilton Academical v. St. Johnstone
Queen of the South v. Brechin City
St. Mirren v. Stranraer
**SECOND DIVISION**
Dumbarton v. Alloa Athletic
Forfar Athletic v. Ayr United
Peterhead v. Partick Thistle
Raith Rovers v. Gretna
Stirling Albion v. Morton
**THIRD DIVISION**
Arbroath v. East Fife
Berwick Rangers v. East Stirlingshire
Cowdenbeath v. Queen's Park
Montrose v. Albion Rovers
Stenhousemuir v. Elgin City
**SATURDAY, AUGUST 20TH, 2005**
**FIRST DIVISION**
Brechin City v. Airdrie United
Dundee v. Queen of the South
Ross County v. Hamilton Academical
St. Johnstone v. St. Mirren
Stranraer v. Clyde
**SECOND DIVISION**
Alloa Athletic v. Raith Rovers
Ayr United v. Peterhead
Gretna v. Stirling Albion
Morton v. Forfar Athletic
Partick Thistle v. Dumbarton
**THIRD DIVISION**
Albion Rovers v. Stenhousemuir
East Fife v. Montrose
East Stirlingshire v. Arbroath
Elgin City v. Cowdenbeath
Queen's Park v. Berwick Rangers
**SATURDAY, AUGUST 27TH, 2005**
**FIRST DIVISION**
Airdrie United v. St. Johnstone
Clyde v. Queen of the South
Hamilton Academical v. Dundee
Ross County v. Stranraer

St. Mirren v. Brechin City
**SECOND DIVISION**
Dumbarton v. Morton
Forfar Athletic v. Peterhead
Gretna v. Ayr United
Partick Thistle v. Raith Rovers
Stirling Albion v. Alloa Athletic
**THIRD DIVISION**
Berwick Rangers v. Elgin City
East Fife v. Cowdenbeath
Montrose v. Arbroath
Queen's Park v. Albion Rovers
Stenhousemuir v. East Stirlingshire
**SATURDAY, SEPTEMBER 10TH, 2005**
**FIRST DIVISION**
Brechin City v. Clyde
Dundee v. Airdrie United
Queen of the South v. St. Mirren
St. Johnstone v. Ross County
Stranraer v. Hamilton Academical
**SECOND DIVISION**
Alloa Athletic v. Forfar Athletic
Ayr United v. Partick Thistle
Morton v. Gretna
Peterhead v. Dumbarton
Raith Rovers v. Stirling Albion
**THIRD DIVISION**
Albion Rovers v. East Fife
Arbroath v. Stenhousemuir
Cowdenbeath v. Berwick Rangers
East Stirlingshire v. Montrose
Elgin City v. Queen's Park
**SATURDAY, SEPTEMBER 17TH, 2005**
**FIRST DIVISION**
Hamilton Academical v. Airdrie United
Ross County v. Brechin City
St. Johnstone v. Dundee
St. Mirren v. Clyde
Stranraer v. Queen of the South
**SECOND DIVISION**
Forfar Athletic v. Dumbarton
Gretna v. Partick Thistle
Morton v. Alloa Athletic
Raith Rovers v. Ayr United
Stirling Albion v. Peterhead
**THIRD DIVISION**
Berwick Rangers v. Arbroath
Cowdenbeath v. Montrose
Elgin City v. Albion Rovers
Queen's Park v. East Stirlingshire
Stenhousemuir v. East Fife
**SATURDAY, SEPTEMBER 24TH, 2005**
**FIRST DIVISION**
Airdrie United v. St. Mirren
Brechin City v. Stranraer
Clyde v. St. Johnstone
Dundee v. Ross County
Queen of the South v. Hamilton Academical
**SECOND DIVISION**
Alloa Athletic v. Gretna
Ayr United v. Morton
Dumbarton v. Stirling Albion
Partick Thistle v. Forfar Athletic

Peterhead v. Raith Rovers
**THIRD DIVISION**
Albion Rovers v. Berwick Rangers
Arbroath v. Cowdenbeath
East Fife v. Queen's Park
East Stirlingshire v. Elgin City
Montrose v. Stenhousemuir
**SATURDAY, OCTOBER 1ST, 2005**
**FIRST DIVISION**
Airdrie United v. Clyde
Brechin City v. Dundee
Hamilton Academical v. St. Mirren
Ross County v. Queen of the South
Stranraer v. St. Johnstone
**SECOND DIVISION**
Alloa Athletic v. Partick Thistle
Gretna v. Dumbarton
Morton v. Peterhead
Raith Rovers v. Forfar Athletic
Stirling Albion v. Ayr United
**THIRD DIVISION**
Berwick Rangers v. Montrose
Cowdenbeath v. Stenhousemuir
East Stirlingshire v. Albion Rovers
Elgin City v. East Fife
Queen's Park v. Arbroath
**FRIDAY, OCTOBER 7TH, 2005**
**FIRST DIVISION**
Ross County v. Airdrie United
**SECOND DIVISION**
Stirling Albion v. Alloa Athletic
**THIRD DIVISION**
East Fife v. Arbroath
**SATURDAY, OCTOBER 8TH, 2005**
**SECOND DIVISION**
Peterhead v. Ayr United
**THIRD DIVISION**
Berwick Rangers v. Elgin City
**SATURDAY, OCTOBER 15TH, 2005**
**FIRST DIVISION**
Clyde v. Hamilton Academical
Dundee v. Stranraer
Queen of the South v. Airdrie United
St. Johnstone v. Brechin City
St. Mirren v. Ross County
**SECOND DIVISION**
Ayr United v. Alloa Athletic
Dumbarton v. Raith Rovers
Forfar Athletic v. Stirling Albion
Partick Thistle v. Morton
Peterhead v. Gretna
**THIRD DIVISION**
Albion Rovers v. Cowdenbeath
Arbroath v. Elgin City
East Fife v. East Stirlingshire
Montrose v. Queen's Park
Stenhousemuir v. Berwick Rangers
**SATURDAY, OCTOBER 22ND, 2005**
**FIRST DIVISION**
Airdrie United v. Stranraer
Clyde v. Ross County
Hamilton Academical v. Brechin City
Queen of the South v. St. Johnstone
St. Mirren v. Dundee

**SECOND DIVISION**
Dumbarton v. Ayr United
Forfar Athletic v. Gretna
Peterhead v. Alloa Athletic
Raith Rovers v. Morton
Stirling Albion v. Partick Thistle
**THIRD DIVISION**
Arbroath v. Albion Rovers
Berwick Rangers v. East Fife
Cowdenbeath v. East Stirlingshire
Montrose v. Elgin City
Stenhousemuir v. Queen's Park
**TUESDAY, OCTOBER 25TH, 2005**
**FIRST DIVISION**
Brechin City v. Queen of the South
St. Johnstone v. Hamilton Academical
Stranraer v. St. Mirren
**SECOND DIVISION**
Alloa Athletic v. Dumbarton
Gretna v. Raith Rovers
Morton v. Stirling Albion
Partick Thistle v. Peterhead
**THIRD DIVISION**
Albion Rovers v. Montrose
East Stirlingshire v. Berwick Rangers
Elgin City v. Stenhousemuir
Queen's Park v. Cowdenbeath
**WEDNESDAY, OCTOBER 26TH, 2005**
**FIRST DIVISION**
Dundee v. Clyde
**SATURDAY, OCTOBER 29TH, 2005**
**FIRST DIVISION**
Airdrie United v. Dundee
Clyde v. Brechin City
Hamilton Academical v. Stranraer
Ross County v. St. Johnstone
St. Mirren v. Queen of the South
**SECOND DIVISION**
Dumbarton v. Peterhead
Forfar Athletic v. Alloa Athletic
Gretna v. Morton
Partick Thistle v. Ayr United
Stirling Albion v. Raith Rovers
**THIRD DIVISION**
Berwick Rangers v. Cowdenbeath
East Fife v. Albion Rovers
Montrose v. East Stirlingshire
Queen's Park v. Elgin City
Stenhousemuir v. Arbroath
**SATURDAY, NOVEMBER 5TH, 2005**
**FIRST DIVISION**
Queen of the South v. Clyde
St. Johnstone v. Airdrie United
Stranraer v. Ross County
**SECOND DIVISION**
Alloa Athletic v. Stirling Albion
Ayr United v. Gretna
Morton v. Dumbarton
Peterhead v. Forfar Athletic
Raith Rovers v. Partick Thistle
**THIRD DIVISION**
Albion Rovers v. Queen's Park
Arbroath v. Montrose
Cowdenbeath v. East Fife
East Stirlingshire v. Stenhousemuir
Elgin City v. Berwick Rangers
**SATURDAY, NOVEMBER 12TH, 2005**
**FIRST DIVISION**
Airdrie United v. Hamilton Academical
Brechin City v. Ross County
Clyde v. St. Mirren
Dundee v. St. Johnstone
Queen of the South v. Stranraer

**SECOND DIVISION**
Alloa Athletic v. Morton
Ayr United v. Raith Rovers
Dumbarton v. Forfar Athletic
Partick Thistle v. Gretna
Peterhead v. Stirling Albion
**THIRD DIVISION**
Albion Rovers v. Elgin City
Arbroath v. Berwick Rangers
East Fife v. Stenhousemuir
East Stirlingshire v. Queen's Park
Montrose v. Cowdenbeath
**TUESDAY, NOVEMBER 15TH, 2005**
**FIRST DIVISION**
Brechin City v. St. Mirren
Dundee v. Hamilton Academical (7.45pm)
**SATURDAY, NOVEMBER 19TH, 2005**
**FIRST DIVISION**
Hamilton Academical v. Queen of the South
Ross County v. Dundee
St. Johnstone v. Clyde
St. Mirren v. Airdrie United
Stranraer v. Brechin City
**SECOND DIVISION**
Ayr United v. Forfar Athletic
**SATURDAY, NOVEMBER 26TH, 2005**
**FIRST DIVISION**
Clyde v. Airdrie United
Dundee v. Brechin City
Queen of the South v. Ross County
St. Johnstone v. Stranraer
St. Mirren v. Hamilton Academical
**SECOND DIVISION**
Forfar Athletic v. Partick Thistle
Gretna v. Alloa Athletic
Morton v. Ayr United
Raith Rovers v. Peterhead
Stirling Albion v. Dumbarton
**THIRD DIVISION**
Berwick Rangers v. Albion Rovers
Cowdenbeath v. Arbroath
Elgin City v. East Stirlingshire
Queen's Park v. East Fife
Stenhousemuir v. Montrose
**SATURDAY, DECEMBER 3RD, 2005**
**FIRST DIVISION**
Airdrie United v. Queen of the South
Brechin City v. St. Johnstone
Hamilton Academical v. Clyde
Ross County v. St. Mirren
Stranraer v. Dundee
**SECOND DIVISION**
Alloa Athletic v. Ayr United
Gretna v. Peterhead
Morton v. Partick Thistle
Raith Rovers v. Dumbarton
Stirling Albion v. Forfar Athletic
**THIRD DIVISION**
Berwick Rangers v. Stenhousemuir
Cowdenbeath v. Albion Rovers
East Stirlingshire v. East Fife
Elgin City v. Arbroath
Queen's Park v. Montrose
**SATURDAY, DECEMBER 10TH, 2005**
**FIRST DIVISION**
Brechin City v. Hamilton Academical
Dundee v. St. Mirren
Ross County v. Clyde
St. Johnstone v. Queen of the South
Stranraer v. Airdrie United
**SATURDAY, DECEMBER 17TH, 2005**
**FIRST DIVISION**
Airdrie United v. Brechin City

Clyde v. Stranraer
Hamilton Academical v. Ross County
Queen of the South v. Dundee
St. Mirren v. St. Johnstone
**SECOND DIVISION**
Ayr United v. Stirling Albion
Dumbarton v. Gretna
Forfar Athletic v. Raith Rovers
Partick Thistle v. Alloa Athletic
Peterhead v. Morton
**THIRD DIVISION**
Albion Rovers v. East Stirlingshire
Arbroath v. Queen's Park
East Fife v. Elgin City
Montrose v. Berwick Rangers
Stenhousemuir v. Cowdenbeath
**SATURDAY, DECEMBER 24TH, 2005**
**SECOND DIVISION**
Alloa Athletic v. Peterhead
**MONDAY, DECEMBER 26TH, 2005**
**FIRST DIVISION**
Brechin City v. Clyde
Dundee v. Airdrie United
Queen of the South v. St. Mirren
St. Johnstone v. Ross County (2.00pm)
Stranraer v. Hamilton Academical
**SECOND DIVISION**
Ayr United v. Dumbarton
Gretna v. Forfar Athletic
Morton v. Raith Rovers
Partick Thistle v. Stirling Albion
**THIRD DIVISION**
Albion Rovers v. Arbroath
East Fife v. Berwick Rangers (2.00pm)
East Stirlingshire v. Cowdenbeath
Elgin City v. Montrose
Queen's Park v. Stenhousemuir
**SATURDAY, DECEMBER 31ST, 2005**
**FIRST DIVISION**
Airdrie United v. St. Johnstone (2.00pm)
Clyde v. Queen of the South
Hamilton Academical v. Dundee (2.00pm)
Ross County v. Stranraer
St. Mirren v. Brechin City
**SECOND DIVISION**
Dumbarton v. Partick Thistle
Forfar Athletic v. Morton (2.00 p.m.)
Raith Rovers v. Alloa Athletic
Stirling Albion v. Gretna
**THIRD DIVISION**
Arbroath v. East Stirlingshire
Berwick Rangers v. Queen's Park
Cowdenbeath v. Elgin City
Montrose v. East Fife
Stenhousemuir v. Albion Rovers
**MONDAY, JANUARY 2ND, 2006**
**FIRST DIVISION**
Hamilton Academical v. Airdrie United
Ross County v. Brechin City
St. Johnstone v. Dundee
St. Mirren v. Clyde
Stranraer v. Queen of the South
**SECOND DIVISION**
Dumbarton v. Morton
Forfar Athletic v. Peterhead (2.00 p.m.)
Gretna v. Ayr United
Partick Thistle v. Raith Rovers
**THIRD DIVISION**
East Fife v. Cowdenbeath
Montrose v. Arbroath
Queen's Park v. Albion Rovers
Stenhousemuir v. East Stirlingshire

**SATURDAY, JANUARY 14TH, 2006**
**FIRST DIVISION**
Airdrie United v. St. Mirren
Brechin City v. Stranraer
Clyde v. St. Johnstone
Dundee v. Ross County
Queen of the South v. Hamilton Academical
**SECOND DIVISION**
Alloa Athletic v. Forfar Athletic
Ayr United v. Partick Thistle
Morton v. Gretna
Peterhead v. Dumbarton
Raith Rovers v. Stirling Albion
**THIRD DIVISION**
Albion Rovers v. East Fife
Arbroath v. Stenhousemuir
Cowdenbeath v. Berwick Rangers
East Stirlingshire v. Montrose
Elgin City v. Queen's Park
**SATURDAY, JANUARY 21ST, 2006**
**FIRST DIVISION**
Airdrie United v. Clyde
Brechin City v. Dundee
Hamilton Academical v. St. Mirren
Ross County v. Queen of the South
Stranraer v. St. Johnstone
**SECOND DIVISION**
Forfar Athletic v. Dumbarton
Gretna v. Partick Thistle
Morton v. Alloa Athletic
Raith Rovers v. Ayr United
Stirling Albion v. Peterhead
**THIRD DIVISION**
Berwick Rangers v. Arbroath
Cowdenbeath v. Montrose
Elgin City v. Albion Rovers
Queen's Park v. East Stirlingshire
Stenhousemuir v. East Fife
**SATURDAY, JANUARY 28TH, 2006**
**FIRST DIVISION**
Clyde v. Hamilton Academical
Dundee v. Stranraer
Queen of the South v. Airdrie United
St. Johnstone v. Brechin City
St. Mirren v. Ross County
**SECOND DIVISION**
Alloa Athletic v. Gretna
Ayr United v. Morton
Dumbarton v. Stirling Albion
Partick Thistle v. Forfar Athletic
Peterhead v. Raith Rovers
**THIRD DIVISION**
Albion Rovers v. Berwick Rangers
Arbroath v. Cowdenbeath
East Fife v. Queen's Park
East Stirlingshire v. Elgin City
Montrose v. Stenhousemuir
**SATURDAY, FEBRUARY 4TH, 2006**
**SECOND DIVISION**
Alloa Athletic v. Partick Thistle
Gretna v. Dumbarton
Morton v. Peterhead
Raith Rovers v. Forfar Athletic
Stirling Albion v. Ayr United
**THIRD DIVISION**
Berwick Rangers v. Montrose
Cowdenbeath v. Stenhousemuir
East Stirlingshire v. Albion Rovers
Elgin City v. East Fife
Queen's Park v. Arbroath
**SATURDAY, FEBRUARY 11TH, 2006**
**FIRST DIVISION**
Brechin City v. Airdrie United
Dundee v. Queen of the South

FALKIRK:
BELL'S FIRST DIVISION CHAMPIONS

Ross County v. Hamilton Academical
St. Johnstone v. St. Mirren
Stranraer v. Clyde
**SECOND DIVISION**
Ayr United v. Alloa Athletic
Dumbarton v. Raith Rovers
Forfar Athletic v. Stirling Albion
Partick Thistle v. Morton
Peterhead v. Gretna
**THIRD DIVISION**
Albion Rovers v. Cowdenbeath
Arbroath v. Elgin City
East Fife v. East Stirlingshire
Montrose v. Queen's Park
Stenhousemuir v. Berwick Rangers
**SATURDAY, FEBRUARY 18TH, 2006**
**FIRST DIVISION**
Airdrie United v. Ross County
Clyde v. Dundee
Hamilton Academical v. St. Johnstone
Queen of the South v. Brechin City
St. Mirren v. Stranraer
**SECOND DIVISION**
Dumbarton v. Alloa Athletic
Forfar Athletic v. Ayr United
Peterhead v. Partick Thistle
Raith Rovers v. Gretna
Stirling Albion v. Morton
**THIRD DIVISION**
Arbroath v. East Fife
Berwick Rangers v. East Stirlingshire
Cowdenbeath v. Queen's Park
Montrose v. Albion Rovers
Stenhousemuir v. Elgin City
**SATURDAY, FEBRUARY 25TH, 2006**
**SECOND DIVISION**
Alloa Athletic v. Raith Rovers
Ayr United v. Peterhead
Gretna v. Stirling Albion
Morton v. Forfar Athletic
Partick Thistle v. Dumbarton
**THIRD DIVISION**
Albion Rovers v. Stenhousemuir
East Fife v. Montrose
East Stirlingshire v. Arbroath
Elgin City v. Cowdenbeath
Queen's Park v. Berwick Rangers
**SATURDAY, MARCH 4TH, 2006**
**FIRST DIVISION**
Brechin City v. St. Mirren
Dundee v. Hamilton Academical
Queen of the South v. Clyde
St. Johnstone v. Airdrie United
Stranraer v. Ross County

**SECOND DIVISION**
Alloa Athletic v. Stirling Albion
Ayr United v. Gretna
Morton v. Dumbarton
Peterhead v. Forfar Athletic
Raith Rovers v. Partick Thistle
**THIRD DIVISION**
Albion Rovers v. Queen's Park
Arbroath v. Montrose
Cowdenbeath v. East Fife
East Stirlingshire v. Stenhousemuir
Elgin City v. Berwick Rangers
**SATURDAY, MARCH 11TH, 2006**
**FIRST DIVISION**
Airdrie United v. Dundee
Clyde v. Brechin City
Hamilton Academical v. Stranraer
Ross County v. St. Johnstone
St. Mirren v. Queen of the South
**SECOND DIVISION**
Dumbarton v. Peterhead
Forfar Athletic v. Alloa Athletic
Gretna v. Morton
Partick Thistle v. Ayr United
Stirling Albion v. Raith Rovers
**THIRD DIVISION**
Berwick Rangers v. Cowdenbeath
East Fife v. Albion Rovers
Montrose v. East Stirlingshire
Queen's Park v. Elgin City
Stenhousemuir v. Arbroath
**SATURDAY, MARCH 18TH, 2006**
**FIRST DIVISION**
Airdrie United v. Hamilton Academical
Brechin City v. Ross County
Clyde v. St. Mirren
Dundee v. St. Johnstone
Queen of the South v. Stranraer
**SECOND DIVISION**
Alloa Athletic v. Morton
Ayr United v. Raith Rovers
Dumbarton v. Forfar Athletic
Partick Thistle v. Gretna
Peterhead v. Stirling Albion
**THIRD DIVISION**
Albion Rovers v. Elgin City
Arbroath v. Berwick Rangers
East Fife v. Stenhousemuir
East Stirlingshire v. Queen's Park
Montrose v. Cowdenbeath
**SATURDAY, MARCH 25TH, 2006**
**FIRST DIVISION**
Hamilton Academical v. Queen of the South
Ross County v. Dundee
St. Johnstone v. Clyde

St. Mirren v. Airdrie United
Stranraer v. Brechin City
**SECOND DIVISION**
Forfar Athletic v. Partick Thistle
Gretna v. Alloa Athletic
Morton v. Ayr United
Raith Rovers v. Peterhead
Stirling Albion v. Dumbarton
**THIRD DIVISION**
Berwick Rangers v. Albion Rovers
Cowdenbeath v. Arbroath
Elgin City v. East Stirlingshire
Queen's Park v. East Fife
Stenhousemuir v. Montrose
**SATURDAY, APRIL 1ST, 2006**
**FIRST DIVISION**
Clyde v. Airdrie United
Dundee v. Brechin City
Queen of the South v. Ross County
St. Johnstone v. Stranraer
St. Mirren v. Hamilton Academical
**SECOND DIVISION**
Ayr United v. Stirling Albion
Dumbarton v. Gretna
Forfar Athletic v. Raith Rovers
Partick Thistle v. Alloa Athletic
Peterhead v. Morton
**THIRD DIVISION**
Albion Rovers v. East Stirlingshire
Arbroath v. Queen's Park
East Fife v. Elgin City
Montrose v. Berwick Rangers
Stenhousemuir v. Cowdenbeath
**SATURDAY, APRIL 8TH, 2006**
**FIRST DIVISION**
Airdrie United v. Queen of the South
Brechin City v. St. Johnstone
Hamilton Academical v. Clyde
Ross County v. St. Mirren
Stranraer v. Dundee
**SECOND DIVISION**
Alloa Athletic v. Ayr United
Gretna v. Peterhead
Morton v. Partick Thistle
Raith Rovers v. Dumbarton
Stirling Albion v. Forfar Athletic
**THIRD DIVISION**
Berwick Rangers v. Stenhousemuir
Cowdenbeath v. Albion Rovers
East Stirlingshire v. East Fife
Elgin City v. Arbroath
Queen's Park v. Montrose
**SATURDAY, APRIL 15TH, 2006**
**FIRST DIVISION**
Airdrie United v. Stranraer

Clyde v. Ross County
Hamilton Academical v. Brechin City
Queen of the South v. St. Johnstone
St. Mirren v. Dundee
**SECOND DIVISION**
Dumbarton v. Ayr United
Forfar Athletic v. Gretna
Peterhead v. Alloa Athletic
Raith Rovers v. Morton
Stirling Albion v. Partick Thistle
**THIRD DIVISION**
Arbroath v. Albion Rovers
Berwick Rangers v. East Fife
Cowdenbeath v. East Stirlingshire
Montrose v. Elgin City
Stenhousemuir v. Queen's Park
**SATURDAY, APRIL 22ND, 2006**
**FIRST DIVISION**
Brechin City v. Queen of the South
Dundee v. Clyde
Ross County v. Airdrie United
St. Johnstone v. Hamilton Academical
Stranraer v. St. Mirren
**SECOND DIVISION**
Alloa Athletic v. Dumbarton
Ayr United v. Forfar Athletic
Gretna v. Raith Rovers
Morton v. Stirling Albion
Partick Thistle v. Peterhead
**THIRD DIVISION**
Albion Rovers v. Montrose
East Fife v. Arbroath
East Stirlingshire v. Berwick Rangers
Elgin City v. Stenhousemuir
Queen's Park v. Cowdenbeath
**SATURDAY, APRIL 29TH, 2006**
**FIRST DIVISION**
Airdrie United v. Brechin City
Clyde v. Stranraer
Hamilton Academical v. Ross County
Queen of the South v. Dundee
St. Mirren v. St. Johnstone
**SECOND DIVISION**
Dumbarton v. Partick Thistle
Forfar Athletic v. Morton
Peterhead v. Ayr United
Raith Rovers v. Alloa Athletic
Stirling Albion v. Gretna
**THIRD DIVISION**
Arbroath v. East Stirlingshire
Berwick Rangers v. Queen's Park
Cowdenbeath v. Elgin City
Montrose v. East Fife
Stenhousemuir v. Albion Rovers

# THE CIS INSURANCE CUP
# DRAW SEASON 2005.06

# THE BELL'S CUP DRAW
# SEASON 2005.06

### 1st ROUND

| | | |
|---|---|---|
| Alloa Athletic | -v- | Arbroath |
| Cowdenbeath | -v- | St. Johnstone |
| Morton | -v- | Ayr United |
| Brechin City | -v- | Partick Thistle |
| Forfar Athletic | -v- | Ross County |
| Hamilton Academical | -v- | Dumbarton |
| East Fife | -v- | Stranraer |
| Stenhousemuir | -v- | Peterhead |
| Berwick Rangers | -v- | Elgin City |
| Raith Rovers | -v- | Airdrie United |
| Montrose | -v- | Clyde |
| East Stirlingshire | -v- | Queen's Park |

Above Ties to be played on Tuesday, 9th August, 2005.

| | | |
|---|---|---|
| Albion Rovers | -v- | Gretna |
| Stirling Albion | -v- | Queen of the South |

Above Ties to be played on Wednesday 10th August, 2005.

### 2nd ROUND

........................................v........................................
........................................v........................................
........................................v........................................
........................................v........................................
........................................v........................................
........................................v........................................
........................................v........................................
........................................v........................................
........................................v........................................
........................................v........................................
........................................v........................................

Ties to be played on Tuesday, 23rd or Wednesday, 24th August, 2005.

### 3rd ROUND

........................................v........................................
........................................v........................................
........................................v........................................
........................................v........................................
........................................v........................................
........................................v........................................

Ties to be played on Tuesday, 20th or Wednesday, 21st September, 2005

### 4th ROUND

........................................v........................................
........................................v........................................
........................................v........................................

Ties to be played on Tuesday, 8th or Wednesday, 9th November, 2005

### SEMI-FINALS

........................................v........................................

Ties to be played on Tuesday, 31st January and Wednesday, 1st February, 2006

### THE CIS INSURANCE CUP FINAL

........................................v........................................

To be played on Sunday, 19th March, 2006

*In the event of a draw after normal time in all rounds, extra-time of 30 minutes (i.e. 15 minutes each way) will take place and thereafter, if necessary, Kicks from the Penalty Mark in accordance with the Rules laid down by The International Football Association Board will be taken.*

### 1st ROUND

| | | |
|---|---|---|
| Raith Rovers | -v- | Elgin City |
| Peterhead | -v- | Berwick Rangers |
| Brechin City | -v- | Clyde |
| Morton | -v- | Gretna |
| Ayr United | -v- | Stirling Albion |
| Dundee | -v- | East Stirlingshire |
| Ross County | -v- | Montrose |
| Arbroath | -v- | Stranraer |
| St. Johnstone | -v- | Alloa Athletic |
| East Fife | -v- | Stenhousemuir |
| St. Mirren | -v- | Forfar Athletic |
| Queen's Park | -v- | Hamilton Academical |
| Partick Thistle | -v- | Cowdenbeath |
| Queen of the South | -v- | Albion Rovers |

**Byes:** Airdrie United & Dumbarton

Above Ties will be played on Saturday, 30th July, 2005

### 2nd ROUND

........................................v........................................
........................................v........................................
........................................v........................................
........................................v........................................
........................................v........................................
........................................v........................................
........................................v........................................
........................................v........................................

Ties to be played on Tuesday, 30th or Wednesday, 31st August, 2005

### 3rd ROUND

........................................v........................................
........................................v........................................
........................................v........................................
........................................v........................................

Ties to be played on Tuesday, 13th or Wednesday, 14th September, 2005

### SEMI-FINALS

........................................v........................................
........................................v........................................

Ties to be played on Tuesday, 27th or Wednesday, 28th September, 2005

### THE BELL'S CUP FINAL

........................................v........................................

To be played on Sunday, 6th November, 2005

*In the event of a draw after normal time in all rounds, extra-time of 30 minutes (i.e. 15 minutes each way) will take place and thereafter, if necessary, Kicks from the Penalty Mark in accordance with the Rules laid down by The International Football Association Board will be taken.*

# ABERDEEN

**ABERDEEN F.C.**
Pittodrie Stadium, Pittodrie Street,
Aberdeen, AB24 5QH
**TELEPHONE NUMBERS**
Ground/General Enquiries (01224) 650400
Football Dept (01224) 650479
Sales & Marketing Dept (01224) 650426
PR Dept (01224) 650406
Community Dept (01224) 650432
Ticket Enquiries 087 1983 1903
Operations Dept (01224) 650405
**FAX** (01224) 644173
**E-MAIL** davidj@afc.co.uk
**E-MAIL 2** feedback@afc.co.uk
**WEBSITE** www.afc.co.uk
**CHAIRMAN** Stewart Milne
**DIRECTORS** Gordon A. Buchan,
Martin J. Gilbert, Hugh Little,
Christopher Gavin, William F. Miller,
Duncan Fraser & Ken Matheson
**EXECUTIVE DIRECTOR** Duncan Fraser
**PRESIDENT** Ian R. Donald
**CLUB SECRETARY** David Johnston
**MANAGER** Jimmy Calderwood
**ASSISTANT MANAGER** Jimmy Nicholl
**DIRECTOR OF FOOTBALL** Willie Miller
**RESERVE COACH** Sandy Clark
**GOALKEEPING COACH** Jim Leighton
**DIRECTOR OF YOUTH DEVELOPMENT**
Chic McLelland
**SENIOR COMMUNITY COACH** Neil Simpson
**COMMUNITY CO-ORDINATOR** Sandy Finnie
**COMMUNITY COACHES** Jim Crawford,
Stuart Glennie & Scott Anderson
**YOUTH COACHES**
U19: Neil Cooper
U17 & U16: Ian Gellie & Ian Fleming
U15: Mark Emslie & Brian Dunn
U14: Raymond Yule & Gary Gibson
U13: Stephen Davidson & Gareth Gentles
**TEAM CAPTAIN** Russell Anderson
**FOOTBALL SAFETY OFFICERS'
ASSOCIATION REPRESENTATIVE /
STADIUM MANAGER**
John Morgan (01224) 650405
**COMMERCIAL MANAGER /
SALES & MARKETING MANAGER**
Ian Riddoch (01224) 650443
**HOSPITALITY MANAGER**
Paul Quick (01224) 650430
**CUSTOMER SERVICES MANAGER**
Peter Roy (01224) 650428
**MEDIA LIAISON PERSON**
Dave Macdermid (01224) 650406
**MATCHDAY PROGRAMME EDITOR**
Malcolm Panton (01224) 650402
**CLUB DOCTORS**
Dr. Derek Gray & Dr. Stephen Wedderburn
**PHYSIOTHERAPISTS**
David Wylie & John Sharp
**GROUNDSMAN** Paul Fiske
**KIT PERSON** Jim Warrender
**CLUB SHOPS**
Pittodrie Club Shop, Pittodrie Stadium,
Aberdeen. Tel 087 1983 1903
Buy on-line at www.afc.co.uk/shop
**OFFICIAL SUPPORTERS CLUB**
The official Association of Aberdeen
Supporters Clubs:
Contact: Peter Roy (01224) 650428
**SHIRT SPONSOR** ADT Fire & Security
**KIT SUPPLIER** Nike

## LIST OF PLAYERS 2005.06

| SQUAD NO. | PLAYERS SURNAME | FIRST NAME | MIDDLE NAME | DATE OF BIRTH | PLACE OF BIRTH | DATE SIGNED | HEIGHT FT INS | WEIGHT ST LBS | POSITION ON PITCH | PREVIOUS CLUB |
|---|---|---|---|---|---|---|---|---|---|---|
| 4 | Anderson | Russell | | 25/10/78 | Aberdeen | 19/07/96 | 6' 1" | 12st 6lb | Def | Dyce Juniors |
| | Bagshaw | Andrew | George | 04/07/88 | Aberdeen | 01/07/04 | 5' 8" | 11st 0lb | Fwd | Aberdeen Youths |
| | Bruce | John | | 16/01/88 | Dundee | 01/07/04 | 5' 9" | 11st 0lb | Fwd | Aberdeen Youths |
| 17 | Byrne | Richard | | 24/09/81 | Dublin | 27/01/05 | 6' 1" | 12st 5lb | Def | Dunfermline Athletic |
| 11 | Clark | Christopher | | 15/09/80 | Aberdeen | 16/08/97 | 5' 9" | 11st 3lb | Mid | Hermes |
| 21 | Considine | Andrew | | 01/04/87 | Torphins | 28/08/03 | 6' 0.5" | 11st 12lb | Def | Aberdeen Youths |
| 23 | Crawford | Stephen | | 09/01/74 | Dunfermline | 31/08/05 | 5' 10.5" | 12st 0lb | Fwd | Dundee United |
| 14 | Dempsey | Gary | | 15/01/81 | Wexford | 08/07/05 | 5' 9" | 11st 8lb | Mid | Dunfermline Athletic |
| 5 | Diamond | Alexander | | 12/03/85 | Alexandria | 12/07/02 | 6' 2" | 11st 7lb | Def | Aberdeen 'S' Form |
| 27 | Donald | David | | 09/11/87 | Aberdeen | 06/01/04 | 5' 7" | 10st 13lb | Def | Glendale |
| 1 | Esson | Ryan | John | 19/03/80 | Aberdeen | 23/10/96 | 6' 1.5" | 13st 3lb | Gk | Rotherham United |
| 19 | Foster | Richard | Martyn | 31/07/85 | Aberdeen | 02/09/98 | 5' 9.5" | 11st 8lb | Mid | Aberdeen Youths |
| 2 | Hart | Michael | | 10/02/80 | Bellshill | 24/01/03 | 5' 11.5" | 12st 2lb | Mid | Livingston |
| 28 | Keily | Willie | John | 25/06/88 | Waterford | 14/07/04 | 5' 7" | 11st 8lb | Fwd | Cherry Orchard |
| 30 | Kelly | Greg | | 28/04/87 | Bellshill | 07/07/04 | 6' 2" | 12st 0lb | Gk | Aberdeen Youths |
| 20 | Langfield | James | | 22/12/79 | Paisley | 22/06/05 | 6' 4" | 13st 0lb | Gk | Dunfermline Athletic |
| 9 | Lovell | Stephen | | 06/12/80 | Amersham | 14/07/05 | 6' 0" | 12st 11lb | Fwd | Dundee |
| 22 | MacAulay | Kyle | Donald | 13/05/86 | Elgin | 25/05/04 | 5' 10" | 11st 12lb | Mid | Aberdeen B.C. |
| 10 | Mackie | Darren | Graham | 05/01/82 | Inverurie | 13/07/98 | 5' 9" | 10st 10lb | Fwd | Aberdeen 'S' Form |
| 26 | Maguire | Chris | | 16/01/89 | Bellshill | 06/01/05 | 5' 7" | 10st 5lb | Fwd | Aberdeen Youths |
| | McInnes | Ashley | | 22/04/87 | Aberdeen | 09/07/03 | 5' 7" | 9st 8lb | Mid | Aberdeen Youths |
| 3 | McNaughton | Kevin | Paul | 28/08/82 | Dundee | 20/07/99 | 5' 10" | 11st 6lb | Def | Aberdeen 'S' Form |
| | McVitie | Neil | | 17/05/89 | Irvine | 03/08/05 | 5' 8.5" | 10st 13lb | Def | Aberdeen Youths |
| 18 | Muirhead | Scott | | 08/05/84 | Paisley | 27/09/01 | 6' 1" | 11st 13lb | Mid | Neilston Thistle |
| | Neill | Brian | | 11/01/88 | Aberdeen | 01/07/04 | 5' 7" | 10st 2lb | Mid | Aberdeen Youths |
| 8 | Nicholson | Barry | | 24/08/78 | Dumfries | 07/06/05 | 5' 7.5" | 10st 12lb | Mid | Dunfermline Athletic |
| | Paton | Michael | | 25/08/89 | Greenock | 30/06/05 | 5' 10" | 11st 3lb | Fwd | Aberdeen Youths |
| 6 | Severin | Scott | Derek | 15/02/79 | Stirling | 05/07/04 | 5' 11" | 12st 12lb | Mid | Hearts |
| | Shields | Gary | | 28/04/88 | Glasgow | 01/07/04 | 5' 5" | 10st 2lb | Fwd | Aberdeen Youths |
| | Skinner | Martin | | 27/02/89 | Aberdeen | 22/02/05 | 5' 11" | 11st 4lb | Mid | Aberdeen Youths |
| 7 | Smith | Jamie | | 20/11/80 | Alexandria | 11/07/05 | 5' 6.5" | 11st 0lb | Fwd | ADO Den Haag |
| 16 | Stewart | John | | 08/03/85 | Bellshill | 13/01/03 | 5' 10" | 9st 9lb | Fwd | Airdrie United |
| | Stewart | Fraser | Hunter | 14/11/88 | Irvine | 06/07/05 | 6' 2" | 12st 7lb | Gk | Aberdeen Youths |
| | Thomas | Mark | | 03/01/88 | Glasgow | 07/07/04 | 5' 8.5" | 10st 0lb | Def | Aberdeen Youths |
| | Thomson | Robert | | 24/05/87 | Bellshill | 09/07/03 | 5' 8" | 10st 3lb | Def | Aberdeen Youths |
| 15 | Winter | Jamie | | 04/08/85 | Dundee | 12/01/05 | 6' 0.5" | 13st 4lb | Mid | Leeds United |

## TICKET INFORMATION

### Season Ticket information

| | Adult | Conc | U12 | 1 Adult 2 Conc | 2 Adult 2 Conc | 1 Adult 2 U12 | 2 Adult 2 U12 |
|---|---|---|---|---|---|---|---|
| MAIN STAND | £370 | £225 | £140 | £708 | £1,078 | £595 | £965 |
| MERKLAND STAND | £230 | £110 | £50 | £395 | £625 | £320 | £550 |
| RDSTAND | £270 | £145 | £80 | £488 | £758 | £405 | £675 |
| RDS CENTRE PADDED | £370 | £225 | £140 | £708 | £1,078 | £595 | £965 |
| SOUTH STAND | £270 | £145 | £80 | £488 | £758 | £405 | £675 |

### Match Ticket information

| | Adult | Conc | U12 |
|---|---|---|---|
| MAIN STAND | £25 | £18 | - |
| MERKLAND STAND | £15 | £8 | £5 |
| RDSTAND | £20 | £15 | - |
| RDS CENTRE PADDED | £25 | £18 | - |
| SOUTH STAND | £20 | £15 | - |

**MILESTONES:**
Year of formation: 1903
Most Capped player: Alex McLeish
No. of Caps: 77
Most League points in a season:
64 (Premier Division – Season 1992/93)
(44 games) (2 Points for a Win)
Most League goals scored by a player in a season:
Benny Yorston (Season 1929/30)
No. of goals scored: 38
Record Attendance: 45,061 (-v- Heart of Midlothian – 13.3
Record Victory: 13-0 (-v- Peterhead – Scottish Cup, 9.2.19
Record Defeat: 0-8 (-v- Celtic - Division 1, 30.1.1965)

## SEASON STATS 2004.05

Figure in bold denotes goal scored. Secondary smaller figure in bold denotes number of goals scored. † denotes opponent's own goal.

| DATE | VENUE | OPPONENTS | ATT | RES | Preece D. | McGuire P. | McNaughton K. | Anderson R. | Diamond A. | Severin S. | Heikkinen M. | Adams D. | Hart M. | Clark C. | Whelan N. | Craig S. | Tosh S. | Morrison S. | Foster R. | Stewart J. | Pasquinelli F. | Muirhead S. | Mackie D. | Esson R. | Winter J. | Kristjansson T. | Byrne R. | Blaha L. | Dempsey G. | Considine A. |
|---|---|---|---|---|---|---|---|---|---|---|---|---|---|---|---|---|---|---|---|---|---|---|---|---|---|---|---|---|---|---|
| 7-Aug | H | Rangers | 19,023 | 0-0 | 1 | 2 | 3 | 4 | 5 | 6 | 7 | 8 | 9 | 10 | 11 | 12 | 13 | 14 | | | | | | | | | | | | |
| 14-Aug | A | Hearts | 13,864 | 0-0 | 1 | 2 | 3 | 4 | 5 | 6 | 7 | 12 | | 10 | 11 | 9 | 8 | | | 13 | | | | | | | | | | |
| 21-Aug | A | Dunfermline Ath. | 8,533 | 1-0 | 1 | 2 | 3 | 4 | 5 | 6 | 7 | 13 | 9 | | **11** | 10 | 8 | | 14 | 12 | | | | | | | | | | |
| 28-Aug | H | Livingston | 13,888 | 2-0 | 1 | 2 | 3 | 4 | 5 | 6 | 7 | 9 | | 12 | | $10^2$ | 8 | | | 11 | 13 | 14 | | | | | | | | |
| 11-Sep | A | Dundee United | 11,595 | 1-1 | 1 | 2 | 3 | 4 | 5 | 6 | 7 | | 9 | 8 | | 10 | 12 | | 14 | 13 | | | 11 | | | | | | | |
| 18-Sep | A | Kilmarnock | 6,686 | †1-0 | 1 | 2 | 3 | 4 | | 6 | | | 9 | 5 | | 10 | 8 | | 7 | | | 12 | 11 | | | | | | | |
| 25-Sep | H | Hibernian | 12,137 | 0-1 | 1 | 2 | 3 | 4 | | 6 | 12 | | 9 | 5 | | 8 | 13 | | 7 | 10 | 14 | | 11 | | | | | | | |
| 2-Oct | H | Dundee | 11,217 | 1-1 | 1 | 2 | 3 | 4 | | 6 | **7** | | 9 | 5 | | 10 | 8 | | | | 11 | | 13 | 14 | 12 | | | | | |
| 16-Oct | H | Inverness Cal.Th. | 9,830 | 3-1 | 1 | 2 | 3 | | 6 | 4 | $9^2$ | | | 5 | 10 | | | | 12 | 8 | | 7 | 14 | 13 | | 11 | | | | |
| 23-Oct | H | Motherwell | 10,737 | 2-1 | 1 | 2 | 3 | 4 | | 6 | 7 | | 9 | 5 | 10 | 12 | | | | 8 | | | 13 | | | 11 | | | | |
| 27-Oct | A | Celtic | 57,060 | 3-2 | 1 | 2 | 3 | 4 | | 6 | | | | 7 | 5 | 10 | | | | 8 | | 13 | **14** | **9** | 11 | 15 | | | | |
| 31-Oct | A | Rangers | 48,918 | 0-5 | | 2 | 3 | 4 | | 6 | | | | 7 | 5 | 10 | 14 | | | 8 | | 13 | 12 | 9 | 11 | 1 | | | | |
| 7-Nov | H | Hearts | 13,055 | 0-1 | 1 | 2 | 3 | 4 | 5 | 6 | | | | 7 | 10 | 9 | | | | 8 | | | 11 | | | | | | | |
| 13-Nov | A | Dunfermline Ath. | 10,398 | †2-1 | 1 | 12 | | 4 | 3 | 6 | 5 | 7 | | | 10 | 9 | | | | 8 | 2 | 13 | 14 | | 11 | | | | | |
| 20-Nov | A | Livingston | 4,270 | 2-0 | 1 | 12 | 3 | 4 | 5 | 6 | 7 | | | | 10 | 9 | | | | 2 | 8 | | 13 | | 11 | | | | | |
| 27-Nov | H | Dundee United | 12,038 | 1-0 | 1 | 2 | 3 | | 5 | 6 | 7 | 13 | | | 10 | 12 | **8** | 4 | 9 | | | | 11 | | | | | | | |
| 4-Dec | H | Kilmarnock | 11,139 | 3-2 | 1 | 2 | 3 | 4 | 5 | 6 | 7 | | | | 12 | **9** | | | | 8 | 13 | 14 | $10^2$ | 11 | | | | | | |
| 11-Dec | A | Hibernian | 13,503 | 1-2 | 1 | 2 | 3 | 4 | 5 | 6 | 7 | | | | | 8 | 9 | | 13 | 14 | 10 | | 11 | 12 | | | | | | |
| 18-Dec | A | Dundee | 7,310 | 0-1 | | | 3 | 4 | 5 | 6 | 7 | 2 | | | | 9 | 12 | | 8 | 14 | 10 | 13 | 11 | 1 | | | | | | |
| 27-Dec | H | Inverness Cal.Th. | 18,250 | 0-0 | 13 | | 3 | 4 | 5 | 6 | 7 | 2 | | | 10 | | | | 8 | 9 | | | 12 | 11 | 1 | | | | | |
| 3-Jan | A | Motherwell | 6,948 | 0-0 | | 2 | 3 | 4 | 5 | | 7 | 13 | 6 | | 10 | 12 | | | 8 | 9 | | 14 | 11 | 1 | | | | | | |
| 16-Jan | H | Celtic | 17,051 | 0-1 | | 2 | 3 | 4 | 5 | | 7 | 8 | 6 | 9 | 10 | 12 | | | | | | | 11 | 1 | 13 | 14 | | | | |
| 23-Jan | A | Rangers | 17,495 | 1-2 | | | 3 | 4 | 5 | | 7 | 2 | | 9 | 10 | | | | 8 | 14 | 13 | | **11** | 1 | | | 6 | 12 | | |
| 29-Jan | A | Hearts | 12,269 | 0-1 | | | 3 | 4 | 5 | | 7 | 2 | | 9 | 10 | | | | 13 | 12 | | | 11 | 1 | | | 6 | 8 | | |
| 12-Feb | A | Dunfermline Ath. | 5,609 | 1-2 | 12 | | 3 | | **5** | | 7 | 10 | 2 | 9 | | | 14 | | | 13 | | 8 | 11 | 1 | | | 6 | 4 | | |
| 19-Feb | H | Livingston | 9,214 | 2-0 | | | 3 | 4 | 5 | | 7 | | 6 | 13 | 10 | 2 | | 14 | | | 9 | | 11 | 1 | | | 8 | 12 | | |
| 2-Mar | A | Dundee United | 6,688 | 2-1 | | 2 | 3 | 4 | **5** | | 7 | | | 10 | 9 | | | | 13 | 12 | | | 11 | 1 | | | 8 | 6 | | |
| 5-Mar | A | Kilmarnock | 5,181 | 1-0 | | | 3 | 4 | | 6 | 7 | | | 10 | 12 | 2 | 13 | | 9 | 14 | | | 11 | 1 | | | 8 | 5 | | |
| 12-Mar | H | Hibernian | 14,465 | 3-0 | 12 | | 3 | **4** | 5 | 6 | 7 | | | 10 | 9 | 2 | | | 8 | 13 | | | 11 | 1 | | | | | | 2 |
| 19-Mar | H | Dundee | 10,474 | 1-1 | | 2 | 3 | 4 | | 6 | 7 | | 5 | 10 | **9** | 12 | | | 13 | | | | 11 | 1 | | | 8 | | | |
| 2-Apr | A | Inverness Cal.Th. | 7,026 | 1-0 | 12 | | 3 | 4 | 5 | 6 | 7 | | | 10 | 9 | | | | 13 | | | | 11 | 1 | | | 8 | | 14 | 2 |
| 9-Apr | H | Motherwell | 10,443 | 1-3 | | 2 | 3 | | 5 | 6 | **7** | 8 | | 10 | 9 | | 14 | | 13 | | | | 11 | 1 | | | | 4 | 12 | |
| 16-Apr | A | Celtic | 59,984 | 2-3 | 13 | | 3 | 4 | 5 | 6 | 7 | | | 10 | | 12 | | | | | 9 | | 11 | 1 | 14 | | 2 | 8 | | |
| 23-Apr | A | Motherwell | 5,063 | 1-0 | | | 3 | 4 | 5 | 6 | 7 | | | | | | | | 14 | | | 8 | 11 | 1 | | | 12 | 13 | | |
| 1-May | H | Rangers | 17,198 | 1-3 | | | 3 | 4 | 5 | 6 | 7 | | | 12 | **10** | 9 | | | 8 | | | | 11 | 1 | | | 2 | 13 | 14 | |
| 8-May | A | Celtic | 59,516 | 0-2 | | | 3 | 4 | 5 | 6 | 7 | | | | 10 | | | | 8 | | | | 11 | 1 | 14 | | 2 | 12 | 13 | 9 |
| 14-May | A | Hibernian | 15,288 | 2-1 | 13 | | 3 | | 5 | 6 | 7 | 12 | | | 10 | | | | 8 | | | | $11^2$ | 1 | 4 | | 2 | | 9 | 14 |
| 22-May | H | Hearts | 16,155 | 2-0 | | 2 | 3 | | 5 | 6 | 7 | | **9** | | 10 | | | | 8 | 14 | | | 11 | 1 | | | **4** | 12 | 13 | |
| **TOTAL FULL APPEARANCES** | | | | | 17 | 22 | 35 | 31 | 29 | 31 | 29 | 16 | 28 | 30 | 18 | 6 | 14 | 6 | 11 | 6 | 5 | 6 | 33 | 21 | 9 | 1 | 11 | 2 | | 1 |
| **TOTAL SUB APPEARANCES** | | | | | 8 | | | 2 | 1 | | 1 | 4 | 4 | 1 | 2 | 7 | 3 | 5 | 14 | 18 | 5 | 8 | 1 | 2 | 3 | 2 | 2 | 6 | 4 | |
| **TOTAL GOALS SCORED** | | | | | | 2 | 1 | 3 | | 1 | 2 | 4 | | | 2 | 4 | 2 | 1 | | 2 | 2 | 3 | 12 | | | | 1 | | | |

## THE DONS' 10 YEAR LEAGUE RECORD

| Season | Div | P | W | D | L | F | A | Pts | Pos |
|---|---|---|---|---|---|---|---|---|---|
| 1995-96 | P | 36 | 16 | 7 | 13 | 52 | 45 | 55 | 3 |
| 1996-97 | P | 36 | 10 | 14 | 12 | 45 | 54 | 44 | 6 |
| 1997-98 | P | 36 | 9 | 12 | 15 | 39 | 53 | 39 | 6 |
| 1998-99 | SPL | 36 | 10 | 7 | 19 | 43 | 71 | 37 | 8 |
| 1999-00 | SPL | 36 | 9 | 6 | 21 | 44 | 83 | 33 | 10 |
| 2000-01 | SPL | 38 | 11 | 12 | 15 | 45 | 52 | 45 | 7 |
| 2001-02 | SPL | 38 | 16 | 7 | 15 | 51 | 49 | 55 | 4 |
| 2002-03 | SPL | 38 | 13 | 10 | 15 | 41 | 54 | 49 | 8 |
| 2003-04 | SPL | 38 | 9 | 7 | 22 | 39 | 63 | 34 | 11 |
| 2004-05 | SPL | 38 | 18 | 7 | 13 | 44 | 39 | 61 | 4 |

## LEADING GOALSCORERS:

| Season | Div | Goals | Player |
|---|---|---|---|
| 1995-96 | P | 9 | S. Booth, J. Miller |
| 1996-97 | P | 15 | W. Dodds |
| 1997-98 | P | 10 | W. Dodds |
| 1998-99 | SPL | 14 | E. Jess |
| 1999-00 | SPL | 9 | A. Stavrum |
| 2000-01 | SPL | 17 | A. Stavrum |
| 2001-02 | SPL | 13 | R. Winters |
| 2002-03 | SPL | 8 | P. Sheerin |
| 2003-04 | SPL | 8 | S. Booth |
| 2004-05 | SPL | 12 | D. Mackie |

### ABERDEEN PLAYING KITS SEASON 2005.06

FIRST KIT · SECOND KIT · THIRD KIT

# CELTIC

## CELTIC F.C.
Celtic Park, Glasgow, G40 3RE

**TELEPHONE NUMBERS**
Ground/General Enquiries 0845 671 1888
Celtic Home Ticketline 0870 060 1888
All other Ticket Enquiries 0870 161 1888
Celtic View (0141) 551 4218
Stadium Catering (0141) 551 9955
Mail Order Hotline 0845 077 1888
Museum (0141) 551 4308
Ticket Hotline Fax (0141) 551 4223
International Enquiries +44 141 627 1888
**FAX** (0141) 551 8106
**E-MAIL** customerservices@celticfc.co.uk
**WEBSITE** www.celticfc.net
**CHAIRMAN** Brian Quinn, C.B.E.

**CELTIC PLC DIRECTORS**
Brian Quinn, C.B.E., Dermot F. Desmond,
Eric J. Riley, Tom Allison,
Eric Hagman C.B.E., Peter T. Lawwell,
Brian J. McBride & Brian Wilson

**CELTIC F.C DIRECTORS**
Eric J. Riley, Peter T. Lawwell, John S. Keane,
Michael A. McDonald & Kevin Sweeney
**CHIEF EXECUTIVE** Peter T. Lawwell
**COMPANY SECRETARY** Robert M. Howat
**FOOTBALL MANAGER** Gordon Strachan
**FOOTBALL ASSISTANT MANAGER**
Garry Pendrey
**RESERVE COACH** Kenny McDowall
**HEAD OF YOUTH** Tommy Burns
**YOUTH TEAM COACH** Willie McStay
**TEAM CAPTAIN** Neil Lennon
**FOOTBALL SAFETY OFFICERS'**
**ASSOCIATION REPRESENTATIVE**
Ronnie Hawthorn (0141) 551 4256
**COMMERCIAL DIRECTOR**
David Thomson (0141) 551 4246
**LOTTERY MANAGER**
John Maguire (0141) 551 4240
**MEDIA LIAISON PERSON**
Iain Jamieson (0141) 551 4235
**MATCHDAY PROGRAMME EDITOR**
Paul Cuddihy
**CLUB DOCTOR** Roddy Macdonald
**PHYSIOTHERAPISTS**
Tim Williamson & Gavin McCarthy
**GROUNDSMAN** John Hayes
**KIT PERSON** John Clark
**CLUB SHOPS**
Superstore, Celtic Park,
Glasgow, G40 3RE Tel (0845) 077 1888.
(9am-6pm Mon-Sat. 10am-5pm Sunday)
21 High Street, Glasgow, G1 1LX
Tel (0141) 552 7630 (9.30am-5.30pm
Mon-Sat. 11.30am-4.30pm Sunday)
Stores also at: Argyle St, Sauchiehall St &
40 Dundas St, Glasgow. Frederick St,
Edinburgh & Glasgow Airport.
The Plaza East Kilbride. Ann St, Belfast.
Bishop St, Derry. Upper Abbey St, Dublin.
**OFFICIAL SUPPORTERS CLUB**
Celtic Supporters Association,
1524 London Road, Glasgow G40 3RJ
Tel (0141) 556 1882/554 6250/554 6342
**SHIRT SPONSOR** Carling
**KIT SUPPLIER** Nike

## LIST OF PLAYERS 2005.06

| SQUAD NO. | PLAYERS SURNAME | FIRST NAME | MIDDLE NAME | DATE OF BIRTH | PLACE OF BIRTH | DATE SIGNED | HEIGHT FT INS | WEIGHT ST LBS | POSITION ON PITCH | PREVIOUS CLUB |
|---|---|---|---|---|---|---|---|---|---|---|
| 17 | Agathe | Didier | | 16/08/75 | St. Pierre La Reunion | 01/09/00 | 5' 11" | 12st 0lb | Fwd | Hibernian |
| | Anderson | Sean | | 15/06/89 | Dundee | 05/07/05 | 6' 1" | 11st 3lb | Mid | Celtic Youths |
| 6 | Balde | Dianbobo | | 05/10/75 | Marseille | 25/07/01 | 6' 3" | 14st 9lb | Def | Toulouse |
| 37 | Beattie | Craig | | 16/01/84 | Glasgow | 04/07/03 | 6' 1" | 12st 12lb | Fwd | Celtic Youths |
| | Bjarnason | Theodor | Elmar | 04/03/87 | Iceland | 06/01/05 | 5' 10" | 11st 3lb | Mid | KR Reykjavik |
| 1 | Boruc | Artur | | 20/02/80 | Siedlce | 19/07/05 | 6' 2" | 14st 0lb | Gk | Legia Warsaw |
| | Caddis | Paul | | 19/04/88 | Irvine | 26/07/04 | 5' 7" | 11st 1lb | Def | Celtic Youths |
| | Cahillane | Paul | | 04/03/89 | Portlaoise | 28/07/05 | 5' 11" | 10st 10lb | Mid | Belvedere |
| 3 | Camara | Mohamed | | 25/06/75 | Conakry | 01/07/05 | 5' 9" | 12st 4lb | Def | Burnley |
| | Carey | Graham | | 20/05/89 | Dublin | 02/08/05 | 6' 0" | 10st 12lb | Mid | Shelbourne |
| | Christie | Gareth | | 08/01/87 | Dublin | 16/07/03 | 6' 0" | 13st 5lb | Def | Home Farm B.C. |
| | Conroy | Ryan | | 28/04/87 | Vale of Leven | 03/07/03 | 5' 10" | 10st 9lb | Fwd | Celtic Youths |
| 49 | Cuthbert | Scott | | 15/06/87 | Alexandria | 16/07/03 | 6' 2" | 14st 0lb | Def | Celtic Youths |
| | Ferry | Simon | | 11/01/88 | Dundee | 19/11/04 | 5' 8" | 11st 0lb | Mid | Celtic 'S' Form |
| | Finnbogason | Kjartan | | 09/07/86 | Iceland | 06/01/05 | 6' 2" | 13st 0lb | Fwd | KR Reykjavik |
| | Fox | Scott | | 28/06/87 | Bellshill | 24/07/03 | 6' 0" | 10st 0lb | Gk | Dundee United |
| 40 | Gardyne | Michael | | 23/01/86 | Dundee | 10/01/02 | 5' 7" | 10st 0lb | Mid/Fwd | Celtic Youths |
| | Grant | Charles | Joseph | 27/01/87 | Bellshill | 14/01/03 | 5' 6" | 10st 3lb | Mid | Celtic Youths |
| | Harris | Ross | | 16/04/85 | Glasgow | 16/01/02 | 5' 11" | 11st 11lb | Fwd | Celtic Youths |
| 10 | Hartson | John | | 05/04/75 | Swansea | 02/08/01 | 6' 1" | 15st 0lb | Fwd | Coventry City |
| | Hepburn | Ross | | 24/05/89 | Glasgow | 03/08/05 | 5' 6" | 10st 9lb | Mid | Celtic Youths |
| | Hutchison | Paul | | 19/05/87 | Wallsend | 16/07/03 | 6' 0" | 12st 6lb | Def | Sunderland |
| 50 | Irvine | Gary | | 17/03/85 | Bellshill | 06/07/01 | 5' 11" | 12st 0lb | Def | Celtic Youths |
| | Jones | Owen | | 07/04/89 | Birmingham | 01/07/05 | 6' 0" | 11st 10lb | Gk | Celtic Youths |
| 41 | Kennedy | John | | 18/08/83 | Bellshill | 20/08/99 | 6' 2" | 13st 7lb | Def | Celtic 'S' Form |
| | Kiely | Timothy | | 07/03/89 | Clonmel | 28/07/05 | 5' 6.5" | 10st 13lb | Fwd | St. Michael's |
| 35 | Lawson | Paul | William | 15/05/84 | Aberdeen | 10/07/00 | 5' 9" | 11st 0lb | Mid | Celtic 'S' Form |
| 18 | Lennon | Neil | Francis | 25/06/71 | Lurgan | 08/12/00 | 5' 9" | 13st 2lb | Mid | Leicester City |
| | Lensky | Jacob | | 06/12/88 | Vancouver | 31/01/05 | 5' 11" | 11st 5lb | Fwd | Surrey United B.C. (Canada |
| 29 | Maloney | Shaun | Richard | 24/01/83 | Mirri | 07/07/99 | 5' 6" | 11st 0lb | Fwd | Celtic Youth Initiative |
| | Marr | Benjamin | Wardlaw | 23/02/89 | Glasgow | 08/08/05 | 5' 8" | 9st 11lb | Mid | Celtic Youths |
| 22 | Marshall | David | James | 05/03/85 | Glasgow | 06/07/01 | 6' 2" | 14st 3lb | Gk | Celtic Youths |
| | McCafferty | Ryan | | 22/04/87 | Falkirk | 13/01/04 | 5' 11" | 10st 10lb | Def | Celtic Youths |
| 46 | McGeady | Aiden | | 04/04/86 | Glasgow | 09/07/02 | 5' 10" | 11st 4lb | Mid | Celtic 'S' Form |
| | McGeough | John | Christopher | 24/05/88 | Glasgow | 07/07/04 | 5' 9" | 11st 0lb | Fwd | Celtic Youths |
| 42 | McGlinchey | Michael | Ryan | 07/01/87 | New Zealand | 09/01/03 | 5' 8" | 9st 6lb | Fwd | Celtic Youths |
| 47 | McGovern | Michael | | 12/07/84 | Enniskillen | 24/07/01 | 6' 2" | 14st 0lb | Gk | Celtic Youths |
| | McGowan | Paul | | 07/11/87 | Bellshill | 16/07/03 | 5' 6" | 10st 8lb | Fwd | Celtic Youths |
| 44 | McManus | Stephen | | 10/09/82 | Lanark | 29/08/99 | 6' 2" | 13st 0lb | Def | Celtic 'S' Form |
| 31 | McParland | Anthony | Patrick | 20/09/82 | Rutherglen | 20/07/99 | 5' 7" | 10st 4lb | Mid | Celtic 'S' Form |
| | Millar | Mark | John | 23/02/88 | Greenock | 26/07/04 | 5' 8" | 9st 12lb | Mid | Celtic Youths |
| 39 | Mulgrew | Charles | Patrick | 06/03/86 | Glasgow | 02/07/02 | 6' 2" | 13st 1lb | Mid | Celtic Youths |
| 25 | Nakamura | Shunsuke | | 24/06/78 | Kanagawa | 01/08/05 | 5' 9" | 11st 0lb | Mid | Reggina |
| | O'Brien | James | John | 28/09/87 | Glasgow | 03/07/03 | 6' 0" | 11st 11lb | Fwd | Celtic Youths |
| 43 | O'Carroll | Diarmuid | | 16/03/87 | Killarney | 16/07/03 | 5' 11" | 11st 11lb | Fwd | Home Farm B.C. |
| 48 | O'Dea | Darren | | 04/02/87 | Dublin | 16/07/03 | 6' 1" | 13st 0lb | Def | Home Farm B.C. |
| 11 | Pearson | Stephen | Paul | 02/10/82 | Lanark | 09/01/04 | 6' 1" | 11st 6lb | Mid | Motherwell |
| 19 | Petrov | Stilian | | 05/07/79 | Bulgaria | 06/08/99 | 5' 10" | 12st 1lb | Mid | CSKA Sofia |
| 38 | Quinn | Rocco | | 07/09/86 | Glasgow | 11/07/02 | 5' 11" | 12st 0lb | Mid | Celtic Youths |
| | Reid | Craig | Robert | 26/02/86 | Irvine | 02/07/02 | 6' 0" | 11st 5lb | Def | Celtic Youths |
| | Richardson | Dean | | 02/03/87 | Bellshill | 03/07/03 | 5' 8" | 10st 8lb | Def | Celtic B.C. |
| | Riley | Nicholas | | 10/05/86 | Edinburgh | 11/07/02 | 5'10" | 9st 11lb | Gk | Celtic Youths |
| | Skinner | Paul | | 03/02/89 | London | 28/07/05 | 6' 2" | 10st 4lb | Gk | Lourdes Celtic |
| | Staunton | Mark | James | 30/01/89 | Alexandria | 12/08/05 | 5' 10" | 11st 8lb | Def | Celtic 'S' Form |
| 9 | Sutton | Christopher | Roy | 10/03/73 | Nottingham | 11/07/00 | 6' 3" | 14st 0lb | Fwd | Chelsea |
| 2 | Telfer | Paul | | 21/10/71 | Edinburgh | 21/07/05 | 5' 9" | 11st 0lb | Def | Southampton |
| 8 | Thompson | Alan | | 22/12/73 | Newcastle | 01/09/00 | 6' 0" | 13st 0lb | Mid | Aston Villa |
| | Traub | Andrew | Leonard | 06/12/88 | Dunfermline | 27/01/05 | 6' 1" | 13st 6lb | Def | Celtic Youths |
| 23 | Varga | Stanislav | | 08/10/72 | Slovakia | 16/07/03 | 6' 4" | 14st 3lb | Def | Sunderland |
| 4 | Virgo | Adam | | 25/01/83 | Brighton | 21/07/05 | 6' 2" | 12st 0lb | Def | Brighton & Hove Albion |
| 33 | Wallace | Ross | | 23/05/85 | Dundee | 13/07/01 | 5' 8" | 10st 2lb | Fwd | Celtic 'S' Form |
| | Walsh | Gary | | 01/07/87 | Dublin | 16/07/03 | 5' 7" | 11st 3lb | Mid | Home Farm B.C. |
| 5 | Wei | Du | | 09/03/82 | China | 31/08/05 | 6' 2" | 13st 7lb | Def | Shanghai Shenhua |
| | Wood | Sandy | | 02/04/86 | Aberdeen | 10/07/03 | 6' 1" | 13st 7lb | Gk | Aberdeen |
| 7 | Zurawski | Maciej | | 12/09/76 | Possnan | 12/07/05 | 5' 10" | 11st 10lb | Fwd | Wisla Krakow SSA |

## TICKET INFORMATION

**Season Ticket information**

| | Adult | U16/65+ | Adult & U16/65+ |
|---|---|---|---|
| SOUTH STAND REAR | £545 | £315 | N/A |
| SOUTH STAND FRONT | £490 | £505 | £505 |
| SOUTH WEST CORNER STAND | £605 | £505 | £505 |
| NORTH STAND UPPER | £525/445/380 | £360* | N/A |
| NORTH STAND LOWER | £410/545/500 | £275/205 | N/A |
| JOCK STEIN STAND UPPER | £525/445 | £380* | N/A |
| JOCK STEIN STAND LOWER | £410/445 | £360/320* | N/A |
| LISBON LIONS STAND UPPER | £445/525 | £380/320* | N/A |
| LISBON LIONS STAND LOWER | £410/445/525 | £160 | £430 |

* 65+ CONCESSION ONLY

**Match Ticket information**

| | Adult | U16/65+ |
|---|---|---|
| SOUTH STAND REAR | £23 | £15 |
| SOUTH STAND FRONT | £23 | £15 |
| SOUTH WEST CORNER STAND | £23 | £15 |
| NORTH STAND UPPER | £23 | N/A |
| NORTH STAND LOWER | £23 | £15 |
| JOCK STEIN STAND LOWER | £23 | N/A |
| LISBON LIONS STAND UPPER | £23 | N/A |
| LISBON LIONS STAND LOWER | £23 | £15 |
| RESTRICTED VIEW | £20 | £15 |

* Please Note: Above prices exclude matches versus Rangers

### MILESTONES:
**Year of formation:** 1888
**Most Capped player:** Paul McStay
**No. of Caps:** 76
**Most League points in a season:**
72 (Premier Division – Season 1987/88) (2 Points for a Wir
103 (SPL – Season 2001/02) (3 Points for a Win)
**Most League goals scored by a player in a season:**
Jimmy McGrory (Season 1935/36)
**No. of goals scored:** 50
**Record Attendance:** 92,000 (-v- Rangers – Division 1, 1.1.1
**Record Victory:** 11-0 (-v- Dundee – Division 1, 26.10.1895)
**Record Defeat:** 0-8 (-v- Motherwell – Division 1, 30.4.1937

# SEASON STATS 2004.05

## SEASON STATS 2004.05

*Figure in bold denotes goal scored. Secondary smaller figure in bold denotes number of goals scored. † denotes opponent's own goal.*

| DATE | VENUE | OPPONENTS | ATT | RES | Marshall D. | Varga S. | Valgaeren J. | McNamara J. | Thompson A. | Petrov S. | Agathe D. | Lennon N. | Sutton C. | Hartson J. | McGeady A. | Camara H. | Pearson S. | Sylla M. | Laursen U. | Beattie C. | Balde D. | Wallace R. | Lambert P. | Juninho O. | McManus S. | Hedman M. | Douglas R. | Bellamy C. | Fernandez D. | Henchoz S. | Maloney S. |
|---|---|---|---|---|---|---|---|---|---|---|---|---|---|---|---|---|---|---|---|---|---|---|---|---|---|---|---|---|---|---|---|
| 8-Aug | H | Motherwell | 56,957 | 2-0 | 1 | 2 | 3 | **4** | 5 | 6 | 7 | 8 | **9** | 10 | 11 | 12 | 13 | 14 | | | | | | | | | | | | | |
| 14-Aug | A | Kilmarnock | 10,526 | 4-2 | 1 | 2 | 3 | 4 | **5²** | 6 | 7 | 8 | 9 | **10²** | 11 | 12 | | | 13 | 14 | | | | | | | | | | | |
| 22-Aug | A | Inverness Cal.Th. | 8,788 | 3-1 | 1 | 2 | 3 | | 5 | **6** | 7 | 8 | 9 | **10²** | | | 13 | | 4 | | 11 | 12 | | | | | | | | | |
| 29-Aug | H | Rangers | 58,763 | 1-0 | 1 | 2 | 14 | 3 | **5** | 6 | 7 | 8 | 9 | 10 | | | 13 | | 4 | 12 | | | | 11 | | | | | | | |
| 11-Sep | H | Dundee | 56,840 | 3-0 | 1 | 2 | 3 | 5 | 7 | 6 | | 8 | | 10 | **9²** | 14 | 13 | 12 | 4 | | | | | 11 | | | | | | | |
| 19-Sep | A | Hibernian | 13,573 | 2-2 | 1 | 2 | 3 | 5 | 6 | 12 | 8 | 7 | **10** | | 9 | 13 | | | 4 | | | | | 11 | | | | | | | |
| 25-Sep | H | Dunfermline Ath. | 56,873 | 3-0 | 1 | **2** | 3 | 5 | 6 | | | 8 | | 10 | 14 | **9²** | 7 | 13 | 4 | 12 | | | | 11 | | | | | | | |
| 3-Oct | A | Dundee United | 10,329 | 3-0 | 1 | 2 | 3 | | 6 | 5 | 8 | **7²** | 10 | | 9 | | 12 | | 4 | 13 | 14 | 11 | | | | | | | | | |
| 16-Oct | H | Hearts | 59,242 | 3-0 | 1 | 2 | | 5 | | 6 | 3 | 8 | 4 | **10** | 14 | **9** | 12 | | | 7 | 13 | **11** | | | | | | | | | |
| 24-Oct | A | Livingston | 6,695 | 4-2 | 1 | 2 | | 3 | | **6** | | 8 | **7** | **10** | 9 | 12 | | | 4 | 11 | 14 | 13 | 5 | | | | | | | | |
| 27-Oct | A | Aberdeen | 57,060 | 2-3 | 1 | 2 | | 3 | | 6 | 7 | 8 | 5 | **10²** | 12 | | 13 | | 4 | 11 | | 9 | | | | | | | | | |
| 30-Oct | A | Motherwell | 10,592 | 3-2 | 1 | | 3 | 2 | 5 | 6 | 7 | 8 | | 10 | **11** | | | | 12 | 4 | 13 | | 9 | | | | | | | | |
| 6-Nov | H | Kilmarnock | 57,268 | 2-1 | 1 | 2 | 3 | 4 | **5** | 6 | 7 | 8 | | 10 | **11** | 9 | | | 12 | | 13 | | | | | | | | | | |
| 13-Nov | H | Inverness Cal.Th. | 56,965 | 3-0 | | 2 | 3 | 5 | 6 | | | 8 | 7 | **10²** | 11 | 9 | 13 | | 4 | | | | 12 | | | 1 | | | | | |
| 20-Nov | A | Rangers | 50,043 | 0-2 | | 2 | 3 | 5 | 7 | 6 | | 8 | 11 | 10 | 13 | 9 | 12 | | 4 | | | | | | | 1 | | | | | |
| 28-Nov | A | Dundee | 9,539 | 2-2 | | 3 | 2 | | | 6 | 7 | 8 | | **10** | 11 | 9 | 5 | | 4 | | | | | | | 1 | | | | | |
| 4-Dec | H | Hibernian | 58,399 | 2-1 | | 2 | 3 | 5 | 7 | 6 | | 8 | 9 | **10²** | 11 | 12 | | | 4 | | | | | | | 1 | | | | | |
| 12-Dec | H | Dunfermline Ath. | 7,650 | 2-0 | | 2 | 3 | 5 | 7 | **6** | | 8 | 9 | 10 | 11 | | | | 4 | | | | | | | 1 | | | | | |
| 18-Dec | H | Dundee United | 56,281 | 1-0 | | 2 | 3 | 5 | 7 | 6 | | 8 | 9 | 10 | 11 | | 13 | | 4 | 14 | | 12 | | | | 1 | | | | | |
| 26-Dec | A | Hearts | 16,163 | 2-0 | | 2 | | 5 | 7 | **6** | | 8 | 9 | 10 | **11** | | 3 | | 4 | | | | | | | 1 | | | | | |
| 2-Jan | H | Livingston | 57,564 | 2-1 | | 2 | | 5 | 7 | 6 | | 8 | **9** | **10** | 11 | | 3 | | 4 | | | 12 | | | | 1 | | | | | |
| 16-Jan | A | Aberdeen | 17,051 | 1-0 | | | | 5 | | 6 | | 8 | **7** | 10 | 11 | 12 | 3 | | 4 | 13 | | 9 | 2 | | | 1 | | | | | |
| 22-Jan | H | Motherwell | 58,244 | 2-0 | | 2 | | 5 | 7 | 6 | | 8 | **9** | 10 | 11 | 13 | 3 | | 4 | | | 12 | | | | 1 | | | | | |
| 30-Jan | A | Kilmarnock | 9,723 | 1-0 | | 2 | | 5 | 7 | 6 | | 8 | **9** | 10 | 11 | 12 | 3 | | 4 | | | | | | | 1 | | | | | |
| 20-Feb | H | Rangers | 58,993 | 0-2 | | 2 | | 5 | 7 | 6 | | 8 | 9 | 10 | 12 | | 3 | | 4 | | | | | | | 1 | 11 | | | |
| 2-Mar | H | Dundee | 56,077 | 3-0 | | 2 | | 5 | 7 | **6** | | 8 | 9 | 10 | 12 | | 3 | | **4²** | | | | | | | 1 | 11 | | | |
| 6-Mar | A | Hibernian | 15,787 | 3-1 | | 2 | | 5 | 7 | 6 | | 8 | 9 | **10** | 12 | | 3 | 13 | 4 | | | | | | | 1 | 11 | | 14 | |
| 12-Mar | A | Dunfermline Ath. | 58,593 | 6-0 | | 2 | | 5 | 7 | **6²** | | 8 | | **10²** | 9 | | 3 | **13** | 4 | | | | | | | 1 | 11 | | 11 | 12 |
| 16-Mar | A | Inverness Cal.Th. | 7,047 | 2-0 | | | 5 | 7 | | 6 | | 8 | | 10 | 9 | | 3 | 12 | 4 | | | | | | | 1 | 11 | | 2 | |
| 19-Mar | A | Dundee United | 10,828 | 3-2 | | 2 | | 5 | 7 | 6 | | 8 | | 12 | 10 | 9 | 3 | | 4 | 13 | | | | | | 1 | **11³** | | | 14 |
| 2-Apr | H | Hearts | 59,551 | 0-2 | 1 | 2 | | 5 | 7 | 6 | | 8 | | 10 | 9 | | | | 4 | 12 | | | | | | | 11 | | 3 | 13 |
| 13-Apr | A | Livingston | 7,750 | 4-0 | 1 | **2** | 3 | 5 | 7 | 6 | | 8 | 9 | **10³** | 13 | | | | 4 | | | | | | | | 11 | | 12 | |
| 16-Apr | H | Aberdeen | 59,984 | 3-2 | 1 | **2** | 3 | 5 | 7 | 6 | 12 | 8 | 14 | **10** | 9 | | | | 4 | | | | | | | | 11 | | 13 | |
| 24-Apr | A | Rangers | 49,593 | 2-1 | 1 | 2 | | 5 | 7 | **6** | 3 | 8 | 9 | 10 | | | | | 12 | 4 | 13 | | | | | | 11 | | | |
| 30-Apr | H | Hibernian | 58,289 | 1-3 | 1 | 2 | 3 | 5 | 7 | 6 | | 8 | | 10 | 9 | | | | 12 | 4 | 13 | | | | | | | | 11 | |
| 8-May | H | Aberdeen | 59,516 | 2-0 | | 2 | 5 | 7 | 6 | 9 | 8 | 11 | **10²** | | | | | | 3 | 12 | 4 | | | | | 1 | | | | |
| 15-May | A | Hearts | 15,927 | 2-1 | | 2 | 5 | **7** | 6 | 3 | 8 | 9 | 10 | | | | | | 12 | 4 | | | | | | 1 | 11 | | | |
| 22-May | A | Motherwell | 12,944 | 1-2 | | 2 | 5 | 7 | 6 | 3 | 8 | **9** | 10 | | | | | | 12 | 4 | | | | | | 1 | 11 | | | |
| **TOTAL FULL APPEARANCES** | | | | | 18 | 34 | 18 | 34 | 32 | 37 | 14 | 38 | 25 | 38 | 20 | 12 | 1 | 1 | 12 | | 34 | 4 | | 9 | 2 | 6 | 14 | 12 | | 2 | 1 |
| **TOTAL SUB APPEARANCES** | | | | | | 1 | | | | | | | 2 | | 2 | 7 | 6 | 7 | 5 | 5 | | 11 | 12 | 4 | 5 | | | | 1 | 4 | 1 |
| **TOTAL GOALS SCORED** | | | | | | | 3 | 1 | 7 | 11 | . | | 12 | 25 | 4 | 8 | | | | 4 | 2 | | 1 | | | | 7 | | |

---

## THE BHOYS' 10 YEAR LEAGUE RECORD

| Season | Div | P | W | D | L | F | A | Pts | Pos |
|---|---|---|---|---|---|---|---|---|---|
| 95-96 | P | 36 | 24 | 11 | 1 | 74 | 25 | 83 | 2 |
| 96-97 | P | 36 | 23 | 6 | 7 | 78 | 32 | 75 | 2 |
| 97-98 | P | 36 | 22 | 8 | 6 | 64 | 24 | 74 | 1 |
| 98-99 | SPL | 36 | 21 | 8 | 7 | 84 | 35 | 71 | 2 |
| 99-00 | SPL | 36 | 21 | 6 | 9 | 90 | 38 | 69 | 2 |
| 00-01 | SPL | 38 | 31 | 4 | 3 | 90 | 29 | 97 | 1 |
| 01-02 | SPL | 38 | 33 | 4 | 1 | 94 | 18 | 103 | 1 |
| 02-03 | SPL | 38 | 31 | 4 | 3 | 98 | 26 | 97 | 2 |
| 03-04 | SPL | 38 | 31 | 5 | 2 | 105 | 25 | 98 | 1 |
| 04-05 | SPL | 38 | 30 | 2 | 6 | 85 | 35 | 92 | 2 |

## LEADING GOALSCORERS:

| Season | Div | Goals | Player |
|---|---|---|---|
| 1995-96 | P | 26 | P. Van Hooijdonk |
| 1996-97 | P | 25 | J. Cadete |
| 1997-98 | P | 16 | H. Larsson |
| 1998-99 | SPL | 29 | H. Larsson |
| 1999-00 | SPL | 25 | M. Viduka |
| 2000-01 | SPL | 35 | H. Larsson |
| 2001-02 | SPL | 29 | H. Larsson |
| 2002-03 | SPL | 28 | H. Larsson |
| 2003-04 | SPL | 30 | H. Larsson |
| 2004-05 | SPL | 25 | J.Hartson |

**CELTIC PLAYING KITS SEASON 2005.06** — FIRST KIT | SECOND KIT | THIRD KIT

# DUNDEE UNITED

**DUNDEE UNITED F.C.**
Tannadice Park, Tannadice Street,
Dundee, DD3 7JW
**TELEPHONE NUMBERS**
Ground/Ticket Office (01382) 833166
Commercial Dept (01382) 832202
**FAX** (01382) 889398
**E-MAIL** admin@dundeeunitedfc.co.uk
**WEBSITE** www.dundeeunitedfc.co.uk
**CHAIRMAN** Eddie H. Thompson
**DIRECTORS**
Gilbert B. Haggart, J.D. Scott Carnegie,
John M. Bennett, Derek W. Robertson &
Stephen E. Thompson
**ASSOCIATE DIRECTORS**
Mike Barile, Peter Cabrelli,
Spence Anderson & Bill Campbell
**COMPANY SECRETARY** Spence Anderson
**MANAGER** Gordon Chisholm
**ASSISTANT MANAGER** Billy Dodds
**FIRST TEAM / RESERVE COACH**
Tony Docherty
**GOALKEEPING COACH** Bobby Geddes
**DIRECTOR OF YOUTH DEVELOPMENT /**
**YOUTH CO-ORDINATOR**
Graeme Liveston
**COMMUNITY COACH** Gordon Grady
**YOUTH TEAM COACHES**
U19: David Bowman
U17: Graeme Liveston
U15: Dougie Robertson
U14: Ian Cathro
U13: Gary Bollan & Kevin McDonald
**CHIEF SCOUT** Graeme Liveston
**TEAM CAPTAIN** Derek McInnes
**FOOTBALL SAFETY OFFICERS'**
**ASSOCIATION REPRESENTATIVE/**
**OPERATIONS MANAGER**
David Anderson (01382) 833166
**COMMERCIAL MANAGER**
Bill Campbell (01382) 832202
**LOTTERY MANAGER**
Mike Barile (01382) 833166
**SALES MANAGER** Ronnie Dare
**COMMERCIAL ASSISTANTS**
Paul Reid & Keith Haggart
**CLUB DOCTOR** Dr. Derek J. McCormack
**PHYSIOTHERAPIST** Jeff Clarke
**STADIUM MANAGER** Ron West
**GROUNDSMAN** Albert Dawson
**KIT PERSON** Ian McIntyre
**CLUB SHOP**
The United Shop, Tannadice Street, Dundee
Tel: 01382 833166 Fax: 01382 889398
Open 9.00am to 5.00pm Mon-Sat.
**OFFICIAL SUPPORTERS CLUB**
Chairman – Angus Falconer
(01224) 249858
email: federationdusc@hotmail.com
**SHIRT SPONSOR** Morning Noon & Night
**KIT SUPPLIER** TFG

## LIST OF PLAYERS 2005.06

| SQUAD NO. | PLAYERS SURNAME | FIRST NAME | MIDDLE NAME | DATE OF BIRTH | PLACE OF BIRTH | DATE SIGNED | HEIGHT FT INS | WEIGHT ST LBS | POSITION ON PITCH | PREVIOUS CLUB |
|---|---|---|---|---|---|---|---|---|---|---|
| 29 | Abbot | Stuart | | 21/06/86 | Dundee | 07/07/03 | 5' 7" | 10st 0lb | Def | Dundee United Youths |
| 35 | Andreoni | Marco | | 12/08/88 | Bellshill | 18/08/04 | 5' 10" | 9st 8lb | Mid | Dundee United Youths |
| 5 | Archibald | Alan | Maxwell | 13/12/77 | Glasgow | 04/06/03 | 6' 0" | 11st 7lb | Def | Partick Thistle |
| 8 | Brebner | Grant | Ian | 06/12/77 | Edinburgh | 27/08/04 | 5' 10" | 11st 13lb | Mid | Hibernian |
| 33 | Burnett | Gregg | | 24/05/87 | Bangour | 29/06/04 | 5' 8" | 9st 12lb | Mid | Dundee United Youths |
| 27 | Callaghan | Barry | | 30/11/86 | Glasgow | 07/07/03 | 5' 8" | 9st 7lb | Fwd | Dundee United Youths |
| 26 | Cameron | Greg | | 10/04/88 | Dundee | 29/06/04 | 5' 9" | 10st 9lb | Mid | Dundee United Youths |
| 6 | Canero | Peter | | 18/01/81 | Glasgow | 08/09/05 | 5' 11" | 11st 4lb | Def | Leicester City |
| 14 | Dodds | William | | 05/02/69 | New Cumnock | 01/01/03 | 5' 8" | 12st 2lb | Fwd | Rangers |
| 41 | Donnelly | Jamie | | 25/05/88 | Irvine | 28/06/05 | 6' 1" | 11st 7lb | Def | Dundee United Youths |
| 12 | Duff | Stuart | | 23/01/82 | Aberdeen | 05/07/99 | 5' 11" | 10st 3lb | Mid | Dundee United B.C. |
| 30 | Easton | William | | 17/07/86 | Rutherglen | 07/07/03 | 5' 7" | 9st 5lb | Fwd | Dundee United Youths |
| | Feeney | Robbie | | 08/09/88 | Broxburn | 28/06/05 | 5' 9" | 11st 9lb | Fwd | Dundee United Youths |
| 20 | Fernandez | David | | 20/01/76 | Coruna | 12/08/05 | 5' 9" | 11st 2lb | Mid | Celtic |
| 42 | Flynn | Matthew | | 15/05/88 | Glasgow | 28/06/05 | 5' 9" | 10st 10lb | Mid | Dundee United Youths |
| 28 | Gardiner | Ross | John | 30/12/86 | Bellshill | 07/07/03 | 5' 11" | 9st 10lb | Fwd | Aberdeen |
| 44 | Gibson | John | Mark | 31/01/89 | Glasgow | 28/06/05 | 6' 3" | 12st 12lb | Gk | Dundee United Youths |
| 36 | Goodwillie | David | | 28/03/89 | Stirling | 01/04/05 | 5' 9" | 11st 2lb | Fwd | Dundee United Youths |
| 40 | Gray | David | | 27/06/88 | Glasgow | 28/06/05 | 5' 8" | 10st 5lb | Fwd | Dundee United Youths |
| 18 | Kenneth | Gary | | 21/06/87 | Dundee | 25/02/04 | 6' 4" | 13st 2lb | Def | Dundee United Youths |
| 7 | Kerr | Mark | | 02/03/82 | Bellshill | 02/07/03 | 5' 11.5" | 10st 11lb | Mid | Falkirk |
| 15 | Mair | Lee | | 09/12/80 | Aberdeen | 10/01/05 | 6' 1" | 12st 3lb | Def | Stockport County |
| 34 | McAleenan | Kieran | | 28/10/87 | Bellshill | 30/06/04 | 5' 7" | 9st 12lb | Def | Dundee United Youths |
| 3 | McCracken | David | | 16/10/81 | Glasgow | 30/06/98 | 6' 2" | 11st 6lb | Def | Dundee United B.C. |
| 4 | McInnes | Derek | | 05/07/71 | Paisley | 17/07/03 | 5' 7" | 11st 5lb | Mid | West Bromwich Albion |
| 10 | McIntyre | James | | 24/05/72 | Alexandria | 06/07/01 | 5' 11" | 11st 5lb | Fwd | Reading |
| 31 | McLean | Euan | | 09/01/86 | Kilmarnock | 21/04/05 | 6' 2" | 13st 10lb | Gk | Sunderland |
| 9 | Miller | Lee | | 18/05/83 | Lanark | 07/06/05 | 6' 2.5" | 11st 7lb | Fwd | Bristol City |
| | O'Byrne | Michael | | 07/09/88 | Glasgow | 28/06/05 | 6' 0" | 11st 7lb | Def | Dundee United Youths |
| 43 | O'Hara | Ryan | | 24/07/89 | Swindon | 11/08/05 | 5' 9" | 9st 8lb | Fwd | Swindon Town |
| 23 | Ritchie | Paul | Simon | 21/08/75 | Kirkcaldy | 09/08/04 | 5' 11" | 12st 0lb | Def | Walsall |
| 25 | Robertson | David | | 23/09/86 | Bangour | 07/07/03 | 5' 10" | 10st 0lb | Mid | Dundee United Youths |
| 11 | Robson | Barry | | 07/11/78 | Aberdeen | 03/01/03 | 5' 11" | 12st 0lb | Mid/Fwd | Inverness Cal. Th. |
| 39 | Russell | William | | 28/02/89 | Bellshill | 28/06/05 | 5' 10" | 10st 0lb | Mid | Dundee United Youths |
| 17 | Samson | Craig | Ian | 01/04/84 | Irvine | 29/07/05 | 6' 2" | 12st 7lb | Gk | Kilmarnock |
| 21 | Samuel | Collin | | 27/08/81 | Manzinilla | 25/07/03 | 5' 9" | 12st 7lb | Mid | Falkirk |
| 1 | Stillie | Derek | | 03/12/73 | Cumnock | 08/07/05 | 6' 0" | 12st 6lb | Gk | Dunfermline Athletic |
| 2 | Wilson | Mark | | 05/06/84 | Glasgow | 02/06/00 | 5' 11" | 11st 13lb | Mid | Dundee United 'S' Form |

## TICKET INFORMATION

**Season Ticket Information**

**Top Tiers**
| | | |
|---|---|---|
| GEORGE FOX PRIME | Adult £380 | Juv/OAP £200 |
| GEORGE FOX PREMIER | Adult £350 | Juv/OAP £200 |
| EAST STAND | Adult £350 | Juv/OAP £200 |

**Lower Tiers**
| | Adult | OAP | U18 | U12 | U8 | Student |
|---|---|---|---|---|---|---|
| GEORGE FOX PRIME | £310 | £160 | £160 | £140 | £120 | £140 |
| GEORGE FOX PREMIER | £310 | £160 | £160 | £140 | £120 | N/A |
| EAST STAND | £310 | £160 | £160 | £140 | £120 | N/A |

**Match Ticket Information**
| | Adults A* | Adults B | Conc. A* | Conc. B |
|---|---|---|---|---|
| **Game Grade** | | | | |
| GEORGE FOX TOP PRIME | £25 | £23 | £13 | £12 |
| GEORGE FOX TOP PREMIER | £23 | £21 | £12 | £11 |
| GEORGE FOX LOWER | £23 | £21 | £12 | £9 |
| EAST TOP | £23 | £21 | £12 | £11 |
| EAST LOWER | £23 | £19 | £12 | £9 |
| JERRY KERR STAND (AWAY) | £23 | £21 | £12 | £11 |
| WEST STAND | £21 | £19 | £11 | £9 |

**MILESTONES:**
**Year of formation:** 1923 (1909 as Dundee Hibs)
**Most Capped player:** Maurice Malpas
**No. of Caps:** 55
**Most League points in a season:**
60 (Premier Division – Season 1986/87) (2 Points for a Win)
67 (First Division – Season 1995/96) (3 Points for a Win)
**Most League goals scored by a player in a season:**
John Coyle (Season 1955/56)
**No. of goals scored:** 41
**Record Attendance:** 28,000 (-v- Barcelona – 16.11.1966)
**Record Victory:** 14-0 (-v- Nithsdale Wanderers – Scottish Cup, 17...
**Record Defeat:** 1-12 (-v- Motherwell – Division 2, 23.1.19...

\* Category A: Celtic, Rangers & possibly selected Cup Ties. Category B: All other SPL clubs

## SEASON STATS 2004.05

| DATE | VENUE | OPPONENTS | ATT | RES | Bullock A. | McCracken D. | Archibald A. | Innes C. | Wilson M. | McInnes D. | Kerr M. | Robson B. | Dodds W. | Grady J. | Scotland J. | Samuel C. | McIntyre J. | Duff S. | Ritchie P. | McLaren A. | Brebner G. | Hirschfeld L. | Jarvie P. | Kerkar K. | Robertson D. | Cameron G. | Crawford S. | Mair L. | Colgan N. | Callaghan B. | Kenneth G. |
|---|---|---|---|---|---|---|---|---|---|---|---|---|---|---|---|---|---|---|---|---|---|---|---|---|---|---|---|---|---|---|---|
| 7-Aug | A | Dunfermline Ath. | 6,474 | 1-1 | 1 | 2 | 3 | 4 | 5 | 6 | 7 | 8 | 9 | 10 | 11 | 12 | **13** | 14 | | | | | | | | | | | | | |
| 15-Aug | H | Dundee | 11,118 | 1-2 | 1 | 2 | **3** | 4 | 5 | 6 | 7 | 8 | 9 | 10 | 12 | 14 | 11 | 13 | | | | | | | | | | | | | |
| 21-Aug | A | Livingston | 3,159 | 1-1 | 1 | 12 | 3 | 4 | 5 | 14 | 7 | 8 | **9** | | 11 | | 10 | 6 | 2 | 13 | | | | | | | | | | | |
| 28-Aug | H | Inverness Cal.Th. | 6,017 | 2-1 | 1 | 2 | 3 | **4** | 5 | | 7 | 8 | 9 | 12 | 11 | | 10 | | 13 | 6 | | | | | | | | | | | |
| 11-Sep | H | Aberdeen | 11,595 | 1-1 | 1 | 2 | 3 | 4 | **5** | 12 | 7 | 8 | 9 | 11 | 14 | | 10 | | 13 | 6 | | | | | | | | | | | |
| 18-Sep | A | Motherwell | 5,091 | 2-4 | 1 | 2 | 3 | 4 | 5 | 6 | 7 | 8 | **11** | 13 | | | 10 | | 12 | 9 | | | | | | | | | | | |
| 25-Sep | A | Kilmarnock | 4,711 | 2-5 | | 2 | 3 | 4 | 5 | 6 | 12 | 8 | **14** | 13 | | | 10 | 7 | 11 | 9 | 1 | | | | | | | | | | |
| 3-Oct | H | Celtic | 10,329 | 0-3 | | 2 | 3 | 4 | 5 | 12 | 13 | 8 | 9 | 11 | | | 10 | 7 | 6 | | 1 | 14 | | | | | | | | | |
| 16-Oct | A | Hibernian | 9,850 | 0-2 | | 3 | 4 | 5 | 6 | 7 | 8 | | 11 | 12 | | | 10 | 9 | 2 | | 1 | 14 | 13 | | | | | | | | |
| 24-Oct | A | Rangers | 46,796 | 1-1 | | 2 | 3 | 4 | 5 | 6 | | 8 | **9** | 11 | | | 10 | 12 | 7 | | 1 | 13 | | | | | | | | | |
| 27-Oct | H | Hearts | 5,723 | 1-1 | | 2 | 3 | 4 | **5** | 6 | | 8 | 9 | 11 | 12 | | 10 | 13 | 7 | | 1 | 14 | | | | | | | | | |
| 30-Oct | H | Dunfermline Ath. | 6,297 | 1-2 | | 2 | 3 | 4 | **5** | 6 | | 8 | 12 | 13 | 11 | | | 7 | 1 | 9 | | | | | | | | | | | |
| 6-Nov | A | Dundee | 9,845 | 0-1 | | 12 | 3 | 4 | 5 | 6 | | 8 | 14 | 11 | 10 | | 13 | 2 | 7 | 1 | 9 | | | | | | | | | | |
| 13-Nov | H | Livingston | 5,507 | 1-0 | **4** | 3 | | | 6 | 7 | 8 | 14 | 11 | 12 | | | 10 | 5 | 2 | 13 | 1 | 9 | | | | | | | | | |
| 23-Nov | A | Inverness Cal.Th. | 1,125 | 1-1 | 4 | 3 | | 5 | 6 | | 8 | 9 | 14 | 11 | 13 | **10** | | 2 | 7 | 1 | 12 | | | | | | | | | | |
| 27-Nov | A | Aberdeen | 12,038 | 0-1 | 4 | 3 | | 5 | 6 | | | 11 | 13 | 14 | 10 | 7 | 2 | 9 | | 1 | 12 | | | | | | | | | | |
| 4-Dec | H | Motherwell | 5,394 | 0-1 | 4 | 3 | | 5 | | | 8 | 14 | 11 | 13 | 12 | 10 | 6 | 2 | 7 | 1 | 9 | | | | | | | | | | |
| 11-Dec | H | Kilmarnock | 5,097 | 3-0 | 1 | | 3 | 4 | 5 | 6 | 9 | **8** | 14 | | 11 | 12 | **10²** | 2 | 7 | | | | | | | 13 | | | | | |
| 18-Dec | A | Celtic | 56,281 | 0-1 | 1 | | 3 | 4 | 5 | 6 | 9 | 8 | 13 | 14 | 12 | 11 | 10 | 2 | 7 | | | | | | | | | | | |
| 27-Dec | H | Hibernian | 10,152 | 1-4 | 1 | 12 | 3 | 4 | 5 | 6 | 9 | 8 | | | **11** | 13 | 10 | 2 | 7 | | | | | | | | | | | |
| 1-Jan | H | Rangers | 10,461 | 1-1 | 1 | **4** | 3 | | 5 | 6 | 9 | 8 | | | 11 | | 10 | 2 | 7 | | | | | | | | | | | |
| 15-Jan | A | Hearts | 10,305 | 2-3 | 1 | 4 | **3** | | 5 | 6 | 9 | **8** | | | 13 | | 10 | 2 | 7 | | | | | | | | 11 | 12 | | | |
| 22-Jan | A | Dunfermline Ath. | 6,578 | 1-1 | 1 | 12 | 3 | | 5 | 6 | 9 | 8 | | | 13 | | 10 | 2 | 7 | | | | | | | | **11** | 4 | | | |
| 29-Jan | H | Dundee | 12,719 | 2-2 | | 4 | 3 | | 5 | 6 | 8 | | 13 | 9 | 14 | | **10** | 7 | 2 | | 12 | | | | | | 11 | 1 | | | |
| 12-Feb | A | Livingston | 4,658 | 2-0 | 1 | | 3 | | 5 | | 7 | | 8 | **9** | | | 10 | 4 | 12 | 6 | | | | | | | **11** | 2 | | | |
| 19-Feb | H | Inverness Cal.Th. | 6,110 | † 1-1 | 1 | | 3 | | 5 | | 7 | 12 | 8 | 9 | 13 | | 10 | 6 | 2 | | 14 | | | | | | 11 | 4 | | | |
| 2-Mar | H | Aberdeen | 6,688 | 1-2 | 1 | | 3 | | 5 | | 7 | 8 | 12 | 9 | **10** | 13 | | 4 | 2 | | 6 | | | | | | 11 | | 14 | | |
| 5-Mar | A | Motherwell | 5,110 | 0-2 | 1 | | 3 | | 5 | 6 | | 8 | 14 | 9 | 10 | 13 | | 4 | | | 6 | | | | | | 11 | | | 12 | |
| 12-Mar | A | Kilmarnock | 4,353 | 0-3 | 1 | | 3 | | 5 | 6 | | 12 | 13 | 9 | 14 | | 10 | 8 | 2 | | 7 | | | | | | 11 | | 4 | | |
| 19-Mar | H | Celtic | 10,828 | 2-3 | 1 | | 3 | | 5 | 12 | 6 | **9** | | 13 | 14 | | 10 | 8 | 2 | | 7 | | | | | | 11 | | 4 | | |
| 2-Apr | A | Hibernian | 11,058 | 2-3 | 1 | | 3 | | 5 | | 6 | 8 | | 9 | **13** | | 10 | 7 | 2 | | | | | | | 12 | 11 | | 4 | | |
| 12-Apr | A | Rangers | 49,302 | 1-0 | 1 | | 3 | | 5 | | 6 | 9 | | 13 | | 11 | 10 | **8** | 2 | | 7 | | | | | | 12 | | 4 | | |
| 16-Apr | H | Hearts | 7,704 | 2-1 | 1 | | 3 | | 5 | | 6 | **9** | | | 11 | 13 | 10 | 8 | 2 | | **7** | | | | | | 12 | | 4 | | |
| 23-Apr | H | Livingston | 7,687 | 1-1 | 1 | | 3 | | 5 | | 6 | 9 | | | 13 | 12 | 10 | 8 | 2 | | | | | | | | **11** | | 4 | | |
| 30-Apr | A | Dundee | 11,263 | 2-1 | 1 | | 3 | | 5 | 13 | 6 | **9** | | 14 | 12 | | 10 | 8 | 2 | | 7 | | | | | | 11 | | 4 | | |
| 7-May | H | Kilmarnock | 6,576 | 1-1 | 1 | | 3 | | 5 | | 6 | **9** | | | 12 | **10** | 8 | 2 | 7 | | | | | | | | 11 | | 4 | | |
| 15-May | H | Dunfermline Ath. | 10,763 | 0-1 | 1 | 13 | 3 | | 5 | 12 | 6 | 9 | | | 10 | | 8 | 2 | 7 | | | | | | | | 11 | | 4 | | |
| 21-May | A | Inverness Cal.Th. | 5,479 | 1-0 | 1 | 2 | 3 | | 5 | 6 | 8 | **9** | | 14 | 12 | | 10 | 13 | 7 | | | | | | | | 11 | | 4 | | |
| **TOTAL FULL APPEARANCES** | | | | | 26 | 19 | 38 | 16 | 37 | 21 | 28 | 34 | 11 | 19 | 11 | 5 | 32 | 21 | 24 | 1 | 31 | 1 | 10 | 4 | | 15 | 3 | 1 | 10 | | |
| **TOTAL SUB APPEARANCES** | | | | | | 5 | | | | 6 | 2 | 2 | 10 | 10 | 18 | 13 | 3 | 4 | | | 5 | 3 | | | 6 | 1 | 2 | 2 | 1 | 1 | 1 |
| **TOTAL GOALS SCORED** | | | | | | 2 | 3 | 1 | 3 | | | | 7 | 2 | 2 | 3 | | 11 | 2 | | | 1 | | | | | 3 | | | |

*...are in bold denotes goal scored. Secondary smaller figure in bold denotes number of goals scored. † denotes opponent's own goal.*

## THE TERRORS' 10 YEAR LEAGUE RECORD

| Season | Div | P | W | D | L | F | A | Pts | Pos |
|---|---|---|---|---|---|---|---|---|---|
| 95-96 | F | 36 | 19 | 10 | 7 | 73 | 37 | 67 | 2 |
| 96-97 | P | 36 | 17 | 9 | 10 | 46 | 33 | 60 | 3 |
| 97-98 | P | 36 | 8 | 13 | 15 | 43 | 51 | 37 | 7 |
| 98-99 | SPL | 36 | 8 | 10 | 18 | 37 | 48 | 34 | 9 |
| 99-00 | SPL | 36 | 11 | 6 | 19 | 34 | 57 | 39 | 8 |
| 00-01 | SPL | 38 | 9 | 8 | 21 | 38 | 63 | 35 | 11 |
| 01-02 | SPL | 38 | 12 | 10 | 16 | 38 | 59 | 46 | 8 |
| 02-03 | SPL | 38 | 7 | 11 | 20 | 35 | 68 | 32 | 11 |
| 03-04 | SPL | 38 | 13 | 10 | 15 | 47 | 60 | 49 | 5 |
| 04-05 | SPL | 38 | 8 | 12 | 18 | 41 | 59 | 36 | 9 |

## LEADING GOALSCORERS:

| Season | Div | Goals | Player |
|---|---|---|---|
| 1995-96 | F | 17 | C. Brewster, G. McSwegan |
| 1996-97 | P | 12 | K. Olofsson |
| 1997-98 | P | 18 | K. Olofsson |
| 1998-99 | SPL | 17 | W. Dodds |
| 1999-00 | SPL | 9 | W. Dodds |
| 2000-01 | SPL | 6 | D. Lilley |
| 2001-02 | SPL | 6 | D. Lilley, J. McIntyre, S. Thompson |
| 2002-03 | SPL | 9 | J. McIntyre |
| 2003-04 | SPL | 10 | J. McIntyre, W. Dodds |
| 2004-05 | SPL | 11 | J. McIntyre |

### DUNDEE UNITED PLAYING KITS SEASON 2005.06

FIRST KIT | SECOND KIT | THIRD KIT

# DUNFERMLINE ATHLETIC

**DUNFERMLINE ATHLETIC F.C.**
East End Park, Halbeath Road,
Dunfermline, Fife, KY12 7RB
**TELEPHONE NUMBERS**
Ground/Secretary (01383) 724295
Ticket Office 0870 300 1201
Ticket Office Fax (01383) 626452
Conference & Banqueting (01383) 741147
Conference & Banqueting Fax (01383) 741411
Pars Superstore (01383) 626737
Pars Personal Health (01383) 623655
Sports Bar (01383) 745514
**FAX** (01383) 723468
**E-MAIL** pars@dafc.co.uk
**WEBSITE** www.dafc.co.uk
**CHAIRMAN** John W. Yorkston
**DIRECTORS** Gavin G. Masterton, C.B.E., F.I.B. (Scot),
John Meiklem, W. Brian Robertson, W.S.,
Francis M. McConnell, SSC.
Edward Smyth & Rodney Shearer
**GENERAL MANAGER** Robin Ozog
**CLUB SECRETARY** Murray Falconer
**DIRECTOR OF FOOTBALL / MANAGER**
Jim Leishman
**FIRST TEAM COACH / RESERVE COACH**
Craig Robertson
**GOALKEEPING COACH** Scott Y. Thomson
**COACHING STAFF** Scott Y. Thomson,
Hamish French & Craig Robertson
**DIRECTOR OF YOUTH DEVELOPMENT**
Craig Robertson
**COMMUNITY COACH / YOUTH
DEVELOPMENT COACH** Hamish French
**YOUTH COACHES**
U19: David Hunter; U17: Hamish French.
U15: Andrew Hutton & Billy Bennett.
U14: Mark O'Donnell.
U13: Frank McAvoy & Derek Nicholson.
U12: Chris Candlish & Gordon Arthur
**CHIEF SCOUT** Alan Morrison
**TEAM CAPTAIN** Scott M. Thomson
**OFFICE ADMINISTRATOR**
Shirley Johnston (01383) 724295
**FOOTBALL SAFETY OFFICERS'
ASSOCIATION REPRESENTATIVE /
STADIUM MANAGER**
David Dickson (01383) 724295
**COMMERCIAL DIRECTOR** Mrs. Karen Brown
**LOTTERY MANAGER** Murray Falconer
**MEDIA LIAISON OFFICER** Stuart Arnott
**MATCHDAY PROGRAMME EDITOR**
Duncan Simpson
**CLUB DOCTOR** Dr. Gerry D. Gillespie
**PHYSIOTHERAPIST** Paul Atkinson (First Team)
**GROUNDSMAN** John Wilson
**KIT PERSON** Andrew Hutton
**FINANCE DIRECTOR** Bill Hodgins
**CONFERENCE & BANQUETING** Robin Ozog
**MARKETING & PR** Tracey Martin
**BUSINESS DEVELOPMENT MANAGER**
Kirsty Brown (01383) 724295
**CLUB SHOP MANAGER** Louise Paton
Club Shop situated at Kingsgate Shopping
Centre. Open 9.00 am – 5.00 pm Mon - Sat
(01383) 626737
Also sitiated at ground - Open matchdays only.
**OFFICIAL SUPPORTERS CLUB**
c/o Mrs. Joan Malcolm, Secretary,
Dunfermline Athletic Supporters Club,
13 South Knowe, Crossgates, KY4 8AW
(01383) 611793
Fod Arms Travel Club –
Linda Cummings (01383) 729909
Lothian68 – John (07719) 564920
Millers Bar – John Angus (01383) 723605
**SHIRT SPONSOR** The Purvis Group
**KIT SUPPLIER** TFG

## LIST OF PLAYERS 2005.06

| SQUAD NO. | PLAYERS SURNAME | FIRST NAME | MIDDLE NAME | DATE OF BIRTH | PLACE OF BIRTH | DATE SIGNED | HEIGHT FT INS | WEIGHT ST LBS | POSITION ON PITCH | PREVIOUS CLUB |
|---|---|---|---|---|---|---|---|---|---|---|
| 33 | Anderson | Christopher | Nicol | 03/08/87 | Broxburn | 05/07/04 | 5' 10" | 11st 5lb | Fwd | Dunfermline Athletic Youths |
| 35 | Armour | David | | 28/08/87 | Paisley | 20/05/04 | 5' 9" | 9st 3lb | Fwd | Dunfermline Athletic Youths |
| 9 | Burchill | Mark | James | 18/08/80 | Broxburn | 06/07/05 | 5' 8" | 10st 7lb | Fwd | Heart of Midlothian |
| 25 | Campbell | Iain | | 28/06/85 | Kirkcaldy | 14/08/02 | 5' 9" | 10st 12lb | Def | Dunfermline Athletic Youths |
| 14 | Donnelly | Simon | Thomas | 01/12/74 | Glasgow | 23/07/04 | 5' 9" | 11st 6lb | Mid/Fwd | St. Johnstone |
| 32 | Dunn | John | | 19/04/87 | Edinburgh | 05/07/05 | 5' 10" | 11st 4lb | Fwd | Dunfermline Athletic Youths |
| 43 | Fenwick | Neil | Peter | 23/06/88 | Edinburgh | 24/06/05 | 6' 0" | 13st 2lb | Mid | Dunfermline Athletic Youths |
| 20 | Halliwell | Bryn | Steven | 01/10/80 | Epsom | 29/06/05 | 6' 1" | 12st 10lb | Gk | Clyde |
| 48 | Halpin | Patrick | | 31/01/88 | Dunfermline | 31/08/05 | 5' 9" | 11st 1lb | Mid | Hibernian |
| 21 | Horsted | Liam | Anthony | 28/10/85 | Portsmouth | 26/08/05 | 6' 0.5" | 12st 6lb | Mid | Portsmouth |
| 44 | Howie | Derek | Greg | 15/03/89 | Glasgow | 10/06/05 | 5' 9" | 11st 3lb | Def | Rangers Youths |
| 16 | Hunt | Noel | | 26/12/82 | Waterford | 28/01/03 | 5' 8" | 11st 5lb | Fwd | Shamrock Rovers |
| 31 | Kay | Clark | Lewis | 06/08/88 | Dunfermline | 05/07/04 | 5' 11" | 10st 1lb | Def | Dunfermline Athletic Youths |
| 19 | Labonte | Aaron | | 27/11/83 | Middlesbrough | 14/07/03 | 5' 10.5" | 10st 10lb | Def | Newcastle United |
| 10 | Makel | Lee | Robert | 11/01/73 | Sunderland | 05/01/05 | 5' 10" | 11st 4lb | Mid | Plymouth Argyle |
| 8 | Mason | Gary | | 15/10/79 | Edinburgh | 22/12/00 | 5' 8.5" | 10st 12lb | Mid | Manchester City |
| 5 | McCunnie | Jamie | | 15/04/83 | Bellshill | 31/08/05 | 5' 10" | 11st 0lb | Mid | Millwall |
| 42 | McDonough | Alan | Douglas | 25/02/88 | Dunfermline | 14/06/05 | 5' 10" | 10st 10lb | Fwd | Dunfermline Athletic Youths |
| 1 | McGregor | Allan | James | 31/01/82 | Edinburgh | 31/08/05 | 6' 3" | 13st 10lb | Gk | Rangers |
| 12 | Morrison | Scott | Alexander | 23/05/84 | Aberdeen | 03/06/05 | 5' 9" | 11st 11lb | Def | Aberdeen |
| 46 | Muhsin | Sean | | 31/07/88 | Dundee | 29/07/05 | 5' 8" | 11st 0lb | Mid | Hibernian Youths |
| 41 | Muir | David | | 06/03/88 | Kirkcaldy | 08/06/05 | 6' 2" | 11st 5lb | Mid | Dunfermline Athletic Youths |
| 30 | Murdoch | Sean | | 31/07/86 | Edinburgh | 12/08/03 | 6' 2" | 11st 10lb | Gk | Hearts Youths |
| 36 | Ogg | Dean | | 07/09/87 | Dunfermline | 20/05/04 | 5' 8" | 10st 2lb | Fwd | Dunfermline Athletic Youths |
| 40 | Paterson | Greg | | 16/09/89 | Dunfermline | 30/06/05 | 6' 4" | 10st 8lb | Gk | Dunfermline Athletic Youths |
| 37 | Phinn | Nicholas | | 14/10/88 | Glasgow | 26/08/05 | 5' 8" | 10st 0lb | Mid | Dunfermline Athletic Youths |
| 23 | Ross | Greg | | 02/05/87 | Edinburgh | 20/05/04 | 6' 1" | 11st 0lb | Def | Dunfermline Athletic Youths |
| 45 | Shaw | Peter | | 03/09/87 | Stirling | 26/07/05 | 6' 2" | 13st 8lb | Gk | St. Johnstone |
| 2 | Shields | Greg | | 21/08/76 | Falkirk | 23/01/04 | 5' 9" | 10st 10lb | Def | Kilmarnock |
| 38 | Smith | Calum | | 11/03/88 | Dunfermline | 08/06/05 | 6' 1" | 10st 2lb | Fwd | Dunfermline Athletic Youths |
| | Tarachulski | Bartosz | | 14/05/75 | Poland | 02/08/05 | 6' 3" | 13st 6lb | Fwd | Yeovil Town |
| 6 | Thomson | Scott | Munro | 29/01/72 | Aberdeen | 06/07/98 | 5' 10" | 11st 4lb | Def/Mid | Raith Rovers |
| 18 | Tod | Andrew | | 04/11/71 | Dunfermline | 08/08/03 | 6' 3" | 12st 10lb | Def | Bradford City |
| 34 | Vinter | Steven | | 05/02/87 | Edinburgh | 20/05/04 | 6' 2" | 10st 6lb | Def | Dunfermline Athletic Youths |
| 39 | Williamson | Iain | James | 12/01/88 | Edinburgh | 29/06/05 | 6' 1" | 11st 3lb | Mid | Dunfermline Athletic Youths |
| 22 | Wilson | Craig | | 28/05/86 | Dunfermline | 06/08/03 | 5' 8" | 10st 2lb | Fwd | Dunfermline Athletic Youths |
| 3 | Wilson | Scott | | 19/03/77 | Edinburgh | 08/08/05 | 6' 2" | 12st 8lb | Def | Rangers |
| 4 | Young | Darren | | 13/10/78 | Glasgow | 10/07/03 | 5' 9" | 11st 11lb | Mid | Aberdeen |
| 11 | Young | Derek | | 27/05/80 | Glasgow | 10/07/03 | 5' 8.5" | 10st 10lb | Mid | Aberdeen |
| | Zambernardi | Yannick | | 03/09/77 | Ajaccio | 30/08/05 | 6' 2" | 12st 4lb | Def | Louviere |

## TICKET INFORMATION

**Season Ticket Information**

| | Adult | 18-21 | Concs. | U18 | U12 |
|---|---|---|---|---|---|
| MAIN STAND | £320 | £185 | £170 | £90 | £55 |
| | Adult | 18-21 | Concs. | U18 | U12 |
| ALL OTHER AREAS | £265 | £150 | £135 | £75 | £40 |
| | Adult | 1 child | 2 child | 3 child | 4 child | OAP |
| FAMILY TICKET | £255 | £35 | £30 | £25 | £10 | £125 |

**Match Ticket Information**

| | Adults | Conc. | U12 |
|---|---|---|---|
| **Category A\*** | | | |
| MAIN STAND | £22 | £15 | £10 |
| ALL OTHER AREAS | £20 | £15 | £10 |
| AWAY STANDS | £22 | £15 | £15 |
| **Category B\*** | | | |
| MAIN STAND | £20 | £14 | £10 |
| ALL OTHER AREAS | £16 | £12 | £8 |
| AWAY STANDS | £19 | £12 | £12 |

## MILESTONES:

**Year of formation:** 1885
**Most Capped player:** Istvan Kozma
**No. of Caps:** Hungary 29 (13 whilst with Dunfermline Athl
**Most League points in a season:**
65 (First Division – Season 1993/94) (2 Points for a Win)
71 (First Division – Seasons 1995/96 and 1999/2000) (3 Points for
**Most League goals scored by a player in a season:**
Bobby Skinner (Season 1925/26)
**No. of goals scored:** 53
**Record Attendance:** 27,816 (-v- Celtic – 30.4.1968)
**Record Victory:** 11-2 (-v- Stenhousemuir – Division 2, 27.9
**Record Defeat:** 0-10 (-v- Dundee – Division 2, 22.3.1947)

* Category A: Celtic& Rangers. Category B: All other SPL clubs

# SEASON STATS 2004.05

## SEASON STATS 2004.05

| DATE | VENUE | OPPONENTS | ATT | RES | Stillie D. | Shields G. | Wilson S. | Skerla A. | Byrne R. | Thomson S.M. | Nicholson B. | Mason G. | Dempsey G. | Hunt N. | Tod A. | Young Darren | Brewster C. | Mehmet B. | Donnelly S. | Young Derek | Labonte A. | Butler T. | Ross G. | Bradley S. | Scullion P. | Campbell I. | Makel L. | Christiansen J. | Hristov G. | Wilson C. | McKeown C. | McGlinchey S. |
|---|---|---|---|---|---|---|---|---|---|---|---|---|---|---|---|---|---|---|---|---|---|---|---|---|---|---|---|---|---|---|---|
| 7-Aug | H | Dundee United | 6,474 | 1-1 | 1 | 2 | 3 | 4 | 5 | 6 | 7 | 8 | | 9 | 10 | **11** | 12 | 13 | 14 | | | | | | | | | | | | | |
| 15-Aug | A | Inverness Cal.Th. | 2,583 | 0-2 | 1 | 2 | 3 | 4 | 5 | 6 | 7 | 8 | | 9 | 10 | | 12 | 11 | 14 | 13 | | | | | | | | | | | | |
| 21-Aug | H | Aberdeen | 8,533 | 0-1 | 1 | 2 | 3 | 4 | | 5 | | 8 | 7 | 10 | 14 | 6 | 11 | 13 | 9 | 12 | | | | | | | | | | | | |
| 29-Aug | A | Kilmarnock | 4,854 | 0-1 | 1 | 2 | | 4 | 3 | 5 | | 8 | 7 | 10 | 14 | 6 | 11 | 9 | | 12 | 13 | | | | | | | | | | | |
| 11-Sep | H | Motherwell | 4,438 | 1-1 | 1 | 2 | 3 | 4 | | 5 | 7 | 8 | 9 | 12 | | 6 | **11** | 10 | 13 | | | | | | | | | | | | | |
| 19-Sep | H | Hearts | 5,883 | 1-0 | 1 | 2 | 3 | 4 | | 5 | **7** | 8 | 9 | | | 6 | 11 | 10 | | | 12 | | | | | | | | | | | |
| 25-Sep | A | Celtic | 56,873 | 0-3 | 1 | 2 | 3 | 4 | | 5 | 7 | 8 | 9 | 13 | | 6 | 11 | 10 | | 12 | 14 | | | | | | | | | | | |
| 2-Oct | H | Hibernian | 7,295 | 1-1 | 1 | 2 | 3 | 4 | | 5 | 7 | | 8 | | 13 | 6 | 11 | 10 | **14** | 12 | 9 | | | | | | | | | | | |
| 16-Oct | A | Livingston | 2,815 | 0-2 | 1 | 2 | 3 | 4 | | 5 | 7 | 12 | 8 | | 14 | 6 | 11 | | 10 | 13 | 9 | | | | | | | | | | | |
| 23-Oct | A | Dundee | 5,456 | 2-1 | 1 | 2 | 3 | 4 | | **5** | 7 | 6 | | | 13 | 14 | 11 | 12 | 10 | **9** | 8 | | | | | | | | | | | |
| 27-Oct | H | Rangers | 8,558 | 1-2 | 1 | 2 | 3 | 4 | | 5 | 7 | 6 | | | 13 | | **11** | 12 | 10 | 9 | 8 | | | | | | | | | | | |
| 30-Oct | A | Dundee United | 6,297 | 2-1 | 1 | | 3 | 4 | 2 | 5 | 7 | 8 | | | 9 | 6 | 11 | 12 | 10 | | 13 | | | | | | | | | | | |
| 6-Nov | H | Inverness Cal.Th. | 4,921 | 1-1 | 1 | 2 | 3 | 4 | 12 | 5 | 7 | 8 | | | 9 | 6 | 11 | 10 | 14 | 13 | | | | | | | | | | | | |
| 13-Nov | A | Aberdeen | 10,398 | 1-2 | 1 | | 3 | | 4 | 5 | 7 | 8 | | | 9 | | 11 | **10** | | 2 | 6 | | | | | | | | | | | |
| 20-Nov | H | Kilmarnock | 4,344 | 4-1 | 1 | | 3 | | | 5 | 7 | 8 | | | 6 | **11** | **9** | 10 | | 2 | 4 | 12 | | | | | | | | | | |
| 27-Nov | A | Motherwell | 5,084 | 1-2 | 1 | 2 | 3 | | | 5 | 7 | 8 | | **11** | | 6 | 9 | 10 | | 4 | 12 | | | | | | | | | | | |
| 4-Dec | A | Hearts | 10,084 | 0-3 | 1 | | 3 | | | 5 | 7 | 8 | 4 | 12 | 11 | 6 | | | | 9 | 2 | 10 | | | | | | | | | | |
| 12-Dec | H | Celtic | 7,650 | 0-2 | 1 | | 3 | | | 5 | 7 | 8 | 4 | 12 | 11 | 6 | | 9 | 10 | | 2 | 13 | | | | | | | | | | |
| 18-Dec | A | Hibernian | 9,859 | 1-2 | 1 | | 3 | 4 | | 5 | 7 | 8 | 9 | 10 | **11** | 6 | | | | 14 | 2 | | | 12 | 13 | | | | | | | |
| 27-Dec | H | Livingston | 5,092 | 0-0 | 1 | | 3 | 4 | | | 7 | 8 | 9 | 13 | 11 | 6 | | | 10 | | 5 | 12 | 2 | | | | | | | | | |
| 1-Jan | H | Dundee | 4,426 | †3-1 | 1 | | 3 | 4 | | | 8 | 13 | 12 | **11²** | 6 | | | | 10 | | 9 | 14 | 2 | | | | | | | | | |
| 15-Jan | A | Rangers | 48,055 | 0-3 | 1 | | | 4 | | | 5 | 7 | 8 | 9 | 12 | 11 | 6 | | | | | 2 | | | 3 | 10 | | | | | | |
| 22-Jan | H | Dundee United | 6,578 | 1-1 | 1 | | | 4 | | 5 | 7 | 8 | 6 | 10 | **11** | | 12 | | | | | 2 | | | 3 | **9** | | | | | | |
| 29-Jan | A | Inverness Cal.Th. | 5,449 | 0-2 | 1 | | | 4 | | 5 | 7 | 8 | 6 | 10 | 11 | 14 | 13 | | | | | 2 | | 12 | 3 | 9 | | | | | | |
| 12-Feb | H | Aberdeen | 5,609 | 2-1 | 1 | | | | | 5 | 7 | 8 | | 10 | 4 | 14 | **11** | **12** | | | | 2 | | | 3 | 6 | 9 | 13 | | | | |
| 19-Feb | A | Kilmarnock | 4,701 | 1-2 | 1 | | | 4 | | 5 | 7 | 8 | | 10 | 3 | 12 | 11 | 13 | | | | 2 | | | | 6 | **9** | 14 | | | | |
| 2-Mar | H | Motherwell | 3,427 | 0-0 | 1 | | 3 | | | 5 | | 8 | | | 4 | 6 | 13 | 10 | 14 | | | 2 | | | 12 | 7 | 9 | 11 | | | | |
| 5-Mar | H | Hearts | 5,935 | 1-1 | 1 | | **3** | | | | 13 | 8 | | | 4 | 6 | 10 | 12 | | | | 2 | | | 5 | 7 | 9 | 11 | | | | |
| 12-Mar | A | Celtic | 58,593 | 0-6 | 1 | | 3 | 4 | | | 7 | | | | 8 | 6 | 10 | | | | | 2 | | | 5 | | 9 | | 11 | 12 | 13 | |
| 19-Mar | H | Hibernian | 7,204 | 1-4 | 1 | | | 4 | | 5 | **7** | | | 13 | 3 | 6 | 8 | 10 | 11 | 2 | | 12 | | | | | 9 | | | | | |
| 2-Apr | A | Livingston | 4,036 | 1-1 | 1 | | 3 | 4 | | 5 | | 8 | | | **12** | 7 | 6 | 13 | 10 | 11 | | | | | | 2 | 9 | | | | | |
| 9-Apr | A | Dundee | 5,995 | 1-2 | 1 | | 3 | 4 | | 5 | | 8 | | 9 | 7 | **6** | 12 | 10 | 11 | | | | | | | 2 | 13 | 14 | | | | |
| 17-Apr | H | Rangers | 8,261 | 0-1 | 1 | | 3 | 4 | | 5 | | 8 | | 9 | | 12 | 10 | 11 | | | | | | | | 2 | 13 | 7 | | | | |
| 23-Apr | H | Inverness Cal.Th. | 4,471 | 0-0 | 1 | | 3 | 4 | | 5 | | 8 | | 9 | 14 | 6 | 13 | 10 | 11 | | | | | | | 2 | 12 | 7 | | | | |
| 30-Apr | A | Livingston | 5,102 | 0-2 | 1 | | 3 | 4 | | 5 | | 8 | | 9 | | 6 | 11 | 10 | 12 | | | | | | | 2 | 7 | 13 | | | | |
| 7-May | H | Dundee | 8,313 | †5-0 | 1 | | 3 | **4** | | 5 | | 8 | | 14 | 10 | **6** | | 12 | **11³** | 13 | | | | | | | 2 | 7 | | 9 | | |
| 15-May | A | Dundee United | 10,763 | †1-0 | 1 | | 3 | 4 | | 5 | | 8 | | | 10 | 6 | | 12 | 11 | | | | | | | | 2 | 7 | | 9 | | |
| 21-May | A | Kilmarnock | 5,100 | 0-4 | 1 | | 3 | 4 | | 5 | | 8 | | | 10 | 6 | 12 | 13 | 11 | 14 | | | | | | | 2 | 7 | | 9 | | |
| **TOTAL FULL APPEARANCES** | | | | | 38 | 13 | 31 | 30 | 5 | 35 | 26 | 34 | 16 | 13 | 24 | 29 | 13 | 16 | 18 | 10 | 9 | 6 | 11 | 1 | | 11 | 11 | 10 | 4 | 4 | | |
| **TOTAL SUB APPEARANCES** | | | | | | | | | 1 | | 1 | 1 | 1 | 10 | 7 | 6 | 1 | 15 | 8 | 7 | 6 | 6 | 3 | 1 | 1 | 2 | | 3 | 4 | 1 | 1 |
| **TOTAL GOALS SCORED** | | | | | | | 2 | 1 | | 1 | 3 | | 1 | 6 | 3 | 3 | 2 | 3 | 4 | | | | | | | 2 | | | |

Figure in bold denotes goal scored. Secondary smaller figure in bold denotes number of goals scored. † denotes opponent's own goal.

## THE PARS' 10 YEAR LEAGUE RECORD

| Season | Div | P | W | D | L | F | A | Pts | Pos |
|---|---|---|---|---|---|---|---|---|---|
| 1995-96 | F | 36 | 21 | 8 | 7 | 73 | 41 | 71 | 1 |
| 1996-97 | P | 36 | 12 | 9 | 15 | 52 | 65 | 45 | 5 |
| 1997-98 | P | 36 | 8 | 13 | 15 | 43 | 68 | 37 | 8 |
| 1998-99 | SPL | 36 | 4 | 16 | 16 | 28 | 59 | 28 | 10 |
| 1999-00 | F | 36 | 20 | 5 | 11 | 66 | 33 | 71 | 2 |
| 2000-01 | SPL | 38 | 11 | 9 | 18 | 34 | 54 | 42 | 9 |
| 2001-02 | SPL | 38 | 12 | 9 | 17 | 41 | 64 | 45 | 6 |
| 2002-03 | SPL | 38 | 13 | 7 | 18 | 54 | 71 | 46 | 5 |
| 2003-04 | SPL | 38 | 14 | 11 | 13 | 45 | 52 | 53 | 4 |
| 2004-05 | SPL | 38 | 8 | 10 | 20 | 34 | 60 | 34 | 11 |

## LEADING GOALSCORERS:

| Season | Div | Goals | Player |
|---|---|---|---|
| 1995-96 | F | 13 | S. Petrie |
| 1996-97 | P | 13 | G. Britton |
| 1997-98 | P | 16 | A. Smith |
| 1998-99 | SPL | 8 | A. Smith |
| 1999-00 | F | 16 | S. Crawford |
| 2000-01 | SPL | 9 | S. Crawford |
| 2001-02 | SPL | 7 | B. Nicholson |
| 2002-03 | SPL | 19 | S. Crawford |
| 2003-04 | SPL | 13 | S. Crawford |
| 2004-05 | SPL | 6 | A. Tod |

DUNFERMLINE ATHLETIC PLAYING KITS SEASON 2005.06

FIRST KIT    SECOND KIT    THIRD KIT

**FALKIRK**

FALKIRK F.C.
The Falkirk Stadium,
Westfield, Falkirk, FK2 9DX
**TELEPHONE NUMBERS**
Ground/Commercial/
Ticket Office/Information Service
(01324) 624121
**FAX** (01324) 612418
**E-MAIL** alexb@falkirkfc.co.uk
**E-MAIL 2** davidw@falkirkfc.co.uk
**E-MAIL 3** post@falkirkfc.co.uk
**WEBSITE** www.falkirkfc.co.uk
**CHAIRMAN** Campbell Christie, C.B.E.
**DIRECTORS**
W. Martin Ritchie O.B.E., Ann M. Joyce,
Graham Crawford, Douglas Paterson,
George Craig, Alexander Miller,
Henry R.E Crosthwaite, Fergus B. Caldwell
& William F.R Anderson
**MANAGING DIRECTOR** George Craig
**COMPANY SECRETARY** David Webster C.A
**SECRETARY**
Alexander Blackwood (01324) 624121
**HEAD COACH** John Hughes
**FIRST TEAM COACH** Brian Rice
**YOUTH CO-ORDINATOR /**
**YOUTH DEVELOPMENT COACH** Eddie May
**COMMUNITY COACH** Tom Elliott
**YOUTH TEAM COACHES**
U19: Eddie May
U17: Alan Sneddon & Willie Irvine
U15: Robert Gouther & Alastair McColl
U14: Alan Bateman & Paul Taylor
U13: Jim Henderson & Tom Herriott
**CHIEF SCOUT** Alan Fraser
**TEAM CAPTAIN** Craig Ireland
**YOUTH INCOME GENERATING MANAGER &**
**COMMERCIAL MANAGER**
Alexander Totten
**WOMENS DEVELOPMENT COACH**
Pauline Hamil
**SCHOOLS DEVELOPMENT COACH**
Tom Elliott
**FOOTBALL SAFETY OFFICERS'**
**ASSOCIATION REPRESENTATIVES**
George Craig & Tom McGunnigle
(01324) 624121
**MEDIA LIAISON PERSON**
Keith Hogg (01324) 624121
**MATCHDAY PROGRAMME EDITOR**
Gordon McFarlane (07801) 798916
**CLUB DOCTORS**
Dr. R. Gillies Sinclair & Dr. Robert Deuchar
**PHYSIOTHERAPIST** Vanessa Smith
**GROUNDSMAN** James Dawson
**KIT PERSON** Steven Sproul
**CLUB SHOP**
47 Glebe Street, Falkirk, FK1 1HX
Tel (01324) 639366. Open Mon. – Sat. 9.30
a.m. – 12 Noon and 1.00 p.m. – 5.00 p.m.
Closed on Wednesday
**OFFICIAL SUPPORTERS CLUB**
Association of Falkirk F.C. Supporters Clubs
Chairman: Gordon McFarlane (01324) 638104
**SHIRT SPONSOR** Central Demolition
**KIT SUPPLIER** TFG

## LIST OF PLAYERS 2005.06

| SQUAD NO. | PLAYERS SURNAME | FIRST NAME | MIDDLE NAME | DATE OF BIRTH | PLACE OF BIRTH | DATE SIGNED | HEIGHT FT INS | WEIGHT ST LBS | POSITION ON PITCH | PREVIOUS CLUB |
|---|---|---|---|---|---|---|---|---|---|---|
| | Allison | Brian | | 23/06/88 | Edinburgh | 03/08/04 | 5' 10" | 11st 7lb | Def | Royston B.C. |
| | Arfield | Scott | | 01/11/88 | Dechmont | 06/11/04 | 5' 10" | 10st 0lb | Mid | Falkirk Form D U 16 |
| 20 | Barr | Darren | | 17/03/85 | Glasgow | 12/07/02 | 5' 10" | 10st 4lb | Mid | Falkirk Form D U 16 |
| | Boyle | Nicholas | James | 28/05/87 | Glasgow | 27/07/04 | 5' 9" | 10st 7lb | Mid | Falkirk Form S |
| | Churchill | Graeme | | 20/07/87 | Glasgow | 27/07/04 | 6' 0" | 11st 0lb | Fwd | Falkirk Form D U 1 |
| | Clements | Dean | | 14/11/88 | Edinburgh | 14/07/05 | 5' 9" | 10st 2lb | Mid | Falkirk Form D U 1 |
| | Currie | David | Walker | 21/11/88 | Forfar | 25/07/05 | 5' 10" | 10st 9lb | Gk | Dundee Youths |
| | Donaldson | Craig | | 06/03/88 | Falkirk | 14/07/05 | 5' 6" | 9st 5lb | Fwd | Falkirk Form D U 1 |
| 11 | Duffy | Darryl | Alexander | 16/04/84 | Glasgow | 05/07/04 | 5' 11" | 12st 1lb | Fwd | Rangers |
| | Easton | David | | 28/11/88 | Edinburgh | 10/08/05 | 6' 3" | 12st 3lb | Gk | Heart of Midlothian Youths |
| 1 | Ferguson | Allan | Thomas | 21/03/69 | Lanark | 04/07/02 | 5' 11" | 13st 0lb | Gk | Airdrieonians |
| | Gibb | Scott | | 16/09/88 | Craigavon | 14/07/05 | 6' 1" | 11st 6lb | Def | Lurgan Town B.C. |
| 27 | Glennan | Matt | | 08/10/78 | Stockport | 21/07/05 | 6' 3" | 14st 10lb | Gk | Carlisle United |
| 8 | Gow | Alan | | 09/10/82 | Glasgow | 01/07/05 | 6' 0" | 12st 0lb | Mid | Airdrie United |
| 17 | Hill | Darren | | 03/12/81 | Falkirk | 07/07/98 | 6' 1.5" | 12st 3lb | Gk | Falkirk B.C. |
| 24 | Hughes | John | | 09/09/64 | Edinburgh | 27/05/04 | 6' 0" | 13st 10lb | Def | Ayr United |
| 6 | Ireland | Craig | Robert | 29/11/75 | Dundee | 15/06/05 | 6' 3" | 13st 9lb | Def | Peterborough United |
| | Johnson | Daryl | George | 17/05/87 | Edinburgh | 25/07/05 | 5' 9" | 11st 0lb | Mid | Cowdenbeath |
| 10 | Latapy | Russell | Nigel | 02/08/68 | Trinidad & Tobago | 02/06/04 | 5' 7" | 11st 4lb | Mid | Dundee United |
| 2 | Lawrie | Andrew | | 24/11/78 | Galashiels | 18/06/96 | 6' 0" | 12st 6lb | Def | Falkirk Form D U 1 |
| | MacAloney | Paul | | 31/01/86 | Bellshill | 08/08/03 | 5' 11" | 11st 2lb | Mid | Livingston |
| 4 | MacKenzie | Scott | | 07/07/70 | Glasgow | 23/08/02 | 5' 9" | 11st 2lb | Mid | St. Mirren |
| 16 | MacSween | Ian | | 07/06/84 | Edinburgh | 10/07/01 | 5' 11.5" | 11st 0lb | Fwd | Falkirk Form D U 1 |
| 29 | Manson | Stephen | | 25/02/86 | Edinburgh | 07/08/03 | 5' 9" | 10st 2lb | Fwd | Hibernian |
| | Mauchline | Scott | | 08/07/87 | Falkirk | 27/07/04 | 5' 11" | 11st 2lb | Fwd | Falkirk Form S |
| | May | Edward | Skillion | 30/08/67 | Edinburgh | 27/05/04 | 5' 10" | 11st 7lb | Def | Berwick Rangers |
| 19 | McBreen | Daniel | James | 23/04/77 | Burnley | 10/09/04 | 6' 1" | 13st 0lb | Fwd | FC Universitatea Craiova |
| 3 | McPherson | Craig | | 27/03/71 | Greenock | 19/05/04 | 5' 10" | 11st 6lb | Mid | Airdrieonians |
| 14 | McStay | Ryan | Michael | 04/12/85 | Bellshill | 12/07/02 | 6' 1" | 10st 0lb | Mid | Falkirk Form D U 16 |
| 15 | Milne | Kenneth | | 26/08/79 | Stirling | 10/06/05 | 6' 2.5" | 12st 8lb | Mid | Partick Thistle |
| | Moffat | Kevin | | 06/08/88 | Edinburgh | 14/07/05 | 5' 5" | 9st 7lb | Fwd | Falkirk Form D U 1 |
| 7 | Moutinho | Pedro | Da Silva | 09/09/79 | Porto | 29/07/04 | 5' 11" | 12st 8lb | Fwd | F.C. Penafiel |
| 28 | O'Donnell | Stephen | | 15/01/86 | Galway | 29/07/05 | 5' 7" | 11st 0lb | Mid | Arsenal |
| 21 | O'Neil | John | Thomas | 06/07/71 | Bellshill | 28/09/03 | 5' 8" | 12st 0lb | Mid | Hibernian |
| | Ramsay | Mark | | 24/01/86 | Dunfermline | 07/08/03 | 5' 7" | 10st 0lb | Mid | Falkirk Form D U 1 |
| | Robertson | Dayne | | 21/06/88 | Edinburgh | 14/07/05 | 5' 8" | 10st 10lb | Fwd | Falkirk Form D U 1 |
| 25 | Rodrigues | Tiago | Jonas | 01/12/83 | Porto | 14/07/05 | 6' 1" | 12st 6lb | Def | FC Infesta |
| 5 | Ross | John | James | 05/06/76 | Falkirk | 10/08/05 | 6' 1" | 12st 4lb | Def | Hartlepool United |
| 18 | Santos | Vitor | Manuel | 10/08/81 | Guimaraes | 14/07/05 | 5' 10" | 10st 2lb | Mid | Academica de Visu |
| 12 | Scally | Neil | | 14/08/78 | Paisley | 19/05/04 | 5' 11" | 12st 7lb | Mid | Dumbarton |
| | Scobbie | Thomas | | 31/03/88 | Falkirk | 27/07/04 | 6' 0" | 11st 0lb | Def | Falkirk Form D U 1 |
| | Storie | Allan | Kenneth | 13/04/88 | Falkirk | 31/08/05 | 5' 7" | 10st 2lb | Fwd | Ipswich Town |
| 9 | Thomson | Andrew | | 01/04/71 | Motherwell | 04/06/04 | 5' 11" | 11st 11lb | Fwd | Partick Thistle |
| 22 | Thomson | Steven | | 23/01/78 | Glasgow | 01/07/05 | 5' 8" | 11st 0lb | Mid | Peterborough United |
| 23 | Twaddle | Marc | Ian | 27/08/86 | Glasgow | 22/08/03 | 6' 1" | 12st 0lb | Mid | Rangers |

### TICKET INFORMATION
**Season Ticket Information**
**Main Stand**

| | |
|---|---|
| Prime Seats (No Concessions) | £320 |
| Adult | £270 |
| Concession | £170 |
| Primary School Child | £85 |

**League Admission Prices**

**Main Stand**
| Adult | £18 | Concession | £12 |
|---|---|---|---|

**North Stand**
| Adult | £18 | Concession | £12 |
|---|---|---|---|

**Temp Stand**
| Adult | £12 | Concession | £8 |
|---|---|---|---|

### MILESTONES:
**Year of formation:** 1876
**Most Capped player:** Alex H. Parker
**No. of Caps:** 14
**Most League points in a season:**
66 (First Division – Season 1993/94) (2 Points for a Win)
81 (First Division – Season 2002/03) (3 Points for a Win)
**Most League goals scored by a player in a season:**
Evelyn Morrison (Season 1928/29)
**No. of goals scored:** 43
**Record Attendance:** 23,100 (-v- Celtic – 21.2.1953 - at Brockville
6,810 (-v- Rangers – 10.9.2005 - at the Falkirk Stadium)
**Record Victory:** 12-1 (-v- Laurieston – Scottish Cup, 23.3.189
**Record Defeat:** 1-11 (-v- Airdrieonians – Division A, 28.4.1951

BANK OF SCOTLAND PREMIERLEAGUE

## SEASON STATS 2004.05

| DATE | VENUE | OPPONENTS | ATT | RES | Hill D. | Lawrie A. | McPherson C. | MacKenzie S. | Campbell M.T. | Sharp J. | O'Neil J.T. | Scally N. | Thomson A. | McStay R.M. | Duffy D.A. | McAnespie K.L. | Moutinho P.D. | Hughes J. | James K.F. | Nicholls D.C. | Latapy R.N. | Ferguson A.T. | Rahim B. | Marshall C.J. | McBreen D.J. | Kernaghan A.N. | Barr D. | Scobbie T. | Henry J. | Ramsay M. |
|---|---|---|---|---|---|---|---|---|---|---|---|---|---|---|---|---|---|---|---|---|---|---|---|---|---|---|---|---|---|---|
| 7-Aug | A | St. Mirren | 3,817 | 0-2 | 1 | 2 | 3 | 4 | 5 | 6 | 7 | 8 | 9 | 10 | 11 | | | 14 | | 16 | | | | | | | | | | |
| 14-Aug | H | Hamilton Academical | 3,423 | 1-1 | 1 | 2 | 3 | 7 | 4 | | | 15 | 9 | | **11** | 12 | | | 5 | 6 | 8 | 10 | | | | | | | | |
| 21-Aug | A | Queen of the South | 2,521 | 3-1 | 1 | 2 | 3 | 4 | | | 7 | 14 | 9 | | **11** | 12 | 15 | | | 6 | 8 | 10 | | | | | | | | |
| 28-Aug | H | Airdrie United | 3,790 | 5-0 | 1 | **2** | 3 | 4 | 5 | | 7 | 14 | 9² | | 11 | 12 | 15 | | | 6 | 8 | 10 | | | | | | | | |
| 4-Sep | A | Partick Thistle | 5,157 | 4-1 | 1 | 2 | 3 | 4 | **5** | | 7 | **14** | 9 | | 11² | | 15 | 16 | | 6 | 8 | 10 | | | | | | | | |
| 11-Sep | H | Raith Rovers | 3,449 | 4-2 | 1 | 2 | 3 | 4 | 5 | | 7 | 14 | 9² | | 11² | 12 | 15 | | | 6 | 8 | 10 | | | | | | | | |
| 18-Sep | A | St. Johnstone | 3,835 | 2-1 | 1 | 2 | 3 | 4 | 5 | | **7** | 14 | 9 | | 11 | 12 | 16 | | | 6 | 8 | 10 | | | | | | | | |
| 25-Sep | H | Clyde | 3,813 | 1-1 | | 2 | 3 | 4 | 5 | | 7 | 14 | **9** | | 11 | 12 | | | | 6 | 8 | 10 | 1 | | | | | | | |
| 2-Oct | A | Ross County | 3,062 | 1-0 | | 2 | 3 | 4 | | | 7 | 14 | 9 | | 11 | | 10 | | 5 | 6 | 8 | | 1 | 16 | | | | | | |
| 16-Oct | A | Hamilton Academical | 2,870 | 1-0 | | 2 | 3 | 4 | | | 7 | | | | 11 | 9 | | | 5 | 6 | 8 | 10 | 1 | | | | | | | |
| 23-Oct | H | St. Mirren | 4,611 | 0-0 | | 2 | 3 | 4 | 5 | | 7 | | 9 | | 11 | 12 | | | | 6 | 8 | 10 | 1 | 16 | | | | | | |
| 30-Oct | A | Airdrie United | 3,247 | 3-1 | | **2** | 3 | 4 | 5 | | 7 | 14 | 9 | | 11 | | | | | 6 | 8 | **10** | 1 | | 15 | | | | | |
| 13-Nov | A | Raith Rovers | 3,050 | 2-0 | | 2 | 3 | 4 | 5 | | 7 | 6 | | 15 | **11** | 16 | 8 | | | | | 10 | 1 | | 12 | **9** | | | | |
| 20-Nov | H | St. Johnstone | 3,439 | 3-1 | | 2 | 3 | 4 | 5 | | 7 | 12 | | | 11 | | | 14 | | 6 | 8 | 10 | 1 | 15 | 9² | | | | | |
| 23-Nov | H | Partick Thistle | 3,335 | 3-0 | | 2 | 3 | 4 | 5 | | 7 | 12 | | | 11 | | | 14 | | 6 | 8 | 10 | 1 | 15 | 9² | | | | | |
| 27-Nov | H | Ross County | 3,182 | 2-2 | | 2 | 3 | **4** | 5 | | 7 | 12 | **14** | | 11 | | | | | 6 | 8 | 10 | 1 | 15 | 9 | | | | | |
| 4-Dec | A | Clyde | 2,859 | 2-0 | | 2 | 3 | **4** | | | 7 | 10 | 14 | | 11 | 12 | | | 5 | 6 | 8 | 15 | 1 | | 9 | | | | | |
| 11-Dec | A | St. Mirren | 4,676 | 1-0 | | 2 | 3 | 14 | | | 7 | 14 | | | 11 | | | | 5 | 6 | 8 | 15 | 10 | 1 | 9 | | | | | |
| 18-Dec | H | Queen of the South | 3,370 | 4-2 | | 2 | 3 | 4 | 5 | | 7 | 12 | | | 11 | | 16 | | | 6 | 8 | 15 | 10 | 1 | 9³ | | | | | |
| 26-Dec | H | Airdrie United | 4,133 | 1-0 | | 2 | 3 | 4 | 5 | | 7 | 14 | 12 | | 11 | | | | | 6 | 8 | 10 | 1 | | 9 | | | | | |
| 29-Dec | A | Partick Thistle | 4,120 | 1-2 | | 2 | 3 | 4 | 5 | 15 | 7 | 14 | 8 | | **11** | | | | | 6 | | 10 | 1 | | 9 | | | | | |
| 1-Jan | H | Raith Rovers | 3,379 | 2-0 | | 2 | 3 | 4 | 5 | | 7 | 8 | **9** | | 11 | | 14 | | | 6 | 16 | 10 | 1 | 15 | | | | | | |
| 15-Jan | A | St. Johnstone | 3,395 | 3-0 | | 2 | 3 | 4 | | | 8 | | 7 | | **11** | 9 | | | 5 | 6 | | 10 | 1 | 16 | | | | | | |
| 29-Jan | A | Ross County | 3,151 | 1-0 | 1 | 2 | 3 | 14 | | | 7 | | 16 | | **11** | 9 | 5 | 6 | | | | 10 | | 12 | 8 | | | | | |
| 12-Feb | H | Hamilton Academical | 3,535 | 1-1 | 1 | 2 | 3 | 4 | 6 | | 14 | 7 | | | 11 | | 5 | | | | | 10 | | 9 | 8 | | | | | |
| 19-Feb | A | Queen of the South | 2,551 | 1-1 | 1 | **2** | 3 | 4 | | | 14 | 7 | | 15 | 11 | | 5 | | | | | 10 | | 9 | 8 | | | | | |
| 5-Mar | H | Partick Thistle | 4,157 | 2-1 | | | 3 | 4 | 14 | | 7 | 8 | 12 | 15 | **11** | | | | 5 | 6 | | 10 | 1 | 9 | 2 | | | | | |
| 12-Mar | A | Airdrie United | 3,111 | 2-2 | | | 3 | 4 | 14 | | 7 | 8 | | 2 | **11** | | | | | 6 | | 10 | 1 | 16 | 15 | 9 | 5 | | | |
| 15-Mar | H | Clyde | 3,834 | 0-0 | | | 3 | 4 | | | 7 | 8 | 12 | 15 | 11 | | | | 5 | 6 | | 10 | 1 | 16 | 9 | 2 | | | | |
| 19-Mar | A | Raith Rovers | 2,369 | 3-3 | | | 3 | | 4 | | 7 | 8 | 12 | 2 | **11** | | | | 5 | 6 | | 10 | 1 | 15 | 9² | | | | | |
| 2-Apr | H | St. Johnstone | 3,748 | 3-0 | | | 3 | 4 | 14 | | 7 | 2 | | 8 | 11 | | | | 5 | 6 | | 10 | 1 | 15 | 9 | 16 | | | | |
| 9-Apr | H | Ross County | 5,272 | 1-0 | | 16 | 3 | 4 | 14 | | 7 | 2 | 12 | **8** | 11 | | | | 5 | 6 | | 10 | 1 | | 9 | | | | | |
| 16-Apr | A | Clyde | 2,090 | 1-0 | | 14 | 3 | 4 | 5 | | 11 | 2 | 12 | 8 | | | | | | 6 | | 10 | 1 | | 9 | 7 | | | | |
| 23-Apr | H | St. Mirren | 4,342 | 1-2 | | 15 | 3 | 4 | 5 | | 7 | 2 | 12 | 8 | **11** | | | | | 6 | | 10 | 1 | | 9 | | | | | |
| 30-Apr | A | Hamilton Academical | 2,300 | 0-1 | | 12 | 3 | 4 | 5 | | 7 | 10 | | 8 | 11 | | | 6 | | | | | 1 | 14 | 9 | 2 | 15 | | | |
| 7-May | H | Queen of the South | 5,067 | 1-2 | | **2** | 3 | 4 | 5 | | | 10 | | 8 | 11 | | | 6 | | | | | 1 | 9 | 7 | 12 | | 14 | 16 | |
| **TOTAL FULL APPEARANCES** | | | | | 10 | 27 | 33 | 34 | 25 | 3 | 30 | 19 | 13 | 10 | 35 | | 12 | 17 | 29 | 12 | 31 | 26 | | 21 | 9 | | | | | |
| **TOTAL SUB APPEARANCES** | | | | | 4 | | | 6 | 1 | 2 | 14 | 11 | 5 | | | 8 | 7 | 2 | | 6 | 1 | | 3 | 12 | 2 | | 2 | 1 | 1 | 1 |
| **TOTAL GOALS SCORED** | | | | | | | | 4 | 1 | | 1 | 9 | 1 | | 17 | 1 | 4 | 2 | 1 | | 3 | 7 | | 13 | | | | | |

…re in bold denotes goal scored. Secondary smaller figure in bold denotes number of goals scored. † denotes opponent's own goal.

## THE BAIRNS' 10 YEAR LEAGUE RECORD

| Season | Div | P | W | D | L | F | A | Pts | Pos |
|---|---|---|---|---|---|---|---|---|---|
| 95-96 | P | 36 | 6 | 6 | 24 | 31 | 60 | 24 | 10 |
| 96-97 | F | 36 | 15 | 9 | 12 | 42 | 39 | 54 | 5 |
| 97-98 | F | 36 | 19 | 8 | 9 | 56 | 41 | 65 | 2 |
| 98-99 | F | 36 | 20 | 6 | 10 | 60 | 38 | 66 | 2 |
| 99-00 | F | 36 | 20 | 8 | 8 | 67 | 40 | 68 | 3 |
| 00-01 | F | 36 | 16 | 8 | 12 | 57 | 59 | 56 | 3 |
| 01-02 | F | 36 | 10 | 9 | 17 | 49 | 73 | 39 | 9 |
| 02-03 | F | 36 | 25 | 6 | 5 | 80 | 32 | 81 | 1 |
| 03-04 | F | 36 | 15 | 10 | 11 | 43 | 37 | 55 | 4 |
| 04-05 | F | 36 | 22 | 9 | 5 | 66 | 30 | 75 | 1 |

## LEADING GOALSCORERS:

| Season | Div | Goals | Player |
|---|---|---|---|
| 1995-96 | P | 6 | P. McGrillen |
| 1996-97 | F | 8 | M. McGraw |
| 1997-98 | F | 8 | D. Moss |
| 1998-99 | F | 17 | M. Keith |
| 1999-00 | F | 14 | S. Crabbe |
| 2000-01 | F | 11 | G. Hutchison |
| 2001-02 | F | 11 | L. Miller |
| 2002-03 | F | 20 | O. Coyle |
| 2003-04 | F | 9 | J. Lee |
| 2004-05 | F | 17 | D. Duffy |

**FALKIRK PLAYING KITS SEASON 2005.06**

FIRST KIT  SECOND KIT  THIRD KIT

# HEART OF MIDLOTHIAN

## HEART OF MIDLOTHIAN F.C.
Tynecastle Stadium, Gorgie Road,
Edinburgh, EH11 2NL

**TELEPHONE NUMBERS**
Reception (0131) 200 7200
Football Dept (0131) 451 8470
Ticket Office (0131) 200 7201
Sales & Marketing (0131) 200 7234
Credit Card Bookings (0131) 200 7201
Superstore (0131) 200 7211
**FAX** 0131 200 7222
**E-MAIL** hearts@homplc.co.uk
**WEBSITE** www.heartsfc.co.uk
**CHAIRMAN** Lord Foulkes of Cumnock
**DIRECTORS**
Stewart Fraser, Sergejus Fedotovas,
David Archer, Liutauras Varanavicius,
Roman Romanov & Julija Goncaruk
**CHIEF EXECUTIVE** Phil Anderton
**COMPANY SECRETARY /**
**FINANCE DIRECTOR**
Stewart Fraser (0131) 200 7270
**MANAGER**
**ASSISTANT MANAGER**
**FIRST TEAM COACH** John McGlynn
**RESERVE COACH** Stephen Frail
**FITNESS COACH** Tom Ritchie
**GOALKEEPING COACH** Malcolm Webster
**DIRECTOR OF YOUTH DEVELOPMENT**
John Murray
**TEAM CAPTAIN** Steven Pressley
**FOOTBALL SAFETY OFFICERS'**
**ASSOCIATION REPRESENTATIVE /**
**FACILITIES & SECURITY MANAGER**
John Boag (0131) 200 7254
**COMMERCIAL DIRECTOR**
Ali Russell (0131) 200 7205
**MEDIA LIAISON OFFICER**
Clare Cowan (0131) 200 7206
**CLUB DOCTOR** Dr. Dewar Melvin
**PHYSIOTHERAPIST** Oliver Findlay
**KIT PERSON** Gordon Paterson
**P.A TO CHIEF EXECUTIVE**
Irene McPhee (0131) 200 7245
**FOOTBALL SECRETARY**
Louise MacKenzie (0131) 451 8470
**SALES & MARKETING**
Ross Easton (0131) 200 7234
**TICKET SUPERVISOR**
Martine Collie (0131) 200 7201
**SUPERSTORE SUPERVISOR**
Gemma Muir (0131) 200 7211
**CLUB SHOP**
Heart of Midlothian Superstore,
Tynecastle Stadium, Gorgie Road, Edinburgh.
Tel (0131) 200 7211. Open 9.30am - 5.30pm
Mon to Sat & on Matchdays
**OFFICIAL SUPPORTERS CLUB**
Heart of Midlothian Federation,
John N. Borthwick, 21/9 Festival Gardens,
Edinburgh, EH11 1RB
**SHIRT SPONSOR** Ukio Bankas
**KIT SUPPLIER** Hummel

## LIST OF PLAYERS 2005.06

| SQUAD NO. | PLAYERS SURNAME | FIRST NAME | MIDDLE NAME | DATE OF BIRTH | PLACE OF BIRTH | DATE SIGNED | HEIGHT FT INS | WEIGHT ST LBS | POSITION ON PITCH | PREVIOUS CLUB |
|---|---|---|---|---|---|---|---|---|---|---|
| 37 | Armstrong | John | William | 25/06/87 | Edinburgh | 08/07/04 | 5' 11" | 11st 10lb | Def | Heart of Midlothian Youths |
| | Armstrong | David | Trevor | 23/01/87 | Lisburn | 14/07/05 | 6' 1" | 12st 2lb | Fwd | Crusaders |
| 13 | Banks | Steven | | 09/12/72 | Hillingdon | 11/08/05 | 5' 11" | 13st 2lb | Gk | Gillingham |
| 36 | Barjaktarevic | Milan | | 12/06/87 | Stockholm | 02/03/04 | 6' 3" | 13st 3lb | Gk | Hammarby |
| 12 | Bednar | Roman | | 26/03/83 | Prague | 29/07/05 | 6' 3" | 13st 3lb | Fwd | Mlada Boleslav |
| 20 | Berra | Christophe | | 31/01/85 | Edinburgh | 26/04/02 | 6' 1" | 12st 10lb | Def | Heart of Midlothian Youths |
| | Bjornsson | Haraldur | | 11/01/89 | Reykjavik | 11/07/05 | 6' 3" | 14st 11lb | Gk | Valur |
| 28 | Brellier | Julien | | 10/01/82 | Echirolles | 05/08/05 | 6' 1" | 12st 8lb | Mid | Venezia |
| 5 | Camazzola | Samuel | Almeida | 30/08/82 | Caxias do Sul | 30/08/05 | 5' 10" | 11st 7lb | Mid | EC Juventude |
| 18 | Cesnauskis | Deividas | | 30/06/81 | Kursenai | 31/01/05 | 5' 11" | 12st 2lb | Fwd | FBK Kaunas |
| | Divine | Alistair | David | 11/04/88 | Edinburgh | 30/06/05 | 5' 11" | 9st 13lb | Mid | Heart of Midlothian Youths |
| 44 | Doherty | Matthew | | 29/04/87 | Londonderry | 28/07/04 | 5' 11" | 11st 7lb | Mid | Carlisle United |
| 41 | Driver | Andrew | David | 12/11/87 | Oldham | 04/07/03 | 5' 8.5" | 10st 10lb | Mid | Heart of Midlothian Youths |
| 26 | Elliot | Calum | | 30/03/87 | Edinburgh | 01/10/03 | 5' 11.5" | 12st 6lb | Fwd | Heart of Midlothian Youths |
| | Forker | Mark | Hugh | 03/04/88 | Co. Donegal | 31/01/05 | 5' 10" | 10st 11lb | Mid | Institute |
| 3 | Fyssas | Panagiotis | | 12/06/73 | Athens | 10/08/05 | 6' 2" | 12st 8lb | Def | Benfica |
| 1 | Gordon | Craig | Sinclair | 31/12/82 | Edinburgh | 26/10/99 | 6' 4" | 12st 2lb | Gk | Heart of Midlothian Youth |
| | Hamilton | Ross | | 10/01/89 | Edinburgh | 30/06/05 | 6' 3" | 11st 11lb | Def | Heart of Midlothian Youth |
| 10 | Hartley | Paul | James | 19/10/76 | Glasgow | 03/06/03 | 5' 8" | 10st 7lb | Fwd | St. Johnstone |
| 9 | Jankauskas | Edgaras | | 12/03/75 | Vilnius | 29/07/05 | 6' 3.5" | 13st 8lb | Fwd | FBK Kaunas |
| | Jonsson | Eggert | Gunnthor | 18/08/88 | Reykjavik | 11/07/05 | 6' 2" | 11st 3lb | Mid | Fyardarbyggd |
| | Lithgow | Alan | | 12/03/88 | Bellshill | 27/05/05 | 6' 2" | 12st 4lb | Def | Heart of Midlothian Youth |
| 25 | MacDonald | Jamie | | 17/04/86 | Broxburn | 15/08/03 | 6' 1" | 11st 2lb | Gk | Musselburgh Athletic Junior |
| | MacDonald | Paul | | 28/05/88 | Glasgow | 10/06/05 | 5' 10" | 11st 11lb | Mid | Heart of Midlothian Youth |
| 11 | Macfarlane | Neil | | 10/10/77 | Dunoon | 08/07/02 | 6' 1" | 13st 1lb | Mid | Airdrieonians |
| 42 | Mackle | Sean | James | 10/04/88 | Belfast | 08/07/05 | 5' 8.5" | 10st 7lb | Mid | Portadown |
| 14 | McAllister | James | Reynolds | 26/04/78 | Glasgow | 04/06/04 | 5' 10" | 11st 0lb | Mid | Livingston |
| | McCusker | Marc | James | 29/07/89 | Rutherglen | 08/07/05 | 5' 11" | 11st 4lb | Fwd | Heart of Midlothian Youth |
| 34 | McLaughlin | Denis | | 05/02/87 | Letterkenny | 08/07/04 | 5' 11" | 11st 13lb | Fwd | Heart of Midlothian Youth |
| 16 | Mikoliunas | Saulius | | 02/05/84 | Vilnius | 25/01/05 | 5' 11" | 12st 1lb | Mid | FBK Kaunas |
| 43 | Mole | Jamie | | 01/06/88 | Newcastle | 08/07/04 | 5' 9.5" | 11st 13lb | Fwd | Newburn B.C. |
| 19 | Neill | John | | 17/08/87 | Bellshill | 06/08/03 | 5' 11" | 11st 4lb | Mid | Hibernian |
| 2 | Neilson | Robbie | | 19/06/80 | Paisley | 25/10/96 | 5' 8" | 11st 0lb | Mid | Rangers B.C. |
| 30 | Pelosi | Marco | Giancarlo | 22/04/86 | Edinburgh | 30/08/02 | 5' 10" | 11st 12lb | Def | Heart of Midlothian Youth |
| 21 | Pospisil | Michal | | 03/05/79 | Prague | 04/08/05 | 6' 0" | 12st 8lb | Fwd | FC Slovan Liberec |
| 4 | Pressley | Steven | John | 11/10/73 | Elgin | 10/07/98 | 6' 0" | 12st 6lb | Def | Dundee United |
| 15 | Simmons | Stephen | Christopher | 27/02/82 | Glasgow | 10/09/97 | 6' 0.5" | 11st 10lb | Mid | Celtic B.C. |
| 23 | Sives | Craig | Stuart | 09/04/86 | Edinburgh | 01/07/02 | 6' 3" | 12st 2lb | Def | Heart of Midlothian Youth |
| 8 | Skacel | Rudolf | | 17/07/79 | Vsti Nad Orlici | 29/07/05 | 5' 10" | 12st 2lb | Mid | Olimpique De Marseille |
| | Slater | Steven | | 10/04/88 | Edinburgh | 08/07/05 | 6' 0" | 10st 13lb | Mid | Heart of Midlothian Youth |
| 29 | Tall | Ibrahim | | 23/06/81 | Aubervilliers | 31/08/05 | 5' 11" | 11st 9lb | Def | Sochaux |
| 38 | Thomson | Jason | | 26/07/87 | Edinburgh | 10/07/03 | 5' 11" | 11st 7lb | Def | Heart of Midlothian Youth |
| 27 | Thorarinsson | Hjalmar | | 16/02/86 | Iceland | 23/05/05 | 6' 0" | 11st 6lb | Fwd | Throttur Reykjavik |
| 24 | Tierney | Garry | | 19/03/86 | Bellshill | 26/01/04 | 5' 11" | 11st 5lb | Def | Musselburgh Athletic Junior |
| 22 | Wallace | Lee | | 01/08/87 | Edinburgh | 08/07/04 | 5' 11" | 11st 12lb | Def | Heart of Midlothian Youth |
| 6 | Webster | Andrew | Neil | 23/04/82 | Dundee | 30/03/01 | 6' 0" | 12st 0lb | Def | Arbroath |
| 17 | Weir | Graham | | 10/07/84 | Harthill | 22/08/00 | 5' 7" | 10st 9lb | Fwd | Heart of Midlothian Youth |

### MILESTONES:
**Year of formation:** 1874
**Most Capped player:** Bobby Walker
**No. of Caps:** 29
**Most League points in a season:**
63 (Premier Division – Season 1991/92) (2 Points for a W
67 (Premier Division – Season 1997/98) (3 Points for a W
**Most League goals scored by a player in a season:**
Barney Battles (Season 1930/31)
**No. of goals scored:** 44
**Record Attendance:** 53,396 (-v- Rangers – 13.2.1932)
**Record Victory:** 21-0 (-v- Anchor – EFA Cup, 1880)
**Record Defeat:** 1-8 (-v- Vale of Leven – Scottish Cup, 188

Category A: Matches against Celtic, Hibernian & Rangers. Category B: All other SPL matches

# SEASON STATS 2004.05

## SEASON STATS 2004.05

Player columns (left to right): Gordon C., Maybury A., Kisnorbo P., Pressley S., Webster A., Hamill J., Neilson R., Stamp P., Hartley P., Pereira R., Weir G., Stewart M., Wyness D., Sloan R., McAllister J., De Vries M., Janczyk N., Macfarlane N., Sives C., Berra C., Elliot C., McKenna K., Miller L., Simmons S., Mikoliunus S., Thorradisson H., Burchill M., Wallace L., Kizys M., Cesnauskis D., Thomson J., McGeown D., Tierney G.

| DATE | VENUE | OPPONENTS | ATT | RES |
|---|---|---|---|---|
| 7-Aug | A | Dundee | 7,770 | 1-0 |
| 14-Aug | H | Aberdeen | 13,864 | 0-0 |
| 21-Aug | H | Kilmarnock | 11,403 | 3-0 |
| 28-Aug | A | Motherwell | 7,095 | 0-2 |
| 12-Sep | H | Rangers | 14,601 | 0-0 |
| 19-Sep | A | Dunfermline Ath. | 5,883 | 0-1 |
| 25-Sep | H | Inverness Cal.Th. | 10,340 | 1-0 |
| 3-Oct | H | Livingston | 10,646 | 0-0 |
| 16-Oct | A | Celtic | 59,242 | 0-3 |
| 24-Oct | H | Hibernian | 16,720 | 2-1 |
| 27-Oct | A | Dundee United | 5,723 | 1-1 |
| 30-Oct | H | Dundee | 10,172 | 3-0 |
| 7-Nov | A | Aberdeen | 13,055 | 1-0 |
| 13-Nov | A | Kilmarnock | 6,129 | 1-1 |
| 20-Nov | H | Motherwell | 10,598 | 0-1 |
| 28-Nov | A | Rangers | 48,494 | 2-3 |
| 4-Dec | H | Dunfermline Ath. | 10,084 | 3-0 |
| 11-Dec | A | Inverness Cal.Th. | 2,011 | 1-1 |
| 26-Dec | H | Celtic | 16,163 | 0-2 |
| 2-Jan | A | Hibernian | 17,259 | 1-1 |
| 15-Jan | H | Dundee United | 10,305 | 3-2 |
| 22-Jan | A | Dundee | 5,780 | 1-1 |
| 25-Jan | A | Livingston | 3,816 | 2-1 |
| 29-Jan | H | Aberdeen | 12,269 | 1-0 |
| 12-Feb | H | Kilmarnock | 9,220 | † 3-0 |
| 19-Feb | A | Motherwell | 7,390 | 1-1 |
| 2-Mar | H | Rangers | 13,842 | 1-2 |
| 5-Mar | A | Dunfermline Ath. | 5,935 | 1-1 |
| 12-Mar | H | Inverness Cal.Th. | 9,822 | 0-2 |
| 19-Mar | H | Livingston | 9,187 | 3-1 |
| 2-Apr | A | Celtic | 59,551 | 2-0 |
| 3-Apr | H | Hibernian | 17,673 | 1-2 |
| 6-Apr | A | Dundee United | 7,704 | 1-2 |
| 23-Apr | A | Hibernian | 16,620 | 2-2 |
| 30-Apr | H | Motherwell | 9,337 | 0-0 |
| 7-May | A | Rangers | 49,342 | † 1-2 |
| 15-May | H | Celtic | 15,927 | 1-2 |
| 22-May | A | Aberdeen | 16,155 | 0-2 |

**TOTAL FULL APPEARANCES** 38 16 17 32 35 25 35 15 32 12 11 5 19 23 7 2 16 2 7 7 17 5 10 5 13 2 7 3

**TOTAL SUB APPEARANCES** 1 ... 7 ... 1 1 4 9 12 10 2 7 2 4 4 5 4 6 1 6 1 4 7 5 1 2 1

**TOTAL GOALS SCORED** 1 3 1 2 1 1 2 1 4 1 2 8 1 3

re in bold denotes goal scored. Secondary smaller figure in bold denotes number of goals scored. † denotes opponent's own goal.

## HE JAM TARTS' 10 YEAR LEAGUE RECORD

| Season | Div | P | W | D | L | F | A | Pts | Pos |
|---|---|---|---|---|---|---|---|---|---|
| 95-96 | P | 36 | 16 | 7 | 13 | 55 | 53 | 55 | 4 |
| 96-97 | P | 36 | 14 | 10 | 12 | 46 | 43 | 52 | 4 |
| 97-98 | P | 36 | 19 | 10 | 7 | 70 | 46 | 67 | 3 |
| 98-99 | SPL | 36 | 11 | 9 | 16 | 44 | 50 | 42 | 6 |
| 99-00 | SPL | 36 | 15 | 9 | 12 | 47 | 40 | 54 | 3 |
| 00-01 | SPL | 38 | 14 | 10 | 14 | 56 | 50 | 52 | 5 |
| 01-02 | SPL | 38 | 14 | 6 | 18 | 52 | 57 | 48 | 5 |
| 02-03 | SPL | 38 | 18 | 9 | 11 | 57 | 51 | 63 | 3 |
| 03-04 | SPL | 38 | 19 | 11 | 8 | 56 | 40 | 68 | 3 |
| 04-05 | SPL | 38 | 13 | 11 | 14 | 43 | 41 | 50 | 5 |

## LEADING GOALSCORERS:

| Season | Div | Goals | Player |
|---|---|---|---|
| 1995-96 | P | 11 | J. Robertson |
| 1996-97 | P | 14 | J. Robertson |
| 1997-98 | P | 14 | J. Hamilton |
| 1998-99 | SPL | 10 | S. Adam |
| 1999-00 | SPL | 13 | G. McSwegan |
| 2000-01 | SPL | 12 | C. Cameron |
| 2001-02 | SPL | 9 | K. McKenna |
| 2002-03 | SPL | 15 | M. De Vries |
| 2003-04 | SPL | 12 | M. De Vries |
| 2004-05 | SPL | 11 | P. Hartley |

HEART OF MIDLOTHIAN PLAYING KITS SEASON 2005.06

FIRST KIT  SECOND KIT  THIRD KIT

# HIBERNIAN

**HIBERNIAN F.C.**
Easter Road Stadium,
12 Albion Place, Edinburgh, EH7 5QG
**TELEPHONE NUMBERS**
Ground (0131) 661 2159
Ticket Office (0131) 661 1875
**FAX GROUND** (0131) 659 6488
**FAX COMMERCIAL** (0131) 652 2202
**E-MAIL** club@hibernianfc.co.uk
**E-MAIL 2** gohagan@hibernianfc.co.uk
**WEBSITES** www.hibernianfc.co.uk
or www.hibs.org.uk
**CHAIRMAN** Roderick McK. Petrie
**DIRECTORS**
Stephen W. Dunn (Non Executive)
Tim Gardiner (Financial Director)
Colin McNeill
(Marketing & Communications Director)
Garry O'Hagan (Director/Club Secretary)
Lord O'Neill of Clackmannanshire
(Non Executive)
**CHIEF EXECUTIVE** Roderick McK. Petrie
**SECRETARY** Garry O'Hagan (0131) 656 7077
**MANAGER** Tony Mowbray
**FIRST TEAM COACH** Mark Venus
**FITNESS COACH** Dougie Fowler
**GOALKEEPING COACH** Ian Westwater
**YOUTH ACADEMY DIRECTOR** John Park
**YOUTH DEVELOPMENT COACH**
Alistair Stevenson
**YOUTH COACHES**
U19: Alistair Stevenson
U17: John Park (Admin: Billy Hendry)
U15:U14:U13: (Admin: Billy Hendry)
**CHIEF SCOUT** John Park
**FOOTBALL SAFETY OFFICERS'
ASSOCIATION REPRESENTATIVE**
James S.Pryde QPM (0131) 656 7089
**COMMERCIAL MANAGER**
Colin McNeill
Tel: (0131) 656 7095 Fax: (0131) 652 2202
**MEDIA LIAISON PERSON**
David Forsyth/Benchmark Media
Tel: (0131) 225 0780 Fax: (0131) 225 0781
**CLUB DOCTORS**
Dr. Tom Schofield & Dr. Duncan Reid
**PHYSIOTHERAPIST** Colin McLelland
**GROUNDSMAN & KIT PERSON** Tam McCourt
**CORPORATE HOSPITALITY MANAGER**
Amanda Vitesse (0131) 656 7073
**COMMERCIAL EXECUTIVE**
Russell Smith (0131) 656 7072
**CONFERENCE & BANQUETING**
Azure Catering (0131) 656 7075
**RETAIL OPERATIONS MANAGER**
Richard Alexander (0131) 656 7097
**COMMUNICATIONS MANAGER**
Elaine Morrison (0131) 656 7085
**CLUB SHOP**
12 Albion Place, Edinburgh. Open Mon.-Sat.
9.00a.m. – 5.00p.m. Home matchdays:
9.30a.m. – 3.00p.m (plus after match).
Tel (0131) 656 7078
e-mail: shopcounter@hibernianfc.co.uk
24 Hour Credit Card Hotline
(0870) 848 1400
**OFFICIAL SUPPORTERS CLUB**
11 Sunnyside Lane, Off Easter Road,
Edinburgh, EH7
**SHIRT SPONSOR** Whyte & Mackay
**KIT SUPPLIER** Le Coq Sportif

## LIST OF PLAYERS 2005.06

| SQUAD NO. | PLAYERS SURNAME | FIRST NAME | MIDDLE NAME | DATE OF BIRTH | PLACE OF BIRTH | DATE SIGNED | HEIGHT FT INS | WEIGHT ST LBS | POSITION ON PITCH | PREVIOUS CLUB |
|---|---|---|---|---|---|---|---|---|---|---|
| 21 | Baillie | Jonathan | | 02/09/85 | Irvine | 25/07/02 | 6' 2" | 12st 9lb | Def | Hibernian Youths |
| 14 | Beuzelin | Guillaume | | 14/04/79 | Ste Adresse | 23/07/04 | 5' 9" | 12st 11lb | Mid | Le Havre |
| 30 | Brown | Alistair | Hugh | 12/12/85 | Irvine | 03/07/02 | 6' 1" | 12st 4lb | Gk | Hibernian Youths |
| 7 | Brown | Scott | | 25/06/85 | Dunfermline | 25/07/02 | 5' 9" | 11st 4lb | Fwd | Hibernian 'S' Form |
| 1 | Brown | Simon | | 03/12/76 | Chelmsford | 23/06/04 | 6' 2" | 15st 0lb | Gk | Colchester United |
| | Bryson | Kyle | Scott | 24/07/87 | Irvine | 21/07/04 | 6' 1" | 11st 9lb | Def | Kilmarnock Youth |
| 4 | Caldwell | Gary | | 12/04/82 | Stirling | 30/01/04 | 5' 11" | 11st 10lb | Def | Newcastle United |
| | Campbell | Ross | Alexander | 03/07/87 | Galashiels | 21/07/04 | 5' 10" | 9st 3lb | Fwd | Hibernian Youths |
| | Chisholm | Ross | Stephen | 14/01/88 | Irvine | 30/01/04 | 5' 9" | 10st 4lb | Def | Hibernian Youths |
| | Crooks | Gary | Alistair | 15/02/87 | Falkirk | 11/09/03 | 5' 8" | 11st 0lb | Mid | St. Johnstone |
| | Cropley | Jordan | | 24/06/89 | Edinburgh | 06/07/05 | 5' 7" | 10st 0lb | Fwd | Hibernian Youths |
| | Curtis | Matthew | Robert | 10/02/89 | Dunfermline | 04/07/05 | 5' 11.5" | 12st 0lb | Gk | Hibernian Youths |
| | Dingwall | Joseph | Michael | 02/10/88 | Edinburgh | 04/07/05 | 5' 10" | 11st 1lb | Def | Hibernian Youths |
| 20 | Fletcher | Steven | | 26/03/87 | Shrewsbury | 04/07/03 | 6' 1" | 12st 0lb | Fwd | Hibernian Youths |
| 11 | Glass | Stephen | | 23/05/76 | Dundee | 10/07/03 | 5' 9.5" | 10st 13lb | Mid/Fwd | Watford |
| | Gray | Damon | | 11/07/88 | Newcastle | 04/07/05 | 5' 9" | 11st 9lb | Fwd | Hibernian Youths |
| 15 | Hogg | Christopher | | 12/03/85 | Middlesbrough | 31/01/05 | 6' 0" | 13st 1lb | Def | Ipswich Town |
| 19 | Konte | Amadou | | 23/01/81 | Bamako | 31/01/05 | 6' 3" | 13st 11lb | Fwd | Cambridge United |
| | Lynch | Sean | | 31/01/87 | Dechmont | 26/07/04 | 5' 10" | 10st 10lb | Mid | Livingston Youths |
| | Mailey | Patrick | | 18/04/88 | Letterkenny | 08/08/05 | 6' 3" | 12st 10lb | Def | Institute |
| 31 | Malkowski | Zbigniew | | 19/01/78 | Olsztyn | 18/07/05 | 6' 2" | 12st 7lb | Gk | Feyenoord |
| | McCaffrey | Dermott | | 29/03/86 | N. Ireland | 30/01/04 | 5' 11" | 10st 12lb | Def | Hibernian Youths |
| | McCann | Kevin | | 11/09/87 | Glasgow | 21/07/04 | 5' 10" | 11st 2lb | Def | Hibernian Youths |
| 18 | McCluskey | Jamie | | 06/11/87 | Bellshill | 16/01/04 | 5' 7" | 8st 8lb | Mid | Hibernian Youths |
| | McCormack | Darren | | 29/09/88 | Edinburgh | 19/07/05 | 6' 0" | 11st 8lb | Def | Hibernian Youths |
| 23 | McDonald | Kevin | Alan | 26/06/85 | Newcastle | 25/07/01 | 5' 10" | 10st 9lb | Mid | Sunderland |
| | McKenzie | Jamie | | 08/05/86 | Kirkcaldy | 04/07/03 | 6' 1" | 12st 10lb | Def | Hibernian Youths |
| 13 | Morrow | Samuel | | 03/03/85 | Derry | 01/07/04 | 6' 0" | 12st 10lb | Fwd | Ipswich Town |
| 3 | Murphy | David | | 01/03/84 | Hartlepool | 28/07/04 | 6' 1" | 13st 8lb | Def | Middlesbrough |
| 16 | Murray | Antonio | | 15/09/84 | Cambridge | 14/01/05 | 5' 9" | 11st 12lb | Mid | Ipswich Town |
| | Mya | Martin | | 06/08/88 | Edinburgh | 19/07/05 | 5' 9" | 10st 6lb | Fwd | Hibernian Youths |
| | Nelson | Kyle | | 05/03/87 | Co. Derry | 27/08/04 | 6' 2" | 14st 4lb | Gk | Glenavon Youths |
| | Nkazi-Tomatala | Ivan | | 31/12/87 | Paris | 06/07/05 | 5' 9" | 10st 12lb | Mid | Wallsend B.C. |
| | Notman | Steven | | 29/09/86 | Edinburgh | 04/07/03 | 5' 11" | 10st 11lb | Mid | Hibernian Youths |
| 9 | O'Connor | Garry | Lawrence | 07/05/83 | Edinburgh | 14/05/99 | 6' 1" | 12st 7lb | Fwd | Salvesen B.C. |
| | Pow | Ryan | | 30/06/87 | Edinburgh | 04/07/03 | 5' 8" | 10st 2lb | Mid | Airdrieonians |
| 10 | Riordan | Derek | George | 16/01/83 | Edinburgh | 14/05/99 | 5' 11" | 10st 8lb | Fwd | Hutchison Vale B.C. |
| | Rossi | Gerard | | 21/05/88 | Edinburgh | 13/07/05 | 5' 7" | 10st 0lb | Fwd | Hibernian Youths |
| 25 | Rudge | Humphrey | | 15/08/77 | Geleen | 09/08/05 | 6' 0" | 12st 0lb | Def | Apollon Limassol |
| 24 | Shields | Jay | | 06/01/85 | Edinburgh | 05/07/01 | 5' 7" | 11st 4lb | Mid | Hibernian Youths |
| 22 | Shiels | Dean | | 01/02/85 | Magherfelt | 09/07/04 | 5' 11" | 9st 10lb | Fwd | Arsenal |
| | Smith | Darren | James | 06/12/86 | Edinburgh | 04/07/03 | 5' 10" | 11st 6lb | Mid | Hibernian Youths |
| 5 | Smith | Gary | | 25/03/71 | Glasgow | 13/07/00 | 6' 0" | 12st 3lb | Def | Aberdeen |
| 17 | Sproule | Ivan | | 18/02/81 | Omagh | 31/01/05 | 5' 8.5" | 10st 5lb | Mid/Fwd | Institute |
| 26 | Stevenson | Lewis | | 05/01/88 | Kirkcaldy | 15/07/05 | 5' 7" | 10st 8lb | Def | Hibernian Youths. |
| 6 | Stewart | Michael | | 26/02/81 | Edinburgh | 30/06/05 | 5' 10" | 12st 5lb | Mid | Manchester United |
| 8 | Thomson | Kevin | | 14/10/84 | Edinburgh | 10/08/01 | 5' 11" | 11st 4lb | Mid | Hibernian Youths |
| | Tolmie | Blair | | 07/08/89 | Edinburgh | 06/07/05 | 6' 1.5" | 10st 12lb | Def | Hibernian Youths. |
| | Venus | Mark | | 06/04/67 | Hartlepool | 23/06/04 | 6' 6" | 12st 12lb | Def | Hornchurch |
| | Weightman | Nicholas | John | 06/04/87 | Lanark | 04/07/03 | 5' 10" | 10st 11lb | Mid | Hibernian Youths. |
| 2 | Whittaker | Steven | Gordon | 16/06/84 | Edinburgh | 01/08/00 | 6' 1" | 13st 9lb | Mid | Star A B.C. |

## TICKET INFORMATION

### Season Ticket Prices

| Stand | Adult | Senior | 15–18 | Student | 14 & Under | 5 & Under |
|---|---|---|---|---|---|---|
| West Stand | £345-320* | £175-125* | £150-100* | £150-100* | £125-65* | £45* |
| Famous Five Upper | £320 | £125 | £100 | £100 | £65 | £45 |
| Famous Five Lower | £295 | £100 | £75 | N/A | £55 | £35 |
| East Stand | £295 | £175 | N/A | £150 | £125 | £105 |

* Special family group price minimum of one adult and one other concessionary price (senior citizen, 15-18/Student, Hibs Kids)

### Match Ticket Information

| Stand | Category A | | Category B | |
|---|---|---|---|---|
| | Adult | Child/Senior | Adult | Child/Senior |
| West Stand | £25 | £10 | £20 | £10 |
| Famous Five Upper | £25 | £10 | £20 | £10 |
| Famous Five Lower (Family Section) | £22 | £10 | £18 | £10 |
| East Stand | £22 | £10 | £18 | £10 |
| South Stand | £25 | £10 | £20 | £10 |

## MILESTONES:

**Year of formation:** 1875
**Most Capped player:** Lawrie Reilly
**No. of Caps:** 38
**Most League points in a season:**
57 (First Division – Season 1980/81) (2 Points for a Win)
89 (First Division – Season 1998/99) (3 Points for a Win)
**Most League goals scored by a player in a season:**
Joe Baker (Season 1959/60)
**No. of goals scored:** 42
**Record Attendance:** 65,840 (-v- Heart of Midlothian – 2)
**Record Victory:** 22-1 (-v- 42nd Highlanders 3.9.1881)
**Record Defeat:** 0-10 (-v- Rangers – 24.12.1898)

Category A: Matches against Celtic, Hearts & Rangers. Category B: All other SPL matches

# SEASON STATS 2004.05

## SEASON STATS 2004.05

| Date | Venue | Opponents | Att | Res | Brown Simon | Murdock C. | Caldwell G. | Murphy D. | Whittaker S. | Glass S. | Beuzelin G. | Brebner G. | Brown Scott | McManus T. | O'Connor G. | Morrow S. | Riordan D. | Shields D. | Shields J. | Smith G. | Dobbie S. | Nicol K. | Baillie J. | Murray I. | Rocastle C. | Fletcher S. | Orman A. | McCluskey J. | McDonald K. | Brown A. | Murray A. | Konte A. | Sproule I. | Thomson K. |
|---|---|---|---|---|---|---|---|---|---|---|---|---|---|---|---|---|---|---|---|---|---|---|---|---|---|---|---|---|---|---|---|---|---|---|---|
| 7-Aug | H | Kilmarnock | 10,933 | 0-1 | 1 | 2 | 3 | 4 | 5 | 6 | 7 | 8 | 9 | 10 | 11 | 12 | 13 | 14 | | | | | | | | | | | | | | | | |
| 14-Aug | A | Motherwell | 5,859 | 2-1 | 1 | 2 | 3 | 4 | 5 | 6 | 7 | 8 | 9 | 10 | 11² | 12 | | 13 | 14 | | | | | | | | | | | | | | | |
| 21-Aug | A | Rangers | 48,702 | 1-4 | 1 | | 2 | 4 | 5 | 6 | 7 | | 9 | | 11 | 12 | 10 | 8 | 14 | 3 | 13 | | | | | | | | | | | | | |
| 28-Aug | H | Dundee | 9,344 | 4-4 | 1 | 2 | 3 | 4 | 5 | 6 | 7 | | 9 | | 11² | 14 | 10 | 8 | | | | 12 | 13 | | | | | | | | | | | |
| 1-Sep | A | Inverness Cal.Th. | 2,011 | 2-1 | 1 | | 2 | 4 | 5 | 7 | 3 | | 9 | | 11 | 10² | 8 | 14 | | 13 | | | 6 | 12 | | | | | | | | | | |
| 19-Sep | H | Celtic | 13,573 | †2-2 | 1 | | 2 | 4 | 5 | 7 | 3 | | 9 | | 11 | | 10 | 8 | 14 | | 12 | | | 6 | | 13 | | | | | | | | |
| 25-Sep | A | Aberdeen | 12,137 | 1-0 | 1 | | 2 | 4 | 5 | 7 | 3 | | | | 11 | | 10 | 8 | 12 | | 13 | | | 6 | | 9 | | | | | | | | |
| 2-Oct | A | Dunfermline Ath. | 7,295 | 1-1 | 1 | | 2 | 4 | 5 | 7 | 3 | | | | 11 | | 10 | 8 | 12 | | | | | 6 | | 9 | | | | | | | | |
| 16-Oct | H | Dundee United | 9,850 | 2-0 | 1 | | 2 | | 5 | 7 | 3 | | | | 11 | | 10 | 8 | | | 14 | | | 6 | 12 | 9 | 4 | 13 | | | | | | |
| 24-Oct | A | Hearts | 16,720 | 1-2 | 1 | | 2 | 4 | 5 | 7 | 3 | | | | 11 | | 10 | 8 | | | 12 | | | 6 | | 9 | | | | | | | | |
| 27-Oct | H | Livingston | 9,087 | 2-1 | 1 | | 2 | 4 | 5 | 7 | 3 | | | | 11 | | 10 | 13 | | | | | | 6 | 8 | 12 | 9 | 14 | | | | | | |
| 30-Oct | A | Kilmarnock | 5,959 | 1-3 | 1 | | 2 | 4 | 5 | 7 | 3 | | | | | | 10 | 13 | | | 12 | | | 6 | 8 | 11 | 9 | 14 | | | | | | |
| 6-Nov | H | Motherwell | 9,931 | 1-0 | 1 | 2 | 4 | | 5 | 7 | 3 | | | | | | 12 | 10 | 9 | | | | | 6 | 8 | 11 | | | | | | | | |
| 14-Nov | H | Rangers | 13,825 | 0-1 | 1 | 2 | 4 | | 5 | 7 | 3 | | | | 11 | 12 | 10 | 9 | | 13 | | | | 6 | 8 | | 14 | | | | | | | |
| 20-Nov | A | Dundee | 5,274 | 4-1 | | | 4 | 2 | 7 | 8 | | | | | 13 | 11 | 10 | 12 | | 3 | | | | 5 | 9 | | 6 | | | | | | | |
| 27-Nov | H | Inverness Cal.Th. | 9,739 | 2-1 | 1 | | 2 | 4 | 3 | 14 | 7 | | | | 13 | 11 | 10 | 9 | | | | | | 5 | 8 | | 6 | 12 | | | | | | |
| 3-Dec | A | Celtic | 58,399 | 1-2 | 1 | | 2 | 4 | 3 | 7 | 6 | | | | 11 | 12 | 10 | 9 | | | | | | 5 | 8 | | 13 | 14 | | | | | | |
| 11-Dec | H | Aberdeen | 13,503 | 2-1 | 1 | | 2 | 4 | 3 | 7 | 6 | | | | 11 | 12 | 10 | 9 | | | | | | 5 | 8 | 14 | 13 | | | | | | | |
| 18-Dec | H | Dunfermline Ath. | 9,859 | 2-1 | 1 | | 2 | 4 | 3 | 7 | 6 | | | | 11 | 14 | 10 | 9 | | | | | | 5 | 8 | | 12 | | 15 | | | | | |
| 27-Dec | A | Dundee United | 10,152 | 4-1 | 1 | | 2 | 4 | 3 | 7 | | | | | 11 | 12 | 10 | 9 | | | | | | 5 | 8 | 13 | 6 | | | | | | | |
| 2-Jan | H | Hearts | 17,259 | 1-1 | 1 | | 2 | 4 | 3 | 7 | | | | | 11 | 12 | 10 | 9 | | | | | | 5 | 8 | | 6 | | | | | | | |
| 15-Jan | A | Livingston | 6,188 | 2-0 | 1 | | 2 | | 5 | 7 | 12 | | | | 11 | 13 | 10 | 9 | | 3 | | | | | 8 | 4 | 14 | | | 6 | | | | |
| 22-Jan | A | Kilmarnock | 12,660 | 3-0 | 1 | | 2 | | 4 | 7 | 12 | | | | 11 | 13 | 10³ | 9 | | 3 | | | | 5 | 8 | | 14 | | | 6 | | | | |
| 2-Feb | A | Rangers | 50,143 | 0-3 | 1 | | 2 | 4 | 5 | 7 | | | | | 11 | 8 | 10 | 9 | | 3 | | | | 6 | 14 | | | | | 13 | 12 | | | |
| 5-Feb | A | Motherwell | 7,453 | 1-1 | 1 | | 2 | 4 | 5 | 7 | | | 12 | | 11 | 8 | 10 | 9 | | 3 | | | | | 13 | | | | | 6 | 14 | | | |
| 9-Feb | H | Dundee | 10,938 | 4-0 | 1 | | 2 | 4 | 5 | 7 | | | 13 | | 11² | 9 | 10 | | | 3 | | | | | 8 | | 14 | | | 6 | 12 | | | |
| ?-Mar | A | Inverness Cal.Th. | 4,443 | 0-3 | 1 | | 2 | 4 | 5 | | | | 9 | | 11 | | 10 | 14 | | 3 | | | | 6 | | 8 | 12 | 7 | | 13 | | | | |
| ?-Mar | H | Celtic | 15,787 | 1-3 | 1 | | 2 | 4 | 5 | | 12 | | 8 | | 11 | | 10 | 9 | | 3 | | | | 6 | | 7 | | | | 13 | 14 | | | |
| 12-Mar | A | Aberdeen | 14,465 | 0-3 | 1 | | 2 | 4 | 5 | 12 | 7 | | 8 | | 11 | | 10 | 9 | | 3 | | | | 6 | | | 13 | | | | 14 | | | |
| 19-Mar | A | Dunfermline Ath. | 7,204 | 4-1 | 1 | | 2 | 4 | 5 | 7 | | | 8 | | 11 | | 10² | 9 | | 3 | | | | 6 | | 12² | 13 | | | 14 | | | | |
| ?-Apr | H | Dundee United | 11,058 | 3-2 | 1 | | 2 | 4 | | 7 | | | 8 | | 11 | 12 | 10 | 9 | 3 | | | | | 6 | | 5 | | | | | | | 13 | |
| 3-Apr | A | Hearts | 17,673 | 2-1 | 1 | | 2 | | 5 | 7 | | | 8 | | 11 | | 10 | 9 | 3 | | | | | 6 | | 14 | | | 4 | 13 | 12 | | | |
| 6-Apr | H | Livingston | 10,637 | 0-3 | 1 | | 2 | 4 | 5 | 7 | | | 8 | | 11 | 13 | 10 | 9 | 3 | | | | | 6 | | | | | | 14 | 12 | | | |
| 13-Apr | H | Hearts | 16,620 | 2-2 | 1 | | 2 | | 5 | 7 | | | 8 | | 11 | 12 | 10 | 9 | 3 | | | | | 6 | | 13 | | | 4 | 6 | | | | |
| 20-Apr | A | Celtic | 58,389 | 3-1 | 1 | | 2 | | 5 | 7 | | | 9 | | 11 | 14 | 10 | 13 | 3 | | | | | 6 | | | | | 4 | 8 | 12 | | | |
| ?-May | A | Motherwell | 8,903 | 2-2 | 1 | | 2 | | 5 | 7 | 12 | | 9 | | 11 | | 10 | 14 | 3 | | | | | 6 | | | | | 4 | 13 | 8 | | | |
| 14-May | H | Aberdeen | 15,288 | 1-2 | 1 | | 2 | | 5 | 7 | 12 | | 9 | | 11 | | 10 | 14 | 3 | | | | | 6 | | | | | 4 | 8 | 13 | | | |
| 22-May | H | Rangers | 16,601 | 0-1 | 1 | | 2 | | 5 | 7 | 4 | | 9 | | 11 | | 10 | 12 | 3 | | | | | 6 | | | | | | | 14 | 13 | 8 | |
| **TOTAL FULL APPEARANCES** | | | | | 38 | 5 | 37 | 27 | 37 | 34 | 21 | 2 | 18 | 2 | 34 | 5 | 36 | 28 | | 19 | | | | 29 | 11 | 11 | 10 | | 10 | 3 | 1 | |
| **TOTAL SUB APPEARANCES** | | | | | | | | | | 2 | 5 | | 2 | | 2 | 17 | 1 | 9 | 6 | 1 | 7 | 1 | 1 | | 2 | 9 | 2 | 10 | 3 | 1 | 2 | 9 | 6 | 3 |
| **TOTAL GOALS SCORED** | | | | | | | 3 | 1 | 1 | 2 | 4 | 1 | | | 14 | 1 | 20 | 5 | | 1 | | | | | 5 | 2 | | | | | 1 | 1 |

Figure in bold denotes goal scored. Secondary smaller figure in bold denotes number of goals scored. † denotes opponent's own goal.

## THE HIBEES' 10 YEAR LEAGUE RECORD

| Season | Div | P | W | D | L | F | A | Pts | Pos |
|---|---|---|---|---|---|---|---|---|---|
| 1995-96 | P | 36 | 11 | 10 | 15 | 43 | 57 | 43 | 5 |
| 1996-97 | P | 36 | 9 | 11 | 16 | 38 | 55 | 38 | 9 |
| 1997-98 | P | 36 | 6 | 12 | 18 | 38 | 59 | 30 | 10 |
| 1998-99 | F | 36 | 28 | 5 | 3 | 84 | 33 | 89 | 1 |
| 1999-00 | SPL | 36 | 10 | 11 | 15 | 49 | 61 | 41 | 6 |
| 2000-01 | SPL | 38 | 18 | 12 | 8 | 57 | 35 | 66 | 3 |
| 2001-02 | SPL | 38 | 10 | 11 | 17 | 51 | 56 | 41 | 10 |
| 2002-03 | SPL | 38 | 15 | 6 | 17 | 56 | 64 | 51 | 7 |
| 2003-04 | SPL | 38 | 11 | 11 | 16 | 41 | 60 | 44 | 8 |
| 2004-05 | SPL | 38 | 18 | 7 | 13 | 64 | 57 | 61 | 3 |

## LEADING GOALSCORERS:

| Season | Div | Goals | Player |
|---|---|---|---|
| 1995-96 | P | 9 | D. Jackson, K. Wright |
| 1996-97 | P | 11 | D. Jackson |
| 1997-98 | P | 9 | S. Crawford |
| 1998-99 | F | 14 | S. Crawford |
| 1999-00 | SPL | 11 | K. Miller |
| 2000-01 | SPL | 11 | M-M. Paatelainen |
| 2001-02 | SPL | 10 | G. O'Connor |
| 2002-03 | SPL | 12 | T. McManus |
| 2003-04 | SPL | 15 | D. Riordan |
| 2004-05 | SPL | 20 | D. Riordan |

HIBERNIAN PLAYING KITS SEASON 2005.06

FIRST KIT  SECOND KIT  THIRD KIT

# INVERNESS CALEDONIAN THISTLE

**INVERNESS CALEDONIAN THISTLE F.C.**
Tulloch Caledonian Stadium,
East Longman, Inverness, IV1 1FF
**TELEPHONE NUMBERS**
Ground/Ticket Office (01463) 222880
Sec. Mobile 07881 770207
**FAX** (01463) 715816
**E-MAIL** jim.falconer@caleythistleonline.com
**WEBSITE** www.caleythistleonline.com
**CHAIRMAN** Kenneth Mackie
**VICE-CHAIRMAN** Graeme Bennett
**DIRECTORS**
Ian MacDonald, Alexander Catto,
Nigel P. Spiller & David Sutherland
**CHIEF EXECUTIVE** Mike Smith
**HONORARY PRESIDENT**
John S. McDonald O.B.E.
**SECRETARY** James Falconer
**PLAYER / MANAGER** Craig Brewster
**ASSISTANT MANAGER** Malcolm Thomson
**FIRST TEAM COACH** Charlie Christie
**DIRECTOR OF FOOTBALL** Graeme Bennett
**RESERVE COACH** John Docherty
**FITNESS COACH** Peter Davidson
**YOUTH & COMMUNITY DEVELOPMENT**
**MANAGER** Danny MacDonald
**ASSISTANT COMMUNITY DEVELOPMENT**
**MANAGER / COMMUNITY DEVELOPMENT**
**CO-ORDINATOR** Fiona McWilliams
**FOOTBALL DEVELOPMENT**
**CO-ORDINATOR** Ronnie Duncan
**SENIOR COMMUNITY COACH** Ally Velzian
**CLUB COACHES** Tony Low & Craig Masterton
**YOUTH COACHES**
U19: Stevie Campbell
U19 Assistant: Scott Kellacher
U17: Danny MacDonald & Tony Low
U15: Ronnie Duncan, Graeme MacDonald &
Charlie Charlesworth
U14: Fiona McWilliams & Ian Polworth
U13: Scott Kellacher & Joe MacMillan
U12: Charlie Christie
U11: Ronnie Duncan
**TEAM CAPTAIN** Stuart Golabek
**FOOTBALL SAFETY OFFICERS'**
**ASSOCIATION REPRESENTATIVE**
John Sutherland M.B.E.
**COMMERCIAL MANAGER** Morven Reid
**LOTTERY MANAGER** Charlie Christie
**MEDIA LIAISON PERSON** Bill McAllister
**MATCHDAY PROGRAMME EDITOR**
Bryan Munro (01463) 230721
email: bryan.munro@lineone.net
**CLUB DOCTORS**
Dr. Ian Smith & Dr. Derek MacLeod
**PHYSIOTHERAPIST** David Brandie
**GROUNDSMAN & KIT PERSON**
Tommy Cumming
**CLUB CHAPLAIN** Rev. Arthur Fraser
**TICKET OFFICE MANAGER** Andrina Robb
**CLUB SHOP**
Situated at Stadium. Open 9.30am - 4.30pm
Monday to Friday and on Home Matchdays
**OFFICIAL SUPPORTERS CLUB**
Secretary, Caledonian Stadium,
East Longman, Inverness, IV1 1FF
**SHIRT SPONSOR** One Touch
**KIT SUPPLIER** Errea

## LIST OF PLAYERS 2005.06

| SQUAD NO. | PLAYERS SURNAME | FIRST NAME | MIDDLE NAME | DATE OF BIRTH | PLACE OF BIRTH | DATE SIGNED | HEIGHT FT INS | WEIGHT ST LBS | POSITION ON PITCH | PREVIOUS CLUB |
|---|---|---|---|---|---|---|---|---|---|---|
| 9 | Bayne | Graham | Patrick | 22/08/79 | Kirkcaldy | 2/6/04 | 6' 1" | 13st | Fwd | Ross County |
| 24 | Black | Ian | George | 14/03/85 | Edinburgh | 30/7/04 | 5' 7.5" | 9st 12lb | Mid | Blackburn Rovers |
| 25 | Brewster | Craig | | 13/12/66 | Dundee | 5/1/05 | 6' 1" | 12st 9lb | Fwd | Dunfermline Athletic |
| 1 | Brown | Mark | | 28/02/81 | Motherwell | 2/8/02 | 6' 1.5" | 13st 2lb | Gk | Motherwell |
| 11 | Carricondo | Juanjo | | 04/05/77 | Barcelona | 29/7/04 | 5' 8" | 10st 7lb | Fwd | Real Jean |
| 32 | Charlesworth | Martin | | 18/04/88 | Inverness | 12/8/05 | 5' 11" | 10st 7lb | Fwd | Elgin City |
| 33 | Clark | Brian | | 01/03/88 | Dundee | 1/7/05 | 5' 11" | 10st 7lb | Mid/Fwd | Dundee |
| 34 | Clark | David | Ewan | 12/01/88 | Inverness | 30/6/05 | 5' 10" | 10st 8lb | Def | Inverness Cal Th Form |
| 17 | Dargo | Craig | Peter | 03/01/78 | Edinburgh | 16/6/05 | 5' 6" | 10st 1lb | Fwd | Kilmarnock |
| 4 | Dods | Darren | | 07/06/75 | Edinburgh | 30/7/04 | 6' 1" | 13st 2lb | Def | St. Johnstone |
| 35 | Donald | Martyn | John | 23/01/88 | Aberdeen | 7/1/05 | 5'11" | 11st 8lb | Fwd | Elgin City |
| 12 | Duncan | Russell | Allan | 15/09/80 | Aberdeen | 3/8/01 | 5' 10" | 11st 7lb | Def/Mid | Forfar Athletic |
| 26 | Finnigan | Christopher | James | 05/04/86 | Glasgow | 11/6/03 | 5' 10" | 11st 0lb | Mid/Fwd | Inverness Cal Th Form DL |
| 23 | Fox | Liam | | 02/02/84 | Edinburgh | 30/7/04 | 5' 11" | 11st 0lb | Mid | Heart of Midlothian |
| 21 | Fraser | Michael | Alan | 08/10/83 | Inverness | 9/1/03 | 6' 3" | 13st 4lb | Gk | Brora Rangers |
| 36 | Gibb | Neil | Alexander | 02/09/88 | Inverness | 30/6/05 | 5' 10" | 10st 7lb | Def | Inverness Cal Th Form |
| 3 | Golabek | Stuart | William | 05/11/74 | Inverness | 27/5/99 | 5' 10" | 11st 0lb | Def | Ross County |
| 10 | Hart | Richard | | 30/03/78 | Inverness | 1/8/02 | 5' 10" | 12st 5lb | Def/Mid | Brora Rangers |
| 16 | Hastings | Richard | Corey | 18/05/77 | Prince George B.C. | 23/8/04 | 5' 11" | 11st 6lb | Def | MVV Maastricht |
| 37 | Jarvie | Darren | James | 29/08/87 | Inverness | 2/6/04 | 5' 11" | 12st 8lb | Def | Inverness Cal Th Form |
| 15 | Keogh | Liam | Michael | 06/09/81 | Aberdeen | 2/8/02 | 5' 9" | 12st 3lb | Mid | St. Mirren |
| 38 | Kerr | Guy | Duncan | 03/04/88 | Edinburgh | 24/5/04 | 6' 2" | 12st 0lb | Def | Dunfermline Athletic |
| 39 | MacLaren | Iain | Ross | 02/03/88 | Inverness | 30/6/05 | 6' 2" | 11 st | Def | Ross County |
| 28 | McAllister | Rory | | 13/05/87 | Aberdeen | 25/8/04 | 6' 1" | 12st 7lb | Fwd | Aberdeen |
| 6 | McBain | Roy | Adam | 07/11/74 | Aberdeen | 4/8/00 | 5' 11" | 11st 5lb | Def/Mid | Ross County |
| 5 | McCaffrey | Stuart | Muir | 30/05/79 | Glasgow | 1/12/00 | 5' 11.5" | 12st 0lb | Def | Aberdeen |
| 40 | McIntyre | Ian | | 23/02/88 | Irvine | 17/1/04 | 5'11" | 12st | GK | Ross County |
| 22 | Morgan | Alan | | 27/11/83 | Musselburgh | 9/8/05 | 6' | 12st 7lb | Def | Blackburn Rover |
| 14 | Munro | Grant | John | 15/09/80 | Inverness | 21/2/00 | 6' 0" | 13st 4lb | Def | Inverness Cal Th Form |
| 20 | Parratt | Tom | | 02/03/86 | Inverness | 5/7/05 | 5'9" | 11st | Def | Birmingham City |
| 18 | Proctor | David | William | 04/05/84 | Bellshill | 7/7/03 | 6' 0" | 11st 2lb | Mid | Hibernian |
| 41 | Ross | Christopher | John | 02/06/88 | Inverness | 30/6/05 | 6' 0" | 10st 0lb | Mid | Inverness Cal Th Form |
| 42 | Rutherford | Martin | | 15/04/87 | Edinburgh | 4/6/04 | 5' 10.5" | 11st 0lb | Def/Mid | Heart of Midlothian |
| 44 | Smith | Jonathon | | 26/11/87 | Inverness | 3/8/04 | 5' 10" | 11st 5lb | Gk | Inverness Cal Th Form DL |
| 43 | Soane | Stuart | | 05/11/87 | Dunfermline | 12/8/04 | 5' 10" | 9st 4lb | Mid | Inverness Cal Th Form DL |
| 45 | Sutherland | Alexander | George | 07/09/87 | Wick | 5/8/04 | 5' 6" | 10st 0lb | Mid | Inverness Cal Th Form |
| 46 | Sutherland | Christopher | Mark | 01/02/88 | Inverness | 30/6/05 | 5'11" | 11st | Fwd | Inverness Cal Th Form |
| 47 | Taylor | Ben | | 08/02/89 | Dundee | 24/8/05 | 5' 9" | 9st 0lb | Def | Dundee Youths |
| 2 | Tokely | Ross | Norman | 08/03/79 | Aberdeen | 3/6/96 | 6' 3" | 14st 6lb | Def/Mid | Huntly |
| 48 | Tulloch | Jamie | | 16/10/88 | Inverness | 30/6/05 | 5' 9" | 11st 2lb | Mid | Inverness Cal Th Form |
| 49 | Watson | David | Allan | 04/01/88 | Dingwall | 7/1/05 | 5'8" | 10st | Mid | Inverness Cal Th Form |
| 7 | Wilson | Barry | John | 16/02/72 | Kirkcaldy | 31/8/03 | 5' 11" | 13st 0lb | Mid/Fwd | Livingston |
| 19 | Wyness | Dennis | | 22/03/77 | Aberdeen | 19/8/05 | 5' 10.5" | 12st 7lb | Fwd | Heart of Midlothian |

### TICKET INFORMATION

**Season Ticket Information**

| | Adult | OAP/Student | Child | Young Blues |
|---|---|---|---|---|
| MAIN STAND | £320 | £195 | £120 | £90 |
| NORTH STAND | £280 | £150 | £80 | £60 |
| KEVIN BISSETT FAMILY ENC. | £200 | £100 | £60 | £45 |

**League Admission Prices**

| | Adults | Conc. |
|---|---|---|
| MAIN STAND (HOME) | £25 | £20 |
| NORTH STAND (HOME) | £20 | £15 |
| KEVIN BISSETT FAMILY ENC. | £15 | £13/7 |
| SOUTH STAND (AWAY END) | £20 | £15 |

### MILESTONES:

**Year of formation:** 1994
**Most League points in a season:**
76 (Third Division – Season 1996/97) (3 Points for a Win)
**Most League goals scored by a player in a season:**
Iain Stewart (Season 1996/97)
**No. of goals scored:** 27
**Record Attendance:** 4,931 (-v- Ross County – 23.1.1996
Telford Street Park) and 7,512 (-v- Rangers - (SPL) – 6.8
at Tulloch Caledonian Stadium)
**Record Victory:** 8-1 (-v- Annan Athletic – Scottish Cup, 2
**Record Defeat:** 1-5 (-v- Morton – First Division, 12.11.19
(-v- Airdrieonians – First Division, 15.4.2000)

## SEASON STATS 2004.05

| DATE | VENUE | OPPONENTS | ATT | RES | Brown M. | Tokely R. | Golabek S. | Munro G. | McCaffrey S. | Duncan R. | Keogh L. | McBain R. | Wilson B. | Hislop S. | Bayne G. | Hart R. | Carricondo J. | Black I. | Prunty B. | Hastings R. | Fox L. | Dods D. | Fraser M. | Thomson D. | Brewster C. | Fetai B. | Proctor D. | McAllister R. |
|---|---|---|---|---|---|---|---|---|---|---|---|---|---|---|---|---|---|---|---|---|---|---|---|---|---|---|---|---|
| ?-Aug | A | Livingston | 3,315 | 0-3 | 1 | 2 | 3 | 4 | 5 | 6 | 7 | 8 | 9 | 10 | 11 | 12 | 13 | 14 | | | | | | | | | | |
| 15-Aug | H | Dunfermline Ath. | 2,583 | 2-0 | 1 | 2 | **3** | 4 | 5 | | 7 | 8 | 12 | 10 | 11 | 6 | **9** | | 13 | | | | | | | | | |
| 22-Aug | H | Celtic | 8,788 | 1-3 | 1 | 2 | 3 | 4 | 5 | | 7 | 8 | **9** | 12 | 11 | 6 | 10 | 14 | 13 | | | | | | | | | |
| 28-Aug | A | Dundee United | 6,017 | 1-2 | 1 | 2 | 3 | 4 | 5 | | 7 | 8 | **9** | 13 | 11 | 6 | 10 | | 12 | | | | | | | | | |
| 1-Sep | H | Hibernian | 2,011 | 1-2 | 1 | 2 | 3 | 4 | 5 | | 7 | 8 | **9** | 12 | 11 | 6 | 10 | 13 | 14 | | | | | | | | | |
| 9-Sep | A | Rangers | 47,063 | 0-1 | 1 | 2 | 3 | 4 | 5 | | 7 | 8 | 9 | 12 | 11 | 6 | 10 | | 13 | | | | | | | | | |
| 25-Sep | A | Hearts | 10,340 | 0-1 | 1 | 2 | 3 | | 5 | 8 | 7 | 12 | 9 | 13 | 11 | 6 | 10 | | 14 | 4 | | | | | | | | |
| ?-Oct | H | Motherwell | 1,438 | 1-1 | 1 | 2 | 3 | 4 | **5** | 8 | 7 | 13 | 9 | | 11 | 6 | 10 | | 12 | | 14 | | | | | | | |
| 16-Oct | H | Aberdeen | 9,830 | 1-3 | 1 | 2 | 3 | 4 | 5 | 7 | 14 | **8** | 9 | | 11 | 6 | 12 | 13 | 10 | | | | | | | | | |
| 23-Oct | A | Kilmarnock | 4,721 | 2-2 | 1 | 2 | 3 | 4 | 5 | 7 | 13 | 8 | **9** | | 11 | 6 | 10 | | | 12 | **14** | | | | | | | |
| 27-Oct | H | Dundee | 1,282 | 2-1 | 1 | 2 | 3 | 4 | | 7 | 12 | 8 | 9 | | **11** | **6** | 10 | | 14 | | | 5 | 15 | | | | | |
| 30-Oct | H | Livingston | 1,284 | 2-0 | 1 | 2 | 3 | 4 | | 7 | 12 | 8 | **9** | | **11** | 6 | 10 | | | | | 5 | | 13 | | | | |
| ?-Nov | A | Dunfermline Ath. | 4,921 | 1-1 | 1 | **2** | 3 | 4 | | 7 | 14 | 8 | 9 | | 11 | 6 | 10 | 13 | | | 12 | 5 | | | | | | |
| 13-Nov | A | Celtic | 56,965 | 0-3 | 1 | | 3 | 4 | 5 | 7 | 8 | | 9 | | 11 | 6 | 10 | | 13 | | 12 | 2 | | | | | | |
| 23-Nov | H | Dundee United | 1,125 | 1-1 | 1 | 2 | 3 | 4 | 13 | 7 | | 8 | 9 | | 11 | 6 | **10** | | | | 12 | 5 | | | | | | |
| 27-Nov | A | Hibernian | 9,739 | 1-2 | 1 | | 3 | 4 | 5 | 7 | 8 | | 9 | | 11 | 6 | **10** | | | | 12 | 2 | | | | | | |
| ?-Dec | H | Rangers | 6,543 | 1-1 | 1 | 2 | 3 | 4 | | 7 | 9 | 8 | | | **11** | 6 | 10 | | 14 | 12 | | 5 | | | | | | |
| 11-Dec | H | Hearts | 2,011 | 1-1 | 1 | 2 | 3 | 4 | 14 | 7 | 9 | 8 | 13 | | 11 | **6** | 10 | | | 12 | | 5 | | | | | | |
| 18-Dec | A | Motherwell | 4,267 | 2-1 | 1 | 2 | 3 | 4 | | 7 | 9 | 8 | 12 | | **11** | **6** | 10 | | | 13 | | 5 | | | | | | |
| 27-Dec | A | Aberdeen | 18,250 | 0-0 | 1 | 2 | 3 | 4 | | 7 | 9 | 8 | | | 11 | 6 | 10 | | 12 | | | 5 | | | | | | |
| ?-Jan | H | Kilmarnock | 1,359 | 0-2 | 1 | 2 | 3 | 4 | | 7 | 9 | 8 | 13 | | 11 | 6 | 10 | | 14 | 12 | | 5 | | | | | | |
| 15-Jan | A | Dundee | 5,567 | 1-3 | 1 | | 3 | 4 | 2 | 7 | 9 | 6 | 8 | | 11 | 12 | 13 | | | | | 5 | | **10** | | | | |
| 22-Jan | A | Livingston | 3,606 | 4-1 | 1 | | 3 | 4 | 2 | **7** | | 8 | | | **11** | **6** | **9** | | 13 | | | 5 | | **10** | 12 | | | |
| 29-Jan | H | Dunfermline Ath. | 5,449 | 2-0 | 1 | 2 | 3 | 4 | | | 14 | **8** | | | 11 | 6 | 9 | | 13 | | | 5 | | **10** | 12 | | | |
| 7-Feb | A | Dundee United | 6,110 | 1-1 | 1 | 2 | 3 | 4 | | 7 | | 8 | **9** | | 11 | 6 | | | | | | 5 | | 10 | | | | |
| ?-Mar | H | Hibernian | 4,443 | 3-0 | 1 | 2 | 3 | 4 | | 7 | | 8 | 9 | | 12 | 6 | **11** | | | | | 5 | | 10 | 13 | 14 | | |
| ?-Mar | A | Rangers | 49,945 | 1-1 | 1 | 2 | 3 | 4 | | 7 | | 8 | 9 | | 11 | 6 | | **13** | | | | 5 | | | 12 | | | |
| 12-Mar | A | Hearts | 9,822 | 2-0 | 1 | 2 | 3 | 4 | | 7 | | 8 | **9** | | 12 | 6 | 11 | | 13 | | 14 | **5** | | | | | | |
| 16-Mar | H | Celtic | 7,047 | 0-2 | 1 | 2 | 3 | 4 | | 7 | | 8 | 9 | | 11 | 6 | 10 | 14 | 12 | | | | | | 13 | | | |
| ?-Apr | H | Aberdeen | 7,026 | 0-1 | 1 | 2 | 3 | 4 | | 7 | | 8 | 9 | | 14 | 6 | 11 | | 13 | | | 5 | | 10 | 12 | | | |
| ?-Apr | A | Kilmarnock | 4,862 | 1-0 | 1 | 2 | 3 | 4 | | | | 8 | **9** | | 11 | 6 | | 7 | | | | 5 | | 10 | | | | |
| 2-Apr | H | Motherwell | 3,746 | 1-0 | 1 | 2 | 3 | 4 | | 12 | | 8 | 9 | | **11** | 6 | | 7 | 10 | | | 5 | | | 13 | 14 | | |
| 16-Apr | H | Dundee | 4,786 | 3-2 | 1 | 2 | | 4 | | 13 | | 8 | 9 | | 14 | 6 | | 7 | 11 | 3 | | 5 | | **10** | 12 | | | |
| 23-Apr | A | Dunfermline Ath. | 4,471 | 0-0 | 1 | 2 | 3 | 4 | | | | 8 | 9 | | 13 | 6 | | 7 | 11 | | | 5 | | 10 | 12 | | | |
| 30-Apr | H | Kilmarnock | 3,108 | 1-2 | 1 | **2** | 3 | | | | | | | | 7 | 11 | 4 | | | | | 5 | | 10 | | 6 | 13 | |
| ?-May | H | Livingston | 3,021 | 0-1 | 1 | 2 | 3 | 4 | | | | | 8 | 9 | 10 | 12 | | 7 | 11 | 13 | | 5 | | | | | | 14 |
| ?-May | A | Dundee | 4,691 | 1-1 | 1 | 2 | 3 | 4 | | 7 | | 8 | | | 10 | 9 | | 11 | 6 | **13** | | 5 | | 12 | | | | 14 |
| ?-May | H | Dundee United | 5,479 | 0-1 | 1 | 2 | 3 | 4 | | | | 13 | | | 10 | 8 | | 7 | 11 | 6 | 9 | 5 | | 12 | | | | 14 |
| **TOTAL FULL APPEARANCES** | | | | | 38 | 34 | 37 | 36 | 14 | 27 | 16 | 31 | 30 | 2 | 32 | 34 | 26 | 7 | 8 | 5 | 1 | 28 | | 11 | | 1 | | |
| **TOTAL SUB APPEARANCES** | | | | | | | 2 | | 2 | 5 | 3 | 6 | 5 | 6 | 3 | 3 | 6 | 19 | 6 | 8 | 1 | 1 | 2 | 8 | 3 | 4 | |
| **TOTAL GOALS SCORED** | | | | | | 2 | 1 | | | 1 | 1 | 2 | 11 | | 6 | 3 | 6 | 1 | | | 2 | 1 | | 4 | | | |

...e in bold denotes goal scored. Secondary smaller figure in bold denotes number of goals scored. † denotes opponent's own goal.

### [INVERNESS CALEDONIAN THIST]LEY THISTLE'S 10 YEAR LEAGUE RECORD

| Season | Div | P | W | D | L | F | A | Pts | Pos |
|---|---|---|---|---|---|---|---|---|---|
| 95-96 | T | 36 | 15 | 12 | 9 | 64 | 38 | 57 | 3 |
| 96-97 | T | 36 | 23 | 7 | 6 | 70 | 37 | 76 | 1 |
| 97-98 | S | 36 | 13 | 10 | 13 | 65 | 51 | 49 | 5 |
| 98-99 | S | 36 | 21 | 9 | 6 | 80 | 48 | 72 | 2 |
| 99-00 | F | 36 | 13 | 13 | 10 | 60 | 55 | 49 | 6 |
| 00-01 | F | 36 | 14 | 12 | 10 | 71 | 54 | 54 | 4 |
| 01-02 | F | 36 | 13 | 9 | 14 | 60 | 51 | 48 | 6 |
| 02-03 | F | 36 | 20 | 5 | 11 | 74 | 45 | 65 | 4 |
| 03-04 | F | 36 | 21 | 7 | 8 | 67 | 33 | 70 | 1 |
| 04-05 | SPL | 38 | 11 | 11 | 16 | 41 | 47 | 44 | 8 |

### LEADING GOALSCORERS:

| Season | Div | Goals | Player |
|---|---|---|---|
| 1995-96 | T | 23 | I. Stewart |
| 1996-97 | T | 27 | I. Stewart |
| 1997-98 | S | 16 | I. Stewart |
| 1998-99 | S | 20 | S. McLean |
| 1999-00 | F | 13 | B. Wilson |
| 2000-01 | F | 24 | D. Wyness |
| 2001-02 | F | 18 | D. Wyness |
| 2002-03 | F | 19 | D. Wyness |
| 2003-04 | F | 14 | P. Ritchie |
| 2004-05 | SPL | 11 | B. Wilson |

**INVERNESS CAL.TH. PLAYING KITS SEASON 2005.06**

FIRST KIT   SECOND KIT   THIRD KIT

# KILMARNOCK

**KILMARNOCK F.C.**

Rugby Park, Rugby Road,
Kilmarnock, KA1 2DP

**TELEPHONE NUMBERS**

Ground & Matchday/Ticket Information
(01563) 545300

**FAX** (01563) 545303

**E-MAIL** aburnett@kilmarnockfc.co.uk

**WEBSITE** www.kilmarnockfc.co.uk

**CHAIRMAN** Michael Johnston

**DIRECTOR** Gordon Jackson, M.S.P

**HONORARY PRESIDENT** Sir John Orr, O.B.E

**SECRETARY, OFFICE ADMINISTRATOR
& MEDIA LIAISON OFFICER**
Mrs Angela Burnett (01563) 545302

**MANAGER** Jim Jefferies

**ASSISTANT MANAGER/
FIRST TEAM COACH** Billy Brown

**RESERVE COACH** Alan Robertson

**FITNESS COACH** Alex MacQueen

**UNDER 21 COACH** Alan Robertson

**COMMUNITY COACH** Paul McDonald

**YOUTH DEVELOPMENT COACH**
Alan Robertson

**YOUTH COACHES**
Paul Clarke & Stuart McLean

**CHIEF SCOUT** John Harvey

**TEAM CAPTAIN** Gary Locke

**FOOTBALL SAFETY OFFICERS'
ASSOCIATION REPRESENTATIVE**
Bob Pitt

**MATCHDAY PROGRAMME EDITOR**
Richard Cairns

**CLUB DOCTOR** Mr. Ivan Brenkel

**PHYSIOTHERAPIST** Alex MacQueen

**GROUNDSMAN** Mark Gallacher

**KIT PERSON** Manson Fowler

**COMMERCIAL ASSISTANT/
MATCHDAY HOSPITALITY**
Anne Clark & Ray Montgomerie
(01563) 545312

**PARK HOTEL**
On site hotel situated at the ground
(01563) 545999
email:enquiries@theparkhotel.uk.com

**SPORTSBAR**
The newly opened Sportsbar is closed on
Matchdays to the public between kick-off
and the final whistle

**CLUB SHOP**
Situated in the Commercial Centre
at the ground. (01563) 545310.
Open Mon to Fri 9 a.m. – 5 p.m.
Saturday home matchdays 10 a.m. – 5.30 p.m.
Saturday away matchdays 10 a.m. – 5 p.m.
buy on-line www.kilmarnockfc.co.uk/shop

**OFFICIAL SUPPORTERS CLUB**
c/o Rugby Park, Kilmarnock, KA1 2DP

**SHIRT SPONSOR**
Seriously Strong Cheddar

**KIT SUPPLIER** TFG

## LIST OF PLAYERS 2005.06

| SQUAD NO. | PLAYERS SURNAME | FIRST NAME | MIDDLE NAME | DATE OF BIRTH | PLACE OF BIRTH | DATE SIGNED | HEIGHT FT INS | WEIGHT ST LBS | POSITION ON PITCH | PREVIOUS CLUB |
|---|---|---|---|---|---|---|---|---|---|---|
| 30 | Adams | James | Stewart | 26/08/87 | Stranraer | 30/06/04 | 6' 1" | 11st 5lb | Mid | Kilmarnock Youth |
| 26 | Bell | Cameron | | 18/09/86 | Dumfries | 30/08/02 | 5' 11" | 12st 4lb | Gk | Queen of the Sou... |
| 9 | Boyd | Kris | | 18/08/83 | Irvine | 25/08/99 | 6' 0" | 12st 12lb | Fwd | Kilmarnock 'S' For... |
| | Bryson | Jordan | | 24/09/88 | Glasgow | 19/08/05 | 5' 9" | 11st 4lb | Fwd | Kilmarnock Youth |
| 24 | Campbell | Robert | Lindsay | 22/07/86 | Glasgow | 15/01/03 | 6' 2" | 12st 8lb | Fwd | Kilmarnock Youth |
| 1 | Combe | Alan | | 03/04/74 | Edinburgh | 02/07/04 | 6' 2" | 13st 2lb | Gk | Bradford City |
| 37 | Cox | David | | 17/03/89 | Lanark | 04/07/05 | 5' 6.5" | 10st 7lb | Fwd | Kilmarnock Youth |
| 31 | Coyne | Thomas | | 30/05/87 | Dundee | 03/09/03 | 6' 0" | 11st 8lb | Fwd | Paisley United |
| 20 | Di Giacomo | Paul | | 30/06/82 | Glasgow | 08/07/98 | 5' 11" | 11st 12lb | Fwd | Kilmarnock Youth |
| 17 | Dillon | Shaun | | 24/08/84 | Greenock | 18/09/00 | 5' 9.5" | 11st 1lb | Def | Kilmarnock Youth |
| 16 | Dodds | Rhian | | 10/03/79 | Irvine | 29/08/03 | 5' 9" | 11st 3lb | Mid | Robert Morris Ur... |
| | Flannigan | Iain | | 15/01/88 | Glasgow | 08/07/05 | 5' 11" | 10st 7lb | Mid | Kilmarnock Youth |
| 6 | Ford | Simon | Gary | 17/11/81 | London | 05/01/05 | 6' 1" | 12st 4lb | Def | Bristol Rovers |
| 2 | Fowler | James | | 26/10/80 | Stirling | 18/10/97 | 5' 9" | 10st 11lb | Def/Mid | Gairdoch B.C. |
| 5 | Greer | Gordon | | 14/12/80 | Glasgow | 31/08/03 | 6' 2" | 12st 5lb | Def | Blackburn Rover... |
| 23 | Hamill | Jamie | | 29/07/86 | Irvine | 16/01/03 | 5' 8" | 11st 2lb | Def | Kilmarnock 'S' For... |
| 3 | Hay | Garry | | 07/09/77 | Irvine | 18/08/95 | 5' 7.5" | 10st 4lb | Def/Mid | Kilmarnock B.C. |
| 11 | Invincibile | Daniele | Anthony | 31/03/79 | Brisbane | 30/07/03 | 5' 11" | 12st 3lb | Mid | Swindon Town |
| 12 | Johnston | Allan | | 14/12/73 | Glasgow | 10/08/04 | 5' 10" | 11st 4lb | Mid | Middlesbrough |
| 22 | Leven | Peter | | 27/09/83 | Glasgow | 15/07/04 | 5' 11" | 12st 13lb | Mid | Rangers |
| 4 | Lilley | David | William | 31/10/77 | Bellshill | 30/01/04 | 6' 1" | 12st 3lb | Def | Partick Thistle |
| 8 | Locke | Gary | | 16/06/75 | Edinburgh | 06/08/02 | 5' 10" | 11st 8lb | Mid | Bradford City |
| 32 | Logan | Peter | | 25/11/88 | Irvine | 13/07/05 | 5' 10" | 11st 7lb | Gk | Kilmarnock Yout... |
| 33 | Loy | Rory | James | 19/03/88 | Dumfries | 30/06/04 | 5' 10" | 10st 7lb | Mid/Fwd | Kilmarnock Yout... |
| 7 | McDonald | Gary | Matthew | 10/04/82 | Irvine | 04/06/99 | 6' 0" | 11st 6lb | Fwd | Kilmarnock Yout... |
| 34 | Mort | Graham | | 17/01/88 | Glasgow | 30/06/04 | 5' 10" | 11st 6lb | Fwd | Kilmarnock Yout... |
| 19 | Murray | Stephen | | 18/04/83 | Bellshill | 20/12/00 | 5' 3.5" | 9st 12lb | Mid/Fwd | Kilmarnock 'S' For... |
| 14 | Naismith | Steven | John | 14/09/86 | Irvine | 30/08/02 | 5' 9" | 10st 3lb | Fwd | Kilmarnock Yout... |
| 15 | Nish | Colin | John | 07/03/81 | Edinburgh | 08/07/03 | 6' 3" | 11st 3lb | Mid | Dunfermline Athle... |
| 35 | Noble | Steven | | 16/04/88 | Paisley | 30/06/04 | 5' 10" | 11st 1lb | Mid | Kilmarnock Yout... |
| 13 | Smith | Graham | | 03/10/82 | Bellshill | 09/06/99 | 6' 2" | 12st 8lb | Gk | Kilmarnock Yout... |
| 10 | Wales | Gary | | 04/01/79 | East Calder | 14/07/04 | 5' 10" | 11st 2lb | Fwd | Gillingham |
| 36 | Wild | Gary | | 12/08/88 | Glasgow | 30/06/04 | 6' 1" | 11st 12lb | Def | Kilmarnock Yout... |
| 18 | Wright | Frazer | | 23/12/79 | East Kilbride | 05/07/05 | 5' 10" | 11st 10lb | Def | Stranraer |

## TICKET INFORMATION

**Season Ticket information**

| Category | East & West Stands | Moffat Stand |
|---|---|---|
| ADULT | £290 | £220 |
| MOFFAT FAMILY | - | £300 2 ADULTS + 2 CHILDREN (U16) |
| STUDENT | £190 | £145 |
| SENIOR CITIZEN | £150 | £105 |
| YOUTH 16/17 | £130 | £80 |
| CHILD U16 | £80 | £45 |

**Match Ticket information**

| Stands | | Cat A | Cat B |
|---|---|---|---|
| WEST/EAST/ | ADULT/OAP | £22 | £18 |
| MOFFAT & NORTH | U16/STUDENTS/OAP £12 | £12 | £12 |

**Please Note:** Under 16's - £5 in Moffat Stand for all Category B matches

**Category A:** Matches against Celtic & Rangers. **Category B:** All other SPL matches

## MILESTONES:

**Year of formation:** 1869

**Most Capped player:** Joe Nibloe

**No. of Caps:** 11

**Most League points in a season:**
58 (Division 2 – Season 1973/74)

**Most League goals scored by a player in a season:**
Harry 'Peerie' Cunningham (Season 1927/28) & Andy Kerr (Season...

**No. of goals scored:** 34

**Record Attendance:** 34,246 (-v- Rangers – August, 1963)

**Record Victory:** 13-2 (-v- Saltcoats – Scottish Cup, 12.9.18...

**Record Defeat:** 0-8 (-v- Rangers and Hibernian – Division 1...

**BANK OF SCOTLAND PREMIERLEAGUE**

## SEASON STATS 2004.05

| DATE | VENUE | OPPONENTS | ATT | RES | Combe A. | Lilley D. | Dindeleux F. | Fowler J. | Hay G. | McDonald G. | Murray S. | Locke G. | Invincible D. | Boyd K. | Wales G. | Joly E. | Leven P. | Dargo C. | Dodds R. | Greer G. | Dillon S. | Naismith S. | Johnston A. | Nish C. | Ford S. | Smith G. | Fontaine L. |
|---|---|---|---|---|---|---|---|---|---|---|---|---|---|---|---|---|---|---|---|---|---|---|---|---|---|---|---|
| -Aug | A | Hibernian | 10,933 | 1-0 | 1 | 2 | 3 | 4 | 5 | 6 | 7 | 8 | 9 | **10** | 11 | 12 | 13 | 14 | | | | | | | | | |
| 4-Aug | H | Celtic | 10,526 | 2-4 | 1 | 2 | 3 | 4 | 5 | **6** | 7 | 8 | | 10 | 11 | | | | | 9 | 12 | 13 | 14 | | | | |
| 1-Aug | A | Hearts | 11,403 | 0-3 | 1 | | 3 | 4 | 5 | 6 | 13 | 8 | 9 | 10 | 11 | 14 | | 12 | | 2 | | 7 | | | | | |
| 9-Aug | H | Dunfermline Ath. | 4,854 | 1-0 | 1 | 2 | 3 | 4 | | 6 | 7 | 8 | | **10** | 11 | 13 | | 12 | | 14 | 5 | | 9 | | | | |
| 1-Sep | A | Livingston | 2,776 | 2-0 | 1 | **2** | 3 | 4 | | 6 | | 8 | **11** | 10 | | 12 | | | | 9 | 5 | | 7 | | | | |
| 8-Sep | H | Aberdeen | 6,686 | 0-1 | 1 | 2 | 3 | 4 | | 6 | 12 | 8 | 11 | 10 | 14 | | | | | 13 | 9 | | 5 | | 7 | | |
| 5-Sep | H | Dundee United | 4,711 | 5-2 | 1 | 2 | 3 | 12 | | 6 | | | 11 | **10**[5] | 13 | | 8 | 9 | 14 | 4 | 5 | | 7 | | | | |
| -Oct | A | Rangers | 46,278 | 0-2 | 1 | 2 | 3 | 4 | | 6 | | 8 | 11 | 10 | | | 5 | 9 | | | | | 7 | 12 | | | |
| 6-Oct | A | Dundee | 4,637 | 1-3 | 1 | 2 | 3 | 4 | | 6 | 7 | 8 | 11 | **10** | | 14 | 5 | 9 | | | 12 | | | 13 | | | |
| 3-Oct | H | Inverness Cal.Th. | 4,721 | 2-2 | 1 | 2 | 3 | | 13 | 6 | **7** | 8 | 11 | 10 | | 12 | 5 | 9 | | **4** | 14 | | | | | | |
| 7-Oct | A | Motherwell | 4,605 | 1-0 | 1 | 2 | 3 | 13 | | 6 | 12 | | 11 | | | | 5 | 10 | | 4 | | | 7 | **9** | 8 | | |
| 0-Oct | H | Hibernian | 5,959 | 3-1 | 1 | 2 | 3 | | 13 | 6 | 7 | | 11 | | | | 5 | **10** | | 4 | 12 | | | **9**[2] | 8 | | |
| -Nov | A | Celtic | 57,268 | 1-2 | | 2 | 3 | 12 | | 6 | | 13 | 11 | | | | 5 | 10 | | 4 | 14 | | 7 | **9** | 8 | | 1 |
| 3-Nov | H | Hearts | 6,129 | 1-1 | 1 | 2 | 3 | 14 | | 6 | | 12 | 11 | | 13 | | **5** | 10 | | 4 | | | 7 | **9** | 8 | | |
| 0-Nov | A | Dunfermline Ath. | 4,344 | 1-4 | 1 | 2 | 12 | | | 6 | 14 | 8 | 11 | | **13** | | 5 | 10 | | 4 | | | 7 | 9 | 3 | | |
| 7-Nov | H | Livingston | 5,389 | 1-3 | 1 | 2 | 3 | 5 | | 6 | 13 | | 10 | | 11 | 12 | | | | 4 | 14 | | **7** | 9 | 8 | | |
| -Dec | A | Aberdeen | 11,139 | 2-3 | 1 | 2 | 3 | | | 7 | | | **11** | 10 | 13 | | 6 | | | 4 | 12 | | 8 | 9 | 5 | | |
| 1-Dec | A | Dundee United | 5,097 | 0-3 | 1 | 2 | 3 | | | 7 | 12 | | 11 | 10 | 14 | | 6 | 13 | | 4 | | | 9 | 8 | 5 | | |
| 9-Dec | H | Rangers | 11,156 | 0-1 | | | 3 | | 2 | 7 | 13 | | 11 | 10 | 12 | | 6 | | 14 | 4 | 8 | | | 9 | 5 | 1 | |
| 7-Dec | H | Dundee | 5,468 | 3-1 | | | 3 | | 2 | 7 | | | **11** | 10 | | | 6 | | | 4 | 8 | | 12 | **9** | **5** | 1 | |
| Jan | A | Inverness Cal.Th. | 1,359 | 2-0 | | | | 14 | 2 | 7 | | 8 | **11**[2] | 10 | 13 | | 5 | | | 4 | 6 | | 12 | 9 | 3 | 1 | |
| 5-Jan | H | Motherwell | 5,225 | 2-0 | 1 | 2 | 3 | | 4 | 7 | | 12 | 11 | **10**[2] | | | 6 | | | | 8 | | 13 | 9 | 5 | | |
| 2-Jan | A | Hibernian | 12,660 | 0-3 | 1 | 2 | | 3 | 4 | 7 | 13 | 8 | 11 | 10 | | | | | 14 | | 6 | | 12 | 9 | 5 | | |
| 0-Jan | H | Celtic | 9,723 | 0-1 | 1 | 2 | | 4 | 7 | | | 8 | 11 | 10 | 14 | | 6 | | | | 9 | | 13 | 12 | 3 | | 5 |
| 2-Feb | A | Hearts | 9,220 | 0-3 | 1 | 2 | 12 | 3 | 13 | 7 | 6 | 8 | | 10 | 14 | | 4 | | | | 11 | 9 | | | | | 5 |
| 9-Feb | H | Dunfermline Ath. | 4,701 | 2-1 | 1 | 2 | | 3 | 4 | 7 | 13 | | 11 | **10** | | | 6 | | | | **9** | 8 | | | 12 | | 5 |
| 6-Feb | A | Rangers | 48,575 | 1-2 | 1 | 2 | | 3 | 4 | 7 | | 8 | 11 | 10 | | 12 | 13 | | | | 9 | 6 | | 14 | 5 | | |
| -Mar | A | Livingston | 1,931 | 1-3 | 1 | 2 | | 3 | 4 | 7 | 14 | 8 | 13 | 10 | | | 6 | | | | 11 | **9** | | 5 | | | |
| -Mar | H | Aberdeen | 5,181 | 0-1 | | 2 | | 3 | 4 | 7 | | | 11 | 10 | | | 6 | 12 | | | 13 | 8 | | 9 | 5 | 1 | |
| 2-Mar | H | Dundee United | 4,353 | 3-0 | | 2 | 3 | 4 | 5 | 7 | | | 12 | **10**[2] | 14 | | 6 | 13 | | | 11 | 8 | 9 | | | 1 | |
| Apr | A | Dundee | 5,494 | 0-1 | 1 | 2 | 3 | 4 | 5 | 7 | 14 | | 9 | 10 | 13 | | 6 | 12 | | | 11 | | 8 | | | | |
| Apr | A | Inverness Cal.Th. | 4,862 | 0-1 | 1 | 2 | 3 | 4 | 5 | 7 | 8 | | | 10 | 9 | | 6 | | | | 11 | 13 | 12 | | | | |
| -Apr | A | Motherwell | 4,999 | 1-1 | 1 | 2 | 3 | 6 | 5 | 9 | | 8 | | 10 | 11 | | **7** | | 4 | | | 12 | | | | | |
| -Apr | H | Dundee | 3,485 | 1-0 | 1 | 2 | 3 | 6 | 5 | 9 | | 8 | 12 | 10 | 11 | | 7 | **13** | 4 | | | 14 | | | | | |
| -Apr | A | Inverness Cal.Th. | 3,108 | 2-1 | 1 | 2 | 3 | 4 | 5 | **7** | | 8 | 10 | | 11 | | 6 | 9 | 13 | | | 14 | 12 | | | | |
| May | A | Dundee United | 6,576 | 1-1 | 1 | 2 | 3 | 6 | 5 | 9 | | 8 | | **12** | 10 | | 7 | | | | 4 | 13 | 14 | 11 | | | |
| -May | H | Livingston | 4,184 | 2-0 | 1 | 2 | | 3 | 5 | 7 | 13 | 8 | | **10** | 11 | | 6 | | 12 | 4 | | 9 | **14** | | | | |
| -May | H | Dunfermline Ath. | 5,100 | 4-0 | 1 | | | 3 | 2 | **7** | 13 | **8** | | **10** | 11 | | 6 | | **5** | 4 | | 9 | 12 | 14 | | | |
| **TOTAL FULL APPEARANCES** | | | | | 32 | 33 | 27 | 24 | 22 | 38 | 8 | 22 | 28 | 29 | 12 | | 29 | 10 | 4 | 19 | 4 | 16 | 19 | 16 | 17 | 6 | 3 |
| **TOTAL SUB APPEARANCES** | | | | | | 2 | 5 | 3 | | 13 | 3 | 3 | 1 | 12 | 6 | 3 | 10 | 4 | 3 | 2 | 8 | 10 | 10 | 1 | | | |
| **TOTAL GOALS SCORED** | | | | | | | | 1 | | 3 | 1 | 1 | 7 | 17 | 2 | | 4 | 2 | 1 | 1 | | | 1 | 3 | 4 | 1 | |

in bold denotes goal scored. Secondary smaller figure in bold denotes number of goals scored. † denotes opponent's own goal.

## [BEL]LIE'S 10 YEAR LEAGUE RECORD

| Season | Div | P | W | D | L | F | A | Pts | Pos |
|---|---|---|---|---|---|---|---|---|---|
| 95-96 | P | 36 | 11 | 8 | 17 | 39 | 54 | 41 | 7 |
| 96-97 | P | 36 | 11 | 6 | 19 | 41 | 61 | 39 | 7 |
| 97-98 | P | 36 | 13 | 11 | 12 | 40 | 52 | 50 | 4 |
| 98-99 | SPL | 36 | 14 | 14 | 8 | 47 | 29 | 56 | 4 |
| 99-00 | SPL | 36 | 8 | 13 | 15 | 38 | 52 | 37 | 9 |
| 00-01 | SPL | 38 | 15 | 9 | 14 | 44 | 53 | 54 | 4 |
| 01-02 | SPL | 38 | 13 | 10 | 15 | 44 | 54 | 49 | 7 |
| 02-03 | SPL | 38 | 16 | 9 | 13 | 47 | 56 | 57 | 4 |
| 03-04 | SPL | 38 | 12 | 6 | 20 | 51 | 74 | 42 | 10 |
| 04-05 | SPL | 38 | 15 | 4 | 19 | 49 | 55 | 49 | 7 |

## LEADING GOALSCORERS:

| Season | Div | Goals | Player |
|---|---|---|---|
| 1995-96 | P | 13 | P. Wright |
| 1996-97 | P | 15 | P. Wright |
| 1997-98 | P | 10 | P. Wright |
| 1998-99 | SPL | 7 | A. McCoist |
| 1999-00 | SPL | 8 | C. Cocard |
| 2000-01 | SPL | 8 | P. Wright |
| 2001-02 | SPL | 7 | T. Johnson |
| 2002-03 | SPL | 12 | K. Boyd |
| 2003-04 | SPL | 15 | K. Boyd |
| 2004-05 | SPL | 17 | K. Boyd |

**KILMARNOCK PLAYING KITS SEASON 2005.06**

FIRST KIT | SECOND KIT | THIRD KIT

# LIVINGSTON

**LIVINGSTON F.C.**
Almondvale Stadium,
Alderstone Road, Livingston,
West Lothian, EH54 7DN
**TELEPHONE NUMBERS**
Ground (01506) 417000
**FAX** (01506) 418888
**E-MAIL** dianne.blair@livingstonfc.co.uk
**WEBSITE** www.livingstonfc.co.uk
**CHAIRMAN** Pearse Flynn
**DIRECTORS**
Anthony K. Kinder, Maurice Smith,
Morris Kaplan, Vivien Kyles
**CHIEF EXECUTIVE** Vivien Kyles
**HONORARY VICE-PRESIDENT**
John L. Bain B.E.M
**SECRETARY** Duncan Bennett (01506) 403340
**MANAGER** Paul Lambert
**ASSISTANT MANAGER** Norrie McWhirter
**RESERVE COACH** Alex Cleland
**GOALKEEPING COACH** Stevie Woods
**DIRECTOR OF YOUTH DEVELOPMENT**
Graeme Robertson
**YOUTH COACHES**
U19: Alex Cleland
**TEAM CAPTAIN** Emmanuel Dorado
**FOOTBALL SAFETY OFFICERS'**
**ASSOCIATION REPRESENTATIVE**
Tom Purdie
**COMMERCIAL DIRECTOR**
Charles Burnett (01506) 417000
**LOTTERY MANAGER** Ray Ballantyne
**MEDIA LIAISON OFFICER**
Duncan Bennett (01506) 403340
**MATCHDAY PROGRAMME EDITOR**
David Stoker (07778 675746)
david@livingstonfc.co.uk
**CLUB DOCTOR** Dr. Gerard Canning
**PHYSIOTHERAPIST** Mairi McPhail
**STADIUM MANAGER**
Paul Mitchell
**GROUNDSMAN** Colin Fraser
**KIT PERSON** Danny Cunning
**PA TO CHIEF EXECUTIVE** Dianne Blair
**PART-TIME PHYSIOTHERAPIST**
Arthur Duncan
**CATERING MANAGER** Allison Ross
**CLUB SHOP**
A wide range of merchandise is available
from both the club shop situated at the
ground and also at the local ASDA
Store. Club shop is also open on home
matchdays 10.30 am - 3.00pm and after
the match. Tel: (01506) 461909
**SUPPORTERS LIAISON MANAGER**
Kay Robertson (01506) 403431
**SHIRT SPONSOR**
Intelligent Finance
**KIT SUPPLIER**
XARA

## LIST OF PLAYERS 2005.06

| SQUAD NO. | PLAYERS SURNAME | FIRST NAME | MIDDLE NAME | DATE OF BIRTH | PLACE OF BIRTH | DATE SIGNED | HEIGHT FT INS | WEIGHT ST LBS | POSITION ON PITCH | PREVIOUS CLUB |
|---|---|---|---|---|---|---|---|---|---|---|
| 16 | Adam | Stephen | | 10/11/86 | Paisley | 09/07/03 | 5' 10" | 11st 6lb | Mid | Livingston Youths |
| 8 | Adams | Derek | Watt | 25/06/75 | Glasgow | 29/07/05 | 5' 10" | 12st 7lb | Mid | Aberdeen |
| | Adamson | Kenneth | | 21/08/88 | Dunfermline | 25/07/05 | 6' 0" | 12st 7lb | Def | Livingston Youths |
| 25 | Barrett | Graham | | 07/06/81 | Dublin | 31/08/05 | 5' 11" | 12st 4lb | Fwd | Coventry City |
| 19 | Boyd | Scott | Robert | 04/06/86 | Bangour | 21/10/02 | 6' 1.5" | 11st 11lb | Def | Livingston Youths |
| 7 | Brittain | Richard | | 24/09/83 | Bangour | 03/08/00 | 5' 9" | 10st 7lb | Mid | Livingston 'S' For |
| 11 | Dair | Jason | | 15/06/74 | Dunfermline | 20/07/04 | 5' 11" | 12st 5lb | Mid/Fwd | Motherwell |
| 9 | Dalglish | Paul | | 18/02/77 | Glasgow | 22/08/05 | 6' 0" | 11st 9lb | Fwd | Linfield |
| | Davidson | Murray | | 07/03/88 | Edinburgh | 17/05/04 | 5' 11" | 9st 5lb | Mid | Livingston Youths |
| 6 | Dorado-Rodriguez | Emmanuel | | 28/03/73 | Brou-Sur-Chanterene | 27/06/02 | 6' 2" | 13st 0lb | Def | Malaga |
| 24 | Dorrans | Graham | | 05/05/87 | Glasgow | 04/07/03 | 5' 9" | 10st 0lb | Mid | Livingston Youths |
| | Droudge | Dene | John | 17/04/89 | Edinburgh | 25/07/05 | 6' 2" | 10st 4lb | Def | Livingston Youth |
| | Geggan | Andrew | | 08/05/87 | Glasgow | 21/08/03 | 5' 8" | 9st 4lb | Def | St. Johnstone |
| | Hamilton | Christopher | | 21/11/87 | Germany | 13/08/03 | 5' 7.5" | 9st 2lb | Mid | Queen's Park |
| 35 | Lambert | Paul | | 07/08/69 | Paisley | 12/08/05 | 5' 11" | 11st 6lb | Mid | Celtic |
| | Mackay | Brian | | 21/03/88 | Vale of Leven | 25/07/05 | 5' 8" | 9st 10lb | Mid | Partick Thistle |
| 3 | Mackay | David | | 02/05/81 | Rutherglen | 19/07/05 | 6' 1" | 13st 3lb | Def | Oxford United |
| | Martin | Thomas | | 04/09/88 | Glasgow | 19/07/05 | 5' 9" | 10st 7lb | Mid | Livingston Youth |
| | McGuigan | Thomas | William | 15/06/87 | Rutherglen | 23/05/05 | 5' 8" | 10st 3lb | Gk | Motherwell |
| 1 | McKenzie | Roderick | | 08/08/75 | Bellshill | 04/08/03 | 6' 0" | 12st 0lb | Gk | Heart of Midlothian |
| | McLaren | Fraser | | 26/09/88 | Edinburgh | 04/06/04 | 5' 10" | 10st 6lb | Mid | Livingston Youth |
| 18 | McLaughlin | Scott | | 20/01/84 | Glasgow | 23/07/02 | 5' 9" | 10st 7lb | Mid | Hamilton Academ |
| 2 | McNamee | David | | 10/10/80 | Glasgow | 31/08/02 | 5' 11" | 10st 7lb | Def | Blackburn Rove |
| 22 | McPake | James | | 24/06/84 | Bellshill | 01/08/00 | 6' 2.5" | 12st 4lb | Fwd | Livingston Youth |
| 20 | Miller | Gary | | 15/04/87 | Glasgow | 29/08/03 | 5' 11.5" | 10st 9lb | Fwd | St. Mirren |
| | Mitchell | Christopher | | 21/07/88 | Stirling | 22/07/04 | 5' 9" | 10st 10lb | Def | St. Johnstone |
| | Monteith | Callum | Douglas | 13/04/88 | Edinburgh | 19/08/05 | 5' 10" | 13st 0lb | Def | Livingston Youth |
| | Monteith | Duncan | | 13/04/88 | Edinburgh | 25/07/05 | 5' 11" | 12st 4lb | Gk | Livingston Youth |
| 10 | Pereira | Ramon | | 12/09/78 | Badajuz | 25/07/05 | 6' 1" | 11st 6lb | Fwd | Heart of Midloth |
| 4 | Pinxten | Harald | | 01/09/77 | Belgium | 25/07/05 | 6' 4" | 14st 8lb | Def | Royal Antwerp |
| 17 | Roy | Ludovic | | 18/08/77 | Tours | 03/06/05 | 6' 1" | 13st 0lb | Gk | Ayr United |
| 14 | Scott | Martin | | 15/02/86 | Livingston | 12/02/00 | 5' 11" | 11st 0lb | Mid | Livingston Youth |
| 12 | Snodgrass | Robert | | 07/09/87 | Glasgow | 09/07/03 | 5' 11.5" | 12st 2lb | Mid | Livingston 'S' Fo |
| 5 | Strong | Gregory | | 05/09/75 | Bolton | 31/01/05 | 6' 2" | 11st 12lb | Def | Boston United |
| 21 | Tesevic | Dubravko | | 18/12/81 | Foca | 26/07/05 | 6' 3" | 12st 7lb | Mid | 1st Vienna |
| 15 | Tierney | Paul | | 15/09/82 | Salford | 11/07/05 | 5' 11" | 11st 6lb | Mid | Manchester Uni |
| | Torrance | Mark | | 06/04/89 | Edinburgh | 25/07/05 | 5' 8" | 9st 10lb | Mid | Livingston Youth |
| 13 | Vincze | Gabor | | 07/09/76 | Ozd | 13/01/05 | 6' 0" | 12st 13lb | Mid | Gyori ETO |
| 23 | Walker | Allan | | 03/01/86 | Edinburgh | 26/07/02 | 5' 10" | 10st 12lb | Mid | Hibernian |
| | Weir | Steven | | 03/10/88 | Harthill | 15/10/04 | 5' 7" | 10st 2lb | Fwd | Livingston Youth |

### TICKET INFORMATION

**Season Ticket information**

| | |
|---|---|
| ADULT | £305/220 |
| PARENT & JUVENILE | £340/240 |
| PARENT & 2 JUVENILES | £370/260 |
| 2 PARENTS & 1 JUVENILE | £635/440 |
| 2 PARENTS & 2 JUVENILES | £660/460 |
| OAP & JUVENILE | £100/150/95 |

**Match Ticket information**

| | Cat A | Cat B | Cat C |
|---|---|---|---|
| ADULT | £23 | £20 | £18 |
| CONCESSIONS | £10 | £10 | £10 |

**MILESTONES:**
**Year of formation:** 1974 (From Seasons 1974/75 to 1994/9 known as Meadowbank Thistle F.C.)
**Most League points in a season:**
55 (Second Division – Season 1986/87) (2 Points for a Win
77 (Second Division – Season 1998/99) (3 Points for a Win
**Most League goals scored by a player in a season:**
John McGachie (Season 1986/87)
**No. of goals scored:** 21
**Record Attendance:** 2,818 (-v- Albion Rovers, 10.8.1974 a Meadowbank Stadium) & 10,024 (-v- Celtic, 18.8.2001 a West Lothian Courier Stadium)
**Record Victory:** 6-0 (-v- Raith Rovers – Second Division, 9.11.1985; -v- Alloa Athletic – First Division, 26.8.2000)
**Record Defeat:** 0-8 (-v- Hamilton Academical – Division 2, 14.12.1974)

Category A: Matches against Celtic & Rangers. Category B: Aberdeen, Hearts & Hibernian. Category C: All other SPL clubs

**BANK OF SCOTLAND PREMIERLEAGUE**

## SEASON STATS 2004.05

| DATE | VENUE | OPPONENTS | ATT | RES | McKenzie R. | McNamee D. | Dorado E. | Rubio O. | McLaughlin S. | Easton C. | Boyack S. | O'Brien B. | Lovell S. | Libbra M. | Lilley D. | Hamilton J. | Bahoken G. | McMenamin C. | Stanik G. | Dair J. | Snodgrass R. | Kernaghan A. | Brittain R. | Snowdon W. | McPake J. | Harding R. | Adam S. | Meldrum C. | Hand J. | Kriston A. | Horvath F. | Vincze G. | Wilson M. | Deloumeaux E. | Strong G. | Nouma P. | Kachloul H. | Dorrans G. |
|---|---|---|---|---|---|---|---|---|---|---|---|---|---|---|---|---|---|---|---|---|---|---|---|---|---|---|---|---|---|---|---|---|---|---|---|---|---|---|---|
| 7-Aug | H | Inverness Cal.Th. | 3,315 | 3-0 | 1 | 2 | 3 | 4 | 5 | 6 | 7 | 8 | 9 | 10 | 11 | 12 | | | | | | | | | | | | | | | | | | | | | | |
| 14-Aug | A | Rangers | 48,102 | 0-4 | 1 | 2 | 3 | 4 | 5 | 6 | 7 | 8 | 9 | 10 | 11 | 14 | 12 | 13 | | | | | | | | | | | | | | | | | | | | |
| 21-Aug | H | Dundee United | 3,159 | 1-1 | 1 | 2 | 3 | 4 | | 6 | 7 | 8 | 9 | | 11 | 10 | 12 | 5 | 13 | | | | | | | | | | | | | | | | | | | |
| 28-Aug | A | Aberdeen | 13,888 | 0-2 | 1 | 2 | 3 | 4 | 13 | 6 | 7 | 8 | 9 | | 11 | 10 | 5 | 12 | | | | | | | | | | | | | | | | | | | | |
| 11-Sep | H | Kilmarnock | 2,776 | 0-2 | 1 | | 3 | 4 | | 6 | | 8 | 7 | 13 | 11 | 10 | 5 | 9 | 2 | | 12 | | | | | | | | | | | | | | | | | |
| 18-Sep | A | Dundee | 4,387 | 0-0 | 1 | 2 | 3 | 4 | | 6 | | 8 | 9 | | 11 | | 10 | 5 | | 7 | | | | | | | | | | | | | | | | | | |
| 25-Sep | H | Motherwell | 3,950 | 2-3 | 1 | | 3 | 4 | 12 | 6 | | 8 | 9 | 14 | 13 | 10 | 11 | 2 | 5 | 7 | | | | | | | | | | | | | | | | | | |
| 3-Oct | A | Hearts | 10,646 | 0-0 | 1 | 2 | 3 | 4 | | 6 | | 8 | 9 | | 13 | 10 | 12 | 5 | 7 | 11 | | | | | | | | | | | | | | | | | | |
| 16-Oct | H | Dunfermline Ath. | 2,815 | †2-0 | 1 | 2 | 3 | 4 | | 6 | | 8 | 9 | | 13 | 10 | | 5 | 7 | 11 | | | | | | | | | | | | | | | | | | |
| 24-Oct | H | Celtic | 6,695 | 2-4 | 1 | 2 | 3 | 4 | 7 | 6 | | 8² | 9 | 14 | 13 | 10 | | 5 | | 11 | | 12 | | | | | | | | | | | | | | | | |
| 27-Oct | A | Hibernian | 9,087 | 1-2 | 1 | | 3 | 4 | 7 | 6 | 14 | 8 | 9 | 13 | 12 | 10 | 5 | | 2 | | | 11 | | | | | | | | | | | | | | | | |
| 30-Oct | A | Inverness Cal.Th. | 1,284 | 0-2 | 1 | 2 | 3 | 4 | | 6 | | 8 | 7 | 13 | 11 | 10 | | 5 | | 12 | | 9 | | | | | | | | | | | | | | | | |
| 7-Nov | H | Rangers | 7,800 | 1-4 | 1 | 2 | 3 | 4 | 7 | 9 | 12 | 8 | | 13 | 14 | 10 | | 5 | | | | 11 | 6 | | | | | | | | | | | | | | | |
| 13-Nov | A | Dundee United | 5,507 | 0-1 | 1 | 2 | 3 | | 5 | 6 | | 8 | 9 | 14 | 11 | 12 | | 10 | | | 4 | 7 | 13 | | | | | | | | | | | | | | | |
| 20-Nov | A | Aberdeen | 4,270 | 0-2 | 1 | 2 | 3 | 12 | 5 | 6 | | 8 | 9 | | 11 | 13 | | 10 | | | 14 | 4 | 7 | | | | | | | | | | | | | | | |
| 27-Nov | H | Kilmarnock | 5,389 | 3-1 | 1 | 2 | | 4 | | 6 | | 8 | | 11 | 10² | | | | 7 | 12 | | 13 | | 9 | 3 | 5 | | | | | | | | | | | | |
| 4-Dec | H | Dundee | 4,009 | 1-0 | 1 | | | 4 | | 6 | 8 | 14 | | 11 | 10 | | | | 2 | 7 | | | | 12 | 13 | 9 | 3 | 5 | | | | | | | | | | |
| 11-Dec | A | Motherwell | 4,363 | 0-0 | 1 | | 3 | 4 | | 6 | | 8 | 9 | | 11 | 10 | | | 2 | 7 | | | | 14 | 13 | 12 | | 5 | | | | | | | | | | |
| 27-Dec | A | Dunfermline Ath. | 5,092 | 0-0 | | 2 | 3 | 4 | 13 | 12 | | 8 | 9 | 14 | | 10 | 5 | | | 7 | | | | | | 11 | | 6 | 1 | | | | | | | | | |
| 2-Jan | A | Celtic | 57,564 | 1-2 | | 2 | 3 | 4 | | | 8 | 11 | 12 | | 10 | 6 | | | 5 | 13 | 9 | | 7 | | | | | 14 | 1 | | | | | | | | | |
| 15-Jan | H | Hibernian | 6,188 | 0-2 | | 2 | 3 | | | | 8 | 9 | | | 10 | 5 | | | 7 | 14 | | | 11 | 4 | | | 1 | 6 | 12 | 13 | | | | | | | | |
| 22-Jan | H | Inverness Cal.Th. | 3,606 | 1-4 | | | 3 | | | | 8 | 9 | | | 13 | 10 | 5 | | 2 | 12 | | | | | | | 1 | 6 | 4 | 11 | 7 | | | | | | | |
| 25-Jan | H | Hearts | 3,816 | 1-2 | 1 | | 3 | 4 | | 13 | | 8 | | | 11 | 2 | | | 12 | 7 | | | 10 | | | | | 6 | 5 | 14 | | 9 | | | | | | |
| 29-Jan | A | Rangers | 48,579 | 0-3 | 1 | | 3 | 4 | | 12 | | 8 | | | 11 | 2 | | | 7 | | 13 | | | | | | | 6 | 5 | | 10 | 9 | | | | | | |
| 2-Feb | H | Dundee United | 4,658 | 0-2 | 1 | 2 | | 4 | | | | 8 | | | 11 | 3 | 10 | | | 7 | | 14 | | 13 | | 12 | | | | | 9 | 6 | 5 | | | | | |
| 9-Feb | A | Aberdeen | 9,214 | 0-2 | 2 | | | | | | | 8 | | | 11 | 3 | 14 | 13 | | 7 | | | | 12 | 1 | 6 | | 10 | | | 9 | 4 | 5 | | | | | |
| 5-Mar | H | Kilmarnock | 1,931 | 3-1 | 1 | 2 | | | | 6 | | 8 | | | | | 12 | 3 | 7 | 13 | | 11 | | | | | | 14 | | 10 | 9 | 4 | 5 | | | | | |
| 12-Mar | A | Dundee | 5,830 | 1-0 | 1 | 2 | | | | 6 | | 8 | | | | | 12 | 3 | 7 | 11 | | | | | | | 13 | | | 10 | 9 | 4 | 5 | | | | | |
| 12-Mar | H | Motherwell | 4,049 | 1-1 | 1 | 2 | 14 | 4 | | 6 | | 8 | | | | | 12 | 3 | 7 | 11 | | | | | | | 13 | | | 10 | 9 | | 5 | | | | | |
| 17-Mar | A | Hearts | 9,187 | 1-3 | 1 | 2 | | | | 6 | | 8 | | | 14 | | 12 | 3 | 7 | 11 | | | | | | | 13 | | | 10 | 9 | 4 | 5 | | | | | |
| 2-Apr | H | Dunfermline Ath. | 4,036 | 1-1 | 1 | 2 | 3 | | | 6 | | 8 | | | | | | 10 | 5 | 11 | | 9 | | | | | | | | 7 | 14 | 4 | | | 12 | | | 13 |
| 13-Apr | H | Celtic | 7,750 | 0-4 | 1 | 2 | 3 | 4 | | 8 | | | | 11 | 5 | | | 7 | | 13 | | | | | | | 10 | | | 6 | | | 12 | 9 | | | | |
| 16-Apr | H | Hibernian | 10,637 | 3-0 | 1 | 2 | 3 | | 13 | 8 | | 11 | | | 5 | 10 | | 7 | | | | 12 | | | | | | | | 6 | 4 | | | 9 | | | | |
| 23-Apr | A | Dundee United | 7,687 | 1-2 | 1 | 2 | 3 | 12 | | 8 | | 11 | | | 5 | 10 | | 7 | | | | | | | | | | | | 6 | 4 | | | 9 | | | | |
| 30-Apr | H | Dunfermline Ath. | 5,102 | 2-0 | 1 | 2 | 3 | | | 12 | | 8 | | | 5 | 10 | | 7 | 14 | | | 13 | | | | | | | | 6 | 4 | | | 9 | | | | |
| 7-May | A | Inverness Cal.Th. | 3,021 | 1-0 | 1 | 2 | 3 | | | 12 | | 8 | | | 5 | 11 | | 7 | | | | | | | | | | | | 6 | 4 | 13 | | 9 | | | | |
| 14-May | A | Kilmarnock | 4,184 | 0-2 | 1 | 2 | 3 | 4 | | 13 | | 8 | | | 11 | | | 10 | 7 | | | | | | | | | | | 6 | 5 | 12 | | 9 | | | | 14 |
| 21-May | H | Dundee | 7,468 | 1-1 | 1 | | 3 | 12 | | 6 | | 8 | | | 11 | 2 | 10 | | 5 | 14 | | | | | | | | | | 7 | 4 | 13 | | 9 | | | | |

| | | TOTAL FULL APPEARANCES | | | 33 | 29 | 30 | 24 | 7 | 24 | 4 | 38 | 19 | 2 | 23 | 17 | 17 | 13 | 18 | 22 | 8 | 4 | 8 | 1 | 7 | 3 | 4 | 5 | 5 | 3 | 6 | 14 | 4 | 13 | 6 | | | 7 |
| | | TOTAL SUB APPEARANCES | | | | 1 | 3 | 3 | 7 | 2 | | 1 | 9 | 8 | 4 | 1 | 9 | 2 | 2 | 9 | | | 5 | | 2 | 8 | | 3 | | 2 | 2 | 2 | | 1 | | 3 | 2 | 1 | 1 |
| | | TOTAL GOALS SCORED | | | | 1 | | | | | | 3 | 8 | 1 | 3 | 4 | | 2 | | 2 | 2 | | | | | | | | | | | 2 | | | 1 | | | | 2 |

*in bold denotes goal scored. Secondary smaller figure in bold denotes number of goals scored. † denotes opponent's own goal.*

**LIVINGSTON PLAYING KITS SEASON 2005.06**

FIRST KIT | SECOND KIT | THIRD KIT

## MOTHERWELL F.C.

Fir Park, Firpark Street,
Motherwell, ML1 2QN

**TELEPHONE NUMBERS**
Ground/Ticket Information (01698) 333333
Hospitality Hotline (01698) 338008/62
Football Dept (01698) 338019
**FAX** (01698) 338001
**E-MAIL** mfcf@motherwellfc.co.uk
**WEBSITE** www.motherwellfc.co.uk
**CHAIRMAN**
William H. Dickie, R.I.B.A., A.R.I.A.S
**DIRECTORS**
John Boyle, Andrew Lapping,
John Swinburne, James McMahon,
Ian Stillie, Martin Rose & Stewart Robertson
**GENERAL MANAGER** Russell Rodger
**HONORARY PRESIDENT**
James C. Chapman, O.B.E.
**SECRETARY**
Stewart Robertson
**MANAGER** Terry Butcher
**ASSISTANT MANAGER / RESERVE COACH**
Maurice Malpas
**HEAD OF YOUTH DEVELOPMENT**
Chris McCart
**COMMUNITY COACH** Bobby Jenks
**ASSISTANT COMMUNITY COACH**
Ian Horne
**YOUTH COACHES**
U19: Chris McCart & Scott Leitch
U17: Graham Ogg, Andy Brown & Ian McIver
U15: Gordon Young & Willie Falconer
U14: Willie Pettigrew & Bill Reside
U13: Willie Devine & Brian Reynolds
U12: Ian Horne & Bobby Jenks
U11: Tom McCafferty & Willie Devine
**CHIEF SCOUT** Bobby Jenks
**TEAM CAPTAIN** Scott Leitch
**OFFICE ADMINISTRATOR** Betty Pryde
**FOOTBALL SAFETY OFFICERS'**
**ASSOCIATION REPRESENTATIVE /**
**FACILITIES MANAGER**
Ken Davies 07762 871049 (Mobile)
**MATCHDAY MEDIA LIAISON PERSON**
Paul Davies
**MATCHDAY PROGRAMME EDITOR**
Graham Barnstaple
**CLUB DOCTOR** Dr. Mark Bonnes
**PHYSIOTHERAPISTS**
John Porteous & Peter Salila
**GROUNDSMAN** Ian Wilson
**KIT PERSON** Alan MacDonald
**HOSPITALITY CO-ORDINATOR**
Wendy McFarlane (01698) 338008
**CLUB SHOP**
Provan Sports, The Well Shop, Fir Park,
Motherwell. Tel: (01698) 338025
Open Tues, Thurs & Fri from
9.30a.m. to 4.00p.m.
Home matchdays 10.00a.m. to 3.00p.m.
Away matchdays 10.00a.m. to 1.00p.m.
**SUPPORTERS CLUB**
c/o Fir Park, Firpark Street,
Motherwell, ML1 2QN
**SHIRT SPONSOR** Zoom Airlines
**KIT SUPPLIER** XARA

# MOTHERWELL

## LIST OF PLAYERS 2005.06

| SQUAD NO. | PLAYERS SURNAME | FIRST NAME | MIDDLE NAME | DATE OF BIRTH | PLACE OF BIRTH | DATE SIGNED | HEIGHT FT INS | WEIGHT ST LBS | POSITION ON PITCH | PREVIOUS CLUB |
|---|---|---|---|---|---|---|---|---|---|---|
| 34 | Alexiou | Peter | Harry | 07/07/87 | Broxburn | 09/07/04 | 6' 0" | 12st 12lb | Gk | Falkirk |
| 41 | Brownlie | Craig | William | 26/05/88 | Bellshill | 09/06/05 | 6' 0" | 12st 8lb | Def | Motherwell Youth |
| 25 | Calder | Douglas | | 01/02/86 | Glasgow | 22/08/03 | 5.11.5" | 11st 11lb | Gk | Hamilton Academical |
| 12 | Clarkson | David | Thomas | 10/09/85 | Bellshill | 02/06/01 | 5' 10.5" | 10st 2lb | Fwd | Motherwell Youth |
| 33 | Coakley | Adam | Thomas | 19/10/87 | Glasgow | 09/01/04 | 5' 9" | 9st 9lb | Fwd | Motherwell Youth |
| 28 | Connolly | Kenneth | | 08/04/87 | Glasgow | 09/06/03 | 5' 10" | 10st 7lb | Mid | Motherwell Youth |
| 2 | Corrigan | Martyn | Alexander | 14/08/77 | Glasgow | 21/01/00 | 5' 11" | 12st 0lb | Def | Falkirk |
| 5 | Craigan | Stephen | James | 29/10/76 | Newtonards | 09/06/03 | 6' 1" | 13st 1lb | Def | Partick Thistle |
| 38 | Donnelly | Alexander | Stevenson | 22/03/88 | Glasgow | 18/05/04 | 6' 1" | 11st 2lb | Mid | Motherwell Youth |
| 27 | Donnelly | Robert | Stevenson | 19/01/87 | Glasgow | 21/01/03 | 6' 1" | 12st 0lb | Mid | Motherwell Youth |
| 21 | Fagan | Shaun | Michael | 22/03/84 | Bellshill | 14/06/00 | 5' 10" | 10st 7lb | Mid | Motherwell Youth |
| 24 | Fitzpatrick | Marc | | 11/05/86 | Lanark | 30/08/02 | 5' 10.5" | 10st 9lb | Def | Motherwell Youth |
| 9 | Foran | Richard | | 16/06/80 | Dublin | 05/07/04 | 6' 0" | 12st 12lb | Fwd | Carlisle United |
| 42 | Forbes | Ross | | 03/03/89 | Glasgow | 09/06/05 | 6' 0" | 10st 6lb | Mid | Motherwell Youth |
| 45 | Gormley | David | Alan | 10/05/88 | Glasgow | 09/06/05 | 5' 10" | 11st 12lb | Fwd | Motherwell Youth |
| 35 | Grant | John | Paul | 25/08/87 | Bellshill | 18/05/04 | 5' 8" | 10st 5lb | Def | Motherwell Youth |
| 16 | Hamilton | James | | 09/02/76 | Aberdeen | 27/01/05 | 6' 0" | 12st 12lb | Fwd | Livingston |
| 3 | Hammell | Steven | | 18/02/82 | Rutherglen | 31/08/99 | 5' 9.5" | 11st 11lb | Def | Motherwell 'X' For |
| 26 | Kane | John | Alexander | 08/06/87 | Glasgow | 27/01/05 | 6' 1" | 10st 8lb | Mid | Hibernian |
| 23 | Keogh | David | John | 29/08/86 | Edinburgh | 09/06/03 | 6' 1.5" | 12st 5lb | Def | Motherwell Youth |
| 4 | Kerr | Brian | | 12/10/81 | Bellshill | 05/07/04 | 5' 10.5" | 11st 5lb | Mid | Newcastle United |
| 22 | Kinniburgh | William | Daniel | 08/09/84 | Glasgow | 14/06/00 | 6' 1.5" | 11st 7lb | Def | Motherwell Youth |
| 8 | Leitch | Donald | Scott | 06/10/69 | Motherwell | 25/06/03 | 5' 10" | 11st 10lb | Mid | Swindon Town |
| 29 | Maguire | Stephen | | 14/02/87 | Bellshill | 09/06/03 | 5' 7" | 9st 8lb | Def/Mid | Motherwell Youth |
| 1 | Marshall | Gordon | George | 19/04/64 | Edinburgh | 04/07/03 | 6' 3" | 14st 1lb | Gk | Kilmarnock |
| 40 | Martin | Alan | Andrew | 01/01/89 | Glasgow | 18/01/05 | 6' 0" | 11st 11lb | Gk | Motherwell Youth |
| 17 | McBride | Kevin | | 14/06/81 | Bellshill | 10/08/04 | 5' 10" | 10st 5lb | Mid | Celtic |
| 6 | McCormack | Alan | | 10/01/84 | Dublin | 29/07/05 | 5' 8" | 10st 0lb | Mid | Preston North En |
| 7 | McDonald | Scott | Douglas | 21/08/83 | Dandenong | 07/01/04 | 5' 8" | 12st 4lb | Fwd | Wimbledon |
| 13 | McDonald | Steven | Alexander | 13/12/79 | Glasgow | 31/08/05 | 6' 6" | 16st 0lb | Def | Sorrento |
| 47 | McLean | Brian | Stuart | 28/02/85 | Rutherglen | 31/08/05 | 6' 2" | 12st 3lb | Def | Rangers |
| 31 | McStay | John | | 10/07/87 | Bellshill | 09/06/03 | 5' 7.5" | 9st 8lb | Fwd | Celtic Youths |
| 18 | Meldrum | Colin | George | 26/11/75 | Kilmarnock | 10/08/05 | 5' 10.5" | 13st 4lb | Gk | Forfar Athletic |
| 46 | Murphy | Jamie | | 28/08/89 | Glasgow | 13/06/05 | 5' 10" | 9st 10lb | Fwd | Motherwell Youth |
| 44 | Murray | Cameron | | 29/04/89 | Bellshill | 09/06/05 | 6' 0" | 10st 0lb | Def | Motherwell Youth |
| 43 | Nixon | David | Thomas | 09/07/88 | Paisley | 09/06/05 | 6' 1" | 12st 9lb | Def | Motherwell Youth |
| 10 | O'Donnell | Philip | | 25/03/72 | Bellshill | 02/01/04 | 5' 10" | 12st 3lb | Mid | Sheffield Wednesd |
| 11 | Paterson | James | Lee | 25/09/79 | Bellshill | 14/07/04 | 5' 11" | 13st 6lb | Mid | Dundee United |
| 30 | Quinn | Mark | James | 13/05/87 | Glasgow | 09/06/03 | 5' 10.5" | 10st 11lb | Def | Motherwell Yout |
| 19 | Quinn | Paul | Charles | 21/07/85 | Lanark | 28/08/00 | 6' 1" | 11st 4lb | Def | Motherwell Youth |
| 39 | Reynolds | Mark | | 07/05/87 | Motherwell | 18/05/04 | 5' 11" | 10st 9lb | Def | Motherwell Yout |
| 32 | Russell | Ryan | | 09/04/87 | Dunfermline | 09/06/03 | 5' 8.5" | 10st 12lb | Fwd | Motherwell Youth |
| 14 | Smith | Andrew | William | 25/09/80 | Lisburn | 05/08/05 | 5' 11" | 11st 10lb | Fwd | Preston North E |
| 37 | Smith | Darren | Lee | 27/03/88 | Lanark | 18/05/04 | 6' 0" | 11st 7lb | Fwd | Motherwell Yout |
| 15 | Smith | Graeme | | 08/06/83 | Edinburgh | 23/06/05 | 6' 0" | 13st 5lb | Gk | Rangers |
| 36 | Soutar | William | Thompson | 12/07/87 | Lanark | 16/01/04 | 5' 11" | 11st 0lb | Def | Motherwell Yout |
| 20 | Wright | Kenneth | Thomas | 01/08/85 | Bellshill | 05/06/01 | 5' 10.5" | 11st 5lb | Fwd | Motherwell Yout |

## TICKET INFORMATION

| | SEASON TICKET | STANDARD ENTRY GATE | PREMIUM ENTRY GATE |
|---|---|---|---|
| **Main Stand** | | | |
| ADULT | £330 | £20 | £24 |
| JUVENILE | £120 | £9 | £11 |
| STUDENT/SENIOR CITIZEN | £185 | £13 | £15 |
| FAMILY ADULT + JUVENILE | - | £26 | - |
| **Cooper Stand** | | | |
| ADULT | £260 | £18 | £20 |
| JUVENILE (U16) | £90 | £7 | £9 |
| STUDENT/SENIOR CITIZEN | £155 | £12 | £14 |
| FAMILY ADULT + JUVENILE | £300 | £23 | £25 |
| **East Stand** | | | |
| ADULT | £240 | £16 | £18 |
| JUVENILE (U16) | £70 | £6 | £8 |
| STUDENT/SENIOR CITIZEN | £130 | £11 | £13 |

## MILESTONES:

**Year of formation:** 1886
**Most Capped player:** Tommy Coyne (Republic of Ireland)
**No. of Caps:** 13
**Most League points in a season:**
66 (Division 1 – Season 1931/32)
**Most League goals scored by a player in a season:**
William McFadyen (Season 1931/32)
**No. of goals scored:** 52
**Record Attendance:**
35,632 (-v- Rangers – Scottish Cup, 12.3.1952)
**Record Victory:** 12-1 (-v- Dundee United – Division 2, 23.1.
**Record Defeat:** 0-8 (-v- Aberdeen – Premier Division, 26.3.

BANK OF SCOTLAND — PREMIERLEAGUE

## SEASON STATS 2004.05

*Note: In the original the player-name columns are printed vertically. The grid below lists, for each match, the shirt numbers worn. **Bold** denotes a goal scored; a small superscript figure denotes the number of goals scored. † denotes an opponent's own goal.*

| DATE | VENUE | OPPONENTS | ATT | RES | Marshall G. | Corrigan M. | Kinniburgh W. | Hammell S. | Craigan S. | Paterson J. | O'Donnell P. | Leitch S. | Fagan S. | Burns A. | Clarkson D. | McDonald S. | Foran R. | Fitzpatrick M. | McBride K. | Partridge D. | Smith D. | Quinn P. | Wright K. | Corr B.J. | Hamilton J. | Britton G. | Kerr B. | Keogh D. |
|---|---|---|---|---|---|---|---|---|---|---|---|---|---|---|---|---|---|---|---|---|---|---|---|---|---|---|---|---|
| 8-Aug | A | Celtic | 56,957 | 0-2 | 1 | 2 | 3 | 4 | 5 | 6 | 7 | 8 | 9 | 10 | 11 | 12 | 13 | 14 | | | | | | | | | | |
| 14-Aug | H | Hibernian | 5,859 | 1-2 | 1 | 2 | 3 | 4 | 5 | 6 | **7** | 8 | 9 | 10 | 13 | 11 | | 14 | | 12 | | | | | | | | |
| 21-Aug | A | Dundee | 4,849 | 2-1 | 1 | 2 | 3 | 4 | 5 | 6 | 7 | 8 | | 13 | 11 | **10²** | 12 | 9 | | | | | | | | | | |
| 28-Aug | H | Hearts | 7,095 | 2-0 | 1 | 2 | 3 | 4 | 5 | | **7** | 8 | | 13 | 11 | 10 | 9 | 12 | | **6** | | | | | | | | |
| 11-Sep | A | Dunfermline Ath. | 4,438 | 1-1 | 1 | 2 | 3 | 4 | 5 | 12 | 7 | 8 | | 13 | 11 | **10** | 9 | | | 6 | | | | | | | | |
| 18-Sep | H | Dundee United | 5,091 | 4-2 | 1 | 2 | 3 | 4 | 5 | 14 | 7 | 8 | 12 | 13 | 11 | **10²** | 9 | | | 6 | | | | | | | | |
| 25-Sep | A | Livingston | 3,950 | 3-2 | 1 | 2 | 3 | 4 | 5 | 13 | 7 | 8 | 12 | | 11 | **10** | 9 | 14 | | 6 | | | | | | | | |
| 3-Oct | A | Inverness Cal.Th. | 1,438 | 1-1 | 1 | 2 | | 4 | 5 | 12 | | 8 | 7 | 13 | 11 | **10** | 9 | | | 6 | 3 | 14 | | | | | | |
| 17-Oct | H | Rangers | 10,946 | 0-2 | 1 | 2 | | 4 | 5 | 12 | 7 | 8 | | | 11 | 10 | 9 | | | 6 | 3 | | | | | | | |
| 23-Oct | A | Aberdeen | 10,737 | 1-2 | 1 | 2 | | 4 | 5 | 12 | 7 | | 8 | 13 | 14 | 11 | 10 | 9 | | 6 | 3 | | | | | | | |
| 27-Oct | H | Kilmarnock | 4,605 | 0-1 | 1 | 2 | | 4 | 5 | 6 | | 8 | | 12 | 13 | 11 | 10 | 9 | | 3 | | | 7 | | | | | |
| 30-Oct | H | Celtic | 10,592 | 2-3 | 1 | **2** | | 4 | 5 | 6 | | 8 | | | 10 | 11 | 9 | | | 3 | | | 7 | | | | | |
| 6-Nov | A | Hibernian | 9,931 | 0-1 | 1 | 2 | | 4 | 5 | 6 | | 8 | | 13 | 10 | 11 | 9 | 12 | | 3 | | | 7 | | | | | |
| 13-Nov | H | Dundee | 4,406 | 3-0 | 1 | 2 | | 4 | 5 | **6²** | | 8 | 12 | 13 | **11** | | | 10 | 9 | 3 | | | 7 | | | | 14 | |
| 20-Nov | A | Hearts | 10,598 | 1-0 | 1 | 2 | | 4 | 5 | 6 | | 8 | | | 12 | 11 | **10** | 9 | | 3 | | | 7 | | | | 13 | |
| 27-Nov | H | Dunfermline Ath. | 5,084 | † 2-1 | 1 | 2 | | 4 | 5 | 9 | | 8 | 14 | | 11 | | 10 | 6 | 7 | 3 | | | | | | | 12 | 13 |
| 4-Dec | A | Dundee United | 5,394 | 1-0 | 1 | 2 | | 4 | 5 | 9 | | 8 | 14 | | 11 | | 10 | 6 | 7 | 3 | | | | | | | 12 | 13 |
| 11-Dec | H | Livingston | 4,363 | 2-0 | 1 | 2 | | | 5 | 9 | **7** | 8 | | | 11 | | 10 | 4 | 6 | 3 | | | | | | | 12 | |
| 18-Dec | H | Inverness Cal.Th. | 4,267 | 1-2 | 1 | 2 | | | 5 | 9 | 7 | 8 | | | **11** | | 10 | 4 | 6 | 3 | | | | | | | 12 | |
| 27-Dec | A | Rangers | 49,909 | 1-4 | | 2 | | 4 | 5 | 9 | | | 13 | | **11** | 10 | 6 | 8 | 3 | | | 7 | 12 | 1 | | | | |
| 3-Jan | H | Aberdeen | 6,948 | 0-0 | | 7 | 13 | 4 | 5 | **7** | | 8 | | | 11 | 9 | 10 | 12 | 6 | 3 | | | | 1 | | | | |
| 15-Jan | A | Kilmarnock | 5,225 | 0-2 | 1 | 2 | | 4 | 5 | | | 8 | 13 | | 11 | 9 | 10 | 12 | 6 | 3 | | | 7 | 14 | | | | |
| 22-Jan | A | Celtic | 58,244 | 0-2 | 1 | 2 | | 4 | 5 | 8 | | | 12 | | 11 | 9 | 10 | 13 | 6 | 3 | | | 7 | 14 | | | | |
| 12-Feb | A | Dundee | 5,746 | 1-2 | 1 | | | 4 | 5 | 9 | 7 | 8 | | | 13 | **11** | 12 | | 6 | 3 | | 2 | | | 10 | | | |
| 15-Feb | H | Hibernian | 7,453 | 1-1 | 1 | | | 4 | **5** | 9 | 7 | 8 | | | 14 | 11 | 13 | 12 | 6 | 3 | | 2 | | | 10 | | | |
| 19-Feb | H | Hearts | 7,390 | 2-0 | 1 | | | 4 | 5 | 9 | | 8 | | | 12 | **11** | **13** | 7 | 6 | 3 | | 2 | | | 10 | | | |
| 2-Mar | A | Dunfermline Ath. | 3,427 | 0-0 | 1 | | | 12 | 4 | 5 | 9 | | | | 11 | 13 | 7 | 6 | 3 | | | 2 | | | 10 | | | |
| 5-Mar | H | Dundee United | 5,110 | 2-0 | 1 | 2 | | 4 | 5 | 9 | 7 | 8 | | | 13 | **11** | 12 | 14 | 6 | 3 | | | | | 10 | | | |
| 12-Mar | A | Livingston | 4,049 | 1-1 | | 2 | | 4 | 5 | 9 | | | 13 | | **11** | 12 | 8 | 7 | 3 | | | 6 | 1 | | 10 | | | |
| 3-Apr | H | Rangers | 10,210 | 2-3 | 1 | **2** | | 4 | 5 | 9 | | 8 | | | 11 | 10 | 12 | 7 | 3 | | | 6 | | | | 13 | | |
| 9-Apr | A | Aberdeen | 10,443 | 3-1 | 1 | | | 4 | 5 | 9 | | 8 | 7 | 13 | **11** | | 6 | 3 | | 2 | | | | | **10** | | 12 | |
| 12-Apr | A | Inverness Cal.Th. | 3,746 | 0-1 | 1 | | | 4 | 5 | 9 | | 8 | 7 | 12 | 11 | | 6 | 3 | | | 13 | 10 | | | | 14 | | |
| 16-Apr | H | Kilmarnock | 4,999 | † 1-1 | | | | 4 | 5 | 9 | | 8 | 7 | | 11 | | 12 | 13 | 3 | | | 2 | 1 | 10 | | 14 | 6 | |
| 23-Apr | H | Aberdeen | 5,063 | 0-1 | 2 | 6 | 4 | 5 | | | 8 | 7 | | | 11 | | 3 | | | 1 | 10 | | 9 | 12 | | | | |
| 30-Apr | A | Hearts | 9,337 | 0-0 | | | 5 | 12 | | 8 | | | 11 | | 9 | 7 | | 3 | 4 | | | 10 | | | 6 | 13 | | |
| 7-May | H | Hibernian | 8,903 | 2-2 | 1 | 2 | 12 | **5²** | 13 | | 8 | | | 14 | 11 | 9 | 7 | | 10 | | | 6 | | | | | | |
| 14-May | A | Rangers | 49,495 | † 1-4 | 1 | 2 | 4 | | | 8 | | 7 | | | 11 | 10 | 9 | 6 | | 3 | | | 13 | | 5 | 12 | | |
| 22-May | H | Celtic | 12,944 | 2-1 | 1 | 2 | 4 | | 5 | 8 | | 7 | | | 13 | **11²** | 9 | 6 | | | | 10 | 12 | 3 | | | | |
| **TOTAL FULL APPEARANCES** | | | | | 33 | 31 | 10 | 32 | 37 | 27 | 18 | 28 | 11 | 4 | 25 | 26 | 25 | 14 | 24 | 29 | | 20 | | 5 | 13 | | 6 | |
| **TOTAL SUB APPEARANCES** | | | | | | 3 | | | | | | 8 | 1 | 12 | 6 | 10 | 1 | 10 | 11 | 1 | 1 | 3 | 7 | 1 | 1 | 3 | 2 | 3 |
| **TOTAL GOALS SCORED** | | | | | | 2 | | 2 | 3 | 3 | | 1 | | | 3 | 15 | 5 | 1 | 5 | | | 1 | | | | | | |

Figure in bold denotes goal scored. Secondary smaller figure in bold denotes number of goals scored. † denotes opponent's own goal.

## THE WELL'S 10 YEAR LEAGUE RECORD

| Season | Div | P | W | D | L | F | A | Pts | Pos |
|---|---|---|---|---|---|---|---|---|---|
| 95-96 | P | 36 | 9 | 12 | 15 | 28 | 39 | 39 | 8 |
| 96-97 | P | 36 | 9 | 11 | 16 | 44 | 55 | 38 | 8 |
| 97-98 | P | 36 | 9 | 7 | 20 | 46 | 64 | 34 | 9 |
| 98-99 | SPL | 36 | 10 | 11 | 15 | 35 | 54 | 41 | 7 |
| 99-00 | SPL | 36 | 14 | 10 | 12 | 49 | 63 | 52 | 4 |
| 00-01 | SPL | 38 | 12 | 7 | 19 | 42 | 56 | 43 | 8 |
| 01-02 | SPL | 38 | 11 | 7 | 20 | 49 | 69 | 40 | 11 |
| 02-03 | SPL | 38 | 7 | 7 | 24 | 45 | 71 | 28 | 12 |
| 03-04 | SPL | 38 | 12 | 10 | 16 | 42 | 49 | 46 | 6 |
| 04-05 | SPL | 38 | 13 | 9 | 16 | 46 | 49 | 48 | 6 |

## LEADING GOALSCORERS:

| Season | Div | Goals | Player |
|---|---|---|---|
| 1995-96 | P | 5 | W. Falconer |
| 1996-97 | P | 11 | T. Coyne |
| 1997-98 | P | 15 | T. Coyne |
| 1998-99 | SPL | 7 | O. Coyle, J. Spencer |
| 1999-00 | SPL | 11 | J. Spencer |
| 2000-01 | SPL | 10 | S. Elliott |
| 2001-02 | SPL | 10 | S. Elliott, J. McFadden |
| 2002-03 | SPL | 13 | J. McFadden |
| 2003-04 | SPL | 13 | D. Clarkson |
| 2004-05 | SPL | 15 | S. McDonald |

MOTHERWELL PLAYING KITS SEASON 2005.06 — FIRST KIT · SECOND KIT · THIRD KIT

# RANGERS

RANGERS F.C.
Ibrox Stadium,150 Edmiston Drive,
Glasgow, G51 2XD
**TELEPHONE NUMBERS**
Main Switchboard (0141) 580 8500
Football Administration (0141) 580 8647
Fax–Football Administration (0141) 419 0600
Ticket Centre 0870 600 1993
Ticket Centre Fax (0141) 580 8504
Customer Services 0870 600 1972
Hospitality 0870 600 1964
Commercial 0870 600 1899
Retail/Mail Order 0870 599 1997
**FAX** (0141) 419 0600
**E-MAIL** lynne_livingstone@rangers.co.uk
**E-MAIL 2** ltarbet@rangers.co.uk
**WEBSITE** www.rangers.co.uk
**CHAIRMAN** David E. Murray
**DIRECTORS**
John McClelland, R. Campbell Ogilvie,
Donald Wilson, David C. King, Martin Bain,
David Jolliffe, John Greig & Alistair Johnston
**ASSOCIATE DIRECTOR** Ian Russell
**CHIEF EXECUTIVE** Martin Bain
**HEAD OF FOOTBALL ADMINISTRATION**
Andrew Dickson
**COMPANY SECRETARY** David Jolliffe
**MANAGER** Alex McLeish
**ASSISTANT MANAGER** Andy Watson
**FIRST TEAM COACH** Jan Wouters
**RESERVE COACH** John Brown
**FITNESS COACH** Frank Nuttall
**GOALKEEPING COACH** Billy Thomson
**COMMUNITY COACH** Craig Mulholland
**YOUTH COACHES**
U19: Ian Durrant
U17 & U16: Peter Weir
U15: Stephen Wright
U14: Drew Todd
U13: Craig Mulholland
**TEAM CAPTAIN** Barry Ferguson
**FOOTBALL SAFETY OFFICERS'**
**ASSOCIATION REPRESENTATIVE /**
**OPERATIONS EXECUTIVE**
Laurence MacIntyre M.B.E. (0141) 580 8630
**MATCHDAY PROGRAMME EDITOR**
Lindsay Herron (Rangers Media Editor in Chief)
**CLUB DOCTOR** Dr. Ian McGuinness
**PHYSIOTHERAPIST** David Henderson
**STADIUM MANAGER** Ross MacAskill
**GROUNDSMAN** David Roxburgh
**KIT PERSON** Jim Bell
**PUBLIC RELATIONS EXECUTIVE**
Carol Patton
**CLUB SHOPS**
1873 Superstore, Ibrox Stadium, Glasgow
G51. Open until 10.00p.m. on Matchdays
and 9.30a.m.-5.30p.m. Mon to Sat,
Sun 11.00a.m. to 5.00p.m.
84-92 Sauchiehall Street, Glasgow.
Open 9.00a.m.-5.30p.m. Mon to Sat
and Sun Noon-4.00p.m.
Unit G5, St Enoch Centre, Glasgow.
Open 9.00a.m.-6.00p.m. Mon, Tue, Wed,
Fri & Sat. 9.00a.m.-8.00p.m Thu & Sun
11.00am-5.00pm
**Additional Shops:** Edinburgh, East Kilbride,
Clydebank, Paisley, Stirling, Falkirk, Ayr,
Kirkcaldy, Inverness, Belfast,
Ballymena, Glasgow & Prestwick Airports
**OFFICIAL SUPPORTERS CLUB**
Worldwide Alliance, Argyle House,
Ibrox Stadium,Glasgow, G51 2XD
**SHIRT SPONSOR** Carling
**KIT SUPPLIER** Umbro

## LIST OF PLAYERS 2005.06

| SQUAD NO. | PLAYERS SURNAME | FIRST NAME | MIDDLE NAME | DATE OF BIRTH | PLACE OF BIRTH | DATE SIGNED | HEIGHT FT INS | WEIGHT ST LBS | POSITION ON PITCH | PREVIOUS CLUB |
|---|---|---|---|---|---|---|---|---|---|---|
| 38 | Adam | Charles | Graham | 10/12/85 | Dundee | 23/01/03 | 6' 1" | 13st 0lb | Mid | Rangers Youths |
| 49 | Agnew | Scott | | 11/07/87 | Irvine | 03/07/03 | 5' 6.5" | 9st 9lb | Mid | Rangers Youths |
| 5 | Andrews | Marvin | | 22/12/75 | San Juan | 21/07/04 | 6' 2" | 14st 7lb | Def | Livingston |
| 3 | Bernard | Olivier | | 14/10/79 | Paris | 01/09/05 | 5' 9" | 12st 8lb | Def | Southampton |
| 4 | Buffel | Thomas | | 19/02/81 | Brugge | 06/01/05 | 5' 9" | 10st 12lb | Mid | Feyenoord |
| 17 | Burke | Christopher | | 02/12/83 | Glasgow | 05/07/00 | 5' 8.5" | 10st 10lb | Mid | Rangers Youths |
| 45 | Campbell | Steven | | 20/08/86 | Kirkcaldy | 04/06/02 | 5' 10" | 10st 8lb | Def | Rangers Youths |
| 42 | Carcary | Derek | | 11/07/86 | Glasgow | 20/08/04 | 5' 6" | 9st 10lb | Fwd | Queen's Park |
| 72 | Craig | Christopher | John | 13/05/89 | Glasgow | 04/07/05 | 5' 5.5" | 10st 4lb | Fwd | Rangers Youths |
| 53 | Crooks | Jason | | 31/01/88 | Glasgow | 30/01/04 | 5' 9.5" | 10st 12lb | Fwd | Rangers Youths |
| 39 | Davidson | Robert | | 25/03/86 | Rutherglen | 04/06/02 | 5' 8.5" | 11st 9lb | Fwd | Rangers Youths |
| 74 | Donald | Michael | | 20/01/89 | Cambridge | 31/08/05 | 5' 9" | 9st 8lb | Def | Rangers Youths |
| 55 | Errislie | Paul | Stephen | 13/03/88 | Aberdeen | 14/06/04 | 5' 10" | 10st 10lb | Mid | Rangers Youths |
| 6 | Ferguson | Barry | | 02/02/78 | Glasgow | 31/02/05 | 5' 11" | 11st 6lb | Mid | Blackburn Rovers |
| 57 | Frizzel | Craig | | 30/06/88 | Edinburgh | 18/08/04 | 5' 11.5" | 10st 11lb | Fwd | Rangers Youths |
| 64 | Gallacher | Scott | | 15/07/89 | Bellshill | 01/07/05 | 6' 1.5" | 12st 1lb | Gk | Rangers Youths |
| 43 | Giacomi | Robert | | 01/08/86 | Toronto | 01/07/05 | 6' 4" | 13st 13lb | Gk | Markham Lightning |
| 47 | Gilmour | Brian | Thomas | 08/05/87 | Irvine | 03/07/03 | 5' 6" | 9st 4lb | Mid | Rangers Youths |
| 61 | Hadden | Scott | | 01/04/89 | Glasgow | 01/07/05 | 5' 7" | 8st 11lb | Fwd | Rangers Youths |
| 62 | Harvey | Ross | | 13/04/89 | Glasgow | 01/07/05 | 6' 1" | 11st 4lb | Def | Rangers Youths |
| 7 | Hemdani | Brahim | | 15/03/78 | Colombes | 04/07/05 | 6' 0" | 11st 9lb | Mid | Marseille |
| 20 | Hutton | Alan | | 30/11/84 | Glasgow | 04/09/00 | 6' 0" | 12st 1lb | Def | Rangers Youths |
| 21 | Jeffers | Francis | | 25/01/81 | Liverpool | 31/08/05 | 5' 10.5" | 11st 4lb | Fwd | Charlton Athletic |
| 46 | Johnston | John | Buchanan | 26/03/87 | Greenock | 03/07/03 | 5' 8" | 10st 8lb | Fwd | Rangers Youths |
| 33 | Kalenga | Marc | Gary | 18/03/85 | Toulouse | 07/10/03 | 6' 0" | 12st 11lb | Mid | Auxerre |
| 63 | Kinniburgh | Steven | Steel | 13/06/89 | Glasgow | 01/07/05 | 5' 11.5" | 11st 2lb | Mid | Rangers Youths |
| 1 | Klos | Stefan | | 16/08/71 | Dortmund | 23/12/98 | 5' 11.5" | 13st 3lb | Gk | BV09 Borussia Dortmund |
| 14 | Kyrgiakos | Sotiris | | 23/07/79 | Trikala | 30/08/05 | 6' 3" | 13st 9lb | Def | Panathinaikos |
| 52 | Lennon | Steven | | 20/01/88 | Irvine | 30/01/04 | 5' 7" | 9st 7lb | Mid | Rangers Youths |
| 26 | Lovenkrands | Peter | | 29/01/80 | Horsholm | 14/06/00 | 5' 10" | 11st 9lb | Fwd | AB Copenhagen |
| 51 | Lowing | Alan | Alexander | 07/01/88 | Rutherglen | 20/05/04 | 5' 10" | 10st 9lb | Def | Rangers Youths |
| 12 | Malcolm | Robert | | 12/11/80 | Glasgow | 01/07/97 | 5' 11.5" | 13st 9lb | Def | Rangers 'S' Form |
| 15 | Maniero | Filippo | | 11/09/72 | Padova | 31/08/05 | 6' 1" | 13st 12lb | Fwd | Torino |
| 44 | McCormack | Ross | | 18/08/86 | Glasgow | 04/06/02 | 5' 9" | 11st 10lb | Fwd | Rangers Youths |
| 37 | McKenzie | Gary | | 15/10/85 | Lanark | 11/03/04 | 6' 3" | 13st 4lb | Def | Rangers Youths |
| 60 | McLachlan | William | | 19/03/89 | Rutherglen | 01/07/05 | 5' 9" | 11st 3lb | Mid | Rangers Youths |
| 58 | McMillan | Jordan | | 16/10/88 | Glasgow | 07/01/05 | 5' 10" | 9st 12lb | Def | Rangers Youths |
| 24 | Murray | Ian | William | 20/03/81 | Edinburgh | 01/07/05 | 6' 0" | 11st 5lb | Mid | Hibernian |
| 31 | Namouchi | Hamed | | 14/02/84 | Cannes | 15/09/03 | 6' 1" | 12st 2lb | Mid | Cannes |
| 50 | Nguessan | Djombo | | 11/08/87 | Ivry Sur Seine | 08/07/05 | 6' 0.5" | 12st 13lb | Mid | Auxerre |
| 23 | Nieto | Federico | | 26/08/83 | Capital Federal | 14/07/05 | 6' 2.5" | 13st 5lb | Fwd | Almagro |
| 10 | Novo | Ignacio | Javier | 26/03/79 | El Ferrol | 09/07/04 | 5' 9" | 10st 8lb | Fwd | Dundee |
| 18 | Pierre Fanfan | Jose Karl | | 26/07/75 | Saint Pol Sur Mer | 22/07/05 | 6' 1" | 14st 0lb | Def | Paris St. Germain |
| 9 | Prso | Dado | | 05/11/74 | Zadar | 07/07/04 | 6' 3" | 14st 0lb | Fwd | AS Monaco |
| 8 | Rae | Alexander | | 30/09/69 | Glasgow | 05/07/04 | 5' 9" | 11st 6lb | Mid | Wolverhampton Wanderers |
| 11 | Rae | Gavin | Paul | 28/11/77 | Aberdeen | 02/01/04 | 6' 0" | 13st 6lb | Mid | Dundee |
| 48 | Reidford | Calum | | 26/05/87 | Glasgow | 03/07/03 | 5' 11" | 12st 4lb | Gk | Rangers 'S' Form |
| 2 | Ricksen | Fernando | | 27/07/76 | Heerlen | 01/07/00 | 5' 9" | 11st 4lb | Def | AZ Aalkmar |
| 41 | Robinson | Lee | David | 02/07/86 | Sunderland | 30/01/04 | 5' 11" | 12st 0lb | Gk | ESH Winning |
| 16 | Rodriguez | Julien | | 11/06/78 | Beziers | 05/08/05 | 6' 0.5" | 13st 5lb | Def | AS Monaco |
| 59 | Sagar | Joseph | Gregory | 04/02/89 | Oldham | 11/07/05 | 5' 11" | 12st 8lb | Gk | Oldham Athletic |
| 36 | Santala | Jukka | | 10/09/85 | Helsinki | 05/01/05 | 6' 4" | 13st 12lb | Def | HJK Helsinki |
| 65 | Shinnie | Andrew | Murray | 17/07/89 | Aberdeen | 08/07/05 | 5' 11" | 11st 0lb | Mid | Rangers Youths |
| 73 | Smith | Christopher | | 31/08/88 | Glasgow | 31/08/05 | 6' 0" | 11st 4lb | Def | Partick Thistle |
| 34 | Smith | Steven | | 30/08/85 | Bellshill | 01/06/02 | 5' 9.5" | 10st 13lb | Def | Rangers Youths |
| 19 | Thompson | Steven | | 14/10/78 | Paisley | 01/01/03 | 6' 2" | 13st 4lb | Fwd | Dundee United |
| 56 | Ure | Martin | | 06/06/88 | Irvine | 23/07/04 | 5' 9" | 10st 13lb | Def | Rangers Youths |
| 25 | Waterreus | Ronald | | 25/08/70 | Eindhoven | 31/01/05 | 6' 1" | 13st 8lb | Gk | Manchester City |
| 40 | Watson | Graeme | | 06/05/86 | Glasgow | 04/06/03 | 5' 8" | 10st 6lb | Def | Rangers Youths |
| 54 | Woods | Samuel | | 06/02/88 | Ascot | 27/08/04 | 5' 8" | 9st 12lb | Mid | Hutchison Vale |

## SEASON TICKET INFORMATION
**Season Ticket Prices**

| | Block | Adult | Conc. | Juv. |
|---|---|---|---|---|
| MAIN STAND (Front) | F/G/O/P | £397 | £282 | £188 |
| | H | £565 | £397 | £220 |
| | J/K/M/N | £538 | £376 | £220 |
| | L (Section MLF) | £596 | £334 | |
| MAIN STAND (Rear) | E | £507 | £356 | £220 |
| | C/D/O/R | £413 | £293 | £188 |
| | A/B/S/T | £382 | £261 | £188 |
| MEMBERS CLUB | Hospitality area only | | | |
| GOVAN (Rear) | 3/4/5 | £554 | £386 | £220 |
| | 2/6 | £507 | £356 | £220 |
| | 1/7 | £465 | £329 | £220 |
| GOVAN (Front) | 2/3/4/5/6 | £418 | £293 | £188 |
| | 1/7/East | £397 | £282 | £188 |
| ENCLOSURE | SE 1/2/3 SW 3/4/5 | £397 | £282 | £188 |
| | SE 4/5 SW1/2 | £397 | £282 | £188 |
| COPLAND (Rear) | 1/2/3/4/5 | £408 | £288 | £188 |
| COPLAND (Front) | 1/2/3/4/5 | £387 | £272 | £188 |

**League Admission prices**

| | | | |
|---|---|---|---|
| (Excluding matches against Celtic) | £22/23 | £12 | £12 |

**MILESTONES:**
**Year of formation:** 1873
**Most Capped player:** Alistair McCoist
**No. of Caps:** 58
**Most League points in a season:**
76 (Division 1 – Season 1920/21) (2 Points for a Win)
97 (Scottish Premier League - Season 2002/2003) (3 Points for a ...
**Most League goals scored by a player in a season:**
Sam English (Season 1931/32)
**No. of goals scored:** 44
**Record Attendance:** 118,567 (-v- Celtic – 2.1.1939)
**Record Victory:** 14-2 (-v- Blairgowrie – Scottish Cup, 20.1.19...
**Record Defeat:** 2-10 (-v- Airdrieonians – 1886)

# SEASON STATS 2004.05

## SEASON STATS 2004.05

| DATE | VENUE | OPPONENTS | ATT | RES | Klos S. | Ricksen F. | Khizanishvili Z. | Boumsong J-A. | Vignal G. | Hughes S. | Rae A. | Burke C. | Prso D. | Novo I. | Lovenkrands P. | Arveladze S. | Andrews M. | Vanoli P. | Thompson S. | Adam C. | Mladenovic D. | Moore C. | Hutton A. | Malcolm R. | Ross M. | Namouchi H. | Ball M. | Smith S. | Davidson R. | Djordjic B. | Buffel T. | McGregor A. | Kyrgiakos S. | Waterreus R. | Ferguson B. | McCormack R. |
|---|---|---|---|---|---|---|---|---|---|---|---|---|---|---|---|---|---|---|---|---|---|---|---|---|---|---|---|---|---|---|---|---|---|---|---|---|---|
| 7-Aug | A | Aberdeen | 19,028 | 0-0 | 1 | 2 | 3 | 4 | 5 | 6 | 7 | 8 | 9 | 10 | 11 | 12 | | | | | | | | | | | | | | | | | | | | |
| 14-Aug | H | Livingston | 48,102 | 4-0 | 1 | 2 | | 4 | 5 | 6² | 7 | | 9 | 10 | 11 | 8 | 3 | 12 | 13 | 14 | | | | | | | | | | | | | | | | |
| 21-Aug | H | Hibernian | 48,702 | 4-1 | 1 | 2 | 3 | 4 | 5 | 6 | 7 | | 9 | 10 | 11 | 8 | | 14 | 13 | | 12 | | | | | | | | | | | | | | | |
| 29-Aug | A | Celtic | 58,763 | 0-1 | 1 | 6 | | 4 | 5 | | 7 | | 11 | 10 | 12 | 9 | | | 13 | | 8 | 3 | 2 | | | | | | | | | | | | | |
| 12-Sep | A | Hearts | 14,601 | 0-0 | 1 | 2 | | 4 | 5 | | | | 9 | 11 | 10 | 14 | 12 | | 7 | 13 | | 8 | 3 | | 6 | | | | | | | | | | | |
| 19-Sep | H | Inverness Cal.Th. | 47,063 | 1-0 | 1 | 2 | 13 | 4 | | | 12 | | 7 | 9 | 10 | 11 | 14 | | 6 | | | 8 | 3 | | 5 | | | | | | | | | | | |
| 26-Sep | A | Dundee | 9,404 | 2-0 | 1 | 2 | 5 | | 4 | 12 | 7 | | 9 | | 14² | 13 | 10 | 3 | 8 | 11 | | | | | 6 | | | | | | | | | | | |
| 3-Oct | H | Kilmarnock | 46,278 | 2-0 | 1 | 2 | | 4 | 5 | 7 | | | 12 | 10 | 11 | 13 | 3 | | 9 | | | | | | 6 | 8 | | | | | | | | | | |
| 17-Oct | A | Motherwell | 10,946 | 2-0 | 1 | 7 | 5 | 4 | 2 | | | 8 | 11² | 10 | | 12 | 3 | | 9 | | | | | | 6 | | 13 | | | | | | | | | |
| 24-Oct | H | Dundee United | 46,796 | 1-1 | 1 | 7 | 5 | 4 | 2 | | | 8 | 11 | 10 | | 9 | 3 | | 12 | | | | | | 6 | | 13 | | | | | | | | | |
| 27-Oct | A | Dunfermline Ath. | 8,558 | 2-1 | 1 | 7 | 5 | 4 | 2 | 12 | | 9 | 11 | 10 | | | 3 | | | | | | | | 6 | | 8 | | | | | | | | | |
| 31-Oct | H | Aberdeen | 48,918 | 5-0 | 1 | 7 | 5 | 4 | 2 | | | 9 | 10² | 11 | | | 3 | | 12 | | | | | 13 | 6 | | 8 | | | | | | | | | |
| 7-Nov | A | Livingston | 7,800 | 4-1 | 1 | 7 | | 4 | 5 | 12 | | | 10 | 11 | 13 | 3 | | | 9 | | | | | 2 | 6 | | 8 | | | | | | | | | |
| 14-Nov | A | Hibernian | 13,825 | 1-0 | 1 | 2 | 5 | 4 | | 12 | | 9 | 10 | 11 | | 3 | | | | | | | | 13 | 6 | | 8 | 7 | | | | | | | | |
| 20-Nov | H | Celtic | 50,043 | 2-0 | 1 | 6 | 5 | 4 | 2 | | 8 | | 9 | 10 | 11 | 12 | 3 | | | | | | | 14 | | 7 | 13 | | | | | | | | | |
| 28-Nov | H | Hearts | 48,494 | †3-2 | 1 | 2 | 5 | 4 | | 13 | 8 | | 9 | 10² | 11 | 3 | | | | | | | | | 6 | 7 | 12 | | | | | | | | | |
| 5-Dec | A | Inverness Cal.Th. | 6,543 | 1-1 | 1 | 2 | 5 | 4 | | 8 | 12 | | 11 | 10 | | 3 | | | | | | | | 7 | | 9 | | 6 | 13 | | | | | | | |
| 11-Dec | H | Dundee | 48,114 | 3-0 | 1 | 2 | 5 | | 4 | | 12 | | 11 | 10 | | 9 | 3 | | | | | 6 | | 7 | | 8 | | 13 | | | | | | | | |
| 19-Dec | A | Kilmarnock | 11,156 | 1-0 | 1 | 6 | | 4 | 5 | | 9 | 13 | 11 | | | 10 | 3 | | | | | 12 | 7 | 2 | | 8 | | | | | | | | | | |
| 27-Dec | H | Motherwell | 49,909 | 4-1 | 1 | 6 | 4 | | 5 | | 12 | | 11 | 10² | | 9 | 3 | | 13 | | | 8 | | 2 | | 7 | | | | | | | | | | |
| 1-Jan | A | Dundee United | 10,461 | 1-1 | 1 | 6 | 4 | | 5 | | 8 | | 11 | | | 9 | 3 | | 10 | | | | | 2 | | 7 | | 12 | | | | | | | | |
| 15-Jan | H | Dunfermline Ath. | 48,055 | 3-0 | 1 | 2 | | | 5 | 14 | 8 | 12 | | | | 3 | | | 11 | | | | | 7 | 4 | 9 | 13 | | | 6 | 10 | | | | | |
| 23-Jan | A | Aberdeen | 17,495 | 2-1 | 1 | 2 | | | 5 | 13 | 8 | | 11 | 10 | | 3 | | | 12 | | | | | 7 | 4 | 14 | | | | 6 | 9 | | | | | |
| 29-Jan | H | Livingston | 48,579 | 3-0 | | 6 | | | | 8 | | | 11 | 10 | | 3 | | | 13 | | | | | 5 | 12 | 2 | | | | 7 | 9 | 1 | 4 | | | |
| 12-Feb | H | Hibernian | 50,143 | 3-0 | | 6 | | | 8 | | 14 | | 11² | 10 | | 13 | 3 | | 12 | | | | | | 2 | | 5 | | | 9 | | 4 | 1 | 7 | | |
| 20-Feb | A | Celtic | 58,993 | 2-0 | | 6 | | | 8 | | 12 | | 11 | 10 | | 3 | | | | | | | | 2 | | | 5 | | | 9 | | 4 | 1 | 7 | | |
| 26-Feb | H | Kilmarnock | 48,575 | 2-1 | | 6 | | | 8 | | 12 | 14 | 11 | 10 | | 3 | | | 13 | | | | | | | | 5 | | | 9 | 4 | 1 | 7 | | | |
| 2-Mar | A | Hearts | 13,842 | 2-1 | | 6 | | | 8 | | | | 11 | 10 | | 3 | | | | | | | | 2 | 12 | 5 | | | | 9 | | 4 | 1 | 7 | | |
| 5-Mar | H | Inverness Cal.Th. | 49,945 | 1-1 | | 6 | | | 8 | | | | | 10 | | 3 | 11 | | | | | 12 | 2 | | | 5 | | 9 | | 4 | 1 | 7 | | | | |
| 13-Mar | A | Dundee | 9,876 | 2-0 | | 6 | | | 8 | | | | 11 | 10 | | 3 | | | 13 | | | | | 9 | 2 | 5 | | | | 12 | | 4 | 1 | 7 | 14 | |
| 3-Apr | A | Motherwell | 10,210 | 3-2 | | 2 | 14 | | 3² | | 8 | | 11 | 10 | 12 | 13 | | | | | | | | 6 | | 9 | 5 | | | | | 4 | 1 | 7 | | |
| 12-Apr | H | Dundee United | 49,302 | 0-1 | | 6 | | | 3 | | 8 | | 11 | 10 | 13 | 12 | | 14 | | | | | | 7 | 2 | 9 | 5 | | | | | 4 | 1 | 7 | | |
| 17-Apr | A | Dunfermline Ath. | 8,261 | 1-0 | | 6 | | | 3 | | | | 11 | 10 | | 12 | | | | | | | | 2 | 13 | 5 | | | | | | 4 | 1 | 7 | | |
| 24-Apr | H | Celtic | 49,593 | 1-2 | | 6 | | | 8 | | | | 11 | 10 | | 3 | | 13 | | | | | | 14 | 2 | 9 | 5 | | | 12 | | 4 | 1 | 7 | | |
| 1-May | A | Aberdeen | 17,198 | 3-1 | | 6 | | | | 5 | | | 11² | 10 | 8 | 12 | 3 | | 13 | | | | | | 2 | | | | | 9 | | 4 | 1 | 7 | | |
| 7-May | H | Hearts | 49,342 | 2-1 | | 2 | | | 5 | | 6 | 14 | 11 | 10 | 8 | 12 | 3 | | 13 | | | | | | | | | | | 9 | | 4 | 1 | 7 | | |
| 14-May | H | Motherwell | 49,495 | 4-1 | | 2 | | | | | 6 | 12 | 11 | 10 | | 9² | 3 | | | | | | | | | | 5 | | | 8² | | 4 | 1 | 7 | | |
| 22-May | A | Hibernian | 16,601 | 1-0 | | 2 | | | | | 6 | | 11 | 10 | | 9 | 3 | | | | | | | | | | 5 | | | 8 | | 4 | 1 | 7 | | |
| **TOTAL FULL APPEARANCES** | | | | | 23 | 38 | 14 | 18 | 29 | 6 | 17 | 7 | 33 | 34 | 12 | 11 | 30 | 3 | 7 | | 6 | 3 | 8 | 19 | 13 | 13 | 12 | 2 | | 4 | 13 | 2 | 15 | 13 | 13 | |
| **TOTAL SUB APPEARANCES** | | | | | | | 2 | | 1 | 5 | 8 | 5 | 1 | 1 | 5 | 13 | | 2 | 17 | 1 | 1 | | 2 | 3 | | 7 | 2 | 2 | 1 | | 2 | | | | 1 |
| **TOTAL GOALS SCORED** | | | | | | | 5 | | 2 | 3 | 1 | | 18 | 19 | 3 | 6 | 4 | 5 | | | | 5 | | | 1 | 2 | | | 4 | | 2 | | | |

*...re in bold denotes goal scored. Secondary smaller figure in bold denotes number of goals scored. † denotes opponent's own goal.*

## THE GERS' 10 YEAR LEAGUE RECORD

| Season | Div | P | W | D | L | F | A | Pts | Pos |
|---|---|---|---|---|---|---|---|---|---|
| 95-96 | P | 36 | 27 | 6 | 3 | 85 | 25 | 87 | 1 |
| 96-97 | P | 36 | 25 | 5 | 6 | 85 | 33 | 80 | 1 |
| 97-98 | P | 36 | 21 | 9 | 6 | 76 | 38 | 72 | 2 |
| 98-99 | SPL | 36 | 23 | 8 | 5 | 78 | 31 | 77 | 1 |
| 99-00 | SPL | 36 | 28 | 6 | 2 | 96 | 26 | 90 | 1 |
| 00-01 | SPL | 38 | 26 | 4 | 8 | 76 | 36 | 82 | 2 |
| 01-02 | SPL | 38 | 25 | 10 | 3 | 82 | 27 | 85 | 2 |
| 02-03 | SPL | 38 | 31 | 4 | 3 | 101 | 28 | 97 | 1 |
| 03-04 | SPL | 38 | 25 | 6 | 7 | 76 | 33 | 81 | 2 |
| 04-05 | SPL | 38 | 29 | 6 | 3 | 78 | 22 | 93 | 1 |

## LEADING GOALSCORERS:

| Season | Div | Goals | Player |
|---|---|---|---|
| 1995-96 | P | 17 | G. Durie |
| 1996-97 | P | 16 | B. Laudrup |
| 1997-98 | P | 32 | M. Negri |
| 1998-99 | SPL | 18 | R. Wallace |
| 1999-00 | SPL | 17 | J. Albertz |
| 2000-01 | SPL | 11 | T. A. Flo |
| 2001-02 | SPL | 17 | T. A. Flo |
| 2002-03 | SPL | 16 | R de Boer, B. Ferguson |
| 2003-04 | SPL | 12 | S. Arveladze |
| 2004-05 | SPL | 19 | I. Novo |

### RANGERS PLAYING KITS SEASON 2005.06

FIRST KIT    SECOND KIT    THIRD KIT

# SCOTTISH PREMIERLEAGUE

## ABERDEEN: PITTODRIE STADIUM

You can reach Pittodrie Stadium by these routes:
**BUSES:** The following buses all depart from the city centre to within a hundred yards of the ground: Nos. 1, 2, and 11.
**TRAINS:** The main Aberdeen station is in the centre of the city and the above buses will then take fans to the ground.
**CARS:** Motor vehicles coming from the city centre should travel along Union Street, then turn into King Street and the park will be on your right, about half a mile further on. Parking on Beach Boulevard and Beach Esplanade.

**CAPACITY:** 21,421 (All Seated)
**PITCH DIMENSIONS:** 115 yds x 72 yds (105 x 66m)

**FACILITIES FOR DISABLED SUPPORTERS:**
There are a total of 26 wheelchair spaces in the home support areas. 20 are located at the front of the Richard Donald stand and 6 at the front of the Merkland Family Stand. There are 7 spaces available in the away support (section Q) in the South Stand. Please telephone 087 1983 1903.

## CELTIC: CELTIC PARK

The following routes may be used to reach Celtic Park:
**BUSES:** The following buses all leave from the city centre and pass within 50 yards of the ground. Nos. 43, 62, and 64.
**TRAINS:** There is a frequent train service from Glasgow Central Low Level station to Bridgeton Cross Station and this is only a ten minute walk from the ground. There is also a train from Queen Street Station (lower level) to Bellgrove Rail Station, approximately 20 minutes walk from the ground.
**CARS:** From the city centre, motor vehicles should travel along London Road and this will take you to the ground. Parking spaces are available in various areas close to the ground. On

matchdays all car parking is strictly limited and is only available to those in possession of a valid car park pass.
**CAPACITY:** 60,355 (All Seated)
**PITCH DIMENSIONS:** 115 yds x 75 yds (105 x 68m)
**FACILITIES FOR DISABLED SUPPORTERS:**
There is provision for 142 wheelchair positions for disabled supporters and their helpers. These are split into 87 in the North Stand, at the front of the lower terracing, 10 in the East Stand, lower terracing and 37 in the South Stand, lower terracing. Celtic fans should contact the club for availability. There is also a provision for 6 away positions in the lower East Stand.

## DUNDEE UNITED: TANNADICE PARK

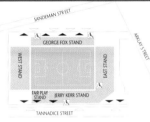

Tannadice Park can be reached by the following routes:
**BUSES:** The following buses leave from the city centre at frequent intervals: Nos. 1a, 18, 19 and 21 from Meadowside and No. 22 from Littlewoods Store, High Street.
**TRAINS:** Trains from all over the country pass through the main Dundee station and fans can then proceed to the ground by the above bus services from stops situated within walking distance of the station.

**CARS:** There is parking in the streets adjacent to the ground.

**CAPACITY:** 14,223 (All Seated)
**PITCH DIMENSIONS:** 110 yds x 72 yds (101 x 66m)
**FACILITIES FOR DISABLED SUPPORTERS:**
George Fox Stand – Lower Tier – Home Supporters.
East Stand – Lower Tier – Home Supporters.
West Stand – Away Supporters.

## DUNFERMLINE ATHLETIC: EAST END PARK

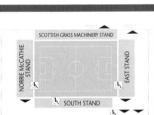

East End Park may be reached by the following routes:
**TRAINS:** There is a regular train service from Edinburgh to either Dunfermline Town or Dunfermline Queen Margaret Stations. The ground is a 15 minute walk from either station.
**BUSES:** Buses destined for Kelty, Perth, St. Andrews and Kirkcaldy all pass close to East End Park.
**CARS:** Car Parking is available in a large car park adjoining the East End of the ground and there are also facilities in various

side streets. Multi-storey car parking approximately 10 minutes walk from the ground.
**CAPACITY:** 11,998 (All Seated)
**PITCH DIMENSIONS:** 115 yds x 70 yds (105 x 64m)
**FACILITIES FOR DISABLED SUPPORTERS:**
12 spaces in East Stand for Away Supporters. 12 spaces in the Norrie McCathie Stand for Home Supporters. 24 seats for helpers.

## FALKIRK: THE FALKIRK STADIUM

The Falkirk Stadium can be reached by the following routes.
**TRAINS:** Take the main Edinburgh-Glasgow service and alight at Grahamston Station. The stadium is approximately 20 minutes walk from here. Alternatively, the bus route from the town centre is the Falkirk to Grangemouth route which is approximately one mile from the stadium.
**BUSES:** The following buses run from Callendar Riggs Bus Station which is in the centre of the town. Bus numbers 3 & 4 (destination Grangemouth) and also numbers 6 and 7 (destination Bo'ness) stop outside the stadium. The Bus Station is appox. 5 min's from Grahamston Railway Station.
**CARS:** Cars from Glasgow and the west should take the M80 then the M876 before joining the M9. Leave the M9 at the exit for B.P. Grangemouth

then turn right at end of the slip road. Follow the road for approximately 200 yards to the Earlsgate roundabout before going under the motorway at the roundabout and then following the Grangemouth to Falkirk Road. The Falkirk Stadium is on the left hand side. Cars travelling from Edinburgh and the east should leave the M9 at Junction 5 and proceed along the road to Falkirk for about 1 mile and the stadium is on your right hand side.
**CAPACITY:** 6,172 (All Seated)
**PITCH DIMENSIONS:** 115 yds x 74 yds (105 x 68m)
**FACILITIES FOR DISABLED SUPPORTERS:**
Accommodation for disabled in new Stand. Toilet facilities also provided.

## HEART OF MIDLOTHIAN: TYNECASTLE STADIUM

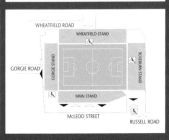

Tynecastle Stadium can be reached by the following routes:
**BUSES:** A frequent service of buses leaves from the city centre, Nos. 1, 2, 3, 4, 33, 34, 35 and 44 all pass the ground.
**TRAINS:** Haymarket Station is about half a mile from the ground.
**CARS:** Car Parking facilities exist in the adjacent side streets in Robertson Avenue and also the Westfield area.

**CAPACITY:** 17,300 (All Seated)
**PITCH DIMENSIONS:** 109 yds x 70 yds (100 x 64m)

**FACILITIES FOR DISABLED SUPPORTERS:**
There are 15 spaces for visiting fans at the Roseburn Stand. Regarding facilities for home supporters, fans should contact the club in advance for availability.

## HIBERNIAN: EASTER ROAD STADIUM

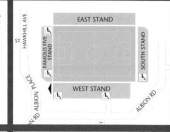

Easter Road Stadium can be reached by the following routes:
**BUSES:** The following Lothian Regional Transport buses depart Princes Street every few minutes and stop in London Road at Easter Road (Nos. 1, 4, 15, 26 and 44). The No. 1 bus travels down Easter Road and stops near the Stadium. The following First Bus Service stop on London Road, at the top of Easter Road (66, 106, 113, 124, 129, X5).
**TRAINS:** Edinburgh Waverley is served by trains from all over the country and adjoins Princes Street. The Stadium is about a 20/25 minute walk from Princes Street.
**CARS:** There are no special parking arrangements for cars in the immediate vicinity of the Stadium. Parking is controlled by a Temporary Traffic

Regulation Order (coned areas). A tow-away scheme is in operation for illegally parked vehicles. Persons with disabilities displaying Orange Badges on their vehicles will be permitted to park on the south side of St. Clair Street under the direction of Parking Attendants/Police.
**CAPACITY:** 17,400 (All Seated)
**PITCH DIMENSIONS:** 115 yds x 70 yds (105 x 64m)
**FACILITIES FOR DISABLED SUPPORTERS:**
Home Supporters: Famous Five (North) Stand / Wheelchair Disabled and Hearing Impaired. West Stand / Wheelchair and Ambulant Disabled and Visually Impaired. Away Supporters: South Stand / Wheelchair and Ambulant Disabled and Hearing and Visually Impaired.

## INVERNESS CALEDONIAN THISTLE: TULLOCH CALEDONIAN STADIUM

You can reach Tulloch Caledonian Stadium by these routes:
**BUSES:** Local services from Farraline Park Bus Station.
**TRAINS:** Nearest Railway station is Inverness which is approximately one mile from the ground.
**CARS:** The Ground is located on North side of A9 Perth/Inverness trunk road and fans should access off the roundabout (first after Perth) before Kessock Bridge. Parking available at Stadium.

**CAPACITY:** 7,512 (All Seated)
**PITCH DIMENSIONS:** 115 yds x 74 yds (105 x 68m)
**FACILITIES FOR DISABLED SUPPORTERS:**
Designated seating at the front of all stands.
Toilet facilities available. Please contact Club Secretary in advance.

## KILMARNOCK: RUGBY PARK

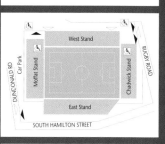

Rugby Park can be reached by the following routes:
**BUSES:** The main bus station, which is served by buses from all over the country, is ten minutes walk from the ground, but there are three local services which run from here to within a two minute walk of the park. These are the Kilmarnock-Saltcoats, Kilmarnock-Ardrossan and Kilmarnock-Largs.
**TRAINS:** Kilmarnock Station is well served by trains from Glasgow and the West Coast, and the station is only 15 minutes walk from the ground.

**CARS:** Car parking is available in the club car park by permit only. Pedestrian entry **ONLY** from Dundonald Road. Visiting supporters enter **ONLY** from Rugby Road Entrance.
**CAPACITY:** 18,128 (All Seated)
**PITCH DIMENSIONS:** 115 yds x 74 yds (105 x 68m)
**FACILITIES FOR DISABLED SUPPORTERS:**
**Contact:** Grace Jamieson, Secretary, Persons with a Disability Association Tel: (01563) 555933

## LIVINGSTON: ALMONDVALE STADIUM

Almondvale Stadium can be reached by the following routes:
**BUSES:** By bus to terminus at Almondvale Shopping Centre. Follow direction signs for St. John's Hospital or Almondvale Stadium and it is a short 5 minute walk.
**TRAINS:** To either Livingston North or South Stations, and by taxi to stadium. Approximate cost is £2.00.

**CARS:** Leave M8 at Livingston Junction (East). Follow signs for St. John's Hospital or the Almondvale Stadium.
**CAPACITY:** 10,005 (All Seated)
**PITCH DIMENSIONS:** 107yds x 75yds (98 x 69m)
**FACILITIES FOR DISABLED SUPPORTERS:**
By prior arrangement with Secretary.

## MOTHERWELL: FIR PARK

The following routes can be used to reach Fir Park:
**BUSES:** Fir Park is less than a quarter of a mile from the main thoroughfare through the town and numerous buses serving Lanarkshire and Glasgow all pass along this road.
**TRAINS:** Motherwell Station is a twenty minute walk from Fir Park, while the station at Airbles Road is only ten minutes away. East Coast access is via Motherwell Central Station on the Glasgow/London East Coast line. Travel from West Coast and Glasgow areas is via the low level Glasgow Central line to Airbles and Motherwell Central. This is a regular service on a 30 minute basis (8 mins & 38 mins past).

**CARS:** Controlled supervised car parking is available in the immediate area of Fir Park. Car park season tickets are available for closest proximity car parks. Away fan car parking is extensive in the grounds of Motherwell College on a day rate basis of £3.00.

**CAPACITY:** 13,664 (All Seated)
**PITCH DIMENSIONS:** 112 yds x 71 yds (102.2 x 65.2m)
**FACILITIES FOR DISABLED SUPPORTERS:**
Area between Main Stand and South Stand. Prior arrangement must be made with Deborah Drummond and a ticket obtained.

## RANGERS: IBROX STADIUM

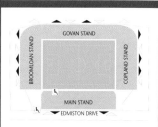

You can reach Ibrox Stadium by these routes:
**BUSES:** The following buses all pass within 300 yards of the Stadium and can be boarded from Glasgow city centre:- Nos. 4, 9A, 23, 23A, 52, 53, 53A, 54A, 54B, 65, 89 and 91.
**UNDERGROUND:** GGPTE Underground station is Ibrox, which is two minutes walk from the Stadium
**CARS:** Motor Vehicles can head for the Stadium from the city centre by joining the M8 Motorway from Waterloo Street. Take the B768 turn-off for Govan. This will then take you to the

ground. A limited number of parking spaces will be available in the Albion Car Park.
**CAPACITY:** 50,444 (All Seated)
**PITCH DIMENSIONS:** 115yds x 75yds (105 x 68m)
**FACILITIES FOR DISABLED SUPPORTERS:**
Special area within stadium and also special toilet facilities provided. The club also have a Rangers Disabled Supporters' Club. Contact: David Milne, Secretary, Disabled Supporters' Club, c/o Ibrox Stadium, Glasgow, G51 2XD. This is free of charge.

# AIRDRIE UNITED

**AIRDRIE UNITED F.C.**

Excelsior Stadium, Broomfield Park,

Airdrie, ML6 8QZ

**TELEPHONE NUMBERS**

Secretary's Business (07710) 230775

Commercial Manager (07949) 976116

Ground (Match Days Only)

(01236) 622000 or (01236) 770147

Club Shop (Match Days Only) (01236) 770147

**FAX** (0141) 221 1497

**E-MAIL** annmarie@airdnieunitedfc.com

**E-MAIL 2** jim@airdnieunitedfc.com

**WEBSITE** www.airdrieunitedfc.com

**CLUB CORRESPONDENCE ADDRESS**

Ms. Anne Marie Ballantyne

Secretary

Airdrie United F.C.

60 St. Enoch Square, Glasgow, G1 4AG

**CHAIRMAN** James W. Ballantyne

**DIRECTORS**

Ann Marie Ballantyne, Gavin W. Speirs,

Mrs. Rose Mary Ballantyne,

John Ballantyne & Walter G. Speirs

**HONORARY PRESIDENT** Ian McMillan

**SECRETARY** Ms. Ann Marie Ballantyne

**MANAGER** Sandy Stewart

**FIRST TEAM COACH** Kenny Brannigan

**YOUTH CO-ORDINATOR** Jimmy Boyle

**YOUTH TEAM COACH**

U19: Jimmy Boyle

**TEAM CAPTAIN** Stephen Docherty

**FOOTBALL SAFETY OFFICERS'**

**ASSOCIATION REPRESENTATIVE**

Alistair Cameron

**COMMERCIAL/LOTTERY MANAGER**

Les Jones

**MEDIA LIAISON PERSON**

James W. Ballantyne

**MATCHDAY PROGRAMME EDITOR**

John O'Brien.

Tel: B (0141) 285 4618

Tel: H (01236) 763824

**CLUB DOCTOR**

Dr. Brian Dunn, M.B., CLB, M.R.C.P.(UK)

**PHYSIOTHERAPIST** Paul Green

**STADIUM MANAGER**

Alistair Cameron. Tel : (01236) 622000

**GROUNDSMAN** John McGuire

**KIT PERSON** John Donnelly

**SEASON TICKET ADMINISTRATOR**

Scott Gilkison

**CLUB SHOP**

Situated at Ground

Open on Home Match Days and on Sundays

between 2.00p.m-4.30pm, Other opening

times listed on club website.

**SUPPORTERS CLUB**

Fans Representative - Veronica McGregor

**SHIRT SPONSOR**

Pertemps

**KIT SUPPLIER**

Pro Star

## LIST OF PLAYERS 2005.06

| PLAYERS SURNAME | FIRST NAME | MIDDLE NAME | DATE OF BIRTH | PLACE OF BIRTH | DATE SIGNED | HEIGHT FT INS | WEIGHT ST LBS | POSITION ON PITCH | PREVIOUS CLUB |
|---|---|---|---|---|---|---|---|---|---|
| Barkey | Kevin | | 05/02/85 | Glasgow | 09/06/05 | 5.8 | 10.7 | Midfield | Motherwell |
| Boyle | Henry | | 06/04/87 | Glasgow | 12/08/05 | 5.7 | 9.11 | Forward | Shettleston Juniors |
| Burrell | Mark | William | 10/01/88 | Lanark | 12/08/05 | 5.10 | 10.3 | Goalkeeper | Motherwell |
| Coyle | Fraser | | 19/02/85 | Glasgow | 05/08/05 | 5.8 | 11.7 | Defender | Rangers |
| Craig | Thomas | | 28/05/87 | Bellshill | 12/08/05 | 6.0 | 14.0 | Defender | East Stirlingshire |
| Cullen | Paul | Francis | 15/04/88 | Lanark | 12/08/05 | 5.9 | 9.10 | Defender | Hamilton A. Form D U1' |
| Docherty | Stephen | | 18/02/76 | Glasgow | 26/07/02 | 5.10 | 12.0 | Def / Mid | Airdrieonians |
| Dunn | David | Hugh | 01/11/81 | Bellshill | 31/01/03 | 5.11 | 12.1 | Midfield | Clyde |
| Gallacher | Christopher | | 23/08/88 | Bellshill | 31/08/05 | 5.8 | 9.7 | Forward | Heart of Midlothian |
| Grant | John | | 24/01/89 | Glasgow | 12/08/05 | 6.1 | 10.10 | Midfield | Queen's Park |
| Hardie | Martin | | 22/04/76 | Alexandria | 04/08/04 | 6.0 | 11.0 | Mid / For | Kilmarnock |
| Hewitt | Terry | | 20/06/88 | Glasgow | 30/09/05 | 6.2 | 11.0 | Defender | Clydebank B.C. |
| Hollis | Lee | James | 12/03/86 | Glasgow | 11/08/03 | 6.0 | 11.0 | Goalkeeper | Hillwood B.C. |
| King | Ross | Kevin | 28/06/88 | Glasgow | 30/09/05 | 5.11 | 10.2 | Midfield | Partick Thistle |
| Lovering | Paul | James | 25/11/75 | Glasgow | 28/05/04 | 5.10 | 11.3 | Defender | St. Johnstone |
| McColl | Alexander | | 07/02/87 | Stirling | 08/08/05 | 5.10 | 11.0 | Defender | Rangers |
| McDougall | Steven | David | 17/06/86 | Paisley | 11/08/03 | 5.11 | 10.6 | Forward | Rangers |
| McGowan | Neil | William | 15/04/77 | Glasgow | 29/08/02 | 5.10 | 11.4 | Defender | K.A. Iceland |
| McKenna | Stephen | | 25/11/85 | Glasgow | 28/05/04 | 6.1 | 12.4 | Midfield | Rangers |
| McKeown | Stephen | James | 17/07/81 | Rutherglen | 29/08/02 | 5.10 | 12.10 | Forward | Airdrieonians |
| McLaren | William | | 06/11/84 | Glasgow | 23/02/04 | 5.9 | 9.0 | Midfield | Benburb Juniors |
| McManus | Allan | William | 17/11/74 | Paisley | 06/06/03 | 6.1 | 13.4 | Defender | Ayr United |
| McPhee | Brian | | 23/10/70 | Glasgow | 08/07/05 | 5.10 | 12.4 | Forward | Hamilton Academical |
| McPherson | Ross | Iain | 27/05/88 | Glasgow | 12/08/05 | 5.8 | 11.12 | Forward | Clydebank B.C. |
| Prunty | Bryan | | 12/01/83 | Coatbridge | 24/08/05 | 5.10 | 11.0 | Forward | Inverness Caledonian Thist |
| Robertson | Stephen | | 16/03/77 | Glasgow | 06/08/05 | 5.10 | 12.2 | Goalkeeper | Ards |
| Stewart | Alexander | | 14/10/65 | Bellshill | 05/08/05 | 5.7 | 11.7 | Defender | Airdrieonians |
| Twigg | Gary | | 19/03/84 | Glasgow | 26/07/05 | 5.8 | 11.10 | Forward | Derby County |
| Wilson | Christopher | Andrew | 02/02/88 | Glasgow | 12/08/05 | 5.10 | 10.8 | Defender | Motherwell |

## TICKET INFORMATION

**Season Ticket information**

| Seated | Adult | £245 Reserved seat |
|---|---|---|
| | Adult | £225 Unreserved seat |
| | OAP/Unemployed | |
| | (Unreserved/Reserved) | £150/170 |
| | Juvenile (12-16) | £90 |
| | Child Under 12 | £40 With parent |
| | Child Over 12 | £60 With parent |
| | Disabled | £100-150 (Variable) |
| | | £170 (Reserved) |

**Match Ticket information**

| Seated | Adult | £15 |
|---|---|---|
| | OAP/Unemployed (with UB40) | £10 |
| | Parent & Child | £22 |
| | Juvenile (12-16) | £7 |

**MILESTONES:**

**Year of formation:**

1965 (From seasons 1965/66 to 2001/02 known as Clydeb

**Most League points in a season:**

58 (Division 1 – Season 1976/77) (2 Points for a Win)

70 (Second Division – Season 2003/04) (3 Points for a W'

**Most League goals scored by a player in a season:**

Ken Eadie (Season 1990/91)

**No. of goals scored:** 29

**Record Attendance:**

14,900 (-v- Hibernian – 10.2.1965 at Kilbowie Park)

5,703 (-v- Morton – 15.5.2004 at Excelsior Stadium)

**Record Victory:** 8-1 (-v- Arbroath – Division 1, 3.1.1977)

**Record Defeat:** 1-9 (-v- Gala Fairydean – Scottish Cup, 1'

## SEASON STATS 2004.05

| DATE | VENUE | OPPONENTS | ATT | RES | McGeown M. | Wilson W.S. | Lovering P.J. | McGowan N.W. | McManus A.W. | Dunn D.H. | Vareille J. | Wilson M. | Coyle O.C. | Gow A. | Roberts M.K. | Docherty S. | McKeown S.J. | Wilson S.W. | Christie K. | Hoey T.G. | Barkey K. | McGroarty C.M. | Hardie M. | McLaren W. | Hollis L.J.M. | McKenna S. | Stewart A. | McDougall S.D. |
|---|---|---|---|---|---|---|---|---|---|---|---|---|---|---|---|---|---|---|---|---|---|---|---|---|---|---|---|---|
| 7-Aug | H | St. Johnstone | 2,365 | 1-0 | 1 | 2 | 3 | 4 | 5 | 6 | **7** | 8 | 9 | 10 | 11 | 12 | 15 | 16 |  |  |  |  |  |  |  |  |  |  |
| 14-Aug | A | Partick Thistle | 4,011 | 2-3 | 1 | 2 | 3 |  | 4 | 6 | 7 | 8 | **9**$^{2}$ |  | 11 | 14 | 10 | 5 | 12 | 16 |  |  |  |  |  |  |  |  |
| 21-Aug | H | Raith Rovers | 2,009 | 1-1 | 1 | 2 | 3 | 4 | 5 | 6 | 7 | 8 | 9 |  | 11 | 14 | **10** |  | 16 | 15 |  |  |  |  |  |  |  |  |
| 28-Aug | A | Falkirk | 3,790 | 0-5 | 1 | 2 | 3 |  | 4 | 10 | 7 | 8 | 9 |  | 11 | 6 |  | 5 |  |  |  |  |  |  |  |  |  |  |
| 4-Sep | H | Queen of the South | 1,652 | 0-1 | 1 | 12 | 3 | 4 | 2 |  | 7 | 8 | 9 |  | 11 | 6 | 10 | 5 |  | 14 |  |  |  |  |  |  |  |  |
| 11-Sep | A | Clyde | 1,680 | 2-1 | 1 | 2 |  | 4 | 6 | 14 | 8 | **9** |  | 11 |  | 10 | 5 | 15 | **7** | 3 | 16 |  |  |  |  |  |  |  |
| 18-Sep | H | Ross County | 1,486 | 1-2 | 1 | 2 |  | 14 | 4 | 6 | 11 | 8 | 9 |  | 12 | **10** | 5 |  | 7 | 3 | 16 |  |  |  |  |  |  |  |
| 25-Sep | A | St. Mirren | 3,569 | 1-1 | 1 |  | 3 | 4 | 14 |  | 8 | 9 | **15** | 2 | 10 | 5 |  | 7 |  | 6 | 11 |  |  |  |  |  |  |  |
| 2-Oct | H | Hamilton Academical | 1,900 | 0-2 | 1 |  | 3 | 4 | 16 | 15 | 8 | 9 |  | 14 | 2 | 10 | 5 |  | 7 |  | 6 | 11 |  |  |  |  |  |  |
| 16-Oct | H | Partick Thistle | 2,548 | 4-2 | 1 | 12 | 3 | 4 |  |  | 8 | 9$^{2}$ | 16 | 15 | 2 | 10 | 5 |  | 7 |  | 6 | **11** |  |  |  |  |  |  |
| 23-Oct | A | St. Johnstone | 2,447 | 1-1 | 1 |  | 3 | 4 | 12 |  | 8 | **9** | 15 | 14 | 2 | 10 | 5 |  | 7 |  | 6 | 11 |  |  |  |  |  |  |
| 30-Oct | H | Falkirk | 3,247 | 1-3 | 1 |  | 3 | 4 | 12 |  | 8 | **9** | 15 | 14 | 2 | 10 | 5 |  | 7 |  | 6 | 11 |  |  |  |  |  |  |
| 6-Nov | A | Queen of the South | 2,022 | 0-1 |  |  | 3 | 4 |  | 16 | 8 | 9 |  | 14 | 2 | 10 | 5 |  | 7 |  | 6 | 11 | 1 |  |  |  |  |  |
| 13-Nov | H | Clyde | 1,862 | 3-1 |  |  | 3 | 4 | 5 | 16 | 14 | 8 | **9** | **10** | **7** |  |  | 15 |  |  | 6 | 11 | 1 |  |  |  |  |  |
| 20-Nov | A | Ross County | 2,173 | 2-1 |  | 12 | **3** | 4 | 5 | 16 |  | 8 | 9 | 10 | 7 | 2 |  |  |  |  | 6 | 11 | 1 |  |  |  |  |  |
| 27-Nov | A | Hamilton Academical | 2,295 | 3-1 |  |  | 3 | 4 |  | 15 | 8 | **9** | **10**$^{2}$ | 7 | 2 |  | 5 |  |  |  | 6 | 11 | 1 |  |  |  |  |  |
| 4-Dec | H | St. Mirren | 2,514 | 3-2 |  |  | 3 | 4 | 12 | 14 | 15 | 8 | 9$^{2}$ | 10 | 7 | 2 |  | 5 |  |  | 6 | 11 | 1 |  |  |  |  |  |
| 11-Dec | H | St. Johnstone | 1,865 | 0-0 | 1 |  | 3 | 4 |  | 6 | 7 | 8 |  | 10 | 2 |  | 5 | 14 |  |  | 6 | 11 |  |  |  |  |  |  |
| 18-Dec | A | Raith Rovers | 1,795 | 2-0 | 1 | 2 | 3 | 4 |  | 15 | 8 | 9 | 10 | 7 |  | 16 | 5 |  | 12 |  | 6 | 11 |  |  |  |  |  |  |
| 26-Dec | A | Falkirk | 4,133 | 0-1 | 1 |  | 3 | 4 | 5 |  | 16 | 8 | 9 | 10 | 7 | 2 |  |  |  |  | 6 | 11 |  |  |  |  |  |  |
| 29-Dec | H | Queen of the South | 1,781 | 2-0 | 1 | 12 | 3 | 4 | 5 | 15 | 16 | 8 | **9** | **10** | 7 | 2 |  |  |  |  | 6 | 11 |  |  |  |  |  |  |
| 1-Jan | A | Clyde | 1,513 | 0-1 | 1 |  | 3 | 4 | 5 |  | 8 | 9 | 10 | 7 | 2 |  |  |  |  |  | 6 | 11 |  |  |  |  |  |  |
| 15-Jan | H | Ross County | 1,512 | 2-1 | 1 |  | 3 | 4 | 5 |  | 16 | 8 | **9** | 10 | 7 | 2 |  |  |  |  | 6 | **11** |  |  |  |  |  |  |
| 22-Jan | A | St. Mirren | 3,047 | 0-1 | 1 | 2 | 3 | 4 | 5 | 14 | 15 | 8 | 9 | 10 | 7 |  |  |  |  |  | 6 | 11 |  |  |  |  |  |  |
| 12-Feb | A | Partick Thistle | 3,791 | 1-1 | 1 |  | 3 | 4 | **5** | 11 | 15 | 8 | 9 | 10 | 7 |  |  |  |  |  | 6 | 16 |  | 2 |  |  |  |  |
| 19-Feb | H | Raith Rovers | 1,599 | 2-1 | 1 |  | 3 | 4 | 5 | 14 | 15 | 8 | 9 | 10 | **7** |  | 16 |  |  |  | 6 | 11 |  | 2 |  |  |  |  |
| 5-Mar | A | Queen of the South | 1,683 | 0-0 | 1 | 12 | 3 | 4 | 5 | 6 | 7 | 8 | 9 | 10 | 15 |  | 11 |  |  |  |  |  |  | 2 |  |  |  |  |
| 8-Mar | H | Hamilton Academical | 1,430 | 1-0 | 1 |  | 3 |  | 5 | 6 | 7 | 8 | 9 | **10** | 15 | 4 | 11 |  |  | 14 |  | 16 |  | 2 |  |  |  |  |
| 12-Mar | H | Falkirk | 3,111 | 2-1 | 1 |  | 3 | 12 | 5 | 14 | 7 | 8 | 9 | **10** | 15 | 4 | **11** |  |  |  | 6 |  |  | 2 |  |  |  |  |
| 19-Mar | H | Clyde | 1,641 | 2-4 | 1 |  | 3 | 4 |  | 7 | 8 | **9** | 10 | 11 | 5 |  |  |  |  |  | 6 | 16 |  | 2 |  |  |  |  |
| 2-Apr | A | Ross County | 2,024 | 1-3 | 1 | 12 |  | 3 | 6 | 11 | 8 | 9 | **10** | 15 | 4 | 7 | 5 |  |  |  |  | 16 |  | 2 |  |  |  |  |
| 9-Apr | A | Hamilton Academical | 2,030 | 1-1 | 1 | 12 | 3 | 6 | 5 |  | 8 | 9 | 10 |  | 2 | 7 |  | **4** |  |  | 11 | 16 |  |  |  |  |  |  |
| 16-Apr | H | St. Mirren | 1,989 | 0-2 | 1 | 2 |  | 3 | 4 | 14 | 15 | 8 | 9 | 10 |  | 6 | 7 |  |  | 12 |  | 11 | 5 |  |  |  |  |  |
| 22-Apr | A | St. Johnstone | 2,239 | 2-1 | 1 | 12 | 3 | 6 | 5 | 14 | 8 |  | **9** |  | 2 |  |  |  |  | 7 |  | 10 | 11 |  |  | 4 |  |  |
| 30-Apr | H | Partick Thistle | 1,747 | 0-1 | 1 | 2 | 3 | 6 | 5 | 14 | 15 | 8 |  | 9 |  | 12 |  |  |  | 7 |  | 10 | 11 |  |  | 4 |  |  |
| 7-May | A | Raith Rovers | 1,296 | 1-0 |  | 12 | 3 | 4 | 5 | 6 | 16 | 8 |  | **10** | 9 | 2 |  |  |  | 15 |  | 11 | 1 |  |  |  | 7 |  |
| **TOTAL FULL APPEARANCES** |  |  |  |  | 30 | 10 | 29 | 30 | 27 | 12 | 12 | 36 | 33 | 23 | 20 | 24 | 18 | 1 | 17 |  | 10 | 2 | 23 | 22 | 6 | 8 | 2 | 1 |
| **TOTAL SUB APPEARANCES** |  |  |  |  | 9 |  | 2 | 3 | 12 | 16 |  |  | 3 | 11 | 4 | 4 | 1 | 1 | 3 | 8 |  | 2 | 5 |  |  |  |  |  |
| **TOTAL GOALS SCORED** |  |  |  |  |  | 1 |  | 1 |  | 1 | 2 | 14 | 9 | 3 |  | 4 |  | 1 |  | 1 | 4 | 3 |  |  |  |  |  |  |

Figure in bold denotes goal scored. Secondary smaller figure in bold denotes number of goals scored. † denotes opponent's own goal.

## THE DIAMONDS' 10 YEAR LEAGUE RECORD

| Season | Div | P | W | D | L | F | A | Pts | Pos |
|---|---|---|---|---|---|---|---|---|---|
| 95-96 | F | 36 | 10 | 10 | 16 | 39 | 58 | 40 | 7 |
| 96-97 | F | 36 | 7 | 7 | 22 | 31 | 59 | 28 | 9 |
| 97-98 | S | 36 | 16 | 12 | 8 | 48 | 31 | 60 | 2 |
| 98-99 | F | 36 | 11 | 13 | 12 | 36 | 38 | 46 | 7 |
| 99-00 | F | 36 | 1 | 28 | 7 | 17 | 82 | 10 | 10 |
| 00-01 | S | 36 | 12 | 11 | 13 | 42 | 43 | 47 | 5 |
| 01-02 | S | 36 | 14 | 9 | 13 | 44 | 45 | 51 | 4 |
| 02-03 | S | 36 | 14 | 12 | 10 | 51 | 44 | 54 | 3 |
| 03-04 | S | 36 | 20 | 10 | 6 | 64 | 36 | 70 | 1 |
| 04-05 | F | 36 | 14 | 8 | 14 | 44 | 48 | 50 | 5 |

## LEADING GOALSCORERS:

| Season | Div | Goals | Player |
|---|---|---|---|
| 1995-96 | F | 11 | J. Grady |
| 1996-97 | F | 8 | J. Grady |
| 1997-98 | S | 13 | C. McDonald |
| 1998-99 | F | 9 | C. McDonald |
| 1999-00 | F | 5 | I. Cameron |
| 2000-01 | S | 8 | A. Burke |
| 2001-02 | S | 9 | A. Burke |
| 2002-03 | S | 18 | J. Vareille |
| 2003-04 | S | 12 | A. Gow, O.Coyle |
| 2004-05 | F | 14 | O.Coyle |

**AIRDRIE UNITED PLAYING KITS SEASON 2005.06**

FIRST KIT | SECOND KIT | THIRD KIT

# BRECHIN CITY

**BRECHIN CITY F.C.**

Glebe Park, Trinity Road,

Brechin, Angus, DD9 6BJ

**TELEPHONE NUMBERS**

Ground (Matchdays Only) (01356) 622856

Sec. Bus. (01356) 625285

Sec. Home (01356) 625691

Sec. Mobile (07803) 089060

Sec. Home Fax (01356) 629292

Sec. Bus. Fax (01356) 625524

**FAX** (01356) 625524

**E-MAIL** secretary@brechincityfc.com

**WEBSITE** www.brechincity.co.uk

**CHAIRMAN** David H. Birse

**VICE-CHAIRMAN**

Hugh A. Campbell Adamson

**MANAGEMENT COMMITTEE**

Martin G. Smith (Treasurer),

Calum I. McK. Brown,

Kenneth W. Ferguson, Stephen D. Mitchell,

Angus A. Fairlie & Andrew D. Allison

**HONORARY PRESIDENT** David H. Will C.B.E

**HONORARY LIFE MEMBERS**

David K. Lindsay & George C. Johnston

**SECRETARY** Kenneth W. Ferguson

**MANAGER** Ian Campbell

**ASSISTANT MANAGER** Bert Paton

**FIRST TEAM COACH** John Young

**BACKROOM STAFF**

Norman Ross, Alan Grieve & Lewis Davidson

**GOALKEEPING COACH** John Ritchie

**TEAM CAPTAIN** Paul Deas

**OFFICE ADMINISTRATOR**

Kenneth W. Ferguson

**FOOTBALL SAFETY OFFICERS'**

**ASSOCIATION REPRESENTATIVE**

Calum Brown (01307) 461222

**COMMERCIAL MANAGER,**

**MEDIA LIAISON OFFICER &**

**MATCHDAY PROGRAMME EDITOR**

Steve Mitchell (01356) 626336

**LOTTERY MANAGER** Angus Fairlie

**CLUB DOCTOR** Dr. Alan Dawson

**PHYSIOTHERAPIST** Tom Gilmartin

**STADIUM MANAGER & CHIEF STEWARD**

Alan Boath

**GROUNDSMAN** Sye Laing

**KIT PERSON** Alan Grieve

**CLUB SHOP**

Glebe Park, Brechin, Angus, DD9 6BJ

Open during Home Matchdays.

Merchandise available online -

www.brechincity.co.uk

**OFFICIAL SUPPORTERS CLUB**

c/o Glebe Park, Brechin, Angus, DD9 6BJ

**SHIRT SPONSOR** Avenue Recruitment

**KIT SUPPLIER** Paulas Benara

## LIST OF PLAYERS 2005.06

| PLAYERS SURNAME | FIRST NAME | MIDDLE NAME | DATE OF BIRTH | PLACE OF BIRTH | DATE SIGNED | HEIGHT FT INS | WEIGHT ST LBS | POSITION ON PITCH | PREVIOUS CLUB |
|---|---|---|---|---|---|---|---|---|---|
| Bollan | Gary | | 24/03/73 | Dundee | 19/07/05 | 5.10 | 14.0 | Defender | Clyde |
| Britton | Gerrard | Joseph | 20/10/70 | Glasgow | 09/09/05 | 6.1 | 13.7 | Forward | Dundee |
| Burns | Alexander | | 04/08/73 | Bellshill | 08/08/05 | 5.8 | 12.0 | Forward | Motherwell |
| Byers | Kevin | | 23/08/79 | Kirkcaldy | 09/06/04 | 5.10 | 11.4 | Midfield | Forfar Athletic |
| Callaghan | Stuart | | 20/07/76 | Calderbank | 10/01/05 | 5.9 | 11.7 | Midfield | Alloa Athletic |
| Deas | Paul | Andrew | 22/02/72 | Perth | 24/01/03 | 5.11 | 12.1 | Defender | Ross County |
| Ferguson | Steven | | 18/05/77 | Edinburgh | 31/01/05 | 5.9 | 12.1 | Midfield | Ayr United |
| Gibson | Graham | | 19/07/80 | Kirkcaldy | 12/03/02 | 6.3 | 11.6 | Forward | Lochore Welfare Juniors |
| Hamilton | Steven | James | 19/03/75 | Baillieston | 30/09/04 | 5.10 | 12.8 | Defender | Forfar Athletic |
| Hampshire | Steven | Gary | 17/10/79 | Edinburgh | 30/08/03 | 5.11 | 11.7 | Midfield | Dunfermline Athletic |
| Hillcoat | John | George | 16/12/70 | Paisley | 16/06/05 | 6.0 | 12.11 | Goalkeeper | Ayr United |
| Johnson | Ian | Grant | 24/03/72 | Dundee | 22/07/03 | 5.11 | 11.3 | Midfield | Montrose |
| King | Charles | Alexander | 15/11/79 | Edinburgh | 18/07/01 | 5.7 | 10.2 | Forward | Livingston |
| McEwan | Craig | George | 03/10/77 | Glasgow | 19/07/05 | 6.2 | 13.8 | Defender | Dumbarton |
| Mitchell | Alistair | Robert | 03/12/68 | Kirkcaldy | 03/07/03 | 5.7 | 11.8 | Forward | St. Mirren |
| Nelson | Craig | Robert | 28/05/71 | Coatbridge | 07/12/04 | 6.1 | 13.8 | Goalkeeper | St. Johnstone |
| Ritchie | Paul | Michael | 25/01/69 | St. Andrews | 19/06/04 | 6.1 | 13.5 | Forward | Inverness Caledonian Thistle |
| Smith | Darren | | 04/06/80 | Edinburgh | 14/07/05 | 5.7 | 10.8 | Forward | Berwick Rangers |
| Strachan | Ryan | | 20/03/87 | Dundee | 06/01/05 | 5.10 | 11.0 | Midfield | Montrose Roselea Juniors |
| Walker | Scott | Edward | 05/03/75 | Glasgow | 30/06/04 | 6.3 | 12.10 | Defender | Hartlepool United |
| White | David | William | 09/08/79 | Edinburgh | 03/07/03 | 6.1.5 | 11.12 | Defender | Cowdenbeath |
| Winter | Craig | John | 30/06/76 | Dunfermline | 12/03/04 | 5.11 | 12.0 | Midfield | Cowdenbeath |

## TICKET INFORMATION
### Season Ticket information

| Seated | Adult | | £185 |
|---|---|---|---|
| | Parent & Juvenile (Under 12) | | £200 |
| | OAP | | £100 |
| | Juvenile | | £60 |

### League Admission Prices

| Seated | Adult | £12 | Juvenile/OAP | £6 |
|---|---|---|---|---|
| Enclosure | Adult | £12 | Juvenile/OAP | £6 |
| Standing | Adult | £12 | Juvenile/OAP | £6 |
| | Parent & Juvenile | | | £15 |

**MILESTONES:**

**Year of formation:** 1906

**Most League points in a season:**

55 (Second Division – Season 1982/83) (2 Points for a Win)

73 (Third Division – Season 2001/02) (3 Points for a Win)

**Most League goals scored by a player in a season:**

Ronald McIntosh (Season 1959/60)

**No. of goals scored:** 26

**Record Attendance:** 8,122 (-v- Aberdeen – 3.2.1973)

**Record Victory:** 12-1 (-v- Thornhill – Scottish Cup, 28.1.17)

**Record Defeat:** 0-10 (-v- Airdrieonians, Albion Rovers and

Cowdenbeath – Division 2, 1937/38)

# SEASON STATS 2004.05

BELL'S SCOTTISH FOOTBALL LEAGUE

## SEASON STATS 2004.05

| DATE | VENUE | OPPONENTS | ATT | RES | Hay D.A. | Smith J. | Deas P.A. | Johnson I.G. | Dennis S. | Walker S.E. | King C.A. | Byers K. | Ritchie P.M. | Templeman C. | Mitchell A.R. | MacNicol S. | Gibson G. | Black R. | Winter C.J. | Jackson C.R. | McLeish K.M. | Nelson C.R. | White D.W. | Hampshire S.G. | McCulloch S.A.J. | Hamilton S.J. | Callaghan S. | Ferguson S. | Sharp J. | Panther E.U.E. |
|---|---|---|---|---|---|---|---|---|---|---|---|---|---|---|---|---|---|---|---|---|---|---|---|---|---|---|---|---|---|---|
| 7-Aug | A | Forfar Athletic | 766 | 0-1 | 1 | 2 | 3 | 4 | 5 | 6 | 7 | 8 | 9 | 10 | 11 | 12 | 15 | 16 | | | | | | | | | | | | |
| **14-Aug** | **H** | **Stirling Albion** | **491** | **0-3** | 1 | | 3 | | 5 | 6 | 7 | 8 | 9 | 10 | | 2 | 11 | 16 | 4 | 14 | 15 | | | | | | | | | |
| 21-Aug | A | Berwick Rangers | 429 | 2-0 | | 2 | 3 | 8 | 5 | 6 | | | 9 | **15**$^{2}$ | | | 14 | | 12 | 11 | 7 | 1 | 4 | 10 | | | | | | |
| **28-Aug** | **H** | **Alloa Athletic** | **428** | **4-0** | | 2 | 3 | 8 | | 4 | 7 | | **9** | 15 | | | **11** | | 14 | 6 | **10** | 1 | 5 | **16** | | | | | | |
| 4-Sep | A | Stranraer | 436 | 2-4 | | 2 | 3 | 10 | 5 | 6 | 14 | | **9** | 12 | | | **11** | | | 8 | 7 | 1 | 4 | 15 | | | | | | |
| **11-Sep** | **H** | **Arbroath** | **559** | **4-1** | | | 3 | | 15 | 6 | **11** | 4 | 9 | **12** | 16 | | **10**$^{2}$ | | 8 | | 2 | 1 | 5 | 7 | | | | | | |
| 18-Sep | A | Morton | 2,432 | 3-0 | | | | | | 6 | 7 | 8 | 9 | **12** | | | **11** | 14 | 4 | 15 | 2 | 1 | 5 | **10** | 3 | | | | | |
| 25-Sep | A | Ayr United | 1,399 | 1-0 | | | 3 | | | 6 | | 8 | **9** | 10 | | | 7 | 16 | 4 | 12 | 15 | 1 | 5 | 11 | | 2 | | | | |
| **2-Oct** | **H** | **Dumbarton** | **503** | **4-0** | | | 3 | 14 | | 6 | | 8 | **9**$^{3}$ | 10 | | | 7 | 15 | 4 | | | 1 | **5** | 11 | 12 | 2 | | | | |
| 16-Oct | A | Stirling Albion | 736 | 5-1 | | | 3 | 12 | | 6 | 15 | **8** | 9 | **10**$^{4}$ | | | 7 | | 4 | 14 | | 1 | 5 | 11 | | 2 | | | | |
| **23-Oct** | **H** | **Forfar Athletic** | **869** | **2-0** | | **2** | 3 | 12 | | 6 | 16 | 8 | 9 | 10 | | | 7 | | **4** | 15 | | 1 | 5 | 11 | | | | | | |
| 30-Oct | A | Alloa Athletic | 474 | 2-2 | | 2 | 3 | | | 6 | 15 | 8 | **9** | **10** | | | 7 | 16 | 4 | | | 1 | 5 | 11 | | | | | | |
| **6-Nov** | **H** | **Stranraer** | **620** | **4-1** | | | 3 | | | **6** | 14 | 8 | 9 | **10**$^{2}$ | | | 7 | | **4** | 15 | 16 | 1 | 5 | 11 | | 2 | | | | |
| 13-Nov | A | Arbroath | 682 | 2-2 | | | 3 | | | 6 | 12 | 8 | **9** | 10 | | | **7** | | 4 | | | 1 | 5 | 11 | | 2 | | | | |
| **27-Nov** | **H** | **Morton** | **989** | **2-1** | | | 3 | 14 | | 6 | 12 | 8 | 9 | **10** | 16 | | **7** | | 4 | | | 1 | 5 | 11 | | 2 | | | | |
| **4-Dec** | **H** | **Ayr United** | **576** | **5-0** | | 14 | 3 | 12 | | **6**$^{2}$ | 16 | 8 | 9 | **10**$^{2}$ | | | 7 | | 4 | | | 1 | **5** | 11 | | 2 | | | | |
| **27-Dec** | **H** | **Forfar Athletic** | **901** | **3-1** | | | 3 | 12 | | 6 | 7 | 8 | **9**$^{2}$ | | 14 | | 10 | | 4 | | 15 | 1 | 5 | **11** | | 2 | | | | |
| **1-Jan** | **H** | **Berwick Rangers** | **515** | **4-1** | | | 3 | 12 | | 6 | **7** | 8 | 9 | | 15 | | 10 | | 4 | 16 | 2 | 1 | 5 | **11**$^{3}$ | | | | | | |
| **8-Jan** | **H** | **Alloa Athletic** | **604** | **2-3** | | | 3 | 8 | | 6 | 7 | 12 | **9** | | 15 | 14 | **10** | | 4 | | 2 | 1 | 5 | 11 | | | | | | |
| 15-Jan | A | Stranraer | 552 | 1-0 | | 12 | 3 | | | 5 | 11 | 16 | 9 | | 14 | | 7 | | 8 | | | 1 | 4 | 10 | | 2 | **6** | | | |
| 29-Jan | A | Morton | 3,004 | 2-0 | | 16 | 3 | | | 5 | 7 | 14 | 9 | | 15 | | 11 | | 8 | | | 1 | 4 | **10**$^{2}$ | | 2 | 6 | | | |
| **9-Feb** | **H** | **Arbroath** | **651** | **4-3** | | 2 | 3 | 8 | | 5 | 7 | | 12 | | 11 | | 14 | | | | | 1 | **4** | **9**$^{2}$ | | 15 | **10** | 6 | | |
| **12-Feb** | **H** | **Dumbarton** | **589** | **0-2** | | 15 | | | | 5 | 7 | 14 | 9 | | 11 | | 12 | 3 | 8 | | | 1 | 4 | 10 | | 2 | 6 | | | |
| 19-Feb | A | Berwick Rangers | 323 | 1-2 | | | 3 | 15 | | 5 | **7** | | 9 | | | | 11 | | 8 | | | 1 | 12 | 10 | | 2 | 6 | | 4 | 14 |
| **26-Feb** | **H** | **Stirling Albion** | **515** | **5-3** | | | 3 | 8 | | | **7** | | 12 | | | | **9** | | 15 | | | 1 | **4** | **10**$^{2}$ | | 2 | 6 | 11 | 5 | 16 |
| -Mar | A | Dumbarton | 548 | 1-1 | | | 3 | 8 | | 16 | 7 | | 12 | | | | 11 | | | | | 1 | 4 | 9 | | 2 | **6** | 10 | 5 | 15 |
| **-Mar** | **H** | **Stranraer** | **606** | **2-1** | | | 3 | 16 | | 14 | 7 | | 9 | | | | 12 | | 8 | | | 1 | 4 | **10**$^{2}$ | | 2 | 6 | 11 | 5 | |
| 2-Mar | A | Alloa Athletic | 522 | 1-1 | | | 3 | | | 6 | 12 | 15 | **9** | | 14 | | 11 | | | | | 1 | | 10 | | 2 | 8 | 4 | 5 | 7 |
| 5-Mar | A | Ayr United | 737 | 1-0 | | | | 8 | | 5 | 7 | 11 | 9 | | 14 | | **12** | | | | | 1 | 4 | 10 | | 2 | 6 | | 3 | 16 |
| 9-Mar | A | Arbroath | 775 | 4-1 | | | 3 | 14 | | 5 | **7** | | | | 12 | | 11 | | 4 | | | 1 | | **9**$^{2}$ | | 2 | 16 | 8 | 6 | **10** |
| **-Apr** | **H** | **Morton** | **1,340** | **1-2** | | | 3 | | | 5 | 7 | | **12** | | 14 | | 10 | | 4 | | | 1 | | 9 | | 2 | 15 | 8 | 6 | 11 |
| -Apr | A | Dumbarton | 777 | 1-1 | | | 3 | 14 | | 5 | 7 | 15 | 9 | | 11 | | 12 | | 4 | | | 1 | | 10 | | 2 | | 8 | **6** | |
| **6-Apr** | **H** | **Ayr United** | **624** | **3-0** | | | 3 | 16 | | 5 | 7 | 12 | **9** | | 8 | | **11** | | 4 | | | 1 | 14 | **10** | | 2 | | | 6 | |
| **3-Apr** | **H** | **Berwick Rangers** | **630** | **1-1** | | | 3 | 12 | | 5 | 7 | 11 | 9 | | 8 | | 15 | | | | | 1 | **14** | 10 | | 2 | | 4 | 6 | |
| 0-Apr | A | Stirling Albion | 667 | 2-1 | | | 3 | 8 | | **6** | **7** | 14 | 12 | | 10 | | 11 | | | | | 1 | 2 | 9 | | | | 4 | 5 | 15 |
| **-May** | **H** | **Forfar Athletic** | **1,074** | **0-3** | | | 4 | 15 | | 3 | 7 | | 16 | | 8 | | 10 | | | | | 1 | 2 | 9 | | 12 | 11 | 6 | 5 | |
| OTAL FULL APPEARANCES | | | | | 2 | 7 | 33 | 10 | 4 | 33 | 24 | 17 | 29 | 11 | 8 | 1 | 28 | 1 | 24 | 3 | 7 | 34 | 27 | 32 | 1 | 22 | 11 | 11 | 13 | 3 |
| OTAL SUB APPEARANCES | | | | | | 4 | | 14 | 1 | 2 | 9 | 8 | 6 | 5 | 11 | 2 | 8 | 6 | 3 | 7 | 4 | | 3 | 2 | 1 | 2 | 2 | | | 5 |
| OTAL GOALS SCORED | | | | | | 1 | | | | 4 | 6 | 1 | 14 | 14 | | | 11 | | 2 | | 1 | | 5 | 17 | | | 3 | | 1 | 1 |

re in bold denotes goal scored. Secondary smaller figure in bold denotes number of goals scored . † denotes opponent's own goal.

## E CITY'S 10 YEAR LEAGUE RECORD

| ason | Div | P | W | D | L | F | A | Pts | Pos |
|---|---|---|---|---|---|---|---|---|---|
| 5-96 | T | 36 | 18 | 9 | 9 | 41 | 21 | 63 | 2 |
| 6-97 | S | 36 | 10 | 11 | 15 | 36 | 49 | 41 | 7 |
| 7-98 | S | 36 | 7 | 11 | 18 | 42 | 73 | 32 | 10 |
| 8-99 | T | 36 | 17 | 8 | 11 | 47 | 43 | 59 | 3 |
| 9-00 | T | 36 | 10 | 18 | 8 | 42 | 51 | 38 | 8 |
| 0-01 | T | 36 | 22 | 6 | 8 | 71 | 36 | 72 | 3 |
| 1-02 | T | 36 | 22 | 7 | 7 | 67 | 38 | 73 | 1 |
| 2-03 | S | 36 | 16 | 7 | 13 | 63 | 59 | 55 | 2 |
| 3-04 | F | 36 | 6 | 9 | 21 | 37 | 73 | 27 | 10 |
| 4-05 | S | 36 | 22 | 6 | 8 | 81 | 43 | 72 | 1 |

## LEADING GOALSCORERS:

| Season | Div | Goals | Player |
|---|---|---|---|
| 1995-96 | T | 8 | A. Ross |
| 1996-97 | S | 7 | S. Kerrigan |
| 1997-98 | S | 7 | C. Feroz |
| 1998-99 | T | 15 | J. Dickson |
| 1999-00 | T | 11 | B. Honeyman |
| 2000-01 | T | 22 | R. Grant |
| 2001-02 | T | 15 | C. Templeman |
| 2002-03 | S | 21 | C. Templeman |
| 2003-04 | F | 5 | C. Templeman |
| 2004-05 | S | 17 | S. Hampshire |

### BRECHIN CITY PLAYING KITS SEASON 2005.06

FIRST KIT | SECOND KIT | THIRD KIT

# CLYDE

## CLYDE F.C.

Broadwood Stadium,
Cumbernauld, G68 9NE

**TELEPHONE NUMBERS**

Ground (01236) 451511

**FAX** (01236) 733490

**E-MAIL** info@clydefc.co.uk

**WEBSITE** www.clydefc.co.uk

**CHAIRMAN** Leonard McGuire

**DIRECTORS**

John D. Taylor, Francis G. Dunn,
James Murray, John Ruddy, David Dalziel
& David J. Boyce

**HONORARY PRESIDENT**

William B. Carmichael

**HONORARY VICE-PRESIDENT**

William J. Dunn

**SECRETARY**

John D. Taylor, A.C.I.B. (B) (01236) 451511
(H) (0141) 633 1010

**MANAGER** Graham Roberts

**PLAYER / ASSISTANT MANAGER** Joe Miller

**COMMUNITY COACH** Jim Strathdee

**YOUTH COACHES**

U19: Chris Hillcoat

U13: Gary O'Rourke

**TEAM CAPTAIN** Paul McHale

**WOMENS DEVELOPMENT COACH**

David Mark

**OFFICE ADMINISTRATOR** Mrs. Lynn Calder

**FOOTBALL SAFETY OFFICERS'
ASSOCIATION REPRESENTATIVE**

Ronnie McCammick

**COMMERCIAL MANAGER** Jack Rolland

**MEDIA LIAISON PERSON** John Ruddy

**MATCHDAY PROGRAMME EDITOR**

John D. Taylor

**CLUB DOCTORS**

Dr. Michael McGavigan,

Dr. Michael McLaughlin & Dr. Frank Dunn

**PHYSIOTHERAPIST** Iain McKinlay

**KIT PERSON** Bill Munro

**CLUB SHOP**

Situated at Ground. Open on Home
Matchdays 1 hour before and for 1 hour after
match. Online Shop -www.clydefc.co.uk

**SUPPORTERS CLUB**

Castlemilk Branch:

Eric Steel (0141) 569 3625

Glasgow Branch:

Andy Peters (07939) 642628

**SHIRT SPONSOR**

**First Choice:**

Front: Optical Express

Back: The Dental Clinic

**Second Choice:**

Front: Dubai Property Centre

**KIT SUPPLIER** TFG

## LIST OF PLAYERS 2005.06

| PLAYERS SURNAME | FIRST NAME | MIDDLE NAME | DATE OF BIRTH | PLACE OF BIRTH | DATE SIGNED | HEIGHT FT INS | WEIGHT ST LBS | POSITION ON PITCH | PREVIOUS CLUB |
|---|---|---|---|---|---|---|---|---|---|
| Allen | Ross | | 21/04/88 | Glasgow | 18/08/05 | 5.11 | 10.0 | Forward | St. Mirren |
| Arbuckle | Gary | | 16/08/84 | Glasgow | 29/07/05 | 5.11 | 12.6 | Forward | Celtic |
| Bartlett | Ross | | 10/10/87 | Lanark | 18/08/05 | 5.7 | 9.10 | Defender | Unattached |
| Bingham | Scott | | 27/08/87 | Los Angeles | 18/08/05 | 5.9 | 10.10 | Defender | Unattached |
| Bouadji | Romuald | | 10/01/83 | Lyon | 28/07/05 | 6.0 | 12.5 | Defender | Carshalton Athletic |
| Bradley | Kevin | | 18/06/86 | Glasgow | 20/07/05 | 5.6 | 9.12 | Forward | Clyde Youths |
| Brawley | William | | 19/03/84 | Motherwell | 11/07/05 | 5.7 | 11.7 | Midfield | Selkirk |
| Brighton | Thomas | | 28/03/84 | Irvine | 05/08/05 | 6.2 | 11.10 | Forward | Rangers |
| Bryson | Craig | James | 06/11/86 | Rutherglen | 02/02/04 | 5.7 | 9.7 | Midfield | East Kilbride Thistle Junior |
| Cherrie | Peter | | 01/10/83 | Bellshill | 20/07/05 | 6.2 | 11.13 | Goalkeeper | Ayr United |
| Dick | Andrew | James | 25/02/86 | Carlisle | 28/07/05 | 6.2 | 10.12 | Midfield | Falkirk |
| Flaherty | Paul | | 13/12/87 | Bellshill | 28/07/05 | 5.11 | 9.5 | Midfield | Clyde Form S |
| Fulton | Michael | Graham | 26/06/88 | Irvine | 18/08/05 | 5.10 | 10.0 | Defender | St. Mirren |
| Harris | Robert | | 28/08/87 | Glasgow | 29/07/05 | 5.8 | 9.2 | Defender | Rangers |
| Hastie | Mark | | 29/06/88 | Irvine | 18/08/05 | 5.6 | 9.0 | Midfield | Queen's Park |
| Higgins | Christopher | | 04/07/85 | Broxburn | 11/07/05 | 6.1 | 11.11 | Defender | Motherwell |
| Hunter | Roddy | | 15/12/84 | Glasgow | 20/07/05 | 5.9 | 9.4 | Midfield | Ayr United |
| Inglis | Raymond | Scott | 31/03/88 | Glasgow | 28/07/05 | 6.0 | 11.5 | Defender | Hamilton Academical |
| Jarvie | Paul | | 14/06/82 | Aberdeen | 28/07/05 | 6.0 | 12.3 | Goalkeeper | Torquay United |
| Kirk | Mark | | 31/05/88 | Bellshill | 18/08/05 | 5.5 | 10.5 | Forward | Unattached |
| MacLennan | Ruari | | 26/03/88 | Livingston | 18/08/05 | 5.9 | 10.3 | Midfield | East Stirlingshire B.C. |
| Malone | Edward | Joseph | 06/04/85 | Edinburgh | 24/08/04 | 5.11 | 10.7 | Midfield | St. Johnstone |
| Marini | Santino | Donato | 26/04/87 | Bellshill | 16/09/05 | 5.11 | 12.0 | Forward | St.Mirren |
| Masterton | Steven | Allan | 02/01/85 | Irvine | 29/07/05 | 6.0 | 13.4 | Midfield | Kilmarnock |
| McGowan | David | | 17/02/88 | Glasgow | 18/08/05 | 6.0 | 11.2 | Midfield | Livingston |
| McGowan | Michael | Valentine | 22/02/85 | Glasgow | 20/07/05 | 5.8 | 11.9 | Defender | Dundee |
| McGregor | Jake | John | 05/05/88 | Edinburgh | 18/08/05 | 5.7 | 10.2 | Midfield | St. Mirren |
| McGregor | Neil | | 17/07/85 | Irvine | 28/07/05 | 6.0 | 11.10 | Defender | Kilmarnock |
| McHale | Paul | | 30/09/81 | Stirling | 20/07/05 | 5.9 | 11.1 | Midfield | Cowdenbeath |
| McKeever | John | Paul | 18/11/87 | Glasgow | 09/08/05 | 5.7 | 8.6 | Midfield | Clyde Form S |
| McKenna | Sean | Barry | 28/07/87 | Bellshill | 28/07/05 | 5.8 | 12.4 | Forward | Queen's Park |
| McKeown | Craig | | 16/03/85 | Aberdeen | 20/07/05 | 6.1 | 13.5 | Defender | Dunfermline Athletic |
| Miller | Joseph | | 08/12/67 | Glasgow | 28/07/05 | 5.7.5 | 10.7 | Midfield | Clydebank |
| O'Donnell | Stephen | James | 10/07/83 | Bellshill | 06/07/05 | 5.11 | 11.3 | Midfield | Boston United |
| Scott | David | Robert | 20/05/88 | Bellshill | 12/08/05 | 6.1 | 11.0 | Goalkeeper | Albion Rovers |
| Trotter | Jaimes | | 21/07/87 | Glasgow | 18/08/05 | 5.7 | 9.0 | Forward | Unattached |
| Williams | Alexander | Boyd | 15/01/83 | Glasgow | 29/07/05 | 5.10 | 11.0 | Forward | Morton |

## TICKET INFORMATION
### Season Ticket information

| Seated | | |
|---|---|---|
| | Adult | £240 |
| | OAP & Students | £120 |
| | Juvenile (Under 18) | £60 |
| | Under 12 | £35 |

### League Admission Prices

| Seated | | |
|---|---|---|
| | Adult | £14 |
| | OAP & Students | £7 |
| | Juvenile (Under 18) | £5 |
| | Parent & 1 Child | £18 |

## MILESTONES:
**Year of formation:** 1877
**Most capped player:** Tommy Ring
**No. of caps:** 12
**Most League points in a season:**
64 (Division 2 – Season 1956/57) (2 Points for a Win)
72 (First Division – Season 2002/03) (3 Points for a Win)
**Most League goals scored by a player in a season:**
Bill Boyd (Season 1932/33)
**No. of goals scored:** 32
**Record Attendance:**
52,000 (-v- Rangers – 21.11.1908 – at Shawfield Stadium)
7,591 (-v- Manchester United – 16.7.2005 (Friendly Match) – at Broadwood Stad
**Record Victory:** 11-1 (-v- Cowdenbeath – Division 2, 6.10.1951)
**Record Defeat:** 0-11 (-v- Dumbarton and Rangers, Scottish Cup)

# SEASON STATS 2004.05

## SEASON STATS 2004.05

Player columns (left to right): Halliwell B.S., Mensing S.R., Bollan G., Balmer S.M., Potter J.P., Sheridan D.S., Arbuckle G., Gibson J.R., Wilford A., Fotheringham K.G., Harty I.M., Gilhaney M., Bryson C.J., Doyle P., Greenhill D., Kerkar K., Walker A., Conway A., Malone E.J., Wilson S.W., Bradley K., Marsiglia M., McKeever J.P., Jones G.A., Burns A., Gardiner C., Espinola M.A., Harris R., Morrison A.J.

| Date | Venue | Opponents | ATT | RES | Hal | Men | Bol | Bal | Pot | She | Arb | Gib | Wil | Fot | Har | Gil | Bry | Doy | Gre | Ker | Wal | Con | Mal | Wls | Bra | Mar | McK | Jon | Bur | Gar | Esp | Hrs | Mor |
|---|---|---|---|---|---|---|---|---|---|---|---|---|---|---|---|---|---|---|---|---|---|---|---|---|---|---|---|---|---|---|---|---|---|
| 7-Aug | H | Partick Thistle | 3,352 | 2-1 | 1 | 2 | 3 | 4 | 5 | 6 | 7 | **8** | 9 | 10 | **11** | 15 | | | | | | | | | | | | | | | | | |
| 14-Aug | A | Raith Rovers | 1,784 | 3-2 | 1 | 2 | 3 | 4 | **5** | 6 | 7 | 8 | 9 | 10 | **11** | 12 | | 14 | | | | | | | | | | | | | | | |
| 21-Aug | H | Ross County | 1,307 | 1-0 | 1 | 2 | 3 | | 5 | 6 | 12 | 8 | **9** | 10 | 11 | 14 | 7 | | | 4 | 15 | | | | | | | | | | | | | |
| 28-Aug | A | Queen of the South | 1,639 | 1-0 | 1 | 2 | 3 | | 5 | 6 | 12 | 8 | 9 | | 11 | 14 | 7 | | | 10 | 4 | 15 | | | | | | | | | | | | |
| 4-Sep | H | St. Mirren | 2,472 | 0-0 | 1 | | | | 5 | 6 | 14 | 8 | 9 | | 11 | 12 | 7 | | 3 | | | 15 | 10 | 4 | | | | | | | | | | |
| 11-Sep | H | Airdrie United | 1,680 | 1-2 | 1 | 2 | | | 5 | | 12 | 8 | 9 | | 11 | 10 | 7 | 14 | 3 | 16 | 6 | | | 4 | | | | | | | | | | |
| 18-Sep | A | Hamilton Academical | 2,017 | 1-0 | 1 | 2 | | | 5 | 6 | 10 | 8 | 9 | | 11 | 12 | | | 3 | | 15 | | | 4 | | | 7 | | | | | | | |
| 25-Sep | A | Falkirk | 3,813 | 1-1 | 1 | 2 | 3 | | 5 | 6 | 10 | 8 | 9 | | **11** | 12 | 7 | | | | | 15 | | 4 | | | | | | | | | | |
| 2-Oct | H | St. Johnstone | 1,456 | 1-0 | 1 | 2 | 3 | | 5 | **6** | 7 | 8 | 9 | | 11 | 12 | | 14 | | | | | 10 | 4 | | | | | | | | | | |
| 15-Oct | H | Raith Rovers | 1,196 | 2-0 | 1 | 2 | | | 5 | 6 | 12 | 8 | 14 | | 11 | 10 | 7 | | 3 | | 15 | **9** | | **4** | | | | | | | | | | |
| 23-Oct | A | Partick Thistle | 4,026 | 0-0 | 1 | 2 | | | 5 | 6 | 7 | 8 | 15 | | 11 | | | | | 16 | | 9 | 10 | 4 | | | | | | | | | | |
| 30-Oct | A | Queen of the South | 1,284 | 2-0 | 1 | 2 | 3 | | 5 | 6 | | 8 | 9 | | $11^2$ | 10 | 7 | | | 16 | 15 | | 4 | | | | | 12 | | | | | | |
| 6-Nov | A | St. Mirren | 3,788 | 0-0 | 1 | 2 | 3 | | 5 | 6 | 15 | 8 | 12 | | 11 | 9 | 7 | | | 16 | | | 10 | 4 | | | | | | | | | | |
| 13-Nov | A | Airdrie United | 1,862 | 1-3 | 1 | 2 | 3 | | 5 | 6 | | 8 | 16 | | 11 | 12 | 7 | **14** | | | 9 | | 10 | 4 | | | | | | | | | | |
| 20-Nov | H | Hamilton Academical | 1,408 | 2-1 | 1 | 2 | 3 | 12 | 5 | 6 | | 8 | 9 | | 11 | 7 | 16 | | | | | 14 | 10 | 4 | | | | | | | | | | |
| 27-Nov | H | St. Johnstone | 2,026 | 0-3 | 1 | 2 | 3 | | 5 | 6 | | 8 | 9 | | 11 | 15 | 7 | | | 16 | | 12 | 10 | 4 | | | | | | | | | | |
| 4-Dec | A | Falkirk | 2,859 | 0-2 | 1 | 2 | 3 | | 5 | 6 | 12 | 8 | 14 | | 11 | 9 | 7 | | | | 15 | | 10 | 4 | | | | | | | | | | |
| 11-Dec | H | Partick Thistle | 1,938 | 1-1 | 1 | 2 | 3 | 4 | 5 | 6 | | 8 | 9 | | 11 | 14 | 7 | | | | | 12 | 10 | | | | | | | | | | | |
| 18-Dec | A | Ross County | 1,939 | 1-0 | 1 | 2 | 3 | 4 | 5 | 6 | | 8 | | | 11 | 12 | 7 | | | | 15 | 9 | 10 | | | | | | | | | | | |
| 1-Jan | H | Airdrie United | 1,513 | 1-0 | 1 | 2 | 3 | | 5 | 6 | 7 | 8 | | | 11 | 12 | | | | | | 15 | 10 | 4 | | | | 9 | | | | | | |
| 15-Jan | A | Hamilton Academical | 1,873 | 1-0 | 1 | 2 | | | 5 | 6 | **7** | 8 | | | 11 | | | | 3 | | | 15 | 10 | 4 | | | | 9 | | | | | | |
| 12-Feb | A | Raith Rovers | 1,394 | 3-3 | 1 | 2 | 3 | | 5 | 6 | | 8 | | | $11^3$ | 16 | | 14 | | | | | 10 | 4 | | | | 9 | | 7 | | | | |
| 19-Feb | H | Ross County | 1,076 | 1-0 | 1 | 2 | 3 | 4 | 5 | 6 | 12 | 8 | | | 11 | 14 | | | | | | 9 | 10 | | | | | | | 7 | | | | |
| 2-Mar | A | Queen of the South | 1,448 | 1-0 | 1 | 2 | 3 | 4 | 5 | | 15 | 8 | | | 11 | 16 | 7 | 14 | | 6 | | | 10 | | | | | | 9 | | | | | |
| 5-Mar | A | St. Mirren | 2,730 | 0-0 | 1 | 2 | 3 | 4 | 5 | 12 | 7 | 8 | | | 11 | 15 | | 14 | | 6 | | | 10 | | | | | | 9 | | | | | |
| 8-Mar | H | St. Mirren | 1,008 | 0-0 | 1 | 2 | 3 | 4 | 5 | | 12 | | | | 11 | 7 | | 14 | | 6 | 8 | 16 | 10 | | | | | | 9 | | | | | |
| 12-Mar | H | Queen of the South | 1,033 | 0-1 | 1 | 2 | 3 | 4 | 5 | 6 | 12 | 8 | | | 11 | 16 | | | | | | 15 | 10 | | | | | | 9 | 7 | | | | |
| 16-Mar | A | Falkirk | 3,834 | 0-0 | 1 | 2 | 3 | 4 | 5 | 6 | | | | 12 | 11 | | | | | | 8 | 15 | 10 | | | | | | 9 | 7 | | | | |
| 19-Mar | A | Airdrie United | 1,641 | 4-2 | 1 | 2 | 3 | 4 | 5 | 6 | 14 | | | | $11^3$ | 8 | | | | | | 12 | 10 | | | | | | 9 | 7 | | | | |
| 22-Mar | H | St. Johnstone | 862 | 1-1 | 1 | 2 | 3 | 4 | 5 | 6 | 12 | | | | 11 | 8 | | | | | | | 10 | | | | | | 9 | **7** | 14 | | | |
| 2-Apr | A | Hamilton Academical | 1,240 | 1-3 | 1 | | | | 5 | 6 | 12 | 8 | | | 11 | 3 | | **14** | | | | | 10 | 4 | | | | | 9 | 7 | 2 | | | |
| 7-Apr | A | St. Johnstone | 1,770 | 0-0 | 1 | | | | 4 | 5 | | 8 | | | 11 | 3 | 10 | | 6 | | | 12 | | | | | | | 9 | 7 | 2 | | | |
| 16-Apr | H | Falkirk | 2,090 | 0-1 | 1 | | | | 5 | | | 8 | | | 11 | 3 | 10 | 4 | | | 6 | | | | | | | | 9 | 7 | 12 | 2 | | |
| 23-Apr | A | Partick Thistle | 2,757 | 0-1 | 1 | | | | 5 | 6 | | 8 | | | 11 | 3 | 4 | | | | | 10 | 12 | | | | | | 9 | 7 | 15 | 2 | | |
| 30-Apr | H | Raith Rovers | 1,122 | 1-0 | 1 | | | | 5 | 6 | | 8 | | | **11** | 3 | 4 | 12 | | | | 15 | 10 | 14 | | | | | 9 | 7 | | 2 | | |
| 7-May | A | Ross County | 2,130 | 1-1 | 1 | | | | 5 | 6 | | 8 | | | | 3 | **4** | 14 | | | | 12 | 10 | 9 | | | | | 9 | | | 2 | 11 | 17 |
| **TOTAL FULL APPEARANCES** | | | | | 36 | 30 | 25 | 12 | 36 | 28 | 12 | 29 | 12 | 33 | 18 | 23 | | | 2 | 2 | 8 | 5 | 27 | 17 | 2 | 1 | | 11 | 15 | 2 | 6 | 1 | |
| **TOTAL SUB APPEARANCES** | | | | | | | | 1 | | | 1 | | 14 | | 6 | | 16 | 5 | 1 | 3 | 6 | 6 | 1 | 2 | 12 | | | 3 | 2 | | 5 | | 1 |
| **TOTAL GOALS SCORED** | | | | | | | 2 | | 2 | 2 | 1 | 1 | | | 15 | 1 | 3 | | | | | 1 | 1 | | | | 1 | 2 | 1 | | | |

Figure in bold denotes goal scored. Secondary smaller figure in bold denotes number of goals scored. † denotes opponent's own goal.

## THE BULLY WEE'S 10 YEAR LEAGUE RECORD

| Season | Div | P | W | D | L | F | A | Pts | Pos |
|---|---|---|---|---|---|---|---|---|---|
| 95-96 | S | 36 | 11 | 12 | 13 | 47 | 45 | 45 | 5 |
| 96-97 | S | 36 | 14 | 10 | 12 | 42 | 39 | 52 | 4 |
| 97-98 | S | 36 | 10 | 12 | 14 | 40 | 53 | 42 | 8 |
| 98-99 | S | 36 | 15 | 8 | 13 | 46 | 42 | 53 | 3 |
| 99-00 | S | 36 | 18 | 7 | 11 | 65 | 37 | 65 | 1 |
| 00-01 | F | 36 | 11 | 14 | 11 | 44 | 46 | 47 | 5 |
| 01-02 | F | 36 | 13 | 10 | 13 | 51 | 56 | 49 | 5 |
| 02-03 | F | 36 | 21 | 9 | 6 | 66 | 37 | 72 | 2 |
| 03-04 | F | 36 | 20 | 9 | 7 | 64 | 40 | 69 | 2 |
| 04-05 | F | 36 | 16 | 12 | 8 | 35 | 29 | 60 | 3 |

## LEADING GOALSCORERS:

| Season | Div | Goals | Player |
|---|---|---|---|
| 1995-96 | S | 21 | E. Annand |
| 1996-97 | S | 21 | E. Annand |
| 1997-98 | S | 8 | P. Brownlie |
| 1998-99 | S | 5 | S. Convery |
| 1999-00 | S | 18 | B. Carrigan |
| 2000-01 | F | 7 | A. Kane |
| 2001-02 | F | 11 | P. Keogh |
| 2002-03 | F | 12 | P. Keogh |
| 2003-04 | F | 15 | I. Harty |
| 2004-05 | F | 15 | I. Harty |

CLYDE PLAYING KITS SEASON 2005.06 — FIRST KIT | SECOND KIT | THIRD KIT

# DUNDEE

**DUNDEE F.C.**
Dens Park Stadium,
Sandeman Street, Dundee, DD3 7JY
**TELEPHONE NUMBERS**
Football Dept./Manager (01382) 826104
Administration/Accounts/
Youth Development (01382) 889966
Commercial/Marketing (01382) 884450
Ticket Office (01382) 889966 (Option 1)
Stadium Manager (01382) 889966
**FAX** Commercial (01382) 832284
**FAX** Football (01382) 828820
**E-MAIL** laura@dundeefc.co.uk
**WEBSITE** www.dundeefc.co.uk
**CHAIRMAN** Robert Brannan
**DIRECTORS**
James M. Marr, Peter Marr, Ross Dow,
Francesco J. Esposito, George Knight &
A. Ritchie Robertson
**CHIEF EXECUTIVE** Peter Marr
**SECRETARY** A. Ritchie Robertson
(01382) 226602
**CLUB SECRETARY / MEDIA LIAISON OFFICER**
Mrs. Laura Hayes
**MANAGER** Alan Kernaghan
**ASSISTANT MANAGER** Billy Kirkwood
**GOALKEEPING COACH** Jim Stewart
**YOUTH CO-ORDINATOR &**
**YOUTH TEAM COACH /**
**COMMUNITY COACH &**
**SCHOOLS DEVELOPMENT** Gordon Wallace
**TEAM CAPTAIN** Barry Smith
**OFFICE ADMINISTRATOR** Laura Hayes
**FOOTBALL SAFETY OFFICERS'**
**ASSOCIATION REPRESENTATIVES**
John Malone
**COMMERCIAL DIRECTOR** Frank Esposito
**FINANCE DIRECTOR**
Ross Dow (01382) 889966
**LOTTERY MANAGER** Graeme Thomson
**MATCHDAY PROGRAMME EDITOR /**
**COMMERCIAL SECRETARY**
Kirsty Cameron
**CLUB DOCTOR**
Dr. Phyllis Windsor, M.D., FRCR., MBE
**PHYSIOTHERAPIST** Jim Law
**MASSEUR** Jack Cashley
**STADIUM MANAGER**
Jim Thomson (01382) 815250
**GROUNDSMAN** Brian Robertson
**KIT PERSON** Neil Cosgrove
**CLUB SHOP**
DFC XARA Shop, situated between Main
Stand and Bobby Cox Stand
**OFFICIAL SUPPORTERS CLUB**
Contact: Norrie Price (01224) 639967
**SHIRT SPONSOR**
The Forfar Roof Truss Company Ltd
**KIT SUPPLIER** XARA

## LIST OF PLAYERS 2005.06

| PLAYERS SURNAME | FIRST NAME | MIDDLE NAME | DATE OF BIRTH | PLACE OF BIRTH | DATE SIGNED | HEIGHT FT INS | WEIGHT ST LBS | POSITION ON PITCH | PREVIOUS CLUB |
|---|---|---|---|---|---|---|---|---|---|
| Allison | Mark | | 22/02/87 | Perth | 29/08/03 | 6.0 | 11.13 | Defender | Dundee Youths |
| Anderson | Iain | William | 23/07/77 | Glasgow | 20/07/04 | 5.8 | 9.7 | Forward | Grimsby Town |
| Bell | Mark | Alexander | 09/03/87 | Dundee | 07/06/04 | 5.7 | 11.9 | Defender | Dundee Form D U16 |
| Black | David | Hugh | 10/04/87 | Dundee | 07/06/04 | 5.8 | 11.0 | Defender | Dundee Form D U16 |
| Brady | Garry | | 07/09/76 | Glasgow | 30/08/02 | 5.8 | 10.10 | Midfield | Portsmouth |
| Craig | Steven | | 05/02/81 | Preston | 16/09/05 | 5.11 | 12.5 | Forward | Aberdeen |
| Deasley | Bryan | | 29/06/88 | Dundee | 20/06/02 | 5.7 | 10.5 | Forward | Dundee Form D U16 |
| Dixon | Paul | Andrew | 22/11/86 | Aberdeen | 03/06/05 | 6.0 | 10.6 | Defender | Monifieth B.C. |
| Eyene | Jacinto | Ela | 02/05/82 | Ecuatorial Guinea | 10/08/05 | 5.5 | 10.4 | Midfield | Alaves |
| Ferguson | Andrew | David | 24/03/85 | Glasgow | 27/07/05 | 5.11 | 12.12 | Forward | Ayr United |
| Fotheringham | Mark | McKay | 22/10/83 | Dundee | 28/08/03 | 5.11 | 12.10 | Midfield | Celtic |
| Gates | Scott | | 14/04/88 | Wegberg | 07/06/04 | 5.7 | 10.3 | Forward | Dundee Form D U16 |
| Hay | Graham | | 11/06/87 | Dundee | 10/07/03 | 6.0 | 11.12 | Defender | Dundee Form S |
| Henderson | Scott | | 25/02/88 | Stafford | 16/09/05 | 5.8 | 11.2 | Defender | Dundee Form D U16 |
| Hendry | Robert | David | 19/01/87 | Dundee | 16/09/05 | 5.8 | 12.6 | Midfield | Dundee Form S |
| Hutchinson | Thomas | Peter | 23/02/82 | Kingston upon Thames | 27/07/05 | 6.2 | 13.0 | Defender | Fulham |
| Jack | Kelvin | Kyron | 29/04/76 | Trinidad | 05/08/04 | 6.3 | 16.0 | Goalkeeper | Reading |
| Keane | Kieren | Ashley | 20/10/82 | London | 12/08/05 | 6.0 | 12.0 | Midfield | Weymouth |
| Kitamirike | Joel | Derick | 05/04/84 | Kampala | 19/01/05 | 5.11 | 12.0 | Defender | Mansfield Town |
| Lynch | Simon | George | 19/05/82 | Montreal | 27/07/05 | 6.0 | 12.2 | Forward | Preston North End |
| Macdonald | Callum | | 31/05/83 | Perth | 08/09/00 | 6.1 | 11.7 | Defender | Dundee Form S |
| Mackay | Paul | Alexander | 20/04/88 | Dundee | 13/07/05 | 5.7 | 9.7 | Midfield | Dundee Form D U16 |
| Madaschi | Adrian | Anthony | 11/07/82 | Perth - Australia | 27/07/05 | 6.2 | 12.5 | Defender | Partick Thistle |
| Mann | Robert | Alexander | 11/01/74 | Dundee | 07/06/04 | 6.3 | 14.7 | Defender | Inverness Caledonian Thistle |
| McCluskey | Stuart | Campbell | 29/10/77 | Bellshill | 16/09/05 | 6.0 | 12.7 | Defender | Morton |
| McDonald | Andrew | James | 06/02/87 | Dundee | 10/07/03 | 5.8 | 9.4 | Midfield | Dundee Form D U16 |
| McDonald | Kevin | David | 04/11/88 | Dundee | 18/11/04 | 6.2 | 13.0 | Midfield | Dundee Form D U16 |
| McManus | Thomas | Kelly | 28/02/81 | Glasgow | 14/01/05 | 5.9 | 10.2 | Forward | Hibernian |
| McNally | Stephen | | 15/03/84 | Dundee | 29/03/02 | 5.9 | 11.10 | Defender | Downfield Juniors |
| Millar | Daniel | John | 17/07/88 | Dundee | 13/07/05 | 6.0 | 10.6 | Defender | Dundee Form D U16 |
| Murray | Scott | Robert | 03/03/88 | Glasgow | 06/08/04 | 6.2 | 12.0 | Goalkeeper | Kilmarnock |
| O'Reilly | Craig | Michael | 20/09/87 | Edinburgh | 13/07/05 | 6.2 | 12.0 | Forward | Raith Rovers |
| Robb | Steven | | 08/03/82 | Perth | 25/08/99 | 5.6 | 9.4 | Midfield | Dundee Form S |
| Roberts | John | Keith | 09/04/88 | Dundee | 13/07/05 | 5.9 | 9.10 | Midfield | Dundee Form D U16 |
| Robertson | Euan | | 25/01/87 | Dundee | 31/01/03 | 5.10 | 11.7 | Midfield | Dundee Form S |
| Robertson | Scott | Ian | 26/12/88 | Dundee | 13/07/05 | 5.11 | 11.7 | Defender | Dundee Form D U16 |
| Robertson | Scott | | 07/04/85 | Dundee | 05/11/98 | 6.0 | 11.4 | Midfield | Dundee Form S |
| Smith | Barry | Martin | 19/02/74 | Paisley | 08/12/95 | 5.10 | 12.0 | Defender | Celtic |
| Soutar | Derek | Robert | 04/06/81 | Dundee | 25/05/99 | 6.1.5 | 12.0 | Goalkeeper | Dundee Form S |
| Swankie | Gavin | | 22/11/83 | Arbroath | 13/07/05 | 5.11 | 11.4 | Forward | Arbroath |
| Watson | Steven | Graham | 07/03/88 | Dundee | 13/07/05 | 5.8 | 10.7 | Forward | Dundee Form D U16 |
| Wilkie | Lee | | 20/04/80 | Dundee | 08/09/98 | 6.4 | 13.0 | Defender | Downfield Juniors |

## TICKET INFORMATION

**Season Ticket information**

**All Areas**

| | | |
|---|---|---|
| Adult | Flexi Seating | £250 (Existing season ticket holders) |
| | | £275 (New season ticket holders) |
| | Allocated Seating | £270 (Existing season ticket holders) |
| | | £295 (New season ticket holders) |
| Juvenile/OAP | Flexi Seating | £120 (Existing season ticket holders) |
| | | £130 (New season ticket holders) |
| | Allocated Seating | £130 (Existing season ticket holders) |
| | | £140 (New season ticket holders) |
| Family Sections | U18 | £95 (Existing/New season ticket holders) |
| | U12 | £60 (Existing/New season ticket holders) |
| | Students | £99 (Existing/New season ticket holders) |

**League Admission Prices**

**All Areas**

| | | |
|---|---|---|
| | Adult | £16 |
| | Concessions/Juvenile | £8 |

**MILESTONES:**
Year of formation: 1893
Most capped player: Alex Hamilton
No. of caps: 24
Most League points in a season:
58 (First Division – Season 1991/92) (2 Points for a Win)
70 (First Division – Season 1997/98) (3 Points for a Win)
Most League goals scored by a player in a season:
Alan Gilzean (Season 1963/64)
No. of goals scored: 32
Record Attendance: 43,024 (-v- Rangers – 1953)
Record Victory:
10-0 (-v- Fraserburgh, 1931; -v- Alloa, 1947;
-v- Dunfermline Athletic, 1947; -v- Queen of the South,
Record Defeat: 0-11 (-v- Celtic – Division 1, 26.10.1895)

## SEASON STATS 2004.05

*Note: the main grid lists each player's shirt number per match. Figures in **bold** denote a goal scored; a secondary smaller bold figure denotes the number of goals scored (e.g. 10² = two goals).*

| DATE | VENUE | OPPONENTS | ATT | RES | Soutar D. | MacDonald C. | Sancho B. | Mann R. | Hernandez J. | Smith B. | Jablonski N. | Robb S. | Brady G. | Lovell S. | Sutton J. | Anderson I. | Fotheringham M. | Barrett N. | McNally S. | Larsen G. | Jack K. | Caballero F. | Hutchison T. | Cerdeira A. | Reilly A. | Wilkie L. | McManus T. | Robertson S. | Kitamarike J. | Conway A. |
|---|---|---|---|---|---|---|---|---|---|---|---|---|---|---|---|---|---|---|---|---|---|---|---|---|---|---|---|---|---|---|
| 7-Aug | H | Hearts | 7,770 | 0-1 | 1 | 2 | 3 | 4 | 5 | 6 | 7 | 8 | 9 | 10 | 11 | 12 | 13 | | | | | | | | | | | | | |
| 15-Aug | A | Dundee United | 11,118 | 2-1 | 1 | 2 | 3 | 4 | 5 | 6 | 13 | 8 | 7 | **10** | 11 | 9 | 14 | 12 | | | | | | | | | | | | |
| 21-Aug | H | Motherwell | 4,849 | 1-2 | 1 | 2 | | 4 | 5 | 3 | 13 | 8 | 7 | **10** | 11 | 9 | 6 | | | 12 | 14 | | | | | | | | | |
| 28-Aug | A | Hibernian | 9,344 | 4-4 | | 7 | 3 | 4 | **5** | 6 | | 12 | 10 | **11** | 9 | 8 | 2 | | | 13 | 1 | | | | | | | | | |
| 11-Sep | A | Celtic | 56,840 | 0-3 | 1 | 7 | 3 | 4 | 5 | 6 | | 13 | 8 | 10 | 11 | 9 | 12 | 2 | | | | | | | | | | | | |
| 18-Sep | H | Livingston | 4,387 | 0-0 | 1 | 2 | 3 | 4 | | 6 | | 7 | 8 | 10 | 11 | 9 | 12 | 5 | | 13 | | | | | | | | | | |
| 26-Sep | H | Rangers | 9,404 | 0-2 | 1 | 7 | 3 | 4 | 5 | 6 | | | 12 | | 11 | 10 | 8 | 2 | | 9 | | | | | | | | | | |
| 2-Oct | A | Aberdeen | 11,217 | 1-1 | 1 | | 3 | 4 | 12 | 6 | | 7 | 14 | 10 | **11** | 9 | 8 | 2 | 5 | | | 13 | | | | | | | | |
| 16-Oct | H | Kilmarnock | 4,637 | 3-1 | 1 | | 3 | 4 | | 6 | 12 | **7** | 8 | 10 | **11** | **9** | | 2 | 5 | 13 | | | 14 | | | | | | | |
| 23-Oct | A | Dunfermline Ath. | 5,456 | 1-2 | 1 | | 3 | 4 | | 6 | | 7 | 8 | 10 | 11 | **9** | | 2 | 5 | 14 | | 12 | 13 | | | | | | | |
| 27-Oct | A | Inverness Cal.Th. | 1,282 | 1-2 | 1 | | 3 | 4 | | 6 | | 7 | | **10** | 11 | | 13 | 2 | 5 | 9 | | 12 | | | | | | | | |
| 30-Oct | A | Hearts | 10,172 | 0-3 | 1 | 9 | | 4 | 5 | 6 | | 7 | | 10 | 12 | | 8 | | 2 | 13 | | 11 | 3 | | | | | | | |
| 6-Nov | H | Dundee United | 9,845 | 1-0 | 15 | 2 | 3 | | | 6 | | 7 | 13 | 10 | **14** | 9 | 8 | | 5 | | 1 | 11 | 4 | | | | | | | |
| 13-Nov | A | Motherwell | 4,406 | 0-3 | 1 | | 3 | | 5 | 6 | | | 10 | 11 | 9 | 7 | | 2 | 12 | | 8 | 4 | 13 | | | | | | | |
| 20-Nov | H | Hibernian | 5,274 | 1-4 | 1 | | 3 | 4 | 5 | 6 | 9 | | 8 | **10** | **14** | | 7 | | 2 | | | 11 | | | 12 | 13 | | | | |
| 28-Nov | H | Celtic | 9,539 | 2-2 | 1 | | 3 | 4 | 5 | 6 | | 9 | 12 | **10²** | | 11 | 7 | 13 | 2 | | | 8 | | | | | | | | |
| 4-Dec | A | Livingston | 4,009 | 0-1 | 1 | 2 | 3 | 4 | 5 | 6 | | 8 | | 10 | 11 | 9 | 7 | | 12 | | | 13 | 14 | | | | | | | |
| 11-Dec | A | Rangers | 48,114 | 0-3 | 1 | | 3 | | 5 | 6 | | 8 | 10 | | | 4 | 2 | 12 | | 11 | 13 | | | | | | | | | |
| 18-Dec | H | Aberdeen | 7,310 | 1-0 | 1 | 5 | 3 | | 6 | 12 | 7 | 8 | 10 | 11 | | 4 | 2 | | 9 | | | | | | | | | | | |
| 27-Dec | A | Kilmarnock | 5,468 | 1-3 | 1 | 7 | 3 | | 5 | 6 | | 9 | 8 | 10 | **11** | 13 | 4 | 2 | | 12 | | | | | | | | | | |
| 1-Jan | H | Dunfermline Ath. | 4,426 | 1-3 | 1 | 7 | | 4 | 6 | | | 9 | | 11 | | 8 | **3** | 2 | 12 | 10 | | | 5 | | | | | | | |
| 15-Jan | A | Inverness Cal.Th. | 5,567 | 3-1 | 1 | 4 | | 14 | 6 | | **7** | | | 11 | | 8 | 3 | 2 | 13 | 10 | | | 5 | **9** | 12 | | | | | |
| 22-Jan | H | Hearts | 5,780 | 1-1 | 1 | 4 | | | 6 | | 7 | | | 11 | | 8 | 3 | 2 | | **10** | | | 5 | **9** | 12 | | | | | |
| 29-Jan | A | Dundee United | 12,719 | 2-2 | 1 | 4 | 2 | 12 | 6 | | 7 | | **10** | 13 | | 8 | 3 | | | 11 | | | 5 | **9** | 14 | | | | | |
| 12-Feb | H | Motherwell | 5,746 | 2-1 | 1 | 4 | 2 | | 6 | | 7 | | **10²** | | | 8 | 3 | | | 11 | | | 5 | **9** | | | | | | |
| 19-Feb | A | Hibernian | 10,938 | 0-4 | 1 | 2 | | | 6 | | 7 | | 10 | 13 | | 8 | | 12 | | 11 | | | 5 | **9** | | 4 | 14 | | | |
| 2-Mar | A | Celtic | 56,077 | 0-3 | 1 | 7 | 2 | 4 | 6 | | 9 | 12 | 10 | 13 | | 8 | 3 | | | 11 | | | 5 | | | | | | | |
| 5-Mar | H | Livingston | 5,830 | 0-1 | 1 | 2 | | 4 | 6 | | 7 | | 10 | 9 | | 8 | 3 | 12 | | 11 | | | 5 | | 13 | | | | | |
| 13-Mar | H | Rangers | 9,876 | 0-2 | 1 | 3 | | 4 | 6 | | 8 | 10 | 13 | | | 2 | | | | 11 | | | 5 | **9** | 12 | 7 | 14 | | | |
| 19-Mar | A | Aberdeen | 10,474 | 1-1 | 1 | 3 | 13 | 4 | 6 | | 9 | 8 | 12 | | | 2 | | | | 11 | | | 5 | **10** | 7 | | | | | |
| 2-Apr | H | Kilmarnock | 5,494 | 1-0 | 1 | 3 | 13 | 4 | 6 | | 9 | 8 | **10** | | | 2 | | | | 12 | | | 5 | 11 | 7 | | | | | |
| 9-Apr | H | Dunfermline Ath. | 5,994 | 2-1 | 1 | 3 | **13** | 4 | 6 | | 7 | 8 | **10** | 9 | | 12 | 2 | | | 14 | | | 5 | 11 | | | | | | |
| 16-Apr | A | Inverness Cal.Th. | 4,786 | 2-3 | 1 | 3 | 5 | 4 | 6 | | 7 | | 10 | **14** | 12 | 8 | 2 | | | 11 | | | | **9** | 13 | 6 | | | | |
| 23-Apr | A | Kilmarnock | 3,485 | 0-1 | 1 | 3 | 2 | 4 | 6 | | 7 | 8 | 10 | 13 | 9 | | 12 | | | 11 | | | 5 | | | | | | | |
| 30-Apr | H | Dundee United | 11,263 | 1-2 | 1 | 2 | | 4 | 6 | | 5 | 7 | **10** | 12 | 8 | | 13 | 14 | | 11 | | | | **9** | 3 | | | | | |
| 7-May | A | Dunfermline Ath. | 8,313 | 0-5 | 1 | 2 | | 4 | 6 | | | 9 | 7 | 14 | 3 | 13 | | 11 | | | | | | 12 | | | | | | |
| 14-May | H | Inverness Cal.Th. | 4,691 | 1-1 | 1 | 3 | **2** | 4 | 6 | | 5 | 8 | 10 | | 9 | 14 | 12 | | | 13 | | | | 11 | 7 | | | | | |
| 21-May | A | Livingston | 7,468 | 1-1 | 1 | **3** | 2 | 4 | 6 | | 8 | | 10 | 12 | 9 | | 7 | 5 | | 13 | | | | 11 | 14 | | | | | |
| **TOTAL FULL APPEARANCES** | | | | | 36 | 32 | 24 | 28 | 13 | 37 | 2 | 32 | 20 | 33 | 20 | 18 | 20 | 25 | 17 | 2 | 2 | 19 | 3 | 1 | 12 | 14 | 1 | 7 | | |
| **TOTAL SUB APPEARANCES** | | | | | 1 | | 3 | 2 | 1 | | 4 | 1 | 6 | | 12 | 2 | 7 | 5 | 4 | 14 | | 9 | 1 | 5 | 2 | | 8 | | 2 | | |
| **TOTAL GOALS SCORED** | | | | | | | | | | 1 | | 2 | 1 | 12 | 8 | 2 | | 2 | | 1 | | | | | | | 4 | | | |

figure in bold denotes goal scored. Secondary smaller figure in bold denotes number of goals scored. † denotes opponent's own goal.

## THE DARK BLUES' 10 YEAR LEAGUE RECORD

| Season | Div | P | W | D | L | F | A | Pts | Pos |
|---|---|---|---|---|---|---|---|---|---|
| 1995-96 | F | 36 | 15 | 12 | 9 | 53 | 40 | 57 | 5 |
| 1996-97 | F | 36 | 15 | 13 | 8 | 47 | 33 | 58 | 3 |
| 1997-98 | F | 36 | 20 | 10 | 6 | 52 | 24 | 70 | 1 |
| 1998-99 | SPL | 36 | 13 | 7 | 16 | 36 | 56 | 46 | 5 |
| 1999-00 | SPL | 36 | 12 | 5 | 19 | 45 | 64 | 41 | 7 |
| 2000-01 | SPL | 38 | 13 | 8 | 17 | 51 | 49 | 47 | 6 |
| 2001-02 | SPL | 38 | 12 | 8 | 18 | 41 | 55 | 44 | 9 |
| 2002-03 | SPL | 38 | 10 | 14 | 14 | 50 | 60 | 44 | 6 |
| 2003-04 | SPL | 38 | 12 | 10 | 16 | 48 | 57 | 46 | 7 |
| 2004-05 | SPL | 38 | 8 | 9 | 21 | 37 | 71 | 33 | 12 |

## LEADING GOALSCORERS:

| Season | Div | Goals | Player |
|---|---|---|---|
| 1995-96 | F | 14 | J. Hamilton |
| 1996-97 | F | 10 | J. O'Driscoll |
| 1997-98 | F | 15 | J. Grady |
| 1998-99 | SPL | 9 | E. Annand |
| 1999-00 | SPL | 13 | W. Falconer |
| 2000-01 | SPL | 14 | J. Sara |
| 2001-02 | SPL | 11 | J. Sara |
| 2002-03 | SPL | 13 | S. Lovell |
| 2003-04 | SPL | 20 | I.Novo |
| 2004-05 | SPL | 12 | S. Lovell |

DUNDEE PLAYING KITS SEASON 2005.06 — FIRST KIT, SECOND KIT, THIRD KIT

# HAMILTON ACADEMICAL

**HAMILTON ACADEMICAL F.C.**
New Douglas Park,
Cadzow Avenue, Hamilton ML3 0FT
**TELEPHONE NUMBERS**
Ground & Secretary (01698) 368650
Stadium Director (01698) 368652
Commercial Manager (01698) 368657
**FAX** (01698) 285422
**E-MAIL** scott.sas@btopenworld.com
**WEBSITE** www.acciesfc.co.uk
**CHAIRMAN** Ronald MacDonald
**VICE-CHAIRMAN** Leslie Gray
**DIRECTORS**
George W. Fairley, Kenneth A. Blake
Brian W. Cairney, Denis Gowans
Arthur T. Lynch, Ronald J. McKinnon &
Scott A. Struthers
**CHIEF EXECUTIVE** George W. Fairley
**HONORARY PRESIDENTS**
Dr. Alexander A. Wilson & Jan W. Stepek
**SECRETARY**
Scott A. Struthers (01698) 368650
**MANAGER** Billy Reid
**FIRST TEAM COACH** Stuart Balmer
**GOALKEEPING COACH** Billy Kerr
**DIRECTOR OF YOUTH DEVELOPMENT**
Leslie Gray
**HEAD OF YOUTH DEVELOPMENT**
John Bean
**YOUTH CO-ORDINATOR**
Scott. A. Struthers
**YOUTH TEAM COACHES**
U19: Gerry McGregor
U17: John Joyce
U16: John Bean & Aiden Byrne
U15: Jamie Duncanson & Murdo MacKinnon
U14: Robert McMillan & Frank McAvoy
U13: Paul Ronald & Alan Henderson
**CHIEF SCOUT** Willie Melville
**TEAM CAPTAIN** Marvyn Wilson
**FOOTBALL SAFETY OFFICERS'**
**ASSOCIATION REPRESENTATIVES**
Scott A. Struthers & Denis Gowans
Tel: (01698) 368650
**COMMERCIAL DIRECTOR** Arthur T. Lynch
**COMMERCIAL MANAGER** Derek McQuade
**MEDIA LIAISON PERSON** Scott A. Struthers
**MATCHDAY PROGRAMME EDITORS**
Scott A. Struthers & Arthur T. Lynch
**PHYSIOTHERAPIST** Avril Downs
**STADIUM MANAGER**
Denis Gowans (01698) 368652
**GROUNDSMAN** Willie Roberts
**KIT PERSON** Jim Kennedy
**CLUB SHOP**
"The Acciesshop",
Hamilton Academical F.C.,
New Douglas Park, Cadzow Avenue,
Hamilton, ML3 0FT
**OFFICIAL SUPPORTERS CLUB**
Jim Galloway, Secretary, HAFC Supporters
Club, 3 Pitcairn Terrace, Burnbank, Hamilton
**SHIRT SPONSOR**
First Choice:
Front: S.L.B & DIY Supplies
Back: Soccersavings
Second Choice:
Front: Hawkhead Carpets
Back: Soccerloans
**KIT SUPPLIER** TFG

## LIST OF PLAYERS 2005.06

| PLAYERS SURNAME | FIRST NAME | MIDDLE NAME | DATE OF BIRTH | PLACE OF BIRTH | DATE SIGNED | HEIGHT FT INS | WEIGHT ST LBS | POSITION ON PITCH | PREVIOUS CLUB |
|---|---|---|---|---|---|---|---|---|---|
| Anson | Scott | Robert | 29/04/89 | Glasgow | 30/08/05 | 6.1 | 10.7 | Forward | Hamilton Acad. Form D U16 |
| Balmer | Stuart | Murray | 20/09/69 | Falkirk | 14/07/05 | 6.1 | 13.7 | Defender | Clyde |
| Bennett | Thomas | McNeill | 12/12/69 | Falkirk | 14/07/05 | 5.11 | 12.6 | Midfield | Kidderminster Harriers |
| Buckley | Sean | Patrick | 07/07/87 | Vale of Leven | 17/08/05 | 6.0 | 13.5 | Forward | Celtic Form D |
| Carrigan | Brian | Eric | 26/09/79 | Glasgow | 18/08/05 | 5.8 | 11.5 | Forward | Raith Rovers |
| Connolly | Stephen | Patrick | 29/11/89 | Glasgow | 30/08/05 | 5.9 | 10.0 | Midfield | Hamilton Acad. Form D U16 |
| Coult | Lewis | Colin | 07/06/88 | Edinburgh | 23/08/05 | 6.3 | 10.0 | Forward | Heart of Midlothian |
| Duncan | Jonathan | Alexander | 12/01/88 | Rutherglen | 18/08/05 | 6.1 | 12.9 | Goalkeeper | Cart Castle B.C. |
| Ferguson | Brown | Alexander | 04/06/81 | Falkirk | 15/06/05 | 5.11 | 11.10 | Midfield | Alloa Athletic |
| Fleming | Derek | Adam | 05/12/73 | Falkirk | 30/06/05 | 5.8 | 10.6 | Midfield | Partick Thistle |
| Galloway | Craig | Thomas | 22/05/88 | Lanark | 29/08/05 | 5.8 | 11.0 | Midfield | Livingston |
| Gibbons | Scott | | 18/06/90 | Glasgow | 23/09/05 | 5.6 | 8.3 | Midfield | Partick Thistle Form D U15 |
| Gilhaney | Mark | | 04/11/84 | Lanark | 03/06/05 | 5.8 | 10.7 | Forward | Clyde |
| Glackin | Ronald | | 06/04/87 | Rutherglen | 17/08/05 | 5.9 | 11.5 | Forward | Clyde Form D Under 15 |
| Hardy | Lee | | 26/11/81 | Blackpool | 21/01/05 | 6.0.5 | 12.4 | Midfield | St. Johnstone |
| Harrison | Greg | | 27/05/88 | Glasgow | 18/08/05 | 5.10 | 10.5 | Midfield | Hamilton Acad. Form D U16 |
| Harty | Ian | McGuinness | 08/04/78 | Bellshill | 07/06/05 | 5.9 | 12.6 | Forward | Clyde |
| Hodge | Sandy | George | 04/10/80 | Lanark | 22/08/03 | 6.3 | 13.5 | Midfield | Queen of the South |
| Jellema | Raymond | James | 27/09/85 | Irvine | 04/06/04 | 5.11 | 11.11 | Goalkeeper | Prestayr B.C. |
| Jones | Graeme | Anthony | 13/03/70 | Gateshead | 04/07/05 | 6.0 | 14.6 | Forward | Clyde |
| Joyce | Craig | | 28/03/88 | Glasgow | 29/08/05 | 5.8 | 10.3 | Midfield | Hamilton Acad. Form D U16 |
| Kenny | Shaun | | 01/08/88 | Glasgow | 29/08/05 | 6.0 | 10.12 | Midfield | Dundee United |
| Keogh | Patrick | Sebastian | 07/05/76 | Glasgow | 10/06/04 | 6.2 | 14.7 | Forward | Clyde |
| Lawley | James | | 23/10/87 | Lanark | 17/08/05 | 5.8.5 | 10.0 | Def / Mid | Hamilton Acad. Form D U16 |
| MacKenzie | Scott | | 07/07/70 | Glasgow | 31/08/05 | 5.9 | 11.2 | Midfield | Falkirk |
| McAlpine | Mark | Ian | 26/06/88 | Glasgow | 18/08/05 | 5.6 | 9.8 | Forward | Hamilton Acad. Form D U16 |
| McArthur | James | McFarlane | 07/10/87 | Glasgow | 03/06/05 | 5.10 | 11.0 | Midfield | Clyde Form D Under 15 |
| McCabe | Ross | | 08/04/88 | Glasgow | 29/08/05 | 6.0 | 11.0 | Defender | Heart of Midlothian Form D |
| McEwan | David | | 26/02/82 | Lanark | 14/02/04 | 6.0 | 12.10 | Goalkeeper | Livingston |
| McGeoghegan | Jamie | | 20/01/87 | Glasgow | 17/08/05 | 6.0.5 | 10.2 | Defender | Celtic Form D Under 16 |
| McJimpsey | Marc | | 30/12/88 | Glasgow | 21/06/05 | 5.6 | 11.0 | Midfield | Motherwell |
| McLaughlin | Mark | | 02/12/75 | Greenock | 10/06/04 | 6.2 | 13.5 | Defender | Clyde |
| McLean | Paul | James | 06/09/88 | Glasgow | 18/08/05 | 5.6 | 9.0 | Midfield | Clyde Form D Under 16 |
| McLenaghan | Gary | Alexander | 29/05/87 | Bellshill | 30/08/05 | 6.2 | 11.6 | Goalkeeper | East Stirlingshire Form S |
| McLenaghan | Ross | | 21/05/89 | Bellshill | 30/08/05 | 5.2 | 8.4 | Midfield | Clyde Form D Under 13 |
| McLeod | Paul | | 22/05/87 | Bellshill | 17/05/05 | 5.10 | 11.2 | Forward | Dundee United Form D U15 |
| Murray | David | Anthony | 25/09/89 | Glasgow | 01/09/05 | 5.9 | 10.1 | Defender | Hamilton Acad. Form D U16 |
| Neil | Alexander | Francis | 09/06/81 | Bellshill | 05/07/05 | 5.9 | 11.0 | Midfield | Mansfield Town |
| Nieto | Gonzalez | Adrian | 19/01/83 | Santiago de Compostela | 09/09/05 | 5.7 | 10.5 | Midfield | Edinburgh City |
| O'Donnell | Paul | David | 27/07/89 | Paisley | 30/08/05 | 6.0 | 11.2 | Midfield | Hamilton Acad. Form D U16 |
| O'Donnell | Ryan | Paul | 07/05/87 | Glasgow | 17/08/05 | 5.10 | 10.2 | Forward | Aberdeen Form D U16 |
| Reid | Christopher | Thomas | 13/08/87 | Glasgow | 09/08/05 | 5.6.5 | 8.11 | Midfield | St. Johnstone Form D U16 |
| Renfrew | Mark | | 01/08/89 | Paisley | 30/08/05 | 5.9 | 10.5 | Forward | Hamilton Acad. Form D U16 |
| Robertson | John | Alexander | 28/03/76 | Irvine | 21/06/05 | 6.0 | 12.6 | Defender | Ross County |
| Sim | Andrew | | 04/02/87 | Lanark | 29/07/05 | 5.4 | 8.0 | Forward | Hamilton Acad. Form D U16 |
| Sweeney | Kevin | Hugh | 26/05/88 | Glasgow | 18/08/05 | 5.6 | 9.0 | Midfield | Airdrie United |
| Thomson | Steven | William | 19/04/73 | Glasgow | 30/06/03 | 6.2 | 12.10 | Defender | Alloa Athletic |
| Tunbridge | Scott | Robert | 26/06/82 | Adelaide | 06/08/05 | 5.10 | 11.4 | Forward | Cumberland United |
| Watson | Christopher | David | 20/03/88 | Glasgow | 18/08/05 | 5.7 | 9.3 | Forward | Hibernian |
| Wilson | Marvyn | | 01/12/73 | Bellshill | 15/06/05 | 5.8 | 11.10 | Midfield | Airdrie United |

## TICKET INFORMATION
### Season Ticket information

| Seated | | |
|---|---|---|
| | Adult | £210 |
| | Student/OAP | £90 |
| | School Children | £50 |

### League Admission Prices

**WEST (MAIN) STAND**

| Seated | | |
|---|---|---|
| | Adult | £14 |
| | Juvenile(U16)/OAP | £6 |

**NORTH STAND**

| Seated | | |
|---|---|---|
| | Adult | £14 |
| | Juvenile(U16)/OAP | £6 |

**MILESTONES:**
**Year of formation:** 1874
**Most capped player:** Colin Miller (Canada)
**No. of caps:** 29
**Most League points in a season:**
57 (First Division – Season 1991/92) (2 Points for a Win)
76 (Third Division – Season 2000/01) (3 Points for a Win)
**Most League goals scored by a player in a season:**
David Wilson (Season 1936/37)
**No. of goals scored:** 35
**Record Attendance:**
28,690 (-v- Hearts – Scottish Cup 3.3.1937 at Douglas Park)
4,280 (-v- Sunderland – Opening of new ground 28.7.2001)
**Record Victory:** 10-2 (-v- Cowdenbeath – Division 1, 15.10.193
**Record Defeat:** 1-11 (-v- Hibernian – Division 1, 6.11.1965)

## SEASON STATS 2004.05

| Date | Venue | Opponents | Att | Res | McEwan D. | Walker R. | Waddell R. | Thomson S.W. | McLaughlin M. | Tunbridge S.R. | Carrigan B.E. | Aitken C.I. | Blackadder R.R. | McPhee B. | Corcoran M.C. | Hamilton D.W. | Convery S. | Keogh P.S. | Hodge S.G. | Ferguson D. | Fyfe I.S. | Lumsden T. | Arbuckle A.P. | Halliday R. | McGlinchey K. | Carney D.R. | Irons S. | McLeod P. | Javary J.P | Cramb C. | Hardy L. | McArthur J. | Rivas F.O. | Mahouve M.D.H. | Jellema R.J. |
|---|---|---|---|---|---|---|---|---|---|---|---|---|---|---|---|---|---|---|---|---|---|---|---|---|---|---|---|---|---|---|---|---|---|---|
| 7-Aug | H | Raith Rovers | 2,176 | †2-0 | 1 | 2 | 3 | 4 | **5** | 6 | 7 | 8 | 9 | 10 | 11 | | | 14 | 15 | 16 | | | | | | | | | | | | | | | |
| 14-Aug | A | Falkirk | 3,423 | 1-1 | 1 | 2 | 11 | 4 | 5 | 6 | **7** | 8 | | | 16 | | | 14 | 15 | 9 | 3 | 10 | | | | | | | | | | | | | | |
| 21-Aug | H | Partick Thistle | 3,543 | 0-1 | 1 | 2 | 3 | 4 | 5 | 6 | 7 | 8 | 14 | | 11 | | | 10 | 16 | 9 | | | | | | | | | | | | | | | |
| 28-Aug | A | St. Mirren | 2,987 | 0-1 | 1 | 2 | 3 | 4 | 5 | | 7 | 15 | | 8 | 10 | 11 | | 6 | 12 | 9 | | | 16 | | | | | | | | | | | | |
| 4-Sep | H | St. Johnstone | 1,904 | 1-1 | 1 | | 16 | 4 | 5 | 3 | | 15 | | 8 | 10 | **11** | | 6 | | 9 | | | 7 | 14 | 2 | | | | | | | | | | | |
| 11-Sep | A | Queen of the South | 1,708 | 1-1 | 1 | | 3 | 4 | | 15 | 16 | 14 | | 8 | 10 | 11 | | 6 | | 9 | 5 | 7 | | **2** | | | | | | | | | | | | |
| 18-Sep | H | Clyde | 2,017 | 0-1 | 1 | | 3 | 4 | | 15 | 16 | 14 | | 8 | 10 | 11 | | 6 | | 9 | 5 | 7 | | 2 | | | | | | | | | | | | |
| 25-Sep | H | Ross County | 1,522 | 1-2 | 1 | | 14 | 4 | | **2** | 7 | 12 | 6 | | 10 | 11 | | 9 | 3 | 5 | 8 | | 16 | | | | | | | | | | | | |
| 2-Oct | H | Airdrie United | 1,900 | 2-0 | 1 | | 8 | 4 | **5** | **2** | | | 15 | 10 | 11 | | 14 | 9 | 3 | | 6 | | | | 7 | | | | | | | | | | | |
| 16-Oct | H | Falkirk | 2,870 | 0-1 | 1 | | 9 | 4 | 5 | 2 | 7 | 8 | | 16 | 11 | 6 | | 3 | | 10 | 12 | 14 | | | | | | | | | | | | | | |
| 23-Oct | A | Raith Rovers | 1,943 | 2-2 | 1 | | 9 | 4 | 5 | 2 | **7²** | 8 | 16 | 12 | 11 | 6 | | 14 | | 10 | 3 | | | | | | | | | | | | | | | |
| 30-Oct | H | St. Mirren | 2,529 | 2-2 | 1 | | 3 | 4 | 5 | **9** | **7** | 8 | 15 | 10 | 11 | | | 12 | | 6 | 2 | | | | | | | | | | | | | | | |
| 6-Nov | A | St. Johnstone | 1,869 | 0-3 | 1 | | 6 | 4 | 5 | 9 | 7 | 15 | 10 | 11 | | | 3 | | | 2 | 14 | 16 | | | | | | | | | | | | | | |
| 13-Nov | H | Queen of the South | 1,592 | 1-0 | 1 | 12 | **8** | **4** | 5 | 9 | 7 | | 11 | 16 | | 10 | | 3 | | 15 | 2 | | 6 | | | | | | | | | | | | | |
| 20-Nov | A | Clyde | 1,408 | 1-2 | 1 | | 8 | 4 | 5 | **9** | 7 | | 11 | 16 | | 10 | | 3 | | 15 | 2 | | 6 | | | | | | | | | | | | | |
| 27-Nov | H | Airdrie United | 2,295 | 1-3 | 1 | | 10 | 4 | 5 | 6 | 7 | | **9** | 11 | | | 3 | | | 15 | 2 | | 8 | | | | | | | | | | | | | |
| 4-Dec | A | Ross County | 2,034 | 1-1 | 1 | | 10 | 4 | 5 | **7** | | 8 | 9 | 11 | | | 3 | 6 | | 12 | | | 15 | | | | | | | | | | | | | |
| 11-Dec | H | Raith Rovers | 1,371 | 1-0 | 1 | | 6 | 4 | 5 | 7 | 16 | 8 | **9** | 11 | 14 | | 15 | 3 | 10 | 2 | | | | | | | | | | | | | | | | |
| 18-Dec | A | Partick Thistle | 3,051 | 1-0 | 1 | | | 4 | 5 | 10 | 16 | | **8** | 11 | 6 | | 9 | 3 | 7 | 2 | | | | | | | | | | | | | | | | |
| 26-Dec | A | St. Mirren | 2,888 | †1-0 | 1 | | | 4 | 5 | 10 | 16 | 15 | 8 | 11 | 6 | | 9 | 3 | 7 | 2 | | | 12 | | | | | | | | | | | | | |
| 29-Dec | H | St. Johnstone | 1,718 | 0-3 | 1 | | | 4 | 5 | 10 | 8 | 15 | | 11 | 6 | | 9 | 3 | 7 | 2 | 14 | | 12 | | | | | | | | | | | | | |
| 3-Jan | A | Queen of the South | 1,790 | 2-1 | 1 | 5 | 14 | 4 | | | | 8 | | **11** | 6 | 7 | 9 | 3 | | 2 | | 15 | | 10 | | **16** | | | | | | | | | | |
| 15-Jan | H | Clyde | 1,873 | 0-1 | 1 | 5 | | 4 | | 14 | | | 8 | 11 | | | 10 | 3 | | 2 | | | 7 | 15 | | 6 | 9 | | | | | | | | | |
| 22-Jan | H | Ross County | 1,476 | 0-1 | 1 | | 4 | | | 7 | | | 16 | 11 | 6 | | 2 | 5 | | | 12 | | | 3 | | | 8 | 9 | 10 | 14 | | | | | | |
| 2-Feb | A | Falkirk | 3,535 | 1-1 | 1 | | 4 | 5 | | 7 | | | 12 | 11 | 15 | | 9 | 3 | | | | | | | | | 6 | | 8 | | 2 | 10 | | | | |
| 19-Feb | H | Partick Thistle | 3,128 | 1-0 | 1 | | 4 | 5 | | 7 | | | 12 | | | | **14** | 3 | 8 | | | | | | | | 6 | 9 | 11 | | 2 | 10 | | | | |
| 5-Mar | A | St. Johnstone | 1,772 | 2-0 | 1 | | 4 | 5 | | 14 | | | **11** | 16 | | | 9 | 3 | 7 | | | | | | | | 6 | **12** | 8 | | 2 | 10 | | | | |
| 12-Mar | A | Airdrie United | 1,430 | 0-1 | 1 | | 4 | 5 | | | | | 12 | 11 | 16 | | | 3 | 7 | | | | | | | | 6 | 9 | 8 | | 2 | 10 | | | | |
| 22-Mar | H | St. Mirren | 1,950 | 1-1 | 1 | | 4 | 5 | | 15 | | | 11 | 16 | | | 9 | 3 | 7 | | | | | | | | 6 | 12 | 8 | | 2 | 10 | | | | |
| 9-Mar | H | Queen of the South | 1,560 | 1-1 | 1 | | 4 | 5 | | | | | 14 | 11 | 16 | | 9 | 3 | 7 | | | | | | | | 6 | 8 | 15 | | 2 | 10 | | | |
| 2-Apr | A | Clyde | 1,240 | 3-1 | 1 | | | 5 | | 15 | | | 16 | 11 | 14 | | **9²** | 3 | | | 4 | | | | | | 6 | | 8 | 7 | 2 | 10 | | | |
| 9-Apr | H | Airdrie United | 2,030 | 1-1 | 1 | | | 5 | | | | | 14 | 11 | | | 12 | 9 | 3 | | 4 | | | | | | 6 | | 8 | 7 | 2 | 10 | | | |
| 16-Apr | A | Ross County | 2,107 | 1-2 | 1 | | | 5 | | | | | 11 | 14 | **15** | | 9 | 3 | 12 | | 4 | | | | | | 6 | | 8 | 7 | 2 | 10 | | | |
| 23-Apr | A | Raith Rovers | 1,474 | 2-0 | 1 | | | | | | | | 16 | 11 | **6** | 15 | **9** | 5 | 7 | | 4 | | | | | | 12 | 8 | 3 | | 2 | 10 | | | |
| 30-Apr | H | Falkirk | 2,300 | 1-0 | 1 | | | 5 | | 14 | | | 12 | | 6 | **9** | | 3 | | | 4 | | | | | | 15 | 8 | 11 | 7 | 2 | 10 | | | |
| 7-May | A | Partick Thistle | 2,845 | 1-1 | | | 14 | 5 | | | | | 8 | | 6 | | 9 | 3 | | | 4 | | | | | | 12 | | 15 | **11** | 7 | 2 | 10 | 1 | |

| | | | | | McEwan D. | Walker R. | Waddell R. | Thomson S.W. | McLaughlin M. | Tunbridge S.R. | Carrigan B.E. | Aitken C.I. | Blackadder R.R. | McPhee B. | Corcoran M.C. | Hamilton D.W. | Convery S. | Keogh P.S. | Hodge S.G. | Ferguson D. | Fyfe I.S. | Lumsden T. | Arbuckle A.P. | Halliday R. | McGlinchey K. | Carney D.R. | Irons S. | McLeod P. | Javary J.P | Cramb C. | Hardy L. | McArthur J. | Rivas F.O. | Mahouve M.D.H. | Jellema R.J. |
|---|---|---|---|---|---|---|---|---|---|---|---|---|---|---|---|---|---|---|---|---|---|---|---|---|---|---|---|---|---|---|---|---|---|---|
| **TOTAL FULL APPEARANCES** | | | | | 35 | 6 | 16 | 30 | 29 | 18 | 16 | 9 | 7 | 18 | 30 | 15 | 4 | 23 | 30 | 16 | 13 | 11 | 3 | 1 | | 6 | | | 11 | 7 | 12 | 5 | 12 | 12 | 1 |
| **TOTAL SUB APPEARANCES** | | | | | | 1 | 3 | 1 | | 2 | 11 | 8 | 4 | 10 | 4 | 10 | 8 | 3 | 2 | 1 | 5 | 3 | 5 | 1 | 2 | 2 | 2 | 2 | 3 | 1 | 1 | | | | |
| **TOTAL GOALS SCORED** | | | | | | | | 1 | 2 | 5 | 4 | | 3 | 3 | 1 | 2 | 4 | | | 1 | | | | | | | 1 | 1 | 2 | 3 | | | |

Figure in bold denotes goal scored. Secondary smaller figure in bold denotes number of goals scored. † denotes opponent's own goal.

## THE ACCIES' 10 YEAR LEAGUE RECORD

| Season | Div | P | W | D | L | F | A | Pts | Pos |
|---|---|---|---|---|---|---|---|---|---|
| 1995-96 | F | 36 | 10 | 6 | 20 | 40 | 57 | 36 | 9 |
| 1996-97 | S | 36 | 22 | 8 | 6 | 75 | 28 | 74 | 2 |
| 1997-98 | F | 36 | 9 | 11 | 16 | 43 | 56 | 38 | 8 |
| 1998-99 | F | 36 | 6 | 10 | 20 | 30 | 62 | 28 | 8 |
| 1999-00 * | S | 36 | 10 | 12 | 14 | 39 | 44 | 29 | 10 |
| 2000-01 | T | 36 | 22 | 10 | 4 | 75 | 30 | 76 | 1 |
| 2001-02 | S | 36 | 9 | 14 | 13 | 49 | 44 | 48 | 5 |
| 2002-03 | S | 36 | 12 | 11 | 13 | 43 | 48 | 47 | 8 |
| 2003-04 | S | 36 | 18 | 8 | 10 | 70 | 47 | 62 | 2 |
| 2004-05 | F | 36 | 12 | 11 | 13 | 35 | 36 | 47 | 7 |

## LEADING GOALSCORERS:

| Season | Div | Goals | Player |
|---|---|---|---|
| 1995-96 | F | 11 | P. Hartley |
| 1996-97 | S | 31 | P. Ritchie |
| 1997-98 | F | 7 | P. Ritchie |
| 1998-99 | F | 11 | G. Wales |
| 1999-00 | S | 6 | D. Henderson, N. Henderson |
| 2000-01 | T | 24 | D. McFarlane |
| 2001-02 | S | 12 | M. Moore |
| 2002-03 | S | 11 | B. McPhee |
| 2003-04 | S | 19 | B. McPhee |
| 2004-05 | F | 5 | S. Tunbridge |

HAMILTON ACADEMICAL PLAYING KITS SEASON 2005.06

FIRST KIT — SECOND KIT — THIRD KIT

* POINTS DEDUCTED FOR FAILING TO FULFIL FIXTURE AGAINST STENHOUSEMUIR F.C. ON SATURDAY, 1ST APRIL, 2000.

# QUEEN OF THE SOUTH

**QUEEN OF THE SOUTH F.C.**
Palmerston Park, Terregles Street,
Dumfries, DG2 9BA
**TELEPHONE NUMBERS**
Ground/Ticket Office/Information Service
(01387) 254853
Football Office Only (01387) 251666
Restaurant (01387) 252241
**FAX** (01387) 240470
**E-MAIL** admin@qosfc.com
**WEBSITE** www.qosfc.com
**CHAIRMAN** David Rae
**VICE-CHAIRMAN** Thomas G. Harkness
**DIRECTORS**
Keith M. Houliston, Craig Paterson &
William Hewitson
**SECRETARY** Margaret Bell (01387) 254853
**MANAGER** Ian Scott
**ASSISTANT MANAGER** Warren Pearson
**FIRST TEAM COACHES**
Brian Reid & Brian McLaughlin
**RESERVE COACH** Stuart Lovell
**COACHING STAFF**
Gordon Hyslop, Fred Smith, Neil Muirhead
Alan Goodwin, Alan Murray, David McCann,
Keith Middlemiss, Scott Solley & Darren Kerr
**YOUTH TEAM COACHES**
U17: Neil Muirhead
U15: Alan Murray & Alan Goodwin
U14: Keith Middlemiss & David McCann
U13: Scott Solley & Darren Kerr
**CHIEF SCOUT** Iain McChesney
**TEAM CAPTAIN** Steven Bowey
**FOOTBALL SAFETY OFFICERS'**
**ASSOCIATION REPRESENTATIVE**
George Galbraith (01387) 254853
**COMMERCIAL MANAGER**
Margaret Heuchan
(B) (01387) 254853 (H) (01556) 504569
**LOTTERY MANAGER** Ian Heuchan
**MEDIA LIAISON PERSON**
Bill Goldie
(H) (01387) 265569
(M) 07733 203171
**MATCHDAY PROGRAMME EDITOR**
Bruce Wright
(B) (01387) 262960
(H) (01387) 252400
**CLUB DOCTORS**
Dr. Andrew Downie & Dr. Bill Balfour
**PHYSIOTHERAPIST** Kenneth Crichton
**GROUNDSMAN** Kevin McCormick
**KIT PERSON** Graeme Maxwell
**BUSINESS DEVELOPMENT MANAGER**
Kenny Crichton
**CLUB SHOP**
Contact: John Paterson
Palmerston Park, Terregles Street,
Dumfries, DG2 9BA
Open 9.00am – 4.00pm Mon. to Fri. and
1.30pm – 5.00pm on home match days.
Also available online - www.qosfc.com
**OFFICIAL SUPPORTERS CLUB**
c/o Palmerston Park, Terregles Street,
Dumfries, DG2 9BA
**SHIRT SPONSOR**
Dumfries Body Repair Centre
**KIT SUPPLIER** Nike

## LIST OF PLAYERS 2005.06

| PLAYERS SURNAME | FIRST NAME | MIDDLE NAME | DATE OF BIRTH | PLACE OF BIRTH | DATE SIGNED | HEIGHT FT INS | WEIGHT ST LBS | POSITION ON PITCH | PREVIOUS CLUB |
|---|---|---|---|---|---|---|---|---|---|
| Barnard | Richard | Michael | 27/12/80 | Frimley | 13/01/05 | 6.2 | 14.8 | Goalkeeper | Aldershot |
| Baty | James | Lea | 28/08/87 | Dumfries | 28/07/04 | 5.7 | 8.5 | Midfield | Queen of the South Form |
| Bowey | Steven | | 10/07/74 | Durham | 14/02/02 | 5.9 | 11.2 | Midfield | Gateshead |
| Burns | Paul | | 18/05/84 | Irvine | 17/06/02 | 5.9 | 9.7 | Midfield | Queen of the South Form S |
| Campbell | Gareth | | 05/10/87 | Irvine | 31/08/04 | 5.10 | 11.5 | Defender | Aberdeen |
| Carr | Christopher | Paul | 14/12/84 | Newcastle | 31/03/05 | 5.10 | 12.2 | Defender | Sheffield Wednesday |
| English | Thomas | | 25/12/83 | Easington | 02/07/04 | 5.10 | 11.13 | Defender | Partick Thistle |
| Gibson | William | | 06/08/84 | Dumfries | 27/09/00 | 5.10 | 10.0 | Midfield | Maxwelltown Thistle |
| Hill | Stuart | David | 26/05/86 | Carlisle | 28/07/04 | 6.4 | 12.7 | Defender | Queen of the South Form D U1 |
| Lovell | Stuart | | 09/01/72 | Sydney | 31/01/05 | 5.10 | 11.10 | Midfield | Livingston |
| Lyle | Derek | | 13/02/81 | Glasgow | 29/10/04 | 5.9 | 11.2 | Forward | Dunfermline Athletic |
| Maxwell | Richard | Graeme | 16/06/87 | Dumfries | 03/09/03 | 5.11 | 10.3 | Defender | Queen of the South Form |
| McColligan | Brian | | 31/10/80 | Glasgow | 06/06/02 | 5.9 | 10.10 | Midfield | Clydebank |
| McGrady | Stuart | Ian | 08/04/85 | Irvine | 17/08/05 | 5.10 | 11.0 | Forward | Ayr United |
| McLaughlin | Brian | | 14/05/74 | Bellshill | 05/06/04 | 5.4 | 9.7 | Midfield | St. Johnstone |
| McNiven | David | | 27/05/78 | Leeds | 06/07/04 | 5.9 | 14.0 | Forward | Leigh R.M.I. |
| O'Neill | John | Joseph | 03/01/74 | Glasgow | 04/06/05 | 5.11 | 12.0 | Midfield | St. Mirren |
| Paton | Eric | John | 01/08/78 | Glasgow | 06/06/02 | 5.10 | 12.0 | Midfield | Clydebank |
| Payne | Stephen | | 23/12/83 | Edinburgh | 08/01/04 | 5.11 | 11.1 | Defender | Aberdeen |
| Reid | Brian | Robertson | 15/06/70 | Paisley | 11/08/03 | 6.3 | 14.2 | Defender | Falkirk |
| Robertson | Scott | | 26/11/87 | Irvine | 16/07/04 | 6.2 | 11.5 | Midfield | Troon Kay Park |
| Scott | Colin | George | 19/05/70 | Glasgow | 03/11/00 | 6.2 | 14.0 | Goalkeeper | Clydebank |
| Thomson | James | | 15/05/71 | Stirling | 23/05/01 | 6.4 | 14.0 | Defender | Arbroath |
| Whorlow | Mark | | 03/07/86 | Dumfries | 26/07/05 | 5.10 | 11.0 | Midfield | Queen of the South Form D U |
| Wood | Garry | Pringle | 18/09/76 | Edinburgh | 05/08/03 | 5.11 | 12.2 | Forward | Berwick Rangers |

## TICKET INFORMATION

**Season Ticket information**

| MAIN STAND | Adult/Under 16 & OAP | £200 / £100 |
|---|---|---|
| EAST STAND | Adult/Under 16 & OAP | £200 / £100 |
| GROUND | Adult/Under 16 & OAP | £200 / £100 |
| EAST STAND | Junior Blues | £45 |

**League Admission Prices**

| MAIN STAND | (no concessions) | £12 |
|---|---|---|
| EAST STAND | Adult/Juvenile & OAP | £12 / £6 |
| STANDING | Adult | £12 |
| | Juvenile, OAP & Unemployed (with UB40) OAP/Family Supplement | £6 |

## MILESTONES:

**Year of formation:** 1919
**Most capped player:** William Houliston
**No. of caps:** 3
**Most League points in a season:**
55 (Second Division – Season 1985/86) (2 Points for a Win)
67 (Second Division – Season 2001/02) (3 Points for a Win)
**Most League goals scored by a player in a season:**
Jimmy Gray (Season 1927/28)
**No. of goals scored:** 37
**Record Attendance:**
26,552 (-v- Hearts – Scottish Cup, 23.2.1952)
**Record Victory:** 11-1 (-v- Stranraer – Scottish Cup, 16.1.1932)
**Record Defeat:** 2-10 (-v- Dundee – Division 1, 1.12.1962)

## SEASON STATS 2004.05

| Date | V | Opponents | Att | Res | Scott Colin | Scott Christopher | English T. | McColligan B. | Reid B.R. | Thomson J. | Bagan D. | Bowey S. | McNiven D. | Armstrong C. | McLaughlin B. | Burns P. | Gibson W. | Payne S. | Paton E.J. | Wood G.P.G. | Craig D.W. | Jaconelli E. | George L.M. | Lyle D. | Barnard R.M. | Bell S.A. | Williams A.B. | Lovell S. | Carr C.P. |
|---|---|---|---|---|---|---|---|---|---|---|---|---|---|---|---|---|---|---|---|---|---|---|---|---|---|---|---|---|---|
| 7-Aug | H | Ross County | 1,910 | 0-1 | 1 | 2 | 3 | 4 | 5 | 6 | 7 | 8 | 9 | 10 | 11 | 14 | 15 | 17 | | | | | | | | | | | |
| 14-Aug | A | St. Johnstone | 2,384 | 3-1 | 1 | | 3 | 4 | 5 | 6 | 7 | 8 | **9** (2) | | 11 | 15 | | | 2 | **10** | | | | | | | | | |
| 21-Aug | H | Falkirk | 2,521 | 1-3 | 1 | | 3 | 4 | 5 | 6 | 7 | 8 | **9** | | 11 | 15 | | 14 | 2 | 10 | | | | | | | | | |
| 28-Aug | H | Clyde | 1,639 | 0-1 | 1 | | 3 | 4 | 5 | 6 | 7 | 8 | 9 | 10 | 11 | | | 14 | 2 | | | | | | | | | | |
| 4-Sep | A | Airdrie United | 1,652 | 1-0 | 1 | | 3 | 4 | 5 | 6 | 7 | 8 | **9** | | 11 | | | | 2 | 10 | | | | | | | | | |
| 11-Sep | H | Hamilton Academical | 1,708 | 1-1 | 1 | | 3 | 4 | 5 | 6 | 7 | 8 | 9 | | 11 | 16 | | 14 | 2 | 10 | 17 | | | | | | | | |
| 18-Sep | A | Partick Thistle | 3,233 | 2-1 | 1 | | 3 | 4 | 5 | 6 | 7 | 8 | 9 | | 11 | 15 | 16 | | 2 | 10 | 17 | | | | | | | | |
| 25-Sep | A | Raith Rovers | 1,491 | 2-1 | 1 | | 3 | 4 | 5 | 6 | 7 | 8 | 9 | | 11 | | | 14 | 2 | 10 | 17 | | | | | | | | |
| 2-Oct | H | St. Mirren | 2,734 | 2-1 | 1 | | 3 | 4 | 5 | 6 | 7 | 8 | **9** | | 11 | | 16 | 14 | 2 | **10** | 17 | | | | | | | | |
| 16-Oct | H | St. Johnstone | 2,059 | 0-1 | 1 | | 3 | 4 | 5 | 6 | 7 | 8 | 9 | | 11 | | | 14 | 2 | 10 | 17 | | | | | | | | |
| 23-Oct | A | Ross County | 2,354 | 0-1 | 1 | | 3 | 4 | 5 | 6 | 7 | 8 | 9 | | 11 | 15 | 16 | 14 | 2 | 10 | | | | | | | | | |
| 30-Oct | A | Clyde | 1,284 | 0-2 | 1 | | 3 | 4 | 5 | 6 | 7 | 8 | 9 | | 11 | 15 | 16 | 14 | 2 | | | | | 10 | | | | | |
| 6-Nov | H | Airdrie United | 2,022 | 1-0 | 1 | | 3 | 4 | 5 | 6 | 7 | 8 | **9** | | 11 | | | 14 | 2 | | | | | 10 | | | | | |
| 13-Nov | A | Hamilton Academical | 1,592 | 0-1 | 1 | | 3 | 4 | 5 | 6 | 7 | 8 | 9 | | 11 | 15 | 16 | | 2 | | 17 | | | 10 | | | | | |
| 20-Nov | H | Partick Thistle | 2,221 | 1-0 | 1 | | 3 | 4 | **5** | 6 | 7 | 8 | 9 | | 11 | 15 | 16 | | 2 | | 17 | | | 10 | | | | | |
| 27-Nov | A | St. Mirren | 2,850 | 2-2 | 1 | | 3 | 4 | 5 | 6 | | 8 | 9 | | 11 | 15 | 16 | 14 | 2 | | | | | 10 | | | | | |
| 4-Dec | H | Raith Rovers | 1,646 | 2-0 | 1 | | 3 | 4 | 5 | 6 | 7 | 8 | 9 | | 11 | 15 | 16 | 14 | 2 | | | | | 10 | | | | | |
| 11-Dec | H | Ross County | 1,588 | 1-0 | 1 | | 3 | 4 | 5 | 6 | 7 | 8 | 9 | | 11 | 15 | 16 | | 2 | | | | | 10 | | | | | |
| 18-Dec | A | Falkirk | 3,370 | 2-4 | 1 | | 3 | 4 | 5 | 6 | 7 | 8 | **9** | | 11 | 15 | | 14 | 2 | | 17 | | | 10 | | | | | |
| 29-Dec | A | Airdrie United | 1,781 | 0-2 | | | 3 | 4 | 5 | 6 | 7 | 8 | 9 | | 11 | | 16 | | 2 | | 17 | | | 10 | | 1 | | | |
| 1-Jan | H | Hamilton Academical | 1,790 | 1-2 | 1 | | 3 | 4 | 5 | 6 | 7 | 8 | 9 | | 11 | 15 | 16 | 14 | 2 | | | | | 10 | | | | | |
| 15-Jan | A | Partick Thistle | 3,257 | 1-3 | 1 | | 3 | | 5 | 6 | 7 | 8 | 9 | | 11 | 15 | | 14 | 2 | | | | | 10 | | | 4 | | |
| 22-Jan | A | Raith Rovers | 1,534 | 1-0 | 1 | | 3 | 4 | 5 | 6 | 7 | 8 | 9 | | 11 | 15 | | | 2 | | | | | 10 | 16 | | | | |
| 29-Jan | H | St. Mirren | 2,016 | 0-0 | 1 | | 3 | 4 | 5 | 6 | 7 | | 9 | | 11 | | | | 2 | | 17 | | | 10 | | | | | |
| 12-Feb | A | St. Johnstone | 1,782 | 0-0 | 1 | | | 4 | 5 | 6 | | 8 | 9 | | 11 | | | | 2 | | | | | 10 | | | | 7 | |
| 19-Feb | H | Falkirk | 2,551 | 1-1 | 1 | | 3 | 4 | 5 | 6 | | 8 | 9 | | 11 | | | 14 | 2 | | | | | 10 | | | | 7 | |
| 2-Mar | H | Clyde | 1,448 | 0-1 | 1 | | 3 | 4 | 5 | 6 | | 8 | 9 | | 11 | 15 | 16 | 14 | 2 | | | | | 10 | | | | 7 | |
| 5-Mar | H | Airdrie United | 1,683 | 0-0 | 1 | | 3 | 4 | 5 | 6 | | 8 | 9 | | 11 | | 16 | 14 | 2 | | 17 | | | 10 | | | | 7 | |
| 12-Mar | A | Clyde | 1,033 | 1-0 | 1 | | 3 | 4 | 5 | 6 | | | **9** | | 11 | 15 | | 14 | 2 | | | | | 10 | | | | 7 | |
| 19-Mar | A | Hamilton Academical | 1,560 | 1-1 | 1 | | 3 | 4 | 5 | 6 | | 8 | 9 | | 11 | 15 | | | 2 | | | | | 10 | | | | 7 | |
| 2-Apr | H | Partick Thistle | 2,589 | 3-1 | 1 | | 3 | 4 | 5 | 6 | | 8 | **9** (2) | | 11 | 15 | | 14 | 2 | | 17 | | | 10 | | | | 7 | |
| 7-Apr | A | St. Mirren | 2,331 | 0-3 | 1 | 18 | 3 | 4 | 5 | 6 | | 8 | 9 | | 11 | 15 | | | 2 | | | | | 10 | | | | 7 | |
| 16-Apr | H | Raith Rovers | 1,361 | 1-1 | 1 | | 3 | 4 | 5 | 6 | | 8 | 9 | | 11 | | 16 | 14 | 2 | | 17 | | | 10 | | | | 7 | |
| 23-Apr | A | Ross County | 2,147 | 1-1 | 1 | | 3 | 4 | | 6 | | 8 | 9 | | 11 | | | 14 | **2** | | 17 | | | 10 | | | | 7 | 5 |
| 30-Apr | H | St. Johnstone | 1,784 | 2-0 | 1 | | 3 | 4 | 5 | 6 | | 8 | 9 | | 11 | 15 | | 14 | **2** (2) | | | | | 10 | | | | 7 | 17 |
| 7-May | A | Falkirk | 5,067 | † 2-1 | 1 | | 3 | 4 | | 6 | | 8 | **9** | | 11 | 15 | | 14 | 2 | | | | | 10 | | | | 7 | 5 |
| **TOTAL FULL APPEARANCES** | | | | | 23 | 1 | 29 | 27 | 21 | 34 | 17 | 34 | 22 | 2 | 25 | 18 | 13 | 10 | 28 | 20 | 18 | 3 | | 22 | 13 | 1 | 1 | 12 | 2 |
| **TOTAL SUB APPEARANCES** | | | | | 1 | | 1 | 5 | | 4 | | 8 | 5 | 5 | 5 | 8 | 7 | 2 | 8 | | | | | 12 | 2 | 1 | 1 | 4 | 1 |
| **TOTAL GOALS SCORED** | | | | | | | | | | | | 3 | 12 | 2 | 1 | 1 | | 1 | 4 | 3 | 1 | | 7 | | | | | |

Figure in bold denotes goal scored. Secondary smaller figure in bold denotes number of goals scored. † denotes opponent's own goal.

## THE DOONHAMERS' 10 YEAR LEAGUE RECORD

| Season | Div | P | W | D | L | F | A | Pts | Pos |
|---|---|---|---|---|---|---|---|---|---|
| 95-96 | S | 36 | 11 | 10 | 15 | 54 | 67 | 43 | 7 |
| 96-97 | S | 36 | 13 | 8 | 15 | 55 | 57 | 47 | 5 |
| 97-98 | S | 36 | 15 | 9 | 12 | 57 | 51 | 54 | 4 |
| 98-99 | S | 36 | 13 | 9 | 14 | 50 | 45 | 48 | 4 |
| 99-00 | S | 36 | 8 | 19 | 9 | 45 | 75 | 33 | 9 |
| 00-01 | S | 36 | 13 | 7 | 16 | 52 | 59 | 46 | 6 |
| 01-02 | S | 36 | 20 | 7 | 9 | 64 | 42 | 67 | 1 |
| 02-03 | F | 36 | 12 | 12 | 12 | 45 | 48 | 48 | 5 |
| 03-04 | F | 36 | 15 | 9 | 12 | 46 | 48 | 54 | 5 |
| 04-05 | F | 36 | 14 | 9 | 13 | 36 | 38 | 51 | 4 |

## LEADING GOALSCORERS:

| Season | Div | Goals | Player |
|---|---|---|---|
| 1995-96 | S | 12 | S. Mallan |
| 1996-97 | S | 13 | S. Mallan |
| 1997-98 | S | 11 | T. Bryce |
| 1998-99 | S | 15 | S. Mallan |
| 1999-00 | S | 13 | S. Mallan |
| 2000-01 | S | 16 | P. Weatherson |
| 2001-02 | S | 19 | J. O'Neill |
| 2002-03 | F | 9 | J. O'Neill |
| 2003-04 | F | 13 | A. Burke |
| 2004-05 | F | 12 | D. McNiven |

### QUEEN OF THE SOUTH PLAYING KITS SEASON 2005.06

FIRST KIT | SECOND KIT | THIRD KIT

# ROSS COUNTY

## ROSS COUNTY F.C.

Victoria Park Stadium, Jubilee Road,
Dingwall, Ross-shire, IV15 9QZ

**TELEPHONE NUMBERS**
Ground/Ticket Office (01349) 860860
Youth Department (01349) 860862

**FAX** (01349) 866277

**E-MAIL** donnie@rosscountyfootballclub.co.uk

**WEBSITE** www.rosscountyfootballclub.co.uk

**CLUB CORRESPONDENCE ADDRESS**
Mr. Donald MacBean
Secretary
Ross County F.C
62 Bayne Drive, Dingwall IV15 9UB

**CHAIRMAN** Peter C. Swanson

**VICE-CHAIRMAN** Gordon M. R. MacRae

**DIRECTORS**
Alastair I. Kennedy, Ronald M. Fraser
& John W. MacGregor

**COMMITTEE**
Donald MacBean, David R. Patience

**HONORARY PRESIDENT**
Roy J. MacGregor

**SECRETARY** Donald MacBean (01349) 860863

**MANAGER** John Robertson

**FIRST TEAM COACH** Donald Park

**DIRECTOR OF FOOTBALL** Alastair Kennedy

**GOALKEEPING COACH** Stuart Garden

**DIRECTOR OF YOUTH DEVELOPMENT**
Calum Grant

**YOUTH CO-ORDINATOR** Graeme Sutherland

**COMMUNITY COACH** Gavin Levey

**YOUTH DEVELOPMENT COACH** Brian Irvine

**YOUTH COACHES**
U19: Gardner Speirs & Brian Irvine
U17: Peter Budge & Andrew Naismith
U15: Martin Bell, Matt McPhee & Martin Rae
U14: Stephen MacLean & Graeme Sutherland
U13: Arthur Jack, Rod Houston & Cameron Stark

**TEAM CAPTAIN** Jim Lauchlan

**OFFICE ADMINISTRATOR** Marie Ewan

**FOOTBALL SAFETY OFFICERS'**
**ASSOCIATION REPRESENTATIVE**
David R. Patience (01463) 222893

**MEDIA LIAISON PERSON**
Alastair Kennedy (01349) 860860

**MATCHDAY PROGRAMME EDITOR**
Bryan Munro (01463) 230721
bryan.munro@lineone.net

**CLUB DOCTOR** Dr. Colin Fettes

**PHYSIOTHERAPIST**
Dougie Sirn & Jan Campbell

**STADIUM MANAGER/GROUNDSMAN**
David Fraser

**KIT PERSON** Susan Wilson

**CLUB SHOP**
Official Ross County F.C. merchandising
available from the Club Shop situated at the
ground. Merchandise also available online -
www.rosscountydirect.com

**OFFICIAL SUPPORTERS CLUB**
George Shiels, 4 Tulloch Place, Dingwall
(01349) 865135

**SHIRT SPONSOR** MacLean Electrical Ltd

**KIT SUPPLIER** XARA

## LIST OF PLAYERS 2005.06

| PLAYERS SURNAME | FIRST NAME | MIDDLE NAME | DATE OF BIRTH | PLACE OF BIRTH | DATE SIGNED | HEIGHT FT INS | WEIGHT ST LBS | POSITION ON PITCH | PREVIOUS CLUB |
|---|---|---|---|---|---|---|---|---|---|
| Anton | Christopher | | 14/04/87 | Perth | 25/07/05 | 5.8 | 10.0 | Defender | St. Johnstone Form S |
| Begg | Scott | Alexander | 15/08/88 | Wick | 27/07/05 | 5.9 | 10.4 | Defender | Ross County Form D U16 |
| Burke | Alexander | | 11/11/77 | Glasgow | 02/06/04 | 5.9 | 10.12 | Forward | Queen of the South |
| Canning | Martin | | 03/12/81 | Glasgow | 28/07/99 | 6.2.5 | 12.10 | Defender | Clydebank |
| Cowan | David | Robert | 05/03/82 | Whitehaven | 12/08/05 | 5.11.5 | 11.2 | Defender | St. Johnstone |
| Cowie | Don | | 15/02/83 | Inverness | 23/08/00 | 5.5 | 8.5 | Midfield | Ross County Form S |
| Djebi-Zadi | Lionel | | 20/05/82 | Lyon | 29/07/05 | 6.3 | 12.7 | Defender | Ca Maureene |
| Duguid | Kevin | Edward | 22/08/88 | Aberdeen | 11/07/05 | 6.0 | 8.11 | Midfield | Ross County Form D U16 |
| Fennessey | Thomas | Harty | 26/03/88 | Coatbridge | 17/08/05 | 6.0 | 11.0 | Midfield | Airdrie United |
| Fraser | Shaun | Martin | 06/03/88 | Glasgow | 27/07/05 | 5.9 | 10.6 | Forward | Partick Thistle |
| Garden | Stuart | Robertson | 10/02/72 | Dundee | 12/07/04 | 5.11.5 | 12.3 | Goalkeeper | Notts County |
| Grant | Alan | | 28/03/88 | Inverness | 21/07/05 | 5.10 | 10.12 | Forward | Ross County Form D U16 |
| Gunn | Craig | | 17/07/87 | Wick | 02/07/04 | 5.11 | 10.7 | Forward | Caithness United |
| Higgins | Sean | | 29/10/84 | Glasgow | 07/08/02 | 5.8.5 | 10.1 | Forward | St. Johnstone |
| Hooks | Neal | | 03/07/87 | Hexham | 10/08/04 | 6.0 | 12.2 | Midfield | Cramlington B.C. |
| Lauchlan | James | Harley | 02/02/77 | Glasgow | 02/01/04 | 6.1 | 12.7 | Defender | Livingston |
| Lindsay | Alan | | 22/02/88 | Bellshill | 11/08/05 | 5.7 | 8.11 | Midfield | Celtic |
| Lombardi | Michele | | 02/08/86 | Irvine | 02/07/04 | 5.10 | 11.5 | Forward | Aberdeen |
| Macadie | Richard | William | 09/04/87 | Wick | 02/07/04 | 5.8 | 10.7 | Midfield | Ross County Form D U1 |
| MacDonald | Neil | MacLeod | 15/06/87 | Dunfermline | 22/08/03 | 5.10 | 11.7 | Defender | Dunfermline Athletic |
| Malin | Joseph | | 13/07/88 | Bellshill | 02/07/04 | 5.10 | 10.1 | Goalkeeper | Celtic |
| McCaldon | Ian | | 14/09/74 | Liverpool | 20/07/05 | 6.3 | 12.4 | Goalkeeper | Chester City |
| McCulloch | Mark | Ross | 19/05/75 | Inverness | 29/07/02 | 5.11 | 13.7 | Midfield | Partick Thistle |
| McGarry | Steven | Thomas | 28/09/79 | Paisley | 29/07/02 | 5.9 | 10.0 | Forward | St. Mirren |
| McGraw | Allan | | 15/06/87 | Glasgow | 10/08/04 | 5.10 | 10.12 | Defender | Partick Thistle |
| McKellar | Scott | | 30/07/87 | Greenock | 20/08/04 | 5.10 | 10.0 | Defender | Partick Thistle |
| McKinlay | Kevin | Donald | 28/02/86 | Stirling | 27/07/05 | 6.0 | 13.10 | Mid / Fwd | Chelsea |
| McSwegan | Gary | John | 24/09/70 | Glasgow | 29/07/04 | 5.7.5 | 12.8 | Forward | Kilmarnock |
| Moffat | Adam | John | 15/05/86 | Glasgow | 30/08/03 | 5.11 | 11.9 | Defender | Rangers |
| Moore | Daniel | Robert | 11/10/88 | Inverness | 11/07/05 | 6.0 | 12.2 | Forward | Ross County Form D U1 |
| Nicolson | Mark | Ross | 25/06/88 | Inverness | 11/07/05 | 6.2 | 11.3 | Midfield | Ross County Form D U1 |
| Niven | David | | 27/12/87 | Glasgow | 19/01/05 | 5.10 | 12.0 | Defender | Ashfield Juniors |
| Nuckowski | Maciej | | 21/03/76 | Bydgoszcz | 09/08/05 | 6.1 | 12.3 | Forward | LKS Lodz |
| Rankin | John | | 27/06/83 | Bellshill | 10/07/03 | 5.8 | 10.8 | Midfield | Manchester United |
| Skinner | Stephen | | 25/04/88 | Inverness | 10/08/05 | 6.0 | 13.0 | Defender | Ross County Form D U1 |
| Stewart | Darren | | 21/09/89 | Paisley | 17/08/05 | 6.1 | 11.7 | Goalkeeper | Celtic |
| Taylor | Stuart | | 26/11/74 | Glasgow | 05/07/04 | 6.1 | 11.10 | Midfield | St. Johnstone |
| Tiernan | Fergus | | 03/01/82 | Nigeria | 29/07/05 | 5.10 | 11.11 | Midfield | Aberdeen |
| Webb | Sean | Michael | 04/01/83 | Dungannon | 14/07/05 | 6.2 | 13.2 | Defender | St. Johnstone |
| Winters | David | | 07/03/82 | Paisley | 09/07/03 | 5.11 | 11.10 | Forward | Dundee United |

## TICKET INFORMATION

### Season Ticket Information

**Seated**
| | |
|---|---|
| Adult | £195 |
| Juvenile/OAP | £100 |
| Juvenile (U16) | £45 |
| Juvenile (U12) | £30 |

**Family Section**
| | |
|---|---|
| Adult | £170 |
| OAP | £90 |
| Juvenile (U16) | £55 |
| Juvenile (U12) | £40 |

**Standing**
| | |
|---|---|
| Adult | £160 |
| OAP | £80 |
| Juvenile (U16) | £45 |
| Juvenile (U12) | £30 |

### League Admission Prices

**Seated**
| | |
|---|---|
| Adult | £14 |
| Juvenile/OAP | £8 |

**Standing**
| | |
|---|---|
| Adult | £12 |
| Juvenile/OAP | £7 |

## MILESTONES:

**Year of formation:** 1929

**Most League points in a season:**
77 (Third Division – Season 1998/99) (3 Points for a Win)

**Most League goals scored by a player in a season:**
Derek Adams (Season 1996/97)

**No. of goals scored:** 22

**Record Attendance:**
8,000 (-v- Rangers – Scottish Cup, 28.2.66)

**Record Victory:**
13-2 (-v- Fraserburgh – Highland League, 1965)

**Record Defeat:**
1-10 (-v- Inverness Thistle – Highland League)

## SEASON STATS 2004.05

| DATE | VENUE | OPPONENTS | ATT | RES | Garden S.R. | Robertson J.A. | McCulloch M.R. | McCunnie J. | Canning M. | Lauchlan J.H. | Rankin J. | Cowie D. | McSwegan G.J. | McGarry S. | Burke A. | Mackay S. | Winters D. | Higgins S. | Malcolm S.R. | Mahood A.S. | Kilgannon S. | Adam C.G. | McKinlay K.D. | Gunn C. | Stewart C. | Tiernan F. | MacDonald N.M. | Taylor S. | Moffat A.J.W. | Kerr S.S. |
|---|---|---|---|---|---|---|---|---|---|---|---|---|---|---|---|---|---|---|---|---|---|---|---|---|---|---|---|---|---|---|
| 7-Aug | A | Queen of the South | 1,910 | 1-0 | 1 | 2 | 3 | 4 | 5 | 6 | 7 | 8 | 9 | 10 | **11** | 15 | 16 | 17 | | | | | | | | | | | | |
| 14-Aug | H | St. Mirren | 2,666 | 1-1 | 1 | 2 | 3 | 4 | 5 | 6 | 7 | 8 | | 10 | **11** | 15 | 9 | 17 | 14 | | | | | | | | | | | |
| 21-Aug | A | Clyde | 1,307 | 0-1 | 1 | 2 | 3 | 4 | 5 | 6 | 7 | 8 | 9 | 10 | 11 | 15 | 16 | | | | 17 | | | | | | | | | |
| 28-Aug | H | Partick Thistle | 2,781 | 0-1 | 1 | 2 | 3 | 4 | 5 | 6 | 7 | 17 | 10 | 11 | 15 | 16 | 9 | | | | 8 | | | | | | | | | |
| 4-Sep | A | Raith Rovers | 1,540 | 2-1 | 1 | 2 | 3 | | 5 | **6** | 7 | 15 | 9 | 16 | 11 | 14 | | 4 | | | 10 | **8** | | | | | | | | |
| 11-Sep | H | St. Johnstone | 2,486 | 0-1 | 1 | 2 | 3 | | 5 | 6 | | 7 | 9 | 16 | 11 | 10 | 17 | | 4 | | | 8 | | | | | | | | |
| 18-Sep | A | Airdrie United | 1,486 | 2-1 | 1 | | 3 | 2 | **5** | 6 | | 7 | 16 | 10 | 11 | 14 | **9** | | | | 4 | 8 | | | | | | | | |
| 25-Sep | A | Hamilton Academical | 1,522 | 2-1 | 1 | 14 | 3 | 2 | | **6** | | 7 | 10 | | 11 | | 9 | **17** | 5 | | 4 | 8 | 16 | | | | | | | |
| 2-Oct | H | Falkirk | 3,062 | 0-1 | 1 | 4 | 3 | 2 | | 6 | | 7 | 16 | 10 | | 9 | 17 | 5 | | | 11 | 8 | 15 | | | | | | | |
| 16-Oct | A | St. Mirren | 2,538 | † 2-3 | 1 | 2 | 3 | 4 | 5 | 6 | | 7 | 16 | 10 | | 9 | 17 | | | | 11 | **8** | | | | | | | | |
| 23-Oct | H | Queen of the South | 2,354 | 1-0 | 1 | 2 | 3 | 4 | 5 | 6 | 16 | **7** | 9 | | | 17 | 10 | 14 | | | 11 | 8 | | | | | | | | |
| 30-Oct | A | Partick Thistle | 2,898 | 0-4 | 1 | | 3 | 2 | 5 | 6 | 15 | 7 | 9 | 16 | 4 | 17 | 10 | | | | 11 | 8 | | | | | | | | |
| 13-Nov | A | St. Johnstone | 2,018 | 1-1 | 1 | 2 | 3 | 16 | 5 | 6 | 7 | 4 | 17 | 8 | | 10 | **9** | 14 | | | 11 | | | | | | | | | |
| 20-Nov | A | Airdrie United | 2,173 | † 1-2 | 1 | 2 | 3 | 4 | 5 | | 7 | 8 | 17 | 10 | 11 | 9 | 6 | | | | 16 | 15 | | | | | | | | |
| 23-Nov | H | Raith Rovers | 1,183 | 1-1 | 1 | 2 | 3 | 14 | 5 | 6 | 7 | 8 | 17 | **10** | 11 | 9 | 4 | | | | 15 | | | | | | | | | |
| 27-Nov | A | Falkirk | 3,182 | 2-2 | | | 3 | | 2 | 6 | 7 | 4 | 17 | **8** | 10 | 14 | 16 | 9 | **5** | | 11 | | | | 1 | | | | | |
| 4-Dec | H | Hamilton Academical | 2,034 | 1-1 | | | 3 | | 2 | 6 | 7 | 4 | 17 | **8** | 10 | 14 | 16 | 9 | **5** | | 11 | | | | 1 | | | | | |
| 12-Dec | A | Queen of the South | 1,588 | 0-1 | | | 3 | 14 | 2 | 6 | 4 | 7 | 16 | 8 | 11 | 15 | 9 | | 5 | | 10 | | | | 1 | | | | | |
| 18-Dec | H | Clyde | 1,939 | 0-1 | | | 3 | 2 | | 6 | 7 | 8 | 9 | 16 | 11 | | 10 | | 5 | | 15 | | | | 1 | | 4 | | | |
| 27-Dec | H | Partick Thistle | 2,844 | 2-1 | | 2 | 3 | 4 | **5** | 6 | 7 | **8** | 9 | 17 | 11 | | 16 | | | | 15 | | | | 1 | | 10 | | | |
| 29-Dec | A | Raith Rovers | 1,127 | 4-1 | | 2 | 3 | 4 | 5 | **6** | 7 | **8** | 9 | 17 | **11** | | 16 | | | | 15 | | | | 1 | | 10 | | | |
| 3-Jan | H | St. Johnstone | 3,105 | 4-0 | | 2 | 3 | | 5 | **6** | 7 | 8 | 16 | 11 | **9**² | 17 | | | | | 10 | | | | 1 | | 4 | 14 | | |
| 15-Jan | A | Airdrie United | 1,512 | 1-2 | | 2 | 3 | | 5 | 6 | 7 | 8 | 16 | 11 | 9 | 17 | | | | | 10 | | | | 1 | | 4 | | | |
| 22-Jan | A | Hamilton Academical | 1,476 | 1-0 | | 2 | 3 | 10 | 5 | 6 | 7 | 8 | | 11 | 9 | | | | | | | | | | 1 | | 4 | | | |
| 29-Jan | H | Falkirk | 3,151 | 0-1 | | 2 | 3 | 10 | 5 | 6 | 7 | 8 | 16 | 11 | 9 | 17 | | | | 14 | | | | 1 | | 4 | | | |
| 19-Feb | A | Clyde | 1,076 | 0-1 | | 2 | 3 | | 5 | 6 | 7 | 8 | 16 | 15 | 9 | 17 | | | | 11 | | | | 1 | | 4 | 10 | | |
| 1-Mar | H | St. Mirren | 1,302 | 0-1 | | 2 | 3 | | 5 | 6 | 7 | 8 | 16 | 11 | 9 | 17 | | | | 15 | | | | 1 | | 4 | 14 | 10 | |
| 5-Mar | H | Raith Rovers | 2,086 | 2-0 | | | 6 | 2 | 5 | | 7 | 8 | 10 | **11** | 9 | 16 | | | | 16 | | | | 1 | | 3 | 4 | 17 | |
| 12-Mar | A | Partick Thistle | 2,939 | 0-0 | | | 6 | 2 | 5 | | 7 | 8 | 10 | 11 | 9 | | | | | 16 | | | | 1 | | | 8 | | |
| 19-Mar | A | St. Johnstone | 1,828 | 2-0 | | | 3 | 2 | **5** | 6 | 7 | | 10 | 11 | 17 | 9 | | | | 16 | | | | 1 | | 8 | 14 | 4 | |
| 2-Apr | H | Airdrie United | 2,024 | 3-1 | | 6 | 3 | 2 | 5 | | 7 | **8** | 10 | 11 | 9² | | | | | 15 | | | | 1 | | 4 | 14 | | 17 |
| 7-Apr | A | Falkirk | 5,272 | 0-1 | | 6 | 3 | 2 | 5 | | | 8 | 10 | 16 | 7 | 9 | | | | 11 | | | | 1 | | 4 | 14 | | 17 |
| 16-Apr | H | Hamilton Academical | 2,107 | 2-1 | | 6 | 3 | 2 | 5 | | 7 | **8** | 10 | 11 | 9 | | | | | 11 | 15 | | | | 1 | | 4 | | 17 |
| 23-Apr | H | Queen of the South | 2,147 | 1-1 | | 6 | 3 | 2 | 5 | | 7 | 8 | **10** | 9 | 16 | 17 | | | | 11 | 15 | | | | 1 | | 4 | | |
| 30-Apr | A | St. Mirren | 3,942 | 0-1 | | 6 | 3 | 2 | 5 | | 7 | 8 | 10 | 9 | 16 | 17 | | | | 11 | | | | 1 | | 4 | 14 | | |
| 7-May | H | Clyde | 2,130 | 1-1 | 18 | 6 | | 5 | | | 7 | 8 | 10 | **15** | 9 | | | | | 3 | | 11 | | | 1 | | 4 | 2 | 14 |
| **TOTAL FULL APPEARANCES** | | | | | 15 | 25 | 36 | 24 | 33 | 28 | 28 | 33 | 10 | 19 | 28 | 3 | 18 | 13 | 10 | | 20 | 8 | 1 | 21 | 16 | 2 | 5 | | |
| **TOTAL SUB APPEARANCES** | | | | | 1 | 1 | | 3 | | 2 | 1 | 7 | 14 | 4 | | 9 | 14 | 13 | 3 | 1 | 9 | 2 | 3 | 1 | | 6 | | 2 | 3 |
| **TOTAL GOALS SCORED** | | | | | | | | | 4 | 4 | | 5 | | 4 | 6 | | 6 | 5 | 1 | | 1 | 2 | | | | | | |

Figure in bold denotes goal scored. Secondary smaller figure in bold denotes number of goals scored. † denotes opponent's own goal.

## THE COUNTY'S 10 YEAR LEAGUE RECORD

| Season | Div | P | W | D | L | F | A | Pts | Pos |
|---|---|---|---|---|---|---|---|---|---|
| 95-96 | T | 36 | 12 | 17 | 7 | 56 | 39 | 53 | 4 |
| 96-97 | T | 36 | 20 | 7 | 9 | 58 | 41 | 67 | 3 |
| 97-98 | T | 36 | 19 | 10 | 7 | 71 | 36 | 67 | 3 |
| 98-99 | T | 36 | 24 | 5 | 7 | 87 | 42 | 77 | 1 |
| 99-00 | S | 36 | 18 | 10 | 8 | 57 | 39 | 62 | 3 |
| 00-01 | F | 36 | 11 | 10 | 15 | 48 | 52 | 43 | 6 |
| 01-02 | F | 36 | 10 | 12 | 14 | 51 | 43 | 52 | 4 |
| 02-03 | F | 36 | 9 | 8 | 19 | 42 | 46 | 35 | 8 |
| 03-04 | F | 36 | 12 | 13 | 11 | 49 | 41 | 49 | 6 |
| 04-05 | F | 36 | 13 | 8 | 15 | 40 | 37 | 47 | 6 |

## LEADING GOALSCORERS:

| Season | Div | Goals | Player |
|---|---|---|---|
| 1995-96 | T | 15 | C. Milne |
| 1996-97 | T | 22 | D. Adams |
| 1997-98 | T | 16 | D. Adams |
| 1998-99 | T | 17 | S. Ferguson, N. Tarrant |
| 1999-00 | S | 13 | G. Shaw |
| 2000-01 | F | 14 | A. Bone |
| 2001-02 | F | 14 | S. Hislop |
| 2002-03 | F | 6 | G. Bayne, S. Ferguson |
| 2003-04 | F | 10 | D. Winters |
| 2004-05 | F | 6 | A. Burke, D. Winters |

ROSS COUNTY PLAYING KITS SEASON 2005.06 — FIRST KIT · SECOND KIT · THIRD KIT

# ST. JOHNSTONE

**ST. JOHNSTONE F.C.**

McDiarmid Park, Crieff Road,

Perth, PH1 2SJ

**TELEPHONE NUMBERS**

Ground (01738) 459090

Ticket Office (01738) 455000

Clubcall (09068) 121559

**FAX** (01738) 625771

**E-MAIL** anyone@saints.sol.co.uk

**E-MAIL 2** karin@saints.sol.co.uk

**WEBSITE** www.stjohnstonefc.co.uk

**CHAIRMAN** Geoffrey S. Brown

**DIRECTORS**

Douglas B. McIntyre, A. Stewart M. Duff

Steven Brown, Steven R. Park

Charles M. Gallagher & Albert J. Ramsay

**MANAGING DIRECTOR/SECRETARY**

A. Stewart M. Duff (01738) 459090

**MANAGER** Owen Coyle

**FIRST TEAM COACH** Jim Weir

**YOUTH CO-ORDINATOR**

Tommy Campbell

**COMMUNITY COACH**

Atholl Henderson

**YOUTH COACHES**

U19: Tommy Campbell

U17: Derek Barron

U15: Derek Simpson

U14: Derek Black

**TEAM CAPTAIN**

Kevin James

**FOOTBALL SAFETY OFFICERS'**

**ASSOCIATION REPRESENTATIVES**

A. Stewart M. Duff (01738) 459090

& George Smith

**SALES EXECUTIVE** Susan Weir

**MARKETING EXECUTIVE** Paul Smith

**MEDIA LIAISON PERSON** A. Stewart M. Duff

**MATCHDAY PROGRAMME EDITOR** David Low

**CLUB DOCTOR** Dr. Alistair McCracken

**PHYSIOTHERAPIST** Nick Summersgill

**HEAD GROUNDSMAN** Chris Smith

**CLUB SHOP**

Open Mon-Fri at Main Reception

at Ground. A shop is also open on matchdays

and is situated at Ormond (South) Stand

**OFFICIAL SUPPORTERS CLUB**

157 Dunkeld Road, Perth

Tel: (01738) 442022

**SHIRT SPONSOR** Megabus.com

**KIT SUPPLIER** XARA

## LIST OF PLAYERS 2005.06

| PLAYERS SURNAME | FIRST NAME | MIDDLE NAME | DATE OF BIRTH | PLACE OF BIRTH | DATE SIGNED | HEIGHT FT INS | WEIGHT ST LBS | POSITION ON PITCH | PREVIOUS CLUB |
|---|---|---|---|---|---|---|---|---|---|
| Anderson | Steven | James | 19/12/85 | Edinburgh | 25/08/04 | 5.11 | 11.4 | Defender | Dundee United |
| Black | Jonathon | | 14/09/88 | Edinburgh | 04/07/05 | 5.9 | 10.5 | Defender | St. Johnstone Form D U16 |
| Campbell | Mark | Thomas | 04/02/78 | Irvine | 02/06/05 | 6.2 | 14.1 | Defender | Falkirk |
| Coyle | Owen | Columba | 14/07/66 | Paisley | 14/07/05 | 5.11 | 10.4 | Forward | Airdrie United |
| Cuthbert | Kevin | Scott | 08/09/82 | Perth | 22/06/05 | 5.11 | 11.0 | Goalkeeper | St. Johnstone B.C. |
| Deery | Patrick | James | 07/10/88 | Stirling | 13/07/05 | 5.10 | 10.7 | Midfield | St. Johnstone Form D U16 |
| Dobbie | Stephen | | 05/12/82 | Glasgow | 07/06/05 | 5.8.5 | 10.4 | Forward | Hibernian |
| Doris | Steven | James | 09/08/88 | Perth | 04/07/05 | 5.11 | 10.11 | Forward | St. Johnstone Form D U16 |
| Dyer | William | | 25/02/87 | Glasgow | 29/06/04 | 5.11 | 10.0 | Defender | Rangers East B.C. |
| Fotheringham | Kevin | George | 13/08/75 | Dunfermline | 25/08/04 | 5.11 | 12.4 | Defender | Clyde |
| Fox | Ross | | 27/02/88 | Falkirk | 04/07/05 | 5.8 | 9.10 | Midfield | St. Johnstone Form D U16 |
| Hannah | David | | 04/08/73 | Coatbridge | 12/06/04 | 5.11.5 | 11.10 | Midfield | Ross County |
| Henry | John | | 31/12/71 | Vale of Leven | 29/07/05 | 5.11 | 10.10 | Midfield | Falkirk |
| Hutton | Blair | David | 28/04/88 | Stirling | 16/06/05 | 5.10 | 10.12 | Goalkeeper | Stirling Albion Form D U14 |
| James | Kevin | Francis | 03/12/75 | Edinburgh | 02/06/05 | 6.7 | 14.7 | Defender | Falkirk |
| Janczyk | Neil | Keith | 07/04/83 | Edinburgh | 02/06/05 | 5.10 | 12.0 | Midfield | Heart of Midlothian |
| MacDonald | Peter | Ian | 17/11/80 | Glasgow | 06/07/04 | 5.9.5 | 11.8 | Forward | Rangers |
| McAnespie | Kieran | Liam | 11/09/79 | Gosport | 07/06/05 | 5.8 | 11.4 | Midfield | Falkirk |
| McCallum | Neil | Stephen | 31/08/87 | Perth | 07/06/05 | 5.7 | 10.0 | Forward | St. Johnstone Form S |
| McCann | Ryan | | 21/09/81 | Bellshill | 31/08/04 | 5.11 | 11.10 | Midfield | Hartlepool United |
| McManus | Steven | | 24/04/87 | Perth | 02/07/03 | 5.8 | 10.7 | Mid/ Fwd | St. Johnstone Form S |
| Mensing | Simon | Ross | 27/06/82 | Wolfenbuttll | 04/07/05 | 6.0 | 13.3 | Defender | Clyde |
| Milne | Steven | | 05/05/80 | Dundee | 17/06/05 | 5.7 | 10.0 | Forward | Plymouth Argyle |
| Moon | Kevin | John | 08/06/87 | Perth | 30/06/04 | 5.7 | 9.0 | Midfield | St. Johnstone Form S |
| Munro | Craig | | 03/06/88 | Glasgow | 24/09/05 | 5.10 | 10.0 | Midfield | Stirling Albion |
| Paston | Mark | Nelson | 13/12/76 | Hastings | 22/08/05 | 6.5 | 14.7 | Goalkeeper | Walsall |
| Paterson | Scott | Thomas | 13/05/72 | Aberdeen | 09/09/05 | 6.2 | 13.1 | Defender | Dundee United |
| Rutkiewicz | Kevin | | 10/08/80 | Glasgow | 02/07/04 | 6.1 | 12.7 | Defender | Aberdeen |
| Scotland | Jason | Kelvin | 18/02/79 | Port of Spain | 24/08/05 | 5.9 | 11.10 | Forward | Dundee United |
| Sheerin | Paul | George | 28/08/74 | Edinburgh | 30/07/04 | 5.10 | 12.8 | Midfield | Aberdeen |
| Sheridan | Darren | Stephen | 08/12/67 | Manchester | 28/07/05 | 5.7 | 11.4 | Midfield | Clyde |
| Stanik | Goran | | 08/09/72 | Skopje | 29/07/05 | 5.9 | 11.0 | Defender | Livingston |
| Stevenson | Ryan | Cairns | 24/08/84 | Irvine | 28/03/02 | 5.11 | 13.7 | Midfield | Chelsea |
| Weir | James | McIntosh | 15/06/69 | Motherwell | 14/07/05 | 6.1 | 12.9 | Defender | Heart of Midlothian |

## TICKET INFORMATION

**Season Ticket Information**

WEST STAND

| | |
|---|---|
| Executive | £305 |
| Adult | £260 |
| OAP/Juvenile | £180 |

EAST STAND

| | |
|---|---|
| Adult | £240 |
| OAP/Juvenile | £85/£45 |
| Parent & Juvenile | £220 |

**League Admission Prices**

WEST STAND

| | |
|---|---|
| Adult | £18 |
| OAP/Juvenile | £10 |

EAST STAND

| | |
|---|---|
| Adult | £16 |
| OAP | £5 |
| Juvenile | £4 |

## MILESTONES:

Year of formation: 1884

Most capped player: Nick Dasovic (Canada)

No. of caps: 26

**Most League points in a season:**

59 (Second Division – Season 1987/88) (2 Points for a Win)

80 (First Division – Season 1996/97) (3 Points for a Win)

**Most League goals scored by a player in a season:**

Jimmy Benson (Season 1931/32)

No. of goals scored: 38

**Record Attendance:**

29,972 (-v- Dundee 10.2.1951 at Muirton Park)

10,545 (-v- Dundee – SPL, 23.05.1999 at McDiarmid Park)

**Record Victory:**

8-1 (-v- Partick Thistle – League Cup, 16.8.1969)

**Record Defeat:** 1-10 (-v- Third Lanark – Scottish Cup, 24.1.190

## SEASON STATS 2004.05

Player columns (left to right): Cuthbert K.S., Tait J.A., Malone E.J., Hannah D., Rutkiewicz K., Maxwell I., Stevenson R.C., Bernard P., Hardy L., Moore M.J., Sheerin P.G., Hay C.D., Marshall C.J., McGregor A.J., Baxter M., Fraser S., Fotheringham M.F., Jackson A.S., Anderson S.J.S., Weir J.M., Webb S.M., Fotheringham K.G., McManus S., McConalogue S., McCann R., Mahood A.S., MacDonald P.I.R., Forsyth R., Linn R.A., McAnespie K.L., Samson C.I., Cowan D.R., Sloan R., Bagan D., Dyer W., Dobbie S.

| Date | Venue | Opponents | Att | Res |
|------|-------|-----------|-----|-----|
| 7-Aug | A | Airdrie United | 2,365 | 0-1 |
| 14-Aug | H | Queen of the South | 2,384 | 1-3 |
| 21-Aug | A | St. Mirren | 3,079 | 1-2 |
| 28-Aug | H | Raith Rovers | 2,574 | 1-0 |
| 4-Sep | A | Hamilton Academical | 1,904 | 1-1 |
| 11-Sep | A | Ross County | 2,486 | 1-0 |
| 18-Sep | H | Falkirk | 3,835 | 1-2 |
| 25-Sep | H | Partick Thistle | 2,763 | 2-1 |
| 2-Oct | A | Clyde | 1,456 | 0-1 |
| 16-Oct | A | Queen of the South | 2,059 | 1-0 |
| 23-Oct | H | Airdrie United | 2,447 | † 1-1 |
| 30-Oct | A | Raith Rovers | 2,089 | 0-1 |
| 6-Nov | H | Hamilton Academical | 1,869 | 3-0 |
| 13-Nov | H | Ross County | 2,018 | 1-1 |
| 20-Nov | A | Falkirk | 3,439 | 1-3 |
| 27-Nov | H | Clyde | 2,026 | 3-0 |
| 5-Dec | A | Partick Thistle | 2,945 | 4-0 |
| 11-Dec | A | Airdrie United | 1,865 | 0-0 |
| 18-Dec | H | St. Mirren | 2,233 | 1-0 |
| 26-Dec | H | Raith Rovers | 2,579 | 2-0 |
| 29-Dec | A | Hamilton Academical | 1,718 | 3-0 |
| 2-Jan | A | Ross County | 3,105 | 0-4 |
| 15-Jan | A | Falkirk | 3,395 | 0-3 |
| 22-Jan | H | Partick Thistle | 2,814 | 1-1 |
| 2-Feb | H | Queen of the South | 1,782 | 0-0 |
| 19-Feb | A | St. Mirren | 2,716 | 1-1 |
| 5-Mar | H | Hamilton Academical | 1,772 | 0-2 |
| 12-Mar | A | Raith Rovers | 1,350 | 2-1 |
| 19-Mar | H | Ross County | 1,828 | 0-0 |
| 22-Mar | A | Clyde | 862 | 1-1 |
| 2-Apr | A | Falkirk | 3,748 | 0-3 |
| 9-Apr | H | Clyde | 1,770 | 0-0 |
| 16-Apr | A | Partick Thistle | 2,310 | 4-0 |
| 23-Apr | H | Airdrie United | 2,239 | 1-2 |
| 30-Apr | A | Queen of the South | 1,784 | 0-2 |
| 7-May | H | St. Mirren | 2,920 | 0-0 |

**TOTAL FULL APPEARANCES:** Cuthbert 5, Tait 13, Malone 3, Hannah 28, Rutkiewicz 16, Maxwell 33, Stevenson 7, Bernard 1, Hardy 11, Moore 19, Sheerin 34, Hay 13, Marshall 1, McGregor 20, Baxter 12, Fraser 1, Jackson 19, Anderson 2, Weir 15, Webb 8, Fotheringham K.G. 4, McManus 4, McConalogue 24, McCann 4, Mahood 26, MacDonald 15, Linn 13, McAnespie 11, Samson 10, Cowan 8, Sloan 4, Bagan 7, Dyer 5

**TOTAL SUB APPEARANCES:** Tait 1, Malone 1, Hannah 4, Maxwell 3, Stevenson 1, Bernard 2, Moore 5, Hay 16, Marshall 1, Fraser 3, Jackson 1, Weir 5, Webb 6, Fotheringham K.G. 1, McCann 3, Mahood 5, MacDonald 2, Linn 3, McAnespie 1, Samson 1, Cowan 1, Sloan 4, Bagan 1, Dyer 2, Dobbie 3

**TOTAL GOALS SCORED:** Malone 1, Maxwell 1, Moore 4, Sheerin 2, Hay 4, McGregor 2, Baxter 2, McConalogue 1, Mahood 2, MacDonald 1, McAnespie 1, Bagan 4, Dyer 1, Dobbie 2

*Figure in bold denotes goal scored. Secondary smaller figure in bold denotes number of goals scored. † denotes opponent's own goal.*

## THE SAINTS' 10 YEAR LEAGUE RECORD

| Season | Div | P | W | D | L | F | A | Pts | Pos |
|--------|-----|---|---|---|---|---|---|-----|-----|
| 1995-96 | F | 36 | 19 | 8 | 9 | 60 | 36 | 65 | 4 |
| 1996-97 | F | 36 | 24 | 8 | 4 | 74 | 23 | 80 | 1 |
| 1997-98 | P | 36 | 13 | 9 | 14 | 38 | 42 | 48 | 5 |
| 1998-99 | SPL | 36 | 15 | 12 | 9 | 39 | 38 | 57 | 3 |
| 1999-00 | SPL | 36 | 10 | 12 | 14 | 36 | 44 | 42 | 5 |
| 2000-01 | SPL | 38 | 9 | 13 | 16 | 40 | 56 | 40 | 10 |
| 2001-02 | SPL | 38 | 5 | 6 | 27 | 24 | 62 | 21 | 12 |
| 2002-03 | F | 36 | 20 | 7 | 9 | 49 | 29 | 67 | 3 |
| 2003-04 | F | 36 | 15 | 12 | 9 | 59 | 45 | 57 | 3 |
| 2004-05 | F | 36 | 12 | 10 | 14 | 38 | 39 | 46 | 8 |

## LEADING GOALSCORERS:

| Season | Div | Goals | Player |
|--------|-----|-------|--------|
| 1995-96 | F | 21 | G. O'Boyle |
| 1996-97 | F | 19 | R. Grant |
| 1997-98 | P | 10 | G. O'Boyle |
| 1998-99 | SPL | 4 | G. Bollan, R. Grant, M. Simao |
| 1999-00 | SPL | 10 | N. Lowndes |
| 2000-01 | SPL | 9 | K. Parker |
| 2001-02 | SPL | 5 | P. Hartley |
| 2002-03 | F | 9 | C. Hay |
| 2003-04 | F | 11 | M-M. Paatelainen |
| 2004-05 | F | 11 | P. MacDonald |

### ST JOHNSTONE PLAYING KITS SEASON 2005.06

| FIRST KIT | SECOND KIT | THIRD KIT |

# ST. MIRREN

## ST. MIRREN F.C.

St. Mirren Park, Love Street,
Paisley, PA3 2EA

**TELEPHONE NUMBERS**
Ground/Administration (0141) 889 2558
Sports Leisure Complex (0141) 849 0609
Commercial/Marketing (0141) 840 1337
**FAX** (0141) 848 6444
**E-MAIL** commercial@saintmirren.net
**WEBSITE** www.saintmirren.net
**CHAIRMAN** Stewart G. Gilmour
**VICE-CHAIRMAN** George P. Campbell
**DIRECTORS**
Bryan A. McAusland, Kenneth D. McGeoch,
James Purves, Allan W. Marshall LL.B.
& Gordon Scott
**HONORARY PRESIDENT**
William Todd, M.B.E., J.P.
**SECRETARY** Allan W. Marshall, LL.B.
**MANAGER** Gus MacPherson
**PLAYER/ASSISTANT MANAGER** Andy Millen
**SPORTS SCIENTIST** Jamie Ramsden
**DIRECTOR OF YOUTH DEVELOPMENT**
Bryan McAusland
**HEAD OF YOUTH DEVELOPMENT**
David Longwell
**SFA COMMUNITY COACH** Frazer Robertson
**YOUTH COACHES**
U19: David Longwell
U17: Jim McGowan
U15: Stephen Adam
U14: Neil Ross
U13: Stephen Oates
U12: Andy Hogg
U11: Stephen Sweeney
**TEAM CAPTAIN** Kevin McGowne
**WOMENS DEVELOPMENT COACH**
Annette Glendinning
**OFFICE ADMINISTRATOR** Kathleen Steel
**FOOTBALL SAFETY OFFICERS'
ASSOCIATION REPRESENTATIVE/
STADIUM MANAGER**
Robert Money (M) (07855) 098921
**COMMERCIAL MANAGER /
LOTTERY MANAGER / MATCHDAY
PROGRAMME EDITOR**
Campbell Kennedy (0141) 840 1337
**CLUB DOCTOR**
Dr. Stewart McCormick, M.B., Ch.B.
**PHYSIOTHERAPIST**
Karen Aston, M.Sc, M.S.C.P.
**HEAD GROUNDSMAN** Tommy Docherty
**KIT PERSON** Jim Munro
**SPORTS COMPLEX /
TICKET OFFICE MANAGER**
Jack Copland
**CLUB SHOP**
Situated in Provan Sports,
23 Causeyside Street, Paisley
(0141) 889 1629
**OFFICIAL SUPPORTERS CLUB**
St. Mirren Supporters' Club,
11 Knox Street, Paisley
**SHIRT SPONSOR**
Front & Back: Braehead Shopping Centre
**KIT SUPPLIER** XARA

## LIST OF PLAYERS 2005.06

| PLAYERS SURNAME | FIRST NAME | MIDDLE NAME | DATE OF BIRTH | PLACE OF BIRTH | DATE SIGNED | HEIGHT FT INS | WEIGHT ST LBS | POSITION ON PITCH | PREVIOUS CLUB |
|---|---|---|---|---|---|---|---|---|---|
| Adam | Charles | Graham | 10/12/85 | Dundee | 31/08/05 | 6.1 | 12.1 | Midfield | Rangers |
| Anderson | Stephen | | 24/03/87 | Paisley | 12/06/04 | 5.10 | 12.11 | Forward | Linwood Rangers B.C. |
| Baird | John | David | 22/08/85 | Rutherglen | 23/07/04 | 5.7 | 10.5 | Forward | Clyde |
| Barron | David | | 10/09/87 | Greenock | 28/07/05 | 5.10 | 12.7 | Midfield | Partick Thistle |
| Broadfoot | Kirk | | 08/08/84 | Irvine | 01/07/02 | 6.2 | 14.1 | Defender | Hibernian |
| Carr | Ryan | | 15/03/88 | Rutherglen | 19/07/05 | 5.8 | 11.1 | Defender | St. Mirren Form D U16 |
| Corcoran | Mark | Christian | 30/11/80 | Perth | 22/07/05 | 5.10 | 11.6 | Forward | Hamilton Academical |
| Docherty | Mark | John | 15/05/88 | Bellshill | 26/08/05 | 5.9 | 10.2 | Midfield | Albion Rovers |
| Gemmill | Scott | | 09/06/87 | Rutherglen | 17/07/03 | 5.10 | 10.0 | Forward | St. Mirren Form D U16 |
| Gillespie | Gary | | 10/04/87 | Paisley | 17/07/03 | 5.10 | 11.4 | Midfield | St. Mirren Form U U16 |
| Harkness | Matthew | | 23/03/87 | Glasgow | 12/06/04 | 5.10 | 10.4 | Defender | St Mirren Form S |
| Hinchcliffe | Craig | Peter | 05/05/72 | Glasgow | 26/06/03 | 5.11 | 12.6 | Goalkeeper | Arbroath |
| Kean | Stewart | | 04/03/83 | Irvine | 11/12/04 | 5.9 | 11.4 | Forward | Ayr United |
| Lappin | Simon | | 25/01/83 | Glasgow | 07/10/99 | 5.11 | 10.0 | Midfield | St. Mirren B.C. |
| Marr | Craig | Andrew | 23/03/88 | Paisley | 16/06/05 | 5.10 | 11.2 | Forward | St. Mirren Form D U15 |
| Martin | David | | 02/02/87 | Paisley | 18/07/03 | 5.9 | 10.7 | Defender | Rangers |
| Maxwell | Ian | | 02/05/75 | Glasgow | 13/07/05 | 6.3 | 12.5 | Defender | St. Johnstone |
| McAusland | Marc | | 13/08/88 | Paisley | 16/06/05 | 6.0 | 10.3 | Defender | St. Mirren Form D U16 |
| McCay | Ryan | John | 04/05/86 | Paisley | 31/08/02 | 5.8 | 10.8 | Midfield | St. Mirren Form S |
| McFarlane | Scott | | 30/07/87 | Paisley | 01/06/04 | 5.6 | 9.0 | Forward | St. Mirren Form D U16 |
| McGinty | Brian | | 10/12/76 | East Kilbride | 31/10/01 | 6.1 | 12.7 | Forward | Cumnock Juniors |
| McGowne | Kevin | | 16/12/69 | Kilmarnock | 10/07/03 | 6.1 | 13.0 | Defender | Partick Thistle |
| McKenna | David | | 19/09/86 | Paisley | 31/03/03 | 5.8 | 11.4 | Forward | St. Mirren Form D U16 |
| McMenamin | Christopher | | 02/01/89 | Glasgow | 27/06/05 | 5.11 | 11.0 | Midfield | St. Mirren Form D U15 |
| Mehmet | Billy | | 03/01/84 | London | 12/08/05 | 6.2 | 13.3 | Forward | Dunfermline Athletic |
| Millen | Andrew | Frank | 10/06/65 | Glasgow | 03/01/04 | 5.11 | 11.4 | Defender | Clyde |
| Milne | Iain | McGarry | 09/01/87 | Paisley | 12/06/04 | 5.8 | 8.8 | Defender | St. Mirren Form D U16 |
| Molloy | Craig | | 26/04/86 | Greenock | 31/08/02 | 5.7 | 10.3 | Midfield | St. Mirren Form D U16 |
| Murray | Hugh | | 08/01/79 | Bellshill | 23/08/02 | 5.10 | 11.9 | Midfield | Mansfield Town |
| Potter | John | Paul | 15/12/79 | Dunfermline | 22/07/05 | 6.0 | 12.0 | Defender | Clyde |
| Reid | Alan | | 21/10/80 | Paisley | 11/03/05 | 5.8 | 11.0 | Forward | Hibernian |
| Reilly | Mark | Francis | 30/03/69 | Bellshill | 10/06/04 | 5.8 | 11.8 | Midfield | St. Johnstone |
| Smith | Wallace | Christopher | 05/03/86 | Glasgow | 03/06/04 | 6.3 | 13.0 | Goalkeeper | St. Mirren Form D U16 |
| Sutton | John | William | 26/12/83 | Norwich | 31/08/05 | 6.2 | 13.10 | Forward | Millwall |
| Van Zanten | David | | 08/05/82 | Dublin | 28/07/03 | 5.10 | 11.0 | Defender | Celtic |
| Weir | Robbie | James | 21/02/88 | Irvine | 16/06/05 | 5.10 | 11.11 | Forward | Ayr United |

## TICKET INFORMATION

### Season Ticket Information

**Main Stand Lower Enclosure**
Adult £210
Juvenile/OAP £130

**LDV North Stand /
Reid Kerr College Family Stand**
Adult £190
OAP £120
Juvenile £70

### League Admission Prices

**Main Stand**
Adult £15
Juvenile/OAP £8

**Lower Enclosure**
Adult £15
Juvenile/OAP £8

**LDV North Stand**
Adult £13
Juvenile/OAP £7
1 Parent & 1 Juvenile £16

**Reid Kerr College Family Stand**
Adult £13
Juvenile/OAP £7
1 Parent & 1 Juvenile £16

## MILESTONES:

**Year of formation:** 1877
**Most capped player:** Iain Munro & Billy Thomson
**No. of caps:** 7
**Most League points in a season:**
62 (Division 2 – Season 1967/68) (2 Points for a Win)
76 (First Division – Season 1999/2000) (3 Points for a Win)
**Most League goals scored by a player in a season:**
Dunky Walker (Season 1921/22)
**No. of goals scored:** 45
**Record Attendance:**
47,438 (-v- Celtic 7.3.1925)
**Record Victory:**
15-0 (-v- Glasgow University – Scottish Cup, 30.1.1960)
**Record Defeat:**
0-9 (-v- Rangers – Division 1, 4.12.1897)

**BELL'S** SCOTTISH FOOTBALL LEAGUE

## SEASON STATS 2004.05

| DATE | VENUE | OPPONENTS | ATT | RES | Hinchcliffe C.R. | Van Zanten D. | Broadfoot K. | Millen A.F. | McGowne K. | Reilly M.F. | Gillies R.C. | Murray H. | Paatelainen M-M. | Annand E. | Lappin S. | Russell A.J. | O'Neill J.J. | Ellis L. | McGinty B. | McCay R.J.J. | Baird J.D. | Crilly M.P. | Kean S. | Dempsie M.W. | Reid A. | McKenna D. | Molloy C. | Woods S.G. | Smith C. |
|---|---|---|---|---|---|---|---|---|---|---|---|---|---|---|---|---|---|---|---|---|---|---|---|---|---|---|---|---|---|
| 7-Aug | H | Falkirk | 3,817 | 2-0 | 1 | 2 | 3 | 4 | 5 | 6 | 7 | 8 | **9** | 10 | 11 | **12** | | | 15 | 16 | | | | | | | | | |
| 14-Aug | A | Ross County | 2,666 | 1-1 | 1 | 2 | 3 | 4 | 5 | 6 | 7 | 8 | 9 | | 11 | **14** | | | 10 | 16 | 15 | | | | | | | | |
| 21-Aug | H | St. Johnstone | 3,079 | 2-1 | 1 | 2 | 3 | 4 | 5 | 6 | 7 | | 9 | | 11 | **8** | | | 10 | 16 | **14** | | | | | | | | |
| 28-Aug | H | Hamilton Academical | 2,987 | 1-0 | 1 | 2 | 3 | 4 | 5 | 6 | | 7 | 9 | | 11 | 8 | | | 10 | 16 | 14 | | | | | | | | |
| 4-Sep | A | Clyde | 2,472 | 0-0 | 1 | 2 | 3 | 4 | 5 | 6 | 7 | 8 | 9 | 10 | 11 | 12 | | 14 | 15 | | | | | | | | | | |
| 11-Sep | H | Partick Thistle | 4,711 | 2-1 | 1 | 2 | 3 | 4 | 5 | 6 | | 7 | **9** | | 11 | **8** | 12 | | 10 | 16 | | | | | | | | | | |
| 18-Sep | A | Raith Rovers | 2,111 | 3-0 | 1 | 2 | 3 | 4 | 5 | 6 | 15 | 7 | **9** | | **11** | 12 | 8 | 16 | 10 | | | | | | | | | | |
| 25-Sep | H | Airdrie United | 3,569 | 1-1 | 1 | 2 | 3 | 4 | 5 | 6 | 15 | 7 | 9 | | 11 | 12 | 8 | | 10 | | | | | | | | | | |
| 2-Oct | A | Queen of the South | 2,734 | 1-2 | 1 | 2 | 3 | 4 | 5 | 6 | 12 | 7 | 9 | | | 8 | 16 | | 10 | | 14 | | | | | | | | |
| 16-Oct | A | Ross County | 2,538 | †3-2 | 1 | 2 | 3 | 4 | 5 | 6 | 7 | 8 | 9 | | 14 | **12** | **11** | | 10 | | 15 | | | | | | | | |
| 23-Oct | A | Falkirk | 4,611 | 0-0 | 1 | 2 | 3 | 4 | 5 | 6 | 7 | 8 | | | 14 | 10 | 11 | 9 | | | 12 | 16 | | | | | | | |
| 30-Oct | A | Hamilton Academical | 2,529 | 2-2 | 1 | 2 | 3 | 4 | 5 | 6 | 7 | 8 | | | 12 | **14** | **10** | 11 | 9 | | | 16 | | | | | | | |
| 6-Nov | H | Clyde | 3,788 | 0-0 | 1 | 2 | 3 | 4 | 5 | 6 | 7 | 8 | | | 11 | 12 | 10 | 15 | 9 | | 14 | | | | | | | | |
| 13-Nov | A | Partick Thistle | 4,949 | 3-0 | 1 | 2 | 3 | 4 | 5 | 6 | | 7 | | | 11 | **9** | **14** | 16 | **10** | | 12 | 8 | | | | | | | |
| 20-Nov | H | Raith Rovers | 3,002 | 1-0 | 1 | 2 | 3 | 4 | 5 | 6 | | 7 | 16 | | 11 | 9 | 12 | 14 | **10** | | | 8 | | | | | | | |
| 27-Nov | H | Queen of the South | 2,850 | 2-2 | 1 | 2 | **3²** | 4 | 5 | 6 | | 7 | 16 | | 11 | 9 | 12 | 14 | **10** | | | 8 | | | | | | | |
| 4-Dec | A | Airdrie United | 2,514 | 2-3 | 1 | 2 | 3 | 4 | 5 | | **7** | 8 | 12 | | | 9 | **14** | 11 | 10 | | 16 | | | | | | | | |
| 11-Dec | H | Falkirk | 4,676 | 0-1 | 1 | 2 | 3 | 4 | 5 | 6 | | 7 | | | 12 | 14 | 8 | 11 | 10 | | | | 16 | | | | | | |
| 18-Dec | A | St. Johnstone | 2,233 | 0-1 | 1 | 2 | 3 | 4 | | 6 | 14 | 7 | | | 11 | 8 | 5 | 12 | 16 | | | | 10 | | | | | | |
| 26-Dec | H | Hamilton Academical | 2,888 | 0-1 | 1 | 2 | 3 | 4 | | 6 | 7 | | | | 11 | 15 | | 12 | 8 | | 16 | 10 | 5 | | | | | | |
| 10-Jan | H | Partick Thistle | 3,779 | 1-1 | 1 | 2 | 3 | 4 | 5 | 6 | 7 | | 12 | | 8 | 14 | 16 | | 10 | 11 | | | 9 | | | | | | |
| 15-Jan | A | Raith Rovers | 1,393 | 0-2 | 1 | 2 | 3 | 4 | 5 | 6 | | 15 | | | 8 | 12 | | 10 | 11 | 16 | 7 | 9 | | | | | | | |
| 22-Jan | H | Airdrie United | 3,047 | 1-0 | 1 | 2 | 3 | 4 | 5 | 6 | 15 | 7 | | | 8 | | 10 | | 12 | 11 | | | 9 | | | | | | |
| 29-Jan | A | Queen of the South | 2,016 | 0-0 | 1 | 2 | 3 | 4 | 5 | 6 | 15 | 7 | | | 8 | 14 | 10 | | 12 | 11 | | | 9 | | | | | | |
| 19-Feb | H | St. Johnstone | 2,716 | 1-1 | 1 | 2 | **3** | 4 | 5 | 6 | 15 | 7 | | | 14 | 12 | 8 | | 10 | 11 | | | 9 | | | | | | |
| 1-Mar | A | Ross County | 1,302 | 1-0 | 1 | 2 | 3 | 4 | 5 | | 7 | 6 | | | 8 | 12 | 10 | 11 | 14 | | | | 9 | | | | | | |
| 5-Mar | H | Clyde | 2,730 | 0-0 | 1 | 2 | 3 | 4 | 5 | 6 | 12 | 7 | | | 8 | 9 | 11 | | 10 | | 14 | 16 | | | | | | | |
| 8-Mar | A | Clyde | 1,008 | 0-0 | 1 | | 3 | 4 | 5 | 6 | 12 | | | | 7 | 9 | 8 | 11 | 10 | | 15 | | | | 2 | | | | |
| 13-Mar | A | Hamilton Academical | 1,950 | 0-0 | 1 | | 3 | 4 | 5 | 6 | 12 | 15 | | | 8 | 9 | 7 | 11 | 10 | | 14 | | | | 2 | | | | |
| 19-Mar | A | Partick Thistle | 3,730 | 0-0 | 1 | | 3 | 4 | 5 | 6 | | 7 | | | 8 | 9 | 14 | 11 | 10 | | 15 | | | | 2 | | | | |
| 2-Apr | H | Raith Rovers | 2,193 | 3-0 | 1 | 5 | 3 | 4 | | 6 | 12 | 7 | | | 8 | **10** | | **11** | 15 | | 14 | | 9 | | 2 | | | | |
| 9-Apr | H | Queen of the South | 2,331 | 3-0 | 1 | 2 | 3 | 4 | | **6** | 12 | **7** | | | 8 | 10 | 5 | 14 | | **11** | | 9 | | | | | 15 | | |
| 16-Apr | A | Airdrie United | 1,989 | 2-0 | 1 | 5 | 3 | 4 | | 6 | | | | | 8 | 10 | 11 | | 12 | **9²** | | 2 | | | | | | | |
| 23-Apr | A | Falkirk | 4,342 | 2-1 | 1 | 2 | **3** | 4 | 5 | 6 | | | | | 8 | **10** | 15 | | 12 | 9 | | | 11 | | 7 | | | 17 | |
| 30-Apr | H | Ross County | 3,942 | 1-0 | | 2 | 3 | 4 | 5 | 6 | 14 | 7 | | | 8 | | | | 10 | | | | 11 | 15 | | | | | 1 |
| 7-May | A | St. Johnstone | 2,920 | 0-0 | | 2 | 3 | 4 | 5 | 6 | | 7 | | | 8 | | 12 | | 14 | | | | 11 | 15 | | | | | 1 |

| | | TOTAL FULL APPEARANCES | | | 34 | 33 | 36 | 36 | 31 | 35 | 11 | 30 | 12 | 1 | 29 | 12 | 19 | 14 | 24 | 6 | 3 | 4 | 14 | 1 | 8 | 1 | | | 2 |
| | | TOTAL SUB APPEARANCES | | | | | | | | | 13 | 2 | 4 | | 5 | 13 | 11 | 8 | 8 | 5 | 18 | 5 | 1 | | 3 | | 1 | | |
| | | TOTAL GOALS SCORED | | | | | 1 | | | 5 | | 1 | 1 | 1 | 4 | | 1 | 5 | 7 | 2 | 4 | | 3 | | 5 | | | | |

ure in bold denotes goal scored. Secondary smaller figure in bold denotes number of goals scored. † denotes opponent's own goal.

### HE BUDDIES' 10 YEAR LEAGUE RECORD

| eason | Div | P | W | D | L | F | A | Pts | Pos |
|---|---|---|---|---|---|---|---|---|---|
| 995-96 | F | 36 | 13 | 8 | 15 | 46 | 51 | 47 | 6 |
| 996-97 | F | 36 | 17 | 7 | 12 | 48 | 41 | 58 | 4 |
| 997-98 | F | 36 | 11 | 8 | 17 | 41 | 53 | 41 | 6 |
| 998-99 | F | 36 | 14 | 10 | 12 | 42 | 43 | 52 | 5 |
| 999-00 | F | 36 | 23 | 6 | 7 | 75 | 39 | 76 | 1 |
| 00-01 | SPL | 38 | 8 | 6 | 24 | 32 | 72 | 30 | 12 |
| 01-02 | F | 36 | 11 | 12 | 13 | 43 | 53 | 45 | 8 |
| 02-03 | F | 36 | 9 | 10 | 17 | 42 | 71 | 37 | 7 |
| 03-04 | F | 36 | 9 | 14 | 13 | 39 | 46 | 41 | 7 |
| 04-05 | F | 36 | 15 | 15 | 6 | 41 | 23 | 60 | 2 |

### LEADING GOALSCORERS:

| Season | Div | Goals | Player |
|---|---|---|---|
| 1995-96 | F | 11 | B. Lavety |
| 1996-97 | F | 15 | M. Yardley |
| 1997-98 | F | 9 | J. Mendes |
| 1998-99 | F | 11 | M. Yardley |
| 1999-00 | F | 19 | M. Yardley |
| 2000-01 | SPL | 10 | R. Gillies |
| 2001-02 | F | 6 | R. Gillies, B. McGinty |
| 2002-03 | F | 12 | M. Cameron |
| 2003-04 | F | 8 | R. Gillies |
| 2004-05 | F | 7 | J. O'Neill |

**ST MIREN PLAYING KITS SEASON 2005.06**

FIRST KIT    SECOND KIT    THIRD KIT

# STRANRAER

**STRANRAER F.C.**
Stair Park, London Road,
Stranraer, DG9 8BS
**TELEPHONE NUMBERS**
Ground (01776) 703271
Secretary's Home/Ticket Office/
Information Service (01776) 702194
**FAX** (01776) 702194
**E-MAIL** grodgers_sfc@yahoo.co.uk
**WEBSITE** www.stranraerfc.org
**CLUB CORRESPONDENCE ADDRESS**
Mr. R.A.G Rodgers
Secretary
Stranraer F.C
28 Springfield Crescent
Stranraer, DG9 7QU
**CHAIRMAN** James Bark
**VICE-CHAIRMAN** James T. Robertson
**COMMITTEE**
George F. Compton, James Hannah,
Alexander McKie, Nigel C. Redhead,
R. A. Graham Rodgers, Barry Critchley,
Bernard J. Duffy, Arthur Campbell &
Thomas L. Sutherland
**HONORARY PRESIDENT** John Carruth
**HONORARY VICE-PRESIDENTS**
J.D. Porter, G. Binnie & P. Muir
**SECRETARY** R. A. Graham Rodgers
**MANAGER** Neil Watt
**ASSISTANT MANAGER** Stuart Millar
**FITNESS COACH** David Johnstone
**TEAM CAPTAIN** Allan Jenkins
**FOOTBALL SAFETY OFFICERS'**
**ASSOCIATION REPRESENTATIVE**
Robert Clanachan
**COMMERCIAL MANAGER**
Brian Reilly (07968) 932257
**LOTTERY MANAGER** Bill Paton
**MATCHDAY PROGRAMME EDITORS**
R. A. Graham Rodgers (01776) 702194
& Brian Reilly (07968) 932257
**CLUB DOCTORS**
Dr. Ranald Spicer, Dr. Niall Balmer
& Dr. Paul Carnaghan
**PHYSIOTHERAPIST** Walter Cannon
**ASSISTANT PHYSIOTHERAPIST**
Jimmy Cooper
**GROUNDSMAN** Murray Gibson
**CLUB SHOP**
Situated at Ground. Open 2.30p.m-3.00pm
and half-time on Matchdays
**OFFICIAL SUPPORTERS CLUB**
Situated in North Strand Street,
Stranraer. (01776) 704121
**SHIRT SPONSOR**
**First Choice:** Stena Line
**Second Choice:** Edinburgh Hill Autos
**KIT SUPPLIER** Nike

## LIST OF PLAYERS 2005.06

| PLAYERS SURNAME | FIRST NAME | MIDDLE NAME | DATE OF BIRTH | PLACE OF BIRTH | DATE SIGNED | HEIGHT FT INS | WEIGHT ST LBS | POSITION ON PITCH | PREVIOUS CLUB |
|---|---|---|---|---|---|---|---|---|---|
| Aitken | Stephen | Smith | 25/09/76 | Glasgow | 10/07/01 | 5.8 | 11.1 | Midfield | Morton |
| Corr | Barry | John | 13/01/81 | Glasgow | 18/06/05 | 6.2 | 13.2 | Goalkeeper | Motherwell |
| Donnachie | Stephen | | 16/02/82 | Bellshill | 20/08/04 | 5.10 | 10.7 | Forward | Bellshill Athletic Juniors |
| Dowie | Andrew | John | 25/03/83 | Bellshill | 30/07/05 | 6.1 | 11.6 | Defender | Partick Thistle |
| Hamilton | David | William | 30/06/80 | Motherwell | 18/06/05 | 6.0.5 | 12.7 | Midfield | Hamilton Academical |
| Henderson | Murray | | 15/06/80 | Lanark | 19/06/03 | 6.3 | 13.0 | Defender | Balmore Amateurs |
| Higgins | Craig | | 24/07/85 | Glasgow | 25/05/05 | 6.2 | 12.6 | Defender | Elgin City |
| Hinds | Leigh | Michael | 17/08/78 | Beckenham | 05/07/05 | 5.10 | 12.1 | Forward | Partick Thistle |
| Jenkins | Allan | David | 07/10/81 | Stranraer | 03/09/98 | 6.1 | 13.0 | Midfield | Ayr Boswell |
| Keddie | Alexander | | 23/01/81 | Glasgow | 04/07/05 | 6.2 | 13.0 | Defender | Shotts Bon Accord Juniors |
| Marshall | Colin | Jenkins | 25/10/84 | Glasgow | 31/08/05 | 5.9 | 11.4 | Midfield | Airdrie United |
| McLean | Scott | James | 17/06/76 | East Kilbride | 07/06/05 | 5.11.5 | 13.6 | Forward | Stirling Albion |
| McPhee | Gary | | 01/10/79 | Glasgow | 25/06/03 | 5.10 | 11.0 | Midfield | Cumbernauld United Junior |
| Moore | Michael | Jordan | 24/03/81 | Paisley | 11/03/05 | 6.2 | 12.7 | Forward | St. Johnstone |
| Morrison | Allan | James | 31/03/82 | Irvine | 23/06/05 | 6.1 | 13.6 | Goalkeeper | Clyde |
| Ross | Ian | | 27/08/74 | Broxburn | 07/06/05 | 5.10 | 11.10 | Midfield | Alloa Athletic |
| Sharp | Lee | | 22/05/75 | Glasgow | 01/08/02 | 5.9 | 12.0 | Midfield | Ayr United |
| Shields | Dene | | 16/09/82 | Edinburgh | 31/08/05 | 6.0 | 12.6 | Forward | Gretna |
| Swift | Stephen | | 21/07/80 | Glasgow | 15/07/03 | 5.11 | 11.7 | Defender | Linlithgow Rose Junior |
| Walker | Paul | | 20/08/77 | Kilwinning | 25/05/05 | 5.7 | 9.7 | Forward | Morton |
| Wingate | Derek | | 26/09/75 | Glasgow | 10/07/01 | 6.2 | 13.0 | Defender | Benburb Juniors |

## TICKET INFORMATION
### Season Ticket information

| | | |
|---|---|---|
| **Seated** | Adult | £170 |
| | Juvenile/OAP | £95 |
| **Standing** | Adult | £145 |
| | Juvenile/OAP | £75 |

### League Admission Prices

| | | |
|---|---|---|
| **Seated** | Adult | £14 |
| | Juvenile/OAP | £8 |
| **Standing** | Adult | £12 |
| | Juvenile/OAP | £6 |

## MILESTONES:
**Year of formation:** 1870
**Most League points in a season:**
56 (Second Division – Season 1993/94) (2 Points for a Win)
79 (Third Division – Season 2003/04) (3 Points for a Win)
**Most League goals scored by a player in a season:**
Derek Frye (Season 1977/78)
**No. of goals scored:** 27
**Record Attendance:**
6,500 (-v- Rangers – 24.1.1948)
**Record Victory:**
7-0 (-v- Brechin City – Division 2, 6.2.1965)
**Record Defeat:**
1-11 (-v- Queen of the South – Scottish Cup, 16.1.1932)

**BELL'S** SCOTTISH FOOTBALL LEAGUE

## SEASON STATS 2004.05

| DATE | VENUE | OPPONENTS | ATT | RES | Meechan K. | Swift S. | Wright F. | Wingate D. | Henderson M. | Fraser J. | Finlayson K.C. | Gaughan K. | Turnbull D. | Graham D. | Sharp L. | McCutcheon G.K. | Gaughan P. | Jenkins A.D. | Aitken S.S. | Crawford B. | McCondichie A.M. | Donnachie S. | Guy G. | McPhee G. | Cruickshank C. | McCaulay M.J.A. | McGovern M. | McManus P.J. | Fox D. | Moore M.J. |
|---|---|---|---|---|---|---|---|---|---|---|---|---|---|---|---|---|---|---|---|---|---|---|---|---|---|---|---|---|---|---|
| ?-Aug | H | Alloa Athletic | 479 | 3-0 | 1 | 2 | | 4 | 5 | 6 | 7 | 8 | 9 | 10² | 11 | 12 | | 14 | | | | | | | | | | | | |
| 4-Aug | A | Morton | 2,653 | 1-3 | 1 | 2 | 3 | 4 | **5** | 12 | 7 | | 9 | 10 | 11 | 14 | 6 | 8 | | 16 | | | | | | | | | | |
| 1-Aug | H | Ayr United | 885 | 2-1 | 1 | 2 | 3 | 4 | 5 | 8 | 7 | 14 | | 10² | 11 | 9 | 6 | | | 15 | | | | | | | | | | |
| 8-Aug | A | Arbroath | 405 | 1-0 | | 2 | 3 | 4 | 5 | 8 | 7 | 9 | | 10 | **11** | 14 | 6 | 12 | | 1 | 16 | | | | | | | | | |
| ?-Sep | H | Brechin City | 436 | 4-2 | | **3** | 4 | 5 | 9 | **7** | 12 | 16 | 10² | 11 | | 6 | 8 | 1 | | 15 | | | | | | | | | | |
| 1-Sep | A | Dumbarton | 841 | 3-1 | | 3 | 4 | 5 | 9 | **7** | 12 | | 10 | 11 | | 6 | 8 | 1 | | **2** | 16 | | | | | | | | | |
| 8-Apr | H | Stirling Albion | 645 | 0-0 | | 2 | 3 | 4 | 5 | 9 | 7 | 12 | | 10 | 11 | 14 | 6 | 8 | 1 | | 16 | | | | | | | | | |
| 8-Sep | A | Forfar Athletic | 524 | 1-0 | | 2 | 3 | | 5 | 9 | 7 | 4 | 8 | 10 | 11 | | 6 | | 1 | | 16 | | | | | | | | | |
| ?-Oct | H | Berwick Rangers | 521 | 2-2 | | 2 | 3 | | 5 | 9 | 7 | 4² | 8 | 10 | 11 | 14 | 6 | | 15 | 1 | | | | | | | | | | |
| 6-Oct | H | Morton | 918 | 1-0 | | 2 | 3 | | 5 | 9 | 7 | 4 | | 10 | 11 | | 6 | | 1 | | 8 | 16 | | | | | | | | |
| 3-Oct | A | Alloa Athletic | 492 | 2-1 | | 2 | 3 | | 5 | 9 | 7 | | 15 | 10² | 11 | | 6 | | 1 | | 8 | 16 | 4 | | | | | | | |
| 0-Oct | A | Arbroath | 503 | 2-1 | | 2 | 3 | | 5 | 9 | **7** | | | 10 | 11 | 14 | 6 | 8 | 1 | | | | 4 | | | | | | | |
| ?-Nov | H | Brechin City | 620 | 1-4 | | 2 | 3 | | **5** | 9 | 7 | 4 | | 10 | 11 | 15 | 6 | 8 | | | 14 | 12 | | | | | | | | |
| 3-Nov | H | Dumbarton | 532 | 1-0 | | 2 | 3 | | 5 | 15 | 7 | 4 | | 10 | 16 | | 6 | 8 | 9 | 1 | **11** | 14 | | | | | | | | |
| 7-Nov | A | Stirling Albion | 678 | 1-1 | | 2 | 3 | | 5 | 9 | 7 | 4 | 12 | **10** | | | 6 | 8 | 14 | 1 | 11 | 16 | | | | | | | | |
| ?-Dec | H | Forfar Athletic | 411 | 1-0 | | 2 | 3 | 4 | 5 | | 7 | 8 | 12 | **10** | | | 6 | | 9 | 1 | 11 | 14 | | | | | | | | |
| 7-Dec | H | Alloa Athletic | 596 | 0-1 | | 2 | | 4 | 5 | | 7 | 8 | 12 | 10 | 11 | | 6 | | 9 | 1 | 15 | 3 | | 20 | | | | | | |
| ?-Jan | A | Ayr United | 1,467 | † 1-0 | | 2 | 3 | 4 | 5 | 9 | 7 | 8 | | 10 | 11 | | 6 | | | | 15 | | | | 1 | | | | | |
| ?-Jan | A | Arbroath | 432 | 4-0 | | 2 | 3 | 4 | **5** | 15 | **7** | 8 | | **10** | 11 | 16 | 6 | | | | 14 | 9 | | | 1 | | | | | |
| 5-Jan | H | Brechin City | 552 | 0-1 | | 2 | 3 | 4 | 5 | | 7 | 8 | | 10 | 11 | 16 | 6 | | | | 9 | | | | 1 | 12 | | | | |
| 9-Jan | H | Stirling Albion | 495 | 0-3 | | | 3 | 4 | 5 | | 7 | 8 | | | 11 | 12 | | 14 | | | 2 | 9 | | | 1 | 10 | | | | |
| ?Feb | A | Forfar Athletic | 453 | 2-1 | | | 3 | 4 | **5** | | 7 | 14 | | | 9 | | **6** | 12 | | | 2 | 8 | | | 1 | 10 | 11 | | | |
| 2-Feb | H | Berwick Rangers | 351 | 1-0 | | | 3 | 4 | 5 | | 7 | 14 | | 16 | 9 | | **6** | 12 | | | 2 | 8 | | | 1 | 10 | 11 | | | |
| 9-Feb | H | Ayr United | 619 | 1-3 | | | 3 | 4 | 5 | | 7 | | | | | | **6** | 9 | 12 | | 2 | 8 | | | 1 | 10 | 11 | | | |
| ?-Feb | A | Morton | 2,592 | 0-2 | | 2 | 3 | 4 | 5 | | 7 | | 15 | | 9 | | 6 | | | | 16 | 8 | | | 1 | 10 | 11 | | | |
| ?-Mar | A | Berwick Rangers | 296 | 2-1 | | 2 | 3 | 4 | 5 | | 7 | | | 12 | 16 | | 6 | | | | 15 | 9 | | | 1 | **10** | **11** | | | |
| ?Mar | A | Brechin City | 606 | 1-2 | | 2 | 3 | 4 | 5 | | 7 | 8 | | 12 | | | 6 | | | | 14 | 9 | | | 1 | **10** | **11** | | | |
| 2-Mar | H | Arbroath | 357 | 3-3 | | 2 | **3** | 4 | 5 | | 7 | **8** | | | | | 6 | | | | | | | | 1 | 10 | 11 | | 9 | |
| 9-Mar | H | Dumbarton | 436 | 2-1 | | 2 | 3 | 4 | 5 | | 7 | | | 12 | | | 6 | | | | | 8 | | | 1 | **10** | **11** | | 9 | |
| ?-Mar | A | Dumbarton | 848 | 1-1 | | **2** | 3 | 4 | 5 | | 7 | | | 12 | | | 6 | 14 | | | | 8 | | | 1 | 10 | 11 | | 9 | |
| ?Apr | A | Stirling Albion | 658 | 1-1 | | 2 | 3 | | 5 | 16 | 7 | 4 | | **11** | | | 6 | | | | | 8 | | | 1 | 10 | | | 9 | |
| ?Apr | A | Berwick Rangers | 363 | 2-1 | | 2 | 3 | 12 | 5 | | **7** | 4 | | 11 | | | 6 | | | | 16 | 8 | | | 1 | 10 | | | 9 | |
| ?-Apr | H | Forfar Athletic | 456 | 0-0 | | 2 | 3 | | 5 | 9 | 7 | 4 | 15 | 11 | | | 6 | 8 | | | 14 | | | | 1 | 10 | | | | |
| ?-Apr | A | Ayr United | 1,367 | 0-0 | | 2 | 3 | | 5 | 14 | 7 | 4 | | 11 | 16 | | 6 | 8 | | | | 9 | | | 1 | 10 | | | | |
| ?-Apr | H | Morton | 2,778 | 1-1 | | 2 | 3 | 12 | 5 | | 7 | 4 | | 11 | | | **6** | 8 | | | | 10 | | | 1 | | 16 | 9 | | |
| ?May | A | Alloa Athletic | 606 | 0-3 | | 2 | 3 | 4 | 5 | | 7 | 8 | | | 14 | 15 | 6 | 12 | | | | | | | 1 | 10 | 11 | 9 | | |
| **TOTAL FULL APPEARANCES** | | | | | 3 | 31 | 35 | 23 | 36 | 15 | 36 | 23 | 4 | 20 | 23 | 4 | 35 | 12 | 3 | 14 | | | 10 | 16 | 2 | | 19 | 15 | 10 | 7 |
| **TOTAL SUB APPEARANCES** | | | | | | | | 2 | | 5 | | 6 | 7 | | 7 | 13 | 1 | | 3 | 8 | | 2 | 8 | 9 | 2 | 1 | | 1 | 1 | |
| **TOTAL GOALS SCORED** | | | | | | 2 | 2 | | 4 | 1 | 5 | 4 | | 14 | 2 | | 5 | | | | | | 2 | | | | 3 | 1 | 2 |

in bold denotes goal scored. Secondary smaller figure in bold denotes number of goals scored . † denotes opponent's own goal.

## THE BLUES' 10 YEAR LEAGUE RECORD

| Season | Div | P | W | D | L | F | A | Pts | Pos |
|---|---|---|---|---|---|---|---|---|---|
| ?5-96 | S | 36 | 8 | 18 | 10 | 38 | 43 | 42 | 8 |
| ?-97 | S | 36 | 9 | 9 | 18 | 29 | 51 | 36 | 8 |
| ?-98 | S | 36 | 18 | 7 | 11 | 62 | 44 | 61 | 1 |
| ?-99 | F | 36 | 5 | 2 | 29 | 29 | 74 | 17 | 10 |
| ?-00 | S | 36 | 9 | 9 | 18 | 47 | 46 | 45 | 6 |
| ?-01 | S | 36 | 15 | 9 | 12 | 51 | 50 | 54 | 4 |
| ?-02 | S | 36 | 10 | 15 | 11 | 48 | 51 | 45 | 7 |
| ?-03 | S | 36 | 12 | 8 | 16 | 49 | 57 | 44 | 9 |
| ?-04 | T | 36 | 24 | 7 | 5 | 87 | 30 | 79 | 1 |
| ?-05 | S | 36 | 18 | 9 | 9 | 48 | 41 | 63 | 2 |

## LEADING GOALSCORERS:

| Season | Div | Goals | Player |
|---|---|---|---|
| 1995-96 | S | 6 | A. Grant |
| 1996-97 | S | 7 | P. McIntyre |
| 1997-98 | S | 11 | G. Young |
| 1998-99 | F | 5 | P. Ronald, G. Young |
| 1999-00 | S | 12 | P. Ronald |
| 2000-01 | S | 13 | I. Harty |
| 2001-02 | S | 16 | I. Harty |
| 2002-03 | S | 12 | I. Harty |
| 2003-04 | T | 24 | M. Moore |
| 2004-05 | S | 14 | D. Graham |

**STRANRAER PLAYING KITS SEASON 2005.06**

FIRST KIT · SECOND KIT · THIRD KIT

# SCOTTISH FOOTBALL LEAGUE FIRST DIVISION

## AIRDRIE UNITED: EXCELSIOR STADIUM

Excelsior Stadium can be reached by the following routes:
**BUSES:** Nos 260 or 15 from Airdrie Town Centre.
**TRAINS:** From Glasgow Queen Street to Airdrie there is a train every 15 minutes. From the station beyond Airdrie, Drumgelloch, there is a train every 30 minutes, then a 10 minute walk to the stadium.
**CARS:** From Glasgow or Edinburgh leave the M8 at Newhouse

junction (A73) and the stadium is 2 1/2 miles north of Newhouse. From Cumbernauld, the stadium is 6 miles south on the A73.
**CAPACITY:** 10,170 (All Seated)
**PITCH DIMENSIONS:** 115 yds x 74 yds (105 x 67m)
**FACILITIES FOR DISABLED SUPPORTERS:**
Disabled facilities are provided in the North, East & South Stands.

## BRECHIN CITY: GLEBE PARK

The following routes may be used to reach Glebe Park:
**BUSES:** Brechin bus station is only a few hundred yards from the ground and buses on the Aberdeen-Dundee and Montrose-Edzell routes stop here.
**TRAINS:** The nearest railway station is Montrose, which is eight miles away. There is a regular Inter-City service from all parts of the country and fans alighting at Montrose can then catch a connecting bus service to Brechin.

**CARS:** Car parking is available in the Brechin City car park, which is capable of holding 50 vehicles. There are also a number of side streets which may be used for this purpose.
**CAPACITY:** 3,060; Seated 1,518, Standing 1,542
**PITCH DIMENSIONS:** 110 yds x 67 yds (101 x 61m)
**FACILITIES FOR DISABLED SUPPORTERS:**
Section of Terracing designated for disabled supporters. Disabled access from both ends of the Ground.

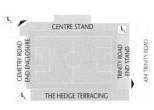

## CLYDE: BROADWOOD STADIUM

The following routes may be used to reach Broadwood Stadium:
**BUSES:** From Buchanan Street Bus Station in Glasgow, fans should board Bus No. 36A (Glasgow to Westfield) or X3.
**TRAINS:** There are regular trains from Queen Street Station, Glasgow to Croy Station. The Stadium is a 15 minute walk from here.

**CARS:** From Glasgow City Centre, fans should take the Stepps By-Pass joining the A80 towards Stirling. Take Broadwood turn-off to Stadium.
**CAPACITY:** 8,006 (All Seated)
**PITCH DIMENSIONS:** 112 yds x 76 yds (102 x 69m)
**FACILITIES FOR DISABLED SUPPORTERS:**
Facilities available in OKI, West and South Stands.

## DUNDEE: DENS PARK

The following routes may be used to reach Dens Park:
**BUSES:** There is a frequent service of buses from the city centre. Nos. 1A and 1B leave from Albert Square and Nos. 18, 19 and 21 leave from Commercial Street.
**TRAINS:** Trains from all over the country pass through the mainline Dundee station and fans can then proceed to the ground by the above buses from stops situated close to the station.

**CARS:** Cars may be parked in the car park (Densfield Park) and local streets adjacent to the ground.

**CAPACITY:** 11,506 (All Seated)
**PITCH DIMENSIONS:** 113 yds x 74 yds (103 x 68m)
**FACILITIES FOR DISABLED SUPPORTERS:**
There is provision for disabled supporters in both the Bobby Cox & Bob Shankly Stands

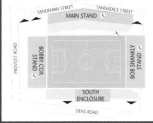

## HAMILTON ACADEMICAL: NEW DOUGLAS PARK

The following routes may be used to reach New Douglas Park:
**BUSES:** Buses from across Lanarkshire and Glasgow pass close to the ground. Buses from across Scotland and the UK call at Hamilton Bus Station 1mile away.
**TRAINS:** Hamilton West Station is situated adjacent to the ground. Normally there are 2 trains per hour to Glasgow, Lanark (change at Motherwell) and Motherwell. A path connects the station to the ground.
**CARS:** Exit M74 at Junction 5 (A725 Coatbridge – East Kilbride

Road goes through this interchange as well). Follow signs for Hamilton Racecourse and Football Traffic. Turn right at lights close to Racecourse and first right again into New Park Street. Stadium is on the left.

**CAPACITY:** 5,396 (All Seated)
**PITCH DIMENSIONS:** 115 yds x 75 yds (105 x 68m)
**FACILITIES FOR DISABLED SUPPORTERS:**
Available trackside and in front row of Main (West) Stand.

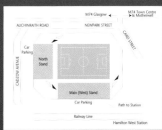

## QUEEN OF THE SOUTH: PALMERSTON PARK

Palmerston Park can be reached by the following routes:
**BUSES:** Buses from Glasgow, Edinburgh, Ayr and Stranraer all pass within a short distance of the park.
**TRAINS:** There is a reasonable service to Dumfries Station from Glasgow on Saturdays, but the service is more limited in midweek. The station is about ³/₄ mile from the ground.
**CARS:** The car park may be reached from Portland Drive or King Street and has a capacity for approximately 174 cars. Please note that the car park is closed 30 minutes prior to kick-off.
**CAPACITY:** 6,412; Seated 3,509, Standing 2,903
**PITCH DIMENSIONS:** 112 yds x 73 yds (102 x 67m)
**FACILITIES FOR DISABLED SUPPORTERS:** Situated in East Stand including toilets.

## ROSS COUNTY: VICTORIA PARK STADIUM

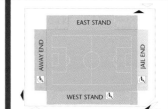

The following routes may be used to reach Victoria Park Stadium:
**BUSES:** Regular buses on a daily basis from Glasgow, Edinburgh and Perth.
**TRAINS:** The nearest mainline station is Inverness and fans travelling from the south should alight and board a train that takes them direct to Dingwall Station.
**CARS:** The major trunk roads, A9 and A96, connect Dingwall with the North, the South and the East.

**CAPACITY:** 6,310, Seated 2,590, Standing 3,720
**PITCH DIMENSIONS:** 115 yds x 74 yds (105 x 68m)
**FACILITIES FOR DISABLED SUPPORTERS:** Areas in Main Stand and Terracing. Toilet facilities are also available.

## ST. JOHNSTONE: McDIARMID PARK

The following routes can be used to reach McDiarmid Park:
**BUSES:** Local services nos. 1 and 2 pass near the ground. Both leave from Mill Street in the town centre.
**TRAINS:** Perth Station is well served by trains from all parts of the country. The station is about 40 minutes walk from the park.
**CARS:** The car park at the park holds 1,500 cars and 100 coaches. Vehicles should follow signs A9 to Inverness on Perth City by-pass, then follow "Football Stadium" signs at Inveralmond Roundabout South onto slip road adjacent to McDiarmid Park. Vehicle charges are £2.00 for cars and no charge for coaches.
**CAPACITY:** 10,723 (All Seated)
**PITCH DIMENSIONS:** 115 yds x 75 yds (105 x 68m)
**FACILITIES FOR DISABLED SUPPORTERS:** Entrance via south end of West Stand and south end of East Stand. Visiting disabled fans should contact the club in advance. Headphones available in West and North Stands for blind and partially sighted supporters.

## ST. MIRREN: ST. MIRREN PARK

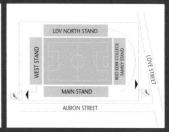

St. Mirren Park can be reached by the following routes:
**BUSES:** All SMT coastal services, plus buses to Johnstone and Kilbarchan, pass within 300 yards of the ground.
**TRAINS:** There is a frequent train service from Glasgow Central Station and all coastal routes pass through Gilmour Street. The ground is about half a mile from the station.
**CARS:** The only facilities for car parking are in the streets surrounding the ground.
**CAPACITY:** 10,752; (All Seated)
**PITCH DIMENSIONS:** 112 yds x 73 yds (102 x 67m)

**FACILITIES FOR DISABLED SUPPORTERS:** Full wheelchair facilities available for visiting supporters in the Caledonia Stand.

## STRANRAER: STAIR PARK

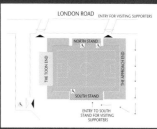

Stair Park can be reached by the following routes:
**BUSES:** Two services pass the park. These are the buses from Glenluce to Portroadie and the Dumfries-Stranraer service.
**TRAINS:** There is a regular service of trains from Ayr and the station is only 1 mile from the ground.
**CARS:** Car parking is available in the Public Park at the ground, where there is space for approximately 50 vehicles and also in the side streets around the park. Signs for away supporters will be displayed and parking situated at Stranraer Academy, McMasters Road.
**CAPACITY:** 6,000; Seated 1,830, Standing 4,170
**PITCH DIMENSIONS:** 110 yds x 70 yds (101 x 64m)
**FACILITIES FOR DISABLED SUPPORTERS:** By prior arrangement with Club Secretary.

ALLOA ATHLETIC F.C.
Recreation Park,
Clackmannan Road, Alloa, FK10 1RY
**TELEPHONE NUMBERS**
Ground (01259) 722695
Sec. Bus. (01324) 619708/626996
Sec. Home. (01259) 722696
**FAX** (01259) 210886
**E-MAIL** fcadmin@alloaathletic.co.uk
**E-MAIL 2** ewen.cameron@acra.gax.gov.uk
**WEBSITE** www.alloaathletic.co.uk
**CLUB CORRESPONDENCE ADDRESS**
Mr. Ewen G. Cameron
Secretary
Alloa Athletic F.C
2B Church Street, Alloa FK10 1DH
**CHAIRMAN** Ian Henderson
**VICE-CHAIRMAN** Patrick Lawlor
**DIRECTORS**
David R. Murray, Robert F. Hopkins
Ewen G. Cameron, Martin Ross
& Michael Mulraney
**HONORARY PRESIDENT** George Ormiston
**HONORARY DIRECTOR** Ronald J. Todd
**SECRETARY** Ewen G. Cameron
**MANAGER** Tom Hendrie
**FIRST TEAM COACH** Gareth Evans
**HEAD OF YOUTH DEVELOPMENT**
Hugh McCann
**YOUTH CO-ORDINATOR** Robert Wilson
**YOUTH COACHES**
U19: Hugh McCann & Robert Campbell
U17: Derek Brown & Eric Syne
U15: Bob Hutton, Jim McKinnon & John Reid
U14: Tom McPake, Stuart MacGregor &
Walter Matthews
**GOALKEEPING COACH** Alistair Jenkins
**TEAM CAPTAIN** Iain Nicolson
**OFFICE ADMINISTRATOR** Jean Davison
**FOOTBALL SAFETY OFFICERS'**
**ASSOCIATION REPRESENTATIVE**
Robert Wilson (01259) 722695
**COMMERCIAL MANAGER** Mike Mulraney
(B) (01259) 722695 Mobile 07770 440795
**MATCHDAY PROGRAMME EDITOR**
John Glencross
(H) (01786) 817362 Mobile 07939 539282
**CLUB DOCTOR** Dr. Clarke Mullen
**PHYSIOTHERAPISTS**
Vanessa Smith & Stuart Murphy
**GROUNDSMAN** John Robertson
**KIT PERSON** Lachie McKinnon
**CLUB SHOP**
Situated adjacent to Refreshment Kiosk
**CLUB SHOP MANAGERS**
Margaret Glencross & Fiona Gordon
**OFFICIAL SUPPORTERS CLUB**
c/o Recreation Park,
Clackmannan Road, Alloa, FK10 1RY
Contact: Charlotte Glass (01259) 216758
**SHIRT SPONSOR**
Front: Machine Tool Engineers (E.K) Ltd
Back: Clackmannanshire Council
**KIT SUPPLIER** Pendle

# ALLOA ATHLETIC

## LIST OF PLAYERS 2005.06

| PLAYERS SURNAME | FIRST NAME | MIDDLE NAME | DATE OF BIRTH | PLACE OF BIRTH | DATE SIGNED | HEIGHT FT INS | WEIGHT ST LBS | POSITION ON PITCH | PREVIOUS CLUB |
|---|---|---|---|---|---|---|---|---|---|
| Barton | Ross | John | 16/10/89 | Bellshill | 27/07/05 | 5.7 | 8.0 | Defender | Airdrie United |
| Bolochoweckyj | Michael | | 04/05/84 | Edinburgh | 30/08/05 | 6.1 | 11.0 | Defender | Ross County |
| Borthwick | John | Derek | 08/08/89 | Edinburgh | 20/08/05 | 6.3 | 12.7 | Forward | Salvesen B.C. |
| Brown | Andrew | Stewart | 11/10/76 | Edinburgh | 10/06/04 | 6.4 | 14.0 | Forward | Stenhousemuir |
| Brown | Daniel | Michael | 16/11/88 | Stirling | 19/07/05 | 5.9 | 10.10 | Midfield | St. Johnstone |
| Brown | Graeme | Robert | 08/11/80 | Johannesburg | 12/03/05 | 5.11 | 13.0 | Forward | Ayr United |
| Caine | David | | 22/07/89 | Bellshill | 27/07/05 | 5.8 | 9.7 | Midfield | Airdrie United |
| Capuano | Giuseppe | | 08/01/89 | Auxerre | 02/09/05 | 5.10 | 11.2 | Defender | Livingston B.C. |
| Carr | Jamie | | 22/03/88 | Glasgow | 19/07/05 | 5.11 | 11.2 | Defender | Alloa Athletic Form D U* |
| Comrie | Alan | MacIver | 05/11/87 | Stirling | 22/07/05 | 5.10 | 11.0 | Midfield | Falkirk |
| Dallas | Allan | | 20/07/88 | Bellshill | 30/08/05 | 5.9 | 11.0 | Defender | Kilmarnock |
| Devanney | Liam | | 27/08/90 | Dunfermline | 30/08/05 | 5.10 | 10.7 | Midfield | Alloa Athletic Form D U* |
| Evans | James | | 27/01/82 | Glasgow | 25/06/03 | 6.0 | 12.10 | Goalkeeper | Bolton Wanderers |
| Ferguson | Mark | | 02/09/90 | Livingston | 27/07/05 | 6.0 | 11.2 | Defender | Alloa Athletic Form D U* |
| Ferguson | Paul | Alan | 19/05/87 | Edinburgh | 24/08/05 | 6.0 | 11.2 | Goalkeeper | Ross County |
| Fleming | Craig | | 09/06/90 | Glasgow | 20/08/05 | 5.10 | 11.1 | Forward | Stenhousemuir Form D U* |
| Forrest | Fraser | Wilson | 14/09/83 | Galashiels | 27/07/05 | 6.2 | 13.0 | Defender | Sauchie Juniors |
| Forrest | Michael | | 02/05/89 | Stirling | 20/08/05 | 6.0 | 11.3 | Defender | Gairdoch United |
| Fusco | Scott | Murray | 26/06/88 | Edinburgh | 19/07/05 | 6.2 | 11.0 | Defender | Alloa Athletic Form D U* |
| Gaffney | Steven | | 20/05/89 | Glasgow | 30/08/05 | 6.0 | 11.0 | Defender | Livingston B.C. |
| Gordon | Steven | Alexander | 30/09/88 | Edinburgh | 20/08/05 | 6.2 | 13.0 | Defender | Stenhousemuir |
| Grant | John | Neil | 10/02/88 | Edinburgh | 20/08/05 | 6.0 | 11.4 | Midfield | Leith Athletic |
| Greenhill | David | | 08/07/85 | Edinburgh | 27/07/05 | 5.7 | 10.0 | Midfield | Clyde |
| Hamilton | Ross | | 17/06/80 | Falkirk | 31/07/00 | 6.1 | 12.8 | Forward | Stenhousemuir |
| Hardie | John | Alexander | 18/01/88 | Glasgow | 20/08/05 | 6.2 | 12.2 | Forward | Alloa Athletic Form D U* |
| Hobb | Graeme | | 06/04/89 | Edinburgh | 20/08/05 | 5.11 | 10.10 | Midfield | Salvesen B.C. |
| Kelly | Francis | | 29/11/88 | Glasgow | 19/07/05 | 5.9 | 10.7 | Forward | Alloa Athletic Form D U* |
| Learmonth | Steven | James | 25/05/86 | Falkirk | 12/05/05 | 5.10 | 10.7 | Defender | B.P. Under 19's |
| MacInnes | Joseph | | 13/09/88 | Edinburgh | 19/07/05 | 6.2 | 11.10 | Defender | Royston B.C. |
| Manson | Elliot | Garrow | 13/09/89 | Falkirk | 27/07/05 | 5.10 | 10.12 | Midfield | Livingston |
| McDougall | Jamie | | 06/04/89 | Bellshill | 02/09/05 | 5.9 | 10.12 | Defender | Rangers S.A.B.C. |
| McDowell | Ben | | 24/02/89 | Livingston | 27/07/05 | 5.9 | 10.11 | Midfield | Polbeth United |
| McGlynn | Gary | Dominic | 24/11/77 | Falkirk | 27/05/05 | 5.11 | 12.0 | Goalkeeper | Montrose |
| McKnight | John | | 21/11/88 | Bangour | 19/07/05 | 6.1 | 11.8 | Midfield | Raith Rovers |
| Montgomery | Craig | | 08/02/89 | Glasgow | 27/07/05 | 5.10 | 10.13 | Midfield | Stenhousemuir |
| Mortimer | Paul | Thomas | 14/02/80 | Falkirk | 23/07/04 | 6.1 | 12.10 | Defender | East Fife |
| Muir | Ross | John | 11/03/88 | Stirling | 22/07/05 | 6.1 | 12.0 | Forward | East Stirlingshire B.C. |
| Nicholson | Barry | | 18/02/89 | Edinburgh | 20/08/05 | 5.11 | 11.0 | Midfield | Hutchison Vale |
| Nicolson | Iain | | 13/10/76 | Glasgow | 30/06/03 | 5.11 | 12.4 | Defender | Ayr United |
| O'Boyle | Connor | | 03/06/90 | Glasgow | 27/07/05 | 6.3 | 11.10 | Goalkeeper | Abronhill Thistle |
| Ovenstone | John | William | 07/10/82 | Kirkcaldy | 23/10/04 | 6.0 | 13.6 | Defender | Glenrothes Juniors |
| Quitongo | Jose | Manuel | 18/11/74 | Luanda | 06/01/05 | 5.7.5 | 10.7 | Forward | Waterford |
| Sloan | Robert | | 14/07/83 | Paisley | 06/08/05 | 5.9 | 11.10 | Midfield | St. Johnstone |
| Sommerville | Andrew | | 25/07/81 | Lanark | 20/08/05 | 6.0 | 10.13 | Defender | Wishaw B.C. |
| Stanton | Patrick | Thomas | 26/01/88 | Edinburgh | 19/07/05 | 5.11 | 11.0 | Midfield | Bankton B.C. |
| Stevenson | James | | 13/07/84 | Glasgow | 02/02/04 | 5.9 | 10.0 | Forward | Real Mallorca |
| Stuart | Michael | John | 21/05/87 | Edinburgh | 19/07/05 | 6.1 | 11.4 | Midfield | Lothian Thistle |
| Swaney | Scott | | 12/10/87 | Edinburgh | 22/07/05 | 5.11 | 10.7 | Defender | Dunfermline Athletic |
| Thomson | Darran | Hunter | 31/01/84 | Edinburgh | 28/07/05 | 5.11 | 11.0 | Defender | Inverness Caledonian This |
| Townsley | Christopher | James | 04/03/85 | Edinburgh | 30/08/05 | 6.1 | 11.8 | Defender | Ross County |
| Walker | Richard | Alan | 08/07/82 | Edinburgh | 13/06/01 | 5.11 | 11.0 | Forward | Whitehill Welfare Col |
| West | Steven | | 21/04/89 | Livingston | 27/07/05 | 5.9 | 10.12 | Goalkeeper | Polbeth United |

### TICKET INFORMATION
**Season Ticket information**

| SEATED | Adult | £150 |
|---|---|---|
| | Juvenile/OAP | £80 |
| STANDING | Adult | £140 |
| | Juvenile/OAP | £70 |

**League Admission Prices**

| SEATED | Adult | £11 |
|---|---|---|
| | Juvenile/OAP | £6 |
| STANDING | Adult | £10 |
| | Juvenile/OAP | £5 |

### MILESTONES:
**Year of formation:** 1883
**Most capped player:** Jock Hepburn
**No. of caps:** 1
**Most League points in a season:**
60 (Division 2 – Season 1921/22)(2 Points for a Win)
76 (Third Division – Season 1997/98)(3 Points for a Win)
**Most League goals scored by a player in a season:**
William Crilley (Season 1921/22)
**No. of goals scored:** 49
**Record Attendance:** 13,000 (-v- Dunfermline Athletic – 26.2.1
**Record Victory:** 9-2 (-v- Forfar Athletic – Division 2, 18.3.193
**Record Defeat:**
0-10 (-v- Dundee – Division 2 and Third Lanark – League Cup

## SEASON STATS 2004.05

| DATE | VENUE | OPPONENTS | ATT | RES | McGlynn G.D. | Walker R.A. | Hill D. | Mortimer P.T. | Bolochoweckyj M. | Townsley C.J. | Nicholas S.A. | Ferguson B.A. | Brown A.S. | Hamilton R. | Daly M. | McLaughlin P.J. | McLeod R. | McMillan A. | McDermott M.R. | Nicolson I. | Callaghan S. | Stevenson J. | Ovenstone J.W. | Evans J. | Calderon J. | Ross I. | Quitongo J.M. | Mackie S.W. | Ebanda H. | Brown G.R. | Thomson D.H. | Learmonth S.J. |
|---|---|---|---|---|---|---|---|---|---|---|---|---|---|---|---|---|---|---|---|---|---|---|---|---|---|---|---|---|---|---|---|---|
| 7-Aug | A | Stranraer | 479 | 0-3 | 1 | 2 | 3 | 4 | 5 | 6 | 7 | 8 | 9 | 10 | 11 | 12 | 14 | 15 | | | | | | | | | | | | | | |
| 14-Aug | H | Forfar Athletic | 446 | 2-3 | 1 | 2 | 3 | 4 | 5 | 6 | 12 | **7** | **9** | 10 | 11 | 8 | | 15 | | | | | | | | | | | | | | |
| 21-Aug | A | Stirling Albion | 1,069 | 0-2 | 1 | 2 | 3 | 4 | 5 | 6 | 7 | 8 | 9 | 10 | | 11 | | | 16 | 12 | | | | | | | | | | | | |
| 28-Aug | A | Brechin City | 428 | 0-4 | 1 | 2 | 3 | | 5 | 4 | 12 | 8 | 9 | 10 | 7 | | 6 | | 15 | 16 | 11 | | | | | | | | | | | |
| 4-Sep | H | Ayr United | 585 | 1-3 | 1 | 14 | | | 5 | 6 | 9 | | | 10 | 8 | 12 | 16 | 7 | 3 | **4** | 11 | | | | | | | | | | | |
| 11-Sep | A | Berwick Rangers | 295 | 3-2 | 1 | 2 | | | 4 | 5 | 6 | 7 | 9 | **10** | 8 | 12 | | | | 3 | **11** | 16 | | | | | | | | | | |
| 19-Sep | H | Dumbarton | 505 | 3-2 | 1 | **2** | | | 4 | 5 | 6 | 7 | | 10 | 8 | 12 | 14 | 15 | 3 | 11 | 9 | | | | | | | | | | | |
| 25-Sep | H | Morton | 1,056 | 1-6 | 1 | 9 | 3 | 4 | 5 | 6 | | | | 8 | 12 | 7 | 14 | 2 | 11 | 10 | | | | | | | | | | | | |
| 2-Oct | A | Arbroath | 431 | 3-0 | 1 | 10 | 3 | 8 | 5 | 6 | | | 9 | | 7 | 4 | | | 14 | 2 | 11³ | 14 | | | | | | | | | | |
| 16-Oct | A | Forfar Athletic | 411 | 1-3 | 1 | 10 | 3 | 8 | 5 | 6 | | **9** | | | 7 | 4 | | | | 2 | 11 | 12 | | | | | | | | | | |
| 23-Oct | H | Stranraer | 492 | 1-2 | 1 | 10 | 3 | 8 | 4 | 5 | | 16 | 9 | | | **7** | | | 15 | 2 | 11 | 12 | 6 | | | | | | | | | |
| 30-Oct | H | Brechin City | 474 | 2-2 | 1 | 10 | | 8 | 4 | 5 | 3 | **9** | | 2 | | | | 16 | | 2 | 11 | 7 | **6** | 12 | | | | | | | | |
| 6-Nov | A | Ayr United | 1,218 | 3-4 | 1 | 10 | | 8 | 4 | 5 | 3 | **9** | | 12 | | | | 16 | | 2 | 11 | 7 | 6 | 1 | | | | | | | | |
| 13-Nov | H | Berwick Rangers | 462 | 2-2 | | 8 | | | 4 | 5 | 3 | **9** | **10** | **12** | | | | 15 | | 2 | 11 | 7 | 6 | 1 | | | | | | | | |
| 20-Nov | A | Dumbarton | 522 | 1-0 | 7 | **3** | 12 | 4 | 5 | | | 9 | | 8 | | | | 15 | | 2 | 11 | 10 | 6 | 1 | | | | | | | | |
| 4-Dec | A | Morton | 2,357 | 2-2 | 7 | 3 | 12 | **4** | 5 | | 14 | **9** | | 8 | | | | | | 2 | 11 | 10 | 6 | 1 | 16 | | | | | | | |
| 18-Dec | H | Arbroath | 435 | 4-2 | 7 | 3 | | **4²** | **5** | | 10 | 9 | 15 | 8 | | | | | | 2 | 11 | 14 | 6 | 1 | 16 | | | | | | | |
| 27-Dec | A | Stranraer | 596 | 1-0 | 7 | | | 4 | 5 | | 3 | 9 | 15 | 8 | | | | | | 2 | 11 | **10** | 6 | 1 | | | | | | | | |
| 1-Jan | A | Brechin City | 604 | 3-2 | 7 | | | 4 | 5 | | 3 | 9 | **10** | 12 | | | | | | 2 | 11 | 8 | 6 | 1 | | | | | | | | |
| 15-Jan | H | Ayr United | 647 | † 5-1 | 7 | | | 4 | 5 | | 8 | **9** | **10** | 12 | | | | | | 2 | | 11 | 6 | 1 | 16 | **3** | 14 | | | | | |
| 29-Jan | H | Dumbarton | 608 | 4-2 | 2 | 14 | 4 | | | **8** | **9** | 10 | 12 | | | | | | | 5 | | 11 | 6 | 1 | | **3** | **7** | 16 | | | | |
| 12-Feb | A | Arbroath | 525 | 1-2 | 2 | | | 4 | 5 | | 8 | 9 | 10 | | | | | | | 3 | | 11 | 6 | 1 | | | 7 | | | | | |
| 19-Feb | A | Stirling Albion | 1,135 | 4-0 | 2 | 14 | | 4 | 5 | | 8 | 9 | 10 | 12 | | | | | | 3 | | 11 | **6** | 1 | | | **7²** | | | | | |
| 26-Feb | H | Forfar Athletic | 516 | 0-2 | | | 3 | | 4 | 5 | 8 | 9 | 10 | 12 | | | | | | 2 | | 11 | 6 | 1 | | | 7 | | 16 | | | |
| 5-Mar | A | Ayr United | 1,003 | 1-1 | 2 | | | 4 | 5 | | 8 | 9 | **10** | | | | | | | 3 | | 11 | 6 | 1 | | | 7 | | | | | |
| 8-Mar | H | Stirling Albion | 626 | 1-1 | 2 | | | 4 | **5** | | 8 | 9 | 10 | | | | | | | 3 | | 11 | 6 | 1 | | | 7 | | | | | |
| 12-Mar | H | Brechin City | 522 | 1-1 | 2 | | | 4 | 5 | | **8** | 9 | 10 | | | | | | | 3 | | 11 | 6 | 1 | | | 7 | | 16 | | | |
| 19-Mar | H | Berwick Rangers | 452 | 2-2 | 2 | | | 4 | 5 | | 8 | 9 | 10 | 14 | | | | | | 12 | | 11 | 6 | 1 | | **3** | **7** | | 16 | | | |
| 26-Mar | A | Morton | 959 | 2-2 | | | | 15 | 4 | 5 | 8 | 16 | 10 | 14 | | | | | | 2 | | 11 | **6** | 1 | | 3 | **7** | | 9 | | | |
| 26-Mar | A | Berwick Rangers | 306 | 1-2 | 2 | | | | 4 | 5 | 8 | | 12 | | | | | | | 10 | | **11** | 6 | 1 | | 12 | 7 | | 9 | 3 | | |
| 2-Apr | A | Dumbarton | 787 | 2-3 | 2 | | | | 4 | 5 | 8 | | **10** | 16 | | | | | | | | 11 | 6 | 1 | | 3 | 7 | | **9** | | | |
| 9-Apr | H | Arbroath | 502 | 2-2 | 2 | | | 15 | 4 | 5 | 8 | | 10 | | | | | | | | | 11 | 6 | 1 | | **3** | 7 | | 9 | | | |
| 16-Apr | A | Morton | 2,721 | 0-2 | 1 | 2 | | 15 | 4 | 5 | 8 | | 10 | | | | | | | | | 11 | 6 | | | 3 | 7 | | 9 | | | |
| 23-Apr | H | Stirling Albion | 921 | 3-0 | 1 | 2 | | | **4** | 5 | 8 | | **10** | | | | | | | 12 | | 11 | 6 | 1 | | 3 | **7** | | 9 | | | |
| 30-Apr | A | Forfar Athletic | 453 | 1-1 | 1 | | 5 | 4 | | 16 | 12 | | 10 | 8 | | | | | | 2 | | 14 | 6 | | **11** | | 7 | | 9 | 3 | | |
| 7-May | H | Stranraer | 606 | 3-0 | 12 | | | 4 | 5 | | **8** | | 10 | | | | | | | 2 | | 14 | 6 | 1 | | **11** | 7 | | 9 | 3 | | 16 |
| **TOTAL FULL APPEARANCES** | | | | | 16 | 32 | 13 | 13 | 34 | 34 | 5 | 26 | 25 | 25 | 16 | 4 | 1 | 2 | 1 | 26 | 16 | 24 | 26 | 20 | 1 | 9 | 16 | | | 8 | 3 | |
| **TOTAL SUB APPEARANCES** | | | | | | 1 | 2 | 6 | | 1 | 2 | 3 | 1 | 3 | 10 | 5 | 3 | 9 | 4 | 3 | 7 | | 1 | 3 | 1 | 1 | 1 | 1 | 2 | | | 1 |
| **TOTAL GOALS SCORED** | | | | | | 1 | 2 | 7 | 3 | | 6 | 8 | 5 | 2 | | 1 | | | | | 6 | 5 | 3 | 3 | | 1 | 5 | 5 | | 2 | |

Figure in bold denotes goal scored. Secondary smaller figure in bold denotes number of goals scored. † denotes opponent's own goal.

## THE WASPS' 10 YEAR LEAGUE RECORD

| Season | Div | P | W | D | L | F | A | Pts | Pos |
|---|---|---|---|---|---|---|---|---|---|
| 95-96 | T | 36 | 6 | 11 | 19 | 26 | 58 | 29 | 9 |
| 96-97 | T | 36 | 16 | 7 | 13 | 50 | 47 | 55 | 4 |
| 97-98 | T | 36 | 24 | 4 | 8 | 78 | 39 | 76 | 1 |
| 98-99 | S | 36 | 13 | 7 | 16 | 65 | 56 | 46 | 5 |
| 99-00 | S | 36 | 17 | 6 | 13 | 58 | 38 | 64 | 2 |
| 00-01 | F | 36 | 7 | 11 | 18 | 38 | 61 | 32 | 10 |
| 01-02 | S | 36 | 15 | 14 | 7 | 55 | 33 | 59 | 2 |
| 02-03 | F | 36 | 9 | 8 | 19 | 39 | 72 | 35 | 9 |
| 03-04 | S | 36 | 12 | 8 | 16 | 55 | 55 | 44 | 7 |
| 04-05 | S | 36 | 12 | 10 | 14 | 66 | 68 | 46 | 6 |

## LEADING GOALSCORERS:

| Season | Div | Goals | Player |
|---|---|---|---|
| 1995-96 | T | 5 | B. Moffat, S. Rixon |
| 1996-97 | T | 12 | W. Irvine |
| 1997-98 | T | 18 | W. Irvine |
| 1998-99 | S | 15 | M. Cameron, W. Irvine |
| 1999-00 | S | 15 | M. Cameron |
| 2000-01 | F | 9 | R. Hamilton |
| 2001-02 | S | 14 | G. Hutchison |
| 2002-03 | F | 8 | R. Sloan |
| 2003-04 | S | 13 | R. Hamilton |
| 2004-05 | S | 8 | A. Brown |

### ALLOA ATHLETIC PLAYING KITS SEASON 2005.06

FIRST KIT | SECOND KIT | THIRD KIT

# AYR UNITED

**AYR UNITED F.C.**
Somerset Park, Tryfield Place, Ayr KA8 9NB
**TELEPHONE NUMBERS**
Ground/Ticket Office (01292) 263435
**FAX** (01292) 281314
**E-MAIL 1** info@aufc.co.uk
**E-MAIL 2** markmeehan@btconnect.com
**WEBSITE** www.ayrunitedfc.co.uk
**CHAIRMAN** Donald R. Cameron
**VICE-CHAIRMAN**
Mark P. Meehan, LL.B, Dip. L.P
**DIRECTORS**
Hugh L. Cameron, Alan G. Murray,
Lewis Grant & Lachlan Cameron
**ASSOCIATE DIRECTOR** Thomas F. Young
**MANAGING DIRECTOR** Lachlan Cameron
**HONORARY PRESIDENT**
William J. Barr, O.B.E, C. Eng., F.I.C.E.,
F.C.I.O.B., F.I. Mgt.
**COMPANY SECRETARY**
Iain Pearson (0141) 331 0533
**MANAGER** Robert Connor
**ASSISTANT MANAGER** Robert Reilly
**RESERVE COACH** Tom Tait
**FITNESS COACH** John Kerr
**DIRECTOR OF YOUTH DEVELOPMENT**
Thomas F. Young
**YOUTH CO-ORDINATOR**
Eric Morris
**YOUTH COACHES**
U13: Tom Robertson
U12: William Hilligan
**CHIEF SCOUT** John Sommerville
**TEAM CAPTAIN** Raymond Logan
**FOOTBALL SAFETY OFFICERS'**
**ASSOCIATION REPRESENTATIVES**
Thomas F. Young (07796) 085682
**COMMERCIAL MANAGERS**
Lachlan Cameron & Hugh Cameron
**LOTTERY MANAGER**
Andrew Downie (M) 07834 903735
**MEDIA LIAISON PERSON**
Mark Meehan 07768 710752
**MATCHDAY PROGRAMME EDITOR**
Duncan Carmichael
**CLUB DOCTOR**
Dr. David Anderson, M.M., Ch. B., 1997 Glas
**PHYSIOTHERAPIST**
John S. Kerr, L.V.M.C. Inst. of H.T.
**STADIUM MANAGER** Thomas F. Young
**GROUNDSMAN** David Harkness
**KIT PERSON** Gus Hollas
**HOSPITALITY/CATERING MANAGER**
Lynne Martin (07952) 723046
**CLUB SHOP**
Open at Ground
9.00am - 5.00p.m. (Weekdays)
and Home Matches 11.00a.m. - 3.00p.m.
**OFFICIAL SUPPORTERS CLUB**
c/o Ayr United F.C.,
Somerset Park, Ayr, KA8 9NB
**SHIRT SPONSOR**
First Choice: G&S Bakers Home Bakery Ayr
Second Choice: Honest Men Trust
**KIT SUPPLIER** TFG

## LIST OF PLAYERS 2005.06

| PLAYERS SURNAME | FIRST NAME | MIDDLE NAME | DATE OF BIRTH | PLACE OF BIRTH | DATE SIGNED | HEIGHT FT INS | WEIGHT ST LBS | POSITION ON PITCH | PREVIOUS CLUB |
|---|---|---|---|---|---|---|---|---|---|
| Boyd | Stuart | | 15/04/78 | Hamilton | 11/03/05 | 5.10 | 10.7 | Mid / Fwd | Glenafton Athletic Junior |
| Buckley | Richard | | 25/01/85 | Rutherglen | 04/03/05 | 6.0 | 11.6 | Defender | Aberdeen |
| Campbell | Martin | | 17/01/81 | Irvine | 05/07/05 | 6.3 | 15.0 | Defender | Irvine Meadow Juniors |
| Casey | Mark | Charles | 09/10/82 | Glasgow | 20/07/05 | 6.0 | 11.11 | Midfield | St. Patricks Athletic |
| Cashmore | Ian | | 19/02/83 | Irvine | 27/06/05 | 5.9 | 11.10 | Forward | Kilwinning Rangers Junior |
| Conway | Craig | Ian | 02/05/85 | Irvine | 03/03/04 | 5.9 | 12.2 | Midfield | Irvine Meadow Juniors |
| Essler | Andrew | | 15/11/76 | Glasgow | 19/07/05 | 5.9 | 11.8 | Defender | Maryhill Juniors |
| Hyslop | Paul | | 12/10/78 | Irvine | 04/07/05 | 6.2 | 13.8 | Midfield | Auchinleck Talbot Junior |
| Johnson | Darren | Michael | 08/03/86 | Irvine | 27/06/05 | 5.11 | 12.10 | Goalkeeper | Girvan Juniors |
| Logan | Raymond | | 20/09/78 | Bellshill | 27/06/05 | 6.1 | 12.5 | Midfield | Pollok Juniors |
| Maisano | John | Marcel | 06/01/79 | Melbourne | 15/06/05 | 5.8 | 10.10 | Midfield | Morton |
| McGeown | Mark | | 10/05/70 | Paisley | 13/06/05 | 5.11 | 11.6 | Goalkeeper | Airdrie United |
| McKinstry | James | Anthony | 03/07/79 | Glasgow | 04/06/05 | 6.0 | 12.7 | Defender | Dumbarton |
| McLaughlin | Barry | John | 19/04/73 | Paisley | 08/07/04 | 6.1 | 13.1 | Defender | Kilmarnock |
| Phillips | Eric | | 30/12/69 | Paisley | 18/08/05 | 6.3 | 14.7 | Goalkeeper | Auchinleck Talbot Junior |
| Ramsay | Douglas | | 26/04/79 | Irvine | 21/07/05 | 5.11 | 12.6 | Midfield | Motherwell |
| Reid | Andrew | James | 26/09/85 | Irvine | 25/01/05 | 6.1 | 12.0 | Forward | Blackburn Rovers |
| Robertson | Christopher | | 12/03/81 | Irvine | 27/06/05 | 6.2 | 11.0 | Defender | Hurlford United Junior |
| Strain | Christopher | Robert | 25/03/80 | Irvine | 22/07/05 | 5.10 | 11.0 | Midfield | Troon Juniors |
| Tait | Thomas | | 08/09/67 | Ayr | 20/10/04 | 5.11 | 13.4 | Midfield | Albion Rovers |
| Vareille | Jerome | | 01/06/74 | Vernoux | 04/07/05 | 6.0 | 12.8 | Forward | Airdrie United |
| Wardlaw | Gareth | William | 07/03/79 | Kirkcaldy | 13/01/05 | 5.11 | 12.7 | Forward | Burntisland Shipyard |
| Weaver | Paul | | 27/02/86 | Irvine | 30/07/05 | 5.7 | 10.13 | Midfield | Blackburn Rovers |

## TICKET INFORMATION

**Season Ticket Prices**

**Seated**
**Centre Stand**
Adult £210
OAP £110
**Wing Stand**
Adult £185
Juvenile/OAP £95
**Family Stand**
Adult/Juvenile £185
Additional Juvenile £50

**Standing**
Ground/Enclosure
Adult £145
Juvenile/OAP £60
Adult & Juvenile £185

**League Admission Prices**

**Seated**

**Main Stand**
Adult £14
Juvenile/OAP £10

**Family Stand**
Adult/Juvenile £12
(Plus £5.00 For
Each Additional Juvenile)

**Standing**
Ground/Enclosure
Adult £10
Juvenile/OAP £5

## MILESTONES:

**Year of formation:** 1910
**Most capped player:** Jim Nisbett
**No. of caps:** 3
**Most League points in a season:**
61 (Second Division – Season 1987/88) (2 Points for a Win)
77 (Second Division – Season 1996/97) (3 Points for a Win)
**Most League goals scored by a player in a season:**
Jimmy Smith (Season 1927/28)
**No. of goals scored:** 66
**Record Attendance:** 25,225 (-v- Rangers – 13.9.1969)
**Record Victory:** 11-1 (-v- Dumbarton – League Cup, 13.8.19[...]
**Record Defeat:** 0-9 (-v- Rangers, Heart of Midlothian,
Third Lanark – Division 1)

# SEASON STATS 2004.05

**BELL'S** SCOTTISH FOOTBALL LEAGUE

## SEASON STATS 2004.05

| DATE | VENUE | OPPONENTS | ATT | RES | Roy L. | Lyle W. | McGrady S.I. | Chaplain S. | McLaughlin B.J. | Smyth M. | Connolly P.M. | Dunning A. | Kean S. | Henderson D.R. | Conway C.I. | Dunlop M. | Ramsay D. | Ferguson A.D. | Burgess R.G. | Cargill A. | Ferguson S. | O'Neill M.A.M. | Craig D.W. | Brown G.R. | Mackay D. | Hillcoat J.G. | Doyle J. | Cherrie P. | McCulloch S.A.J. | Gilmour N. | Tait T. | Wardlaw G.W.R. | Nesovic A. | Reid A.J. | Buckley R. | Boyd S. | Johnson D.M. | Crawford S. | Templeton P.J.J. |
|---|---|---|---|---|---|---|---|---|---|---|---|---|---|---|---|---|---|---|---|---|---|---|---|---|---|---|---|---|---|---|---|---|---|---|---|---|---|---|---|---|
| 7-Aug | A | Dumbarton | 1,016 | 0-1 | 1 | 2 | 3 | 4 | 5 | 6 | 7 | 8 | 9 | 10 | 11 | 12 | | 14 | 16 | | | | | | | | | | | | | | | | | | | | |
| 14-Aug | H | Berwick Rangers | 1,342 | 2-1 | 1 | 2 | 3 | 4 | | 7 | **10** | 9 | 11 | | 6 | 8 | | **5** | 12 | 14 | 15 | | | | | | | | | | | | | | | | | | |
| 21-Aug | A | Stranraer | 885 | 1-2 | 1 | 2 | 4 | 5 | 7 | 10 | **9** | 11 | | 3 | 14 | 16 | | 8 | 15 | 6 | | | | | | | | | | | | | | | | | | | |
| 28-Aug | H | Morton | 2,264 | 2-0 | 1 | 2 | 16 | 5 | 4 | 12 | **10²** | 11 | 7 | 3 | 8 | 15 | | | 6 | | | | 9 | | | | | | | | | | | | | | | | |
| 4-Sep | A | Alloa Athletic | 585 | 3-1 | 1 | 2 | 15 | 6 | 5 | 4 | **10** | 11 | **7²** | 3 | 8 | 14 | | | 9 | 16 | | | | | | | | | | | | | | | | | | | |
| 11-Sep | H | Forfar Athletic | 1,386 | 3-3 | 1 | 2 | 14 | 6 | 5 | 4 | **10²** | 11 | **7** | 3 | 8 | | | | 9 | 18 | | | | | | | | | | | | | | | | | | | |
| 18-Sep | H | Arbroath | 481 | 0-0 | | 2 | 15 | 6 | 5 | 4 | 16 | | 10 | 11 | 7 | 3 | 8 | 14 | | 9 | 1 | | | | | | | | | | | | | | | | | | |
| 25-Sep | H | Brechin City | 1,399 | 0-1 | 1 | 2 | 6 | 5 | 4 | 12 | 10 | 11 | 7 | 3 | 8 | 9 | 16 | | | 14 | | | | | | | | | | | | | | | | | | | |
| 2-Oct | A | Stirling Albion | 1,022 | 1-1 | 1 | 2 | 15 | 5 | 4 | 10 | 16 | | 11 | 7 | 3 | 6 | **9** | 12 | | 8 | | | | | | | | | | | | | | | | | | | |
| 16-Oct | A | Berwick Rangers | 403 | 1-0 | 1 | 2 | 8 | 6 | 5 | 4 | 10 | 7 | **9** | 11 | 3 | 16 | | 14 | | | | | | | | | | | | | | | | | | | | | |
| 23-Oct | H | Dumbarton | 1,468 | 0-1 | 1 | 2 | 8 | 6 | 5 | 4 | 10 | 7 | 9 | 11 | 3 | 16 | 12 | 15 | | | | | | | | | | | | | | | | | | | | | |
| 30-Oct | A | Morton | 3,232 | 1-0 | 2 | | 5 | | 10 | | **11** | | | 3 | 8 | 9 | 12 | | | | 6 | 1 | 4 | 7 | 14 | | | | | | | | | | | | | | |
| 6-Nov | H | Alloa Athletic | 1,218 | 4-3 | 2 | | 5 | **4** | 10 | | **9²** | | | 3 | 7 | 12 | | | 8 | 1 | 6 | 11 | 15 | 16 | | | | | | | | | | | | | | | |
| 13-Nov | A | Forfar Athletic | 518 | 3-2 | 2 | 15 | 5 | **4** | 10 | 9 | | | | 3 | 7 | 12 | | | 1 | 6 | 11 | 8 | 14 | | | | | | | | | | | | | | | | |
| 27-Nov | H | Arbroath | 1,189 | 1-1 | 2 | | 5 | 4 | 9 | 11 | 7 | 3 | | | | | | | 1 | **6** | | 8 | 15 | | | | | | | | | | | | | | | | |
| 4-Dec | A | Brechin City | 576 | 0-5 | 2 | | 5 | 4 | 9 | 11 | 7 | 3 | | | | | | | 1 | 6 | 14 | 8 | | | | | | | | | | | | | | | | | |
| 18-Dec | H | Stirling Albion | 1,288 | 3-2 | 1 | 2 | 16 | 5 | 4 | 11 | 7 | 9 | 15 | | 3 | | 6 | **14²** | 8 | | | | | | | | | | | | | | | | | | | | |
| 27-Dec | A | Dumbarton | 1,118 | 1-1 | 1 | 2 | 6 | 5 | 4 | **10** | 11 | 7 | 12 | | 17 | 3 | 8 | 9 | | | | | | | | | | | | | | | | | | | | | |
| 1-Jan | H | Stranraer | 1,467 | 0-1 | 12 | 6 | 15 | 5 | 4 | 8 | 11 | 7 | 3 | | 1 | | | | 2 | 10 | | | | | | | | | | | | | | | | | | | |
| 3-Jan | H | Morton | 2,455 | 2-1 | 12 | 6 | 16 | 5 | 4 | **8** | 11 | 7 | 3 | | **9** | 15 | | | 1 | | | | | 2 | 10 | | | | | | | | | | | | | | |
| 15-Jan | A | Alloa Athletic | 647 | †1-5 | 2 | 6 | | 5 | | 12 | 11 | 7 | 4 | | 9 | | | 14 | | 1 | 15 | | 3 | 8 | 10 | | | | | | | | | | | | | | |
| 29-Jan | A | Arbroath | 426 | 0-2 | 1 | 4 | 6 | 5 | | 8 | | 17 | 15 | 9 | | | 16 | | | 2 | | | 3 | 10 | 14 | | | | | | | | | | | | | | |
| 12-Feb | A | Stirling Albion | 711 | 0-2 | 1 | 2 | 3 | 10 | 5 | 4 | 8 | 11 | 7 | | 12 | | | | | 14 | | | 16 | 6 | 9 | | | | | | | | | | | | | | |
| 19-Feb | A | Stranraer | 619 | 3-1 | **2** | 12 | 7 | 5 | 4 | 10 | 11 | | 3 | | | | | | | 16 | **6** | | 8 | **9** | 15 | | | | | | | | | | | | | | |
| 26-Feb | H | Berwick Rangers | 1,019 | 0-1 | 1 | 2 | 12 | 11 | 5 | 4 | 10 | 7 | 3 | | | | | | 14 | 6 | | 8 | 9 | 16 | | | | | | | | | | | | | | |
| 5-Mar | H | Alloa Athletic | 1,003 | 1-1 | 1 | 3 | 5 | 4 | **8** | | | | 11 | 12 | | | | | 10 | 16 | 6 | 9 | 7 | 2 | | | | | | | | | | | | | | |
| 12-Mar | A | Morton | 2,448 | 1-2 | 1 | 3 | 5 | **4** | 8 | 6 | 7 | 15 | | | | | | 17 | | 12 | 9 | 11 | 2 | 10 | | | | | | | | | | | | | | |
| 15-Mar | H | Brechin City | 737 | 0-1 | 2 | 16 | 5 | 4 | 12 | 3 | 11 | 8 | 14 | | 1 | | | | 6 | 9 | 7 | 10 | | | | | | | | | | | | | | | | | |
| 19-Mar | A | Forfar Athletic | 490 | 0-1 | 1 | 2 | 12 | 5 | 4 | 9 | 3 | 11 | | | | | | | 6 | | 7 | 10 | 17 | | | | | | | | | | | | | | | | |
| 26-Mar | H | Forfar Athletic | 1,076 | 1-0 | 12 | 11 | **10** | 5 | 4 | 9 | 3 | 7 | | | | | | | 1 | 15 | 6 | | 2 | 8 | | | | | | | | | | | | | | | |
| 2-Apr | H | Arbroath | 1,115 | 2-2 | 12 | 11 | **10** | 5 | 4 | 9 | 3 | 7 | 14 | | | | | | 1 | | 6 | | 2 | **8** | | | | | | | | | | | | | | | |
| 9-Apr | H | Stirling Albion | 1,046 | 0-3 | 2 | 11 | 10 | 5 | 4 | 9 | 3 | 7 | 15 | | 14 | | | | 1 | | 6 | | 12 | 8 | | | | | | | | | | | | | | | |
| 16-Apr | A | Brechin City | 624 | 0-3 | 2 | 10 | 5 | 4 | 12 | 3 | 9 | | | | 1 | 11 | | | 6 | | | 7 | 8 | | 15 | | | | | | | | | | | | | | |
| 23-Apr | H | Stranraer | 1,367 | 0-0 | 1 | 2 | 7 | 4 | 15 | 11 | 3 | 9 | 15 | | | | | | 10 | | 6 | | 16 | 5 | 8 | | | | | | | | | | | | | | |
| 30-Apr | A | Berwick Rangers | 425 | 1-2 | 1 | 2 | 11 | 14 | 5 | 4 | **9** | 3 | 12 | | | | | | 10 | | 6 | | 16 | 7 | 8 | | | | | | | | | | | | | | |
| 7-May | H | Dumbarton | 1,236 | 1-1 | 1 | 2 | 11 | 5 | **4** | 7 | 16 | 3 | 15 | | | | | | 6 | | 9 | | 12 | 10 | | | | | | | | | | | | | | | |
| **TOTAL FULL APPEARANCES** | | | | | 22 | 29 | 19 | 16 | 34 | 33 | 27 | 3 | 14 | 29 | 22 | 24 | 14 | 10 | 1 | 2 | 1 | 5 | 9 | 7 | 5 | 10 | 3 | 22 | 11 | 1 | 3 | 9 | 10 | 1 | | | | |
| **TOTAL SUB APPEARANCES** | | | | | 4 | 7 | 7 | | 7 | 1 | 1 | | 4 | 5 | 16 | 3 | 2 | 5 | 2 | 6 | 1 | 2 | 4 | 1 | 1 | 3 | 4 | | 5 | 2 | | | 1 | 1 | | | | |
| **TOTAL GOALS SCORED** | | | | | | | 1 | | 2 | | 4 | 7 | 10 | 1 | 3 | | | 3 | 1 | | | | 2 | | 3 | | | 1 | | | | | | | | |

*Figure in bold denotes goal scored. Secondary smaller figure in bold denotes number of goals scored. † denotes opponent's own goal.*

## THE HONEST MEN'S 10 YEAR LEAGUE RECORD

| Season | Div | P | W | D | L | F | A | Pts | Pos |
|---|---|---|---|---|---|---|---|---|---|
| 95-96 | S | 36 | 11 | 12 | 13 | 40 | 40 | 45 | 6 |
| 96-97 | S | 36 | 23 | 8 | 5 | 61 | 33 | 77 | 1 |
| 97-98 | F | 36 | 10 | 10 | 16 | 40 | 56 | 40 | 7 |
| 98-99 | F | 36 | 19 | 5 | 12 | 66 | 42 | 62 | 3 |
| 99-00 | F | 36 | 10 | 18 | 8 | 42 | 52 | 38 | 7 |
| 00-01 | F | 36 | 19 | 12 | 5 | 73 | 41 | 69 | 2 |
| 01-02 | F | 36 | 13 | 13 | 10 | 53 | 44 | 52 | 6 |
| 02-03 | F | 36 | 12 | 9 | 15 | 34 | 44 | 45 | 6 |
| 03-04 | F | 36 | 6 | 13 | 17 | 37 | 58 | 31 | 9 |
| 04-05 | S | 36 | 11 | 9 | 16 | 39 | 54 | 42 | 8 |

## LEADING GOALSCORERS:

| Season | Div | Goals | Player |
|---|---|---|---|
| 1995-96 | S | 5 | B. Bilsland, I. English |
| 1996-97 | S | 14 | S. Kerrigan |
| 1997-98 | F | 10 | L. D'Jaffo |
| 1998-99 | F | 18 | G. Hurst |
| 1999-00 | F | 14 | G. Hurst |
| 2000-01 | F | 18 | E. Annand |
| 2001-02 | F | 14 | E. Annand |
| 2002-03 | F | 7 | S. Kean |
| 2003-04 | F | 9 | S. Kean |
| 2004-05 | S | 10 | S. Kean |

### AYR UNITED PLAYING KITS SEASON 2005.06

FIRST KIT  SECOND KIT  THIRD KIT

# DUMBARTON

**DUMBARTON F.C.**

Strathclyde Homes Stadium, Dumbarton

Castle, Castle Road, Dumbarton, G82 1JJ

**TELEPHONE NUMBERS**

Ground (01389) 762569

Sec. Bus. (01389) 723510

Sec. Home (01389) 602567

Sec. Mobile 07796 881002

**FAX** (01389) 762629

**E-MAIL** david_prophet58@hotmail.com

**E-MAIL 2** dumbarton.footballclub@btopenworld.com

**WEBSITE** www.dumbartonfootballclub.com

**CHAIRMAN** Neil Rankine

**VICE CHAIRMAN** Colin J. Hosie

**DIRECTORS**

John G. MacFarlane, Callum L. Hosie

Donald McK. MacIntyre, Sidney S. Collumbine

Allan T. Jardine, Stephen Lynch,

Andrew Gemmell & Jack Gammie

**CHIEF EXECUTIVE** John G. MacFarlane

**HONORARY PRESIDENTS**

Ian A. Bell, J.P. & Douglas S. Dalgleish

**SECRETARY** J. David Prophet

**COMPANY SECRETARY** Gilbert Lawrie

**MANAGER** Paul Martin

**ASSISTANT MANAGER** John Gallagher

**GOALKEEPING COACH** Jim Gallacher

**YOUTH COACH**

U19: John Richardson

**CHIEF SCOUT** Willie Hughes

**TEAM CAPTAIN** Paul Ronald

**OFFICE ADMINISTRATOR** Freida McMahon

**FOOTBALL SAFETY OFFICER'S**

**ASSOCIATION REPRESENTATIVE**

Martin Love

(M) 07713 151023 (H) (01389) 602866

**COMMERCIAL MANAGER**

John G. MacFarlane

(M) 07837 540770 (H) (01389) 758905

**LOTTERY MANAGER**

George Park (01389) 763651

**MEDIA LIAISON PERSON** Colin J. Hosie

**MATCHDAY PROGRAMME EDITOR**

Graeme Robertson (0131) 441 5451

**CLUB DOCTOR** Dr. Neil MacKay, MBC, HB

**PHYSIOTHERAPIST**

Lindsay Smart, Chartered Physiotherapist

**GROUND MAINTENANCE** Apex Groundcare

**KIT PERSON** Steven Hunter

**CLUB SHOP**

Situated in ground. Open on home matchdays

and 10.00 a.m. – 4.00 p.m. Mon-Fri

**OFFICIAL SUPPORTERS CLUB**

c/o Dumbarton FC,

Strathclyde Homes Stadium, Castle Road,

Dumbarton, G82 1JJ

**SHIRT SPONSOR** Laphroaig

**KIT SUPPLIER** Vandanel

## LIST OF PLAYERS 2005.06

| PLAYERS SURNAME | FIRST NAME | MIDDLE NAME | DATE OF BIRTH | PLACE OF BIRTH | DATE SIGNED | HEIGHT FT INS | WEIGHT ST LBS | POSITION ON PITCH | PREVIOUS CLUB |
|---|---|---|---|---|---|---|---|---|---|
| Allan | James | | 21/09/79 | Glasgow | 22/01/05 | 5.10 | 11.0 | Midfield | Stirling Albion |
| Allan | Richard | | 04/02/88 | Paisley | 15/09/05 | 5.9 | 10.6 | Midfield | Queen's Park |
| Anderson | Karl | William | 26/03/82 | Irvine | 01/09/04 | 5.11 | 11.0 | Defender | Knightswood Juveniles |
| Ballantyne | Graeme | John | 19/01/88 | Bellshill | 15/09/05 | 5.9 | 10.0 | Goalkeeper | Morton |
| Bannerman | Scott | John | 21/03/79 | Edinburgh | 11/07/05 | 5.7 | 11.0 | Defender | Morton |
| Borris | Ryan | Edward | 07/06/83 | Paisley | 07/06/04 | 5.11 | 11.0 | Forward | St. Peters Juveniles |
| Boyce | Kieran | | 12/07/87 | Alexandria | 20/06/05 | 5.10 | 11.0 | Midfield | Stenhousemuir |
| Brittain | Craig | | 10/01/74 | Glasgow | 14/06/97 | 5.5 | 10.0 | Defender | Ashfield Juniors |
| Burden | Stephen | | 14/06/88 | Greenock | 20/06/05 | 5.9 | 10.5 | Midfield | Greenock Juniors Colts |
| Cannon | Craig | | 01/05/87 | Vale of Leven | 15/09/05 | 6.1.5 | 11.7 | Midfield | St. Johnstone |
| Connell | Graham | | 31/10/74 | Glasgow | 04/06/05 | 5.10 | 11.7 | Midfield | Berwick Rangers |
| Cosh | Christopher | John | 09/01/88 | Alexandria | 20/06/05 | 5.9 | 11.0 | Defender | Gretna |
| Deas | Ryan | | 08/09/87 | Glasgow | 20/06/05 | 5.8 | 9.3 | Midfield | Goldenhill B.C. |
| Dempsie | Mark | William | 19/10/80 | Bellshill | 09/02/05 | 6.1 | 12.10 | Defender | St. Mirren |
| Dillon | John | Peter | 16/12/78 | Vale of Leven | 30/07/99 | 5.7 | 10.5 | Midfield | Clyde |
| Dornan | Scott | Thomas | 30/04/87 | Glasgow | 20/06/05 | 5.10 | 10.0 | Defender | Clyde |
| Ferry | Daniel | | 31/01/77 | Glasgow | 20/05/05 | 5.8 | 10.0 | Midfield | Queen's Park |
| Fitzpatrick | Steven | | 11/08/87 | Glasgow | 18/08/05 | 5.11 | 10.1 | Forward | Paisley United |
| Gaughan | Kevin | | 06/03/78 | Glasgow | 31/08/05 | 6.1 | 13.4 | Defender | Stranraer |
| Gemmell | John | O'Neill | 06/09/84 | Glasgow | 26/01/05 | 6.3 | 14.0 | Forward | Partick Thistle |
| Gentile | Christopher | | 09/09/81 | Glasgow | 04/07/05 | 6.0 | 12.0 | Midfield | Kilsyth Rangers Junior |
| Gledhill | Dean | | 06/06/87 | Swindon | 20/06/05 | 5.10 | 11.0 | Defender | Glen Lusset B.C. |
| Grindlay | Stephen | John | 13/03/82 | Vale of Leven | 02/08/02 | 6.2 | 13.12 | Goalkeeper | Dumbarton Academy |
| Jamieson | Sean | | 20/07/87 | Greenock | 18/08/05 | 6.0 | 11.2 | Defender | Port Glasgow Juniors |
| Love | Andrew | Robert | 16/05/88 | Dumbarton | 20/06/05 | 5.11 | 10.0 | Midfield | St. Mirren |
| Lynn | Christopher | | 12/09/88 | Glasgow | 20/06/05 | 5.11 | 11.0 | Defender | Stenhousemuir |
| MacDonald | Kevin | Graham | 05/02/83 | Glasgow | 23/07/05 | 6.0 | 11.7 | Midfield | Motherwell |
| McLenaghan | David | | 16/04/87 | Glasgow | 04/07/05 | 5.6 | 10.3 | Midfield | East Kilbnde Thistle Junior |
| McMillan | Garry | | 25/11/88 | Paisley | 04/07/05 | 5.10 | 10.7 | Forward | Barrhead B.C. |
| McNaught | David | Andrew | 24/03/88 | Alexandria | 13/07/05 | 5.11 | 11.0 | Forward | Clyde |
| McQuilken | Paul | | 22/06/81 | Glasgow | 04/07/05 | 5.10 | 11.0 | Forward | Kilsyth Rangers Junior |
| Robinson | Robert | | 11/04/88 | Alexandria | 20/06/05 | 5.10 | 10.7 | Defender | St. Mirren |
| Rodgers | Andrew | | 18/10/83 | Falkirk | 14/06/04 | 5.10.5 | 10.1 | Forward | Falkirk |
| Ronald | Paul | | 19/07/71 | Glasgow | 31/01/04 | 6.2 | 12.10 | Forward | Airdrie United |
| Russell | Iain | Thomas | 14/11/82 | Dumfries | 31/01/03 | 5.10 | 11.0 | Forward | Motherwell |
| Scott | Christopher | John | 02/04/87 | Paisley | 18/08/05 | 5.10 | 10.7 | Midfield | Kilbarchan Thistle |
| Smith | James | | 11/07/78 | Glasgow | 19/07/05 | 6.3 | 13.0 | Defender | Brechin City |
| Strain | James | Joseph | 30/12/86 | Bellshill | 15/09/05 | 6.1 | 11.0 | Forward | East Kilbride Thistle |
| Walker | Robert | | 16/06/82 | Glasgow | 30/01/05 | 6.0 | 13.4 | Defender | Hamilton Academical |
| Wight | John | Campbell | 11/12/73 | Alexandria | 04/08/00 | 6.0 | 13.0 | Goalkeeper | Beith Juniors |
| Young | Paul | | 10/07/88 | Glasgow | 04/07/05 | 6.0 | 10.5 | Defender | Barrhead B.C. |

### TICKET INFORMATION

**Season Ticket information**

**Seated**

| | |
|---|---|
| Adult | £135 |
| Juvenile 13-16 years/OAP | £70 |
| Parent & Juvenile | £170 |
| Juvenile up to 12 years | £45 |
| Premier Seat | £150 |
| Parent + 2 children | £200 |
| Parent + 3 children | £230 * |
| 2Parents + 1 child | £295 |
| 2Parents + 2 children | £330 |
| 2Parents + 3 children | £360 * |

* Any additional child above quantity of three add £30 per child

**League Admission Prices**

**Seated**

| | |
|---|---|
| Adult | £11 |
| Juvenile/OAP | £6 |

### MILESTONES:

**Year of formation:** 1872

**Most capped players:** J. Lindsay and J.McAulay

**No. of caps:** 8 each

**Most League points in a season:**

53 (First Division – Season 1986/87) (2 Points for a Win)

61 (Third Division – Season 2001/02) (3 Points for a Win)

**Most League goals scored by a player in a season:**

Kenneth Wilson (Season 1971/72)

**No. of goals scored:** 38

**Record Attendance:** 18,001 (-v- Raith Rovers – 2.3.1957 at Boghead Park) and 2,011 (-v- Morton – 3.1.2004 at Strathclyde Homes Stadium)

**Record Victory:** 13-2 (-v- Kirkintilloch – Scottish Cup)

**Record Defeat:** 1-11 (-v- Ayr United/Albion Rovers)

## SEASON STATS 2004.05

| DATE | VENUE | OPPONENTS | ATT | RES | Grindlay S.J. | McEwan C.G. | Brittain C. | McKinstry J.A. | Dobbins I.A. | Donald B. | Dunn R. | Ronald P. | Herd G.R.W. | Rodgers A. | Dillon J.P. | Borris R.E. | Boyle C.T. | Bradley M. | Bonar S.A. | Russell I.T. | Annand E. | Holmes G. | Allan D. | McGroarty C.M. | Wight J.C. | Walker R. | Allan J. | Gemmell J.O. | Dempsie M.W. | Anderson K.W. |
|---|---|---|---|---|---|---|---|---|---|---|---|---|---|---|---|---|---|---|---|---|---|---|---|---|---|---|---|---|---|---|
| 7-Aug | H | Ayr United | 1,016 | 1-0 | 1 | 2 | 3 | 4 | 5 | 6 | 7 | 8 | 9 | 10 | **11** | | | 14 | 15 | 16 | | | | | | | | | | |
| 14-Aug | A | Arbroath | 505 | 2-0 | 1 | 2 | 3 | 4 | 5 | 6 | | 8 | 16 | 15 | 9 | 11 | | 14 | | | 7 | **10²** | | | | | | | | |
| 21-Aug | H | Morton | 1,670 | 0-3 | 1 | 2 | 3 | 4 | 5 | 6 | 7 | 16 | 9 | 10 | 11 | 14 | | | 15 | 8 | | | | | | | | | | |
| 28-Aug | H | Forfar Athletic | 723 | 0-1 | 1 | 2 | 3 | 4 | 5 | 6 | 14 | 8 | 16 | | 11 | | | | | | 7 | 10 | 9 | 15 | | | | | | |
| 4-Sep | A | Berwick Rangers | 412 | 4-0 | 1 | 2 | 3 | 4 | 5 | **15** | 16 | 6 | | 10 | 11 | | | | | | 14 | 8 | **9³** | 7 | | | | | | |
| 11-Sep | H | Stranraer | 841 | 1-3 | 1 | 2 | 3 | 4 | 5 | 6 | 15 | | | 10 | 11 | | | 14 | 7 | 16 | **9** | 8 | | | | | | | | |
| 18-Sep | A | Alloa Athletic | 505 | 2-3 | 1 | 2 | 3 | | 5 | | 16 | 6 | | **10** | 11 | | 15 | | 12 | | **7** | 9 | 8 | 4 | | | | | | |
| 25-Sep | H | Stirling Albion | 990 | 1-1 | 1 | | 3 | 4 | | 15 | 16 | 10 | | | 6 | | | | 2 | | **7** | 9 | 8 | 5 | 11 | | | | | |
| 2-Oct | A | Brechin City | 503 | 0-4 | 1 | | 3 | 14 | 8 | 15 | | 6 | | | | | | | 7 | 10 | 9 | 16 | 5 | 11 | | | | | | |
| 16-Oct | A | Arbroath | 716 | 1-3 | 1 | **2** | 3 | 4 | 5 | | | 16 | | 11 | 12 | 6 | | | 7 | 10 | 9 | 8 | | 15 | | | | | | |
| 23-Oct | A | Ayr United | 1,468 | 1-0 | 1 | 2 | 3 | 4 | 5 | 9 | | **16** | | 15 | 6 | | | | 7 | 10 | 12 | 8 | | 11 | | | | | | |
| 30-Oct | A | Forfar Athletic | 486 | 2-0 | 1 | 2 | 3 | 4 | | 6 | **9²** | 10 | | | 11 | | | | 7 | 16 | | 8 | 5 | 15 | | | | | | |
| 6-Nov | H | Berwick Rangers | 790 | 3-1 | 1 | 2 | 3 | 4 | 5 | 9 | 15 | **10** | | 11 | 6 | | | | 7 | 16 | 12 | **8** | | | | | | | | |
| 13-Nov | A | Stranraer | 532 | 0-1 | 1 | 2 | | 4 | 5 | 6 | 9 | 8 | | 11 | | | | | 7 | 16 | 12 | | 3 | | | | | | | |
| 30-Nov | H | Alloa Athletic | 522 | 0-1 | 1 | 2 | 3 | 4 | 5 | 8 | 9 | 16 | | 15 | 11 | 6 | | | 7 | 10 | | 12 | | | | | | | | |
| 4-Dec | A | Stirling Albion | 688 | 0-1 | | 3 | 4 | 5 | 6 | 8 | | 9 | | 11 | 7 | 14 | 15 | | 2 | 10 | | 12 | | | | | | | | |
| 27-Dec | H | Ayr United | 1,118 | 1-1 | | 2 | 3 | 4 | 5 | 6 | 8 | 16 | | 11 | 14 | | | | 7 | **10** | 9 | | | | | 1 | | | | |
| 1-Jan | A | Morton | 2,764 | 0-3 | | 2 | 3 | 4 | 5 | 6 | 8 | 16 | | 11 | 12 | | | | 7 | 10 | 9 | 15 | | | | 1 | | | | |
| 3-Jan | H | Forfar Athletic | 714 | 1-1 | | 2 | 3 | 4 | 5 | 6 | | **12** | | 10 | 11 | 8 | 14 | | 7 | 9 | | 16 | | | | 1 | | | | |
| 15-Jan | A | Berwick Rangers | 322 | 3-0 | | 2 | 3 | 4 | 5 | 6 | | **10** | | **11** | 14 | 8 | 15 | | 7 | **9** | | | | | | 1 | | | | |
| 29-Jan | A | Alloa Athletic | 608 | 2-4 | | 2 | | **4** | 5 | | | **11** | | 3 | 8 | 10 | 14 | | 7 | 9 | | | | | 1 | 6 | | 12 | 15 | |
| 5-Feb | H | Stirling Albion | 981 | 0-2 | 1 | 2 | **15** | 4 | 5 | | 6 | | | 8 | 7 | | 12 | | 14 | 8 | | | | | 3 | 11 | 10 | | | |
| 12-Feb | H | Brechin City | 589 | 2-0 | 1 | 2 | 3 | **8** | | 6 | | | | 10 | | | | | 7 | **9** | | | | | 4 | 11 | 16 | 5 | | |
| 19-Feb | H | Morton | 1,508 | 3-0 | 1 | 2 | 3 | 8 | | 16 | | 6 | | 10 | 12 | | 14 | | **7²** | | | | | | 4 | 11 | 9 | 5 | | |
| 26-Feb | A | Arbroath | 502 | 1-2 | 1 | | 3 | 8 | | 2 | | 6 | | 16 | 10 | | | | 7 | **9** | | | | | 4 | 11 | 15 | 5 | | |
| 1-Mar | H | Brechin City | 548 | 1-1 | 1 | **2** | 3 | 16 | | 8 | | | | 9 | 10 | 12 | | | 7 | | | | | | 4 | 11 | 15 | 5 | | |
| 5-Mar | H | Berwick Rangers | 690 | 1-1 | 1 | **2** | 3 | 8 | | 14 | | 6 | | 7 | 10 | | | | 16 | 9 | | | | | 4 | 11 | 15 | 5 | | |
| 12-Mar | A | Forfar Athletic | 443 | 0-6 | 1 | 2 | 3 | 8 | | 6 | | | | 7 | 10 | 12 | | | 16 | 9 | | | | | 4 | 11 | 15 | 5 | | |
| 19-Mar | A | Stranraer | 436 | 1-2 | 1 | **2** | 3 | | | | 6 | | | 16 | 14 | 10 | 8 | | 7 | 12 | | | | | 4 | 11 | 9 | 5 | | |
| 26-Mar | H | Stranraer | 848 | 1-1 | 1 | 2 | 3 | 15 | | | 6 | | | 16 | | 10 | 8 | | **7** | 9 | | | | | 4 | | 11 | 5 | | |
| 2-Apr | H | Alloa Athletic | 787 | 3-2 | 1 | 2 | 3 | 16 | | | 6 | | | 14 | | 11 | 8 | | **7³** | 9 | | | | | 4 | | 12 | 10 | 5 | |
| 9-Apr | H | Brechin City | 777 | 1-1 | 1 | 2 | 3 | | | 6 | 8 | | | 15 | **16** | | 10 | | 7 | 12 | | | | | 4 | 11 | 9 | 5 | | |
| 16-Apr | A | Stirling Albion | 705 | 0-3 | 1 | 2 | 3 | | | 6 | 8 | | | 16 | 14 | 12 | 10 | | | 11 | | | | | 4 | 7 | 9 | 5 | | |
| 23-Apr | A | Morton | 3,229 | 0-0 | 1 | 2 | 3 | 10 | 6 | | | 16 | | 11 | 7 | 8 | 14 | | | 9 | | | | | 4 | | 15 | 5 | | |
| 30-Apr | H | Arbroath | 1,192 | 3-0 | 1 | 2 | 3 | 15 | 6 | | 8 | | | **11** | 7 | **12** | | | 10 | 9 | | | | | 4 | | **14** | 5 | | |
| 7-May | A | Ayr United | 1,236 | 1-1 | | | | | 9 | 14 | 7 | | 16 | | 15 | 6 | 3 | 4 | | 10 | | | | | 1 | 11 | **8** | 5 | 2 | |
| **TOTAL FULL APPEARANCES** | | | | | 30 | 31 | 32 | 28 | 24 | 19 | 8 | 18 | 2 | 17 | 26 | 7 | 18 | 3 | 15 | 25 | 22 | 8 | 4 | 4 | 6 | 16 | 10 | 8 | 14 | 1 |
| **TOTAL SUB APPEARANCES** | | | | | | 1 | 4 | 2 | 4 | 6 | 5 | 1 | | 14 | 5 | 9 | 4 | 12 | 2 | 7 | 6 | 4 | 1 | 2 | | | | 2 | 8 | |
| **TOTAL GOALS SCORED** | | | | | | 4 | 2 | | 1 | 2 | 1 | | 6 | | 4 | | | | 2 | | 11 | 7 | 1 | | | | | | 2 | |

Figure in bold denotes goal scored. Secondary smaller figure in bold denotes number of goals scored. † denotes opponent's own goal.

## THE SONS' 10 YEAR LEAGUE RECORD

| Season | Div | P | W | D | L | F | A | Pts | Pos |
|---|---|---|---|---|---|---|---|---|---|
| 95-96 | F | 36 | 3 | 2 | 31 | 23 | 94 | 11 | 10 |
| 96-97 | S | 36 | 9 | 8 | 19 | 44 | 66 | 35 | 9 |
| 97-98 | T | 36 | 7 | 10 | 19 | 42 | 61 | 31 | 10 |
| 98-99 | T | 36 | 16 | 9 | 11 | 53 | 40 | 57 | 4 |
| 99-00 | T | 36 | 15 | 8 | 13 | 53 | 51 | 53 | 6 |
| 00-01 | T | 36 | 13 | 6 | 17 | 46 | 49 | 45 | 6 |
| 01-02 | T | 36 | 18 | 7 | 11 | 59 | 48 | 61 | 2 |
| 02-03 | S | 36 | 13 | 9 | 14 | 48 | 47 | 48 | 6 |
| 03-04 | S | 36 | 18 | 6 | 12 | 56 | 41 | 60 | 3 |
| 04-05 | S | 36 | 11 | 9 | 16 | 43 | 53 | 42 | 7 |

## LEADING GOALSCORERS:

| Season | Div | Goals | Player |
|---|---|---|---|
| 1995-96 | F | 5 | M. Mooney |
| 1996-97 | S | 7 | H. Ward |
| 1997-98 | T | 10 | C. McKinnon |
| 1998-99 | T | 17 | P. Flannery |
| 1999-00 | T | 14 | P. Flannery |
| 2000-01 | T | 17 | P. Flannery |
| 2001-02 | T | 18 | P. Flannery |
| 2002-03 | S | 8 | P. Flannery, G. McCutcheon |
| 2003-04 | S | 10 | I. Russell |
| 2004-05 | S | 11 | I. Russell |

**DUMBARTON PLAYING KITS SEASON 2005.06**

FIRST KIT — SECOND KIT — THIRD KIT

# FORFAR ATHLETIC

**FORFAR ATHLETIC F.C.**
Station Park,
Carseview Road,
Forfar, DD8 3BT

**TELEPHONE NUMBERS**
Ground (01307) 463576/462259
Sec. Home. (01307) 464924
Sec. Bus. (01307) 475519
Sec. Bus. Fax (01307) 466956
**FAX** (01307) 466956
**E-MAIL** pat@ramsayladders.co.uk
**WEBSITE** www.forfarathletic.co.uk

**CLUB CORRESPONDENCE ADDRESS**
Mr. David McGregor
Secretary
Forfar Athletic F.C.
6 Westfield Crescent, Forfar DD8 1EG

**CHAIRMAN**
David McGregor

**VICE-CHAIRMAN**
Neill McK. Wilson

**DIRECTORS**
Alastair S. Nicoll, Michael S. McEwan,
Gordon Menmuir (Treasurer)
Ronald Blair & James Farquhar

**HONORARY PATRON**
Rt. Hon. Lord Lyell of Kinnordy

**SECRETARY**
David McGregor

**COMPANY SECRETARIES**
Blackadders

**MANAGER**
Raymond Farningham

**ASSISTANT MANAGER**
George Shaw

**TEAM CAPTAIN**
Steven Bonar

**MEDIA LIAISON PERSON**
David McGregor

**MATCHDAY PROGRAMME EDITOR**
Kevin Candy (07841) 703055

**CLUB DOCTORS**
Dr. Peter Dick & Dr. Susan Woodruffe

**PHYSIOTHERAPIST**
Brian McNeill

**ASSISTANT PHYSIOTHERAPIST**
Donald Ritchie

**GROUNDSMAN/KIT PERSON**
Martin Gray

**OFFICIAL SUPPORTERS CLUB**
c/o Mrs. Yvonne Nicoll,
7 Fyfe Jamieson, Forfar
Tel: Home (01307) 467255

**SHIRT SPONSOR**
Universal Telecom

**KIT SUPPLIER**
Paulas Benara

## LIST OF PLAYERS 2005.06

| PLAYERS SURNAME | FIRST NAME | MIDDLE NAME | DATE OF BIRTH | PLACE OF BIRTH | DATE SIGNED | HEIGHT FT INS | WEIGHT ST LBS | POSITION ON PITCH | PREVIOUS CLUB |
|---|---|---|---|---|---|---|---|---|---|
| Barr | Darren | | 17/03/85 | Glasgow | 26/08/05 | 5.10 | 10.4 | Midfield | Falkirk |
| Bonar | Steven | Andrew | 20/05/79 | Glasgow | 15/01/05 | 5.9.5 | 10.6 | Midfield | Dumbarton |
| Brown | Michael | | 07/11/79 | Stranraer | 06/06/01 | 6.1 | 12.8 | Goalkeeper | Partick Thistle |
| Cameron | Martin | George | 16/06/78 | Dunfermline | 12/08/05 | 6.1 | 13.12 | Forward | Shamrock Rovers |
| Connolly | Charles | | 18/07/85 | Glasgow | 09/09/05 | 6.0 | 10.4 | Defender | Albion Rovers |
| Conway | Aaron | | 29/03/85 | Dundee | 28/06/05 | 5.10 | 10.7 | Forward | Dundee |
| Donald | Barry | | 24/12/78 | Glasgow | 27/05/05 | 6.1 | 12.0 | Midfield | Dumbarton |
| Dubourdeau | Francois | | 12/04/80 | Angouleme | 26/08/05 | 6.3 | 13.0 | Goalkeeper | Dundee |
| Dunn | David | Walter | 01/03/84 | Edinburgh | 20/07/04 | 6.2 | 11.10 | Defender | Heart of Midlothian |
| Florence | Steven | | 28/10/71 | Dundee | 18/07/03 | 5.6 | 11.0 | Defender | Arbroath |
| Forrest | Edward | Alexander | 17/12/78 | Edinburgh | 15/06/04 | 6.0 | 12.0 | Defender | Partick Thistle |
| Fraser | Alan | Douglas | 10/10/63 | Musselburgh | 09/08/05 | 6.0 | 14.10 | Goalkeeper | Dumbarton |
| Gribben | Darren | | 27/03/86 | Bellshill | 31/08/05 | 5.11 | 10.12 | Forward | Cowdenbeath |
| King | David | William | 13/07/79 | Falkirk | 28/05/04 | 6.0 | 12.0 | Midfield | Arbroath |
| Lowing | David | | 04/09/83 | Paisley | 02/07/03 | 6.0 | 10.0 | Defender | St. Mirren |
| Lunan | Paul | James | 20/09/82 | Dundee | 04/08/01 | 5.10 | 10.0 | Midfield | Dundee Violet Juniors |
| McClune | David | James | 08/02/83 | Glasgow | 03/07/03 | 5.7 | 10.0 | Defender | St. Johnstone |
| Murdoch | Sean | | 31/07/86 | Edinburgh | 31/08/05 | 6.0 | 10.7 | Goalkeeper | Dunfermline Athletic |
| Rattray | Alan | Raymond | 08/06/79 | Dundee | 16/11/96 | 5.10 | 11.0 | Defender | Dundee Violet Juniors |
| Sellars | Barry | Michael | 06/12/75 | Arbroath | 02/11/00 | 6.1 | 12.10 | Midfield | Clyde |
| Tosh | Paul | James | 18/10/73 | Arbroath | 28/06/01 | 6.1 | 13.4 | Forward | Raith Rovers |
| Voigt | Jon | Werner | 06/10/86 | Arbroath | 19/07/05 | 6.0 | 11.7 | Forward | Dundee |
| Waddell | Richard | | 04/02/81 | Falkirk | 04/02/05 | 5.11 | 11.0 | Forward | Hamilton Academical |

### TICKET INFORMATION
**Season Ticket information**

| SEATED | Adult | £150 |
|---|---|---|
| | Juvenile/OAP | £75 |
| | Juvenile (U12) | £40 |
| STANDING | Adult | £140 |
| | Juvenile/OAP | £70 |
| | Juvenile (U12) | £40 |

**League Admission Prices**

| SEATED | Adult | £11 |
|---|---|---|
| | Juvenile/OAP | £5.50 |
| STANDING | Adult | £10 |
| | Juvenile/OAP | £5 |

### MILESTONES:
**Year of formation:** 1885
**Most League points in a season:**
63 (Second Division – Season 1983/84) (2 Points for a Win)
80 (Third Division – Season 1994/95) (3 Points for a Win)
**Most League goals scored by a player in a season:**
Dave Kilgour (Season 1929/30)
**No. of goals scored:** 45
**Record Attendance:** 10,800 (-v- Rangers – 7.2.1970)
**Record Victory:** 14-1 (-v- Lindertis – Scottish Cup, 1.9.1888)
**Record Defeat:** 2-12 (-v- King's Park – Division 2, 2.1.1930)

# SEASON STATS 2004.05

## SEASON STATS 2004.05

| DATE | VENUE | OPPONENTS | ATT | RES | Brown M. | Rattray A.R. | Lowing D. | Forrest E.A. | King D.W. | McClune D.J. | Sellars B.M. | Lunan P.J. | Tosh P.J. | Shields P.M. | Stein J. | Booth M. | King M. | Maher M.N. | Clark N. | Cameron D. | Ferrie N. | Creer A.W. | Davidson H.N. | Florence S. | Dunn D.W. | Bonar S.A. | Waddell R. | McAlpine J.C. | McKenzie D. |
|---|---|---|---|---|---|---|---|---|---|---|---|---|---|---|---|---|---|---|---|---|---|---|---|---|---|---|---|---|---|
| 7-Aug | H | Brechin City | 766 | 1-0 | 1 | 2 | 3 | 4 | 5 | 6 | **7** | 8 | 9 | 10 | 11 | | | | | | | | | | | | | | |
| 14-Aug | A | Alloa Athletic | 446 | 3-2 | 1 | 2 | 3 | 4 | 5 | 6 | 7 | 8 | $9^{2}$ | 10 | 14 | 11 | 15 | | | | | | | | | | | | |
| 21-Aug | H | Arbroath | 696 | 5-0 | 1 | 2 | 3 | 4 | **5** | 6 | 7 | 8 | 9 | $10^{2}$ | 11 | 14 | 15 | 16 | | | | | | | | | | | |
| 28-Aug | A | Dumbarton | 723 | 1-0 | 1 | 2 | 3 | 4 | 5 | 6 | 7 | 8 | 9 | 10 | 11 | 14 | 15 | | | | | | | | | | | | |
| 4-Sep | H | Stirling Albion | 841 | 0-2 | 1 | 2 | 3 | 4 | 5 | 6 | | 8 | 9 | 10 | 11 | 7 | 14 | | 15 | 16 | | | | | | | | | |
| 11-Sep | A | Ayr United | 1,386 | 3-3 | 1 | 2 | 3 | 4 | 5 | 6 | 7 | 14 | $9^{2}$ | 10 | 11 | 8 | 16 | | | | | | | | | | | | |
| 18-Sep | H | Berwick Rangers | 435 | 1-1 | | 2 | 3 | 4 | 5 | 6 | | 8 | 9 | **10** | 11 | 7 | | | 15 | 16 | 1 | | | | | | | | |
| 25-Sep | H | Stranraer | 524 | 0-1 | | 2 | 3 | 4 | 5 | 6 | 7 | 8 | 9 | 10 | 11 | 12 | | | 15 | 14 | 1 | | | | | | | | |
| 2-Oct | A | Morton | 2,736 | 1-2 | | 2 | 3 | 4 | 5 | 6 | 7 | 8 | 9 | **10** | 11 | | | 14 | | 16 | 1 | | | | | | | | |
| 16-Oct | H | Alloa Athletic | 411 | 3-1 | | 2 | 3 | 4 | 5 | **6** | 7 | | 9 | 10 | 11 | | | 14 | 15 | 16 | | 1 | 8 | | | | | | |
| 23-Oct | A | Brechin City | 869 | 0-2 | | 2 | 3 | 4 | 5 | 6 | 7 | | 9 | 10 | 11 | | | | 15 | | | 1 | 8 | | | | | | |
| 30-Oct | H | Dumbarton | 486 | 0-2 | | 2 | | 4 | 5 | 6 | 7 | | 9 | 10 | 11 | | | 14 | 15 | 16 | | 1 | 8 | 3 | | | | | |
| 6-Nov | A | Stirling Albion | 756 | 1-3 | | 2 | | 4 | 5 | 6 | 7 | 8 | **9** | 10 | 11 | 12 | | 14 | | 16 | | 1 | | 3 | | | | | |
| 13-Nov | H | Ayr United | 518 | 2-3 | | **2** | 3 | 4 | 5 | | 7 | **8** | 9 | 10 | 11 | | | | 15 | | | 1 | 6 | | | | | | |
| 20-Nov | A | Berwick Rangers | 294 | 0-1 | 1 | 2 | 3 | 4 | 5 | 6 | 7 | 8 | 9 | 10 | 11 | | | 14 | 15 | | | | | | | | | | |
| 4-Dec | A | Stranraer | 411 | 0-1 | 1 | 2 | 3 | 4 | 5 | 6 | 7 | 8 | 9 | 10 | 11 | 12 | | | | | | | | | | | | | |
| 27-Dec | H | Brechin City | 901 | 1-3 | 1 | 2 | 3 | 4 | | 6 | | 8 | 9 | 10 | 11 | | | 14 | 15 | 16 | | 7 | | 5 | | | | | |
| 1-Jan | A | Arbroath | 825 | 2-0 | 1 | 2 | 3 | 4 | | 6 | 7 | 8 | | **10** | **11** | | | 14 | | 16 | | | | 5 | | | | | |
| 8-Jan | A | Dumbarton | 714 | 1-1 | 1 | 2 | 3 | 4 | | 6 | 7 | 8 | 9 | 10 | 11 | 12 | | | 15 | 16 | | | | 5 | | | | | |
| 15-Jan | H | Stirling Albion | 501 | 4-1 | 1 | | 3 | 4 | | | | 8 | 9 | $10^{3}$ | 11 | | | | 15 | 16 | | | | 5 | 2 | | | | |
| 29-Jan | H | Berwick Rangers | 435 | 0-2 | 1 | 2 | 3 | 4 | 5 | 6 | 7 | 8 | 9 | | 11 | 12 | | | 15 | 16 | | | | | | | | | |
| 5-Feb | H | Stranraer | 453 | 1-2 | 1 | | 3 | 4 | 5 | **6** | 7 | 8 | 9 | 10 | 11 | 12 | | 14 | | 16 | | | | | 2 | | | | |
| 12-Feb | A | Morton | 2,244 | 0-4 | 1 | 2 | 3 | 4 | 5 | 6 | 7 | 8 | 9 | 10 | 11 | | | | 15 | 16 | | | | | | | | | |
| 19-Feb | H | Arbroath | 758 | 1-1 | 1 | 2 | 3 | 4 | | 6 | 7 | 8 | 9 | **10** | 11 | | | | | | | | | 5 | | | | | |
| 26-Feb | A | Alloa Athletic | 516 | 2-0 | 1 | 2 | 3 | 4 | | 6 | 7 | $8^{2}$ | 9 | 10 | 11 | | | 14 | | 16 | | | | 5 | 2 | | | | |
| 5-Mar | A | Stirling Albion | 537 | 2-3 | 1 | 2 | 3 | 4 | | 6 | 7 | 8 | **9** | **10** | 11 | | | 14 | | 16 | | | | 5 | 2 | | | | |
| 12-Mar | H | Morton | 555 | 2-0 | 1 | 2 | 3 | 4 | | 6 | 7 | 8 | 9 | **10** | | 12 | | | | 16 | | | | 5 | 2 | **11** | | | |
| 22-Mar | H | Dumbarton | 443 | 6-0 | 1 | 2 | 3 | 4 | | 6 | 7 | 8 | 9 | $10^{3}$ | 11 | 12 | | | 15 | 16 | | | | 5 | | | | | |
| 29-Mar | H | Ayr United | 490 | 1-0 | 1 | 2 | 3 | 4 | | 6 | 7 | 8 | 9 | **10** | 11 | 12 | | | | 16 | | | | 5 | | | | | |
| 2-Apr | A | Ayr United | 1,076 | 0-1 | 1 | 2 | 3 | 4 | | 6 | 7 | 8 | 9 | 10 | 11 | 12 | | 14 | | 16 | | | | 5 | | | | | |
| 9-Apr | A | Berwick Rangers | 369 | 1-1 | 1 | 2 | 3 | 4 | | 6 | 7 | 8 | 9 | **10** | 11 | 12 | | 14 | | | | | | 5 | | | | | |
| 16-Apr | H | Morton | 1,064 | 0-0 | 1 | 2 | | 4 | | 6 | | 8 | 9 | 10 | 11 | | | | | 16 | | | | 5 | | | | | |
| 16-Apr | A | Stranraer | 456 | 0-0 | 1 | 2 | 3 | 4 | | 6 | 7 | 8 | 9 | 10 | 11 | 12 | | | | 16 | | | | 5 | | | | | |
| 23-Apr | A | Arbroath | 697 | 2-1 | 1 | 2 | 3 | 4 | | 6 | 7 | 8 | 9 | $10^{2}$ | 11 | | | 14 | | 16 | | 6 | | 5 | | | | | |
| 30-Apr | H | Alloa Athletic | 453 | 1-1 | | 2 | 3 | 4 | | 6 | 7 | 8 | 9 | 10 | **11** | | | | 15 | 16 | | 1 | | 5 | | | | 4 | |
| 7-May | A | Brechin City | 1,074 | 3-0 | 1 | 2 | 3 | 4 | | 6 | 7 | 8 | 9 | **10** | 11 | 12 | | | | 16 | | | | 5 | | | | | 14 |
| **TOTAL FULL APPEARANCES** | | | | | 27 | 17 | 30 | 35 | 16 | 34 | 25 | 33 | 28 | 33 | 23 | 11 | 9 | | 1 | 4 | 5 | 11 | 7 | 17 | 14 | 14 | 1 | 1 | |
| **TOTAL SUB APPEARANCES** | | | | | | | | 1 | | | | 3 | 2 | 3 | 8 | 7 | 17 | 11 | 5 | 4 | | 7 | 5 | 1 | | | 1 | 1 | 1 |
| **TOTAL GOALS SCORED** | | | | | | | | | 1 | 1 | 5 | 3 | 13 | 20 | 4 | 3 | | | | | | | | 1 | | | | |

*…re in bold denotes goal scored. Secondary smaller figure in bold denotes number of goals scored. † denotes opponent's own goal.*

## THE LOONS' 10 YEAR LEAGUE RECORD

| Season | Div | P | W | D | L | F | A | Pts | Pos |
|---|---|---|---|---|---|---|---|---|---|
| 95-96 | S | 36 | 11 | 7 | 18 | 37 | 61 | 40 | 9 |
| 96-97 | T | 36 | 19 | 10 | 7 | 74 | 45 | 67 | 2 |
| 97-98 | S | 36 | 12 | 10 | 14 | 51 | 61 | 46 | 7 |
| 98-99 | S | 36 | 8 | 7 | 21 | 48 | 70 | 31 | 10 |
| 99-00 | T | 36 | 17 | 9 | 10 | 64 | 40 | 61 | 3 |
| 00-01 | S | 36 | 10 | 10 | 16 | 48 | 52 | 40 | 8 |
| 01-02 | S | 36 | 15 | 8 | 13 | 51 | 47 | 53 | 3 |
| 02-03 | S | 36 | 14 | 9 | 13 | 55 | 53 | 51 | 4 |
| 03-04 | S | 36 | 12 | 11 | 13 | 49 | 57 | 47 | 6 |
| 04-05 | S | 36 | 13 | 8 | 15 | 51 | 45 | 47 | 5 |

## LEADING GOALSCORERS:

| Season | Div | Goals | Player |
|---|---|---|---|
| 1995-96 | S | 12 | G. Higgins |
| 1996-97 | T | 17 | B. Honeyman |
| 1997-98 | S | 14 | M. McLauchlan |
| 1998-99 | S | 10 | R. Brand |
| 1999-00 | T | 16 | S. Milne |
| 2000-01 | S | 9 | W. Stewart |
| 2001-02 | S | 19 | P. Tosh |
| 2002-03 | S | 15 | M. Bavidge |
| 2003-04 | S | 18 | P. Tosh |
| 2004-05 | S | 20 | P. Shields |

### FORFAR ATHLETIC PLAYING KITS SEASON 2005.06

FIRST KIT — SECOND KIT — THIRD KIT

# GRETNA F.C.

GRETNA F.C.
Raydale Park, Dominion Road,
Gretna, DG16 5AP.
**TELEPHONE NUMBERS**
Ground (01461) 337602
Sec. Home & Fax (01387) 811820
Sec. Mobile 07769 685524
**GROUND FAX** (01461) 338047
**E-MAIL** info@gretnafootballclub.co.uk
**WEBSITE** www.gretnafootballclub.co.uk
**CHAIRMAN** Ron MacGregor MA(Hons), FIHM
**VICE-CHAIRMAN**
Mrs. Helen S. MacGregor MSR, DCR
**DIRECTORS**
Brooks G. Mileson, Paul J.H Grootendorst
Ms. Debra A. Wicks, Mark C. Hampson
(Non-Executive) & Graeme R. Muir
(Non-Executive)
**PRESIDENT** Brian Fulton
**HONORARY LIFE PRESIDENT** Tom Kerr
**HONORARY LIFE MEMBERS**
John Smith & Jack Gass
**SECRETARY**
Mrs Helen S. MacGregor MSR, DCR
**MANAGER** Rowan Alexander
**ASSISTANT MANAGER** David Irons
**RESERVE COACH & FITNESS COACH**
David Holdsworth
**GOALKEEPING COACHES**
Alan Main & David Wylie
**YOUTH ACADEMY DIRECTORS**
Viv Busby & David Holdsworth
**HEAD OF YOUTH DEVELOPMENT**
Danny Lennon
**YOUTH CO-ORDINATOR** Bobby Paterson
**HEAD COMMUNITY COACH** Tom Cowan
**YOUTH DEVELOPMENT /**
**COMMUNITY COACHES**
Peter Osgood & Kevin Somerville
**YOUTH COACHES**
U19: Danny Lennon & David Farrell
U17: David Farrell & John Feenie
U15: Derek McWilliams
U14: David McLenaghan
U13: Neil Graham
**HEAD OF COMMUNITY & EDUCATION**
Graeme Muir
**YOUTH ADMINISTRATOR** Karen Jackson
**CHIEF SCOUT** David Wylie
**TEAM CAPTAIN** Chris Innes
**OFFICE MANAGER** Lynne Hampson
**GROUNDSMAN/FOOTBALL SAFETY**
**OFFICERS' ASSOCIATION REPRESENTATIVE**
Paul Barnett
**COMMERCIAL & OPERATIONS DIRECTOR**
Ms. Debra Wicks
**MEDIA LIAISON PERSONS**
Jon Tait & Ron MacGregor
**MATCHDAY PROGRAMME EDITOR** Jon Tait
**CLUB DOCTOR**
Dr. Fiona Vernon M.B, CH.B, D.R.C.O.G, M.R.C.G.P
**PHYSIOTHERAPIST** Michael McLaughlan
**STADIUM MANAGER** Mark Hampson
**GROUNDSMAN** Paul Barnett
**KIT PERSON** John Bryden
**CLUB SHOP**
Situated at Ground. (01461) 337602
Open on Home Matchdays 1.00 p.m. to 5.00 p.m.
Contact: Alan Watson (01387) 251550
**SUPPORTERS CLUB**
Secretary: Richard Wharton, 31 Lindisfarne
Street, Carlisle CA1 2ND Tel No. (01228) 547761
**SHIRT SPONSOR** Wm. Armstrong Group
**KIT SUPPLIER** Nike

## LIST OF PLAYERS 2005.06

| PLAYERS SURNAME | FIRST NAME | MIDDLE NAME | DATE OF BIRTH | PLACE OF BIRTH | DATE SIGNED | HEIGHT FT INS | WEIGHT ST LBS | POSITION ON PITCH | PREVIOUS CLUB |
|---|---|---|---|---|---|---|---|---|---|
| Aitken | Andrew | Robert | 02/02/78 | Dumfries | 18/05/04 | 6.0 | 12.7 | Defender | Queen of the South |
| Baldacchino | Ryan | | 13/01/81 | Leicester | 02/01/04 | 5.10 | 10.8 | Midfield | Carlisle United |
| Banks | Martin | Wales | 23/05/88 | Paisley | 21/06/05 | 6.0 | 10.2 | Midfield | St. Mirren Form D U15 |
| Bannon | Sean | | 29/06/88 | Carlisle | 24/06/05 | 6.2 | 12.0 | Forward | Pirelli F.C. |
| Berkeley | Matthew | Anthony | 03/08/87 | Manchester | 14/09/04 | 5.11 | 10.10 | Forward | Burnley |
| Bingham | David | Thomas | 03/09/70 | Dunfermline | 16/06/04 | 5.10 | 10.13 | Forward | Inverness Caledonian Thistle |
| Birch | Mark | | 05/01/77 | Stoke on Trent | 21/08/03 | 5.11 | 13.2 | Defender | Carlisle United |
| Boyd | Mark | Edward | 22/10/81 | Carlisle | 30/07/04 | 5.9 | 12.6 | Midfield | Carlisle United |
| Bryan | Anthony | | 13/04/86 | Glasgow | 24/06/04 | 6.3 | 12.0 | Defender | Lennox B.C. |
| Campagna | Mario | | 28/08/89 | Harrogate | 22/06/05 | 5.9 | 10.10 | Midfield | Barnsley |
| Collins | Derek | Joseph | 15/04/69 | Glasgow | 31/01/05 | 5.9 | 11.0 | Defender | Morton |
| Davis | Marc | | 13/08/89 | Glasgow | 17/08/05 | 5.7 | 10.4 | Defender | Cumbernauld Colts |
| Deuchar | Kenneth | Robert | 06/07/80 | Stirling | 08/07/04 | 6.3 | 13.10 | Forward | East Fife |
| Dunglinson | Daniel | Scott | 24/05/87 | Dumfries | 24/06/04 | 5.7 | 9.7 | Midfield | Falkirk |
| Faulds | Nicholas | Samuel | 26/11/89 | Irvine | 17/08/05 | 6.0 | 11.7 | Defender | Ayr United |
| Ferrie | Chris | Patrick | 20/07/89 | Dundee | 22/06/05 | 5.6 | 9.5 | Midfield | Harraby Catholic |
| Fleming | Greg | William | 27/09/86 | Dunfermline | 03/06/05 | 6.3 | 12.10 | Goalkeeper | Livingston |
| Gilfillan | Bryan | James | 14/09/84 | Cardenden | 21/08/04 | 6.0 | 11.2 | Defender | Cowdenbeath |
| Grady | James | | 14/03/71 | Paisley | 05/08/05 | 5.7 | 10.8 | Forward | Dundee United |
| Graham | David | | 02/06/83 | Stirling | 28/01/05 | 5.9 | 11.0 | Forward | Stranraer |
| Grainger | Daniel | Leslie | 28/07/86 | Carlisle | 19/10/02 | 6.0 | 12.0 | Defender | Penrith |
| Heed | Martin | John | 07/01/89 | Dagenham | 20/07/05 | 5.5 | 9.0 | Midfield | Billericay Town |
| Heggie | Craig | | 27/01/89 | Rutherglen | 17/08/05 | 5.7 | 9.0 | Forward | Glasgow United |
| Henderson | Niall | Joseph | 07/02/88 | Craigavon | 28/07/04 | 5.9 | 10.3 | Midfield | Lurgan Town |
| Inglis | Alan | Stuart | 20/02/87 | Carlisle | 25/05/05 | 5.11 | 11.0 | Defender | Queen of the South |
| Innes | Christopher | | 13/07/76 | Broxburn | 28/01/05 | 6.1 | 13.3 | Defender | Dundee United |
| Kerr | David | | 09/03/89 | Paisley | 20/08/05 | 6.1 | 11.0 | Defender | St. Mirren B.C. |
| Leith | Paul | | 11/03/89 | Glasgow | 17/08/05 | 5.9 | 10.7 | Midfield | Kilmarnock |
| Macphail | Dylan | | 30/07/90 | Irvine | 20/08/05 | 5.8 | 9.8 | Forward | Gretna B.C. |
| Maddison | Lee | Robert | 05/10/72 | Bristol | 29/08/03 | 6.2 | 12.11 | Defender | Carlisle United |
| Main | Alan | David | 05/12/67 | Elgin | 28/07/04 | 5.11.5 | 13.9 | Goalkeeper | Livingston |
| Marshall | Craig | | 23/04/90 | Glasgow | 17/08/05 | 5.8 | 9.6 | Mid / Fwd | Stepford B.C. |
| Marshall | Scott | Robertson | 23/02/88 | Glasgow | 18/01/05 | 5.9 | 10.2 | Midfield | Rangers East B.C. |
| Mathieson | David | James | 18/01/78 | Dumfries | 02/08/02 | 6.0 | 12.10 | Goalkeeper | Queen of the South |
| McBride | Martin | Anthony | 21/05/86 | Glasgow | 24/06/04 | 5.11 | 11.0 | Midfield | Partick Thistle |
| McGill | Mark | Joseph | 27/02/89 | Glasgow | 21/06/05 | 5.9 | 10.8 | Defender | Gretna Form S |
| McGuffie | Ryan | | 22/07/80 | Dumfries | 05/08/02 | 6.2 | 12.6 | Def / Mid | Newcastle United |
| McQuilken | James | Charles | 03/10/74 | Glasgow | 20/12/04 | 5.10 | 11.2 | Defender | St. Johnstone |
| Mennie | Aidan | | 11/01/89 | Bellshill | 22/09/05 | 5.8 | 10.0 | Midfield | Hibernian |
| Mooty | James | | 07/03/89 | Bellshill | 17/08/05 | 5.7 | 8.11 | Midfield | Stirling Albion |
| Morgan | Steven | | 12/09/90 | Livingston | 17/08/05 | 6.0 | 11.7 | Midfield | Armadale Sports Club |
| Mulgrew | Bryan | Anthony | 15/11/87 | Glasgow | 14/09/04 | 5.11 | 10.5 | Defender | Benburb Juniors |
| Nicholls | David | Clarkson | 05/04/72 | Bellshill | 14/01/05 | 6.1 | 13.2 | Midfield | Falkirk |
| Orr | Allan | James | 12/05/88 | Glasgow | 11/01/05 | 5.7 | 10.0 | Forward | Rangers |
| Poulter | Robert | John | 02/02/86 | Sheffield | 01/07/05 | 6.1 | 13.10 | Goalkeeper | Sheffield Wednesday |
| Prokas | Richard | | 22/01/76 | Penrith | 05/08/03 | 5.10 | 12.0 | Midfield | Workington |
| Robinson | Dan | | 21/05/89 | Penrith | 24/06/05 | 5.10 | 10.10 | Forward | Appleby Under 16's |
| Robinson | Daniel | Michael | 17/05/88 | Carlisle | 22/06/05 | 5.11 | 12.0 | Defender | Newton Rigg |
| Shaw | Stuart | John | 17/07/89 | Whitehaven | 30/08/05 | 5.10 | 11.0 | Midfield | Calder Lions |
| Silk | Andrew | Michael | 25/11/90 | Livingston | 17/08/05 | 5.9 | 10.0 | Goalkeeper | Dunfermline Athletic |
| Skelton | Gavin | Richard | 27/03/81 | Carlisle | 31/07/02 | 5.10 | 12.10 | Defender | Gretna |
| Sloan | Lewis | | 22/06/87 | Dumfries | 22/07/05 | 5.8 | 10.4 | Midfield | Kilmarnock |
| Smith | Andrew | Mark | 27/11/68 | Aberdeen | 27/05/04 | 6.1 | 13.8 | Forward | Clyde |
| Studholme | Jonathan | | 19/07/89 | Carlisle | 22/06/05 | 5.9 | 10.6 | Midfield | Preston North End |
| Tosh | Steven | William | 27/04/73 | Kirkcaldy | 22/01/05 | 5.11 | 12.0 | Midfield | Aberdeen |
| Townsley | Derek | Johnstone | 21/01/73 | Carlisle | 19/01/04 | 6.5 | 14.7 | Midfield | Oxford United |
| Welch | Ross | Christopher | 11/12/89 | Lanark | 17/08/05 | 5.6 | 9.0 | Midfield | Kirkfield United |

## MILESTONES:
**Year of formation:** 1946
**Most League points in a season:**
98 (SFL Third Division – Season 2004/05 – 3 Points for a Win)
**Most League goals scored by a player in a season:**
Kenny Deuchar (Season 2004/05)
**No. of goals scored:** 38
**Record Attendance:**
3,000 (-v- Dundee United – Scottish Cup 17.1.2005)
**Record Victory:**
20-0 (-v- Silloth – Carlisle & District League,1962)
**Record Defeat:**
2-9 (-v- Ashton United – Unibond League Division 1 – 28.10.2000)

# SEASON STATS 2004.05

| DATE | VENUE | OPPONENTS | ATT | RES | Mathieson D.J. | Birch M. | Skelton G.R. | Prokas R. | Aitken A.R. | Holdsworth D.G. | Baldacchino R. | Galloway M.A. | Smith A.M. | Bingham D.T. | Townsley D.J. | Deuchar K.R.J. | McGuffie R. | Cosgrove S. | Gilfillan B.J. | Boyd M.E. | McQuilken J.C. | Lennon D.J. | Irons D.J. | Gordon W. | Wake B.C. | Nicholls D.C. | Tosh S.W. | Innes C. | Graham D. | Collins D.J. | Shields D. | Main A.D. | Grainger D.L. |
|---|---|---|---|---|---|---|---|---|---|---|---|---|---|---|---|---|---|---|---|---|---|---|---|---|---|---|---|---|---|---|---|---|---|---|
| 7-Aug | H | Albion Rovers | 646 | 6-0 | 1 | 2 | 3 | 4 | 5 | 6 | 7 | | **8** | 9 | **10[2]** | 11 | **12** | 14 | **15** | | | | | | | | | | | | | | |
| 14-Aug | A | East Stirlingshire | 276 | 2-1 | 1 | 2 | 3 | 4 | **5** | 6 | 7 | | 8 | 9 | 10 | **11** | 12 | 14 | | | | | | | | | | | | | | | |
| 21-Aug | H | Montrose | 501 | 1-0 | 1 | 2 | **3** | 4 | 5 | 6 | 7 | | 8 | 9 | 10 | 11 | 12 | 14 | | | 15 | | | | | | | | | | | | |
| 28-Aug | A | Queen's Park | 496 | 2-3 | 1 | 2 | 3 | 4 | 5 | 6 | **7** | | 8 | 9 | **10** | | 12 | 14 | | | 11 | 15 | | | | | | | | | | | |
| 4-Sep | H | Cowdenbeath | 568 | 2-1 | 1 | 2 | 15 | 5 | | | 7 | 16 | **9** | 10 | | 12 | 8 | | | | 3 | 4 | 6 | 11 | | | | | | | | | |
| 11-Sep | A | Peterhead | 861 | 1-1 | 1 | 2 | 11 | 5 | | 7 | 14 | 9 | 10 | | 12 | 8 | | | 16 | | 3 | 4 | 6 | | | | | | | | | | |
| 18-Sep | H | East Fife | 457 | †5-1 | 1 | 2 | 11 | 5 | | | 10 | | 9 | **9[3]** | 8 | 15 | 4 | 14 | 3 | | | 6 | 12 | | | | | | | | | | | |
| 25-Sep | H | Elgin City | 574 | 3-0 | 1 | 2 | 11 | 5 | | | **10[2]** | | | 9 | 8 | 14 | 4 | | 3 | | | 6 | 12 | | | | | | | | | | | |
| 2-Oct | A | Stenhousemuir | 373 | 3-0 | 1 | 2 | 11 | 5 | | 7 | **10[2]** | | | 9 | 8 | | 4 | | 3 | | | 6 | 12 | | | | | | | | | | | |
| 16-Oct | H | East Stirlingshire | 468 | 8-1 | 1 | **2** | 11 | 5 | | 7 | 10 | 15 | **9[3]** | 8 | 16 | **4** | | | 3 | | | 6 | **12** | | | | | | | | | | | |
| 23-Oct | A | Albion Rovers | 326 | 6-2 | 1 | **2** | 11 | 5 | | 7 | **10[2]** | | 9 | 8 | | 4 | | 3 | 15 | 6 | | | 12 | | | | | | | | | | | |
| 30-Oct | H | Queen's Park | 706 | 4-1 | 1 | 2 | **11** | 5 | | 7 | 10 | 14 | **9** | 8 | | 4 | | 3 | | 6 | | | 12 | | | | | | | | | | | |
| 6-Nov | A | Cowdenbeath | 322 | 8-0 | 1 | **2[3]** | 11 | 5 | | 7 | **10[2]** | 14 | 9 | 8 | | 4 | | 3 | | 6 | | | | | | | | | | | | | | |
| 13-Nov | H | Peterhead | 2,200 | 2-1 | 1 | 2 | 11 | 5 | | 7 | **10[2]** | 14 | 9 | 8 | | 4 | | 3 | | 6 | | | | | | | | | | | | | | |
| 20-Nov | H | Albion Rovers | 627 | 6-2 | 1 | 2 | 11 | 5 | | 7 | 10 | 14 | **9[5]** | 8 | | 4 | | 3 | | 6 | | | | | | | | | | | | | | |
| 27-Nov | A | East Fife | 551 | 3-1 | 1 | 2 | 11 | 5 | | 7 | 10 | | 9 | 8 | | 4 | | 3 | | 6 | | | | | | | | | | | | | | |
| 4-Dec | A | Elgin City | 505 | 3-1 | 1 | 2 | 11 | 5 | 16 | 7 | 14 | 10 | | **9[2]** | 8 | 15 | 4 | | 3 | | 6 | | | | | | | | | | | | | |
| 18-Dec | H | Stenhousemuir | 1,078 | 3-0 | 1 | 2 | 11 | 5 | | 7 | 10 | 16 | | 9 | 8 | | 4 | | 3 | | 6 | | | | | | | | | | | | | |
| -Jan | A | Montrose | 592 | 3-2 | 1 | 2 | 11 | 5 | | 7 | 10 | 16 | | **9[2]** | 8 | | 4 | | 3 | | 6 | | | | | | | | | | | | | |
| -Jan | A | Queen's Park | 803 | 1-1 | 1 | 2 | 11 | 5 | | | 10 | 7 | | 9 | 8 | 16 | 4 | | 3 | | 6 | | | | | | | | | | | | | |
| 15-Jan | H | Cowdenbeath | 738 | 2-0 | 1 | 2 | **11** | 5 | | | 12 | 10 | | 9 | 8 | | 4 | | 3 | | | | | | | | 7 | | | | | | | |
| 22-Jan | A | Peterhead | 1,207 | 2-4 | 1 | **2** | 11 | 5 | | | 12 | 10 | | 9 | 8 | | 4 | | 3 | | 6 | | | | | | 14 | 7 | | | | | | |
| 29-Jan | H | East Fife | 828 | 4-0 | 1 | 2 | 11 | 5 | | | 10 | 16 | | **9[3]** | 8 | | 4 | | 3 | | | | | | | | 15 | 7 | **6** | 12 | | | | |
| 5-Feb | H | Elgin City | 809 | 2-1 | 1 | | 11 | 4 | 5 | | 10 | 6 | | 9 | 8 | | | | 3 | | | | | | | | 7 | | 12 | 2 | 14 | | | |
| 12-Feb | A | Stenhousemuir | 416 | 4-1 | 1 | 2 | 11 | 5 | | | 14 | 10 | 6 | **9[3]** | 8 | | 4 | | 3 | | | | | | | | 15 | 7 | | 12 | | | | |
| 19-Feb | H | Montrose | 913 | 4-1 | 1 | **2** | 11 | 5 | | | 10 | 6 | | **9[2]** | 8 | | 4 | | 3 | | | | | | | | 15 | 7 | | 14 | | 16 | | |
| -Mar | A | Cowdenbeath | 339 | 1-0 | 1 | 2 | 11 | 5 | | 7 | 10 | | | 9 | 8 | | 14 | | 3 | | | | | | | | | **4** | | 6 | 16 | | | 15 |
| -Mar | A | East Stirlingshire | 185 | 4-0 | 1 | | 11 | 5 | | 7 | 10 | | | 9 | 16 | | 8 | | 3 | | | | | | | | **14** | 4 | | 6 | 12 | 2 | | |
| 2-Mar | H | Queen's Park | 978 | 4-0 | 1 | | **11[2]** | | 7 | | **10[2]** | | | 9 | 8 | | | | 3 | | 6 | | | | | | 15 | 4 | | 5 | 12 | 2 | | |
| 9-Mar | H | Peterhead | 1,538 | 6-1 | 1 | | 11 | 5 | | 7 | 10 | | | **9[3]** | **8[2]** | | 16 | | 3 | | | | | | | | 15 | 4 | | 6 | 14 | 2 | | |
| -Apr | A | East Fife | 723 | 2-0 | 1 | | 11 | 5 | | 7 | 10 | 16 | | 9 | 8 | | | | 3 | | | | | | | | 15 | 4 | | **6** | 14 | 2 | | |
| -Apr | H | Stenhousemuir | 908 | 7-0 | 1 | 14 | 11 | 5 | | 7 | 12 | 10 | | **9[2]** | 8 | | 15 | | 3 | | | | | | | | | 4 | 6 | | | 2 | | |
| 16-Apr | A | Elgin City | 503 | 6-2 | | 2 | 11 | 5 | | | **10[3]** | 15 | 11 | 14 | | | | | | | | | | | | | 8 | 4 | 6 | 12 | | | 1 | 3 |
| 23-Apr | A | Montrose | 462 | 4-0 | | 2 | 11 | 5 | | | 10 | **14** | **9[2]** | 8 | | | | | | | 3 | | | | | | | **4** | 6 | 12 | | | 1 | 16 |
| -Apr | H | East Stirlingshire | 1,585 | 1-0 | | 2 | 11 | 3 | | 7 | 10 | 5 | 9 | 8 | | | | | | | 12 | | | | | | 15 | 4 | 6 | | | 1 | | |
| -May | A | Albion Rovers | 519 | 5-0 | | | 11 | | 7 | **7[2]** | 14 | 10 | 5 | 9 | **8[2]** | | 4 | | | 16 | | 12 | | | | | | 6 | | 2 | | | 1 | 3 |
| **TOTAL FULL APPEARANCES** | | | | | 32 | 29 | 35 | 5 | 34 | 4 | 29 | 4 | 6 | 36 | 9 | 30 | 30 | | 21 | 1 | 29 | 2 | 19 | 1 | | 3 | 13 | 11 | | 7 | | 4 | 2 |
| **TOTAL SUB APPEARANCES** | | | | | | 1 | | 1 | | 1 | | 2 | 6 | | | 11 | 6 | 6 | 6 | 5 | 1 | 3 | 1 | | 6 | 9 | | 11 | | 3 | | 1 | |
| **TOTAL GOALS SCORED** | | | | | | 7 | 12 | 2 | | | 9 | 1 | 3 | 27 | 5 | 38 | 8 | 1 | 6 | | 2 | | | | | 3 | 2 | 1 | 2 | | | |

Figure in bold denotes goal scored. Secondary smaller figure in bold denotes number of goals scored. † denotes opponent's own goal.

## THE BLACK AND WHITES' LEAGUE RECORD

Season 2002-03 was the club's first season in membership of SFL

| Season | Div | P | W | D | L | F | A | Pts | Pos |
|---|---|---|---|---|---|---|---|---|---|
| 02-03 | T | 36 | 11 | 12 | 13 | 50 | 50 | 45 | 6 |
| 03-04 | T | 36 | 20 | 8 | 8 | 59 | 39 | 68 | 3 |
| 04-05 | T | 36 | 32 | 2 | 2 | 130 | 29 | 98 | 1 |

## LEADING GOALSCORERS:

Season 2002-03 was the club's first season in membership of SFL

| Season | Div | Goals | Player |
|---|---|---|---|
| 2002-03 | T | 10 | M. Dobie |
| 2003-04 | T | 17 | M.Cameron |
| 2004-05 | T | 38 | K.Deuchar |

### GRETNA PLAYING KITS SEASON 2005.06

FIRST KIT    SECOND KIT    THIRD KIT

# MORTON

**MORTON F.C.**
Cappielow Park, Sinclair Street,
Greenock, PA15 2TY
**TELEPHONE NUMBERS**
Ground/Ticket Office (01475) 723571
**FAX** (01475) 781084
**E-MAIL** info@gmfc.net
**E-MAIL 2** chiefexec@gmfc.net
**WEBSITE** www.gmfc.net
**CHAIRMAN** Douglas D. F. Rae
**DIRECTORS**
Iain D. Brown, James McColl,
W. Arthur M. Montford &
Crawford McL. Rae
**CHIEF EXECUTIVE**
Gillian Donaldson (07713) 624369
**COMPANY SECRETARY**
Mrs Mary Davidson
**MANAGER** Jim McInally
**ASSISTANT MANAGER** Martin Clark
**YOUTH COACHES**
U17: Joe Harkins
U15: Robert Ahlfeld
U13: George Wall
**CHIEF SCOUT** Pat Gardner
**TEAM CAPTAIN** Stewart Greacen
**OFFICE ADMINISTRATOR** Tony Cowden
**FOOTBALL SAFETY OFFICERS'**
**ASSOCIATION REPRESENTATIVE**
Peter Copland
**COMMERCIAL MANAGER &**
**MATCHDAY PROGRAMME EDITOR**
Susan Gregory
**LOTTERY MANAGER** Heather Arthur
**MEDIA LIAISON PERSON**
Gillian Donaldson
**CLUB DOCTORS**
Dr. R. Craig Speirs, M.B., Ch.B
& Dr. Fraser Gray, M.B., Ch.B
**PHYSIOTHERAPIST** Paul Kelly B.Sc. SRP
**STADIUM DIRECTOR** Crawford Rae
**GROUNDSMAN** Mark Farrell
**KIT PERSON** Andy Bryan
**CLUB SHOP**
Morton F.C. Cappielow Park,
Sinclair Street, Greenock, PA15 2TY.
Opening Hours Mon - Fri 12 noon - 4pm.
Also open on Home Matchdays
**OFFICIAL SUPPORTERS CLUB**
Morton Supporters Club,
Regent Street, Greenock
**SHIRT SPONSOR**
**First Choice:**
Front: Millions – The Tiny Tasty Chewy Sweets
**Second Choice:**
Front: Halfpounders - Bags of Confectionery
for everyone
**Third Choice:**
Front: Millions – The Tiny Tasty Chewy Sweets
Back: Buchanan's - The fine taste of Scotland
**KIT SUPPLIER** Vandanel

## LIST OF PLAYERS 2005.06

| PLAYERS SURNAME | FIRST NAME | MIDDLE NAME | DATE OF BIRTH | PLACE OF BIRTH | DATE SIGNED | HEIGHT FT INS | WEIGHT ST LBS | POSITION ON PITCH | PREVIOUS CLUB |
|---|---|---|---|---|---|---|---|---|---|
| Adam | John | | 26/12/84 | Falkirk | 27/09/04 | 6.1 | 12.8 | Midfield | Rangers |
| Finlayson | Kevin | Charles | 07/12/79 | Glasgow | 16/05/05 | 5.9 | 10.11 | Midfield | Stranraer |
| Fulton | Michael | | 25/04/84 | Greenock | 13/09/05 | 5.8 | 11.0 | Midfield | Greenock High School FP |
| Gilbride | Alan | | 03/03/88 | Greenock | 24/06/05 | 6.2 | 12.0 | Defender | Morton Form D U16 |
| Gonet | Stefan | | 11/11/81 | Paisley | 23/03/05 | 6.3 | 12.6 | Goalkeeper | Ross County |
| Graham | Brian | | 23/11/87 | Glasgow | 24/06/05 | 6.1 | 11.0 | Forward | Hillington B.C. |
| Greacen | Stewart | | 31/03/82 | Lanark | 20/06/03 | 6.2 | 14.0 | Defender | Forfar Athletic |
| Harding | Ryan | | 27/04/84 | Edinburgh | 11/03/05 | 6.3 | 13.0 | Defender | Livingston |
| Keenan | Dean | Matthew | 15/10/85 | Glasgow | 26/05/04 | 5.11 | 11.0 | Midfield | Pollok United |
| Lilley | Derek | Symon | 09/02/74 | Paisley | 03/06/05 | 5.11 | 12.7 | Forward | Livingston |
| Macgregor | David | George | 09/06/81 | Greenock | 03/08/01 | 5.11 | 11.10 | Midfield | Morton Form S |
| MacLeod | David | | 19/09/88 | Greenock | 24/06/05 | 5.8 | 10.7 | Defender | Morton Form D U16 |
| McAlister | James | Duncan | 02/11/85 | Rothesay | 01/06/04 | 5.10 | 13.0 | Forward | Linwood Rangers |
| McGurn | David | Edward | 14/09/80 | Glasgow | 26/05/04 | 6.1 | 13.3 | Goalkeeper | Hillwood B.C. |
| McLaren | Andrew | | 05/06/73 | Glasgow | 06/07/05 | 5.10.5 | 12.0 | Forward | Dundee United |
| McLaughlin | Scott | Bonner | 20/01/84 | Glasgow | 31/08/05 | 5.9 | 10.8 | Midfield | Livingston |
| McLean | Kenneth | | 17/11/84 | Glasgow | 04/01/05 | 5.8 | 10.3 | Forward | Hillwood Juveniles |
| Millar | Christopher | Alexander | 30/03/83 | Glasgow | 13/07/04 | 5.9 | 10.3 | Midfield | Celtic |
| Stark | John | Paul | 03/06/86 | Glasgow | 12/11/04 | 6.2 | 13.0 | Goalkeeper | Greenock Juniors |
| Templeman | Christopher | | 12/01/80 | Kirkcaldy | 10/12/04 | 6.5 | 14.4 | Forward | Brechin City |
| Walker | Alexander | | 25/04/84 | Bellshill | 06/07/05 | 6.0 | 11.0 | Midfield | Rangers |
| Walker | Jason | | 21/03/84 | Barrow in Furness | 23/07/04 | 5.9 | 11.7 | Forward | Dundee |
| Weatherson | Peter | Joseph | 29/05/80 | North Shields | 24/06/03 | 6.0 | 12.10 | Forward | Queen of the South |

## TICKET INFORMATION

**Season Ticket Information**

**Seated**
Grandstand
(Sections A & B numbered seats)
Adult £190
Concessions £95
Parent & Juvenile £210

Grandstand
(Sections C & D numbered seats)
Adult £205

**Standing**
Adult £160
Concessions £80
Child (15 & under) £40
Parent & Juvenile £190

**League Admission Prices**

**Seated**
Grandstand (Sections A,B,E & F)
Adult £13
Concessions £7
Parent & Juvenile £16

**Standing**
Adult £11
Concessions £6
Child (15 & under) £2
Parent & Juvenile £13

## MILESTONES:
**Year of formation:** 1874
**Most capped player:** Jimmy Cowan
**No. of caps:** 25
**Most League points in a season:**
69 (Division 2 – Season 1966/67) (2 Points for a win)
72 (Third Division - Season 2002/03) (3 Points for a win)
**Most League goals scored by a player in a season:**
Allan McGraw (Season 1963/64)
**No. of goals scored:** 58
**Record Attendance:** 23,500 (-v- Celtic – 1922)
**Record Victory:**
11-0 (-v- Carfin Shamrock – Scottish Cup, 13.11.1886)
**Record Defeat:** 1-10 (-v- Port Glasgow Athletic, 5.5.1884)

# SEASON STATS 2004.05

**BELL'S** SCOTTISH FOOTBALL LEAGUE

## SEASON STATS 2004.05

*Figure in bold denotes goal scored. Secondary smaller figure in bold denotes number of goals scored. † denotes opponent's own goal.*

| DATE | VENUE | OPPONENTS | ATT | RES | Coyle C.R. | Collins D.J. | McCulloch M.R. | McCluskey S.C. | Greacen S. | Maisano M.M. | Millar C.A. | Maisano J.M. | Williams A.B. | Diack I.G. | Walker P. | Walker J. | McAlister J.D. | Weatherson P.J. | Hawke W.R. | Bannerman S.J. | Keenan D.M. | McLean K. | McGurn D.E. | Adam J. | Mahood A.S. | Templeman C. | Dilton S. | McLaughlin S. | McLaren A. | Harding R. |
|---|---|---|---|---|---|---|---|---|---|---|---|---|---|---|---|---|---|---|---|---|---|---|---|---|---|---|---|---|---|---|
| 7-Aug | A | Berwick Rangers | 907 | 1-2 | 1 | 2 | 3 | 4 | 5 | 6 | 7 | 8 | 9 | 10 | 11 | | **14** | 15 | 16 | | | | | | | | | | | |
| 14-Aug | H | Stranraer | 2,653 | †3-1 | 1 | 2 | 3 | 4 | 5 | | 7 | 8 | **9** | | | 16 | 11 | **6** | 15 | 10 | 14 | | | | | | | | | |
| 21-Aug | A | Dumbarton | 1,670 | 3-0 | 1 | 2 | 3 | 4 | **5** | | 7 | 8 | 9 | | | 16 | **11** | 6 | **15** | 10 | 12 | | | | | | | | | |
| 28-Aug | A | Ayr United | 2,264 | 0-2 | 1 | 2 | 3 | 4 | 5 | | 7 | 8 | 15 | | | 16 | 11 | 6 | 10 | 9 | 14 | | | | | | | | | |
| 4-Sep | H | Arbroath | 2,360 | 2-1 | 1 | 2 | 3 | | 5 | | 7 | 8 | 9 | 12 | 15 | | 6 | $10^2$ | | | 4 | 11 | | | | | | | | |
| 11-Sep | A | Stirling Albion | 1,831 | 1-1 | 1 | 2 | 3 | | 5 | 6 | **7** | 8 | 12 | | | 11 | 9 | 10 | | | 4 | | | | | | | | | |
| 18-Sep | H | Brechin City | 2,432 | 0-3 | 1 | 2 | 3 | | 5 | 6 | 7 | 8 | 10 | | 12 | 14 | 11 | 9 | | | 4 | | | | | | | | | |
| 25-Sep | A | Alloa Athletic | 1,056 | 6-1 | 1 | 2 | 12 | 3 | 5 | 6 | **7** | **8** | 10 | | | $15^2$ | 11 | $9^2$ | | | 14 | 4 | | | | | | | | |
| 2-Oct | H | Forfar Athletic | 2,736 | 2-1 | 1 | 2 | 12 | 3 | 5 | 6 | **7** | 8 | 10 | | | 15 | 11 | **9** | | | 14 | 4 | | | | | | | | |
| 16-Oct | A | Stranraer | 918 | 0-1 | 1 | 2 | 15 | 4 | 5 | 6 | 11 | 8 | 14 | | 16 | 10 | 3 | 9 | | | 7 | | | | | | | | | |
| 23-Oct | H | Berwick Rangers | 2,720 | 2-0 | | 2 | 3 | 4 | 5 | 6 | 7 | **8** | 9 | 12 | 16 | **10** | 11 | | | | | 14 | | 1 | | | | | | |
| 30-Oct | H | Ayr United | 3,232 | 0-1 | | 2 | | 4 | 5 | 6 | 7 | | 14 | 8 | 11 | 10 | | 12 | 3 | | | 1 | | | | | | | | |
| 6-Nov | A | Arbroath | 857 | †3-0 | | 2 | | 4 | 5 | | 7 | | 9 | 15 | **8** | 12 | 11 | **10** | | 14 | 3 | | 1 | 6 | | | | | | |
| 13-Nov | H | Stirling Albion | 3,020 | 3-0 | | 2 | | 4 | 5 | 15 | **7** | 14 | 9 | | **8** | **12** | 11 | 10 | | | 3 | | 1 | 6 | | | | | | |
| 27-Nov | A | Brechin City | 989 | †1-2 | | 2 | | 4 | 5 | | 7 | 15 | 9 | | 11 | 12 | 8 | 10 | | | 3 | | 1 | 6 | 14 | | | | | |
| 4-Dec | H | Alloa Athletic | 2,357 | 2-2 | | 2 | | | 5 | | 7 | **10** | 14 | | **8** | 9 | 11 | 12 | | | 3 | | 1 | 6 | 4 | | | | | |
| 27-Dec | A | Berwick Rangers | 968 | 2-2 | 1 | 2 | | | **5** | **7** | | 14 | | | 8 | 10 | 11 | | | 16 | 3 | | | 6 | 4 | 9 | | | | |
| 1-Jan | H | Dumbarton | 2,764 | 3-0 | 1 | 2 | 4 | | | **7** | | | | | 8 | 10 | 11 | **5** | 16 | | | 20 | 12 | 6 | 9 | 3 | | | | |
| 3-Jan | A | Ayr United | 2,455 | 1-2 | 1 | 2 | 4 | | | 7 | | | | | **8** | 10 | 11 | 5 | 14 | 15 | | | 12 | 6 | 9 | 3 | | | | |
| 15-Jan | H | Arbroath | 2,689 | 2-0 | | 2 | 4 | 5 | | 7 | | | | | 8 | 12 | 11 | 10 | | | 14 | | 1 | 16 | 6 | **9** | 3 | | | |
| 26-Jan | A | Stirling Albion | 1,075 | 1-1 | | 2 | | 4 | 5 | | 7 | 16 | | | 8 | 14 | 11 | 10 | | | 15 | | 1 | | 6 | 9 | 3 | | | |
| 29-Jan | H | Brechin City | 3,004 | 0-2 | | | | 4 | 5 | | 7 | 16 | | | 8 | 10 | 11 | 14 | | | 2 | | 1 | 6 | | 9 | 3 | 15 | | |
| 12-Feb | H | Forfar Athletic | 2,244 | 4-0 | | | | 4 | 5 | | 7 | 15 | | | 8 | 12 | 11 | **3** | | 2 | 14 | | 1 | | 6 | $9^3$ | | 10 | | |
| 19-Feb | A | Dumbarton | 1,508 | 0-3 | | | | 4 | 5 | | 7 | 16 | | | 8 | 12 | 11 | 3 | | 2 | | | 1 | 14 | 6 | 9 | | 10 | | |
| 26-Feb | H | Stranraer | 2,592 | 2-0 | | | | 4 | | | 7 | 10 | | | 8 | | 11 | 5 | | 2 | | | 1 | | | 3 | 6 | $9^2$ | | |
| 5-Mar | A | Arbroath | 832 | 1-0 | | | | 4 | 5 | | **7** | 8 | | | | 14 | 11 | 6 | | 2 | | | 1 | 16 | | 12 | 3 | 10 | 9 | |
| 13-Mar | A | Forfar Athletic | 555 | 0-2 | | | | 4 | 5 | | 7 | 6 | | | | 14 | 11 | 12 | | 2 | | | 1 | 16 | | 8 | 3 | 10 | 9 | |
| 12-Mar | H | Ayr United | 2,448 | 2-1 | | | | | 5 | | **7** | 6 | | | 14 | | 11 | 2 | | | | | 1 | | | 8 | 3 | 10 | 9 | 4 |
| 19-Mar | H | Stirling Albion | 2,764 | 2-0 | | | | | 5 | | 7 | 14 | | | 6 | 12 | 11 | 2 | | | | | 1 | 15 | | 8 | 3 | 10 | 9 | **4** |
| 23-Mar | A | Alloa Athletic | 959 | 2-2 | | | | | 5 | | **7** | 14 | | | 6 | | 11 | **2** | | | | | 1 | | | 8 | 3 | 10 | 9 | 4 |
| 2-Apr | A | Brechin City | 1,340 | 2-1 | | | | | 5 | | 7 | 6 | | | 14 | | **11** | 2 | | | | | 16 | 9 | | 8 | 3 | 10 | **8** | 4 |
| 9-Apr | A | Forfar Athletic | 1,064 | 0-0 | | | | | 5 | | 7 | 6 | | | 14 | | 11 | | | 2 | | | 1 | | | 9 | 3 | 10 | 8 | 4 |
| 16-Apr | H | Alloa Athletic | 2,721 | 2-0 | | | | | 5 | | **7** | 14 | | | **6** | | 11 | | | 2 | | | 1 | 15 | 16 | 9 | 3 | 10 | 8 | 4 |
| 23-Apr | A | Dumbarton | 3,229 | 0-0 | | | | | 5 | | 7 | | | | 6 | 12 | 11 | 2 | | | | | 1 | 15 | | 9 | 3 | 10 | 8 | 4 |
| 30-Apr | A | Stranraer | 2,778 | 1-1 | | | | | 5 | | 7 | 15 | | | 6 | 12 | 11 | **2** | | | | | 1 | | | 9 | 3 | 10 | 8 | 4 |
| 7-May | H | Berwick Rangers | 2,475 | 4-2 | | | | | 5 | | | $12^2$ | | | 6 | | 11 | 2 | 16 | 15 | 7 | | 1 | | | **9** | **3** | 10 | 8 | 4 |
| **TOTAL FULL APPEARANCES** | | | | | 14 | 21 | 8 | 22 | 32 | 9 | 34 | 19 | 12 | 1 | 20 | 11 | 35 | 26 | 4 | 6 | 15 | 1 | 22 | 6 | 8 | 18 | 17 | 14 | 12 | 9 |
| **TOTAL SUB APPEARANCES** | | | | | | 3 | | | 1 | | 11 | 5 | 3 | 11 | 16 | 1 | 6 | 2 | 10 | 5 | | | 1 | 9 | 3 | 1 | | 1 | |
| **TOTAL GOALS SCORED** | | | | | | | 1 | 2 | 11 | 6 | 1 | | | | 5 | 6 | 2 | 11 | | | | | | 6 | 1 | | 3 | 1 |

## THE TON'S 10 YEAR LEAGUE RECORD

| Season | Div | P | W | D | L | F | A | Pts | Pos |
|---|---|---|---|---|---|---|---|---|---|
| 95-96 | F | 36 | 20 | 7 | 9 | 57 | 39 | 67 | 3 |
| 96-97 | F | 36 | 12 | 9 | 15 | 42 | 41 | 45 | 8 |
| 97-98 | F | 36 | 12 | 10 | 14 | 47 | 48 | 46 | 5 |
| 98-99 | F | 36 | 14 | 7 | 15 | 45 | 41 | 49 | 6 |
| 99-00 | F | 36 | 10 | 20 | 6 | 45 | 61 | 36 | 8 |
| 00-01 | F | 36 | 9 | 8 | 19 | 34 | 61 | 35 | 9 |
| 01-02 | S | 36 | 7 | 14 | 15 | 48 | 63 | 35 | 10 |
| 02-03 | T | 36 | 21 | 9 | 6 | 67 | 33 | 72 | 1 |
| 03-04 | S | 36 | 16 | 11 | 9 | 66 | 58 | 59 | 4 |
| 04-05 | S | 36 | 18 | 8 | 10 | 60 | 37 | 62 | 3 |

## LEADING GOALSCORERS:

| Season | Div | Goals | Player |
|---|---|---|---|
| 1995-96 | F | 14 | D. Lilley |
| 1996-97 | F | 15 | D. Lilley |
| 1997-98 | F | 10 | W. Hawke |
| 1998-99 | F | 9 | K. Thomas |
| 1999-00 | F | 9 | H. Curran |
| 2000-01 | F | 9 | R. Matheson |
| 2001-02 | S | 8 | S. Bannerman |
| 2002-03 | T | 23 | A. Williams |
| 2003-04 | S | 15 | A. Williams |
| 2004-05 | S | 11 | C.Millar, P.Weatherson |

**MORTON PLAYING KITS SEASON 2005.06**

FIRST KIT　　SECOND KIT　　THIRD KIT

# PARTICK THISTLE

**PARTICK THISTLE F.C.**

Firhill Stadium, 80 Firhill Road,

Glasgow, G20 7AL

**TELEPHONE NUMBERS**

Ground/Ticket Office/Commercial

(0141) 579 1971

Jagsline (09068) 666474

**FAX** (0141) 945 1525

**E-MAIL** mail@ptfc.co.uk

**E-MAIL 2** tonia@ptfc.co.uk

**WEBSITE** www.ptfc.co.uk

**CHAIRMAN** T. Brown McMaster

**VICE-CHAIRMAN** Allan Cowan

**DIRECTORS**

Thomas Hughes, James Oliver,

Edward Prentice, Norman Springford,

Gordon D. Peden, Ronald S. Gilfillan

& Grant A. Bannerman

**ASSOCIATE DIRECTORS**

Robert W. Reid, Les Hope & John Lambie

**HONORARY VICE-PRESIDENT**

Robert W. Reid

**SECRETARY / OFFICE ADMINISTRATOR**

Antonia Kerr

**MANAGER** Richard Campbell

**ASSISTANT MANAGER** Jimmy Bone

**GOALKEEPING COACH** Tom Scott

**TEAM CAPTAIN** Marc Smyth

**COMMERCIAL MANAGER &**

**MEDIA LIAISON OFFICER**

Michael Max (0141) 579 1971

**LOTTERY MANAGER** Bobby Briggs

**MATCHDAY PROGRAMME EDITOR**

Tom Hosie

**CLUB DOCTOR** Dr Alan W. Robertson

**PHYSIOTHERAPIST** George Hannah

**GROUNDSMAN** George Furze

**KIT PERSON** Ricky Roughan

**CHIEF STEWARD** Brian McKigen

**SHOP MANAGERESS** Liz Gordon

**CLUB SHOP**

80 Firhill Road, Glasgow, G20 7AL

Tel (0141) 579 1971.

Open each Matchday:

12.30p.m. - 4.30p.m.

Upstairs office shop open daily:

9.00 a.m. - 4.30 p.m.

**OFFICIAL SUPPORTERS CLUB**

c/o Firhill Stadium,

80 Firhill Road,

Glasgow, G20 7AL

**SHIRT SPONSOR** D.H. Morris

**KIT SUPPLIER** TFG

## LIST OF PLAYERS 2005.06

| PLAYERS SURNAME | FIRST NAME | MIDDLE NAME | DATE OF BIRTH | PLACE OF BIRTH | DATE SIGNED | HEIGHT FT INS | WEIGHT ST LBS | POSITION ON PITCH | PREVIOUS CLUB |
|---|---|---|---|---|---|---|---|---|---|
| Arthur | Kenneth | | 07/12/78 | Bellshill | 01/06/97 | 6.3 | 13.8 | Goalkeeper | Possilpark Y.M.C.A. |
| Brady | Darren | Simon | 04/11/81 | Glasgow | 27/01/05 | 5.11 | 11.0 | Midfield | Raith Rovers |
| Cameron | Ian | | 23/05/88 | Glasgow | 11/07/05 | 5.10 | 11.2 | Midfield | Partick Thistle Form D U16 |
| Carter | Jonathan | | 02/12/87 | Glasgow | 10/06/04 | 6.1 | 12.5 | Defender | Partick Thistle Form D U16 |
| Cassidy | Paul | John | 18/11/86 | Glasgow | 02/07/03 | 5.11 | 10.7 | Midfield | Partick Thistle Form D U16 |
| Craig | David | William | 11/06/69 | Glasgow | 31/08/05 | 6.2 | 13.0 | Defender | Brechin City |
| Dorrans | Graham | | 05/05/87 | Glasgow | 31/08/05 | 5.10 | 11.0 | Forward | Livingston |
| Gibson | Andrew | Stewart | 02/03/82 | Glasgow | 03/07/00 | 5.10 | 10.9 | Mid / Fwd | Partick Thistle B.C. |
| Gibson | James | Robert | 19/02/80 | Bellshill | 02/06/05 | 5.7 | 11.3 | Midfield | Clyde |
| Gibson | William | | 01/08/81 | Bellshill | 09/07/04 | 5.10.5 | 11.13 | Midfield | Rangers |
| Gillies | Richard | Charles | 24/08/76 | Glasgow | 02/06/05 | 5.10 | 12.2 | Forward | St. Mirren |
| Haswell | Kenneth | Andrew | 29/02/88 | Glasgow | 10/06/04 | 6.1 | 11.11 | Defender | Celtic Form D Under 16 |
| Kilgannon | Sean | David | 08/03/81 | Stirling | 20/07/05 | 5.11 | 12.5 | Midfield | Ross County |
| McConalogue | Stephen | | 16/06/81 | Glasgow | 26/01/05 | 5.9 | 11.7 | Forward | St. Johnstone |
| McCulloch | Scott | Anderson | 29/11/75 | Cumnock | 19/07/05 | 6.0 | 14.5 | Defender | Ayr United |
| McDevitt | Gary | | 12/03/88 | Glasgow | 05/01/05 | 5.9 | 11.0 | Defender | Partick Thistle Form D U11 |
| McGoldrick | John | Lowe | 30/06/88 | Bellshill | 04/06/04 | 5.11 | 11.4 | Forward | Partick Thistle Form D U16 |
| Murray | Grant | Robert | 29/08/75 | Edinburgh | 23/06/03 | 5.10 | 12.0 | Defender | St. Johnstone |
| Nicholas | Steven | Arthur | 08/07/81 | Stirling | 11/07/05 | 5.10 | 12.0 | Forward | East Fife |
| Roberts | Mark | Kingsley | 29/10/75 | Irvine | 19/08/05 | 5.11 | 11.10 | Forward | Airdrie United |
| Santala | Jukka | | 10/09/85 | Helsinki | 04/08/05 | 6.2 | 13.0 | Defender | Rangers |
| Smyth | Marc | | 27/12/82 | Edinburgh | 30/05/05 | 6.0 | 11.7 | Defender | Ayr United |
| Snowdon | William | Robert | 07/01/83 | Colchester | 11/03/05 | 5.11 | 11.10 | Defender | Livingston |
| Stewart | Colin | James | 10/01/80 | Middlesbrough | 19/08/05 | 6.3 | 12.12 | Goalkeeper | Ross County |
| Stewart | Mark | Gordon | 22/06/88 | Glasgow | 10/06/04 | 5.7 | 10.6 | Forward | Celtic Form D Under 1 |
| Strachan | Adam | | 24/02/87 | Glasgow | 26/11/03 | 5.10.5 | 11.0 | Forward | Partick Thistle Form D U1 |

## TICKET INFORMATION

**Season Ticket Information**

**Seated**

| | |
|---|---|
| Adult | £225 |
| OAP/U16/Student | £115 |
| U12 | £60 |

**League Admission Prices**

| | |
|---|---|
| Adult | £13 |
| OAP/U16/Student | £7 |

**MILESTONES:**

**Year of formation:** 1876

**Most capped player:** Alan Rough

**No. of caps:** 53

**Most League points in a season:**

57 (First Division – Season 1991/92) (2 Points for a Win)

75 (Second Division – Season 2000/01) (3 Points for a Win)

**Most League goals scored by a player in a season:**

Alex Hair (Season 1926/27)

**No. of goals scored:** 41

**Record Attendance:** 49,838 (-v- Rangers – 18.2.1922)

**Record Victory:**

16-0 (-v- Royal Albert – Scottish Cup, 17.1.1931)

**Record Defeat:** 0-10 (-v- Queen's Park – Scottish Cup, 3.12.188

# SEASON STATS 2004.05

## SEASON STATS 2004.05

| DATE | VENUE | OPPONENTS | ATT | RES | Arthur K. | Gibson W. | Howie W. | Murray G.R. | Dowie A.J. | Fulton S. | Mitchell J.M. | Fleming D.A. | Escalas J.A.R. | Hinds L.M. | Anis J-Y. | Wilkinson A.G. | Panther E.U.E. | Oné A. | Milne K. | Madaschi A.A. | Strachan A. | Britton G.J. | Ross I. | McLaren M. | Gibson A.S. | Ross A.C. | McConalogue S. | Brady D.S. | Snowdon W.R. | Bennett N.R. | Paterson S.T. | Stewart M.G. | Cameron I. |
|---|---|---|---|---|---|---|---|---|---|---|---|---|---|---|---|---|---|---|---|---|---|---|---|---|---|---|---|---|---|---|---|---|---|---|
| 7-Aug | A | Clyde | 3,352 | 1-2 | 1 | 2 | 3 | 4 | 5 | 6 | 7 | 8 | **9** | 10 | 11 | 16 | 16 | | 17 | | | | | | | | | | | | | | |
| 14-Aug | H | Airdrie United | 4,011 | 3-2 | 1 | 2 | 16 | 4 | | 6 | **7** | 8 | **9** | **10** | 11 | 5 | 15 | | | | | 3 | | | | | | | | | | | |
| 21-Aug | A | Hamilton Academical | 3,543 | 1-0 | 1 | 2 | | 4 | 5 | 6 | 7 | 8 | **9** | 9 | 11 | | 15 | 17 | 3 | | | | | | | | | | | | | | |
| 28-Aug | A | Ross County | 2,781 | 1-0 | 1 | 2 | 14 | 4 | 5 | 6 | 7 | 8 | | **10** | 11 | | 17 | 9 | 3 | | | | | | | | | | | | | | |
| 4-Sep | H | Falkirk | 5,157 | 1-4 | 1 | 2 | 11 | 4 | | 6 | 7 | 8 | 9 | 10 | | | 14 | 17 | 3 | 5 | | | | | | | | | | | | |
| 11-Sep | A | St. Mirren | 4,711 | 1-2 | 1 | 2 | 11 | 4 | 5 | 6 | 7 | 8 | **9** | 10 | | | 3 | 17 | 14 | | | | | | | | | | | | | | |
| 18-Sep | H | Queen of the South | 3,233 | 1-2 | 1 | | 7 | 4 | 5 | 6 | | 8 | **9** | 11 | 15 | | 2 | 10 | 14 | 3 | 17 | | | | | | | | | | | | |
| 25-Sep | A | St. Johnstone | 2,763 | 1-2 | 1 | | 14 | 4 | 5 | | 8 | 9 | 7 | 17 | 2 | 6 | | 10 | **11** | 3 | | 16 | | | | | | | | | | | |
| 2-Oct | H | Raith Rovers | 3,059 | 2-0 | 1 | | | 4 | 5 | 14 | 8 | 9 | 17 | 7 | 2 | **6** | **10** | 11 | 3 | | | | | | | | | | | | | | |
| 16-Oct | A | Airdrie United | 2,548 | 2-4 | 1 | 16 | | 4 | 5 | 14 | 8 | **9** | 17 | 7 | 2 | 6 | 10 | 11 | **3** | | | | | | | | | | | | | | |
| 23-Oct | H | Clyde | 4,026 | 0-0 | 1 | 2 | | 3 | 6 | 7 | 8 | 9 | 10 | | | 4 | 14 | 11 | 5 | | | | | | | | | | | | | | |
| 30-Oct | H | Ross County | 2,898 | 4-0 | 1 | 2 | | 4 | 3 | 6 | 7 | 8 | **9**² | 10 | | | 14 | **17** | 11 | **5** | | 16 | | | | | | | | | | | |
| 13-Nov | H | St. Mirren | 4,949 | 0-3 | 1 | 2 | | 4 | 3 | 6 | 7 | 8 | 9 | 10 | | | 16 | 17 | 11 | 5 | | | 14 | | | | | | | | | | |
| 20-Nov | A | Queen of the South | 2,221 | 0-1 | 1 | 2 | | 4 | 3 | 6 | | 8 | 9 | 10 | 7 | | 17 | 14 | | 5 | | | 11 | 16 | | | | | | | | | |
| 23-Nov | A | Falkirk | 3,335 | 0-3 | 1 | | 8 | 4 | 3 | 6 | | 15 | 9 | 10 | | 2 | | 14 | | 5 | 17 | | 11 | 7 | | | | | | | | | |
| 27-Nov | A | Raith Rovers | 2,452 | 0-0 | 1 | 7 | | 4 | 5 | 6 | | 8 | 9 | 10 | | 2 | | | 14 | 17 | | 3 | 11 | | | | | | | | | | |
| 4-Dec | H | St. Johnstone | 2,945 | 0-4 | 1 | | | 4 | 3 | 6 | | 8 | 9 | 10 | | 7 | | 15 | 5 | | | 11 | 14 | | | | | | | | | | |
| 11-Dec | A | Clyde | 1,938 | 1-1 | 1 | | | 4 | 3 | | 16 | 8 | 9 | 10 | | | 2 | | 11 | 5 | | 6 | 7 | | | | | | | | | | |
| 18-Dec | H | Hamilton Academical | 3,051 | 0-1 | 1 | 2 | | 4 | 3 | | 16 | 8 | 9 | 10 | | | 15 | 11 | 5 | 17 | | 6 | 7 | | | | | | | | | | |
| 27-Dec | A | Ross County | 2,844 | 1-2 | 1 | 8 | | 2 | 5 | 15 | 7 | 6 | **9** | 10 | | 4 | | 16 | 11 | 3 | | | 14 | | | | | | | | | | |
| 29-Dec | H | Falkirk | 4,120 | 2-1 | 1 | 16 | | 4 | | | 7 | 6 | 9 | 14 | 2 | 17 | **8**² | 3 | 5 | 11 | | 10 | | | | | | | | | | | |
| 1-Jan | A | St. Mirren | 3,779 | 1-1 | 1 | 16 | | 4 | | | 7 | **6** | 9 | 14 | 2 | | 8 | 3 | 5 | 11 | | | 10 | | | | | | | | | | |
| 15-Jan | H | Queen of the South | 3,257 | ††3-1 | 1 | | | 4 | 14 | 7 | 6 | 9 | 17 | 2 | | | **8** | 3 | 5 | 10 | | | 11 | 15 | | | | | | | | | |
| 22-Jan | A | St. Johnstone | 2,814 | 1-1 | 1 | 15 | | 4 | 6 | 14 | | 9 | **16** | 2 | | | 8 | 3 | 5 | 11 | | | 7 | 10 | | | | | | | | | |
| 29-Jan | H | Raith Rovers | 3,181 | 4-1 | 1 | 2 | | 4 | 14 | 6 | | 11 | 17 | 8 | | | 9 | 3 | 5 | | | | 7 | **10** | **16**² | | | | | | | | |
| 12-Feb | H | Airdrie United | 3,791 | 1-1 | 1 | 2 | | 4 | 5 | 6 | | **11** | 14 | 8 | | | 9 | 3 | | | | | 7 | 10 | 15 | 16 | | | | | | | |
| 19-Feb | A | Hamilton Academical | 3,128 | 0-1 | 1 | | 2 | 4 | | | 3 | 11 | 17 | | | | 9 | 5 | 16 | | | | 7 | 10 | 8 | 6 | | | | | | | |
| 5-Mar | A | Falkirk | 4,157 | 1-2 | 1 | 14 | **2** | 4 | | 7 | 6 | | 16 | | | | 9 | 3 | 5 | 17 | | | 8 | 10 | 11 | | | | | | | | |
| 13-Mar | H | Ross County | 2,939 | 0-0 | 1 | | 5 | 6 | | 10 | 16 | 9 | 15 | | | | 3 | | 11 | | | 7 | 8 | 14 | 4 | 2 | | | | | | | |
| 19-Mar | H | St. Mirren | 3,730 | 0-0 | 1 | | 5 | 4 | | 7 | 11 | 9 | 17 | | | 16 | 3 | | | | | 14 | 8 | 10 | 6 | 2 | | | | | | | |
| 2-Apr | A | Queen of the South | 2,589 | 1-3 | 1 | 14 | | 4 | 5 | 7 | 11 | | 16 | | | | 9 | 3 | 6 | | | | 10 | **17** | 8 | 2 | | | | | | | |
| 9-Apr | A | Raith Rovers | 1,403 | 1-2 | | | 7 | 4 | | | 15 | **16** | 8 | | | | | 3 | 5 | 11 | | 14 | 10 | 9 | 6 | 2 | 1 | | | | | | |
| 16-Apr | H | St. Johnstone | 2,310 | 0-4 | 1 | 7 | | 2 | | | 6 | 9 | 16 | | | | | 3 | 5 | | | 11 | 15 | 10 | 8 | 14 | | 4 | | | | | |
| 23-Apr | H | Clyde | 2,757 | 1-0 | 1 | 8 | | | | 3 | | 7 | 2 | | | 9 | 6 | | | | | 11 | 16 | **10** | 4 | 5 | | | 17 | | | | |
| 30-Apr | A | Airdrie United | 1,747 | 1-0 | 1 | 8 | | 14 | | 3 | | 9 | 2 | | | | | 5 | 16 | | | 7 | 11 | 10 | 6 | 4 | | | | 15 | | |
| 7-May | H | Hamilton Academical | 2,845 | †1-1 | 1 | 4 | | | | 3 | | 10 | 2 | | | | 15 | 6 | | | | 7 | 11 | 9 | 8 | 5 | | | | | 16 | 17 |
| **TOTAL FULL APPEARANCES** | | | | | 35 | 22 | 4 | 31 | 26 | 16 | 17 | 32 | 27 | 24 | 14 | 9 | 6 | 15 | 26 | 26 | 6 | | 6 | 5 | 11 | 11 | 8 | 10 | 7 | 1 | 1 | | |
| **TOTAL SUB APPEARANCES** | | | | | | 6 | 3 | 1 | 1 | 3 | 4 | 3 | 3 | 12 | 2 | 2 | 8 | 12 | 4 | 1 | 7 | 1 | 1 | 4 | 2 | 3 | 4 | 1 | 1 | | | 2 | 2 |
| **TOTAL GOALS SCORED** | | | | | | | | | 1 | 2 | 10 | 4 | | 1 | 2 | 6 | 1 | 2 | | | | | | 1 | 4 | | | | | | |

Figure in bold denotes goal scored. Secondary smaller figure in bold denotes number of goals scored. † denotes opponent's own goal.

## THE JAGS' 10 YEAR LEAGUE RECORD

| Season | Div | P | W | D | L | F | A | Pts | Pos |
|---|---|---|---|---|---|---|---|---|---|
| 95-96 | P | 36 | 8 | 6 | 22 | 29 | 62 | 30 | 9 |
| 96-97 | F | 36 | 12 | 12 | 12 | 49 | 48 | 48 | 6 |
| 97-98 | F | 36 | 8 | 12 | 16 | 45 | 55 | 36 | 9 |
| 98-99 | S | 36 | 12 | 7 | 17 | 36 | 45 | 43 | 8 |
| 99-00 | S | 36 | 12 | 14 | 10 | 42 | 44 | 46 | 5 |
| 00-01 | S | 36 | 22 | 9 | 5 | 66 | 32 | 75 | 1 |
| 01-02 | F | 36 | 19 | 9 | 8 | 61 | 38 | 66 | 1 |
| 02-03 | SPL | 38 | 8 | 11 | 19 | 37 | 58 | 35 | 10 |
| 03-04 | SPL | 38 | 6 | 8 | 24 | 39 | 67 | 26 | 12 |
| 04-05 | F | 36 | 10 | 9 | 17 | 38 | 52 | 39 | 9 |

## LEADING GOALSCORERS:

| Season | Div | Goals | Player |
|---|---|---|---|
| 1995-96 | P | 5 | A. Lyons, R. McDonald |
| 1996-97 | F | 11 | D. Moss |
| 1997-98 | F | 6 | J. Stirling |
| 1998-99 | S | 10 | R. Dunn |
| 1999-00 | S | 5 | R. Dunn |
| 2000-01 | S | 16 | S. McLean |
| 2001-02 | F | 12 | G. Britton |
| 2002-03 | SPL | 16 | A. Burns |
| 2003-04 | SPL | 15 | J. Grady |
| 2004-05 | F | 10 | J. Escalas |

**PARTICK THISTLE PLAYING KITS SEASON 2005.06**

FIRST KIT | SECOND KIT | THIRD KIT

# PETERHEAD

**PETERHEAD F.C.**

Balmoor Stadium,

Lord Catto Park,

Balmoor Terrace,

Peterhead, AB42 1EU

**TELEPHONE NUMBERS**

Ground (01779) 478256

Sec. Bus. (01224) 820851

Sec. Home. (01779) 476870

Sec. Mob. 07740 105457

**FAX** (01779) 490682

**E-MAIL** georgemoore@tiscali.co.uk

**WEBSITE** www.peterheadfc.org.uk

**CLUB CORRESPONDENCE ADDRESS**

Mr. G.Moore

Secretary,

Peterhead F.C.

23 Willowbank Road,

Peterhead, AB42 2FG

**CHAIRMAN** Rodger G. Morrison

**VICE-CHAIRMAN** George Watson

**DIRECTORS**

Gerry Gaffney & Charles M. Donaldson

**GENERAL MANAGER**

Dave Watson (M) 07774 615820

**COMMITTEE**

Dave Watson, Arthur Duncan & George Moore

**SECRETARY** George Moore

**MANAGER** Iain Stewart

**ASSISTANT MANAGER** Paul Mathers

**FIRST TEAM COACH** Shaun McSkimming

**CHIEF SCOUT** Andy Gibson

**TEAM CAPTAIN** Robert Raeside

**OFFICE ADMINISTRATOR / TREASURER**

Shona Aird

**FOOTBALL SAFETY OFFICERS'**

**ASSOCIATION REPRESENTATIVE**

Arthur Duncan (01779) 477201

**MEDIA LIAISON PERSONS**

Dave Watson (01224) 771100 &

George Moore 07740 105457

**MATCHDAY PROGRAMME EDITOR**

Ken Duncan (01779) 476373

**CLUB DOCTOR** Dr. Ian Small

**PHYSIOTHERAPIST** Sandy Rennie

**GROUNDSMAN** Bill Spence

**KIT PERSON** Robert Buchan

**OFFICIAL SUPPORTERS CLUB**

c/o Balmoor Stadium,

Peterhead, AB42 1EU

**SHIRT SPONSOR** L&N

**KIT SUPPLIER** ProStar

## LIST OF PLAYERS 2005.06

| PLAYERS SURNAME | FIRST NAME | MIDDLE NAME | DATE OF BIRTH | PLACE OF BIRTH | DATE SIGNED | HEIGHT FT INS | WEIGHT ST LBS | POSITION ON PITCH | PREVIOUS CLUB |
|---|---|---|---|---|---|---|---|---|---|
| Bavidge | Martin | Mitchell | 30/04/80 | Aberdeen | 24/07/03 | 6.1 | 13.7 | Forward | Forfar Athletic |
| Buchan | Martin | James | 03/04/77 | Manchester | 23/01/04 | 5.11 | 12.7 | Midfield | Stockport County |
| Cameron | Douglas | James | 08/02/83 | Dundee | 19/01/05 | 5.10 | 12.8 | Midfield | Dundee |
| Duncan | Robert | | 08/03/83 | Peterhead | 01/08/03 | 5.11 | 11.0 | Forward | Aberdeen |
| Farquhar | John | Graham | 31/07/85 | Aberdeen | 28/08/04 | 5.11 | 10.7 | Goalkeeper | Wilsons X1 Juniors |
| Gibson | Keith | | 01/05/81 | Dundee | 26/03/04 | 6.0 | 12.4 | Midfield | Montrose |
| Good | Iain | David | 09/08/77 | Glasgow | 24/07/03 | 6.1 | 12.0 | Defender | Forfar Athletic |
| Hagen | David | James | 05/05/73 | Edinburgh | 10/06/04 | 5.11 | 13.12 | Forward | Clyde |
| Hegarty | Christopher | James | 24/07/84 | Dundee | 13/07/05 | 5.8 | 11.0 | Midfield | Dundee |
| Linn | Robert | Alexander | 10/10/85 | Dundee | 13/10/04 | 5.8 | 10.7 | Forward | Dundee |
| Mathers | Paul | | 17/01/70 | Aberdeen | 30/05/02 | 6.0 | 12.7 | Goalkeeper | Berwick Rangers |
| McCafferty | John | | 21/03/85 | Dundee | 13/07/05 | 5.10 | 11.9 | Goalkeeper | East Fife |
| Michie | Scott | David | 22/08/83 | Aberdeen | 08/07/04 | 5.10 | 11.7 | Forward | Aberdeen |
| Perry | Mark | George | 07/02/71 | Aberdeen | 31/01/03 | 6.1 | 12.10 | Defender | Ross County |
| Raeside | Robert | | 07/07/72 | Petersburg - S.A. | 09/08/02 | 6.2 | 13.10 | Defender | Alloa Athletic |
| Robertson | Colin | David | 13/07/85 | Dundee | 30/08/04 | 5.10 | 11.0 | Midfield | Wilsons X1 Juniors |
| Shand | Calvin | David | 09/11/83 | Edinburgh | 06/06/05 | 6.0 | 11.6 | Defender | Cowdenbeath |
| Sharp | Graeme | Malcolm | 03/05/84 | Fraserburgh | 13/07/05 | 5.10 | 11.0 | Midfield | Montrose |
| Stewart | Graeme | John | 02/04/82 | Aberdeen | 11/07/03 | 6.1 | 12.8 | Midfield | Inverness Caledonian Thistle |
| Stewart | Iain | Angus | 23/10/69 | Dundee | 27/06/02 | 5.7 | 10.5 | Forward | Inverness Caledonian Thistle |
| Tully | Craig | | 07/01/76 | Stirling | 21/05/04 | 6.0 | 12.10 | Defender | Elgin City |
| Wood | Martin | | 20/08/82 | Aberdeen | 13/07/05 | 5.10 | 13.0 | Forward | Montrose |
| Youngson | Allan | | 29/09/84 | Aberdeen | 08/06/04 | 5.9 | 11.3 | Def / Mid | Dundee |

## TICKET INFORMATION

### Season Ticket Information

**Seated**

Adult — £130

Adult & Juvenile — £195

OAP — £65

**Standing**

Adult — £110

Juvenile/OAP — £55

### League Admission Prices

**Seated**

Adult — £10

Juvenile/OAP — £5

**Standing**

Adult — £10

Juvenile/OAP — £5

**MILESTONES:**

**Year of formation:** 1891

**Most League points in a season:**

89 (Highland League – Season 1989/90 (3 Points for a Win)

78 (SFL Third Division – Season 2004/05 (3 Points for a Win)

**Most League goals scored by a player in a season:**

Iain Stewart (Season 2001/02)

**No. of goals scored:** 23

**Record Attendance:**

6,310 (-v- Celtic – 1948 at Recreation Park)

2,200 (-v- Aberdeen – 6.7.2002 – at Balmoor Stadium)

**Record Victory:**

17-0 (-v- Fort William – Season 1998/99)

**Record Defeat:** 0-13 (-v- Aberdeen, Scottish Cup, Season 1923/2...

BELL'S SCOTTISH FOOTBALL LEAGUE

## SEASON STATS 2004.05

| DATE | VENUE | OPPONENTS | ATT | RES | Mathers P. | Tully C. | Good I.D. | Raeside R. | Perry M.G. | Gibson K. | Campbell C. | Buchan M.J. | Michie S.D. | Bavidge M.M. | Hagen D.J. | Tindal K.D. | Youngson A. | Johnston M.A. | Robertson S. | Milne D.D. | Stewart G.J. | Linn R.A. | McSkimming S.P. | Shand R. | Cameron D. | Thompson B.C. | Hegarty C.J. | Stewart I.A. | Robertson C. | Duncan R. |
|---|---|---|---|---|---|---|---|---|---|---|---|---|---|---|---|---|---|---|---|---|---|---|---|---|---|---|---|---|---|
| 7-Aug | H | East Stirlingshire | 561 | 5-0 | 1 | 2$^2$ | 3 | 4 | 5 | 6 | 7 | 8 | 9 | 10 | 11 | 12 | 14 | 15 | | | | | | | | | | | | |
| 14-Aug | A | Montrose | 379 | 1-0 | 1 | 2 | | 4 | 5 | 6 | 7 | 8 | 9 | 10 | 11 | | 14 | 3 | 12 | | | | | | | | | | | |
| 21-Aug | H | Elgin City | 688 | 2-1 | 1 | 2 | | 4 | 5 | 6 | 7 | 8 | 9 | 10 | 11 | | | 3 | 12 | | | | | | | | | | | |
| 28-Aug | A | Albion Rovers | 351 | 1-0 | 1 | 2 | | 4 | 5 | 6 | 7 | 8 | 9 | 10 | 11 | | 12 | | **3** | | | | | | | | | | | |
| 4-Sep | H | East Fife | 507 | 2-0 | 1 | 2 | 3 | 4 | 5 | 6 | 14 | 8 | 9$^2$ | 10 | 11 | 12 | | | | | 7 | 16 | | | | | | | | |
| 11-Sep | H | Gretna | 861 | 1-1 | 1 | 2 | 3 | 4 | 5 | 6 | | 8 | 9 | 10 | 11 | | | | | | 15 | 7 | | | | | | | | |
| 18-Sep | A | Stenhousemuir | 307 | 2-1 | 1 | 2 | 3 | 4 | 5 | 6 | 12 | 8 | 9$^2$ | 10 | 11 | | 14 | | | | 7 | 15 | | | | | | | | |
| 25-Sep | H | Cowdenbeath | 582 | 3-1 | 1 | 2 | 3 | 4 | 5 | 6 | 12 | 8 | 9$^2$ | 10 | 11 | | 14 | | | | 7 | 15 | | | | | | | | |
| 2-Oct | A | Queen' Park | 625 | 2-1 | 1 | 2 | 3 | 4 | 5 | 6 | 12 | 8 | 9 | 10 | 11 | | 14 | | | | 7 | | | | | | | | | |
| 16-Oct | H | Montrose | 626 | 3-2 | 1 | 2 | 3 | 4 | 5 | 6 | 7 | 8 | 9 | 10 | 11 | | | 15 | 14 | | 12 | | | | | | | | | |
| 23-Oct | A | East Stirlingshire | 281 | 2-1 | 1 | 2 | 3 | 4 | 5 | 6 | 7 | 8 | 9$^2$ | 10 | 11 | | 14 | 15 | | | 12 | | | | | | | | | |
| 30-Oct | H | Albion Rovers | 729 | †4-1 | 1 | 2 | | 4 | 5 | 6 | | 8 | 9$^2$ | 10 | 11 | 12 | 14 | | | 3 | 7 | | | | | | | | | |
| 6-Nov | A | East Fife | 410 | 2-0 | 1 | 2 | 15 | 4 | 5 | 6 | 14 | 8 | 9 | 10 | 11 | 12 | | | | 3 | 7 | | | | | | | | | |
| 13-Nov | A | Gretna | 2,200 | 1-2 | 1 | 2 | 3 | 4 | 5 | 6 | 7 | 8 | 15 | 10 | 11 | | | | | | | 9 | | | | | | | | |
| 30-Nov | H | Stenhousemuir | 499 | 5-0 | 1 | 2 | 3 | 4 | 5 | 6 | | 8 | 9 | 10$^4$ | 11 | | 12 | | | | 7 | 14 | 16 | | | | | | | |
| 4-Dec | A | Cowdenbeath | 201 | 4-0 | 1 | 2 | 3 | 4 | 5 | 6 | | 8 | 9$^3$ | 10 | 11 | | 12 | | | 7 | | 15 | 16 | | | | | | | |
| 18-Dec | H | Queen' Park | 569 | 2-2 | 1 | 2 | 3 | 4 | 5 | 6 | | 8 | 9 | 10 | 11 | | 14 | | | 12 | 7 | | | | | | | | | |
| 27-Dec | H | East Stirlingshire | 647 | 3-0 | 1 | 2 | 3 | 4 | 5 | 12 | 14 | 8 | 9 | 10 | 11 | | | | | 15 | 6 | 7 | | | | | | | | |
| 3-Jan | A | Albion Rovers | 306 | 4-0 | 1 | 2 | 3 | 4 | 5 | 12 | 7 | 8$^2$ | 16 | 10 | 11 | | | | | 14 | 6 | 9 | | | | | | | | |
| 15-Jan | H | East Fife | 587 | 0-0 | 1 | 2 | 3 | 4 | 5 | 14 | | 8 | 15 | 10 | 11 | | | | | 7 | 6 | 9 | | | | | | | | |
| 22-Jan | H | Gretna | 1,207 | 4-2 | 1 | 2 | 3 | 4 | 5 | 12 | 7 | 8 | 9 | 10 | | | | | | | 6 | 14 | | | | | | | 11 | |
| 29-Jan | A | Stenhousemuir | 394 | 1-1 | 1 | 2 | 3 | 4 | 5 | 12 | 7 | 8 | 9 | 10 | | | | | | | 6 | 14 | | | | | | | 11 | |
| 5-Feb | H | Cowdenbeath | 563 | 1-1 | 1 | 2 | 3 | 4 | 5 | 6 | 15 | 8 | 9 | 10 | | | 14 | | | | 7 | 12 | | | | | | | 11 | |
| 12-Feb | A | Queen' Park | 454 | 1-1 | 1 | 2 | 3 | 4 | 5 | 6 | 7 | 8 | 9 | 10 | | | 14 | | | | 12 | 16 | | | | | | | 11 | |
| 26-Feb | A | Montrose | 467 | 2-0 | 1 | 2 | 3 | 4 | 5 | 6 | | 8 | 9$^2$ | 15 | 11 | | 14 | | | | 16 | 10 | | 7 | | | | | | |
| 1-Mar | H | Elgin City | 611 | 3-0 | 1 | 2 | 3 | 4 | 5 | 6 | 12 | 8 | 9 | 14 | 11 | | | | | | 15 | 10 | | 7 | | | | | | |
| 5-Mar | A | East Fife | 495 | 2-1 | 1 | 2 | 3 | 4 | 5 | 6 | 12 | 8 | 9 | 14 | **11** | | | | | | 15 | 10 | | 7 | | | | | | |
| 8-Mar | A | Elgin City | 383 | †2-2 | 1 | 2 | 3 | 4 | 5 | 6 | | 8 | 9 | 14 | 11 | | 15 | | | | 16 | 10 | | 7 | | | | | | |
| 12-Mar | H | Albion Rovers | 532 | 2-3 | 1 | 2 | | 4 | 5 | 6 | 7 | 8 | 12 | 9 | 11 | | | | | 3 | 15 | 10 | 14 | | | | | | | |
| 19-Mar | A | Gretna | 1,538 | 1-6 | 1 | 2 | 3 | 4 | 5 | 6 | 12 | 8 | 14 | 10 | 11 | | | | | | 15 | 9 | | | | | | | | |
| 2-Apr | A | Stenhousemuir | 523 | 1-1 | | 2 | | 4 | 5 | 6 | 15 | 8 | 9 | 10 | 11 | | 14 | | | 3 | 7 | 12 | | | 1 | | | | | |
| 9-Apr | H | Queen' Park | 479 | 1-1 | | 2 | | 4 | 5 | 6 | 15 | 8 | 9 | | 11 | | 14 | | | 3 | 7 | 10 | 12 | | 1 | | | | | |
| 16-Apr | A | Cowdenbeath | 153 | 0-4 | | 2 | 3 | 4 | 5 | | 12 | 8 | 9 | 10 | 11 | | | | | | 6 | 15 | 7 | | 1 | | | | | |
| 23-Apr | A | Elgin City | 507 | 2-0 | 1 | 2 | 3 | 4 | 5 | | | 8 | 9 | 10 | 11 | | 14 | | | | 6 | 12 | **7** | | | | | | | |
| 30-Apr | H | Montrose | 702 | 4-1 | 1 | 2 | 3 | 4 | 5 | | | 8 | 9 | 10 | 11 | | | | | | **6$^2$** | 7 | | | | | | 15 | 12 | 16 |
| 7-May | A | East Stirlingshire | 192 | 5-1 | 1 | 2 | | 4 | | | | 8 | 9 | **10$^2$** | 11 | | 12 | | | | 7 | 6 | | | | | 3 | 14 | 5 | 15 |
| **TOTAL FULL APPEARANCES** | | | | | 33 | 34 | 31 | 32 | 34 | 27 | 12 | 35 | 30 | 31 | 25 | | 14 | 10 | | 13 | 14 | | 13 | 3 | 4 | | 1 | | | |
| **TOTAL SUB APPEARANCES** | | | | | | 1 | 1 | | | 5 | 11 | 1 | 6 | 5 | 1 | 2 | 17 | 5 | 3 | 1 | 8 | 13 | 3 | 1 | | 3 | 1 | 2 | | 1 |
| **TOTAL GOALS SCORED** | | | | | | 7 | 4 | | | | 1 | 8 | 21 | 13 | 3 | | | 2 | 1 | 1 | | 6 | 6 | | | 4 | | 1 | 1 | |

Figure in bold denotes goal scored. Secondary smaller figure in bold denotes number of goals scored. † denotes opponent's own goal.

## THE BLUE TOON'S 10 YEAR LEAGUE RECORD

Season 2000-01 was the club's first season in membership of SFL

| Season | Div | P | W | D | L | F | A | Pts | Pos |
|---|---|---|---|---|---|---|---|---|---|
| 2000-01 | T | 36 | 13 | 10 | 13 | 46 | 46 | 49 | 5 |
| 2001-02 | T | 36 | 17 | 5 | 14 | 63 | 52 | 56 | 4 |
| 2002-03 | T | 36 | 20 | 8 | 8 | 76 | 37 | 68 | 4 |
| 2003-04 | T | 36 | 18 | 7 | 11 | 67 | 37 | 61 | 4 |
| 2004-05 | T | 36 | 23 | 9 | 4 | 81 | 38 | 78 | 2 |

## LEADING GOALSCORERS:

Season 2000-01 was the club's first season in membership of SFL

| Season | Div | Goals | Player |
|---|---|---|---|
| 2000-01 | T | 11 | C. Yeats |
| 2001-02 | T | 19 | I. Stewart |
| 2002-03 | T | 21 | I. Stewart |
| 2003-04 | T | 18 | M. Johnston |
| 2004-05 | T | 21 | S. Michie |

PETERHEAD PLAYING KITS SEASON 2005.06 — FIRST KIT · SECOND KIT · THIRD KIT

# RAITH ROVERS

**RAITH ROVERS F.C.**
Stark's Park, Pratt Street,
Kirkcaldy, Fife, KY1 1SA
**TELEPHONE NUMBERS**
Ground (01592) 263514
**FAX** (01592) 642833
**E-MAIL** office@raithroversfc.com
**E-MAIL 2** bob.mullen@raithroversfc.com
**WEBSITE** www.raithroversfc.com
**DIRECTORS**
Mario Caira, Eric W. Drysdale,
William H. Gray, Colin C. McGowan,
Alexander Short & James Miller
**HONORARY PRESIDENT** John Urquhart
**SECRETARY** Robert Mullen
**MANAGER** Gordon Dalziel
**FIRST TEAM COACH** Shaun Dennis
**YOUTH CO-ORDINATOR** John Drysdale
**YOUTH DEVELOPMENT COACHES**
John Gavin, Iain Milligan, Ben Reekie &
Henry Smith
**YOUTH COACHES**
U17: George Gemmell & Ged Chapman
**TEAM CAPTAIN** Todd Lumsden
**FOOTBALL SAFETY OFFICERS'**
**ASSOCIATION REPRESENTATIVE**
Bill Brown (01592) 263514
**COMMERCIAL MANAGER**
John Drysdale (07962) 023683
**HOSPITALITY MANAGER** Tom Smith
**MATCHDAY PROGRAMME EDITOR**
John Drysdale
**WEBSITE NEWS EDITOR** Jim Foy
**CLUB PHOTOGRAPHER**
Tony Fimister (01592) 201645
**PHYSIOTHERAPIST** Don Lennox
**DISABILITY LIAISON** Elizabeth Drysdale
**GROUNDSMAN** John Murray
**KIT PERSON** Linda Patrick
**CLUB SHOP**
South Stand Shop situated within Stand.
Open during Office Hours 9.00 a.m. to 5.00 p.m.
and on Home Matchdays 2.00 p.m. to 5.00 p.m.
**OFFICIAL SUPPORTERS CLUB**
c/o Fraser Hamilton, 22 Tower Terrace,
Kirkcaldy, Fife
**SHIRT SPONSOR**
First Choice:
Front: Bar Itza
Back: F.F.D.R - All Trades Building Contractor
Second Choice:
Front: Ceramic Tile Warehouse
**KIT SUPPLIER** XARA

## LIST OF PLAYERS 2005.06

| PLAYERS SURNAME | FIRST NAME | MIDDLE NAME | DATE OF BIRTH | PLACE OF BIRTH | DATE SIGNED | HEIGHT FT INS | WEIGHT ST LBS | POSITION ON PITCH | PREVIOUS CLUB |
|---|---|---|---|---|---|---|---|---|---|
| Annand | Edward | | 24/03/73 | Glasgow | 28/06/05 | 5.11 | 13.1 | Forward | Dumbarton |
| Bagan | David | | 26/04/77 | Irvine | 02/09/05 | 5.7 | 10.7 | Midfield | St. Johnstone |
| Batchelor | Blair | | 24/03/88 | Falkirk | 26/07/05 | 5.7 | 10.7 | Midfield | St. Johnstone |
| Brown | Alistair | | 12/12/85 | Irvine | 25/07/05 | 6.1 | 12.4 | Goalkeeper | Hibernian |
| Campbell | Richard | | 15/01/88 | Edinburgh | 02/08/05 | 6.2 | 11.6 | Defender | Edina Hibs |
| Crabbe | Scott | | 12/08/68 | Edinburgh | 28/06/05 | 5.9 | 11.8 | Midfield | Albion Rovers |
| Crilly | Mark | Patrick | 23/05/80 | Glasgow | 22/06/05 | 5.11 | 11.7 | Midfield | St. Mirren |
| Cunningham | Dean | | 02/03/88 | Kirkcaldy | 09/09/05 | 5.8 | 11.6 | Midfield | Dunfermline Athletic |
| Davidson | Ian | | 14/01/84 | Kirkcaldy | 29/07/04 | 6.0 | 10.7 | Defender | Scarborough |
| Ellis | Laurence | | 07/11/79 | Edinburgh | 27/05/05 | 5.11 | 11.7 | Defender | St. Mirren |
| Fairbairn | Brian | | 07/04/83 | Broxburn | 29/07/05 | 5.10 | 11.7 | Forward | East Fife |
| Ferguson | Derek | | 31/07/67 | Glasgow | 27/05/05 | 5.8.5 | 11.2 | Midfield | Hamilton Academical |
| Gilfillan | Jamie | | 28/08/86 | Kirkcaldy | 30/08/04 | 5.10 | 11.7 | Forward | Kirkcaldy Y.M.C.A. Juniors |
| Hall | Stuart | Matthew | 09/02/87 | Kirkcaldy | 20/08/04 | 6.1 | 11.0 | Goalkeeper | Ballingry Rovers Juniors |
| Hilland | Paul | | 28/07/83 | Glasgow | 26/08/05 | 6.1 | 13.0 | Defender | Clyde |
| Jablonski | Neil | | 09/03/83 | Kirkcaldy | 30/06/05 | 6.1 | 12.12 | Midfield | Dundee |
| Jaconelli | Emilio | | 05/06/83 | Lanark | 22/06/05 | 5.8 | 12.5 | Forward | Queen of the South |
| Leiper | Colin | | 05/02/87 | Kirkcaldy | 01/09/04 | 6.2 | 11.0 | Midfield | Whitburn Juniors |
| Liddle | Christopher | | 03/09/88 | Broxburn | 30/07/05 | 5.11 | 11.2 | Defender | Falkirk Form D Under 14 |
| Lumsden | Todd | | 06/02/78 | Consett | 18/05/05 | 6.2 | 12.5 | Defender | Hamilton Academical |
| Lyle | William | | 14/04/84 | Irvine | 09/08/05 | 5.10 | 10.7 | Defender | Ayr United |
| McLeod | Christopher | | 28/01/84 | Edinburgh | 01/06/05 | 6.2 | 12.7 | Defender | Arbroath |
| McManus | Paul | John | 26/12/82 | Kirkcaldy | 06/07/05 | 5.10 | 10.5 | Forward | Stranraer |
| McMurray | John | Michael | 20/06/88 | Lanark | 02/08/05 | 5.8 | 11.0 | Defender | Hareleeshill B.C. |
| Silvestro | Christopher | | 16/03/79 | Bellshill | 25/05/05 | 5.7 | 11.4 | Midfield | Albion Rovers |
| Tulloch | Stephen | | 04/12/87 | Edinburgh | 06/10/04 | 6.1 | 13.0 | Defender | Dalkeith Thistle Juniors |
| Wilcox | Colin | James | 12/07/87 | Perth | 16/09/05 | 6.0 | 10.7 | Defender | Kinnoull Juniors |
| Wilson | Derek | | 01/11/88 | Bangour | 02/08/05 | 5.10 | 10.10 | Midfield | Linlithgow B.C. |
| Wilson | Scott | William | 20/04/82 | Bellshill | 28/06/05 | 6.3 | 11.2 | Defender | Clyde |

## TICKET INFORMATION
### Season Ticket Information

Seated

| | | |
|---|---|---|
| MAIN STAND & SOUTH STAND | Adult | £220 |
| | Juvenile/OAP | £100 |
| | Child (Primary School) | £50 |
| | Parent & Juvenile | £270 |

### League Admission Prices

Seated

| | | |
|---|---|---|
| MAIN STAND, SOUTH STAND & NORTH STAND | Adult | £12 |
| | Juvenile/OAP | £6 |

**MILESTONES:**
**Year of formation:** 1883
**Most capped player:** David Morris
**No. of caps:** 6
**Most League points in a season:**
65 (First Division - Season 1992/93) (2 Points for a Win)
69 (First Division - Season 1994/95) (3 Points for a Win)
**Most League goals scored by a player in a season:**
Norman Heywood (Season 1937/38)
**No. of goals scored:** 42
**Record Attendance:** 31,306 (-v- Hearts – Scottish Cup, 7.2.1953)
**Record Victory:** 10-1 (-v- Coldstream – Scottish Cup, 13.2.195...)
**Record Defeat:** 2-11 (-v- Morton – Division 2, 18.3.1936)

# SEASON STATS 2004.05

BELL'S
SCOTTISH FOOTBALL LEAGUE

## SEASON STATS 2004.05

Players (columns, left to right): Pounoussamy R.J.F., Rivas F.O., McAlpine J.C., Hajovsky T., Davidson I., Brady D.S., Young L.P., Sacko H., Hagan P., Ebanda H., Lusamba N., Boyle J., Smart J., Ouattara M., Bartholome A., O'Reilly C., Tagro B., Malcolm C., Berthelot D., Perry J.J., Daly W.J.P., Martin J., Maxwell D.R., Millar P.T., Dennis S., Raffell B.J., Mendy M., Leiper C., McMullen P., Tulloch S., Murtagh C., Jablonski N., Crabbe S., Fullerton E.J., McGowan M., Clarke P., Hall S.M., Gilfillan J.

| DATE | VENUE | OPPONENTS | ATT | RES |
|---|---|---|---|---|
| 7-Aug | A | Hamilton Academical | 2,176 | 0-2 |
| 14-Aug | H | Clyde | 1,784 | † 2-3 |
| 21-Aug | A | Airdrie United | 2,009 | 1-1 |
| 28-Aug | A | St. Johnstone | 2,574 | 0-1 |
| 4-Sep | H | Ross County | 1,540 | 1-2 |
| 11-Sep | A | Falkirk | 3,449 | 2-4 |
| 18-Sep | H | St. Mirren | 2,111 | 0-3 |
| 25-Sep | H | Queen of the South | 1,491 | 1-2 |
| 2-Oct | A | Partick Thistle | 3,059 | 0-2 |
| 16-Oct | A | Clyde | 1,196 | 0-2 |
| 23-Oct | H | Hamilton Academical | 1,943 | 2-2 |
| 30-Oct | H | St. Johnstone | 2,089 | 1-0 |
| 13-Nov | H | Falkirk | 3,050 | 0-2 |
| 20-Nov | A | St. Mirren | 3,002 | 1-1 |
| 23-Nov | A | Ross County | 1,183 | 1-1 |
| 27-Nov | H | Partick Thistle | 2,452 | 0-0 |
| 4-Dec | A | Queen of the South | 1,646 | 0-2 |
| 12-Dec | A | Hamilton Academical | 1,371 | 0-1 |
| 18-Dec | H | Airdrie United | 1,795 | 0-2 |
| 26-Dec | A | St. Johnstone | 2,579 | 0-2 |
| 29-Dec | H | Ross County | 1,127 | 1-4 |
| 1-Jan | A | Falkirk | 3,379 | 0-2 |
| 15-Jan | H | St. Mirren | 1,393 | 2-0 |
| 22-Jan | A | Queen of the South | 1,534 | 0-1 |
| 29-Jan | A | Partick Thistle | 3,181 | 1-4 |
| 12-Feb | H | Clyde | 1,394 | 3-3 |
| 19-Feb | A | Airdrie United | 1,599 | 1-2 |
| 5-Mar | A | Ross County | 2,086 | 0-2 |
| 12-Mar | H | St. Johnstone | 1,350 | 1-2 |
| 19-Mar | H | Falkirk | 2,369 | 3-3 |
| 2-Apr | A | St. Mirren | 2,193 | 0-3 |
| 9-Apr | H | Partick Thistle | 1,403 | 2-1 |
| 16-Apr | A | Queen of the South | 1,361 | 1-1 |
| 23-Apr | A | Hamilton Academical | 1,474 | 0-2 |
| 30-Apr | A | Clyde | 1,122 | 0-1 |
| 7-May | H | Airdrie United | 1,296 | 0-1 |

**TOTAL FULL APPEARANCES:** 9 14 6 6 25 19 6 19 1 13 1 … 29 29 26 5 4 1 26 6 9 19 2 19 12 8 8 5 10 10 10 12 4 … 10 1

**TOTAL SUB APPEARANCES:** 2 5 1 9 3 4 5 1 1 4 1 10 1 14 2 1 3 1 3 1 7 1 1 1

**TOTAL GOALS SCORED:** 1 1 4 2 1 1 1 4 1 2 1 2 4

Figure in bold denotes goal scored. Secondary smaller figure in bold denotes number of goals scored. † denotes opponent's own goal.

## THE ROVERS' 10 YEAR LEAGUE RECORD

| Season | Div | P | W | D | L | F | A | Pts | Pos |
|---|---|---|---|---|---|---|---|---|---|
| 1995-96 | P | 36 | 12 | 7 | 17 | 41 | 57 | 43 | 6 |
| 1996-97 | P | 36 | 6 | 7 | 23 | 29 | 73 | 25 | 10 |
| 1997-98 | F | 36 | 17 | 9 | 10 | 51 | 33 | 60 | 3 |
| 1998-99 | F | 36 | 8 | 11 | 17 | 37 | 57 | 35 | 8 |
| 1999-00 | F | 36 | 17 | 11 | 8 | 55 | 40 | 59 | 5 |
| 2000-01 | F | 36 | 10 | 8 | 18 | 41 | 55 | 38 | 7 |
| 2001-02 | F | 36 | 8 | 11 | 17 | 50 | 62 | 35 | 8 |
| 2002-03 | S | 36 | 16 | 11 | 9 | 53 | 36 | 59 | 1 |
| 2003-04 | F | 36 | 8 | 10 | 18 | 37 | 57 | 34 | 8 |
| 2004-05 | F | 36 | 3 | 7 | 26 | 26 | 67 | 16 | 10 |

## LEADING GOALSCORERS:

| Season | Div | Goals | Player |
|---|---|---|---|
| 1995-96 | P | 9 | C. Cameron |
| 1996-97 | P | 5 | P. Duffield, D. Lennon |
| 1997-98 | F | 10 | P. Hartley, K. Wright |
| 1998-99 | F | 8 | C. Dargo |
| 1999-00 | F | 12 | C. Dargo |
| 2000-01 | F | 9 | P. Tosh |
| 2001-02 | F | 19 | I. Novo |
| 2002-03 | S | 7 | K. Hawley |
| 2003-04 | F | 13 | J. Sutton |
| 2004-05 | F | 4 | P. Clarke, J. Martin, H. Sacko |

RAITH ROVERS PLAYING KITS SEASON 2005.06

FIRST KIT · SECOND KIT · THIRD KIT

# STIRLING ALBION

**STIRLING ALBION F.C.**

Forthbank Stadium, Springkerse,

Stirling, FK7 7UJ

**TELEPHONE NUMBERS**

Ground/Ticket Office (01786) 450399

**FAX** (01786) 448400

**E-MAIL** stirlingalbion.footballclub@virgin.net

**CHAIRMAN** Peter McKenzie

**VICE-CHAIRMAN** Peter Gardiner, C.A.

**DIRECTORS**

Duncan B. MacGregor & John L. Smith

**SECRETARY** Mrs. Marlyn Hallam

**HEAD COACH** Allan Moore

**FIRST TEAM COACHES**

David Gemmell & Mark McNally

**DIRECTOR OF YOUTH DEVELOPMENT**

John L. Smith

**YOUTH CO-ORDINATOR &**

**YOUTH DEVELOPMENT COACH**

Stuart Taylor

**YOUTH COACHES**

U19: David Gemmell

U15: Paul Donnelly

U14: Mike Kerr & Paul Chalmers

U13: Ian McConnell & Tommy Smith

**FOOTBALL SAFETY OFFICERS'**

**ASSOCIATION REPRESENTATIVE**

Alistair Caw (01786) 812520

**COMMERCIAL MANAGER**

Mrs. Marlyn Hallam

**MATCHDAY PROGRAMME EDITOR**

Graham Hamilton

(Stirling Albion Supporters Trust)

**CLUB DOCTOR**

Dr. Duncan MacGregor

**GROUND MAINTENANCE**

Greentech, Bandbeath Ind. Est., Throsk

**KIT PERSON** Stuart McColl

**CLUB SHOP**

Situated at Forthbank Stadium.

Open Mon to Fri and Home Matchdays.

**OFFICIAL SUPPORTERS CLUB**

Stephen Torrance, Secretary,

Forthbank Stadium, Springkerse,

Stirling, FK7 7UJ

**SHIRT SPONSOR** Prudential

**KIT SUPPLIER** Vandanel

## LIST OF PLAYERS 2005.06

| PLAYERS SURNAME | FIRST NAME | MIDDLE NAME | DATE OF BIRTH | PLACE OF BIRTH | DATE SIGNED | HEIGHT FT INS | WEIGHT ST LBS | POSITION ON PITCH | PREVIOUS CLUB |
|---|---|---|---|---|---|---|---|---|---|
| Aitken | Christopher | Ian | 31/03/81 | Glasgow | 28/01/05 | 5.10 | 11.6 | Midfield | Hamilton Academical |
| Bell | Andrew | Robert | 16/01/87 | Glasgow | 30/08/04 | 5.11 | 10.6 | Midfield | Kilmarnock |
| Bell | Steven | Andrew | 24/02/85 | Glasgow | 20/05/05 | 6.1 | 11.7 | Midfield | Queen of the South |
| Boyack | Steven | | 04/09/76 | Edinburgh | 06/07/05 | 5.11 | 12.3 | Midfield | Blackpool |
| Brophy | Christopher | | 16/03/87 | Glasgow | 17/08/04 | 5.6 | 9.6 | Forward | Stirling Albion Form D U16 |
| Brown | Andrew | Kenneth | 24/04/88 | Broxburn | 24/08/05 | 6.0 | 12.0 | Midfield | Airdrie United |
| Brown | Mark | Alexander | 21/11/87 | Glasgow | 24/08/05 | 5.7 | 10.4 | Forward | Queen of the South |
| Bryce | Graham | | 21/06/88 | Bellshill | 24/08/05 | 5.9 | 9.5 | Defender | Dundee United |
| Christie | Scott | James | 13/11/87 | Falkirk | 24/12/03 | 5.10 | 9.0 | Goalkeeper | Stirling Albion Form D U16 |
| Connolly | Patrick | Martin | 25/06/70 | Glasgow | 30/07/05 | 5.11 | 11.0 | Forward | Ayr United |
| Devine | Stewart | | 11/04/84 | Edinburgh | 13/07/00 | 5.10 | 10.2 | Midfield | Stirling Albion Youth |
| Donnelly | Paul | | 23/09/87 | Bangour | 17/08/04 | 5.8 | 9.0 | Midfield | Stirling Albion Form D U16 |
| Dunn | Robert | | 28/06/79 | Glasgow | 21/01/05 | 5.10 | 11.0 | Mid / Fwd | Dumbarton |
| Forbes | David | | 03/02/87 | Glasgow | 17/08/04 | 5.11 | 10.3 | Midfield | Stirling Albion Form D U16 |
| Forsyth | Ross | David | 20/11/82 | Glasgow | 06/07/05 | 5.11 | 11.4 | Defender | St. Johnstone |
| Fraser | John | | 17/01/78 | Dunfermline | 23/07/05 | 5.11 | 12.6 | Midfield | Stranraer |
| Giacomi | Robert | | 01/08/86 | Toronto | 23/09/05 | 6.3 | 13.9 | Goalkeeper | Rangers |
| Graham | Andrew | | 22/09/83 | Glasgow | 06/07/05 | 6.1 | 13.0 | Defender | Glasgow Amateurs |
| Hay | Christopher | Drummond | 28/08/74 | Glasgow | 10/08/05 | 5.6 | 13.0 | Forward | St. Johnstone |
| Hay | Paul | | 14/11/80 | Glasgow | 16/03/01 | 5.10 | 11.7 | Midfield | Clyde |
| Hogarth | Myles | | 30/03/75 | Falkirk | 11/03/03 | 6.2.5 | 12.7 | Goalkeeper | Alloa Athletic |
| Honeyman | David | Lee | 01/02/88 | Rinteln | 24/08/05 | 5.8 | 10.5 | Forward | Dundee United |
| Hutchison | Steven | | 01/08/85 | Stirling | 23/07/01 | 5.11 | 10.7 | Forward | Rangers |
| McKinlay | Lewis | Alexander | 28/11/89 | Stirling | 24/08/05 | 6.1 | 12.6 | Midfield | Stirling Albion Form D U15 |
| McNally | Mark | | 10/03/71 | Motherwell | 25/07/02 | 5.11 | 12.7 | Defender | Clydebank |
| McSkimming | Robert | Scott | 25/02/87 | Bellshill | 23/08/04 | 5.7 | 10.0 | Midfield | Raith Rovers |
| Millar | John | Duncan | 18/06/87 | Stirling | 12/08/05 | 5.11 | 12.5 | Forward | Stirling Albion Form D U16 |
| Nugent | Paul | Brian | 04/04/83 | Alexandria | 30/11/01 | 5.11 | 11.0 | Defender | Clyde |
| O'Brien | David | | 24/01/84 | Stirling | 20/07/01 | 5.10 | 10.8 | Midfield | Denny Amateurs |
| Roycroft | Sean | | 29/08/85 | Stirling | 29/08/03 | 6.0 | 11.0 | Forward | Stirling Albion Form D U16 |
| Scotland | Christopher | James | 22/03/85 | Stirling | 14/08/02 | 5.11.5 | 12.0 | Defender | Stirling Albion Form D U16 |
| Taggart | Nathan | | 28/08/87 | Glasgow | 30/08/04 | 5.6 | 10.7 | Midfield | Stirling Albion Form D U16 |
| Thomson | David | Angus | 15/05/88 | Stirling | 24/08/05 | 6.0 | 12.1 | Goalkeeper | Alloa Athletic Form D U16 |
| Turnbull | David | | 05/09/80 | Durban | 05/08/05 | 6.1 | 13.5 | Forward | Stranraer |
| Wilson | Douglas | John | 27/05/84 | Stirling | 20/07/01 | 5.7 | 9.3 | Midfield | Stirling Albion Form D U16 |

## TICKET INFORMATION

**Season Ticket Information**

**Seated**
| | |
|---|---|
| Adult | £180 |
| Juvenile/OAP | £100 |
| Young Red | £80 |

**League Admission Prices**

**Seated**
| | |
|---|---|
| Adult | £10 |
| Juvenile | £6 |

**Standing**
| | |
|---|---|
| Adult | £9 |
| Juvenile/OAP | £5 |

## MILESTONES:

**Year of formation:** 1945

**Most League points in a season:**

59 (Division 2 – Season 1964/65)(2 Points for a Win)

81 (Second Division – Season 1995/96)(3 Points for a Win)

**Most League goals scored by a player in a season:**

Joe Hughes (Season 1969/70)

**No. of goals scored:** 26

**Record Attendance:**

26,400 (-v- Celtic – Scottish Cup, 11.3.1959 at Annfield Park)

3,808 (-v- Aberdeen – Scottish Cup, 17.2.1996 at Forthbank Stadiu

**Record Victory:** 20-0 (-v- Selkirk – Scottish Cup, 8.12.1984)

**Record Defeat:** 0-9 (-v- Dundee United – Division 1, 30.12.1967)

# SEASON STATS 2004.05

## SEASON STATS 2004.05

| DATE | VENUE | OPPONENTS | ATT | RES | Hogarth M. | Nugent P.B. | Devine S. | McNally M. | Rowe J.G. | MacDonald K.G. | Hay P. | Ferguson C.W. | McLean S.J. | Glancy M.P. | O'Brien D. | Allan J. | Neville B. | Scotland C.J. | Cummings D.D. | Gethins C. | Hutchison S. | Prentice M.J. | Wilson D.J. | Galloway M.A. | Gibson A.S. | Roycroft S. | Canning M. | Di Giacomo P. | Dunn R. | Aitken C.I. | Ferguson W. | Forbes D. | Christie S.J. | Taggart N. |
|---|---|---|---|---|---|---|---|---|---|---|---|---|---|---|---|---|---|---|---|---|---|---|---|---|---|---|---|---|---|---|---|---|---|---|---|
| 7-Aug | H | Arbroath | 706 | 5-2 | 1 | 2 | 3² | 4 | 5 | 6 | 7 | 8 | 9 | 10 | 11 | | | 12 | 15 | 16 | | | | | | | | | | | | | | |
| 14-Aug | A | Brechin City | 491 | 3-0 | 1 | 2 | | 4 | 5 | 6 | 7 | 8 | 9² | 10 | 11 | | | 3 | 12 | | | | | | | | | | | | | | | |
| 21-Aug | H | Alloa Athletic | 1,069 | 2-0 | 1 | 2 | | 4 | 5 | 6 | 7 | 8 | 9 | 10 | 11 | | | 3 | 14 | 12 | 16 | | | | | | | | | | | | | |
| 28-Aug | H | Berwick Rangers | 695 | 3-1 | 1 | 2 | | 4 | 5 | 6 | 7 | 8 | 9² | 10 | 11 | | 16 | 3 | | 12 | 15 | | | | | | | | | | | | | |
| 4-Sep | A | Forfar Athletic | 841 | 2-0 | 1 | 2 | 3. | | 5 | 6 | 7 | 8 | 9 | 10 | 11 | | | 4 | 12 | | 16 | | | | | | | | | | | | | |
| 11-Sep | H | Morton | 1,831 | 1-1 | 1 | 2 | 8 | 4 | 5 | 6 | 7 | | 9 | 10 | 11 | | | 3 | 12 | 15 | | | | | | | | | | | | | | |
| 18-Sep | A | Stranraer | 645 | 0-0 | 1 | 2 | 3 | | 5 | 6 | 7 | 8 | 9 | 10 | 11 | | | 4 | 12 | 14 | | 16 | | | | | | | | | | | | |
| 25-Sep | A | Dumbarton | 990 | 1-1 | 1 | 2 | 3 | | 5 | 6 | 7 | 8 | | 10 | 11 | 14 | | 4 | 9 | 12 | | | | 15 | | | | | | | | | | |
| 2-Oct | H | Ayr United | 1,022 | 1-1 | 1 | 2 | 3 | | 5 | 12 | 7 | 8 | 9 | 10 | 11 | | | 4 | 14 | 6 | | 15 | | | | | | | | | | | | |
| 16-Oct | H | Brechin City | 736 | 1-5 | 1 | 2 | 15 | 4 | 5 | 6 | | 8 | 9 | 10 | 11 | | | 3 | 14 | 7 | | | 16 | | | | | | | | | | | |
| 23-Oct | A | Arbroath | 620 | 1-2 | 1 | 2 | 3 | 4 | | | 8 | 10 | 7 | 11 | 16 | | | 5 | 9 | 14 | 15 | 6 | | | | | | | | | | | | |
| 30-Oct | A | Berwick Rangers | 453 | 1-0 | 1 | 2 | 3 | | 5 | 6 | | 9 | 10 | 11 | | 4 | | | | 12 | | 8 | | | | | | | | | | | | |
| 6-Nov | H | Forfar Athletic | 756 | 3-1 | 1 | 2 | 3 | | 5 | 6 | 7 | | 9 | 10 | | 11 | 4 | | | 12 | | 15 | 8 | 16 | | | | | | | | | | |
| 13-Nov | A | Morton | 3,020 | 0-3 | 1 | 2 | 3 | | 5 | 6 | | | 9 | 10 | 16 | 11 | 4 | | | | | 8 | 15 | | | | | | | | | | | |
| 20-Nov | H | Berwick Rangers | 551 | 0-1 | | | 6 | | 3 | 8 | | 9 | 10 | 11 | | 4 | 14 | | 12 | 5 | | | | | | | | | | | | | | |
| 27-Nov | H | Stranraer | 678 | 1-1 | 1 | 2 | | 4 | | | 6 | 8 | 9 | 12 | 11 | 16 | | | 10 | | | | | 15 | 5 | 7 | 3 | | | | | | | |
| 4-Dec | H | Dumbarton | 688 | 1-0 | 1 | 2 | | 4 | | | 5 | 8 | 9 | 12 | 11 | 16 | | | | 10 | | | | 15 | 6 | 7 | 3 | | | | | | | |
| 18-Dec | A | Ayr United | 1,288 | 2-3 | 1 | 2 | 3 | 4 | | | 14 | 12 | 9 | 10 | 11 | | | | | | | | | 16 | 6 | 7 | 5 | | | | | | | |
| 27-Dec | H | Arbroath | 755 | 0-3 | 1 | 2 | 3 | 4 | | | 15 | 6 | 9 | 12 | 11 | 10 | | 5 | | | | | | 16 | 8 | 7 | | | | | | | | |
| 15-Jan | A | Forfar Athletic | 501 | 1-4 | 1 | | | 16 | 4 | 5 | 7 | 3 | 8 | | 11 | | 2 | | | | 12 | | 9 | | | | | 6 | 10 | | | | | |
| 26-Jan | H | Morton | 1,075 | 1-1 | 1 | 4 | 3 | | | | 8 | 2 | 15 | | 14 | 11 | | 5 | | | | 7 | | | | | | 6 | 9 | 10 | | | | |
| 29-Jan | A | Stranraer | 495 | 3-0 | 1 | 5 | 3 | | | | 8 | 2 | | | 12 | 11 | | 4 | | 14 | | 7 | | | | | | 6 | 9² | 10 | 16 | | | |
| 5-Feb | A | Dumbarton | 981 | 2-0 | 1 | 5 | 3 | | | | 8 | 2 | | | 12 | 11 | | 4 | | 15 | | 7 | | | | | | 6 | 9 | 10² | 14 | | | |
| 12-Feb | H | Ayr United | 711 | 2-0 | 1 | 5 | 3 | | | | 8 | 2 | | | 12 | 11 | | 4 | | | | 7 | | | | | | 6 | 9 | 10 | 15 | 16 | | |
| 19-Feb | H | Alloa Athletic | 1,135 | 0-4 | 1 | 5 | 3 | | | | 8 | 2 | | | 12 | 11 | | 4 | | | | 7 | | | | | | 6 | 9 | 10 | 14 | | | |
| 26-Feb | A | Brechin City | 515 | 3-5 | 1 | 5 | | 4 | | | 7 | 2 | 8 | | 16 | | | | 15 | | | | | | | | | 11 | 9 | 10 | 6 | | 3 | |
| 5-Mar | H | Forfar Athletic | 537 | 3-2 | 1 | 5 | 3 | 4 | | | 7 | 2 | | | 11 | | | | 16 | | | 15 | | | | | | 8 | 9 | 10 | 6 | | | |
| 8-Mar | A | Alloa Athletic | 626 | 1-1 | 1 | 2 | 3 | 5 | | | 7 | | | | 11 | | | 4 | | | | | | | | | | 6 | 9 | 10 | 8 | | | |
| 12-Mar | A | Berwick Rangers | 366 | 2-2 | 1 | 2 | 3 | 5 | | 6 | 7 | 14 | 9 | | 11 | | | 4 | | | 12 | | | | | | | 8 | | 10 | | 15 | | |
| 19-Mar | A | Morton | 2,764 | 0-2 | 1 | 2 | 3 | 5 | | 8 | 7 | 15 | | | 11 | | | 4 | | | 12 | | | | | | | 6 | 9 | 10 | | | | |
| 2-Apr | H | Stranraer | 658 | 1-1 | 1 | 5 | 3 | 4 | | 6 | 2 | | | | 12 | 11 | | | | | | 7 | | | | | | 16 | 9 | 10 | 8 | | | |
| 9-Apr | A | Ayr United | 1,046 | 3-0 | 1 | 5 | 3 | 4 | | 6 | 2 | 15 | 10 | | 11 | | | | | | | 12 | | | | | | 14 | 9 | 7 | 8 | | | |
| 16-Apr | H | Dumbarton | 705 | 3-0 | 1 | 5 | 3 | 4 | | 6 | 2 | 14 | | | 11 | | | 16 | | | | 7 | | | | | | 12 | 9 | 10 | 8 | | | |
| 23-Apr | A | Alloa Athletic | 921 | 0-3 | 1 | 5 | 3 | 4 | | 6 | 2 | 15 | | | 11 | | | | | | 16 | 7 | | | | | | 12 | 9 | 10 | 8 | | | |
| 30-Apr | H | Brechin City | 667 | 1-2 | | 5 | 3 | | | 2 | 6 | | | | 11 | | | 4 | | | 15 | 7 | | | | | | 14 | 9 | 10 | 8 | | 1 | 16 |
| 7-May | A | Arbroath | 535 | 2-3 | 1 | 5 | | | 12 | 2 | 15 | | | | 11 | | | 4 | | | 8 | 7 | | | | | | 6 | 9 | 10 | 14 | | 3 | |
| **TOTAL FULL APPEARANCES** | | | | | 35 | 35 | 26 | 21 | 14 | 27 | 33 | 17 | 18 | 18 | 33 | 3 | 5 | 21 | 1 | 3 | 4 | | 11 | 8 | 5 | 3 | 12 | 16 | 16 | 8 | | 2 | 1 |
| **TOTAL SUB APPEARANCES** | | | | | | 2 | | | 4 | 1 | 7 | | 10 | 1 | 6 | 2 | 4 | 5 | 9 | 12 | 1 | 12 | 1 | 2 | | 5 | | | 5 | 2 | | 1 | |
| **TOTAL GOALS SCORED** | | | | | | | 2 | 5 | 1 | 1 | 4 | | 10 | 6 | 6 | | | 2 | | | 3 | | | | | | 6 | 7 | 3 | | | |

re in bold denotes goal scored. Secondary smaller figure in bold denotes number of goals scored. † denotes opponent's own goal.

## THE ALBION'S 10 YEAR LEAGUE RECORD

| Season | Div | P | W | D | L | F | A | Pts | Pos |
|---|---|---|---|---|---|---|---|---|---|
| 95-96 | S | 36 | 24 | 9 | 3 | 83 | 30 | 81 | 1 |
| 96-97 | F | 36 | 12 | 10 | 14 | 54 | 61 | 46 | 7 |
| 97-98 | F | 36 | 8 | 10 | 18 | 40 | 56 | 34 | 10 |
| 98-99 | S | 36 | 12 | 8 | 16 | 50 | 63 | 44 | 6 |
| 99-00 | S | 36 | 11 | 18 | 7 | 60 | 72 | 40 | 7 |
| 00-01 | S | 36 | 5 | 17 | 14 | 34 | 50 | 32 | 10 |
| 01-02 | T | 36 | 9 | 10 | 17 | 45 | 68 | 37 | 9 |
| 02-03 | T | 36 | 15 | 11 | 10 | 50 | 44 | 56 | 5 |
| 03-04 | T | 36 | 23 | 8 | 5 | 78 | 27 | 77 | 2 |
| 04-05 | S | 36 | 14 | 9 | 13 | 56 | 55 | 51 | 4 |

## LEADING GOALSCORERS:

| Season | Div | Goals | Player |
|---|---|---|---|
| 1995-96 | S | 25 | S. McCormick |
| 1996-97 | F | 9 | A. Bone |
| 1997-98 | F | 13 | A. Bone |
| 1998-99 | S | 20 | A. Bone |
| 1999-00 | S | 17 | A. Graham |
| 2000-01 | S | 5 | C. Feroz, A. Graham |
| 2001-02 | T | 17 | A. Williams |
| 2002-03 | T | 10 | S. Nicholas |
| 2003-04 | T | 21 | S. McLean |
| 2004-05 | S | 10 | S. McLean |

### STIRLING ALBION PLAYING KITS SEASON 2005.06

FIRST KIT | SECOND KIT | THIRD KIT

# SCOTTISH FOOTBALL LEAGUE SECOND DIVISION

## ALLOA ATHLETIC: RECREATION PARK

Recreation Park can be reached by the following routes:
**BUSES:** There are three main services which stop outside the ground. These are the Dunfermline-Stirling, Stirling-Clackmannan and Falkirk-Alloa buses.
**TRAINS:** The nearest railway station is Stirling, which is seven miles away. Fans would have to connect with an inter-linking bus service to reach the ground from here.

**CARS:** Car Parking is available in the car park adjacent to the ground and this can hold 175 vehicles.
**CAPACITY:** 3,100; Seated 400, Standing 2,700
**PITCH DIMENSIONS:** 110 yds x 75 yds (101 x 69m)
**FACILITIES FOR DISABLED SUPPORTERS:**
Accommodation for wheelchairs and invalid carriages in front of Stand. Disabled toilets are also available.

## AYR UNITED: SOMERSET PARK

Somerset Park can be reached by the following routes:
**BUSES:** There are several buses from the town centre with a frequency approximately every five minutes. Fans should board buses bound for Dalmilling, Whitletts or any bus passing Ayr Racecourse. The ground is only a ten minute walk from the town centre.
**TRAINS:** There is a half hourly train service from Glasgow to either Ayr or Newton-on-Ayr. The ground is a ten minute walk from both stations.
**CARS:** A77 to Ayr and at Whitletts Roundabout, take third exit

(A719) and follow until after Ayr Racecourse. Take first right at traffic lights then left and right into Somerset Road. Car parking facilities are available at Craigie Road, Ayr Racecourse and also at Somerset Road car parks.
**CAPACITY:** 10,185; Seated 1,597, Standing 8,588
**PITCH DIMENSIONS:** 110 yds x 72 yds (101 x 66m)
**FACILITIES FOR DISABLED SUPPORTERS:**
Enclosure and toilet facilities for wheelchairs. Match commentary available for blind persons at all first team matches. Disabled access from both ends of the Ground.

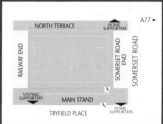

## DUMBARTON: STRATHCLYDE HOMES STADIUM

Strathclyde Homes Stadium can be reached by the following routes:
**BUSES:** There are two main services which pass close to the ground. These are bound for Helensburgh and Balloch from Glasgow.
**TRAINS:** The train service from Glasgow Queen Street and Glasgow Central Low Level both pass through Dumbarton East Station (fans best choice) situated just under a ten minute walk from the ground.
**CARS:** Follow A82 then A814 Helensburgh/Dumbarton sign

post. Follow road for about 1 mile. Pass under Dumbarton East Railway Bridge and take second right – Victoria Street (also signposted Dumbarton Castle). The car park at the stadium holds 400 cars and 6 coaches.
**CAPACITY:** 2,020 (All Seated)
**PITCH DIMENSIONS:** 114 yds x 75 yds (104 x 69m)
**FACILITIES FOR DISABLED SUPPORTERS:**
20 Wheelchair spaces are accommodated at the front of the stand. Contact the Club Secretary in advance regarding availability.

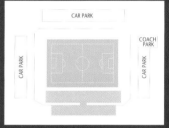

## FORFAR ATHLETIC: STATION PARK

Station Park can be reached by the following routes:
**BUSES:** There is a regular service of buses departing from Dundee City Centre into Forfar. The bus station in the town is about half a mile from the ground. There is also a local service.
**TRAINS:** The nearest railway station is Dundee (14 miles away) and fans who travel to here should then board a bus for Forfar from the city centre. Arbroath station is also about 14 miles away.

**CARS:** There are car parking facilities in adjacent streets to the ground and also in the Market Muir car park.

**CAPACITY:** 5,177 Seated 739, Standing 4,438
**PITCH DIMENSIONS:** 113 yds x 70 yds (103 x 64m)
**FACILITIES FOR DISABLED SUPPORTERS:**
Ramp entrance via Main Stand.

## GRETNA: RAYDALE PARK

Raydale Park can be reached by the following routes:
**BUSES:** Buses between Carlisle and Annan and Dumfries serve Gretna.
**TRAINS:** Gretna Station is on the Glasgow-Carlisle line. Raydale Park is approximately one mile south-west of the station.
**CARS:** From the North: Leave M74 at sign for Old Blacksmith's Shop Visitor sign (B7076). Go through Springfield into Gretna Green. Turn left and left again. Go through traffic lights into Gretna. Through roundabout take B721 at Crossways Inn. After ¼ mile turn left into Dominion Road. Raydale Park is on your right. From the South: 8 miles north of Carlisle look for

the Old Blacksmith's Shop Visitor Centre sign. Take B7076 to Gretna. In Gretna turn left at Crossways Inn and go on the Annan Road for ¼ mile. Turn left into Dominion Road and Raydale Park is on your right. From the West: Leave A75 at sign for Gretna (B721). Turn left into Gretna and right into Dominion Road. Raydale Park is on your right.
**CAPACITY:** 3,000; Seated 1,318 Standing 1,682
**PITCH DIMENSIONS:** 113 yds x 74 yds (103 x 68m)
**FACILITIES FOR DISABLED SUPPORTERS:**
Toilets and ramps in place. Further information available from Secretary.

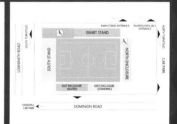

## MORTON: CAPPIELOW PARK

Cappielow Park may be reached by the following routes:
**BUSES:** Services from Glasgow stop just outside the park. There are also services from Port Glasgow and Gourock.
**TRAINS:** The nearest local station is Cartsdyke and is a five minute walk from the ground. There are two to three trains every hour from Glasgow and from Gourock.

**CARS:** Car parking is available adjacent to the ground.
**CAPACITY:** 11,589; Seated 6,039, Standing 5,550
**PITCH DIMENSIONS:** 110 yds x 70 yds (100 x 64m)
**FACILITIES FOR DISABLED SUPPORTERS:** Seating facilities below Grandstand. Disabled toilets located at Main Entrance. Disabled Access and facilities within Club Hospitality areas.

## PARTICK THISTLE: FIRHILL STADIUM

The following routes may be used to reach Firhill Stadium:
**BUSES:** Buses from the city centre all pass near the ground: No's. 40, 61, 109 and 119 and the frequency of the buses is just under 10 minutes from Hope Street.
**TRAINS:** The nearest railway stations are Glasgow Queen Street and Glasgow Central and buses from the centre of the city pass within 100 yards of the ground.
**UNDERGROUND:** The nearest Strathclyde PTE Underground station is St.George's Cross and supporters walking from here should pass through Cromwell Street into Maryhill Road and walk up this road as far as Firhill Street. The ground is on the right. The Kelvinbridge

Underground Station is also not far from the ground and supporters from here should walk along Great Western Road as far as Napiershill Street and then follow this into Maryhill Road.
**CARS:** Street parking near the ground is somewhat limited. Supporters Buses can park in Panmure Street under Police direction.
**CAPACITY:** 13,141; Seated 10,921; Standing 2,220
**PITCH DIMENSIONS:** 115 yds x 75 yds (105 x 68m)
**FACILITIES FOR DISABLED SUPPORTERS:** Covered places are available for 17 supporters in front of the Main Stand (North area). A total of 14 spaces are available in front of the North Stand for visiting disabled fans. Prior arrangement must be made with the Secretary and a ticket obtained.

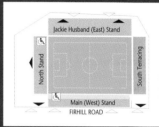

## PETERHEAD: BALMOOR STADIUM

Balmoor Stadium can be reached by the following routes:
**BUSES:** Buses leave Aberdeen city centre every hour for Peterhead. Travel time 1 hour.
**TRAINS:** The nearest train station is Aberdeen. From Aberdeen you would have to travel by bus to Peterhead. Travel time 1 hour.
**CARS:** From Aberdeen city centre: Take A90 to Peterhead, at first roundabout approaching Peterhead take a left at McDonalds to St. Fergus (still on A90). Continue on this road to

next roundabout - go straight on to the next T-junction. Take right A980 back into Peterhead - continue on A980 through next roundabout and Balmoor Stadium is about ½ mile past the roundabout on the right hand side.
**CAPACITY:** 3,150; Seated 990, Standing 2,160
**PITCH DIMENSIONS:** 110 yds x 70 yds (101 x 64m)
**FACILITIES FOR DISABLED SUPPORTERS:** Designated area in new stand. Lift at main entrance for access to Main Stand.

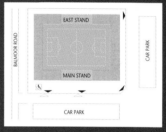

## RAITH ROVERS: STARK'S PARK

The following routes may be used to reach Stark's Park:
**BUSES:** The main bus station in Kirkcaldy is also within 15 minutes walking distance of the ground, but the Edinburgh, Dunfermline and Leven services pass close by the park.
**TRAINS:** Kirkcaldy railway station is served by trains from Dundee, Edinburgh and Glasgow (via Edinburgh) and the ground is within 10-15 minutes walking distance of the station.
**CARS:** Car parking is available in the Esplanade, which is on the south side of the ground and in Beveridge Park, which is on

the north side of the ground. Follow signs for Football traffic.
**CAPACITY:** 8,473 (All Seated)
**PITCH DIMENSIONS:** 113 yds x 70 yds (103 x 64m)
**FACILITIES FOR DISABLED SUPPORTERS:**
By prior arrangement with Disability Liaison Officer or General Manager. North Stand – Away Supporters. South Stand – Home Supporters. Limited disabled parking immediately adjacent to North Stand. By prior arrangement, Matchday Hospitality can be arranged for disabled supporters.

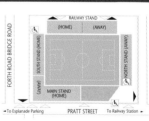

## STIRLING ALBION: FORTHBANK STADIUM

Forthbank Stadium can be reached by the following routes:
**BUSES:** From Goosecroft Bus Station, Stirling.
**TRAINS:** The nearest station is Stirling Railway Station, which is approximately 2 miles from the ground.
**CARS:** Follow signs for A91 St. Andrews/Alloa. Car Parking is available in the club car park. Home support in West Car Park

and visiting support in East Car Park.

**CAPACITY:** 3,808, Seated 2,508, Standing 1,300
**PITCH DIMENSIONS:** 110 yds x 74 yds (101 x 68m)
**FACILITIES FOR DISABLED SUPPORTERS:**
Disabled access, toilets and spaces for 36.

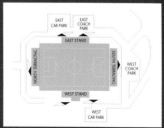

# ALBION ROVERS

**ALBION ROVERS F.C.**

Cliftonhill Stadium, Main Street,

Coatbridge, ML5 3RB

**TELEPHONE NUMBERS**

Ground (01236) 606334/607041

Sec. Home (01236) 421686

Sec. Bus (01236) 762775

Sec. Mob 07977 470379

**FAX** (01236) 606334

**E-MAIL** john_reynolds@hotmail.com

**E-MAIL 2** jimmy_lindsay66@hotmail.com

**WEBSITE** www.albionrovers.com

**CHAIRMAN** Frank Meade

**VICE-CHAIRMAN** David T. Shanks, B.Sc.

**DIRECTORS**

Robert Watt, David Wright,

Thomas Young & Lew McWilliam

**GENERAL MANAGER &**

**OFFICE ADMINISTRATOR** John Reynolds

**SECRETARY** David T. Shanks, B.Sc.

**HEAD COACH** Jim Chapman

**DIRECTOR OF YOUTH DEVELOPMENT/**

**YOUTH CO-ORDINATOR** Jimmy Lindsay

**COMMUNITY COACH** William McNab

**YOUTH TEAM COACHES**

U19: Jimmy Lindsay

U17: Derek Frye

U16: Willie McNab

U15: John Bell

**TEAM CAPTAIN** Scott Friel

**FOOTBALL SAFETY OFFICERS'**

**ASSOCIATION REPRESENTATIVE**

John Reynolds 07719 736287

**COMMERCIAL MANAGER** Brian Kennedy

**MEDIA LIAISON PERSON** John Reynolds

**MATCHDAY PROGRAMME EDITOR**

Bill Walker 07855 492122

**PHYSIOTHERAPIST** Derek Kelly

**STADIUM MANAGER** John Reynolds

**GROUNDSMAN** Hugh McBride

**KIT PERSON** Wilma McBride

**CLUB SHOP**

Cliftonhill Stadium, Main Street,

Coatbridge, ML5 3RB. Open one hour prior

to kick-off at first team home matches.

**OFFICIAL SUPPORTERS CLUB**

John Smith, 45 Blair Road, Coatbridge

(01236) 420417

**SHIRT SPONSOR** Reigart

**KIT SUPPLIER** Pro Star

## LIST OF PLAYERS 2005.06

| PLAYERS SURNAME | FIRST NAME | MIDDLE NAME | DATE OF BIRTH | PLACE OF BIRTH | DATE SIGNED | HEIGHT FT INS | WEIGHT ST LBS | POSITION ON PITCH | PREVIOUS CLUB |
|---|---|---|---|---|---|---|---|---|---|
| Alexander | Jason | | 22/08/88 | Bangour | 14/07/05 | 5.10 | 12.0 | Forward | Hibernian |
| Baird | James | | 04/02/89 | Ayr | 14/07/05 | 5.8 | 10.5 | Midfield | Ayr United |
| Black | Daniel | | 22/01/86 | New Plymouth | 08/07/03 | 5.11 | 13.0 | Defender | Heart of Midlothian Form |
| Bonnar | Martin | Michael | 12/01/79 | Bellshill | 27/07/05 | 5.8 | 10.3 | Mid / Fwd | Queen's Park |
| Brown | Scott | | 22/02/89 | Edinburgh | 14/07/05 | 5.9 | 11.0 | Forward | Hibernian |
| Chisholm | Iain | | 29/08/85 | Glasgow | 27/07/05 | 5.9 | 10.4 | Forward | Tower Hearts |
| Creaney | Philip | | 12/02/83 | Bellshill | 20/07/05 | 5.11.5 | 11.7 | Midfield | Falkirk |
| Creer | Alan | | 12/11/86 | Rutherglen | 30/07/05 | 6.2 | 14.8 | Goalkeeper | Wishaw Juniors |
| Dewar | Neil | | 10/01/89 | Glasgow | 14/07/05 | 5.8 | 10.5 | Forward | Heart of Midlothian |
| Donachy | Stephen | | 08/07/83 | Glasgow | 18/08/05 | 5.9 | 10.2 | Midfield | Harmony Row |
| Donnelly | Ciaran | Anthony | 30/04/86 | East Kilbride | 27/07/05 | 5.11 | 12.4 | Midfield | Aberdeen |
| Douglas | Ian | | 03/08/87 | Broxburn | 07/07/04 | 5.9 | 9.6 | Forward | Falkirk |
| Ewings | Jamie | | 04/08/84 | Bellshill | 20/07/05 | 6.0 | 11.0 | Goalkeeper | Motherwell |
| Franch | Thomas | | 12/07/83 | Lanark | 27/07/05 | 5.10 | 11.0 | Forward | Symington Tinto |
| Friel | Scott | | 21/04/85 | Glasgow | 14/01/05 | 5.10 | 11.2 | Midfield | Dublin City |
| Hardie | Craig | | 16/07/88 | Glasgow | 07/07/04 | 5.9 | 12.0 | Midfield | Heart of Midlothian |
| Houston | Scott | John | 04/05/85 | Irvine | 27/07/05 | 5.9 | 12.7 | Defender | Troon Juniors |
| Inglis | Jason | | 08/09/88 | Edinburgh | 14/07/05 | 5.10 | 10.2 | Defender | Heart of Midlothian |
| Lennon | Gordon | | 15/02/83 | Larne | 29/07/05 | 6.1 | 11.2 | Defender | Harmony Row |
| Lennox | Thomas | | 02/02/84 | Lanark | 22/07/05 | 5.9 | 10.2 | Midfield | Queen of the South |
| Love | Robert | | 26/02/89 | Irvine | 20/07/05 | 5.7 | 10.0 | Forward | Ayr United |
| Lygate | Darren | | 04/07/89 | Hamilton | 14/07/05 | 6.1 | 10.5 | Midfield | Heart of Midlothian |
| Mackie | Ross | | 22/03/88 | Glasgow | 14/07/05 | 6.3 | 10.0 | Forward | Lenzie B.C. |
| Mathie | Graeme | Ross | 17/10/82 | Lanark | 06/09/05 | 6.1 | 11.6 | Defender | East Fife |
| Macdonald | Scott | McKenzie | 25/01/88 | Glasgow | 14/07/05 | 6.0 | 11.7 | Defender | Heart of Midlothian |
| McGhee | Graham | Henry | 24/09/81 | Coatbridge | 27/07/05 | 6.1 | 12.10 | Defender | East Stirlingshire |
| Middleton | Alan | | 01/01/88 | Irvine | 14/07/05 | 6.1 | 11.5 | Midfield | Ayr United |
| Monaghan | Christopher | | 21/05/89 | Bellshill | 14/07/05 | 5.11 | 10.5 | Defender | Gartsherrie B.C. |
| Noble | Steven | | 21/08/86 | Edinburgh | 27/07/05 | 5.10 | 10.7 | Midfield | Hibernian |
| O'Neil | Kevin | | 16/05/86 | Edinburgh | 27/07/05 | 6.2 | 13.0 | Defender | Hibernian |
| Paterson | Scott | | 21/04/88 | Bellshill | 07/07/04 | 5.9 | 10.0 | Defender | Albion Rovers Form D U |
| Preston | Fraser | | 18/04/87 | Edinburgh | 14/07/05 | 5.10 | 10.0 | Defender | Falkirk Form S |
| Quinn | Mark | | 03/09/88 | Glasgow | 18/08/05 | 5.11 | 10.7 | Goalkeeper | Partick Thistle Form D U |
| Reid | Alan | | 12/07/88 | Glasgow | 18/08/05 | 5.11 | 11.4 | Midfield | Hibernian |
| Reid | Graeme | | 05/02/88 | Bellshill | 07/07/04 | 5.5 | 8.7 | Midfield | Albion Rovers Form D U |
| Reid | Stephen | | 20/01/81 | Irvine | 27/07/05 | 5.6 | 10.8 | Forward | Auchinleck Talbot Junior |
| Selkirk | Andrew | | 12/09/86 | Glasgow | 17/07/02 | 5.10 | 11.5 | Midfield | Albion Rovers Form D U |
| Sichi | Lee | | 11/01/83 | Glasgow | 27/07/05 | 5.8 | 10.4 | Forward | Drumchapel United |
| Sideserf | Mark | | 11/08/88 | Glasgow | 14/07/05 | 5.10 | 9.2 | Defender | Gretna |
| Stewart | Paul | | 19/08/88 | Glasgow | 21/09/04 | 5.5 | 9.0 | Forward | Hibernian |
| Thompson | Bruce | David | 01/04/89 | Vale of Leven | 14/07/05 | 5.8 | 10.0 | Forward | Partick Thistle |
| Wallace | George | | 03/03/82 | Irvine | 30/07/05 | 6.1 | 12.5 | Forward | Auchinleck Talbot Junior |
| Wallace | Neil | | 13/06/87 | Edinburgh | 07/07/04 | 5.9 | 10.0 | Defender | Heart of Midlothian |
| Wilson | Lee | | 01/10/81 | Stirling | 31/01/05 | 6.1 | 12.2 | Forward | Dunipace Juniors |
| Young | Craig | | 13/06/78 | Inverness | 27/07/05 | 5.11 | 12.0 | Forward | Dalziel A.F.C. |

## SEASON TICKET INFORMATION

### Season Ticket Information

| Seated | Adult | £120 |
|---|---|---|
| | OAP/Unemployed | £70 |
| | 12-16 Years Unaccompanied | £30 |
| | Under 12's | FREE |
| | (when accompanied by a paying adult) | |

### League Admission Prices

| Seated | Adult | £10 |
|---|---|---|
| | OAP/Unemployed | £5 |
| Standing | Adult | £10 |
| | OAP/Unemployed | £5 |

## MILESTONES:

**Year of formation:** 1882

**Most capped player:** John White

**No. of caps:** 1

**Most League points in a season:**

54 (Division 2 – Season 1929/30)(2 Points for a win)

70 (Third Division – Season 2002/03)(3 Points for a win)

**Most League goals scored by a player in a season:**

John Renwick (Season 1932/33)

**No. of goals scored:** 41

**Record Attendance:** 27,381 (-v- Rangers 8.2.1936)

**Record Victory:** 12-0 (-v- Airdriehill – Scottish Cup, 3.9.1887

**Record Defeat:** 1-11 (-v- Partick Thistle – League Cup, 11.8.1

## SEASON STATS 2004.05

| DATE | VENUE | OPPONENTS | ATT | RES | Peat M. | Paterson A. | Stirling J. | Black D. | McGowan J. | McLaren G. | McKenzie M. | Boyle J. | Yardley M. | Bradford J. | Mercer J. | McManus P.J. | Patrick R. | Silvestro C. | Fahey C. | Crabbe S. | McCaul G. | Smith J.A. | Connolly C. | Selkirk A. | McLaughlin P.J. | Potter K.A. | Fleming G. | Friel S. | Wallace N. | McNulty S. | Wilson L. | Gordon W. | Richardson G.S. | Thomson D.H. | Douglas I. | Preston F. |
|---|---|---|---|---|---|---|---|---|---|---|---|---|---|---|---|---|---|---|---|---|---|---|---|---|---|---|---|---|---|---|---|---|---|---|---|---|---|
| 7-Aug | A | Gretna | 646 | 0-6 | 1 | 2 | 3 | 4 | 5 | 6 | 7 | 8 | 9 | 10 | 11 | | | 14 | 15 | | | | | | | | | | | | | | | | | |
| 14-Aug | H | East Fife | 384 | 2-0 | 1 | | 3 | 4 | 5 | 6 | 7 | 8 | 9 | 10 | 11 | 14² | 2 | | | | | | | | | | | | | | | | | | | |
| 21-Aug | A | Queen's Park | 505 | 1-1 | | | 3 | 4 | 5 | 6 | 7 | | 9 | 10 | 11 | | | | 8 | 2 | 1 | 14 | 15 | | | | | | | | | | | | | |
| 28-Aug | H | Peterhead | 351 | 0-1 | 12 | 3 | 2 | 5 | 6 | 7 | | 9 | 10 | 11 | | | 15 | 8 | 1 | 14 | | 4 | | | | | | | | | | | | | | |
| 4-Sep | H | Montrose | 330 | 1-1 | | | 3 | 4 | | 5 | 7 | | 9 | 12 | | 10 | 6 | 8 | 1 | | 11 | | 2 | | | | | | | | | | | | | |
| 11-Sep | H | Stenhousemuir | 339 | 1-0 | | | 3 | 4 | | 5 | 7 | | 9 | 11 | 10 | 6 | 8 | 1 | | | 2 | | | | | | | | | | | | | | | |
| 18-Sep | A | Elgin City | 450 | 0-1 | | | 3 | 4 | | 5 | 7 | 12 | 9 | 11 | 10 | 6 | 8 | 1 | | 14 | | | | | | | | | | | | | | | | |
| 25-Sep | H | East Stirlingshire | 225 | 3-3 | | | 3² | 4 | 5 | 6 | 7 | | 9 | | 11 | 10 | 15 | 2 | 1 | 14 | 8 | | 16 | | | | | | | | | | | | | |
| 2-Oct | A | Cowdenbeath | 243 | 0-2 | | 2 | 3 | 4 | 5 | 6 | 7 | 14 | | 11 | 10 | 8 | | 1 | 9 | 12 | | | | | | | | | | | | | | | | |
| 16-Oct | A | East Fife | 396 | 0-1 | 1 | 2 | 3 | 4 | | 5 | 7 | 6 | | | 10 | 8 | | | 9 | 11 | | 12 | | | | | | | | | | | | | | |
| 23-Oct | H | Gretna | 326 | 2-6 | 1 | 12 | 3 | 4 | 5 | 6 | 7 | 11 | | 16² | 10 | 8 | 2 | | 9 | | | 15 | | | | | | | | | | | | | | |
| 30-Oct | A | Peterhead | 729 | 1-4 | 1 | 2 | 3 | 4 | 5 | 6 | 7 | 15 | 12 | 11 | 10 | 14 | 8 | | 9 | | | | | | | | | | | | | | | | | |
| 6-Nov | H | Montrose | 245 | 1-2 | 2 | 3 | 4 | | 5 | 7 | 14 | 9 | 12 | | 10 | 6 | 8 | 1 | 11 | | | | | | | | | | | | | | | | | |
| 13-Nov | A | Stenhousemuir | 318 | 0-3 | 2 | 3 | 4 | | 5 | 7 | 15 | 9 | 12 | | 10 | | 8 | 1 | 11 | | | 5 | 16 | | | | | | | | | | | | | |
| 20-Nov | A | Gretna | 627 | † 2-6 | 2 | 3 | 4 | | 6 | 7 | | 9 | 11 | 10 | | | 8 | 1 | | | | 5 | | | | | | | | | | | | | | |
| 27-Nov | H | Elgin City | 262 | 2-2 | 2 | 3 | | | 7 | | | 12 | 11 | 10 | | 8 | 1 | 9 | 6 | 4 | | | 5 | 16 | | | | | | | | | | | | |
| 4-Dec | A | East Stirlingshire | 262 | 1-1 | 2 | 3 | | | 7 | | | 9 | 11 | 10 | | 8 | 1 | | 6 | | | | 5 | 4 | | | | | | | | | | | | |
| 18-Dec | H | Cowdenbeath | 303 | 2-3 | | 3 | 4 | | 6 | 7 | 8 | | 11 | 10 | | | 2 | 1 | | | | 12 | 9 | 5 | | | | | | | | | | | | |
| 1-Jan | H | Peterhead | 306 | 0-4 | | 3 | 4 | | 5 | 7 | 15 | | 9 | 11 | | | 8 | 1 | | | | 2 | 6 | 14 | | 16 | | | | | | | | | | |
| 15-Jan | A | Montrose | 269 | 1-0 | 3 | | | | 7 | | | | 10 | 11 | 15 | 8 | 1 | | | | | 2 | 14 | 6 | 9 | 4 | 5 | | | | | | | | | |
| 29-Jan | A | Elgin City | 380 | 1-1 | 2 | 3 | | | 7 | | | | 10 | 11 | 15 | 8 | 1 | | | | | 12 | 6 | 9 | 4 | 5 | | | | | | | | | | |
| 5-Feb | H | East Stirlingshire | 350 | 1-1 | 2 | 4 | | | 12 | | | | 10 | 11 | | 8 | 1 | | | | | 6 | 7 | 5 | 3 | 9 | 14 | | | | | | | | | |
| 12-Feb | A | Cowdenbeath | 254 | 2-1 | | 8 | 4 | | | | | | 10 | 11 | 7 | | 1 | 15 | | | | 6 | 9 | 2 | 5 | 3 | 12 | 14 | | | | | | | | |
| 19-Feb | A | Queen's Park | 497 | 3-0 | | 8 | 4 | | 12 | | | | 10 | 11² | 5 | 7 | 1 | | | | | 6 | 2 | | 3 | 9 | 14 | 16 | | | | | | | | |
| 5-Mar | H | Queen's Park | 355 | 0-4 | | 8 | 4 | | 12 | | | | 9 | 11 | 5 | 7 | 1 | | | | | 6 | 15 | 2 | 3 | 10 | 14 | | | | | | | | | |
| 8-Mar | H | Montrose | 307 | 1-2 | 17 | 8 | 4 | | | | | | 9 | 11 | | 7 | 14 | | | | | 15 | 6 | 2 | 3 | 5 | 10 | | | | | | | | | |
| 15-Mar | H | Stenhousemuir | 222 | 1-1 | 1 | 8 | 4 | | 7 | | | | | 11 | 5 | | | 11 | | | | 6 | 15 | 2 | 12 | 3 | 9 | 10 | | | | | | | | |
| 22-Mar | A | Peterhead | 532 | 3-2 | 1 | 8 | 4 | | 12 | | | | 7 | 5 | | 11 | | | | | 6 | 14 | 2 | | | 9 | 10 | 15 | 3 | | | | | | | |
| 29-Mar | A | Stenhousemuir | 370 | 1-1 | 1 | 6 | | | 7 | | | | 11 | 8 | | 5 | | | | | 4 | 2 | | | 9 | 10 | 16 | 3 | | | | | | | | |
| 12-Mar | H | East Fife | 316 | 0-6 | | 8 | 4 | | 7 | | | | 11 | 5 | 1 | | | | | | 14 | 2 | 3 | 9 | 10 | 6 | | | | | | | | | | |
| 2-Apr | H | Elgin City | 246 | 2-0 | | 3 | 6 | 7 | | | | 9 | 11 | 5 | 1 | | | | | | 4 | 2 | | 10 | 8 | | | | | | | | | | | |
| 9-Apr | H | Cowdenbeath | 323 | 1-4 | | 3 | 6 | 7 | | | | 9 | 11 | 5 | 1 | | | | 16 | | 4 | 2 | | 12 | 10 | 8 | | | | | | | | | | |
| 23-Apr | A | East Stirlingshire | 285 | 2-0 | | 6 | 4 | 7 | | | | | 5 | 8 | 1 | | | | 11 | | | 2 | 3 | 10² | 9 | | | 14 | | | | | | | | |
| 23-Apr | H | Queen's Park | 353 | 1-2 | | 8 | 4 | | | | | | 11 | 7 | 1 | | | 9 | | | 6 | 14 | 5 | 2 | 3 | 10 | 15 | 12 | | | | | | | | |
| 30-Apr | A | East Fife | 568 | 1-1 | | 6 | 4 | | 12 | | | | 10 | 11 | 16 | 7 | 1 | | | | 2 | 8 | | 5 | 3 | 14 | | 9 | | | | | | | | |
| 7-May | H | Gretna | 519 | 0-5 | | 8 | 4 | | 7 | | | | 12 | 11 | 1 | | | | | | 5 | 6 | | 2 | 3 | 10 | 16 | 9 | 15 | | | | | | | |
| **TOTAL FULL APPEARANCES** | | | | | 8 | 12 | 35 | 30 | 8 | 17 | 28 | 5 | 8 | 20 | 25 | 15 | 19 | 27 | 28 | 7 | 8 | 2 | 7 | 6 | 3 | 16 | 4 | 16 | 5 | 11 | 11 | 10 | | 3 | 2 | |
| **TOTAL SUB APPEARANCES** | | | | | 1 | 2 | | | 5 | | 5 | 2 | 6 | | | 2 | 7 | | | 3 | 5 | | 3 | 6 | 1 | 1 | 6 | | 1 | 1 | 1 | 5 | 5 | | 2 | 1 |
| **TOTAL GOALS SCORED** | | | | | | | 4 | | | | 1 | | 7 | 5 | 6 | 1 | | | | 1 | 1 | | | | 1 | 1 | 1 | | | 6 | 2 | | 1 | |

e in bold denotes goal scored. Secondary smaller figure in bold denotes number of goals scored. † denotes opponent's own goal.

### THE WEE ROVERS' 10 YEAR LEAGUE RECORD

| Season | Div | P | W | D | L | F | A | Pts | Pos |
|---|---|---|---|---|---|---|---|---|---|
| 95-96 | T | 36 | 7 | 8 | 21 | 37 | 74 | 29 | 10 |
| 96-97 | T | 36 | 13 | 10 | 13 | 50 | 47 | 49 | 5 |
| 97-98 | T | 36 | 13 | 5 | 18 | 60 | 73 | 44 | 5 |
| 98-99 | T | 36 | 12 | 8 | 16 | 43 | 63 | 44 | 7 |
| 99-00 | T | 36 | 5 | 24 | 7 | 33 | 75 | 22 | 10 |
| 00-01 | T | 36 | 12 | 9 | 15 | 38 | 43 | 45 | 7 |
| 01-02 | T | 36 | 16 | 11 | 9 | 51 | 42 | 59 | 3 |
| 02-03 | T | 36 | 20 | 10 | 6 | 62 | 36 | 70 | 3 |
| 03-04 | T | 36 | 12 | 4 | 20 | 66 | 75 | 40 | 8 |
| 04-05 | T | 36 | 8 | 10 | 18 | 40 | 78 | 34 | 9 |

### LEADING GOALSCORERS:

| Season | Div | Goals | Player |
|---|---|---|---|
| 1995-96 | T | 12 | G. Young |
| 1996-97 | T | 11 | W. Watters |
| 1997-98 | T | 13 | W. Watters |
| 1998-99 | T | 10 | D. Lorimer |
| 1999-00 | T | 7 | I. Diack |
| 2000-01 | T | 6 | M. Booth |
| 2001-02 | T | 11 | C. McLean |
| 2002-03 | T | 10 | J. Mercer |
| 2003-04 | T | 18 | P. McManus |
| 2004-05 | T | 7 | J. Bradford |

### ALBION ROVERS PLAYING KITS SEASON 2005.06

FIRST KIT — SECOND KIT — THIRD KIT

# ARBROATH

## ARBROATH F.C.

Gayfield Park,
Arbroath, Angus, DD11 1QB

**TELEPHONE NUMBERS**
Ground/Ticket Office/Club Shop
(01241) 872157
Sec. Home (01241) 872394
Sec. Bus. (01382) 344695
**FAX** (01241) 431125
**E-MAIL** afc@gayfield.fsnet.co.uk
**E-MAIL 2** garycallon@onetel.com
**WEBSITE** www.arbroathfc.co.uk

**CHAIRMAN** John D. Christison
**VICE-CHAIRMAN** Michael I. Caird
**DIRECTORS**
R. Alan Ripley (Treasurer),
Malcolm L. Fairweather,
Dr. Gary J. Callon,
Mark R. Davies & Ian J. Angus
**HONORARY PRESIDENTS**
Ian Stirling, George Johnston, Bert Pearson,
Jim Leslie, Duncan Ferguson, Jim King,
Rusty Smith & Charles Kinnear
**HONORARY PATRONS**
Earl of Airlie, Lord Inchcape & Lord Fraser
**SECRETARY** Dr. Gary J. Callon
**MANAGER** John McGlashan
**DIRECTOR OF YOUTH DEVELOPMENT**
Michael I. Caird
**YOUTH CO-ORDINATOR** Mike Cargill
**YOUTH TEAM COACHES**
U19: Mike Cargill & Mark Anderson
U17: Willie Anderson
**TEAM CAPTAIN** Marc McCulloch
**OFFICE ADMINISTRATOR** Mike Cargill
**FOOTBALL SAFETY OFFICERS'**
**ASSOCIATION REPRESENTATIVE**
William Scorgie (01241) 878778
**COMMERCIAL & LOTTERY MANAGER**
Malcolm Fairweather (01241) 434765
**MEDIA LIAISON PERSON** Mike Cargill
**MATCHDAY PROGRAMME EDITOR**
Ian Angus
**CLUB DOCTOR** Dr. Dick Spiers
**PHYSIOTHERAPIST** John Cooper
**STADIUM MANAGER** Michael Caird
**GROUNDSMAN** Peter Clarke
**KIT PERSON** Margaret Reid
**CHIROPODIST** Alexander McKinnon
**CLUB SHOP**
Contact: Karen Fleming (07947 302625)
Gayfield Park, Arbroath, DD11 1QB.
Open on home matchdays.
**SHIRT SPONSOR** AllStar's International
**KIT SUPPLIER** Errea

## LIST OF PLAYERS 2005.06

| PLAYERS SURNAME | FIRST NAME | MIDDLE NAME | DATE OF BIRTH | PLACE OF BIRTH | DATE SIGNED | HEIGHT FT INS | WEIGHT ST LBS | POSITION ON PITCH | PREVIOUS CLUB |
|---|---|---|---|---|---|---|---|---|---|
| Anderson | Craig | Duncan | 21/02/88 | Dundee | 20/08/05 | 5.11 | 11.0 | Midfield | Arbroath Form D U16 |
| Anderson | Graham | | 25/07/88 | Dundee | 20/08/05 | 6.0 | 11.10 | Defender | Arbroath Form D U16 |
| Bishop | James | David | 14/01/85 | Dundee | 06/07/04 | 6.1 | 12.6 | Defender | Dunfermline Athletic |
| Black | Roddy | | 22/02/78 | Dundee | 28/05/05 | 5.10 | 12.7 | Midfield | Brechin City |
| Brazil | Alan | | 05/07/85 | Edinburgh | 20/07/04 | 5.10 | 13.0 | Forward | Aston Villa |
| Cairns | Mark | Henry | 25/09/69 | Edinburgh | 06/07/05 | 6.0 | 13.7 | Goalkeeper | Bo'ness United Juniors |
| Cargill | Christopher | James | 30/05/86 | Dundee | 13/08/05 | 6.3 | 13.6 | Goalkeeper | Arbroath Victoria Junior |
| Clarke | Patrick | | 18/05/85 | Edinburgh | 31/08/05 | 5.11 | 10.4 | Forward | Raith Rovers |
| Collier | James | Stewart | 17/12/86 | Aberdeen | 01/06/04 | 6.1 | 13.0 | Forward | Aberdeen |
| Cook | Steven | Derek | 13/06/85 | Dundee | 26/05/05 | 5.10 | 11.0 | Midfield | Dundee |
| Cormack | Peter | Robert | 08/06/74 | Southport | 27/07/05 | 6.1 | 12.0 | Defender | Bo'ness United Juniors |
| Davidson | Hugh | Norman | 03/08/80 | Dundee | 06/07/05 | 6.1 | 12.4 | Midfield | Forfar Athletic |
| Dobbins | Ian | Alexander | 24/08/83 | Bellshill | 31/08/05 | 6.2 | 12.7 | Defender | Dumbarton |
| Duncan | Graeme | | 16/03/88 | Dundee | 20/08/05 | 6.2 | 12.0 | Defender | Arbroath Form D U16 |
| Gordon | Ross | MacDonald | 19/11/88 | Dundee | 20/08/05 | 5.7 | 10.1 | Defender | Arbroath Form D U16 |
| Inglis | Neil | David | 10/09/74 | Glasgow | 06/07/04 | 6.1 | 12.2 | Goalkeeper | Berwick Rangers |
| Jackson | Christopher | Robert | 29/10/73 | Edinburgh | 24/06/05 | 5.9.5 | 12.0 | Midfield | Brechin City |
| Kane | David | Darren | 30/07/87 | Dundee | 20/08/05 | 5.9 | 11.8 | Midfield | Forfar Athletic |
| King | Mathu | | 26/03/84 | Bellshill | 26/05/05 | 6.0 | 12.0 | Forward | Forfar Athletic |
| Macdonald | Gordon | | 28/05/89 | Dundee | 20/08/05 | 6.0 | 11.12 | Forward | Camoustie Panmure B.C. |
| MacGregor | Scott | Charles | 22/12/88 | Glasgow | 20/08/05 | 6.2 | 12.7 | Defender | Stonehaven Youth |
| Masson | Terry | | 03/07/88 | Dundee | 20/08/05 | 5.8 | 10.12 | Midfield | Dundee |
| McCulloch | Marc | Raymond | 14/03/80 | Edinburgh | 31/01/05 | 5.10 | 12.0 | Midfield | Morton |
| McKibben | Philip | Neil | 04/04/87 | Aberdeen | 20/08/05 | 5.11 | 11.7 | Midfield | Albion B.C. |
| McMullan | Kevin | Andrew | 15/06/83 | Kirkcaldy | 25/05/04 | 5.9 | 11.0 | Defender | Newburgh Juniors |
| Miller | Greg | Allan | 01/04/76 | Glasgow | 18/06/04 | 5.8 | 11.1 | Midfield | Brechin City |
| Myles | Barry | Allan | 29/04/89 | Dundee | 27/08/05 | 6.1 | 11.6 | Defender | Fairmuir B.C. |
| Peat | Mark | | 13/03/82 | Bellshill | 08/09/05 | 6.1 | 13.1 | Goalkeeper | Albion Rovers |
| Reilly | Andrew | | 25/05/86 | Dundee | 29/07/05 | 5.9 | 11.0 | Midfield | Dundee |
| Rennie | Steven | | 03/08/81 | Stirling | 30/06/03 | 6.2 | 12.10 | Defender | Falkirk |
| Russell | Nicholas | John | 31/01/87 | Dundee | 20/08/05 | 6.3 | 12.12 | Goalkeeper | Brechin City Form S |
| Smith | Nicky | William | 31/07/87 | Arbroath | 30/07/05 | 6.0 | 11.2 | Midfield | Arbroath Form S |
| Stein | Jay | | 13/01/80 | Dunfermline | 26/05/05 | 5.9 | 11.0 | Midfield | Forfar Athletic |
| Warren | Garry | Stewart | 01/07/86 | Dundee | 08/08/05 | 5.11 | 10.0 | Forward | Arbroath Form S |
| Watson | Paul | | 22/11/85 | Dundee | 01/02/05 | 6.2 | 11.10 | Defender | Forfar West End Junio |
| Webster | Martin | James | 07/05/87 | Dundee | 20/08/05 | 6.1 | 11.4 | Forward | Brechin City Form S |

### TICKET INFORMATION
#### Season Ticket Information

| Seated | Adult | £160 |
|---|---|---|
| | Juvenile | £80 |
| | OAP | £75 |
| Standing | Adult | £160 |
| | Juvenile | £50 |
| | OAP | £75 |
| | Juvenile under 12 Years | £20 |

#### League Admission Prices

| Seated | Adult | £9 |
|---|---|---|
| | Juvenile/OAP | £5 |
| Standing | Adult | £9 |
| | Juvenile/OAP & Unemployed with UB40 | £5 |
| | Parent & Child | £12 |

**MILESTONES:**
Year of formation: 1878
Most capped player: Ned Doig
No. of caps: 2
Most League points in a season:
57 (Division 2 – Season 1966/67) (2 Points for a Win)
68 (Third Division – Season 1997/98) (3 Points for a Win)
Most League goals scored by a player in a season:
David Easson (Season 1958/59)
No. of goals scored: 45
Record Attendance: 13,510 (-v- Rangers – Scottish Cup, 23.2.19
Record Victory: 36-0 (-v- Bon Accord – Scottish Cup, 12.9.18
Record Defeat: 1-9 (-v- Celtic – League Cup, 25.8.1993)

# SEASON STATS 2004.05

## SEASON STATS 2004.05

*Figure in bold denotes goal scored. Secondary smaller figure in bold denotes number of goals scored. † denotes opponent's own goal.*

| Date | Venue | Opponents | Att | Res | Inglis N.D. | McMullan K. | Beith G. | Renwick M.J. | Bishop J.D.G. | Cusick J.J. | Miller G.A. | MacDonald S. | McLean D.W. | Brazil A. | Swankie G. | McAulay J. | Farquharson P. | Henslee G. | Cook S. | McLeod C. | Collier J.S. | Woodcock T.M. | Rennie S. | Donaldson E.G. | Millar M. | Fraser S. | McGlashan J. | Diack I.G. | McCulloch M.R. | Coyle C.R. | Watson P. |
|---|---|---|---|---|---|---|---|---|---|---|---|---|---|---|---|---|---|---|---|---|---|---|---|---|---|---|---|---|---|---|---|---|
| -Aug | A | Stirling Albion | 706 | 2-5 | 1 | 2 | 3 | 4 | 5 | 6 | 7 | 8 | **9** | 10 | 11 | 12 | 14 | **15** | | | | | | | | | | | | | |
| 4-Aug | H | Dumbarton | 505 | 0-2 | 1 | 2 | | | 5 | 6 | 7 | 8 | 9 | 10 | 11 | | 14 | | | | 3 | 4 | 15 | | | | | | | | |
| 1-Aug | A | Forfar Athletic | 696 | 0-5 | | 2 | 3 | 4 | | | 7 | 8 | 9 | | 11 | | | 16 | 10 | 14 | 5 | 15 | 1 | 6 | | | | | | | |
| 8-Aug | H | Stranraer | 405 | 0-1 | | 2 | 3 | | 5 | | 7 | 8 | 9 | 14 | 11 | | | 16 | 10 | 15 | 6 | 1 | 4 | | | | | | | | |
| -Sep | A | Morton | 2,360 | 1-2 | | 2 | 3 | | 5 | | 7 | 8 | 9 | | 11 | | | 14 | **10** | 15 | 6 | 1 | 4 | 16 | | | | | | | |
| 1-Sep | A | Brechin City | 559 | 1-4 | | 2 | | | 5 | 7 | | 8 | | 15 | 11 | 14 | 9 | 10 | 16 | 6 | 1 | 4 | 3 | | | | | | | | |
| 8-Sep | H | Ayr United | 481 | 0-0 | 1 | 2 | | | | 6 | 7 | 8 | | | 11 | | 9 | 10 | 5 | | 4 | 3 | | | | | | | | | |
| 5-Sep | A | Berwick Rangers | 335 | 3-0 | 1 | 2 | | | | 6 | 7 | 8 | **9²** | 15 | 11 | | | 10 | 5 | | 4 | 3 | | | | | | | | | |
| -Oct | H | Alloa Athletic | 431 | 0-3 | 1 | 2 | 14 | | | 6 | 7 | 8 | 9 | 15 | 11 | | | 10 | 5 | 16 | 4 | 3 | | | | | | | | | |
| 5-Oct | A | Dumbarton | 716 | 3-1 | 1 | **2** | | | | 6 | 7 | 8 | 9 | 16 | **11²** | 12 | | 10 | 15 | 5 | 4 | 3 | | | | | | | | | |
| 3-Oct | H | Stirling Albion | 620 | 2-1 | 1 | 2 | | | | 6 | **7** | 8 | **9** | | 11 | | | 10 | 5 | | 4 | 3 | | | | | | | | | |
| 0-Oct | A | Stranraer | 503 | 1-2 | 1 | 2 | | | | 6 | 7 | 8 | **9** | | 11 | | | 10 | 5 | | 4 | 3 | | | | | | | | | |
| -Nov | H | Morton | 857 | 0-3 | 1 | 2 | | | | 6 | 7 | 8 | 9 | | 11 | | | 10 | 5 | | 4 | 3 | 15 | | | | | | | | |
| 3-Nov | H | Brechin City | 682 | 2-2 | 1 | 2 | | | | 6 | 7 | 8 | 9 | **16** | 11 | | | 10 | 5 | | 4 | 3 | 15 | | | | | | | | |
| 7-Nov | A | Ayr United | 1,189 | 1-1 | 1 | 2 | | | | 6 | 7 | 8 | 9 | | 11 | | 16 | 10 | 5 | | 4 | 3 | 14 | | | | | | | | |
| -Dec | A | Berwick Rangers | 450 | 1-1 | 1 | 2 | | | | 6 | 14 | 8 | 9 | 16 | 11 | | | 10 | 5 | | 4 | 3 | | | | | | | | | |
| 3-Dec | A | Alloa Athletic | 435 | 2-4 | 1 | 2 | | | | 6 | 14 | 8 | 9 | | 11 | | | 10 | 5 | | 3 | 7 | 4 | | | | | | | | |
| 7-Dec | A | Stirling Albion | 755 | 3-0 | 1 | 2 | | | | 6 | 15 | 4 | **9²** | 8 | 11 | | 14 | 10 | 5 | | 3 | 7 | | | | | | | | | |
| -Jan | H | Forfar Athletic | 825 | 0-2 | 1 | 2 | | | | 6 | 4 | 8 | | 16 | 11 | | 14 | 10 | 5 | | 3 | 7 | | | | | | | | | |
| -Jan | H | Stranraer | 432 | 0-4 | 1 | 2 | | | | 6 | 14 | 12 | 9 | 8 | 11 | | | 10 | 5 | | 3 | 7 | 4 | | | | | | | | |
| 5-Jan | A | Morton | 2,689 | 0-2 | 1 | 2 | | | | 6 | 14 | 8 | **9** | 16 | 11 | | | **10** | 5 | | 4 | 3 | 7 | | | | | | | | |
| 9-Jan | H | Ayr United | 426 | 2-0 | 1 | | | | | 7 | 2 | 12 | **9** | | 11 | | 8 | **10** | 16 | 5 | 4 | 3 | | | | | 6 | | | | |
| Feb | A | Berwick Rangers | 309 | 3-2 | 1 | 14 | | | | 7 | 2 | 12 | 9 | | 11 | | | 10 | 5 | | 4 | 3 | | | | | 6 | 8 | 15 | | |
| Feb | A | Brechin City | 651 | 3-4 | 1 | 14 | | | 5 | | 2 | | 9 | | 11 | | | 10 | | 15 | 4 | 3 | | | | | 6 | 8 | 7 | | |
| 2-Feb | H | Alloa Athletic | 525 | 2-1 | 1 | 12 | | | 14 | 16 | 2 | | 9 | | 11 | | | 10 | 5 | | 4 | 3 | | | | | 6 | 8 | 7 | | |
| 9-Feb | A | Forfar Athletic | 758 | 1-1 | 1 | 12 | | | 15 | 14 | 2 | | 9 | | 11 | | | 10 | 5 | | 4 | 3 | | | | | 6 | 8 | 7 | | |
| 6-Feb | H | Dumbarton | 502 | 2-1 | 1 | 12 | | | | 14 | 2 | | 9 | | 11 | | | 10 | 5 | | 4 | 3 | | | | | 6 | 8 | 7 | | |
| Mar | H | Morton | 832 | 0-1 | 1 | | | | | 4 | 2 | | 9 | | 11 | | | 10 | 15 | 5 | | 3 | | | | | 6 | 8 | 7 | | |
| 2-Mar | A | Stranraer | 357 | 3-3 | 1 | 4 | | | | 8 | **2** | | 9 | | 11 | | | 10 | 5 | | | 3 | | | | | 6 | 14 | 7 | | |
| 9-Mar | H | Brechin City | 775 | 1-4 | 1 | 8 | | | 15 | 12 | 2 | | 9 | | 11 | | | 10 | 5 | | 4 | 3 | | | | | 6 | 14 | 7 | | |
| Apr | A | Ayr United | 1,115 | 2-2 | | | 3 | | | 12 | 7 | 2 | 9 | 14 | 11 | | | 10 | 5 | | 4 | | | | | | 6 | 8 | | 1 | |
| Apr | A | Alloa Athletic | 502 | 2-2 | 18 | 3 | | | | 7 | 12 | 2 | 9 | | 11 | | | 10 | 16 | 5 | 4 | | | | | | 6 | 8 | | 1 | |
| 6-Apr | H | Berwick Rangers | 460 | 2-0 | | 3 | | | | 7 | 2 | | 9 | | 11 | | | 10 | 15 | 5 | 4 | | | | | | 6 | 8 | | 1 | |
| 0-Apr | A | Dumbarton | 697 | 0-3 | | 3 | | | | 12 | | 2 | 9 | 14 | 11 | | | 10 | 5 | 15 | 4 | | | | | | 6 | 8 | 7 | 1 | |
| 3-Apr | H | Forfar Athletic | 1,192 | 1-2 | | 3 | | | | 12 | 7 | 2 | 9 | | 11 | | | 10 | 16 | 5 | 4 | | | | | | 6 | 8 | | 1 | |
| May | H | Stirling Albion | 535 | 3-2 | 1 | 7 | | | | 6 | | 2 | 9 | 16 | 11 | 12 | | 10 | 5 | | 4 | | | | | | 8 | | | | 3 |
| **TOTAL FULL APPEARANCES** | | | | | 27 | 29 | 4 | 1 | 25 | 18 | 21 | 21 | 9 | 28 | 34 | 5 | 34 | 1 | 34 | 4 | 28 | 24 | 8 | 2 | 11 | 11 | 11 | 5 | 1 | | |
| **TOTAL SUB APPEARANCES** | | | | | 1 | 5 | 2 | | 6 | 8 | 3 | 6 | 6 | 3 | 3 | 8 | 1 | 11 | 5 | | 3 | 1 | | | | | 2 | 1 | | |
| **TOTAL GOALS SCORED** | | | | | | | | | 5 | 3 | 1 | 1 | | 5 | 7 | 4 | 1 | 11 | 1 | 4 | 1 | | | | | | 2 | 3 | | |

## THE RED LITCHIES' 10 YEAR LEAGUE RECORD

| Season | Div | P | W | D | L | F | A | Pts | Pos |
|---|---|---|---|---|---|---|---|---|---|
| 95-96 | T | 36 | 13 | 13 | 10 | 41 | 41 | 52 | 5 |
| 96-97 | T | 36 | 6 | 13 | 17 | 31 | 52 | 31 | 10 |
| 97-98 | T | 36 | 20 | 8 | 8 | 67 | 39 | 68 | 2 |
| 98-99 | S | 36 | 12 | 8 | 16 | 37 | 52 | 44 | 7 |
| 99-00 | S | 36 | 11 | 11 | 14 | 52 | 55 | 47 | 4 |
| 00-01 | S | 36 | 15 | 13 | 8 | 54 | 38 | 58 | 2 |
| 01-02 | F | 36 | 14 | 6 | 16 | 42 | 59 | 48 | 7 |
| 02-03 | F | 36 | 3 | 6 | 27 | 30 | 77 | 15 | 10 |
| 03-04 | S | 36 | 11 | 10 | 15 | 41 | 57 | 43 | 8 |
| 04-05 | S | 36 | 10 | 8 | 18 | 49 | 73 | 38 | 9 |

## LEADING GOALSCORERS:

| Season | Div | Goals | Player |
|---|---|---|---|
| 1995-96 | T | 8 | S. McCormick, D. Pew |
| 1996-97 | T | 5 | B. Grant |
| 1997-98 | T | 16 | W. Spence |
| 1998-99 | S | 12 | C. McGlashan |
| 1999-00 | S | 16 | C. McGlashan |
| 2000-01 | S | 10 | S. Mallan |
| 2001-02 | F | 6 | G. Bayne, J. McGlashan, S. Mallan |
| 2002-03 | F | 4 | J. Cusick, M. McDowell |
| 2003-04 | S | 10 | J. McGlashan |
| 2004-05 | S | 11 | G. Henslee |

### ARBROATH PLAYING KITS SEASON 2005.06

FIRST KIT | SECOND KIT | THIRD KIT

# BERWICK RANGERS

## BERWICK RANGERS F.C.

Shielfield Park, Shielfield Terrace,
Tweedmouth, Berwick-Upon-Tweed, TD15 2EF

**TELEPHONE NUMBERS**
Ground/Ticket Office (01289) 307424
Club Sec. Home (01289) 307623
24 Hour Hotline (09068) 800697
**FAX** (01289) 309424
**E-MAIL** dennis@mccleary133.fsnet.co.uk
**WEBSITE** www.berwickrangers.co.uk
**CHAIRMAN** Robert L. Wilson
**VICE-CHAIRMAN** W. Moray McLaren
**DIRECTORS**
John H. Hush, Peter McAskill,
Ian R. Smith, Robert J. Darling
Craig Forsyth & Brian J. Porteous
**GENERAL MANAGER** Jimmy Crease
**HONORARY PRESIDENT**
Rt. Hon. Alan Beith M.P.
**CLUB SECRETARY** Dennis J. McCleary
**COMPANY SECRETARY**
Ross Hood (Morison's Solicitors)
**MANAGER** John Coughlin
**PLAYER/COACH** Ian Little
**GOALKEEPING COACH** Alex Connon
**YOUTH DEVELOPMENT OFFICER &**
**YOUTH CO-ORDINATOR** David Buglass
**YOUTH TEAM MANAGERS**
U19: Drew Thomson
U17: Richard Young
U15: Stephen Lennon
**CHIEF SCOUT** Bill Barclay
**TEAM CAPTAIN** David Murie
**OFFICE ADMINISTRATOR &**
**FINANCE OFFICER** J. Neil Simpson
**FOOTBALL SAFETY OFFICERS**
**ASSOCIATION REPRESENTATIVE**
Craig Forsyth
**COMMERCIAL MANAGER**
Conrad Turner (01289) 307969
**MEDIA LIAISON OFFICER**
John Coughlin (07769) 700657
**MATCHDAY PROGRAMME EDITOR**
Dennis McCleary (01289) 307623
**CLUB DOCTOR**
Dr. W.A. Fortune MB, BS, FRCOG
**HONORARY CLUB PARAMEDIC**
Paul Ross R.Para, EMT. P Assoc EU
**PHYSIOTHERAPISTS**
Kerry Sneddon B. Sc & Jamie Dougall
**STADIUM MANAGER & GROUNDSMAN**
Ross Aitchison
**KIT PERSON** Ian Oliver
**CHIEF STEWARD** John Dodds
**CLUB SHOP**
Supporters Shop situated within the ground.
Open during first team home Matchdays.
**OFFICIAL SUPPORTERS CLUB**
c/o Shielfield Park, Tweedmouth,
Berwick-Upon-Tweed, TD15 2EF
(01289) 307424
**SHIRT SPONSOR**
Front: 247ink.com(Red Shark)
Back: Buccleuch Group
**KIT SUPPLIER**
TFG

## LIST OF PLAYERS 2005.06

| PLAYERS SURNAME | FIRST NAME | MIDDLE NAME | DATE OF BIRTH | PLACE OF BIRTH | DATE SIGNED | HEIGHT FT INS | WEIGHT ST LBS | POSITION ON PITCH | PREVIOUS CLUB |
|---|---|---|---|---|---|---|---|---|---|
| Ainslie | Jordan | | 14/09/89 | Ashington | 12/08/05 | 6.0 | 12.5 | Midfield | Tweedmouth Juniors |
| Ainslie | Kieran | | 04/03/89 | Ashington | 12/08/05 | 6.0 | 13.0 | Defender | Berwick Rangers Juniors |
| Aitchison | Ross | | 06/06/87 | Edinburgh | 17/08/05 | 5.11 | 11.0 | Midfield | Eyemouth United |
| Arthur | Robbie | | 12/08/86 | Edinburgh | 25/07/05 | 5.7 | 10.9 | Forward | Livingston |
| Avery | Dean | | 08/05/89 | Alnwick | 12/08/05 | 5.10 | 10.3 | Goalkeeper | Berwick Rangers Juniors |
| Brown | Robert | | 23/05/89 | Alnwick | 12/08/05 | 5.9 | 9.8 | Midfield | Berwick Rangers Juniors |
| Brown | Robin | | 21/11/89 | Melrose | 12/08/05 | 6.1 | 12.5 | Forward | Tweedmouth Juniors |
| Brown | Tony | | 18/09/87 | Alnwick | 17/08/05 | 5.9 | 9.0 | Midfield | Shilbottle |
| Chisholm | Bruce | | 21/08/88 | Galashiels | 17/08/05 | 6.2 | 13.0 | Forward | Greenlaw A.F.C. |
| Connelly | Gordon | | 01/11/76 | Glasgow | 04/07/02 | 6.0 | 12.7 | Midfield | Queen of the South |
| Cowan | Mark | | 16/01/71 | Edinburgh | 17/06/03 | 6.0 | 13.0 | Defender | Alloa Athletic |
| Coyle | Craig | Robert | 06/09/80 | Edinburgh | 25/07/05 | 5.11 | 12.0 | Goalkeeper | Arbroath |
| Darling | Ross | | 09/10/89 | Melrose | 12/08/05 | 5.7 | 10.0 | Midfield | Tynecastle East B.C. |
| Dickson | Jamie | | 06/08/87 | Edinburgh | 18/08/05 | 5.11 | 12.7 | Defender | Eyemouth United |
| Fawcett | Chris | | 20/03/88 | Ashington | 17/08/05 | 5.11 | 11.0 | Forward | Cramlington Juniors |
| Gibson | Jamie | | 26/10/89 | Melrose | 12/08/05 | 6.0 | 11.0 | Forward | Easthouses B.C. |
| Gordon | Kevin | Mervyn | 01/05/77 | Tranent | 29/01/04 | 5.10 | 10.12 | Mid/ Fwd | Cowdenbeath |
| Greenhill | Gary | James | 16/06/85 | Kirkcaldy | 06/01/05 | 5.11 | 11.4 | Midfield | Dunfermline Athletic |
| Greenlees | Peter | | 19/09/87 | Ashington | 17/08/05 | 5.11 | 11.0 | Defender | Berwick Under 16's |
| Hastie | Andrew | | 17/11/87 | Ashington | 17/08/05 | 5.10 | 11.6 | Defender | Highfield United |
| Haynes | Kevin | | 17/05/81 | Ashington | 16/06/05 | 6.1 | 13.4 | Forward | Dunbar United |
| Horn | Robert | David | 03/08/77 | Edinburgh | 02/06/04 | 6.0 | 12.7 | Defender | Forfar Athletic |
| Hutchison | Gareth | William | 04/06/72 | Edinburgh | 05/06/03 | 5.11 | 11.10 | Forward | Alloa Athletic |
| Jess | Alan | | 12/10/89 | Edinburgh | 12/08/05 | 5.7 | 8.6 | Defender | Tweedmouth Juniors |
| Johnstone | Steven | | 23/11/87 | Broxburn | 17/08/05 | 5.11 | 12.7 | Forward | Livingston United Juniors |
| Little | Ian | James | 10/12/73 | Edinburgh | 25/05/04 | 5.8 | 10.10 | Forward | Alloa Athletic |
| Macpherson | Tom | | 06/09/87 | Hexham | 17/08/05 | 6.3 | 12.5 | Defender | Morpeth Town Juniors |
| McGarty | Mark | | 03/08/82 | Bangour | 11/11/04 | 5.10 | 12.0 | Midfield | Dunfermline Athletic |
| McGroarty | Christopher | Martin | 06/02/81 | Bellshill | 26/07/05 | 5.10 | 11.0 | Midfield | East Stirlingshire |
| McLean | Andrew | | 20/10/89 | Melrose | 12/08/05 | 6.0 | 11.8 | Midfield | Tynecastle B.C. |
| McLeish | Kevin | Michael | 03/12/80 | Edinburgh | 20/01/05 | 5.10 | 12.0 | Midfield | Brechin City |
| McNicoll | Grant | | 07/09/77 | Edinburgh | 30/07/97 | 5.11 | 11.1 | Defender | Heart of Midlothian |
| Miller | Grant | | 21/03/89 | Galashiels | 12/08/05 | 5.10 | 11.0 | Goalkeeper | Hutchison Vale B.C. |
| Murie | David | | 02/08/76 | Edinburgh | 14/06/01 | 5.9 | 11.0 | Defender | Morton |
| Neill | Kristian | | 25/05/89 | Berwick upon Tweed | 18/08/05 | 5.8 | 10.0 | Midfield | Berwick Rangers Juniors |
| O'Connor | Gary | | 07/04/74 | Newtongrange | 02/06/04 | 6.3 | 14.0 | Goalkeeper | East Fife |
| Peoples | Callum | Stuart | 21/05/89 | Galashiels | 12/08/05 | 6.1 | 11.7 | Midfield | Heart of Midlothian |
| Pitman | Darren | | 17/04/89 | Greenwich | 12/08/05 | 5.8 | 11.0 | Defender | Tweedmouth Juniors |
| Punton | Ben | | 07/01/89 | Berwick upon Tweed | 12/08/05 | 6.0 | 12.0 | Defender | Berwick Rangers Juniors |
| Robertson | James | | 10/06/88 | Edinburgh | 17/08/05 | 5.11 | 11.0 | Midfield | Salvesen B.C. |
| Senior | David | | 20/08/89 | Ashington | 12/08/05 | 5.11 | 11.11 | Defender | Berwick Rangers Juniors |
| Shields | Jay | | 06/01/85 | Edinburgh | 31/08/05 | 5.7 | 11.4 | Midfield | Hibernian |
| Simpson | Johny | | 14/02/89 | Huntington | 12/08/05 | 5.10 | 11.5 | Forward | Tweedmouth Juniors |
| Simpson | Sean | | 12/03/89 | Ashington | 12/08/05 | 5.10 | 13.2 | Forward | Berwick Rangers Juniors |
| Stalker | Russell | | 27/07/88 | Alnwick | 17/08/05 | 6.0 | 11.12 | Goalkeeper | Belford B.C. |
| Swanson | Daniel | | 28/12/86 | Edinburgh | 09/08/05 | 5.6 | 9.3 | Forward | Leith Athletic |
| Tait | Fraser | | 02/03/89 | Ashington | 12/08/05 | 6.1 | 11.0 | Defender | Alnwick Town Juniors |
| Vitorino | Bruno | Miguel | 03/02/81 | Portalegre | 29/07/05 | 5.10 | 10.12 | Forward | Farne A.F.C. |
| Walton | Sean | | 14/04/89 | St. Peters Port | 12/08/05 | 5.9 | 10.0 | Midfield | Tweedmouth Juniors |
| Weddell | Peter | | 19/01/88 | Ashington | 18/08/05 | 5.9 | 11.7 | Midfield | Shilbottle |
| Windram | Jack | | 29/04/88 | Edinburgh | 17/08/05 | 5.9 | 10.0 | Forward | Eyemouth Under 17's |
| Wood | Paul | | 11/10/89 | Ashington | 17/08/05 | 5.8 | 11.0 | Midfield | Berwick Rangers Juniors |
| Young | Christopher | David | 16/01/88 | Edinburgh | 17/08/05 | 6.0 | 13.4 | Defender | Ayton Amateurs |

## TICKET INFORMATION

### Season Ticket Information
Tickets for seated or standing valid for all Bell's Third Division games

| Seated & Standing | Adult | £130 |
|---|---|---|
| | Concessions | £65 |

(Includes Juvenile/OAP/Unemployed with UB40/Registered Disabled)
Schoolchild Season Tickets available via club. Equates to £2 per League game

### League Admission Prices

| Seated & Standing | Adult | £10 |
|---|---|---|
| | Concessions | £5 |

N.B. All fans for Stand enter via either Ground 'A' or 'B' and transfer to Stand(s).

## MILESTONES:

**Year of formation:** 1881
**Most League points in a season:**
54 (Second Division – Season 1978/79)(2 Points for a Win)
66 (Third Division – Season 1999/2000)(3 Points for a Win)
**Most League goals scored by a player in a season:**
Ken Bowron (Season 1963/64)
**No. of goals scored:** 33
**Record Attendance:** 13,365 (-v- Rangers – 28.1.1967)
**Record Victory:**
8-1 (-v- Forfar Athletic (H) – Division 2, 25.12.1965)
8-1 (-v- Vale of Leithen – Scottish Cup at Innerleithen, 17.12.19
**Record Defeat:**
1-9 (-v- Hamilton Academical – First Division, 9.8.1980)

BELL'S — SCOTTISH FOOTBALL LEAGUE

## SEASON STATS 2004.05

| DATE | VENUE | OPPONENTS | ATT | RES | O'Connor G. | Murie D. | Seaton A.M. | Cowan M. | Horn R.D. | Connell G. | Connelly G. | Forrest G.I. | Hutchison G.W.M. | Gordon K.M. | Hampshire P.C. | Little I.J. | Smith D. | Neil M. | McNicoll G. | Smith E.H. | Clarke P. | McGarty M. | McKeown C. | MacSween I. | Greenhill G.J. | McLeish K.M. | Britton G.J. | McCann G.J. |
|---|---|---|---|---|---|---|---|---|---|---|---|---|---|---|---|---|---|---|---|---|---|---|---|---|---|---|---|---|
| 7-Aug | H | Morton | 907 | 2-1 | 1 | 2 | 3 | 4 | 5 | 6 | 7 | **8** | 9 | 10 | 11 | 14 | | | | | | | | | | | | |
| 14-Aug | A | Ayr United | 1,342 | 1-2 | 1 | 2 | 3 | 4 | 5 | 6 | | 8 | **9** | 10 | 11 | 14 | 7 | 12 | 12 | | | | | | | | | |
| 21-Aug | H | Brechin City | 429 | 0-2 | 1 | 2 | 3 | | 5 | 6 | | 8 | 9 | 10 | 11 | 13 | 15 | 7 | 4 | 14 | | | | | | | | |
| 28-Aug | A | Stirling Albion | 695 | 1-3 | 1 | | 3 | 4 | 5 | | 7 | | **9** | 6 | 11 | 10 | 14 | 8 | | 2 | | | | | | | | |
| 4-Sep | H | Dumbarton | 412 | 0-4 | 1 | 2 | 3 | 5 | 4 | 6 | | 7 | 9 | 10 | 11 | 13 | 15 | 8 | 12 | | | | | | | | | |
| 11-Sep | H | Alloa Athletic | 295 | 2-3 | 1 | 2 | **3** | 5 | 4 | | 7 | 6 | 9 | 13 | | 10 | **11** | 8 | | | | | | | | | | |
| 18-Sep | A | Forfar Athletic | 435 | 1-1 | 1 | 2 | 3 | 5 | | | 7 | 6 | **9** | | 10 | 14 | 11 | 8 | | 4 | | | | | | | | |
| 25-Sep | H | Arbroath | 335 | 0-3 | 1 | 2 | 3 | 5 | | 6 | 7 | | 9 | 12 | 10 | 11 | 8 | | | | | | | | | | | |
| 2-Oct | A | Stranraer | 521 | 2-2 | 1 | 2 | 3 | 5 | 4 | 6 | **7** | 14 | 9 | | 12 | **10** | 11 | 8 | | | | | | | | | | |
| 16-Oct | H | Ayr United | 403 | 0-1 | 1 | 2 | 3 | 5 | 4 | 6 | 7 | 14 | 9 | 13 | 12 | 10 | 11 | 8 | | | | | | | | | | |
| 23-Oct | A | Morton | 2,720 | 0-2 | 1 | 2 | | 5 | 4 | 6 | 7 | 11 | 9 | 15 | 3 | 10 | 12 | 8 | | | | | | | | | | |
| 30-Oct | H | Stirling Albion | 453 | 0-1 | 1 | 2 | | 5 | 4 | 6 | 12 | 8 | 9 | 7 | 3 | | 11 | | 15 | 10 | | | | | | | | |
| 6-Nov | A | Dumbarton | 790 | 1-3 | 1 | 2 | 15 | 5 | 4 | 6 | | 12 | | **10** | 3 | 7 | 11 | | 13 | | 9 | 8 | | | | | | |
| 13-Nov | A | Alloa Athletic | 462 | 2-2 | 1 | 2 | 3 | 5 | | 6 | 15 | | 14 | 10 | | 7 | **11²** | | 4 | | 9 | 8 | | | | | | |
| 20-Nov | A | Stirling Albion | 551 | 1-0 | 1 | 2 | 3 | 5 | | 6 | 15 | | 14 | 10 | | 7 | 11 | | 4 | | 9 | 8 | | | | | | |
| 30-Nov | H | Forfar Athletic | 294 | 1-0 | 1 | 2 | 3 | 5 | | 6 | 15 | | 14 | 10 | | 7 | 11 | | 4 | | 9 | **8** | | | | | | |
| 4-Dec | A | Arbroath | 450 | 1-1 | 1 | | 3 | 5 | | 6 | 2 | | 14 | 7 | | 10 | 11 | | 4 | | 9 | **8** | | | | | | |
| 27-Dec | H | Morton | 968 | 2-2 | 1 | 2 | 3 | 5 | | 6 | 7 | | 9 | | | **14** | 11 | | 10 | | 8 | 4 | | | | | | |
| 1-Jan | A | Brechin City | 515 | 1-4 | 1 | 2 | 3 | 5 | | 6 | | | 9 | 7 | 13 | | 11 | | 14 | 10 | **8** | 4 | | | | | | |
| 15-Jan | H | Dumbarton | 322 | 0-3 | 1 | 2 | 3 | 5 | | | | | 9 | 12 | | 6 | 11 | | 10 | 8 | 4 | 7 | 14 | | | | | |
| 29-Jan | A | Forfar Athletic | 435 | 2-0 | 1 | 2 | **3** | 5 | | 6 | 7 | | 12 | | | 10 | | | 9 | 8 | **4** | 14 | 13 | 11 | | | | |
| 5-Feb | H | Arbroath | 309 | 2-3 | 1 | 2 | 3 | 5 | | 6 | 7 | | **9** | | | 10 | 12 | | 4 | | | | | 11 | | | | |
| 12-Feb | A | Stranraer | 351 | 0-1 | 1 | 2 | 3 | 5 | 4 | 6 | 12 | | 9 | 15 | | 8 | | | | | | | | 13 | 7 | | | |
| 19-Feb | H | Brechin City | 323 | 2-1 | 1 | 2 | 3 | 5 | | 6 | 7 | | **9** | | | 10 | 11 | | 4 | | | | | 8 | | | | |
| 26-Feb | A | Ayr United | 1,019 | 1-0 | 1 | 2 | 3 | 5 | | 6 | **7** | | 9 | | | 10 | 11 | | 4 | | | | 12 | 8 | | | | |
| 1-Mar | H | Stranraer | 296 | 1-2 | 1 | 2 | 3 | 5 | | 6 | 7 | | 9 | | | 10 | **11** | | 4 | | | | 12 | 8 | | | | |
| 5-Mar | A | Dumbarton | 690 | 1-1 | 1 | 2 | 3 | | 5 | 6 | **7** | | 9 | | | 10 | 11 | | | | | | | 8 | | | | |
| 12-Mar | H | Stirling Albion | 366 | 2-2 | 1 | 2 | **3** | 5 | | 6 | 7 | | 14 | 9 | 11 | 10 | | | | | | | | 8 | | | | |
| 19-Mar | H | Alloa Athletic | 452 | 2-2 | 1 | 2 | 3 | 5 | | 6 | | | 7 | 9 | 11 | **10** | | | 4 | | | | 14 | | 13 | 8 | 15 | |
| 26-Mar | H | Alloa Athletic | 306 | 2-1 | 1 | 2 | 3 | 5 | 4 | 6 | | | 7 | 9 | 12 | 10 | **11** | | | | | | 14 | | 13 | 8 | | |
| 2-Apr | H | Forfar Athletic | 369 | 1-1 | 1 | 2 | 3 | 5 | 4 | | | | 7 | 9 | 12 | 10 | 11 | | | | | | 15 | 6 | | 8 | | |
| 9-Apr | H | Stranraer | 363 | 1-2 | 1 | 2 | 3 | | 5 | 6 | | | 7 | 9 | 11 | | | | 4 | | | | 14 | | 12 | 10 | **8** | |
| 16-Apr | A | Arbroath | 460 | 0-2 | 1 | 2 | 3 | 5 | | 6 | 7 | | 12 | 9 | | 10 | 11 | | | | | | | | | 8 | | |
| 23-Apr | A | Brechin City | 630 | 1-1 | 1 | 2 | | 5 | | 6 | 7 | | 9 | | | 10 | 11 | | | | 3 | | | 12 | | 8 | | |
| 30-Apr | H | Ayr United | 425 | 2-1 | 1 | 2 | | 5 | | 6 | 7 | | 14 | 9 | | 11 | | | 4 | | 3 | | | | 10 | 8 | | |
| 7-May | A | Morton | 2,475 | 2-4 | | 2 | | 5 | 13 | 6 | 7 | | **12** | 9 | 15 | 11 | | | 4 | | 3 | | | | 10 | 8 | | 1 |
| **TOTAL FULL APPEARANCES** | | | | | 35 | 34 | 30 | 33 | 16 | 31 | 20 | 9 | 21 | 25 | 13 | 24 | 26 | 9 | 17 | 3 | 10 | 14 | 4 | 1 | 4 | 16 | | 1 |
| **TOTAL SUB APPEARANCES** | | | | | 1 | | 1 | | | 5 | 3 | 9 | 5 | 6 | 7 | 5 | 1 | 3 | 3 | | 3 | | 6 | 5 | | 1 | | |
| **TOTAL GOALS SCORED** | | | | | 3 | | | 4 | 1 | 8 | 6 | | 4 | 8 | | | | 1 | 3 | 1 | | | | 1 | | | | |

Figure in bold denotes goal scored. Secondary smaller figure in bold denotes number of goals scored. † denotes opponent's own goal.

## THE BORDERERS' 10 YEAR LEAGUE RECORD

| Season | Div | P | W | D | L | F | A | Pts | Pos |
|---|---|---|---|---|---|---|---|---|---|
| 95-96 | S | 36 | 18 | 6 | 12 | 64 | 47 | 60 | 3 |
| 96-97 | S | 36 | 4 | 11 | 21 | 32 | 75 | 23 | 10 |
| 97-98 | T | 36 | 10 | 12 | 14 | 47 | 55 | 42 | 6 |
| 98-99 | T | 36 | 12 | 14 | 10 | 53 | 49 | 50 | 5 |
| 99-00 | T | 36 | 19 | 8 | 9 | 53 | 30 | 66 | 2 |
| 00-01 | S | 36 | 14 | 12 | 10 | 51 | 44 | 54 | 3 |
| 01-02 | S | 36 | 12 | 11 | 13 | 44 | 52 | 47 | 6 |
| 02-03 | S | 36 | 13 | 10 | 13 | 43 | 48 | 49 | 5 |
| 03-04 | S | 36 | 14 | 6 | 16 | 61 | 67 | 48 | 5 |
| 04-05 | S | 36 | 8 | 10 | 18 | 40 | 64 | 34 | 10 |

## LEADING GOALSCORERS:

| Season | Div | Goals | Player |
|---|---|---|---|
| 1995-96 | S | 13 | W. Irvine |
| 1996-97 | S | 6 | P. Forrester |
| 1997-98 | T | 10 | P. Forrester |
| 1998-99 | T | 12 | M. Leask |
| 1999-00 | T | 9 | M. Anthony |
| 2000-01 | S | 14 | G. Wood |
| 2001-02 | S | 9 | G. Wood |
| 2002-03 | S | 12 | A. Burke, G. Wood |
| 2003-04 | S | 22 | G. Hutchison |
| 2004-05 | S | 8 | G. Hutchison, D. Smith |

### BERWICK RANGERS PLAYING KITS SEASON 2005.06

FIRST KIT | SECOND KIT | THIRD KIT

**COWDENBEATH F.C.**

Central Park, High Street,

Cowdenbeath, KY4 9QQ

**TELEPHONE NUMBERS**

Ground/Ticket Office/Information Service

(01383) 610166

Sec. Home (01383) 513013

**FAX** (01383) 512132

**E-MAIL** bluebrazil@cowdenbeathfc.com

**WEBSITE** www.cowdenbeathfc.com

**CHAIRMAN** Gordon McDougall

**VICE-CHAIRMAN** Albert V. Tait

**DIRECTORS**

Ian Fraser, Brian Watson,

Dr. Robert Brownlie, John Johnston,

Robert Johnston, Graham Thompson ,

Joseph J. Macnamara,

Thomas W. Ogilvie & Ross Hamilton

**GENERAL MANAGER** Joseph J. Macnamara

**HONORARY LIFE MEMBER** Brenda Solomon

**SECRETARY** Thomas W. Ogilvie

**MANAGER** Mixu Paatelainen

**DIRECTOR OF YOUTH DEVELOPMENT**

Gordon McDougall

**YOUTH CO-ORDINATOR** Brian Welsh

**YOUTH TEAM COACHES**

U19: Gary McAlpine, Carlo Crolla & David Stewart

U17: Jim Ward & Craig Muir

U15: Brian Welsh, Gary Miller & David Liddle

U14: Phillip Kidd & Steven Forrest

U13: Steven McLeish & Robert Hart

U12: Grant Letham & Tony Baldwin

**TEAM CAPTAIN** Innes Ritchie

**WOMEN'S DEVELOPMENT COACH**

Graham Thompson

**OFFICE ADMINISTRATOR**

Kathryn Nellies

**FOOTBALL SAFETY OFFICERS'**

**ASSOCIATION REPRESENTATIVE**

Aaron Turnbull

**COMMERCIAL & LOTTERY MANAGER**

Joseph Macnamara

**MATCHDAY PROGRAMME EDITOR**

Andrew Mullen (01383) 611644

**CLUB DOCTOR** Dr. Robert Brownlie

**PHYSIOTHERAPIST** Neil Bryson

**GROUNDSMAN** Gordon McDougall Jnr.

**KIT PERSON** Bert Johnston

**CLUB SHOP**

Situated at Stadium. Open 10.00 a.m. – 3.00 p.m.

and on Home Matchdays. Merchandise also

available on-line at www.cowdenbeathfc.com

**OFFICIAL SUPPORTERS CLUB**

Central Park, High Street,

Cowdenbeath, KY4 9QQ

**SHIRT SPONSOR** Panda Print

**KIT SUPPLIER** Paulas Benara

## LIST OF PLAYERS 2005.06

| PLAYERS SURNAME | FIRST NAME | MIDDLE NAME | DATE OF BIRTH | PLACE OF BIRTH | DATE SIGNED | HEIGHT FT INS | WEIGHT ST LBS | POSITION ON PITCH | PREVIOUS CLUB |
|---|---|---|---|---|---|---|---|---|---|
| Anderson | Craig | | 05/05/88 | Edinburgh | 02/08/04 | 5.10 | 10.0 | Midfield | Hutchison Vale |
| Arbuckle | Scott | | 03/03/89 | Kirkcaldy | 18/08/05 | 6.1 | 10.7 | Forward | Blue Brazil B.C. |
| Baird | Stuart | | 26/07/82 | Kirkcaldy | 07/01/05 | 6.2 | 13.8 | Defender | Kirkcaldy Y.M.C.A. |
| Baxter | Mark | | 16/04/85 | Perth | 31/08/05 | 5.8 | 11.6 | Defender | St. Johnstone |
| Bouglas | Dale | | 23/01/87 | Dunfermline | 21/08/03 | 5.10 | 10.0 | Defender | Raith Rovers Form D U1 |
| Buchanan | Liam | | 27/03/85 | Edinburgh | 02/07/02 | 5.8 | 10.8 | Midfield | Heart of Midlothian |
| Campbell | Murray | Iain | 26/11/89 | Kirkcaldy | 18/08/05 | 5.10 | 10.6 | Midfield | Woodside B.C. |
| Carlin | Andrew | | 06/01/81 | Glasgow | 06/06/03 | 6.1 | 13.8 | Goalkeeper | Stenhousemuir |
| Clark | William | Robert | 13/07/89 | Kirkcaldy | 18/08/05 | 5.7 | 11.0 | Defender | Woodside B.C. |
| Connelly | Jamie | | 14/05/89 | Kirkcaldy | 18/08/05 | 6.0 | 10.5 | Goalkeeper | Woodside B.C. |
| Crolla | Jacob | Aaron | 08/10/87 | Kirkcaldy | 14/05/04 | 5.11 | 9.10 | Forward | Raith Rovers Form D U1 |
| Crookston | Michael | Douglas | 24/11/88 | Kirkcaldy | 20/01/05 | 5.9 | 9.6 | Forward | Cairneyhill Y.F.C. |
| Cusick | John | James | 16/01/75 | Kirkcaldy | 01/06/05 | 5.11 | 14.0 | Midfield | East Fife |
| Donnachie | Ryan | | 18/10/89 | Dunfermline | 18/08/05 | 5.9 | 11.0 | Defender | Blue Brazil B.C. |
| Downs | Robert | | 22/04/79 | Glasgow | 23/06/05 | 5.11 | 12.0 | Forward | Arthurlie Juniors |
| Dunsmore | Scott | | 09/06/87 | Lanark | 11/08/05 | 5.9 | 10.7 | Midfield | Paisley United |
| Fusco | Gary | George | 01/06/82 | Edinburgh | 22/07/02 | 6.1 | 11.5 | Midfield | Musselburgh Athletic Junior |
| Fyfe | Robert | James | 03/05/88 | Dunfermline | 02/08/04 | 6.0 | 11.0 | Defender | Dunfermline Athletic |
| Gilbertson | John | | 19/12/86 | Edinburgh | 12/03/05 | 6.1 | 11.7 | Goalkeeper | Glenrothes Juniors |
| Glynn | Daniel | | 27/04/87 | Edinburgh | 28/01/05 | 6.0 | 10.5 | Defender | Raith Rovers |
| Gray | Liam | | 22/02/87 | Edinburgh | 26/08/04 | 5.10 | 11.7 | Goalkeeper | Hibernian |
| Guild | Graeme | | 10/05/88 | Kirkcaldy | 04/08/04 | 5.8 | 9.10 | Midfield | Cowdenbeath Form D U1 |
| Guy | Graham | | 15/08/83 | Bellshill | 04/08/05 | 5.10 | 11.0 | Defender | Stranraer |
| Hay | David | Alexander | 02/01/80 | Edinburgh | 23/06/05 | 6.4 | 14.0 | Goalkeeper | Brechin City |
| Hill | Douglas | | 16/01/85 | Edinburgh | 29/07/05 | 6.0 | 12.2 | Defender | Alloa Athletic |
| Howitt | Kyle | | 16/06/87 | Dundee | 28/01/05 | 5.8 | 9.7 | Midfield | Raith Rovers |
| Hughes | Christopher | John | 21/04/89 | Dunfermline | 18/08/05 | 6.1 | 12.4 | Midfield | Cowdenbeath Form D U1 |
| Jackson | Andrew | Steven | 09/01/88 | Falkirk | 31/08/05 | 5.10 | 9.7 | Forward | St. Johnstone |
| Jahn | Simon | | 14/11/87 | Broxburn | 21/08/03 | 5.9 | 11.0 | Forward | Cairneyhill B.C. |
| Krobot | Lukas | | 31/10/83 | Prostesov | 23/09/05 | 5.11 | 12.9 | Defender | Couper Angus Juniors |
| Mauchlen | Iain | | 11/06/79 | Irvine | 24/07/01 | 5.7 | 10.10 | Mid / Fwd | Oakley United Juniors |
| McAndrew | Steven | | 27/02/88 | Kirkcaldy | 26/01/05 | 5.11 | 10.0 | Defender | Cowdenbeath Form S |
| McAvinue | Paul | | 25/01/88 | Lille | 04/08/04 | 6.0 | 11.0 | Defender | Cowdenbeath Form D U1 |
| McBride | Kevin | James | 12/04/80 | Glasgow | 28/07/05 | 5.11 | 10.9 | Defender | Glenafton Athletic Junior |
| McCaffery | Jonathan | | 21/09/87 | Glasgow | 10/11/03 | 5.6 | 9.0 | Defender | Raith Rovers Form D U1 |
| McCallum | Ryan | | 20/12/86 | Edinburgh | 13/05/03 | 6.1 | 11.0 | Forward | Fernieside B.C. |
| McConnachie | Scott | | 09/08/88 | Edinburgh | 02/08/04 | 5.10 | 10.4 | Defender | Cowdenbeath Form D U1 |
| McGregor | Darren | | 07/08/85 | Edinburgh | 16/08/03 | 5.11 | 12.0 | Defender | Leith Athletic |
| McIlvean | Ross | | 13/09/88 | Dunfermline | 20/01/05 | 6.0 | 10.6 | Defender | Rosyth Recreation Junior |
| Millar | Marc | | 10/04/69 | Dundee | 01/03/05 | 5.10 | 12.5 | Midfield | Arbroath |
| Niven | Johnnie | | 05/08/88 | Edinburgh | 26/01/05 | 5.6 | 10.7 | Midfield | Royston B.C. |
| Paatelainen | Markus | | 23/01/83 | Valkeakosken | 08/09/05 | 6.0 | 12.7 | Midfield | Aberdeen |
| Paatelainen | Mika-Matti | Petteri | 03/02/67 | Helsinki | 26/08/05 | 6.0 | 14.7 | Forward | St. Mirren |
| Paterson | Ross | | 10/05/88 | Dumfries | 09/08/04 | 5.9 | 10.1 | Midfield | Hibernian |
| Richardson | Stuart | | 26/08/88 | Edinburgh | 20/01/05 | 5.9 | 10.0 | Midfield | Aberdour B.C. |
| Ritchie | Innes | | 24/08/73 | Edinburgh | 16/09/03 | 6.1 | 14.4 | Defender | Arbroath |
| Saddler | Matthew | David | 25/12/88 | Kirkcaldy | 08/08/05 | 5.8 | 9.9 | Defender | Dunfermline Athletic |
| Scott | Craig | | 15/08/87 | Edinburgh | 21/07/04 | 5.6.5 | 9.0 | Forward | Bayswater City S.C. |
| Shepherd | Martyn | John | 21/11/89 | Dunfermline | 18/08/05 | 6.1 | 11.4 | Defender | Blue Brazil B.C. |
| Stevenson | Mark | | 05/04/88 | Edinburgh | 04/08/04 | 6.1 | 10.12 | Forward | Hutchison Vale B.C. |
| Stewart | Alistair | | 02/03/90 | Edinburgh | 18/08/05 | 5.4 | 9.0 | Midfield | Salvesen B.C. |
| Stewart | Neil | | 28/03/88 | Dundee | 25/08/05 | 5.10 | 11.0 | Forward | Arbroath |
| Stewart | Sean | David | 01/07/88 | Dunfermline | 02/08/04 | 5.10 | 10.5 | Midfield | Cowdenbeath Form D U |
| Thomas | Jamie | | 25/02/87 | Edinburgh | 02/08/04 | 6.1 | 10.5 | Midfield | Hibernian |
| Ward | John | | 25/11/77 | Dundee | 19/07/05 | 6.4 | 13.7 | Defender | Tayport Juniors |
| Wilson | David | | 22/01/86 | Glasgow | 28/07/05 | 5.11 | 11.3 | Defender | Partick Thistle |
| Young | Kyle | | 18/02/89 | Manchester | 18/08/05 | 6.0 | 11.7 | Midfield | Woodside B.C. |

### TICKET INFORMATION

#### Season Ticket Information

| Seated | Adult | £145 |
|---|---|---|
| | Juvenile/OAP | £60 |
| | (Including all cup ties) | |

#### League Admission Prices

| Seated & Standing | Adult | £9 |
|---|---|---|
| | Juvenile/OAP | £4 |

### MILESTONES:

**Year of formation:** 1881

**Most capped player:** Jim Paterson

**No. of caps:** 3

**Most League points in a season:**

60 (Division 2 – Season 1938/39)(2 Points for a Win)

76 (Third Division – Season 2000/01)(3 Points for a Win)

**Most League goals scored by a player in a season:**

Rab Walls (Season 1938/39)

**No. of goals scored:** 54

**Record Attendance:** 25,586 (-v- Rangers – 21.9.1949)

**Record Victory:** 12-0 (-v- Johnstone – Scottish Cup, 21.1.192

**Record Defeat:** 1-11 (-v- Clyde – Division 2, 6.10.1951)

**BELL'S** SCOTTISH FOOTBALL LEAGUE

## SEASON STATS 2004.05

Player columns (left to right): Carlin A., Shand C.D., Campbell A.M., Gilfillan B.J., McKeown J.P., Ritchie I., Mauchlen I., McHale P.S., Scott C., Mowat D., Burns J.P., Buchanan L., Kelly J.P., McCallum R., Gollasch S., Fusco G.G., McGregor D., Shields D., Gray C., Fleming A., Miller D., Findlay S., Williams D., Gibson N., Bathgate S., Gribben D., McEwen M., Cargill A., Newall C., Fraser S., Baird S., Bain J., Kelly P., Millar M., Howitt K., Carruth J., Mallan S.P.

| DATE | VENUE | OPPONENTS | ATT | RES |
|---|---|---|---|---|
| -Aug | A | Queen`s Park | 490 | † 2-3 |
| 4-Aug | H | Stenhousemuir | 233 | 0-6 |
| 1-Aug | A | East Fife | 555 | 1-1 |
| 8-Aug | H | East Stirlingshire | 232 | 2-1 |
| -Sep | A | Gretna | 568 | 1-2 |
| 1-Sep | H | Elgin City | 275 | 3-1 |
| 8-Sep | A | Montrose | 351 | 1-3 |
| 5-Sep | A | Peterhead | 582 | 1-3 |
| -Oct | H | Albion Rovers | 243 | 2-0 |
| 6-Oct | A | Stenhousemuir | 300 | 2-2 |
| 3-Oct | H | Queen`s Park | 280 | 2-1 |
| 0-Oct | A | East Stirlingshire | 637 | 2-0 |
| -Nov | H | Gretna | 322 | 0-8 |
| 3-Nov | A | Elgin City | 336 | 4-0 |
| 0-Nov | H | Montrose | 145 | 0-0 |
| -Dec | H | Peterhead | 201 | 0-4 |
| 3-Dec | A | Albion Rovers | 303 | 3-2 |
| 7-Dec | A | Queen`s Park | 568 | 3-2 |
| -Jan | H | East Fife | 454 | 1-1 |
| -Jan | H | East Stirlingshire | 212 | 3-2 |
| 5-Jan | A | Gretna | 738 | 0-2 |
| 9-Jan | A | Montrose | 292 | 2-1 |
| Feb | A | Peterhead | 563 | 1-1 |
| 2-Feb | H | Albion Rovers | 254 | † 1-2 |
| 9-Feb | A | East Fife | 671 | 1-1 |
| Mar | H | Gretna | 339 | 0-1 |
| 2-Mar | A | East Stirlingshire | 204 | 1-2 |
| 5-Mar | H | Elgin City | 149 | 1-1 |
| 9-Mar | A | Elgin City | 338 | 0-2 |
| 2-Mar | H | Stenhousemuir | 173 | 0-2 |
| Apr | H | Montrose | 199 | 0-0 |
| Apr | A | Albion Rovers | 323 | 4-1 |
| 5-Apr | H | Peterhead | 153 | 4-0 |
| 4-Apr | H | East Fife | 348 | 4-2 |
| -Apr | A | Stenhousemuir | 360 | 1-1 |
| May | H | Queen`s Park | 346 | 1-0 |

**TOTAL FULL APPEARANCES:** 29 25 21 1 33 30 19 28 1 12 2 18 5 13 1 33 13 18 2 5 3 1 22 26 2 7 1 2 9 2 10 1 1

**TOTAL SUB APPEARANCES:** 1 1 7 1 2 1 13 19 7 1 3 2 3 5 5 2 4 5 1 1 1 2 1

**TOTAL GOALS SCORED:** 1 2 2 1 5 1 7 1 2 4 1 8 4 12

*in bold denotes goal scored. Secondary smaller figure in bold denotes number of goals scored. † denotes opponent's own goal.*

## THE BLUE BRAZIL'S 10 YEAR LEAGUE RECORD

| Season | Div | P | W | D | L | F | A | Pts | Pos |
|---|---|---|---|---|---|---|---|---|---|
| 5-96 | T | 36 | 10 | 8 | 18 | 45 | 59 | 38 | 8 |
| 5-97 | T | 36 | 10 | 9 | 17 | 38 | 51 | 39 | 7 |
| 7-98 | T | 36 | 12 | 2 | 22 | 33 | 57 | 38 | 8 |
| 3-99 | T | 36 | 8 | 7 | 21 | 34 | 65 | 31 | 9 |
| 9-00 | T | 36 | 15 | 12 | 9 | 59 | 43 | 54 | 5 |
| 0-01 | T | 36 | 23 | 7 | 6 | 58 | 31 | 76 | 2 |
| 1-02 | S | 36 | 11 | 11 | 14 | 49 | 51 | 44 | 8 |
| 2-03 | S | 36 | 8 | 12 | 16 | 46 | 57 | 36 | 10 |
| 3-04 | T | 36 | 15 | 10 | 11 | 46 | 39 | 55 | 5 |
| 4-05 | T | 36 | 14 | 9 | 13 | 54 | 61 | 51 | 3 |

## LEADING GOALSCORERS:

| Season | Div | Goals | Player |
|---|---|---|---|
| 1995-96 | T | 11 | D. Scott |
| 1996-97 | T | 6 | G. Wood |
| 1997-98 | T | 6 | W. Stewart |
| 1998-99 | T | 7 | W. Stewart |
| 1999-00 | T | 13 | M. McDowell |
| 2000-01 | T | 10 | M. McDowell |
| 2001-02 | S | 17 | G. Brown |
| 2002-03 | S | 10 | G. Brown, K. Gordon |
| 2003-04 | T | 12 | D. Shields |
| 2004-05 | T | 12 | D. Gribben |

### COWDENBEATH PLAYING KITS SEASON 2005.06

FIRST KIT  SECOND KIT  THIRD KIT

## EAST FIFE

**EAST FIFE F.C.**
First 2 Finance Bayview Stadium,
Harbour View, Methil, Leven,
Fife, KY8 3RW
**TELEPHONE NUMBER**
Ground/Commercial (01333) 426323
**FAX** (01333) 426376
**E-MAIL** derrick@eastfife.org
**E-MAIL 2** jdbrown@icscotland.net
**E-MAIL 3** eastfife@tiscali.co.uk
**WEBSITE** www.eastfifefc.org
**CLUB CORRESPONDENCE ADDRESS**
Mr. J. Derrick Brown,
Chairman/Secretary,
East Fife F.C.
Lyncol, Largo Road, Leven, Fife KY8 4TB
**CHAIRMAN** J. Derrick Brown
**VICE-CHAIRMAN** David Hamilton
**DEPUTY CHAIRMAN** David Marshall
**DIRECTORS**
David McK. Stevenson,
Ian Johnson, Kenneth R. MacKay,
Andrew Hain & Elizabeth Brown
**ASSOCIATE DIRECTORS**
Douglas Briggs & James Stewart
**CHIEF EXECUTIVE** J. Derrick Brown
**HONORARY VICE-PRESIDENTS**
John Fleming & James Drysdale
**SECRETARY** J. Derrick Brown
**MANAGER** James Moffat
**ASSISTANT MANAGER** Greg Shaw
**RESERVE COACH** Kevin Bain
**GOALKEEPING COACH** David Westwood
**DIRECTORS OF YOUTH DEVELOPMENT**
David Hamilton & Andrew Hain
**YOUTH TEAM COACHES**
U19: Harvey Munn & Alex Blyth
**TEAM CAPTAIN** Kevin Bain
**WOMEN'S DEVELOPMENT COACH**
David Hamilton
**OFFICE ADMINISTRATOR /
STADIUM MANAGERESS**
Leona Guidi
**FOOTBALL SAFETY OFFICERS'
ASSOCIATION REPRESENTATIVE**
David Marshall (01333) 426323/351486
**CORPORATE & COMMERCIAL DIRECTOR**
Andrew Hain (01333) 425750 / (01592) 771451
**HOSPITALITY & CATERING DIRECTOR**
Elizabeth Brown
**LOTTERY MANAGER** John Band
**MEDIA LIAISON PERSON** J. Derrick Brown
**MATCHDAY PROGRAMME EDITORS**
Jim Stewart & Fiona McKay
**MATCHDAY DIRECTOR** Kenneth R. MacKay
**SURGEON**
Ivan Brenkell, M.B., Ch.B., F.R.C.S.
**CLUB DOCTORS**
Douglas Ross & Howard Stevens
**PHYSIOTHERAPIST** Ian Barrett
**GROUNDSMEN**
David Marshall & David Montador
**KIT PERSON** David Marshall
**CLUB SHOP**
A Club Shop is situated within the Ground.
Goods available via post and online:
www.eastfife.org
**OFFICIAL SUPPORTERS CLUB**
c/o First 2 Finance Bayview Stadium,
Harbour View, Methil, Leven,
Fife, KY8 3RW
**SHIRT SPONSOR**
**First Choice:**
The Adam Smith College, Fife
**Second Choice:**
Pinpoint - Protecting people at work
**KIT SUPPLIER** Paulas Benara

### LIST OF PLAYERS 2005.06

| PLAYERS SURNAME | FIRST NAME | MIDDLE NAME | DATE OF BIRTH | PLACE OF BIRTH | DATE SIGNED | HEIGHT FT INS | WEIGHT ST LBS | POSITION ON PITCH | PREVIOUS CLUB |
|---|---|---|---|---|---|---|---|---|---|
| Bain | Kevin | | 19/09/72 | Kirkcaldy | 30/01/04 | 6.0 | 12.7 | Midfield | Peterhead |
| Beith | Gavin | | 07/10/81 | Dundee | 31/01/05 | 5.10 | 10.10 | Midfield | Arbroath |
| Bissett | Scott | | 31/07/88 | Kirkcaldy | 03/08/05 | 6.0 | 10.0 | Forward | Hill of Beath Swifts |
| Bradford | John | | 15/12/79 | Irvine | 23/07/05 | 6.0 | 12.7 | Forward | Albion Rovers |
| Brash | Kristofer | | 01/03/83 | Dundee | 15/06/04 | 5.9 | 9.7 | Midfield | Peterhead |
| Campbell | Andrew | Mark | 15/03/79 | Edinburgh | 25/05/05 | 6.0 | 12.7 | Defender | Cowdenbeath |
| Cargill | Stuart | | 01/12/88 | Kirkcaldy | 12/07/05 | 5.8 | 10.7 | Midfield | Glenrothes Strollers |
| Crawford | Robert | Edward | 26/01/87 | Dunfermline | 28/04/04 | 5.11 | 11.2 | Midfield | Dunfermline Athletic |
| Cusick | Brendan | | 26/07/87 | Dunfermline | 15/07/05 | 5.11 | 11.7 | Forward | Aberdour U'19's |
| Dammer | Kyle | Ewan | 27/09/87 | Kirkcaldy | 18/06/04 | 6.3 | 13.6 | Defender | Thornton B.C. |
| Davies | Gordon | | 24/01/87 | Kirkcaldy | 03/08/05 | 6.0 | 11.0 | Defender | Greig Park Rangers |
| Dodds | John | George | 16/12/81 | Edinburgh | 24/05/04 | 6.3 | 14.7 | Goalkeeper | Queen of the South |
| Doig | Robert | David | 10/05/87 | Kirkcaldy | 07/05/05 | 5.9 | 10.12 | Forward | East Fife Form S |
| Donaldson | Euan | Gordon | 20/08/75 | Falkirk | 01/06/05 | 5.11 | 11.0 | Defender | Arbroath |
| Findlay | Scott | | 16/10/83 | Perth | 02/08/05 | 6.4 | 14.7 | Goalkeeper | Cowdenbeath |
| Ford | Daniel | | 07/04/89 | Kirkcaldy | 12/07/05 | 6.0 | 11.7 | Defender | Burntisland Shipyard |
| Fortune | Stephan | | 06/03/88 | Kirkcaldy | 23/07/05 | 6.0 | 11.0 | Midfield | Livingston |
| Graham | James | Ross | 03/06/71 | Baillieston | 25/05/05 | 6.3 | 13.7 | Midfield | Montrose |
| Grant | Scott | | 09/08/87 | Kirkcaldy | 03/08/05 | 5.11 | 12.0 | Mid / Fwd | Forfar Athletic |
| Hampshire | Paul | Christopher | 20/09/81 | Edinburgh | 14/07/05 | 6.0 | 12.0 | Midfield | Musselburgh Athletic Junior |
| Hodge | Robert | | 31/03/87 | Kirkcaldy | 28/04/04 | 6.0 | 11.2 | Forward | Thornton Y.F.C. U' 15's |
| Ireland | Derek | | 02/09/87 | Kirkcaldy | 19/07/05 | 5.9 | 10.5 | Midfield | Greig Park Rangers |
| Johnston | Craig | | 24/07/87 | Kirkcaldy | 15/07/05 | 5.10 | 11.0 | Forward | Leven Royals |
| Johnston | Craig | | 29/06/85 | Perth | 21/07/04 | 6.0 | 12.0 | Defender | St. Johnstone |
| Kelly | Gary | Patrick | 01/09/81 | Falkirk | 17/06/04 | 5.11 | 11.9 | Midfield | Stirling Albion |
| Logie | Robert | William | 23/09/87 | Perth | 09/05/05 | 6.2 | 13.6 | Goalkeeper | Dunfermline Athletic |
| Lumsden | Craig | McDonald | 26/04/84 | Kirkcaldy | 11/07/02 | 6.1 | 12.0 | Defender | Dunfermline Athletic |
| Martin | John | | 04/05/85 | Kirkcaldy | 29/07/05 | 6.1 | 11.7 | Midfield | Raith Rovers |
| McDonald | Greig | James | 12/05/82 | Dunfermline | 06/03/03 | 6.1 | 13.0 | Defender | Dunfermline Athletic |
| McKay | Grant | John | 24/05/86 | Kirkcaldy | 30/04/04 | 5.10 | 11.0 | Defender | Dunfermline Athletic |
| McLeod | Euan | | 12/08/88 | Perth | 12/07/05 | 6.0 | 11.7 | Defender | Fossoway Star |
| Mills | Graeme | | 30/01/87 | Kirkcaldy | 28/06/04 | 5.9 | 10.0 | Midfield | Thornton Y.F.C. |
| Mitchell | Eoghainn | | 19/07/87 | Dunfermline | 03/08/05 | 6.1 | 11.7 | Defender | Inverkeithing United |
| Mitchell | Jonathon | Andrew | 22/06/81 | Dundee | 03/07/03 | 5.10 | 11.7 | Midfield | Tayport Juniors |
| Morrison | Scott | John | 22/10/81 | Glasgow | 02/07/04 | 6.2 | 12.0 | Goalkeeper | Drymen United |
| Noble | Stuart | William | 14/10/83 | Edinburgh | 02/09/05 | 6.0 | 13.7 | Forward | Fulham |
| Paliczka | Sean | | 25/04/84 | Galashiels | 24/05/04 | 5.10 | 10.7 | Forward | Innerleven Vale |
| Pelosi | Marco | Giancarlo | 22/04/86 | Edinburgh | 29/07/05 | 5.11 | 12.7 | Defender | Heart of Midlothian |
| Port | Graeme | | 13/04/86 | York | 03/08/05 | 5.11 | 10.7 | Midfield | Dunfermline Athletic |
| Samson | Christopher | | 26/12/87 | Kirkcaldy | 12/07/05 | 5.9 | 11.0 | Midfield | Greig Park Rangers |
| Simpson | Gregor | | 02/08/87 | Kirkcaldy | 31/12/04 | 5.10 | 13.0 | Midfield | East Fife Form S |
| Smart | Craig | | 26/11/78 | Kirkcaldy | 25/05/05 | 5.10 | 11.12 | Forward | Montrose |

### TICKET INFORMATION

#### Season Ticket Information

| Seated | Adult | £144 |
|---|---|---|
| | Juvenile /OAP | £76 |
| | Parent & Juvenile | £190 |
| | Parent & 2 Juveniles | £225 |

#### League Admission Prices

| Seated | Adult | £9 |
|---|---|---|
| | Juvenile /OAP | £5 |

### MILESTONES:
**Year of formation:** 1903
**Most capped player:** George Aitken
**No. of caps:** 5
**Most League points in a season:**
57 (Division 2 – Season 1929/30)(2 Points for a Win)
71 (Third Division – Season 2002/03)(3 Points for a Win)
**Most League goals scored by a player in a season:**
Henry Morris (Season 1947/48)
**No. of goals scored:** 41
**Record Attendance:**
22,515 (-v- Raith Rovers – 2.1.1950 at Bayview Park – old Stadium)
1,996 (-v- Queen's Park – 10.5.2003 at Bayview Stadium – new Stadium)
**Record Victory:** 13-2 (-v- Edinburgh City – Division 2, 11.12.1937)
**Record Defeat:** 0-9 (-v- Heart of Midlothian – Division 1, 5.10.1957)

## SEASON STATS 2004.05

| DATE | VENUE | OPPONENTS | ATT | RES | Dodds J.G.W. | Lumsden C.M. | McDonald I. | Bain K. | Hall M. | Kelly G.P. | Herkes J. | McDonald G.J. | Fairbairn B. | Tarditi S. | Brash K. | Paliczka S. | Mitchell J.A. | Byle L. | Renwick M.J. | Mathie G.R. | Steele K.J. | Morrison S.J. | Colquhoun D. | Duncan F.T.D. | Linton S.P. | Crawford R.E.W. | Gaughan P. | Nicholas S.A. | Ferguson J.N. | Boyle J. | Beith G. | McCafferty J. |
|---|---|---|---|---|---|---|---|---|---|---|---|---|---|---|---|---|---|---|---|---|---|---|---|---|---|---|---|---|---|---|---|---|---|
| 7-Aug | H | Montrose | 437 | 1-0 | 1 | 2 | 3 | 4 | 5 | 6 | 7 | 8 | 9 | **10** | 11 | | | 14 | 16 | | | | | | | | | | | | | |
| 14-Aug | A | Albion Rovers | 384 | 0-2 | 1 | 2 | 3 | 4 | 5 | 6 | 11 | 8 | 9 | 10 | | | | | 16 | 7 | 14 | | | | | | | | | | | |
| 21-Aug | H | Cowdenbeath | 555 | 1-1 | 1 | | 3 | 4 | 5 | 6 | 7 | 8 | **9** | 10 | 11 | 16 | 15 | | | | 2 | | | | | | | | | | | | |
| 28-Aug | H | Stenhousemuir | 468 | 0-0 | 1 | | | 4 | | 5 | 8 | 7 | | 10 | 16 | 9 | | | 6 | 2 | 3 | 11 | | | | | | | | | | | |
| 4-Sep | A | Peterhead | 507 | 0-2 | | | | 4 | | 5 | 6 | 7 | 15 | 10 | 14 | 9 | | | 8 | 2 | 3 | 11 | 1 | 16 | | | | | | | | | |
| 11-Sep | H | East Stirlingshire | 425 | 1-0 | | | | 4 | | | 8 | 7 | | 9 | 16 | 3 | | | 6 | 2 | 5 | 11 | 1 | **10** | | | | | | | | | |
| 18-Sep | A | Gretna | 457 | 1-5 | | | | 4 | 5 | | 8 | 7 | | 9 | 16 | 3 | | | 6 | 2 | | 11 | 1 | 10 | 12 | | | | | | | | |
| 25-Sep | H | Queen's Park | 445 | 1-4 | | | | 4 | | | 8 | 7 | | 9 | **16** | 3 | | | 6 | 2 | | 11 | 1 | 10 | | 5 | 14 | | | | | | |
| 2-Oct | A | Elgin City | 558 | 1-2 | | | | 4 | | 14 | | **7** | | 10 | | 3 | | | 8 | 2 | | 11 | 1 | 9 | | 5 | | | | | | | |
| 16-Oct | H | Albion Rovers | 396 | 1-0 | | | | | | | 6 | 7 | | 11 | 16 | 3 | | | 8 | 2 | | | 1 | **10** | 5 | | | 4 | 9 | | | | |
| 22-Oct | A | Montrose | 435 | 1-2 | | | | | | | 6 | 7 | | 11 | 16 | 3 | | 15 | 8 | 2 | | | 1 | 10 | 5 | | | 4 | 9 | | | | |
| 30-Oct | A | Stenhousemuir | 382 | 2-5 | | | | | 14 | | 6 | 7 | | 11 | | 3 | | 15 | 8 | 2 | | | 1 | 10 | 5 | | | 4 | 9 | | | | |
| 6-Nov | H | Peterhead | 410 | 0-2 | | | | 4 | | 5 | 8 | 7 | 14 | 11 | 10 | | | 15 | | 6 | 2 | | 1 | | 3 | | | | | | | | |
| 13-Nov | A | East Stirlingshire | 364 | 1-1 | | | | 4 | | | 8 | 7 | 14 | 11 | 10 | | | 16 | | 6 | 2 | 15 | 1 | | 3 | | | 5 | 9 | | | | |
| 27-Nov | H | Gretna | 551 | 1-3 | | | | 4 | | 6 | 8 | | 5 | 11 | | 15 | | 7 | | 10 | 1 | | | 3 | | | | 9 | | | | | |
| 4-Dec | A | Queen's Park | 575 | 2-1 | | | | 4 | | 5 | | **8** | **11** | 16 | 3 | | 7 | 10 | | 2 | | 15 | 1 | | | | | 9 | | | | | |
| 27-Dec | H | Montrose | 784 | 1-0 | | | | 4 | | 5 | 6 | 15 | 8 | **11** | 16 | 3 | 7 | 10 | 14 | 2 | | | 1 | | | | | 9 | | | | | |
| Jan | A | Cowdenbeath | 454 | 1-1 | | | | 4 | | 5 | 8 | | | 11 | 16 | 3 | 7 | 10 | 6 | 2 | | | 1 | | | | | 9 | | | | | |
| Jan | H | Stenhousemuir | 491 | 2-0 | | | | **4** | | 5 | 8 | | 14 | **11** | 9 | 3 | 7 | 10 | 6 | 2 | | 15 | 1 | | | | | 16 | | | | | |
| 15-Jan | A | Peterhead | 587 | 0-0 | | | | 4 | | 5 | 8 | | | 11 | | 3 | 7 | 10 | | 2 | | | 1 | | | | | 9 | | | | | |
| 29-Jan | A | Gretna | 828 | 0-4 | | | | 4 | | 5 | 8 | | | 11 | | 3 | 7 | 10 | 14 | 2 | 12 | 15 | 1 | | | | | 9 | | | | | |
| Feb | H | Queen's Park | 601 | 0-1 | | | | 4 | | 5 | | | 8 | | 12 | 15 | 10 | 6 | 2 | 3 | 7 | 1 | | | | | | 9 | | 11 | 14 | | |
| 12-Feb | A | Elgin City | 379 | 1-2 | | | | 4 | | 5 | | | 8 | | 12 | 7 | 10 | 6 | 2 | 3 | 15 | 1 | | | | | | 9 | | 16 | 11 | | |
| 5-Feb | H | East Stirlingshire | 441 | 2-0 | | | | 4 | | | 8 | | 5 | | 11 | | 7 | 6 | 2 | 3 | | | | | | | | 9 | | | 10 | | |
| 19-Feb | H | Cowdenbeath | 671 | 1-1 | | | | 4 | | | 8 | | 5 | | 11 | | **7** | 6 | 2 | 3 | | | | | | | | 9 | | | 10 | 12 | |
| Mar | H | Peterhead | 495 | 1-2 | | | | 4 | | | 6 | | 8 | 14 | | | 7 | | 2 | 5 | 11 | 1 | | 3 | | | | 9 | | | 15 | 10 | |
| 12-Mar | A | Stenhousemuir | 334 | 2-1 | | | | 4 | | | 6 | | **8** | | | 15 | 7 | | 2 | 5 | | | 1 | | 3 | | | 9 | | | 11 | 10 | 21 |
| 19-Mar | A | East Stirlingshire | 315 | 0-1 | | | | 4 | | | 6 | | 8 | 15 | 16 | | 7 | | 2 | 5 | | | | 3 | | | | 9 | | | 11 | 10 | 1 |
| Mar | A | Albion Rovers | 316 | 6-0 | | | | 4 | | | 6 | | **8** | **11** | 3 | **7**³ | 15 | | 2 | 5 | | | | | | | | 9 | | | 10 | | 1 |
| 6-Mar | H | Elgin City | 456 | 2-0 | | | | 4 | | | 6 | | **8** | 11 | 9 | 3 | **7** | **15** | 2 | 5 | | | | | | | | 9 | | | 10 | | 1 |
| Apr | H | Gretna | 723 | 0-2 | | | | 4 | | | 6 | | 8 | 11 | 3 | | 7 | 16 | 2 | 5 | | | | | | | | 9 | | 15 | 10 | | 1 |
| Apr | H | Elgin City | 466 | 1-2 | | | | 4 | | | 6 | | 8 | 11 | 3 | | 7 | | 2 | 5 | | | | | | | | 9 | | 16 | 10 | | 1 |
| 16-Apr | A | Queen's Park | 451 | 1-2 | 1 | | | 4 | | | 6 | | 8 | 7 | 3 | | 16 | **10** | 2 | 5 | | | | | | | | 9 | | | 11 | | |
| 3-Apr | A | Cowdenbeath | 348 | 2-4 | 1 | | **4** | | | | 6 | | 8 | 11 | 3 | | 7 | 10 | 2 | 5 | | | | | | | | 9 | | 15 | | | |
| 9-Apr | H | Albion Rovers | 568 | 1-1 | 1 | 2 | | 4 | | | 8 | | 6 | | 3 | | **10** | 14 | | | | | | | | | | 9 | 7 | | 11 | | |
| May | A | Montrose | 496 | 2-2 | 1 | 4 | | 5 | | | 6 | | | | 3 | | 7 | **10** | 8 | | | | | 2 | | | 12 | 9 | 14 | | 11 | | |
| | | **TOTAL FULL APPEARANCES** | | | 8 | 32 | 3 | 16 | 5 | 34 | 14 | 22 | 25 | 9 | 25 | 14 | 20 | 18 | 32 | 17 | 9 | 23 | 7 | 10 | 2 | | 4 | 25 | 1 | 6 | 10 | 5 |
| | | **TOTAL SUB APPEARANCES** | | | | | 2 | | | 1 | 3 | 3 | 9 | 5 | 8 | 7 | 4 | | 1 | 5 | | 1 | 1 | | 2 | | | 3 | 4 | 2 | 1 |
| | | **TOTAL GOALS SCORED** | | | 2 | | | | | 1 | 5 | 6 | 2 | | 4 | 5 | 1 | | | | | 3 | 1 | | | | 9 | | | 1 | | |

Figure in bold denotes goal scored. Secondary smaller figure in bold denotes number of goals scored . † denotes opponent's own goal.

## THE FIFERS' 10 YEAR LEAGUE RECORD

| Season | Div | P | W | D | L | F | A | Pts | Pos |
|---|---|---|---|---|---|---|---|---|---|
| 95-96 | S | 36 | 19 | 10 | 7 | 50 | 29 | 67 | 2 |
| 96-97 | F | 36 | 2 | 8 | 26 | 28 | 92 | 14 | 10 |
| 97-98 | S | 36 | 14 | 6 | 16 | 51 | 59 | 48 | 6 |
| 98-99 | S | 36 | 12 | 6 | 18 | 42 | 64 | 42 | 9 |
| 99-00 | T | 36 | 17 | 11 | 8 | 45 | 39 | 59 | 4 |
| 00-01 | T | 36 | 15 | 8 | 13 | 49 | 46 | 53 | 4 |
| 01-02 | T | 36 | 11 | 7 | 18 | 39 | 56 | 40 | 8 |
| 02-03 | T | 36 | 20 | 11 | 5 | 73 | 37 | 71 | 2 |
| 03-04 | S | 36 | 11 | 8 | 17 | 38 | 45 | 41 | 9 |
| 04-05 | T | 36 | 10 | 8 | 18 | 40 | 56 | 38 | 8 |

## LEADING GOALSCORERS:

| Season | Div | Goals | Player |
|---|---|---|---|
| 1995-96 | S | 11 | R. Scott |
| 1996-97 | F | 4 | M. Dyer, P. Ronald |
| 1997-98 | S | 11 | M. Dyer |
| 1998-99 | S | 13 | B. Moffat |
| 1999-00 | T | 11 | B. Moffat |
| 2000-01 | T | 8 | S. Kerrigan |
| 2001-02 | T | 11 | P. McManus |
| 2002-03 | T | 20 | K. Deuchar |
| 2003-04 | S | 11 | K. Deuchar |
| 2004-05 | T | 9 | S. Nicholas |

### EAST FIFE PLAYING KITS SEASON 2005.06

FIRST KIT | SECOND KIT | THIRD KIT

**EST. 1881**

**EAST STIRLINGSHIRE F.C.**

Firs Park,

Firs Street,

Falkirk, FK2 7AY

**TELEPHONE NUMBERS**

Ground (01324) 623583

Sec. Home (01324) 551099

Sec. Mobile 07739 209648

Head Coach (at ground) (01324) 623583

(Monday & Thursday evenings only)

**FAX** (01324) 637862

**E-MAIL** lestshirefc@aol.com

**E-MAIL 2** chaletom@aol.com

**WEBSITE** www.eaststirlingshire.com

**CHAIRMAN** Alan J. Mackin

**VICE-CHAIRMAN** Douglas W. Morrison

**DIRECTORS**

Alexander M. McCabe, John M. D. Morton

& Alexander S.H. Forsyth

**CHIEF EXECUTIVE / SECRETARY &**

**OFFICE ADMINISTRATOR**

Leslie G. Thomson

**HEAD COACH** Dennis Newall

**ASSISTANT COACH** Gordon Wylde

**CHIEF SCOUT** Billy Gibson

**TEAM CAPTAIN** Paul Tyrrell

**FOOTBALL SAFETY OFFICERS'**

**ASSOCIATION REPRESENTATIVE**

Robert Jack

**COMMERCIAL MANAGER &**

**MEDIA LIAISON PERSON**

Leslie G. Thomson (01324) 623583

**MATCHDAY PROGRAMME EDITOR**

Tadek Kopszywa

**GROUNDSMAN/KIT PERSON**

James Wilson

**CLUB SHOP**

Situated at ground. Open Mon-Fri

10.00a.m. - 2.00p.m. (except Wednesday)

and on all Home Matchdays

**SHIRT SPONSOR**

**First Choice:**

Littlewoods Football Pools - *be lucky*

**Second Choice:**

Meikle & Co – HR Consultants

**KIT SUPPLIER** Pro Star

# EAST STIRLINGSHIRE

## LIST OF PLAYERS 2005.06

| PLAYERS SURNAME | FIRST NAME | MIDDLE NAME | DATE OF BIRTH | PLACE OF BIRTH | DATE SIGNED | HEIGHT FT INS | WEIGHT ST LBS | POSITION ON PITCH | PREVIOUS CLUB |
|---|---|---|---|---|---|---|---|---|---|
| Blair | Steven | | 04/01/86 | Glasgow | 30/07/05 | 6.0 | 12.0 | Midfield | Newcastle United |
| Brand | Andrew | Gerard | 17/04/83 | Glasgow | 23/07/05 | 5.11 | 12.5 | Midfield | Knightswood Juveniles |
| Diack | Iain | Gordon | 17/02/81 | Glasgow | 27/07/05 | 6.0 | 11.6 | Forward | Arbroath |
| Dymock | Steven | William | 02/12/83 | Glasgow | 24/06/05 | 6.0 | 11.4 | Forward | Harmony Row |
| Gaughan | Paul | | 27/09/80 | Glasgow | 30/07/05 | 6.3 | 14.6 | Defender | Stranraer |
| Gillespie | Aaron | John | 21/11/84 | Stirling | 27/07/05 | 6.2 | 13.5 | Goalkeeper | Sauchie Juniors |
| Graham | Alastair | Slowey | 11/08/66 | Glasgow | 30/07/05 | 6.3 | 15.7 | Forward | Queen's Park |
| Jackson | Derek | | 29/08/65 | Alloa | 28/01/05 | 6.1 | 13.8 | Goalkeeper | Sauchie Juniors |
| Lejman | Karl | | 19/04/80 | Falkirk | 30/09/05 | 6.0 | 11.0 | Midfield | Fauldhouse United Juniors |
| Livingstone | Scott | Alan | 05/04/80 | Falkirk | 31/08/02 | 6.0 | 11.2 | Midfield | Stirling Albion |
| Mackay | Jamie | Andrew | 02/09/81 | Glasgow | 23/07/05 | 6.0 | 13.10 | Defender | Dumbarton |
| Miller | Christopher | Thomas | 19/11/82 | Paisley | 28/07/04 | 5.8 | 12.6 | Defender | Stenhousemuir |
| Oates | Stephen | John | 02/01/84 | Falkirk | 30/05/03 | 6.0 | 9.7 | Midfield | Zeneca Juveniles |
| Owen | Adam | | 05/09/80 | Wrexham | 28/09/05 | 5.9 | 12.0 | Defender | Lex X1 |
| Ross | Peter | James | 02/05/85 | Melbourne | 23/08/05 | 6.0 | 10.12 | Midfield | Camelon Juniors |
| Smith | Jordan | Anthony | 02/02/82 | Bellshill | 28/09/05 | 6.2 | 13.12 | Defender | Arbroath |
| Sobolewski | Henry | | 18/09/85 | Falkirk | 30/07/05 | 5.9 | 12.0 | Midfield | Sauchie Juniors |
| Thywissen | Carl | Erich | 28/02/78 | Leicester | 06/08/04 | 6.2 | 13.0 | Midfield | Fossum I.F. |
| Tyrrell | Mark | | 21/03/83 | Stirling | 13/05/05 | 5.10 | 11.5 | Defender | Kilsyth Amateurs |
| Tyrrell | Paul | | 11/04/80 | Stirling | 28/01/05 | 5.10 | 13.0 | Midfield | Kilsyth Amateurs |
| Ure | Derek | | 20/07/84 | Falkirk | 19/02/02 | 5.9 | 10.0 | Forward | Zeneca Juveniles |
| Walker | John | | 12/12/73 | Glasgow | 06/09/05 | 5.7 | 11.0 | Midfield | Carnoustie Panmure Juniors |

## TICKET INFORMATION

### Season Ticket Information

| Seated or Standing | Adult | £120 |
|---|---|---|
| | Concessions * | £60 |
| | Family Ticket | £150 |

### League Admission Prices

| Seated | Adult | £11 |
|---|---|---|
| | Juvenile/OAP | £6.50 |
| Standing | Adult | £9 |
| | Concessions * | £4.50 |

\* Concessionary Tickets allow OAPS, Juveniles, UB40 holders, Students and people with long term illness to be admitted to ground at the stated concessionary price. Production of DSS Benefit book or similar documentary proof required.

## MILESTONES:

**Year of formation:** 1881

**Most capped player:** Humphrey Jones

**No. of caps:** 5 (for Wales)

**Most League points in a season:**
55 (Division 2 – Season 1931/32) (2 Points for a Win)
59 (Third Division – Season 1994/95) (3 Points for a Win)

**Most League goals scored by a player in a season:**
Malcolm Morrison (Season 1938/39)

**No. of goals scored:** 36

**Record Attendance:** 11,500 (-v- Hibernian – 10.2.1969)

**Record Victory:**
10-1 (-v- Stenhousemuir – Scottish Cup, 1.9.1888)

**Record Defeat:** 1-12 (-v- Dundee United – Division 2, 13.4.1936)

**BELL'S** — SCOTTISH FOOTBALL LEAGUE

## SEASON STATS 2004.05

| DATE | VENUE | OPPONENTS | ATT | RES | Mitchell A.M. | Harvey D. | McGhee G.H. | Mackay J.A. | Newall C. | McAuley S. | Ross P. | Moffat A.J. | Donaldson R. | Dunbar J. | Miller C.T. | Leishman J.N. | Baldwin C.J. | Ure D. | Gilpin R.S. | Parks G.J. | Denham G.P. | Livingstone S.A. | Robertson J. | Findlay G. | Stewart W.P. | Thywissen C.E. | Oates S. | Peutherer S. | Walker J. | Diack I.G. | McGroarty C.M. | Rae D.P. | Jackson D. | Tyrell P. | Gerrard D. | Walker N. | Tyrell M. |
|---|---|---|---|---|---|---|---|---|---|---|---|---|---|---|---|---|---|---|---|---|---|---|---|---|---|---|---|---|---|---|---|---|---|---|---|---|---|---|
| 7-Aug | A | Peterhead | 561 | 0-5 | 1 | 2 | 3 | 4 | 5 | 6 | 7 | 8 | 9 | 10 | 11 | 12 | | | 15 | 16 | | | | | | | | | | | | | | | | | |
| 14-Aug | H | Gretna | 276 | 1-2 | | 2 | 5 | 16 | 4 | | 6 | 8 | 10 | 7 | 3 | 12 | 11 | 9 | 1 | 14 | | | | | | | | | | | | | | | | | |
| 21-Aug | A | Stenhousemuir | 405 | 0-6 | 1 | 2 | 3 | 5 | 4 | 7 | 14 | 8 | 9 | 6 | | 12 | 11 | 10 | | 15 | | | | | | | | | | | | | | | | | |
| 28-Aug | A | Cowdenbeath | 232 | 1-2 | | 2 | 3 | 4 | | 8 | 7 | 15 | 9 | 10 | | 16 | 12 | 1 | | 5 | 6 | **11** | | | | | | | | | | | | | | | |
| 4-Sep | H | Elgin City | 617 | 0-1 | | 2 | 3 | 4 | 8 | | 7 | | 9 | 11 | | 10 | 1 | 12 | 5 | 6 | | | 14 | 15 | | | | | | | | | | | | | |
| 11-Sep | A | East Fife | 425 | 0-1 | | 2 | 3 | 5 | 4 | | 7 | | 9 | 10 | | 16 | 1 | | 6 | 11 | 15 | | 8 | | | | | | | | | | | | | | |
| 18-Sep | H | Queen's Park | 335 | 0-5 | | 2 | 3 | 4 | 5 | | 7 | 15 | 9 | 10 | | 12 | 1 | | 6 | 11 | 15 | | 8 | | | | | | | | | | | | | | |
| 25-Sep | A | Albion Rovers | 225 | 3-3 | | 2 | 3 | 5 | | | 15 | 6 | 9 | | | **10** | 1 | 15 | | 11 | **7** | | 8 | 4 | 16 | | | | | | | | | | | | |
| 2-Oct | H | Montrose | 247 | 1-1 | | 2 | 3 | | | | 6 | | 9 | 12 | | **10** | 1 | | 5 | 11 | **7** | | 8 | 4 | | | | | | | | | | | | | |
| 16-Oct | A | Gretna | 468 | 1-8 | | 2 | 3 | 15 | | | 6 | | | 10 | | **9** | 1 | 14 | 5 | 7 | 11 | 12 | 8 | 4 | | | | | | | | | | | | | |
| 23-Oct | H | Peterhead | 281 | 1-2 | 1 | 2 | 3 | 8 | | | | 9 | 12 | | | **10** | | | 5 | 6 | **11** | | 7 | 4 | 14 | | | | | | | | | | | | |
| 30-Oct | H | Cowdenbeath | 637 | 0-2 | 1 | 2 | 3 | 8 | 12 | | | 10 | | | | **11** | 15 | 5 | 6 | 9 | | | 7 | 4 | 14 | | | | | | | | | | | | |
| 6-Nov | A | Elgin City | 502 | 3-1 | 1 | 2 | 3 | 4 | | 6 | | 9 | 10 | | | 15 | | | 11 | 8 | | | **7²** | 5 | | | | 12 | | | | | | | | | |
| 13-Nov | H | East Fife | 364 | 1-1 | 1 | 2 | 3 | 4 | | 15 | 6 | 9 | 10 | | | 14 | | | 11 | 8 | | | 7 | **5** | | | | 12 | | | | | | | | | |
| 27-Nov | H | Queen's Park | 457 | 0-0 | 1 | 2 | 6 | 5 | | 12 | 16 | 9 | 15 | | | 10 | | | 3 | 11 | | | 8 | 4 | | 7 | | | | | | | | | | | |
| 4-Dec | H | Albion Rovers | 262 | 1-1 | 1 | 2 | 6 | 4 | | 14 | | 9 | | | | **10** | | | 3 | **11** | | | 8 | 5 | | 7 | 10 | | | | | | | | | | |
| 27-Dec | A | Peterhead | 647 | 0-3 | 1 | 2 | 3 | 5 | | 8 | 12 | 9 | | | | 11 | 14 | | | | | | 7 | 4 | | 6 | 10 | | | | | | | | | | |
| 3-Jan | A | Cowdenbeath | 212 | 2-3 | 1 | 2 | | **4** | | 16 | 14 | 10 | | | | 11 | | | 12 | | | | 3 | **8** | | 7 | 5 | | 6 | 9 | | | | | | | | |
| 15-Jan | H | Elgin City | 191 | 0-3 | | | 6 | 5 | | 7 | | | 14 | | | 10 | 1 | | 2 | 11 | | | 8 | 4 | | 9 | 3 | 16 | | | | | | | | | |
| 29-Jan | H | Queen's Park | 317 | 3-1 | | 2 | | | | 14 | 7 | 9 | | | | 16 | | | 5 | 3 | | | 4 | | | 6 | **10** | **11²** | | 1 | 8 | | | | | | |
| 5-Feb | A | Albion Rovers | 350 | 1-1 | | 2 | | | | 7 | | 9 | | | | 10 | | | 5 | 3 | 14 | | 15 | **4** | | 6 | 11 | 12 | 1 | 8 | | | | | | | |
| 12-Feb | H | Montrose | 198 | 1-2 | | 2 | | 4 | 15 | 7 | | 9 | | | | **10** | | | 5 | 3 | 11 | 16 | | 6 | | | 12 | 1 | 8 | | | | | | | | |
| 15-Feb | A | East Fife | 441 | 0-2 | | 2 | 3 | | | 12 | 10 | | | | | 11 | | | 5 | | 14 | | | | | 7 | 1 | 8 | 4 | 9 | | | | | | | |
| 19-Feb | A | Stenhousemuir | 422 | 2-3 | 21 | | | | | 2 | | **9** | | | | 10 | | | 5 | **3** | | | | 4 | | 11 | 7 | 1 | 8 | 4 | | 6 | | | | | |
| 5-Mar | A | Montrose | 270 | 1-4 | 1 | | 3 | | | 6 | | 9 | | | | 11 | 10 | | 5 | | 14 | | 4 | | | **8** | 15 | | 7 | | | 2 | | | | | |
| 12-Mar | A | Elgin City | 394 | 0-0 | 4 | | | | | 16 | | 9 | | | | 3 | 10 | 14 | 5 | | | | | 6 | | 11 | | | 1 | 8 | | 7 | | | | | |
| 19-Mar | H | Gretna | 185 | 0-4 | | 2 | 12 | | | 7 | | 9 | | | | 10 | | | 5 | 3 | | | 4 | | | 11 | | | 1 | 8 | | 6 | | | | | |
| 22-Mar | H | Cowdenbeath | 204 | 2-1 | | 2 | 12 | | | 7 | | 9 | | | | 10 | | | 5 | 3 | | | 4 | | | **11** | | | 1 | 8 | | 6 | | | | | |
| 26-Mar | H | Stenhousemuir | 211 | 3-2 | | 2 | 16 | | | | 7 | **9** | | | | 10 | 14 | 5 | 3 | | | | 12 | 4 | | | **11** | | | 1 | 8 | | 6 | | | | |
| 29-Mar | H | East Fife | 315 | 1-0 | | 4 | 3 | | | 7 | | 9 | | 8 | | **10** | | | 2 | | | | | 6 | | | 11 | | 1 | | | 5 | | | | | |
| 2-Apr | A | Queen's Park | 486 | 0-2 | | 2 | 3 | 14 | | 7 | | 9 | | | | 10 | | | 11 | | 12 | | 6 | | | 4 | 8 | 15 | 1 | | | 5 | | | | | |
| 5-Apr | A | Montrose | 329 | 1-4 | | 2 | 3 | 15 | | | 9 | | | | | **10** | | | 6 | | | 7 | | 4 | | | 11 | | 1 | 8 | | 5 | | | | | |
| 16-Apr | H | Albion Rovers | 285 | 0-2 | | 6 | 4 | | | 7 | | | | | | 9 | | | 3 | | | | 5 | 8 | | | 11 | 12 | 1 | 10 | | 2 | | | | | |
| 23-Apr | H | Stenhousemuir | 242 | 1-4 | | 3 | 14 | | | | | 9 | | | | | | | 11 | | 10 | | 6 | **5** | | 4 | | | 1 | 7 | | 2 | | | | | |
| 30-Apr | A | Gretna | 1,585 | 0-1 | | 3 | | | | 12 | | 9 | | | | | | | 2 | | 10 | | 7 | 4 | | | 6 | | 1 | 11 | | 8 | | | | | |
| 7-May | H | Peterhead | 192 | 1-5 | 1 | 3 | 14 | | | 12 | | **9** | | | | | | | 2 | | 10 | | | 7 | | | 6 | | 1 | 11 | | 8 | | | | | |
| **TOTAL FULL APPEARANCES** | | | | | 12 | 29 | 27 | 16 | 8 | 5 | 21 | 4 | 29 | 11 | 2 | | | 7 | 26 | 9 | | | 16 | 30 | 15 | 3 | | | 19 | 20 | | 19 | 5 | 16 | 2 | 15 | 15 | 1 |
| **TOTAL SUB APPEARANCES** | | | | | 1 | | 3 | 5 | 1 | 6 | 10 | 2 | | 4 | | 3 | 2 | 8 | | 9 | | | 1 | 8 | 1 | 2 | | 3 | 2 | | 6 | | | | | | |
| **TOTAL GOALS SCORED** | | | | | | | 1 | | | 1 | 2 | 1 | | 6 | | | 1 | 7 | | | | 3 | 3 | | 1 | 5 | | | | | | 1 |

*Figure in bold denotes goal scored. Secondary smaller figure in bold denotes number of goals scored. † denotes opponent's own goal.*

## THE SHIRE'S 10 YEAR LEAGUE RECORD

| Season | Div | P | W | D | L | F | A | Pts | Pos |
|---|---|---|---|---|---|---|---|---|---|
| 1995-96 | T | 36 | 11 | 11 | 14 | 58 | 62 | 44 | 7 |
| 1996-97 | T | 36 | 8 | 9 | 19 | 36 | 58 | 33 | 9 |
| 1997-98 | T | 36 | 17 | 6 | 13 | 50 | 48 | 57 | 4 |
| 1998-99 | T | 36 | 9 | 13 | 14 | 50 | 48 | 40 | 8 |
| 1999-00 | T | 36 | 11 | 18 | 7 | 28 | 50 | 40 | 7 |
| 2000-01 | T | 36 | 10 | 7 | 19 | 37 | 69 | 37 | 8 |
| 2001-02 | T | 36 | 12 | 4 | 20 | 51 | 58 | 40 | 7 |
| 2002-03 | T | 36 | 2 | 7 | 27 | 32 | 105 | 13 | 10 |
| 2003-04 | T | 36 | 2 | 2 | 32 | 30 | 118 | 8 | 10 |
| 2004-05 | T | 36 | 5 | 7 | 24 | 32 | 88 | 22 | 10 |

## LEADING GOALSCORERS:

| Season | Div | Goals | Player |
|---|---|---|---|
| 1995-96 | T | 21 | P. Dwyer |
| 1996-97 | T | 9 | G. Inglis |
| 1997-98 | T | 13 | D. Watt |
| 1998-99 | T | 8 | W. McNeill |
| 1999-00 | T | 9 | G. Higgins, S. Laidlaw |
| 2000-01 | T | 16 | S. Hislop |
| 2001-02 | T | 11 | K. Gordon |
| 2002-03 | T | 5 | J. Leishman, D. Ure |
| 2003-04 | T | 9 | D. Ure |
| 2004-05 | T | 7 | J. Robertson |

**EAST STIRLINGSHIRE PLAYING KITS SEASON 2005.06** — FIRST KIT / SECOND KIT / THIRD KIT

ELGIN CITY F.C.

**ELGIN CITY F.C.**
Borough Briggs,
Borough Briggs Road, Elgin, IV30 1AP
**TELEPHONE NUMBERS**
Ground (01343) 551114
Sec. Home (01343) 546312
Sec. Bus (01343) 822541
**FAX** (01343) 547921
**E-MAIL** elgincityfc@ukonline.co.uk
**CHAIRMAN** Denis J. Miller
**DIRECTORS**
Ronald W. McHardy, John R. Meichan,
John A. Milton, Norman J. Green,
James A. Farquhar,
Ronald A. Thomson & Roy J. Laing
**SECRETARY** John A. Milton
**MANAGER** David Robertson
**ASSISTANT MANAGER &**
**DIRECTOR OF YOUTH DEVELOPMENT**
Kenny Black
**COACHING STAFF** John Wood
**YOUTH DEVELOPMENT &**
**COMMUNITY COACH** Scott Paton
**YOUTH CO-ORDINATOR** Graeme Porter
**YOUTH TEAM COACHES**
U19: John Wood
U17: Bob Scott
U15: Gordon Nicolson,
Joe Mackay & Robbie Hope
U13/Primary School Select:
Scott Paton & Graham Steele
**TEAM CAPTAIN** Jamie McKenzie
**OFFICE MANAGER /**
**MATCHDAY PROGRAMME EDITOR**
Kevin Cruickshank
**OFFICE ADMINISTRATOR** Audrey Fanning
**FOOTBALL SAFETY OFFICERS'**
**ASSOCIATION REPRESENTATIVE**
Steven Hamilton (07773) 525375
**CLUB DOCTOR** Dr. Alan Rodger, MB, ChB
**PHYSIOTHERAPIST** Leigh Thomas
**STADIUM MAINTENANCE MANAGER**
Bob Cruickshank
**CLUB SHOP**
Situated at Stadium (01343) 551114
Mon-Fri 9.00a.m.-5.00p.m.
Home Matchdays 10.00a.m.-5.00p.m.
**OFFICIAL SUPPORTERS CLUB**
Borough Briggs, Borough Briggs Road,
Elgin, IV30 1AP
President: Cecil Jack
**SHIRT SPONSOR** Robertson Group Ltd
**KIT SUPPLIER** Errea

## LIST OF PLAYERS 2005.06

| PLAYERS SURNAME | FIRST NAME | MIDDLE NAME | DATE OF BIRTH | PLACE OF BIRTH | DATE SIGNED | HEIGHT FT INS | WEIGHT ST LBS | POSITION ON PITCH | PREVIOUS CLUB |
|---|---|---|---|---|---|---|---|---|---|
| Booth | Mark | | 07/03/80 | Coatbridge | 07/07/05 | 5.10 | 12.0 | Midfield | Forfar Athletic |
| Bremner | Fraser | | 24/03/85 | Elgin | 09/07/03 | 5.11 | 11.7 | Midfield | Elgin City Form S |
| Cumming | Stuart | Alexander | 30/01/85 | Aberdeen | 07/07/05 | 5.11 | 11.7 | Defender | Blackburn Rovers |
| Dempsie | Allan | Henry | 05/11/82 | Bellshill | 07/07/05 | 5.11 | 11.0 | Defender | Hibernian |
| Dickson | Hugh | | 28/08/81 | Downpatrick | 07/07/05 | 6.1 | 11.7 | Defender | Linfield |
| Duff | Murray | Thomas | 25/05/87 | Edinburgh | 31/08/04 | 5.11 | 10.4 | Midfield | East End Villa |
| Easton | Stewart | | 10/10/81 | Coatbridge | 20/07/05 | 5.10 | 11.7 | Midfield | Stenhousemuir |
| Gardiner | Christopher | | 05/01/86 | Bellshill | 28/07/05 | 6.0 | 11.7 | Forward | Heart of Midlothian |
| Gray | Alexander | Charles | 21/03/88 | Aberdeen | 11/08/04 | 5.6 | 9.9 | Defender | Elgin City Form S |
| Hind | David | Scott | 15/03/82 | Inverness | 14/07/05 | 6.1 | 11.7 | Defender | Inverness Caledonian Thistle |
| Johnston | Martin | Alan | 24/06/78 | Aberdeen | 14/07/05 | 6.2 | 12.0 | Forward | Cove Rangers |
| Kaczan | Paul | | 03/02/83 | Bellshill | 23/07/05 | 6.1 | 12.0 | Defender | Partick Thistle |
| Kelly | Darryn | Paul | 19/01/88 | Greenock | 10/08/04 | 6.0 | 10.0 | Defender | Banchory B.C. |
| Lennox | Anthony | | 29/04/88 | Glasgow | 25/08/04 | 5.11 | 11.0 | Forward | Sheddocksly B.C. |
| McKenzie | Jamie | | 29/11/80 | Bellshill | 06/02/04 | 5.8 | 11.6 | Midfield | Stenhousemuir |
| McKenzie | Stuart | | 06/01/88 | Aberdeen | 10/08/04 | 6.1 | 10.4 | Goalkeeper | Albion B.C. |
| Melrose | Gary | George | 18/04/88 | Bangour | 18/11/04 | 5.6 | 9.3 | Midfield | Livingston |
| Muir | Alan | Scott | 05/11/86 | Paisley | 29/07/05 | 5.8 | 11.0 | Midfield | St. Mirren |
| Napier | Paul | Alexander | 17/06/87 | Aberdeen | 25/08/04 | 5.5 | 9.0 | Midfield | Banks O' Dee Juniors |
| Nelson | Adam | Edgar | 24/07/84 | Edinburgh | 14/07/05 | 5.11 | 12.0 | Midfield | Blackburn Rovers |
| Ralph | Jamie | Innes | 21/02/88 | Fraserburgh | 11/08/04 | 5.11 | 10.3 | Defender | Albion B.C. |
| Read | Calum | Daniel | 05/01/88 | Northampton | 25/08/04 | 5.11 | 11.10 | Defender | Elgin City Form S |
| Reid | Philip | George | 03/04/87 | Aberdeen | 26/07/05 | 6.0 | 11.0 | Forward | Motherwell |
| Renton | Keiron | Desmond | 13/02/84 | Edinburgh | 14/07/05 | 6.2 | 13.0 | Goalkeeper | Blackburn Rovers |
| Robertson | David | Alexander | 17/10/68 | Aberdeen | 31/08/05 | 5.11 | 13.0 | Defender | Montrose |
| Scullion | James | Patrick | 02/03/86 | Dunfermline | 27/07/05 | 6.2 | 13.0 | Defender | Dunfermline Athletic |
| Vigurs | Iain | Angus | 07/05/88 | Aberdeen | 31/08/04 | 5.6 | 10.2 | Defender | Albion B.C. |
| Vigurs | Patrick | Scott | 06/08/86 | Dartford | 31/08/04 | 6.0 | 11.5 | Midfield | Elgin City Form X |
| Wood | Garry | John | 27/01/88 | Aberdeen | 05/08/04 | 6.0 | 12.5 | Midfield | Albion B.C. |

## TICKET INFORMATION

**Season Ticket Prices**

| Seated | Adult | £180 |
|---|---|---|
| | Juvenile/OAP | £100 |
| Standing | Adult | £140 |
| | Juvenile/OAP | £70 |

**League Admission Prices**

| Seated | Adult | £11 |
|---|---|---|
| | Juvenile/OAP | £6.50 |
| Standing | Adult | £9 |
| | Juvenile/OAP | £4.50 |

## MILESTONES:

**Year of formation:** 1893
**Most capped player:** Douglas Grant (Scotland Amateur International)
**Most League points in a season:**
55 (Highland League - Season 1967/68) (2 Points for a Win)
81 (Highland League - Season 1989/90) (3 Points for a Win)
47 (SFL Third Division - Season 2001/02) (3 Points for a Win)
**Most League goals scored by a player in a season:**
Alex Bone (Season 2003/04)
**No. of goals scored:** 15
**Record Attendance:** 12,608 (-v- Arbroath – 17.2.1968)
**Record Victory:** 18-1 (-v- Brora Rangers – North of Scotland Cup – 6.2.1
**Record Defeat:** 1-14 (-v- Heart of Midlothian – Scottish Cup – 4.2.19

# SEASON STATS 2004.05

## SEASON STATS 2004.05

| DATE | VENUE | OPPONENTS | ATT | RES | Renton K.D. | Cumming S.A. | Dempsie A.H. | Kaczan P. | Dickson H. | Black S.T. | Martin W.M. | Nelson A.E. | Bone A.S.F. | Reid P.G. | Roddie A.R. | Napier P.A. | Bremner F. | Harty M.J. | Vigurs I.A. | McKenzie J. | McDonald J.N. | McKendrick K. | Higgins C. | Lennox A. | Wood G.J. | Melrose G.G. | Vigurs P.S. | Allison J.C. | Donnachie S. | Thomson D.H. | Huckins M. |
|---|---|---|---|---|---|---|---|---|---|---|---|---|---|---|---|---|---|---|---|---|---|---|---|---|---|---|---|---|---|---|---|---|
| 7-Aug | A | Stenhousemuir | 267 | 2-0 | 1 | 2 | 3 | 4 | 5 | 6 | 7 | 8 | 9² | 10 | 11 | | | 14 | | | | | | | | | | | | | |
| 14-Aug | H | Queen's Park | 523 | 1-0 | 1 | 2 | 3 | 4 | 5 | 6 | 7 | 8 | 9 | 10 | **11** | 12 | | | | | | | | | | | | | | | |
| 21-Aug | A | Peterhead | 688 | 1-2 | 1 | 2 | 3 | 4 | **5** | | 7 | 8 | 9 | 10 | 11 | 12 | 6 | | | | | | | | | | | | | | |
| 28-Aug | H | Montrose | 555 | 1-3 | 1 | 2 | 3 | 4 | 5 | | 7 | 8 | **9** | | 11 | | 6 | 10 | 12 | | | | | | | | | | | | |
| 4-Sep | A | East Stirlingshire | 617 | 1-0 | 1 | 5 | 2 | 4 | | | 10 | 8 | | | 11 | 15 | 7 | 9 | 3 | 6 | 14 | | | | | | | | | | |
| 11-Sep | A | Cowdenbeath | 275 | 1-3 | 1 | 5 | 2 | **4** | 12 | | 10 | 8 | | | 11 | 14 | 7 | 9 | 3 | 6 | | | | | | | | | | | |
| 18-Sep | H | Albion Rovers | 450 | 1-0 | 1 | 2 | 3 | 4 | 5 | | 10 | **8** | | | 11 | 15 | 7 | 9 | 6 | | | | | | | | | | | | |
| 25-Sep | A | Gretna | 574 | 0-3 | 1 | 2 | 3 | 4 | 5 | | 10 | 8 | | | | 15 | 7 | 9 | 11 | 6 | 16 | 14 | | | | | | | | | |
| 2-Oct | H | East Fife | 558 | 2-1 | 1 | 2 | 3 | 4 | 5 | | 10 | 8 | | 9 | | 15 | 7 | 11 | 12 | **6** | 14 | | | | | | | | | | |
| 16-Oct | A | Queen's Park | 507 | 1-0 | 1 | 2 | | | 5 | | | 8 | | 9 | 11 | 10 | 7 | **3** | 12 | 6 | | | | 4 | 14 | 15 | | | | | |
| 23-Oct | H | Stenhousemuir | 622 | 1-1 | 1 | 2 | | 4 | | | | 8 | **9** | | 11 | 5 | 7 | 10 | 3 | 6 | | | | | | 12 | | | | | |
| 30-Oct | A | Montrose | 447 | 0-2 | 1 | 2 | | 4 | | | | 8 | 9 | | 11 | 3 | 7 | 10 | 12 | 6 | | | 5 | | 16 | | | | | | |
| 6-Nov | H | East Stirlingshire | 502 | 1-3 | 1 | | | 4 | | | 10 | 8 | 9 | | 11 | 16 | 6 | 7 | 3 | | | | 2 | 5 | 15 | 14 | | | | | |
| 13-Nov | H | Cowdenbeath | 336 | 0-4 | 1 | 5 | | 4 | | 6 | 10 | | 9 | | 11 | 15 | 7 | 8 | 3 | | | | 2 | | 12 | 14 | | | | | |
| 27-Nov | A | Albion Rovers | 262 | 2-2 | 1 | 2 | | 4 | | 6 | 10 | 8 | | | 11 | 16 | 7 | 3 | | | | | 5 | 15 | 9 | | | | | | |
| 4-Dec | H | Gretna | 505 | 1-3 | 1 | 2 | | 4 | | 6 | 10 | 8 | | 7 | 11 | 14 | | 3 | 15 | | | | 5 | 16 | 9 | | | | | | |
| 27-Dec | A | Stenhousemuir | 329 | 0-4 | 1 | 2 | | 4 | 5 | | | | | 7 | 11 | | 3 | 6 | | | | | | 16 | 15 | 9 | 12 | | | | |
| 8-Jan | H | Montrose | 446 | 2-2 | 1 | 2 | | 4 | 5 | 7 | 10 | 8 | | 15 | 11 | | 3 | 6 | | | | | | 14 | | 9 | | | | | |
| 15-Jan | A | East Stirlingshire | 191 | 3-0 | 1 | | 3 | **4** | 5 | 11 | 10 | 8 | | | | | 7 | 6 | | | | | 2 | | | | | | | 9 | |
| 29-Jan | H | Albion Rovers | 380 | 1-1 | 1 | 7 | 3 | 4 | 5 | | 10 | 8 | | | **14** | | 11 | 6 | | | | | 2 | | | | | | | 9 | |
| 5-Feb | A | Gretna | 809 | 1-2 | 1 | 2 | | 4 | 3 | | 10 | 8 | | | **11** | 14 | | 7 | | | | | 6 | | | | | 15 | | 9 | |
| 12-Feb | H | East Fife | 379 | 2-1 | 1 | 2 | | 4 | 5 | | | | 12 | | | | 7 | **11** | 6 | | | | | | | | 14 | 9 | 3 | | |
| -Mar | A | Peterhead | 611 | 0-3 | 1 | 2 | 3 | | 5 | | 10 | 8 | 12 | | | 14 | | 6 | | | | | | 15 | | | | 4 | | 9 | 11 |
| -Mar | H | East Stirlingshire | 394 | 0-0 | 1 | 4 | 3 | 16 | 8 | | 10 | | | | 14 | | 15 | 7 | | | | | 6 | 5 | 9 | | 2 | | | | 11 |
| -Mar | H | Peterhead | 383 | 2-2 | 1 | 2 | 3 | 4 | | 6 | 10 | 7 | | | 14 | 11 | | 9 | 8 | | | | 5 | | | | | | | | |
| 2-Mar | A | Montrose | 308 | 0-2 | 1 | 2 | 3 | 4 | 5 | | 10 | 8 | | | 15 | 11 | 14 | 7 | | | | | 6 | | 16 | | 9 | | | | |
| 5-Mar | A | Cowdenbeath | 149 | 1-1 | 1 | | 3 | | 5 | | 10 | 8 | | | 11 | | 6 | **7** | | | | | 4 | | 9 | | | 2 | 16 | | |
| 19-Mar | H | Cowdenbeath | 338 | 2-0 | 1 | 2 | 3 | | 5 | | 10 | **8** | | | 15 | 11 | 16 | 6 | 9 | | | | 4 | | | 7 | | 12 | | | |
| 22-Mar | H | Queen's Park | 354 | †1-0 | 1 | 2 | 3 | | 5 | | 10 | 8 | | | 11 | | 14 | 6 | 9 | | | | 4 | | | 7 | | 15 | 12 | | |
| 6-Mar | A | East Fife | 456 | 0-2 | 1 | 2 | | 5 | 3 | | 10 | 8 | 9 | | 11 | 14 | | 7 | | | | | 6 | 15 | | | | | | | |
| -Apr | A | Albion Rovers | 246 | 0-2 | 1 | 2 | | 5 | 3 | | 10 | 8 | 9 | | 11 | 15 | 6 | 14 | | | | | 7 | | | | | | | 12 | |
| -Apr | A | East Fife | 466 | 2-1 | 1 | 2 | 3 | | 5 | | 10 | 8 | | | 15 | | 6 | 11 | | | | | 7 | | | | | 9 | | | |
| 6-Apr | H | Gretna | 503 | 2-6 | 1 | 2 | 3 | | 5 | | 10² | 8 | | | 15 | 14 | 7 | 11 | | | | | 6 | | | 16 | | 9 | | | |
| 13-Apr | H | Peterhead | 507 | 0-2 | 1 | 2 | 3 | | 5 | | 10 | 8 | | | 16 | 11 | 12 | 6 | 9 | | | | 4 | | | 14 | | 9 | | | |
| 20-Apr | A | Queen's Park | 581 | 0-1 | 1 | 2 | 3 | | 5 | | 10 | 8 | | | 15 | 11 | 17 | 7 | 9 | | | | 4 | | | 16 | | | | | |
| -May | H | Stenhousemuir | 314 | 4-2 | 1 | 2 | 3 | | 5 | | 10 | 8 | | | 12 | 11 | **14** | 6 | 7 | | | | 4 | | | | 15 | 9² | | | |
| **TOTAL FULL APPEARANCES** | | | | | 36 | 33 | 24 | 25 | 30 | 4 | 33 | 34 | 4 | 13 | 24 | 4 | 23 | 31 | 8 | 28 | | 2 | 18 | 2 | | 4 | 3 | 10 | 3 | |
| **TOTAL SUB APPEARANCES** | | | | | | | 1 | 1 | | | | | | 10 | 2 | 22 | 3 | 1 | 5 | | | 3 | 1 | 2 | 9 | 5 | 7 | 3 | 1 | 1 |
| **TOTAL GOALS SCORED** | | | | | | 1 | 1 | 3 | 4 | | 9 | 1 | 3 | 1 | 3 | 1 | | 4 | | 3 | | | 1 | | | | | 3 | | |

Score in bold denotes goal scored. Secondary smaller figure in bold denotes number of goals scored. † denotes opponent's own goal.

## THE BLACK AND WHITES' 10 YEAR LEAGUE RECORD

Season 2000-01 was the club's first season in membership of SFL

| Season | Div | P | W | D | L | F | A | Pts | Pos |
|---|---|---|---|---|---|---|---|---|---|
| 2000-01 | T | 36 | 5 | 7 | 24 | 29 | 65 | 22 | 10 |
| 2001-02 | T | 36 | 13 | 8 | 15 | 45 | 47 | 47 | 6 |
| 2002-03 | T | 36 | 5 | 13 | 18 | 33 | 63 | 28 | 9 |
| 2003-04 | T | 36 | 6 | 7 | 23 | 48 | 93 | 25 | 9 |
| 2004-05 | T | 36 | 12 | 7 | 17 | 39 | 61 | 43 | 6 |

## LEADING GOALSCORERS:

Season 2000-01 was the club's first season in membership of SFL

| Season | Div | Goals | Player |
|---|---|---|---|
| 2000-01 | T | 6 | Colin Milne, D. Ross |
| 2001-02 | T | 12 | I. Gilzean |
| 2002-03 | T | 6 | K. Steele |
| 2003-04 | T | 15 | A. Bone |
| 2004-05 | T | 9 | W. Martin |

### ELGIN CITY PLAYING KITS SEASON 2005.06

FIRST KIT    SECOND KIT    THIRD KIT

# MONTROSE

**MONTROSE F.C.**

Links Park Stadium, Wellington Street, Montrose, DD10 8QD

**TELEPHONE NUMBERS**
Ground/Commercial (01674) 673200
Office Admin. Home (01674) 672314
Office Admin. Bus. (01356) 626766
**FAX** (01674) 677311
**E-MAIL** montrosefootballclub@tesco.net
**WEBSITE** www.montrosefc.co.uk
**CHAIRMAN** John F. Paton
**VICE-CHAIRMAN** Robert McB. Ritchie
**DIRECTORS**
John D. Crawford, David I. Tait & Malcolm J. Watters
**ASSOCIATE DIRECTORS**
Andrew G. Stephen, David G. Skene & J. Kennedy Pratt
**COMPANY SECRETARY** John F. Paton
**MANAGER** Henry Hall
**FIRST TEAM COACH** Ian Gilzean
**FITNESS COACH** Scott Shepherd
**GOALKEEPING COACH** Jim Butter
**CHIEF SCOUT** Ian Cochrane
**CLUB CAPTAIN** Stuart Ferguson
**TEAM CAPTAIN** Steven Kerrigan
**ASSISTANT SECRETARY /**
**OFFICE ADMINISTRATOR**
Andrew Stephen
**FOOTBALL SAFETY OFFICERS'**
**ASSOCIATION REPRESENTATIVE**
Robert Ritchie
**COMMERCIAL REPRESENTATIVE**
Mrs Glynis Crawford
(B) (01674) 673200 (H) (01674) 673758
**LOTTERY MANAGER**
Alan Pirie
**MEDIA LIAISON PERSON**
Jon Blackwood
**MATCHDAY PROGRAMME EDITOR**
Andrew Stephen
(B) (01356) 626766 (H) 01674 672314
**PHYSIOTHERAPIST** Scott Shepherd
**STADIUM MANAGER & KIT PERSON**
Brian Leiper
**GROUNDSMAN** Ron Marquis
**CLUB SHOP**
Situated at Stadium (01674) 673200
Open 2.00pm - 5.00pm on Home Matchdays
**OFFICIAL SUPPORTERS CLUB**
c/o Simone Bradford, Secretary
16 Mount Avenue, Montrose
**SHIRT SPONSOR** Bon Accord Glass
**KIT SUPPLIER** Vandanel

## LIST OF PLAYERS 2005.06

| PLAYERS SURNAME | FIRST NAME | MIDDLE NAME | DATE OF BIRTH | PLACE OF BIRTH | DATE SIGNED | HEIGHT FT INS | WEIGHT ST LBS | POSITION ON PITCH | PREVIOUS CLUB |
|---|---|---|---|---|---|---|---|---|---|
| Butter | James | Ross | 14/12/66 | Dundee | 23/07/04 | 6.1 | 12.12 | Goalkeeper | East Fife |
| Cargill | Andrew | | 02/09/75 | Dundee | 06/07/05 | 5.6.5 | 10.8 | Midfield | Ayr United |
| Dodds | Kerr | | 05/05/85 | Edinburgh | 31/01/05 | 5.10 | 11.7 | Midfield | Ross County |
| Donachie | Barry | James | 21/12/79 | Dundee | 18/01/03 | 5.8 | 12.0 | Defender | Brechin City |
| Doyle | Paul | | 26/09/84 | Bellshill | 06/07/05 | 5.10.5 | 11.6 | Defender | Clyde |
| Ferguson | Stuart | | 09/11/80 | Bangour | 03/08/00 | 5.10 | 10.5 | Def / Mid | Forfar Athletic |
| Fotheringham | Martyn | Fraser | 23/03/83 | Perth | 14/06/05 | 5.10 | 11.3 | Midfield | St. Johnstone |
| Fraser | Stephen | | 01/03/85 | Glasgow | 12/07/05 | 5.11 | 11.0 | Midfield | St. Johnstone |
| Hall | Euan | Stuart | 19/08/85 | Dundee | 23/12/03 | 5.8 | 10.10 | Midfield | St. Johnstone |
| Hankinson | Michael | Richard | 04/07/83 | Dundee | 31/08/02 | 6.1 | 11.7 | Goalkeeper | Tayport Juniors |
| Henslee | Greig | Robert | 13/01/83 | Dundee | 14/07/05 | 5.10 | 12.0 | Midfield | Arbroath |
| Kerrigan | Steven | Paul | 29/09/70 | Wolverhampton | 30/05/01 | 5.10 | 11.7 | Midfield | East Fife |
| Martin | William | McLean | 21/08/81 | Glasgow | 14/06/05 | 6.1 | 11.10 | Forward | Elgin City |
| Mackenzie | Jamie | | 08/05/86 | Kirkcaldy | 29/07/05 | 6.1 | 12.10 | Defender | Hibernian |
| McLean | Duncan | William | 07/08/83 | Dundee | 01/02/05 | 5.10 | 11.6 | Forward | Arbroath |
| Reid | Andrew | William | 06/03/85 | Aberdeen | 06/07/05 | 6.1 | 14.7 | Goalkeeper | Hibernian |
| Russell | James | Alan | 05/02/84 | London | 31/08/05 | 6.1 | 12.0 | Midfield | Dundee East Craigie Junior |
| Smith | Elliott | Harvey | 23/12/83 | Edinburgh | 28/02/05 | 5.10 | 11.0 | Defender | Berwick Rangers |
| Smith | Robert | | 15/09/85 | Aberdeen | 31/08/05 | 6.2 | 12.2 | Defender | Dundee East Craigie Junior |
| Stephen | Neil | Andrew | 03/07/84 | Dundee | 30/01/04 | 6.2 | 12.7 | Defender | Dundee North End Junior |
| Watson | Calum | Neil | 18/02/84 | Montrose | 04/03/04 | 5.11 | 12.4 | Forward | Montrose Roselea Junior |
| Webster | Kevin | Scott | 21/01/83 | Dundee | 29/03/02 | 5.9 | 10.0 | Midfield | Dundee |

### TICKET INFORMATION

**Season Ticket Prices**
**Seated or Standing**

| | |
|---|---|
| Adult | £145 |
| Juvenile/OAP | £80 |
| Family (1 Adult & 1 Juvenile) | £150 |

**League Admission Prices**

**Seated or Standing**

| | |
|---|---|
| Adult | £9 |
| Juvenile/OAP | £4.50 |
| Family (1 Adult & 1 Juvenile) | £12 |

### MILESTONES:
**Year of formation:** 1879
**Most capped player:** Sandy Keiller
**No. of caps:** 6 (2 whilst with Montrose)
**Most League points in a season:**
53 (Division 2 - Season 1974/75) &
(Second Division - Season 1984/85) (2 Points for a win)
67 (Third Division - Season 1994/95) (3 Points for a win)
**Most League goals scored by a player in a season:**
Brian Third (Season 1972/73)
**No. of goals scored:** 28
**Record Attendance:** 8,983 (-v- Dundee – 17.3.1973)
**Record Victory:** 12-0 (-v- Vale of Leithen – Scottish Cup, 4.1.19
**Record Defeat:** 0-13 (-v- Aberdeen, 17.3.1951)

## SEASON STATS 2004.05

| DATE | VENUE | OPPONENTS | ATT | RES | Hankinson M. | Donachie B.J.T. | Budd A.D. | Stephen N.A. | Smith G. | Kerrigan S.P. | Webster K.S. | Smart C. | Watson C.N. | Spink D. | Sharp G. | Smith D.A.M. | Hall E.S. | Brenner K. | Jones D. | Morrice K.M. | O'Reilly C. | Doyle P. | Wood M. | Dodds K. | Greenhill D. | Ferguson S. | Butter J.R. | Slater M.P. | Graham J.R. | McLean D. | Fraser S. | Smith E.H. |
|---|---|---|---|---|---|---|---|---|---|---|---|---|---|---|---|---|---|---|---|---|---|---|---|---|---|---|---|---|---|---|---|---|---|
| 7-Aug | A | East Fife | 437 | 0-1 | 1 | 2 | 3 | 4 | 5 | 6 | 7 | 8 | 9 | 10 | 11 | 12 | 14 | 16 | | | | | | | | | | | | | | |
| 14-Aug | H | Peterhead | 379 | 0-1 | 1 | 2 | 3 | | 5 | 4 | | 10 | 9 | 6 | 11 | 7 | 8 | 15 | 12 | 14 | | | | | | | | | | | | |
| 21-Aug | A | Gretna | 501 | 0-1 | 1 | 2 | 3 | | 5 | 4 | 7 | 10 | 9 | 6 | | | 8 | 16 | 12 | | 11 | | | | | | | | | | | |
| 28-Aug | A | Elgin City | 555 | 3-1 | 1 | 2 | 3 | | 5 | 6 | 7 | 10 | | | 15² | | 8 | | | | 11 | 4 | 9 | 12 | | | | | | | | |
| 4-Sep | H | Albion Rovers | 330 | †1-1 | 1 | 2 | | | 5 | 6 | 15 | 10 | 16 | | 7 | | 8 | | | | 11 | 3 | 9 | 12 | 4 | | | | | | | |
| 11-Sep | A | Queen's Park | 406 | 2-1 | 1 | 2 | 12 | | 5 | 6 | 15 | 10 | 9 | 14 | 11 | 7 | | | | | | 4 | 3 | 8 | | | | | | | | |
| 18-Sep | H | Cowdenbeath | 351 | 3-1 | 1 | 2 | | | 5 | 6 | 7 | 9³ | | 14 | 11 | 10 | | | | | 16 | 4 | 3 | 8 | | | | | | | | |
| 25-Sep | H | Stenhousemuir | 360 | 0-2 | 1 | 2 | | | 5 | 6 | 7 | 9 | | 14 | 11 | 10 | | | | | 16 | 4 | 3 | 8 | 12 | | | | | | | |
| 2-Oct | A | East Stirlingshire | 247 | 1-1 | 1 | 2 | | | 5 | 6 | 7 | | 11 | 8 | 15 | 10 | | | | | 16 | 4 | 9 | | 14 | 3 | | | | | | |
| 16-Oct | A | Peterhead | 626 | 2-3 | 1 | 2 | 12 | | | 6 | 7 | | 15 | | 11 | 10 | | | | | 16 | 5 | 9 | 4 | 8 | 3 | | | | | | |
| 23-Oct | H | East Fife | 435 | 2-1 | 12 | | | | 5 | 6 | 7 | 10 | 15 | | 11 | | | | | | | 4 | 9 | 2 | 8 | 3 | 1 | | | | | |
| 30-Oct | H | Elgin City | 447 | 2-0 | | 2 | | | 5 | 6 | 7 | 10 | 15 | | 11 | 14 | | | | | 16 | 4 | 9 | | 8 | 3 | 1 | | | | | |
| 6-Nov | A | Albion Rovers | 245 | 2-1 | | 2 | | | 5 | 6 | 7 | 8 | 14 | 16 | 11 | 10 | | | | | | 4 | 9 | 12 | | 3 | 1 | | | | | |
| 13-Nov | H | Queen's Park | 410 | 2-4 | | 2 | | | 5 | 6 | 7² | 8 | 14 | | 11 | 10 | | | | | | 4 | 9 | 12 | | 3 | 1 | | 16 | | | |
| 30-Nov | A | Cowdenbeath | 145 | 0-0 | | 2 | 15 | | 5 | | 7 | 8 | | 12 | | 14 | | | | | 11 | 4 | 9 | 6 | | 3 | 1 | | 10 | | | |
| 4-Dec | A | Stenhousemuir | 309 | 1-1 | | 2 | 11 | | 5 | | 7 | 8 | | | | | 15 | 10 | | | 16 | 4 | 9 | | | 3 | 1 | | | | | |
| 27-Dec | A | East Fife | 784 | 0-1 | | 2 | | | 5 | | 7 | 8 | 16 | | 12 | | 10 | | | | | 4 | 9 | 11 | 15 | 3 | 1 | | | | | |
| 1-Jan | H | Gretna | 592 | 2-3 | | 2 | 10 | | 5 | 6 | 12 | 14 | 16 | | 11 | | 8 | | | | | 4 | 9 | 7 | | 3 | 1 | | | | | |
| 3-Jan | A | Elgin City | 446 | 2-2 | | 2 | | | 5 | 6 | 7 | 8 | 15 | | 11 | 16 | | | | | | 4 | 9 | 10 | | 3 | 1 | | | | | |
| 15-Jan | H | Albion Rovers | 269 | 0-1 | | 2 | | | 5 | 6 | 7 | 8 | 15 | | 11 | 10 | | | | | | 4 | 9 | 16 | | 3 | 1 | 14 | | | | |
| 22-Jan | A | Queen's Park | 575 | 0-1 | | | | | 5 | 6 | | 8 | 14 | | 12 | 10 | | | | | | 4 | 9 | 2 | 7 | 3 | 1 | 11 | 15 | | | |
| 29-Jan | H | Cowdenbeath | 292 | 1-2 | | 2 | | | 5 | 6 | | 8 | 10 | | 11 | | | | | | | 4 | 9 | 7 | 15 | 3 | 1 | 12 | | | | |
| 5-Feb | H | Stenhousemuir | 305 | 0-3 | | 2 | | | 5 | | | 8 | 10 | 14 | 11 | 15 | | | | | | 4 | 12 | 7 | | 3 | 1 | 6 | | 9 | | |
| 12-Feb | A | East Stirlingshire | 198 | 2-1 | 1 | 2 | | | 5 | | 7 | 8 | 15 | 12 | 11 | 16 | | | | | | 4 | 9 | 6 | | 3 | | | 10 | | | |
| 19-Feb | A | Gretna | 913 | 1-4 | | 2 | | | 5 | | 7 | | 15 | | 11 | 14 | | | | | | 4 | 9 | 6 | | 3 | 1 | 12 | 10 | 8 | | |
| 26-Feb | H | Peterhead | 467 | 0-2 | | 2 | | | | | 7 | | 15 | 12 | 11 | 16 | | | | | | 5 | 9 | | | 3 | 1 | 8 | 10 | 6 | 4 | |
| 2-Mar | H | East Stirlingshire | 270 | 4-1 | | 2 | | | | | 7² | 8 | 15 | | 11 | | | | | | | 5 | 9 | 12 | | 3 | 1 | | 10² | 6 | 4 | |
| 8-Mar | A | Albion Rovers | 307 | 2-1 | | 2 | | 6 | | | 7 | 8 | 15 | | 14 | | | | | | | 5 | 9 | 12 | | 3 | 1 | | 10 | 11 | 4 | |
| 12-Mar | H | Elgin City | 308 | 2-0 | | 2 | | | 5 | | 7 | 8 | 15 | | 11 | | | | | | | 6 | 9 | 12 | | 3 | 1 | 14 | 10 | | 4 | |
| 19-Mar | H | Queen's Park | 377 | 2-0 | | 2 | | | 5 | | 7 | 8 | 10 | | 12 | | | | | | | | 9 | 11 | | 3 | 1 | 14 | 6 | | 4 | |
| 2-Apr | A | Cowdenbeath | 199 | 0-0 | | 2 | | | 5 | | 7 | 8 | 10 | | 11 | 15 | 12 | | | | | 6 | 9 | | | 3 | 1 | 16 | | | 4 | |
| 9-Apr | H | East Stirlingshire | 329 | 4-1 | | | | | 5 | | 7 | 8 | | | 11 | 14 | | | | | | 6 | 9 | 2 | | 3 | 1 | 16 | 10 | | 4 | |
| 16-Apr | A | Stenhousemuir | 263 | 1-0 | | 2 | | | 5 | | | 8 | 16 | | 11 | 7 | | | | | | | 9 | 6 | | 3 | 1 | 15 | 10 | | 4 | |
| 23-Apr | H | Gretna | 462 | 0-4 | | 2 | | | 5 | | 7 | 8 | | 4 | 11 | 10 | | | | | | | 9 | 6 | | 1 | | 14 | | | 3 | |
| 30-Apr | A | Peterhead | 702 | 1-4 | 1 | 2 | | | 5 | | 7 | 8 | | 4 | 11 | 14 | 10 | | | | | | 9 | 6 | | | | 12 | | 16 | 3 | |
| 7-May | H | East Fife | 496 | 2-2 | | 2 | | | 5 | | 7 | 8 | 10 | 4 | 11² | 15 | 12 | | | | | | 9 | | | 1 | | | 15 | 6 | 3 | |
| **TOTAL FULL APPEARANCES** | | | | | 12 | 33 | 6 | 33 | 1 | 21 | 28 | 31 | 10 | 7 | 27 | 1 | 19 | | | | 4 | 28 | 29 | 19 | 8 | 25 | 24 | 4 | | 8 | 7 | 11 |
| **TOTAL SUB APPEARANCES** | | | | | 1 | 2 | 1 | | | 3 | 1 | 17 | 9 | 6 | 11 | 6 | 3 | 2 | 1 | 6 | 1 | 7 | 4 | 1 | | | | | 4 | 7 | 2 | 1 |
| **TOTAL GOALS SCORED** | | | | | | | | | 2 | 1 | 6 | 14 | 2 | | 7 | 1 | | | | | 2 | 5 | | 1 | 1 | | | | 4 | | |

Figure in bold denotes goal scored. Secondary smaller figure in bold denotes number of goals scored. † denotes opponent's own goal.

## THE GABLE ENDIES' 10 YEAR LEAGUE RECORD

| Season | Div | P | W | D | L | F | A | Pts | Pos |
|---|---|---|---|---|---|---|---|---|---|
| 95-96 | S | 36 | 5 | 5 | 26 | 33 | 86 | 20 | 10 |
| 96-97 | T | 36 | 12 | 7 | 17 | 46 | 62 | 43 | 6 |
| 97-98 | T | 36 | 10 | 8 | 18 | 53 | 80 | 38 | 9 |
| 98-99 | T | 36 | 8 | 6 | 22 | 42 | 74 | 30 | 10 |
| 99-00 | T | 36 | 10 | 19 | 7 | 39 | 54 | 37 | 9 |
| 00-01 | T | 36 | 6 | 8 | 22 | 31 | 65 | 26 | 9 |
| 01-02 | T | 36 | 16 | 7 | 13 | 43 | 39 | 55 | 5 |
| 02-03 | T | 36 | 7 | 12 | 17 | 35 | 61 | 33 | 7 |
| 03-04 | T | 36 | 12 | 12 | 12 | 52 | 63 | 48 | 6 |
| 04-05 | T | 36 | 13 | 7 | 16 | 47 | 53 | 46 | 6 |

## LEADING GOALSCORERS:

| Season | Div | Goals | Player |
|---|---|---|---|
| 1995-96 | S | 16 | C. McGlashan |
| 1996-97 | T | 11 | C. McGlashan |
| 1997-98 | T | 20 | C. McGlashan |
| 1998-99 | T | 7 | S. Taylor |
| 1999-00 | T | 12 | S. Taylor |
| 2000-01 | T | 7 | J. Mitchell |
| 2001-02 | T | 13 | S. Laidlaw |
| 2002-03 | T | 8 | S. Kerrigan |
| 2003-04 | T | 14 | S. Michie |
| 2004-05 | T | 14 | C. Smart |

### MONTROSE PLAYING KITS SEASON 2005.06

FIRST KIT    SECOND KIT    THIRD KIT

# QUEEN'S PARK

**QUEENS PARK F.C.**
The National Stadium,
Hampden Park, Mount Florida,
Glasgow, G42 9BA
**TELEPHONE NUMBERS**
Office (0141) 632 1275
Stadium Operations (0141) 620 4000
Sec. Home (0141) 638 0905
**FAX** (0141) 636 1612
**E-MAIL** secretary@queensparkfc.co.uk
**E-MAIL 2** jbalmain@queensparkfc.co.uk
**WEBSITE** www.queensparkfc.co.uk
**PRESIDENT**
Garry M. Templeman
**COMMITTEE**
A. Kenneth C. Harvey, Malcolm D. Mackay,
David McNeil, David Gordon B.Acc., ACMA
(Treasurer), James M. Hastie LL.B,
Dr. Alan S. Hutchison B.Sc., M.B., ChB.,
F.R.C.P. Glas, F.R.C., P.A.T.H.,
Keith McAllister, Ross Caven MBA, M.Sc,
B.Sc & James Nicholson
**HONORARY PATRON**
The Lord Macfarlane of Bearsden KT
**SECRETARY** Alistair MacKay
**HEAD COACH** William Stark
**ASSISTANT COACH** Robert Dickson
**RESERVE COACH** David McCallum
**GOALKEEPING COACH** Ronnie Cant
**HEAD OF YOUTH DEVELOPMENT**
Ian Cairns
**YOUTH DEVELOPMENT COACH**
Tommy Wilson
**YOUTH TEAM COACHES**
U19: Keith MacKenzie & Robert Kelly
U17: Billy Ogilvie
U13: Willie Neil
**CLUB CAPTAIN** Richard Sinclair
**OFFICE ADMINISTRATORS**
Mrs. Janice Balmain & Mrs. Susan Kennedy
**FOOTBALL SAFETY OFFICERS'**
**ASSOCIATION REPRESENTATIVE/**
**MEDIA LIAISON OFFICER**
Alistair MacKay (0141) 632 1275
**COMMERCIAL DIRECTOR** Johnathan Whelan
**MATCHDAY PROGRAMME EDITORS**
David B. Stirling & Logan Taylor
**CLUB DOCTOR** Dr. Alan S. Hutchison
**PHYSIOTHERAPISTS**
Robert C. Findlay & Andrew Myles
**GROUNDSMEN**
Steve Bache & Scott McCreadie
**KIT PERSON** Billy Ogilvie
**CLUB SHOP**
Home matches only – Hampden Park
(Kiosk within BT Scotland Stand). Open 2.15p.m. –
3.00p.m. and 4.45pm – 5.00pm on Home
Matchdays. Mail Orders may be obtained through
the Secretary of the Official Supporters Club.
**OFFICIAL SUPPORTERS CLUB**
c/o Secretary, Keith McAllister,
58 Brunton Street,
Glasgow, G44 3NQ
**SHIRT SPONSOR**
Barr Irn Bru – Original and Best
**KIT SUPPLIER** DIADORA

## LIST OF PLAYERS 2005.06

| PLAYERS SURNAME | FIRST NAME | MIDDLE NAME | DATE OF BIRTH | PLACE OF BIRTH | DATE SIGNED | HEIGHT FT INS | WEIGHT ST LBS | POSITION ON PITCH | PREVIOUS CLUB |
|---|---|---|---|---|---|---|---|---|---|
| Agostini | Damiano | Pietro | 22/11/78 | Irvine | 13/03/98 | 6.1 | 13.7 | Defender | East Fife |
| Anderson | Alex | | 24/06/88 | Glasgow | 26/08/04 | 5.7 | 10.6 | Defender | Partick Thistle |
| Bowers | Richard | | 16/06/87 | Glasgow | 12/05/05 | 5.11 | 10.10 | Forward | St. Johnstone Form D U16 |
| Cairney | Paul | | 29/08/87 | Glasgow | 08/08/05 | 5.9 | 10.0 | Midfield | Hillwood B.C. |
| Campbell | Ross | | 17/03/87 | Glasgow | 27/08/04 | 6.2 | 11.7 | Defender | Queen's Park Form D U15 |
| Canning | Steven | | 06/05/83 | Glasgow | 31/07/01 | 5.11 | 12.2 | Midfield | Queen's Park Form X |
| Clark | Ross | | 07/02/83 | Rutherglen | 31/07/01 | 5.9 | 11.0 | Midfield | Queen's Park Form X |
| Close | Gary | | 29/09/88 | Bellshill | 26/08/04 | 5.10 | 10.0 | Defender | Queen's Park Form D U16 |
| Colquhoun | Christopher | | 06/01/88 | Glasgow | 26/08/04 | 6.1 | 11.3 | Forward | St. Mirren Form D U16 |
| Copland | Kevin | | 04/01/87 | Paisley | 05/09/05 | 5.6 | 9.12 | Defender | St. Mirren |
| Cowie | Alexander | Fraser | 16/05/86 | Glasgow | 12/05/05 | 6.0 | 11.10 | Goalkeeper | Giffnock North |
| Crawford | David | | 30/06/85 | Glasgow | 28/08/03 | 6.2 | 11.7 | Goalkeeper | Dundee B.C. |
| Daily | James | | 11/10/87 | Glasgow | 27/08/04 | 6.3 | 11.7 | Defender | Queen's Park B.C. |
| Doran | Paul | | 09/05/87 | Glasgow | 05/09/05 | 6.0 | 11.2 | Defender | St. Johnstone B.C. |
| Dunlop | Michael | | 05/11/82 | Glasgow | 19/08/05 | 6.1 | 11.12 | Defender | Ayr United |
| Felvus | Bryan | | 16/01/86 | Bellshill | 30/06/04 | 5.6 | 10.4 | Forward | Hamilton Acad. Form D U14 |
| Ferry | Mark | | 19/01/84 | Glasgow | 24/09/04 | 5.11 | 11.13 | Midfield | St. Johnstone |
| Galloway | Stephen | | 02/05/88 | Paisley | 27/08/04 | 5.10 | 10.2 | Forward | St. Mirren B.C. |
| Gibson | Stephen | | 17/10/87 | Glasgow | 27/08/04 | 5.10 | 12.4 | Midfield | Queen's Park Form D U15 |
| Harty | Alan | | 28/03/88 | Bellshill | 27/08/04 | 6.0 | 10.9 | Defender | Queen's Park Form D U16 |
| Harvey | Paul | Edward | 28/08/68 | Glasgow | 30/08/03 | 5.9 | 11.7 | Midfield | Airdrie United |
| Kane | Alan | | 12/12/87 | Glasgow | 29/08/05 | 5.10 | 10.10 | Forward | Gretna |
| Kettlewell | Stuart | | 04/06/84 | Glasgow | 16/08/02 | 6.0 | 11.0 | Midfield | Lenzie Youth Club |
| Koukos | Markos | | 08/06/88 | Glasgow | 05/09/05 | 6.0 | 10.11 | Goalkeeper | Weirs B.C. |
| Lennon | Sean | | 25/10/87 | Bellshill | 27/08/04 | 5.7 | 9.7 | Defender | Queen's Park Form D U15 |
| Livingston | Anthony | | 15/08/86 | Glasgow | 28/08/03 | 5.8 | 10.5 | Midfield | Queen's Park Form D U16 |
| McBride | Joseph | | 01/05/88 | Glasgow | 27/08/04 | 5.8 | 10.0 | Midfield | Queen's Park Form D U16 |
| McBride | Sean | | 01/05/88 | Glasgow | 27/08/04 | 5.8 | 10.2 | Midfield | Queen's Park Form D U16 |
| McCallum | David | John | 07/09/77 | Bellshill | 31/01/03 | 5.10 | 10.10 | Midfield | Partick Thistle |
| McCann | Liam | Shane | 28/02/86 | Glasgow | 20/09/05 | 5.10 | 13.10 | Midfield | Raith Rovers |
| McClory | Paul | | 26/11/87 | Bellshill | 27/08/04 | 5.6 | 9.2 | Midfield | Queen's Park Form D U15 |
| McGinty | Andrew | | 19/07/84 | Glasgow | 16/08/02 | 6.0 | 12.0 | Defender | Cumbernauld United Junior |
| McLaughlin | David | | 20/02/87 | Glasgow | 27/08/04 | 6.1 | 10.4 | Forward | Motherwell |
| Molloy | Shaun | | 14/06/85 | Glasgow | 28/07/04 | 6.0 | 12.7 | Defender | Dundee United |
| Paton | Paul | Raymond | 18/04/87 | Paisley | 04/06/05 | 5.10 | 10.7 | Midfield | St. Mirren |
| Proctor | Kevin | James | 28/02/82 | Bellshill | 09/09/05 | 5.11 | 10.10 | Forward | Pollok Juniors |
| Quinn | Anthony | Thomas | 09/09/81 | Glasgow | 30/06/04 | 6.2 | 13.5 | Midfield | Kirkintilloch Rob Roy Junior |
| Reilly | Steven | James | 29/08/81 | Glasgow | 22/07/03 | 6.0 | 12.10 | Defender | Stirling Albion |
| Sinclair | Richard | | 20/05/82 | Glasgow | 25/05/00 | 5.10 | 12.0 | Defender | Queen's Park Form S |
| Strachan | Stewart | | 19/03/89 | Paisley | 08/08/05 | 5.11 | 11.7 | Goalkeeper | Ayr United Form D U16 |
| Trouten | Alan | | 08/11/85 | Rutherglen | 30/06/04 | 5.7 | 10.3 | Midfield | Morton |
| Waters | David | Anthony | 01/10/88 | Glasgow | 27/08/04 | 5.9 | 9.7 | Midfield | Queen's Park Form D U15 |
| Weatherston | David | | 25/08/86 | Paisley | 30/06/04 | 5.9 | 10.0 | Forward | Queen's Park B.C. |
| Weir | John | | 05/04/85 | Glasgow | 28/08/03 | 6.1 | 12.0 | Midfield | Queen's Park Form D U17 |
| Whelan | Jonathan | | 10/10/72 | Liverpool | 30/11/01 | 6.0 | 12.3 | Midfield | Berwick Rangers |

## TICKET INFORMATION

**Season Ticket Prices**

**BT Scotland Stand**

| | |
|---|---|
| Adult | £135 |
| Juvenile (over 12 & under 16) / OAP | £40 |
| Parent & Juvenile | £145 |
| For each additional Juvenile (4 Juveniles Max) | £10 |
| Juvenile (under 12) | £25 |

**League Admission Prices**

**BT Scotland Stand**

| | |
|---|---|
| Adult | £9 |
| Juvenile (under 16) / OAP | £2 |
| Parent & Juvenile | £10 |
| For each additional Juvenile | £1 |

## MILESTONES:

**Year of formation:** 1867
**Most capped player:** Walter Arnott
**No. of caps:** 14
**Most League points in a season:**
57 (Division 2 – Season 1922/23)(2 Points for a Win)
69 (Third Division – Season 1999/2000)(3 Points for a Win)
**Most League goals scored by a player in a season:**
William Martin (Season 1937/38)
**No. of goals scored:** 30
**Ground Record Attendance:** 149,547 (Scotland v England – 17.4.19
**Club Record Attendance:** 95,772 (-v- Rangers – 18.1.1930)
**Record Victory:** 16-0 (-v- St. Peters – Scottish Cup, 29.8.1885)
**Record Defeat:** 0-9 (-v- Motherwell – Division 1, 29.4.1930)

## SEASON STATS 2004.05

| DATE | VENUE | OPPONENTS | ATT | RES | McCue B. | Blair B. | McCallum D.J. | Rushford G.D. | Reilly S.J. | Molloy S. | Clark R. | Harvey P.E. | Graham A.S. | Carroll F.A. | Clarke D. | Sloan T. | Trouten A. | McGovern S. | Agostini D.P. | Weatherston D. | Bonnar M.M. | Felvus B. | Crawford D. | Kettlewell S. | Sinclair R. | Weir J. | Ferry M. | Whelan J. | McGinty A. | Livingston A. | Ferry D. | Quinn A.T.P. | Bowers R. | Canning S. |
|---|---|---|---|---|---|---|---|---|---|---|---|---|---|---|---|---|---|---|---|---|---|---|---|---|---|---|---|---|---|---|---|---|---|---|
| 7-Aug | H | Cowdenbeath | 490 | 3-2 | 1 | 2 | 3 | 4 | 5 | 6 | 7 | 8 | 9 | 10² | 11 | 14 | | | | 16 | | | | | | | | | | | | | | |
| 14-Aug | A | Elgin City | 523 | 0-1 | | 2 | 4 | 5 | 6 | 7 | 8 | 9 | 11 | 10 | | | | | 3 | | | | 1 | | | | 12 | | 16 | | | | | |
| 21-Aug | H | Albion Rovers | 505 | 1-1 | | 11 | 3 | 4 | 5 | 6 | **7** | 8 | 9 | 10 | | | 2 | | | 16 | | 15 | 1 | 12 | | | | | | | | | | |
| 28-Aug | H | Gretna | 496 | 3-2 | | 11 | 3 | 4 | 5 | 6 | 7 | 8 | 9 | **10** | | | 2 | | | 12 | | 14 | 1 | 16 | | | | | | | | | | |
| 4-Sep | A | Stenhousemuir | 410 | 1-1 | | 11 | | 4 | | 6 | | | 9 | 10 | | | 2 | | 3 | 16 | | 14 | 1 | 8 | 5 | 7 | | | | | | | | |
| 11-Sep | H | Montrose | 406 | 1-2 | | 11 | | 4 | | 6 | 8 | 15 | 9 | 10 | | | 2 | | 3 | 16 | | 14 | 1 | 7 | 5 | | | | | | | | | |
| 18-Sep | A | East Stirlingshire | 335 | †† 5-0 | | 11 | | 4 | | 6 | 8 | 12 | 9 | 10² | | | 2 | | 3 | | | 14 | 1 | 7 | 5 | | | | 16 | | | | | |
| 25-Sep | A | East Fife | 445 | 4-1 | | 11 | 6 | 4 | | 12 | 8 | 15 | 9³ | 10 | | | 2 | | 3 | | | | 1 | 7 | 5 | | | | 16 | | | | | |
| 2-Oct | H | Peterhead | 625 | 1-2 | | 11 | 6 | 4 | 5 | 8 | | | 9 | 10 | | | 2 | | 3 | | | 14 | 1 | 7 | | | | | 16 | | | | | |
| 16-Oct | H | Elgin City | 507 | 0-1 | | | 3 | 4 | | 8 | 6 | | 9 | 10 | | | 2 | | 5 | | | | 1 | 7 | | 11 | | | | | | | | |
| 23-Oct | A | Cowdenbeath | 280 | 1-2 | | | 3 | 4 | | 8 | 6 | 16 | | 10 | | | 2 | | 5 | | | 9 | 1 | 7 | | 11 | | | | | | | | |
| 30-Oct | A | Gretna | 706 | 1-4 | 7 | | | 4 | 3 | 8 | 6 | | 9 | 10 | | | 2 | | | 15 | | | 1 | | 5 | | 11 | | | | | | | |
| 6-Nov | H | Stenhousemuir | 491 | † 4-3 | 12 | | | 4 | 15 | 3 | 8² | 6 | 9 | 10 | | | 2 | | | | | 14 | 1 | 7 | 5 | | **11** | | | | | | | |
| 13-Nov | H | Montrose | 410 | 4-2 | 15 | | | 4 | 3 | 8 | 6 | | 9 | 10 | | | 2 | | | | | 14 | 1 | 7 | 5 | | **11²** | | | | | | | |
| 27-Nov | H | East Stirlingshire | 457 | 0-0 | | | 12 | 4 | 3 | 8 | 6 | | 9 | 10 | | | 2 | | | 16 | | 14 | 1 | 7 | 5 | | 11 | | | | | | | |
| 4-Dec | H | East Fife | 575 | 1-2 | | 6 | | 4 | 3 | 8 | 6 | | 9 | 10 | | | 2 | | | 15 | | 14 | 1 | 7 | 5 | | 11 | | | | | | | |
| 18-Dec | A | Peterhead | 569 | 2-2 | 10 | 5 | | 4 | 3 | 8 | 6 | | **9** | | | | 2 | | | | | | 1 | 7 | | | 11 | | 12 | | 14 | | 16 | |
| 27-Dec | H | Cowdenbeath | 568 | 2-3 | | 5 | 4 | | | 8 | 6 | | 9 | 10 | | | 2² | | | 16 | | | 1 | 7 | 3 | | 11 | | 15 | | | 14 | | |
| 3-Jan | H | Gretna | 803 | 1-1 | | 9 | 4 | | | 8 | 6 | 12 | | 10 | | | 2 | | | | | | 1 | **7** | 5 | | | | 3 | | | | | |
| 15-Jan | A | Stenhousemuir | 356 | 0-0 | | 6 | 4 | | | 8 | | | 9 | 10 | | | 2 | | | | | | 1 | 7 | 5 | | 11 | | 3 | | | | | |
| 22-Jan | H | Montrose | 575 | 1-0 | | 6 | 4 | | 3 | 8 | | | 12 | **10** | | | 2 | | | | | | 1 | 7 | 5 | | 11 | | 9 | | | | | |
| 29-Jan | A | East Stirlingshire | 317 | 1-3 | | 6 | 4 | | 3 | 8 | | | **9** | 10 | | | 2 | | | | | | 1 | 7 | 5 | | 11 | 12 | 16 | 2 | | | | |
| 5-Feb | A | East Fife | 601 | 1-0 | | | 4 | | 3 | 8 | 6 | | | 10 | | | 2 | | | | | 7 | 1 | | 5 | | **11** | | 9 | | | | | |
| 12-Feb | H | Peterhead | 454 | 1-1 | | | 3 | | | 8 | 6 | | | 10 | | | 2 | | | 16 | | 7 | 1 | | 5 | | 11 | 4 | 9 | | | | | |
| 19-Feb | H | Albion Rovers | 497 | 0-3 | | | 3 | | | 8 | 6 | | | 10 | | | 2 | | | 16 | | 7 | 1 | | 5 | | 11 | 4 | 15 | 9 | | | | |
| 1-Mar | A | Albion Rovers | 355 | 4-0 | | | 4 | | | 3 | **6** | | | 10² | | | 2 | | | | | | 1 | 7 | | **11** | 5 | | | | 9 | 8 | | |
| 5-Mar | H | Stenhousemuir | 512 | 0-0 | | | 4 | | | 3 | 6 | 16 | | 10 | | | 2 | | | | | | 1 | 7 | 14 | **11** | 5 | | | | 9 | 8 | | |
| 12-Mar | A | Gretna | 978 | 0-4 | | | 12 | | | 15 | 9 | 6 | | 14 | 10 | | 2 | | | | | | 1 | 7 | 4 | **11** | 5 | | | | 3 | 8 | | |
| 19-Mar | A | Montrose | 377 | 0-2 | | | 4 | | | 3 | 8 | 6 | | 9 | 10 | | 2 | | | 16 | | | 1 | 7 | 5 | 11 | | | | | | | | |
| 22-Mar | A | Elgin City | 354 | 0-1 | | | 4 | | | 3 | 8 | 6 | | 10 | | | 2 | | | 15 | | | 1 | 7 | 5 | | | 12 | 16 | 9 | 11 | | | |
| 2-Apr | H | East Stirlingshire | 486 | 2-0 | | | | 4 | | 3 | 7 | 6 | 14 | 10 | | | | 15 | | | | | 1 | | 5 | | 9 | | 16 | 2 | | **8** | **11** | |
| 9-Apr | A | Peterhead | 479 | 1-1 | | | | 4 | | | 7 | 6 | | 10 | | | | 3 | | | | | 1 | | 9 | | | | 16 | 2 | 8 | **11** | 14 | |
| 16-Apr | H | East Fife | 451 | 2-1 | | | | 4 | | | **7** | 6 | 10 | | | | | 3 | | | | | 1 | 14 | 5 | | 9 | | 12 | 2 | 8 | **11** | 15 | |
| 23-Apr | A | Albion Rovers | 353 | †† 2-1 | | | | 4 | | 3 | 7 | 6 | | 10 | | | 2 | | | | | | 1 | 15 | | | 9 | | 5 | | 11 | 8 | | |
| 30-Apr | H | Elgin City | 581 | 1-0 | | 15 | | | 3 | 7 | 6 | | | **10** | | | 2 | 4 | 11 | | | | 1 | 12 | | | 9 | | 5 | 2 | 8 | | | |
| 7-May | A | Cowdenbeath | 346 | 0-1 | | | | | | 6 | 14 | | | 10 | | | 2 | 4 | | | | | 1 | 7 | 5 | | 9 | | 3 | | 8 | 11 | | |
| **TOTAL FULL APPEARANCES** | | | | | 1 | 16 | 7 | 24 | 13 | 26 | 33 | 27 | 20 | 33 | 2 | | 31 | 1 | 10 | 2 | | 4 | 34 | 23 | 24 | 1 | 26 | 3 | 4 | | 17 | 10 | 4 | |
| **TOTAL SUB APPEARANCES** | | | | | | 2 | 3 | 1 | 2 | | | 3 | 7 | | 1 | 2 | | 3 | 5 | 3 | 16 | | | 5 | 1 | | 3 | 5 | 2 | 6 | 1 | | | 2 |
| **TOTAL GOALS SCORED** | | | | | | | 1 | | | 1 | 6 | 2 | 5 | 14 | | | 3 | | | | | 2 | | 2 | | | 7 | | | | 1 | 2 | |

Figure in bold denotes goal scored. Secondary smaller figure in bold denotes number of goals scored. † denotes opponent's own goal.

## THE SPIDERS' 10 YEAR LEAGUE RECORD

| Season | Div | P | W | D | L | F | A | Pts | Pos |
|---|---|---|---|---|---|---|---|---|---|
| 95-96 | T | 36 | 12 | 12 | 12 | 40 | 43 | 48 | 6 |
| 96-97 | T | 36 | 9 | 9 | 18 | 46 | 59 | 36 | 8 |
| 97-98 | T | 36 | 10 | 11 | 15 | 42 | 55 | 41 | 7 |
| 98-99 | T | 36 | 11 | 11 | 14 | 41 | 46 | 44 | 6 |
| 99-00 | T | 36 | 20 | 9 | 7 | 54 | 37 | 69 | 1 |
| 00-01 | S | 36 | 10 | 10 | 16 | 28 | 40 | 40 | 9 |
| 01-02 | T | 36 | 9 | 8 | 19 | 38 | 53 | 35 | 10 |
| 02-03 | T | 36 | 7 | 11 | 18 | 39 | 51 | 32 | 8 |
| 03-04 | T | 36 | 10 | 11 | 15 | 41 | 53 | 41 | 7 |
| 04-05 | T | 36 | 13 | 9 | 14 | 51 | 50 | 48 | 4 |

## LEADING GOALSCORERS:

| Season | Div | Goals | Player |
|---|---|---|---|
| 1995-96 | T | 6 | S. Edgar, K. McGoldrick |
| 1996-97 | T | 7 | D. Ferry |
| 1997-98 | T | 8 | S. Edgar, J. Mercer |
| 1998-99 | T | 7 | S. Edgar |
| 1999-00 | T | 13 | M. Gallagher |
| 2000-01 | S | 7 | M. Gallagher |
| 2001-02 | T | 5 | S. Canning, R. Jackson |
| 2002-03 | T | 8 | J. Gemmell |
| 2003-04 | T | 7 | S. Reilly |
| 2004-05 | T | 14 | F. Carroll |

### QUEEN'S PARK PLAYING KITS SEASON 2005.06

FIRST KIT | SECOND KIT | THIRD KIT

# STENHOUSEMUIR

## LIST OF PLAYERS 2005.06

| PLAYERS SURNAME | FIRST NAME | MIDDLE NAME | DATE OF BIRTH | PLACE OF BIRTH | DATE SIGNED | HEIGHT FT INS | WEIGHT ST LBS | POSITION ON PITCH | PREVIOUS CLUB |
|---|---|---|---|---|---|---|---|---|---|
| Arbuckle | Andrew | Paul | 06/02/85 | Munster | 09/09/05 | 5.10 | 11.2 | Defender | Hamilton Academical |
| Carroll | Frank | Andrew | 30/01/81 | Glasgow | 14/06/05 | 5.8 | 11.10 | Forward | Queen's Park |
| Collins | Lee | | 03/02/74 | Bellshill | 07/06/04 | 5.8 | 11.0 | Midfield | Stranraer |
| Cramb | Colin | | 23/06/74 | Lanark | 20/06/05 | 6.0 | 13.0 | Forward | Hamilton Academical |
| Denham | Greig | Paterson | 05/10/76 | Glasgow | 20/06/05 | 6.2 | 13.3 | Defender | East Stirlingshire |
| Fahey | Christopher | | 28/06/78 | Coatbridge | 27/06/05 | 6.0 | 12.6 | Goalkeeper | Albion Rovers |
| Fallon | Steven | | 08/05/79 | Paisley | 20/05/04 | 5.8.5 | 12.0 | Defender | Queen's Park |
| Henderson | Robbie | | 11/10/82 | Bellshill | 09/06/04 | 6.1 | 13.2 | Defender | Morton |
| Kerrigan | Steven | John | 09/10/72 | Bellshill | 26/03/04 | 6.0 | 12.10 | Forward | Berwick Rangers |
| MacIntosh | Ewan | | 31/01/88 | Edinburgh | 01/08/05 | 5.11 | 11.0 | Defender | Tynecastle Hearts |
| McAlpine | Joseph | Charles | 12/09/81 | Glasgow | 04/07/05 | 5.10 | 11.8 | Midfield | Forfar Athletic |
| McBride | John | Paul | 28/11/78 | Hamilton | 29/07/04 | 5.10 | 12.0 | Midfield | Partick Thistle |
| McCulloch | William | | 02/04/73 | Baillieston | 04/06/03 | 6.1 | 13.7 | Goalkeeper | Stranraer |
| McGregor | Steven | | 08/02/82 | Dundee | 07/06/04 | 6.1 | 12.7 | Midfield | Campsie Black Watch |
| McGrillen | Paul | Alexander | 19/08/71 | Glasgow | 12/07/04 | 5.9 | 11.0 | Forward | Bellshill Juniors |
| McInally | David | | 03/03/81 | Glasgow | 29/07/04 | 5.8 | 10.8 | Midfield | Cowdenbeath |
| McKenzie | Marc | David | 11/07/85 | Glasgow | 27/07/05 | 5.6 | 10.0 | Midfield | Albion Rovers |
| McKeown | John | Paton | 21/04/81 | Glasgow | 04/07/05 | 6.4.5 | 13.10 | Defender | Cowdenbeath |
| Menzies | Craig | | 10/07/86 | Paisley | 28/02/05 | 5.10 | 11.0 | Midfield | Stenhousemuir Form DU1 |
| Mercer | James | | 30/07/74 | Glasgow | 07/06/05 | 6.5 | 13.6 | Midfield | Albion Rovers |
| Morrison | David | James | 02/01/86 | Falkirk | 09/07/03 | 6.1 | 10.7 | Midfield | Stenhousemuir Form DU1 |
| Murphy | Paul | David | 01/08/85 | Peterhead | 14/05/02 | 6.1 | 11.0 | Midfield | Celtic B.C. |
| Nicoll | Kevin | | 16/06/86 | Glasgow | 22/08/05 | 6.1 | 11.7 | Defender | Hamilton Academical |
| Renwick | Michael | John | 29/02/76 | Edinburgh | 07/06/05 | 5.10 | 12.0 | Defender | East Fife |
| Savage | Joseph | Gerard | 22/05/84 | Bellshill | 16/01/04 | 6.1 | 11.0 | Forward | Bo'ness United Juniors |
| Sinclair | Thomas | | 22/05/87 | Glasgow | 08/08/03 | 5.8 | 12.2 | Midfield | Stenhousemuir B.C. |
| Templeton | David | Cooper | 07/01/89 | Glasgow | 24/08/05 | 5.8 | 8.12 | Forward | Aberdeen |

**MILESTONES:**

**Year of formation:** 1884

**Most League points in a season:**

50 (Division 2 – Season 1960/61) (2 Points for a Win)

64 (Second Division – Season 1998/99) (3 Points for a Win)

**Most League goals scored by a player in a season:**

Evelyn Morrison (Season 1927/28) & Robert Murray (Season 1936/3...

**No. of goals scored:** 31

**Record Attendance:** 12,500 (-v- East Fife – 11.3.1950)

**Record Victory:** 9-2 (-v- Dundee United – Division 2, 16.4.1937)

**Record Defeat:** 2-11 (-v- Dunfermline Athletic – Division 2, 27.9.1930)

## SEASON STATS 2004.05

| Date | Venue | Opponents | Att | Res | McCulloch W. | Fallon S. | McInally D. | Murphy P.D. | Henderson R. | McBride J.P. | Lauchlan M.T. | Morrison D.J. | Kerrigan S. | Davidson R.T. | McGrillen P.A. | Savage J.G. | Knox K. | Collins L. | McGregor S. | Sinclair T. | Smith A. | Gardiner M.J. | Ogunmade D. | Easton S. | McCulloch G. | Menzies C. | Struthers K. | Kirkham J. | Orr D. | Morrison M. | Miles C. |
|---|---|---|---|---|---|---|---|---|---|---|---|---|---|---|---|---|---|---|---|---|---|---|---|---|---|---|---|---|---|---|---|---|
| 7-Aug | H | Elgin City | 267 | 0-2 | 1 | 2 | 3 | 4 | 5 | 6 | 7 | 8 | 9 | 10 | 11 | 12 | 14 | | | | | | | | | | | | | | |
| 4-Aug | A | Cowdenbeath | 233 | 6-0 | 1 | | 3 | 4 | 5 | **6** | 7 | | | 10 | 12 | **11**[3] | 9 | 2 | **8** | 14 | 15 | | | | | | | | | | |
| 21-Aug | H | East Stirlingshire | 405 | 6-0 | 1 | | 3 | 4 | 5 | **6** | 7 | | | 10 | | 11 | **9**[3] | 2 | **8** | 14 | 15 | | | | | | | | | | |
| 28-Aug | A | East Fife | 468 | 0-0 | 1 | 2 | 3 | | 5 | 6 | 7 | | | 10 | 11 | | 9 | 4 | 8 | | 16 | | | | | | | | | | |
| 6-Sep | H | Queen's Park | 410 | 1-1 | 1 | 2 | 3 | | 5 | 6 | 7 | | | 10 | 11 | | 9 | 4 | **8** | 14 | 16 | | | | | | | | | | |
| 1-Sep | A | Albion Rovers | 339 | 0-1 | 1 | 2 | 3 | 12 | 5 | 10 | 7 | | 14 | | 11 | | 9 | 4 | 8 | 6 | 16 | | | | | | | | | | |
| 8-Sep | H | Peterhead | 307 | 1-2 | 1 | 7 | 3 | 4 | | 6 | 10 | | 9 | | 11 | 15 | 2 | | 8 | | | | | 12 | 5 | | | | | | |
| 25-Sep | A | Montrose | 360 | †2-0 | 1 | 2 | 3 | 10 | 6 | | **14** | 7 | | 12 | 11 | | 9 | 4 | 8 | | 5 | | | | | | | | | | |
| 2-Oct | H | Gretna | 373 | 0-3 | 1 | 2 | 3 | 7 | 6 | 10 | 12 | | 9 | | 11 | | | 4 | 8 | | 5 | | | | | 15 | | | | | |
| 6-Oct | H | Cowdenbeath | 300 | 2-2 | 1 | | 3 | 4 | 6 | 10 | **7** | | 9 | | 11 | 12 | 2 | | **8** | 14 | | | | | 5 | | | | | | |
| 3-Oct | A | Elgin City | 622 | 1-1 | 1 | 15 | 3 | 4 | 6 | 10 | 7 | | 9 | | 11 | | 2 | | **8** | | | | | | 5 | | | | | | |
| 0-Oct | H | East Fife | 382 | 5-2 | 1 | 2 | 3 | | 6 | 10 | **7** | | 9 | | **14**[2] | **11**[2] | | 4 | 8 | | 5 | | | | | | | | | | |
| -Nov | A | Queen's Park | 491 | 3-4 | 1 | 2 | 3 | | 6 | 10 | **7** | | 9 | | **4** | 11 | | 5 | 8 | 16 | 12 | 15 | | | | | | | | | |
| 3-Nov | H | Albion Rovers | 318 | 3-0 | 1 | 2 | | 4 | 3 | 6 | 7 | | | **10** | 11 | | **9** | 12 | **8** | 15 | 5 | | | | | | | | | | |
| 0-Nov | A | Peterhead | 499 | 0-5 | 1 | 2 | 15 | 4 | 3 | 6 | 7 | | 9 | 10 | 11 | 12 | 14 | | 8 | | 5 | | | | | | | | | | |
| -Dec | H | Montrose | 309 | 1-1 | 1 | 2 | 3 | | 6 | 7 | 16 | | | 10 | **11** | | 9 | 4 | 8 | | | | | 5 | | | | | | | |
| 8-Dec | H | Gretna | 1,078 | 0-3 | 1 | 2 | 11 | 15 | 3 | 6 | 8 | 7 | | | 12 | 10 | 4 | | 9 | | 5 | | | | 16 | | | | | | |
| 7-Dec | H | Elgin City | 329 | 4-0 | 1 | 11 | 3 | 10 | | 6 | 7 | 15 | | | | **9**[2] | 2 | | 8 | 5 | 16 | | | 4 | | | | | | | |
| -Jan | A | East Fife | 491 | 0-2 | 1 | 11 | 3 | 5 | | 6 | 7 | | | | 12 | 10 | 2 | | 8 | 9 | | | | 4 | | | | | | | |
| 5-Jan | H | Queen's Park | 356 | 0-0 | 1 | | 3 | | 6 | | 10 | 7 | | | 12 | 11 | 9 | 2 | 8 | 5 | | | | 4 | | | | | | | |
| 9-Jan | H | Peterhead | 394 | 1-1 | 1 | | 3 | | 6 | | 10 | 7 | | | 11 | | 9 | 2 | 8 | 5 | 16 | | | 4 | | | | | | | |
| -Feb | A | Montrose | 305 | 3-0 | 1 | 2 | 3 | | 6 | | 10 | 7 | 12 | | **11**[2] | 9 | | | 8 | 5 | 14 | | | 4 | | | | | | | |
| 2-Feb | H | Gretna | 416 | 1-4 | 1 | 2 | 3 | | 6 | | 10 | 7 | | | 11 | 9 | | | 8 | 5 | 15 | | | 4 | | 16 | | | | | |
| 9-Feb | H | East Stirlingshire | 422 | 3-2 | 1 | 2 | 3 | | 6 | 14 | 10 | 7 | | | **11**[3] | 9 | | | 8 | 5 | 12 | | | 4 | | | | | | | |
| -Mar | A | Queen's Park | 512 | 0-0 | 1 | 2 | 12 | 6 | | 3 | 10 | 7 | | | | 9 | | | 5 | 8 | 11 | | | 4 | | 15 | 16 | | | | |
| -Mar | A | Albion Rovers | 222 | 1-1 | 1 | 2 | 9 | | 6 | 3 | 10 | | | | 11 | **16** | | | 5 | 8 | | | | 4 | | 7 | | | | | |
| 2-Mar | H | East Fife | 334 | 1-2 | 1 | 2 | 9 | | 6 | 3 | 10 | | | | 11 | 12 | | | 5 | 8 | | | | 4 | | 15 | 7 | | | | |
| 5-Mar | A | East Stirlingshire | 211 | 2-3 | 1 | | 9 | | | 3 | 10 | 16 | | | 11 | | | 6 | 8 | 5 | | | | 4 | | 2 | 7 | 17 | | | |
| 9-Mar | H | Albion Rovers | 370 | 1-1 | | | 3 | 14 | | 10 | 16 | | 9 | | 11 | | | 6 | 8 | 5 | | | | 12 | 4 | 2 | 7 | 1 | | | |
| 2-Mar | A | Cowdenbeath | 173 | †2-0 | 1 | | 3 | | 8 | 6 | 10 | | | | 11 | 9 | | | 7 | 5 | | | | 4 | | 2 | | | | | |
| -Apr | A | Peterhead | 523 | 1-1 | 1 | | 3 | | 8 | 6 | 10 | 12 | 16 | | 11 | 9 | | | 7 | 5 | | | | 4 | | 2 | | | | | |
| -Apr | A | Gretna | 908 | 0-7 | 1 | | | 5 | 3 | 10 | 6 | | | | 11 | 9 | | | 8 | | | | | 4 | | 2 | 7 | 12 | | | |
| 6-Apr | H | Montrose | 263 | 0-1 | 1 | | | 6 | 3 | | 7 | | | | 11 | 9 | 2 | | 4 | 10 | 5 | | | 8 | | 12 | 15 | | | | |
| 3-Apr | H | East Stirlingshire | 242 | 4-1 | | | 6 | | 3 | | 7 | | | | 11 | 9 | | | 5 | 8 | | | | 4 | | 2 | 12 | | 17 | | |
| 0-Apr | H | Cowdenbeath | 360 | 1-1 | | | 15 | 6 | 3 | | 8 | | | | 11 | 9 | | | 5 | 10 | | | | 4 | | 2 | 7 | 1 | | | |
| -May | A | Elgin City | 314 | 2-4 | 1 | | 10 | 6 | 5 | | 8 | | | | 11 | 9 | | | 7 | | | | | 4 | | 2 | | 3 | 15 | | |
| **TOTAL FULL APPEARANCES** | | | | | 34 | 23 | 27 | 29 | 25 | 32 | 23 | 7 | 10 | 8 | 32 | 24 | 19 | 22 | 16 | 12 | 16 | | | 14 | 11 | 5 | 4 | 1 | 1 | 1 | |
| **TOTAL SUB APPEARANCES** | | | | | 1 | 3 | 3 | 1 | 1 | 3 | 4 | | 6 | 2 | 6 | 3 | | 3 | 9 | 4 | 3 | 1 | 2 | 1 | 4 | 3 | 1 | 1 | | | 1 |
| **TOTAL GOALS SCORED** | | | | | | | | | | 4 | 2 | | | 5 | 18 | 9 | 1 | | 4 | 1 | 2 | | | | | | | | | |

Figure in bold denotes goal scored. Secondary smaller figure in bold denotes number of goals scored. † denotes opponent's own goal.

### THE WARRIORS' 10 YEAR LEAGUE RECORD

| Season | Div | P | W | D | L | F | A | Pts | Pos |
|---|---|---|---|---|---|---|---|---|---|
| 5-96 | S | 36 | 14 | 7 | 15 | 51 | 49 | 49 | 4 |
| 6-97 | S | 36 | 11 | 11 | 14 | 49 | 43 | 44 | 6 |
| 7-98 | S | 36 | 10 | 10 | 16 | 44 | 53 | 40 | 9 |
| 8-99 | T | 36 | 19 | 7 | 10 | 62 | 42 | 64 | 2 |
| 9-00 | S | 36 | 10 | 18 | 8 | 44 | 59 | 38 | 8 |
| 0-01 | S | 36 | 12 | 6 | 18 | 45 | 63 | 42 | 7 |
| 1-02 | S | 36 | 8 | 12 | 16 | 33 | 57 | 36 | 9 |
| 2-03 | S | 36 | 12 | 11 | 13 | 49 | 51 | 47 | 7 |
| 3-04 | S | 36 | 7 | 4 | 25 | 28 | 65 | 25 | 10 |
| 4-05 | T | 36 | 10 | 12 | 14 | 58 | 58 | 42 | 7 |

### LEADING GOALSCORERS:

| Season | Div | Goals | Player |
|---|---|---|---|
| 1995-96 | S | 10 | M. Mathieson |
| 1996-97 | S | 14 | I. Little |
| 1997-98 | S | 15 | I. Little |
| 1998-99 | T | 11 | R. Hamilton |
| 1999-00 | S | 8 | M. Mooney |
| 2000-01 | S | 18 | I. English |
| 2001-02 | S | 7 | W. Irvine |
| 2002-03 | S | 9 | M. Booth |
| 2003-04 | S | 5 | A. Brown |
| 2004-05 | T | 18 | P. McGrillen |

STENHOUSEMUIR PLAYING KITS SEASON 2005.06

FIRST KIT    SECOND KIT    THIRD KIT

# SCOTTISH FOOTBALL LEAGUE THIRD DIVISION

## ALBION ROVERS: CLIFTONHILL STADIUM

The following routes can be used to reach Cliftonhill Stadium:
**BUSES:** The ground is conveniently situated on the main Glasgow-Airdrie bus route and there is a stop near the ground. Local buses serving most areas of Coatbridge and Airdrie pass by the stadium every few minutes.
**TRAINS:** The nearest railway station is Coatdyke on the Glasgow-Airdrie line and the ground is a ten minute walk from there. The frequency of service is 15 minutes.

**CARS:** Vehicles may park in Hillcrest Avenue, Albion Street and East Stewart Street, which are all adjacent to the ground.
**CAPACITY:** 1,238; Seated 538, Standing 700
**PITCH DIMENSIONS:** 110 yds x 72 yds (101 x 66m)
**FACILITIES FOR DISABLED SUPPORTERS:**
Access from East Stewart Street with toilet facilities and space for wheelchairs, cars etc. Advanced contact with club advised – this area is uncovered.

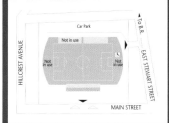

## ARBROATH: GAYFIELD PARK

The following routes may be used to reach Gayfield Park:
**BUSES:** Arbroath is on the main route from both Glasgow and Edinburgh to Aberdeen. Buses from these three cities, plus Stirling, Dundee and Perth all stop at Arbroath Bus Station at hourly intervals. There is also a local service between Dundee-Arbroath and Montrose and this service is half hourly until 7.00 p.m. Between 7.00 p.m. and 10.45 p.m. the service is hourly. The bus station is 10 minutes walk from the ground.
**TRAINS:** Abroath is on the Inter-City 125 route from London to Aberdeen and there are frequent local services between

Arbroath, Dundee and Edinburgh. Trains also travel north from Glasgow, Stirling and Perth. The station is a 15 minute walk from the ground.
**CARS:** There is free parking for 500 cars just next to the ground in Queen's Drive.
**CAPACITY:** 4,165; Seated 860, Standing 3,305
**PITCH DIMENSIONS:** 115 yds x 71 yds (105 x 65m)
**FACILITIES FOR DISABLED SUPPORTERS:**
Enclosure at east and west ends of Stand with wide steps to take a wheelchair. Toilet facilities are also available.

## BERWICK RANGERS: SHIELFIELD PARK

Shielfield Park can be reached by the following routes:
The ground is approximately 1 1/2 miles south of Berwick town centre and is situated in Shielfield Terrace, Tweedmouth (signposted).
**BUSES:** The local bus route from the town centre is the Prior Park service and the nearest stop is Shielfield Terrace, only yards from the ground.
**TRAINS:** The railway station is Berwick, which is situated on the East Coast line and a frequent service operates at various stages during the day. The ground is 1 1/2 miles (approx.) from

the station and a taxi service operates from there or alternatively, fans can take the local bus service as detailed.
**CARS:** There is a large car park at the rear of the ground.

**CAPACITY:** 4,131; Seated 1,366, Standing 2,765
**PITCH DIMENSIONS:** 110 yds x 70 yds (101 x 64m)
**FACILITIES FOR DISABLED SUPPORTERS:**
Supporters should enter via gate adjacent to ground turnstiles (see ground plan) or via official entrance.

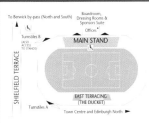

## COWDENBEATH: CENTRAL PARK

You can get to Central Park by the following routes:
**BUSES:** A limited Edinburgh-Cowdenbeath service stops just outside the ground on matchdays and a frequent service of Dunfermline-Ballingry buses also stop outside the ground, as does the Edinburgh-Glenrothes service.
**TRAINS:** There is a regular service of trains from Edinburgh and Glasgow (via Edinburgh) which call at Cowdenbeath and the station is only 400 yards from the ground.
**CARS:** Car parking facilities are available in the public car park

adjacent to the ground for 190 cars. There are also another 300 spaces at the Stenhouse Street car park, which is 200 yards from the ground.

**CAPACITY:** 4,370; Seated 1,431, Standing 2,939
**PITCH DIMENSIONS:** 107 yds x 65 yds (98 x 59m)
**FACILITIES FOR DISABLED SUPPORTERS:**
Direct access from car park into designated area within ground. Toilet and catering facilities also provided.

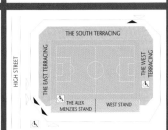

## EAST FIFE: FIRST 2 FINANCE BAYVIEW STADIUM

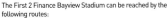

The First 2 Finance Bayview Stadium can be reached by the following routes:
**BUSES:** A regular service from Kirkcaldy to Leven passes close to the ground, as does the Leven to Dunfermline service. The Leven bus terminus is approximately 2/3 mile from the ground (5 minutes walk).
**TRAINS:** The nearest railway station is Kirkcaldy (8 miles away), and fans will have to catch an inter-linking bus service from

just outside the station to the ground.
**CARS:** There are Car Parking facilities available for both Home and Away fans at the ground.
**CAPACITY:** 1,992 (All Seated)
**PITCH DIMENSIONS:** 115 yds x 75 yds (105 x 69m)
**FACILITIES FOR DISABLED SUPPORTERS:**
Area available at both Home & Away Sections of the Stand. Spaces for 12 wheelchairs

## EAST STIRLINGSHIRE: FIRS PARK

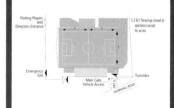

The following routes may be used to reach Firs Park:
**BUSES:** All buses running from the town centre pass close by the ground. The Grangemouth via Burnbank Road and Tamfourhill via Kennard Street services both stop almost outside the ground.
**TRAINS:** Passengers should alight at Grahamston Station and the ground is then five minutes walk.

**CARS:** Car parking is available in the adjacent side streets. There are also spaces available in the car park adjacent to the major stores around the ground.
**CAPACITY:** 781; Seated 245, Standing 536
**PITCH DIMENSIONS:** 109 yds x 71 yds (100x 65m)
**FACILITIES FOR DISABLED SUPPORTERS:**
By prior arrangement with Secretary.

## ELGIN CITY: BOROUGH BRIGGS

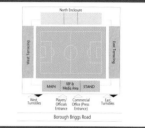

Borough Briggs can be reached by the following routes:
**BUSES:** Elgin Bus Station is situated in the town centre, which is only half a mile from Borough Briggs. Regular connections to and from Aberdeen and Inverness.
**TRAINS:** Elgin Railway Station is situated approximately one mile south of the stadium. Regular connections to and from Aberdeen and Inverness.
**CARS:** Elgin is situated on the A96, 38 miles east of Inverness

and 67 miles west of Aberdeen. From the south, leave A9 at Aviemore and take the A95 as far as Craigellachie then take A941 to Elgin.

**CAPACITY:** 4,962; Seated 480, Standing 4,482
**PITCH DIMENSIONS:** 111 yds x 72 yds (101 x 66m)
**FACILITIES FOR DISABLED SUPPORTERS:**
An area is designated in the south east enclosure.

## MONTROSE: LINKS PARK

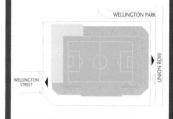

Links Park can be reached by the following routes:
**BUSES:** An hourly service of buses from Aberdeen and Dundee stop in the town centre and it is a 15 minute walk from here to the ground.
**TRAINS:** Montrose is on the Inter-City 125 route from London to Aberdeen and also on the Glasgow-Aberdeen route. There is a regular service and the station is about 15 minutes walk from the ground.

**CARS:** Car parking is available in the car park at the ground and there are numerous side streets all round the park which can be used if necessary.
**CAPACITY:** 3,292; Seated 1,334, Standing 1,958
**PITCH DIMENSIONS:** 113 yds x 70 yds (103 x 64m)
**FACILITIES FOR DISABLED SUPPORTERS:**
Area set aside for wheelchairs and designated area in new stand.

## QUEEN'S PARK FC: THE NATIONAL STADIUM, HAMPDEN PARK

The following routes may be used to reach The National Stadium, Hampden Park:
**BUSES:** Services to approach Mount Florida end of Stadium: From City Centre: 5, 5A, 5B, M5, M14, 31, 37, 66, 66A, 66B, 66C; From Govan Cross; 34; From Drumchapel: 96, 97, Circular Service: 89, 90; G.C.T. Service: 1; Services to approach King's Park end of Stadium; From City Centre: 12, 12A, 74; Circular Service: 89, 90; G.C.T. Service: 19.
**TRAINS:** There are two stations within five minutes walk of the ground. Mount Florida Station, on the Cathcart Circle, and King's Park Station. A 15 minute service runs from Glasgow Central.

**CARS:** Car and Coach parking facilities are available in the car park in Letherby Drive, which is capable of holding 200 vehicles. Side streets can also be used. Free car parking at all Queen's Park matches.
**CAPACITY:** 52,025 (All Seated)
**PITCH DIMENSIONS:** 115 yds x 75 yds (105 x 68m)
**FACILITIES FOR DISABLED SUPPORTERS:**
Disabled facilities are situated in the BT Scotland Stand as follows: West Front (44 places & 44 helpers), West Section A (21 places & 21 helpers), Ambulant/Blind (55 places), East Front (44 places & 44 helpers), East Section G (21 places & 21 helpers), Ambulant/Blind (55 places)

## STENHOUSEMUIR: OCHILVIEW PARK

Ochilview Park can be reached by the following routes:
**BUSES:** There are regular bus services from Falkirk.
**TRAINS:** The nearest station is Larbert, which is about 1 mile away from the ground.
**CARS:** There is a large car park on the north side of the ground.

**CAPACITY:** 3,776; Seated 626, Standing 3,150
**PITCH DIMENSIONS:** 110 yds x 72 yds (101 x 66m)
**FACILITIES FOR DISABLED SUPPORTERS:**
Accommodation for disabled in Norway Stand. Toilet facilities also provided.

## JULY

Swedish defender Johan Mjallby leaves Celtic to sign for Spanish club Levante on a free transfer.

Kilmarnock sign goalkeeper Alan Combe on a free transfer from Bradford City.

Rangers sign Spanish striker Nacho Novo from Dundee for £450,000.

Billy Reid, formerly assistant to Alan Kernaghan, is appointed as the new manager of Clyde.

Crystal Palace sign Argentinian goalkeeper Julian Speroni from Dundee for £750,000.

Spanish midfielder Mikel Arteta leaves Rangers to return to his homeland and sign for Real Sociedad in a £2.6 million deal.

Tony Mowbray's reign as Hibernian manager gets off to a disappointing start when the Easter Road club lose 2-1 on aggregate to Lithuanian side Vetra Vilnius in the UEFA Intertoto Cup.

Hearts sign Scotland midfielder Michael Stewart on a season long loan from Manchester United.

Celtic pay Wolverhampton Wanderers a fee of £1.5 million to sign Senegalese international striker Henri Camara on a season long loan.

**Other transfers in July include:** Goran Stanik (Raith Rovers to Livingston), David Rowson (Partick Thistle to Northampton Town), Liam Miller (Celtic to Manchester United), David McNiven (Leigh RMI to Queen of the South), Roland Edge (Hibernian to Hull City), John Sutton (Millwall to Dundee), Gary McSwegan (Kilmarnock to Ross County), Stephen McConalogue (Clyde to St. Johnstone), Steven MacLean (Rangers to Sheffield Wednesday), Gary Wales (Gillingham to Kilmarnock), Michael Moore (Stranraer to St. Johnstone), Peter Leven (Rangers to Kilmarnock), Jim Paterson (Dundee United to Motherwell), Iain Anderson (Grimsby Town to Dundee), Jason Lee (Falkirk to Boston United), Charlie Miller (Dundee United to Brann Bergen), Derek Lilley (Boston United to Livingston), Matthew Doherty (Carlisle United to Hearts), Neil Barrett (Portsmouth to Dundee), Jordan Tait (Ayr United to St. Johnstone), Pedro Moutinho (Penafiel to Falkirk), David Murphy (Middlesbrough to Hibernian), Leigh Hinds (Aberdeen to Partick Thistle).

## AUGUST

Rangers midfielder Alex Rae is handed a five match suspension by UEFA for kicking CSKA Moscow player Serghei Dadu in the head during the first leg of the Ibrox club's Champions League Third Qualifying Round tie.

Kenny Brannigan resigns as Head Coach of Queen's Park following a touchline fracas with a supporter during a match at Elgin City.

Rangers sign French full-back Gregory Vignal on a season long loan from Liverpool.

Aberdeen sign English striker Noel Whelan on a free transfer from Derby County.

Kilmarnock sign former Scotland winger Allan Johnston on a free transfer from Middlesbrough.

Scotland's Under-21 side lose 4-2 to Hungary in a friendly match in Dunaferr.

Scotland lose 3-0 to Hungary at Hampden in a friendly international, their biggest home defeat since 1973. Steve Kirk resigns as manager of Arbroath after the club suffer a fifth consecutive defeat of the season in a 5-0 loss to Forfar Athletic.

Sunderland sign defender Neil Collins from Dumbarton for £25,000.

Rangers fail to reach the Group Stage of the Champions League, losing 3-2 on aggregate to CSKA Moscow in the Third Qualifying Round after a 1-1 draw with the Russian Champions at Ibrox.

Dunfermline Athletic are eliminated from the UEFA Cup in the Second Qualifying Round, losing 4-3 on aggregate to Icelandic side Hafnarfjordur following a 2-1 defeat in the Second Leg of the tie at McDiarmid Park. The visitors declined to play the match on the Fife club's artificial playing pitch at East End Park.

Campbell Money is dismissed as manager of Ayr United after they lose four of their first five matches of the season. He is immediately replaced by Mark Shanks.

Billy Stark is named as the new Head Coach of Queen's Park.

Celtic sign Brazilian international midfielder Juninho from Middlesbrough on a free transfer.

**Other transfers in August include:** Martin Hardie (Kilmarnock to Ayr United), Chris Armstrong (Rochdale to Queen of the South), Eric Joly (Mons to Kilmarnock), Bryan Prunty (Aberdeen to Inverness Caledonian Thistle), Brian Gilfillan (Cowdenbeath to Gretna), Grant Brebner (Hibernian to Dundee United), Eddie Annand (St. Mirren to Dumbarton), Ed Malone (St. Johnstone to Clyde), Charlie Adam (Rangers to Ross County).

## SEPTEMBER

David Murray resumes the position of Rangers Chairman, returning to the job two years after stepping back to hand the reins at Ibrox to John McClelland.

Scotland's Under-21 side slip to a 3-1 defeat against their Spanish counterparts in a friendly international in Alcoi.

Scotland's friendly international against Spain in Valencia is abandoned after 59 minutes because of an electrical storm resulting in floodlight failure with the teams level at 1-1. FIFA later rule the fixture will stand as an official result.

Garry O'Connor scores for Scotland's Under-21's as they are held 1-1 by Slovenia in their opening European Under-21 Championship qualifying match at McDiarmid Park.

Scotland's bid to qualify for the 2006 World Cup Finals gets off to a disappointing start with an uninspiring 0-0 draw with Slovenia at Hampden.

John McCormack is dismissed as manager of Morton with the club fourth in the Second Division, six points behind the leaders.

Harry Cairney is named as the new manager of Arbroath.

Claude Anelka is relieved of his duties as Head Coach of Raith Rovers after the First Division side collect just one point from their first eight League games of the season.

Celtic begin their campaign in the Group Stage of the Champions League with successive 3-1 defeats, at home to Barcelona and away to AC Milan.

Rangers and Hearts both defeat Portuguese opposition to reach the inaugural Group Stage of the revamped UEFA Cup. Alex McLeish's side defeat Maritimo in a penalty shoot-out after the Second Leg of their First Round tie at Ibrox while Hearts defeat Sporting Braga 5-3 on aggregate.

Hearts Chief Executive, Chris Robinson, agrees to sell his 19.6 per cent stake in the club to Lithuanian businessman Vladimir Romanov.

**September transfers include:** Thomas Butler (Sunderland to Dunfermline Athletic), Jean-Louis Valois (Clyde to Burnley), Chris McGroarty (St. Mirren to Dumbarton), David Craig (Ayr United to Queen of the South), Gary Liggett (Glenavon to Falkirk).

## OCTOBER

Keith Wright is dismissed as manager of Cowdenbeath with the club struggling near the foot of the Third Division.

Paul Smith is dismissed as manager of Berwick Rangers after seven years in charge of the Shielfield Park club.

Scotland's Under-21 side lose 2-0 to Norway in a European Under-21 Championship qualifier at Broadwood.

Scotland's World Cup qualifying hopes suffer a serious blow when they lose 1-0 to Norway at Hampden.

Gordon Dalziel is named as the new manager of Raith Rovers.

Dave Baikie, the former Arbroath manager, leaves Tayport Juniors to become the new manager of Cowdenbeath.

A goalless draw with Moldova in Chisinau leaves Scotland's Under-21 side at the bottom of their European Under-21 Championship qualifying group after three games.

Scotland's miserable start to their World Cup qualifying campaign continues with a dismal 1-1 draw against Moldova in Chisinau which sparks angry protests from supporters against Head Coach, Berti Vogts. Steven Thompson scores Scotland's goal.

Sandy Clark, the former Partick Thistle, Hearts, Hamilton Academical and St. Johnstone manager, is named as the new boss of Berwick Rangers.

Former Celtic, Nottingham Forest, Dundee United and Scotland midfielder Jim McInally is named as the new manager of Morton.

JULY - Celtic pay Wolverhampton Wanderers a fee of £1.5 million to sign Senegalese international striker Henri Camara on a season long loan.

AUGUST - Kilmarnock sign former Scotland winger Allan Johnston on a free transfer from Middlesbrough.

SEPTEMBER - David Murray resumes the position of Rangers Chairman, returning to the position two years after stepping down and handing the reins at Ibrox to John McClelland.

OCTOBER - Jim McInally is named as the new manager of Morton.

NOVEMBER - Berti Vogts finally bows to pressure by resigning as manager of Scotland.

DECEMBER - Walter Smith is named as the new manager of Scotland.

JANUARY - Scotland captain Barry Ferguson returns to Rangers from Blackburn Rovers.

Celtic slump to a third consecutive defeat in their Champions League group, losing 3-0 to Shakhtar Donetsk in Ukraine.

Rangers begin their UEFA Cup Group Stage campaign with a facile 5-0 win over Amica Wronki in Poland while Hearts start with a 3-0 defeat to Feyenoord in Holland.

Craig Levein resigns as Head Coach of Hearts to become the new manager of Leicester City.

## NOVEMBER

Berti Vogts finally bows to pressure by resigning as manager of Scotland after two and a half years in the job.

John Robertson, Hearts record goalscorer, resigns as manager of Inverness Caledonian Thistle to return to Tynecastle to replace Craig Levein as the club's new Head Coach.

Falkirk win The Bell's Cup Final at McDiarmid Park when they come from behind to defeat Ross County 2-1.

Scotland's Under-21 side lose 2-1 to Sweden in a friendly international at Falkirk.

Tommy Burns is caretaker manager of Scotland as they lose 4-1 to Sweden in a friendly international at Easter Road. Celtic defeat Shakhtar Donetsk 1-0 at Parkhead then take another point in the Group Stage of the Champions League with a creditable 1-1 draw against Barcelona in the Nou Camp.

Hearts lose 1-0 at Murrayfield to German club Schalke 04 but defeat Basel 2-1 in Switzerland to maintain their hopes of progress from the Group Stage of the UEFA Cup. Rangers record a second consecutive win in their UEFA Cup group when they defeat Grazer of Austria 3-0 at Ibrox.

Allan Preston is sacked as manager of Livingston, along with his assistant Alan Kernaghan, after a seventh consecutive defeat leaves the West Lothian club at the bottom of the SPL.

Craig Brewster is allowed to leave Dunfermline Athletic to become the new Player/Manager of Inverness Caledonian Thistle.

Ray Stewart resigns as manager of Forfar Athletic following a 5-1 defeat at home to Montrose in the First Round of the Tennent's Scottish Cup.

Former Rangers and Scotland captain Richard Gough is named as the new manager of Livingston.

## DECEMBER

Walter Smith is named as the new manager of Scotland. The former Rangers and Everton boss agrees a four year contract with the SFA.

Brian Fairley resigns as manager of Dumbarton to take charge of Forfar Athletic. He is immediately replaced at Boghead by former Queen's Park coach Paul Martin.

Scotland's Future international team lose 3-0 to Germany in a Future Cup match in Mannheim.

Celtic fail to secure a place in the UEFA Cup when they finish bottom of their Champions League group after a 0-0 draw with AC Milan at Parkhead.

Rangers are unable to clinch one of the three qualifying places in their five team UEFA Cup group after losing their final two matches, 1-0 to AZ Alkmaar in Holland and then 2-0 to French club Auxerre at Ibrox.

Hearts finish bottom of their UEFA Cup group after losing their final fixture 1-0 to Ferencvaros at Murrayfield.

Derek Whyte and Gerry Britton are dismissed as co-managers of Partick Thistle after a 1-0 home defeat to Hamilton Academical leaves the Firhill club second bottom of the Bell's First Division. Former manager John Lambie is installed as caretaker boss.

**December transfers include:** Craig Nelson (St. Johnstone to Brechin City), Chris Templeman (Brechin City to Morton), Stewart Kean (Ayr United to St. Mirren), Theodor Bjarnason (KR Reykjavik to Celtic), Kjarten Finnbogason (KR Reykjavik to Celtic), Bojan Djordjic (Manchester United to Rangers).

## JANUARY

Rangers sell French international defender Jean-Alain Boumsong to Newcastle United for £8 million just six months after signing the player from Auxerre on a Bosman free transfer.

Dick Campbell resigns as manager of Brechin City to become the new boss of

FEBRUARY - Terry Butcher celebrates as Motherwell claim a place in The CIS Insurance Cup Final for the first time in 50 years.

MARCH - Rangers win The CIS Insurance Cup for the 24th time.

Partick Thistle. His twin brother Ian replaces him in charge at Glebe Park.

Leicester City manager Craig Levein signs Dutch striker Mark de Vries and Republic of Ireland defender Alan Maybury from his former club Hearts. Dundee United sign Scotland striker Stevie Crawford from Plymouth Argyle for £80,000.

Kevin McAllister resigns as Albion Rovers manager after 15 games without a win. Youth Development Coach, Jimmy Lindsay, is placed in temporary charge at Cliftonhill.

Hearts sign striker Lee Miller on loan from Bristol City for the rest of the season.

Greek international defender Sotirios Kyrgiakos joins Rangers on loan from Panathinaikos for the rest of the season with the option of a further two year permanent transfer.

Celtic sign Welsh international striker Craig Bellamy on loan from Newcastle United for the rest of the season.

Scotland captain Barry Ferguson returns to Rangers from Blackburn Rovers for £4.5 million, 18 months after he left Ibrox for Ewood Park in a £7.5 million deal.

Wolverhampton Wanderers striker Henri Camara's loan deal at Celtic is terminated as he joins Southampton in a similar arrangement for the rest of the season.

Rangers sign Dutch goalkeeper Ronald Waterreus from Manchester City for £100,000 to replace Stefan Klos, who will miss the rest of the season after suffering a knee ligament injury in training.

**Other January transfers include:** Stuart Callaghan (Alloa Athletic to Brechin City), Paul McManus (Albion Rovers to Stranraer), Steve Tosh (Aberdeen to Gretna), Francisco Rivas (Raith Rovers to Hamilton Academical), David Graham (Stranraer to Gretna), Dene Shields (Cowdenbeath to Gretna), Jamie Winter (Leeds United to Aberdeen), Lars Hirschfeld (Dundee United to Leicester City), Greg Strong (Boston United to Livingston), Ivan Sproule (Institute to Hibernian), Colin Murdock (Hibernian to Crewe Alexandra), Stuart Lovell (Livingston to Queen of the South), Amadou Konte (Cambridge United to Hibernian), Chris Hogg (Ipswich Town to Hibernian), Eric Deloumeaux (Coventry City to Livingston), Steven Boyack (Livingston to Boston United).

## FEBRUARY

Motherwell claim a place in The CIS Insurance Cup Final for the first time in 50 years when they defeat Hearts 3-2 after extra-time in a thrilling Semi-Final at Easter Road.

Rangers secure the right to face Motherwell in The CIS Insurance Cup Final when they sweep aside Dundee United 7-1 in the second Semi-Final at Hampden.

Scotland's Under-21 side lose 2-1 to Northern Ireland in a friendly international in Belfast.

Hearts pull out of their proposed sale of Tynecastle Stadium to property developers CALA Homes after accepting assurances from prospective new owner Vladimir Romanov that he can secure the financial future of the club.

Rangers record their first victory over Celtic at Parkhead under Alex McLeish's management, the 2-0 win putting them three points clear at the top of the SPL table.

Ian Durrant leaves his position as first team coach at Kilmarnock to return to his former club Rangers as a youth team coach.

## MARCH

Mark Shanks resigns as manager of Ayr United with the club placed fifth in the Bell's Second Division. Coaches Robert Connor, Robert Reilly and Jim Dempsey take temporary charge at Somerset Park.

Gretna clinch promotion from the Bell's Third Division with nine games to spare when a Steve Tosh goal earns them a 1-0 win at Cowdenbeath.

Peterhead's 2-2 draw at Elgin City secures the second promotion place from the Bell's Third Division with eight games still remaining.

Raith Rovers are relegated from the Bell's First Division with seven games of the season still to go when they lose 2-1 at home to St. Johnstone.

Ian McCall is dismissed as manager of Dundee United after a 3-0 defeat at Kilmarnock sees the Tannadice club slip to the bottom of the Bank of Scotland Premierleague. His assistant Gordon Chisholm is placed in temporary charge.

Rangers win The CIS Insurance Cup for the 24th time when they defeat Motherwell 5-1 in the Final at Hampden.

Scotland's Under-21 side lose 2-0 to Italy in Pavia in a European Under-21 Championship qualifying match.

Walter Smith's first game in charge of Scotland ends in a 2 0 defeat to Italy in a World Cup qualifying match in Milan.

**March transfers include:** Michael Moore (St. Johnstone to Stranraer), Graeme Brown (Ayr United to Alloa Athletic).

## APRIL

John Connolly is dismissed as manager of St. Johnstone after a 3-0 defeat at Falkirk leaves the club in seventh place in the Bell's First Division. Jim Weir is placed in temporary charge at McDiarmid Park.

Falkirk secure the Bell's First Division title and promotion to the Bank of Scotland Premierleague when a 1-0 home win over Ross County leaves them 16 points clear of nearest rivals Clyde with four games remaining.

Gretna clinch the Bell's Third Division title with a 7-0 defeat of Stenhousemuir at Raydale Park.

Dundee United come from behind to defeat Hibernian 2-1 in the first Tennent's Scottish Cup Semi-Final at Hampden.

Celtic secure their place in the Tennent's Scottish Cup Final when they defeat Hearts 2-1 at Hampden in the second Semi-Final.

Owen Coyle leaves Airdrie United to become the new Player/Manager of St. Johnstone.

Brechin City clinch promotion from the Bell's Second Division with three games remaining when they defeat Ayr United 3-0 at Glebe Park.

Tony Smith resigns as co-manager of Stenhousemuir, leaving Des McKeown in sole charge at Ochilview.

Partick Thistle suffer a second successive relegation, dropping out of the Bell's First Division with two games of the campaign remaining despite a 1-0 home win over Clyde.

Brechin City clinch the Bell's Second Division title with a 1-1 draw at home to Berwick Rangers who are relegated to the Third Division as a result.

Billy Reid resigns as manager of Clyde after rejecting the offer of a new contract at Broadwood. Stuart Balmer is placed in temporary charge of the first team.

Stranraer secure promotion from the Bell's Second Division on the penultimate day of the campaign with a 1-1 draw at home to nearest rivals Morton who needed a victory to retain their hopes of going up in their place.

Arbroath are relegated from the Bell's Second Division when they lose 3-0 to Dumbarton at the Strathclyde Homes Stadium, leaving Ayr United safe despite a 2-1 defeat at Berwick.

## MAY

David Hay is dismissed as manager of Dunfermline Athletic after a 2-0 defeat at Livingston see the club slip to the bottom of the Bank of Scotland Premierleague with three games of the campaign remaining. Director of Football, Jim Leishman, is placed in temporary charge at East End Park.

Robert Connor is named new manager of Ayr United on a permanent basis.

John Robertson resigns as Head Coach of Hearts after just seven months in the job, rejecting the offer of a new role as Assistant Head Coach

from the club. Coach John McGlynn and captain Steven Pressley are placed in temporary charge at Tynecastle.

Sandy Clark resigns as manager of relegated Berwick Rangers after just seven months in charge at Shielfield Park to take up a coaching position with Aberdeen.

Former St. Mirren Manager, John Coughlin, is named as the new boss of Berwick Rangers.

Jim Leishman is named new Manager of Dunfermline Athletic on a permanent basis after all but securing their Bank of Scotland Premierleague safety with two victories as caretaker boss.

Livingston announce that Richard Gough will resign his position as Manager following the last game of the season. Former Scotland and Celtic captain Paul Lambert will take charge at Almondvale at the beginning of June.

Clyde appoint former Rangers and England defender Graham Roberts as their new Manager with former Celtic winger Joe Miller as his assistant.

Dundee are relegated from the Bank of Scotland Premierleague following a 1-1 draw at Livingston in their final match of the campaign.

Rangers clinch the Bank of Scotland Premierleague title in dramatic fashion on the final day of the campaign. Their 1-0 win over Hibernian at Easter Road sees them finish one point ahead of Celtic who concede two late goals to lose 2-1 to Motherwell at Fir Park.

Gordon Chisholm is named Dundee United Manager on a permanent basis in the wake of the Tannadice club avoiding relegation from the Bank of Scotland Premierleague.

Martin O'Neill reveals he will resign as Celtic manager at the end of the month in order to spend more time with his wife as she battles serious illness.

Celtic announce that Gordon Strachan will replace Martin O'Neill as manager from 1st June.

The Scottish Football League's Annual General Meeting sees the introduction of play-offs to decide some promotion and relegation issues with effect from season 2005/06.

Celtic win the Tennent's Scottish Cup for the 33rd time with a 1-0 win over Dundee United in the Final at Hampden.

## JUNE

Billy Reid is named as the new manager of Hamilton Academical, replacing Allan Maitland who was unable to take the job on a full-time basis.

Dundee United sign striker Lee Miller from Bristol City for £225,000.

Scotland's Under-21 side can only draw 0-0 with Moldova at Firhill in a disappointing European Under-21 Championship qualifier.

Scotland record the first victory of their World Cup qualifying campaign when they defeat Moldova 2-0 at Hampden with goals from Christian Dailly and James McFadden.

Scotland goalkeeper, Robert Douglas, leaves Celtic to sign for Leicester City on a free transfer.

Scotland's Under-21 side lose 3-2 to Belarus in Minsk in their European Under-21 Championship qualifier.

Scotland pick up another World Cup qualifying point with a goalless draw against Belarus in Minsk.

Alex Smith is dismissed as manager of Ross County after the club change their mind on handing him a new contract.

Hibernian captain Ian Murray leaves Easter Road to join Rangers on a free transfer.

Rangers sign French midfielder Brahim Hemdani on a free transfer from Marseille.

Celtic captain Jackie McNamara leaves the Parkhead club after failing to agree a new contract and signs for Wolverhampton Wanderers on a free transfer.

Albion Rovers name former player Jim Chapman as their new manager.

Livingston are fined £15,000 by The Scottish Premier League for signing Moroccan international Hassan Kachloul on amateur status when they would have been entitled to sign him as a professional.

Mohamed Camara becomes Gordon Strachan's first signing for Celtic when the Guinean international defender joins the Parkhead club from Burnley on a free transfer.

John Robertson is named as the new manager of Ross County and appoints Donald Park as his assistant.

Hibernian sign Scotland international midfielder Michael Stewart on a free transfer from Manchester United.

George Burley is named as the new manager of Hearts. The former Scotland defender signs a two year contract at Tynecastle.

**Other June transfers include:**
Momo Sylla (Celtic to Leicester City), Ian Ross (Alloa Athletic to Stranraer), Paul McManus (Stranraer to Raith Rovers), Graeme Smith (Rangers to Motherwell), Fraser Wright (Stranraer to Kilmarnock), Tony Bullock (Dundee United to Gillingham), Steven Thomson (Peterborough United to Falkirk), Steven O'Donnell (Boston United to Clyde), Simon Mensing (Clyde to St. Johnstone), Billy Brawley (Selkirk to Clyde), Stephen Dobbie (Hibernian to St. Johnstone).

**STEPHEN HALLIDAY**
(The Scotsman)

APRIL - Owen Coyle leaves Airdrie United to become the new Manager of St. Johnstone.

MAY - Alex McLeish celebrates Rangers clinching the Bank of Scotland Premierleague title in dramatic fashion on the final day of the campaign.

MAY - Martin O'Neill bows out as Celtic manager after the Parkhead club win the Scottish Cup for the 33rd time with a 1-0 win over Dundee United in the Final at Hampden.

JUNE - Christian Dailly celebrates his goal for Scotland against Moldova in the World Cup qualifying tie at Hampden.

Rangers -
Bank of Scotland Scottish Premierleague
Champions 2004.05

Falkirk -
Bell's SFL First Division Champions 2004.05

Brechin City -
Bell's SFL Second Division Champions 2004.05

Gretna -
Bell's SFL Third Division Champions 2004.05

# SCOTTISH PREMIER LEAGUE & SCOTTISH FOOTBALL LEAGUE FINAL TABLES 2004.05

## BANK OF SCOTLAND PREMIERLEAGUE

| | P | W | D | L | F | A | PTS |
|---|---|---|---|---|---|---|---|
| RANGERS | 38 | 29 | 6 | 3 | 78 | 22 | 93 |
| CELTIC | 38 | 30 | 2 | 6 | 85 | 35 | 92 |
| HIBERNIAN | 38 | 18 | 7 | 13 | 64 | 57 | 61 |
| ABERDEEN | 38 | 18 | 7 | 13 | 44 | 39 | 61 |
| HEARTS | 38 | 13 | 11 | 14 | 43 | 41 | 50 |
| MOTHERWELL | 38 | 13 | 9 | 16 | 46 | 49 | 48 |
| KILMARNOCK | 38 | 15 | 4 | 19 | 49 | 55 | 49 |
| INVERNESS CALEDONIAN THISTLE | 38 | 11 | 11 | 16 | 41 | 47 | 44 |
| DUNDEE UNITED | 38 | 8 | 12 | 18 | 41 | 59 | 36 |
| LIVINGSTON | 38 | 9 | 8 | 21 | 34 | 61 | 35 |
| DUNFERMLINE ATHLETIC | 38 | 8 | 10 | 20 | 34 | 60 | 34 |
| DUNDEE | 38 | 8 | 9 | 21 | 37 | 71 | 33 |

## BELL'S SFL FIRST DIVISION

| | P | W | D | L | F | A | PTS |
|---|---|---|---|---|---|---|---|
| FALKIRK | 36 | 22 | 9 | 5 | 66 | 30 | 75 |
| ST. MIRREN | 36 | 15 | 15 | 6 | 41 | 23 | 60 |
| CLYDE | 36 | 16 | 12 | 8 | 35 | 29 | 60 |
| QUEEN OF THE SOUTH | 36 | 14 | 9 | 13 | 36 | 38 | 51 |
| AIRDRIE UNITED | 36 | 14 | 8 | 14 | 44 | 48 | 50 |
| ROSS COUNTY | 36 | 13 | 8 | 15 | 40 | 37 | 47 |
| HAMILTON ACADEMICAL | 36 | 12 | 11 | 13 | 35 | 36 | 47 |
| ST. JOHNSTONE | 36 | 12 | 10 | 14 | 38 | 39 | 46 |
| PARTICK THISTLE | 36 | 10 | 9 | 17 | 38 | 52 | 39 |
| RAITH ROVERS | 36 | 3 | 7 | 26 | 26 | 67 | 16 |

## BELL'S SFL SECOND DIVISION

| | P | W | D | L | F | A | PTS |
|---|---|---|---|---|---|---|---|
| BRECHIN CITY | 36 | 22 | 6 | 8 | 81 | 43 | 72 |
| STRANRAER | 36 | 18 | 9 | 9 | 48 | 41 | 63 |
| MORTON | 36 | 18 | 8 | 10 | 60 | 37 | 62 |
| STIRLING ALBION | 36 | 14 | 9 | 13 | 56 | 55 | 51 |
| FORFAR ATHLETIC | 36 | 13 | 8 | 15 | 51 | 45 | 47 |
| ALLOA ATHLETIC | 36 | 12 | 10 | 14 | 66 | 68 | 46 |
| DUMBARTON | 36 | 11 | 9 | 16 | 43 | 53 | 42 |
| AYR UNITED | 36 | 11 | 9 | 16 | 39 | 54 | 42 |
| ARBROATH | 36 | 10 | 8 | 18 | 49 | 73 | 38 |
| BERWICK RANGERS | 36 | 8 | 10 | 18 | 40 | 64 | 34 |

## BELL'S SFL THIRD DIVISION

| | P | W | D | L | F | A | PTS |
|---|---|---|---|---|---|---|---|
| GRETNA | 36 | 32 | 2 | 2 | 130 | 29 | 98 |
| PETERHEAD | 36 | 23 | 9 | 4 | 81 | 38 | 78 |
| COWDENBEATH | 36 | 14 | 9 | 13 | 54 | 61 | 51 |
| QUEEN'S PARK | 36 | 13 | 9 | 14 | 51 | 50 | 48 |
| MONTROSE | 36 | 13 | 7 | 16 | 47 | 53 | 46 |
| ELGIN CITY | 36 | 12 | 7 | 17 | 39 | 61 | 43 |
| STENHOUSEMUIR | 36 | 10 | 12 | 14 | 58 | 58 | 42 |
| EAST FIFE | 36 | 10 | 8 | 18 | 40 | 56 | 38 |
| ALBION ROVERS | 36 | 8 | 10 | 18 | 40 | 78 | 34 |
| EAST STIRLINGSHIRE | 36 | 5 | 7 | 24 | 32 | 88 | 22 |

# SCOTTISH PREMIER LEAGUE & SCOTTISH FOOTBALL LEAGUE RESERVE & YOUTH LEAGUES - **FINAL TABLES 2004.05**

## THE SCOTTISH PREMIER LEAGUE RESERVE LEAGUE

| | P | W | D | L | F | A | PTS |
|---|---|---|---|---|---|---|---|
| CELTIC | 22 | 15 | 5 | 2 | 46 | 13 | 50 |
| LIVINGSTON | 22 | 14 | 2 | 6 | 36 | 21 | 44 |
| RANGERS * | 21 | 9 | 8 | 4 | 38 | 25 | 35 |
| ABERDEEN | 22 | 10 | 5 | 7 | 24 | 21 | 35 |
| DUNFERMLINE ATHLETIC | 22 | 11 | 1 | 10 | 33 | 31 | 34 |
| KILMARNOCK | 22 | 10 | 3 | 9 | 30 | 42 | 33 |
| DUNDEE UNITED | 22 | 9 | 5 | 8 | 26 | 29 | 32 |
| HIBERNIAN | 22 | 8 | 6 | 8 | 36 | 40 | 30 |
| HEARTS | 22 | 7 | 6 | 9 | 31 | 31 | 27 |
| MOTHERWELL | 22 | 6 | 4 | 12 | 27 | 30 | 22 |
| INVERNESS CALEDONIAN THISTLE * | 21 | 5 | 5 | 11 | 31 | 41 | 20 |
| DUNDEE | 22 | 1 | 2 | 19 | 19 | 53 | 5 |

* Rangers v Inverness Cal. Th. fixture not played. Inverness Cal. Th. failed to fulfil fixture.

## SFL RESERVE LEAGUE EAST

| | P | W | D | L | F | A | PTS |
|---|---|---|---|---|---|---|---|
| ST. JOHNSTONE | 12 | 11 | 0 | 1 | 40 | 4 | 33 |
| COWDENBEATH | 12 | 6 | 0 | 6 | 24 | 26 | 18 |
| MONTROSE | 12 | 6 | 0 | 6 | 21 | 24 | 18 |
| FORFAR ATHLETIC | 12 | 5 | 2 | 5 | 28 | 26 | 17 |
| ARBROATH | 12 | 5 | 2 | 5 | 22 | 22 | 17 |
| EAST FIFE | 12 | 3 | 1 | 8 | 16 | 37 | 10 |
| RAITH ROVERS | 12 | 2 | 3 | 7 | 16 | 28 | 9 |

## SFL RESERVE LEAGUE WEST

| | P | W | D | L | F | A | PTS |
|---|---|---|---|---|---|---|---|
| FALKIRK | 20 | 13 | 4 | 3 | 53 | 18 | 43 |
| ST. MIRREN | 20 | 13 | 3 | 4 | 53 | 25 | 42 |
| GRETNA | 20 | 11 | 2 | 7 | 39 | 35 | 35 |
| MORTON | 20 | 10 | 4 | 6 | 44 | 41 | 34 |
| PARTICK THISTLE | 20 | 10 | 3 | 7 | 63 | 41 | 33 |
| AIRDRIE UNITED | 20 | 8 | 5 | 7 | 43 | 37 | 29 |
| AYR UNITED | 20 | 6 | 7 | 7 | 31 | 32 | 25 |
| STRANRAER | 20 | 6 | 5 | 9 | 37 | 53 | 23 |
| QUEEN'S PARK | 20 | 6 | 4 | 10 | 25 | 38 | 22 |
| STENHOUSEMUIR | 20 | 5 | 3 | 12 | 31 | 51 | 18 |
| ALBION ROVERS | 20 | 1 | 2 | 17 | 14 | 62 | 5 |

## THE SCOTTISH PREMIER LEAGUE UNDER 19 YOUTH DIVISION

| | P | W | D | L | F | A | PTS |
|---|---|---|---|---|---|---|---|
| CELTIC | 22 | 16 | 2 | 4 | 52 | 17 | 50 |
| MOTHERWELL | 22 | 15 | 3 | 4 | 37 | 11 | 48 |
| HEARTS | 22 | 15 | 2 | 5 | 45 | 22 | 47 |
| LIVINGSTON | 22 | 11 | 5 | 6 | 35 | 25 | 38 |
| RANGERS | 22 | 10 | 6 | 6 | 46 | 22 | 36 |
| DUNDEE | 22 | 11 | 2 | 9 | 43 | 45 | 35 |
| DUNDEE UNITED | 22 | 9 | 3 | 10 | 34 | 29 | 30 |
| HIBERNIAN | 22 | 8 | 4 | 10 | 29 | 38 | 28 |
| KILMARNOCK | 22 | 5 | 5 | 12 | 33 | 44 | 20 |
| ABERDEEN | 22 | 5 | 5 | 12 | 29 | 50 | 20 |
| DUNFERMLINE ATHLETIC | 22 | 3 | 5 | 14 | 20 | 44 | 14 |
| INVERNESS CALEDONIAN THISTLE | 22 | 2 | 2 | 18 | 23 | 79 | 8 |

## SFL UNDER 19 YOUTH DIVISION

| | P | W | D | L | F | A | PTS |
|---|---|---|---|---|---|---|---|
| ST. JOHNSTONE | 18 | 13 | 4 | 1 | 58 | 25 | 43 |
| ST. MIRREN | 18 | 13 | 1 | 4 | 62 | 29 | 40 |
| PARTICK THISTLE | 18 | 12 | 2 | 4 | 43 | 19 | 38 |
| HAMILTON ACADEMICAL | 18 | 12 | 1 | 5 | 39 | 31 | 37 |
| FALKIRK | 18 | 12 | 0 | 6 | 60 | 34 | 36 |
| ROSS COUNTY | 18 | 10 | 4 | 4 | 49 | 27 | 34 |
| CLYDE | 18 | 10 | 4 | 4 | 49 | 35 | 34 |
| STENHOUSEMUIR | 18 | 10 | 2 | 6 | 46 | 38 | 32 |
| COWDENBEATH | 18 | 8 | 3 | 7 | 38 | 38 | 27 |
| GRETNA | 18 | 7 | 5 | 6 | 34 | 29 | 26 |
| ALLOA ATHLETIC | 18 | 7 | 3 | 8 | 32 | 28 | 24 |
| QUEEN OF THE SOUTH | 18 | 6 | 4 | 8 | 31 | 35 | 22 |
| EAST FIFE | 18 | 6 | 2 | 10 | 22 | 33 | 20 |
| ARBROATH | 18 | 4 | 4 | 10 | 29 | 46 | 16 |
| QUEEN'S PARK | 18 | 4 | 4 | 10 | 29 | 50 | 16 |
| ALBION ROVERS | 18 | 3 | 3 | 12 | 20 | 48 | 12 |
| FORFAR ATHLETIC | 18 | 2 | 5 | 11 | 16 | 55 | 11 |
| ELGIN CITY | 18 | 1 | 5 | 12 | 19 | 41 | 8 |
| STIRLING ALBION | 18 | 2 | 2 | 14 | 24 | 59 | 8 |

## SFL UNDER 17 YOUTH DIVISION

| | P | W | D | L | F | A | PTS |
|---|---|---|---|---|---|---|---|
| MORTON | 18 | 15 | 1 | 2 | 62 | 18 | 46 |
| AYR UNITED | 18 | 13 | 1 | 4 | 49 | 25 | 40 |
| ROSS COUNTY | 18 | 11 | 4 | 3 | 55 | 24 | 37 |
| RAITH ROVERS | 18 | 10 | 6 | 2 | 41 | 26 | 36 |
| FALKIRK | 18 | 11 | 2 | 5 | 58 | 28 | 35 |
| HAMILTON ACADEMICAL | 18 | 11 | 2 | 5 | 37 | 28 | 35 |
| COWDENBEATH | 18 | 9 | 5 | 4 | 45 | 34 | 32 |
| AIRDRIE UNITED | 18 | 9 | 5 | 4 | 39 | 39 | 32 |
| GRETNA | 18 | 9 | 2 | 7 | 39 | 33 | 29 |
| ELGIN CITY | 18 | 8 | 3 | 7 | 42 | 28 | 27 |
| QUEEN'S PARK | 18 | 7 | 4 | 7 | 46 | 48 | 25 |
| ST. MIRREN | 18 | 7 | 3 | 8 | 34 | 40 | 24 |
| ALLOA ATHLETIC | 18 | 6 | 3 | 9 | 42 | 40 | 21 |
| STENHOUSEMUIR | 18 | 5 | 3 | 10 | 27 | 31 | 18 |
| BERWICK RANGERS | 18 | 4 | 1 | 13 | 24 | 53 | 13 |
| ALBION ROVERS | 18 | 4 | 1 | 13 | 33 | 71 | 13 |
| ARBROATH | 18 | 3 | 3 | 12 | 26 | 50 | 12 |
| QUEEN OF THE SOUTH | 18 | 3 | 0 | 15 | 26 | 65 | 9 |
| STIRLING ALBION | 18 | 1 | 1 | 16 | 23 | 67 | 4 |

# THE CIS INSURANCE CUP COMPETITION
## SEASON 2004.05

### FIRST ROUND
Tuesday, 10th August, 2004

**STENHOUSEMUIR 2**     **ARBROATH 1**
J.P. McBride, L. Collins     J. Cusick

Stenhousemuir: W. McCulloch, K. Knox, D. McInally, P. Murphy, A. Smith, (A. Armit), (J. Savage), R. Henderson, M. Lauchlan, L. Collins, S. Kerrigan, J.P. McBride, P. McGrillen
Substitutes not used: R. Davidson, S. McGregor, D. Orr
Arbroath: N. Inglis, K. McMullan, G. Henslee, S. Rennie, (S. Cook), J. Bishop, J. Cusick, G. Miller, S. MacDonald, D. McLean, A. Brazil, (J. Collier), G. Swankie
Substitutes not used: J. McAulay, P. Farquharson, T. Woodcock
Referee: Willie Young Attendance: 145

**AIRDRIE UNITED 3**     **EAST FIFE 0**
J. Vareille, O. Coyle,
M. Roberts

Airdrie United: M. McGeown, W. Wilson, P. Lovering, A. McManus, S. Wilson, D. Dunn, J. Vareille, (K. Barkey), M. Wilson, (S. Docherty), O. Coyle, A. Gow, (S. McKeown), M. Roberts.
Substitutes not used: K. Christie, L. Hollis
East Fife: J. Dodds, C. Condie, I. McDonald, C. Lumsden, (S. Linton), M. Hall, L. Byle, J. Herkes, G. Kelly, B. Fairbairn, S. Tarditi, K. Brash, (J. Mitchell).
Substitutes not used: R. Crawford, S. Paliczka, S. Morrison
Referee: Dougie McDonald Attendance: 1,054

**DUMBARTON 1**     **ROSS COUNTY 3**
I. Russell     A. Burke (3)

Dumbarton: S. Grindlay, C. McEwan, C. Brittain, J. McKinstry, I. Dobbins, B. Donald, S. Bonar, P. Ronald, (G. Herd), A. Rodgers, I. Russell, J. Dillon, (C. Boyle)
Substitutes not used: R. Borris, R. Dunn, N. Binnie
Ross County: S. Garden, J. Robertson, M. McCulloch, J. McCunnie, (S. Mackay), M. Canning, J. Lauchlan, J. Rankin, D. Cowie, G. McSwegan, (D. Winters), S. McGarry, (S. Higgins), A. Burke
Substitutes not used: S. Malcolm, J. McCafferty
Referee: Iain Brines Attendance: 437

**STRANRAER 2**     **RAITH ROVERS 1**
L. Sharp, D. Turnbull     F. Rivas

Stranraer: K. Meechan, S. Swift, F. Wright, D. Wingate, M. Henderson, A. Jenkins, K. Finlayson, S. Aitken, D. Turnbull, D. Graham, L. Sharp
Substitutes not used: K. Gaughan, G. McCutcheon, B. Crawford, P. Gaughan, A. McCondichie
Raith Rovers: D. Berthelot, M. Ouattara, (C. Leiper), A. Benaissa, (J. Boyle), T. Hajovsky, J. Smart, F. Rivas, D. Brady, J. McAlpine, L. Young, (P. Hagan), H. Sacko, C. O'Reilly
Substitutes not used: C. Malcolm, R. Pounoussamy
Referee: Tom Brown Attendance: 393

**PETERHEAD 3**     **EAST STIRLINGSHIRE 2**
M. Bavidge, S. Michie (2)     D. Ure, G. Parks

Peterhead: P. Mathers, C. Tully, S. McSkimming, (A. Youngson), I. Good, M. Perry, K. Gibson, C. Campbell, (M. Johnston), M.J. Buchan, S. Michie, M. Bavidge, D. Hagen
Substitutes not used: K. Tindal, C. Bain, R. Buchanan

East Stirlingshire: R. Gilpin, D. Harvey, (J. Leishman), C. Miller, C. Newall, G. McGhee, P. Ross, J. Dunbar, A. Moffat, D. Ure, (G. Parks), R. Donaldson, (G. Findlay), C. Baldwin
Substitutes not used: G. Denham, A. Mitchell
Referee: Ian Frickleton Attendance: 482

**BRECHIN CITY 5**     **COWDENBEATH 2**
          (AET -2-2 After 90 Minutes)
C. Templeman (2),     B. Gilfillan, I. Mauchlen
P. Ritchie, G. Gibson (2)

Brechin City: D. Hay, J. Smith, (K. McLeish), S. Walker, I.G. Johnson, S. Dennis, D. White, S. MacNicol, (G. Gibson), C. Winter, (K. Byers), P. Ritchie, C. Templeman, C. King
Substitutes not used: R. Black, S. Vanderdeyl
Cowdenbeath: A. Carlin, C. Shand, A. Campbell, (P. McHale), B. Gilfillan, D. McGregor, I. Ritchie, I. Mauchlen, (C. Scott), G. Fusco, D. Shields, L. Buchanan, (C. Gray), D. Mowat
Substitutes not used: J.P. Kelly, A. Fleming
Referee: Alan Freeland Attendance: 304

**FALKIRK 4**     **MONTROSE 1**
D. Duffy (2), R. Latapy,     D. Jones
S. MacKenzie

Falkirk: D. Hill, A. Lawrie, (K. McAnespie), C. McPherson, M. Campbell, (R. McStay), J. Hughes, K. James, S. MacKenzie, D. Nicholls, A. Thomson, R. Latapy, D. Duffy, (P. Moutinho)
Substitutes not used: N. Scally, J. Hutchison
Montrose: M. Hankinson, B. Donachie, A. Budd, S. Kerrigan, N. Stephen, D. Spink, K. Webster, (R. Lindsay), E. Hall, C. Watson, (K. Bremner), C. Smart, S. Lannen, (D. Jones)
Substitutes not used: K. Morrice, J. Butter
Referee: Kevin Toner Attendance: 1,379

**BERWICK RANGERS 3**     **ELGIN CITY 2**
G. McNicoll, D. Smith,     A. Bone, W. Martin
P. Hampshire

Berwick Rangers: G. O'Connor, D. Murie, E. Smith, (A. Seaton), M. Cowan, (R. Horn), G. McNicoll, G. Connell, (P. Hampshire), M. Neil, G. Forrest, G. Hutchison, I. Little, D. Smith
Substitutes not used: J. Birrell, R. Godfrey
Elgin City: K. Renton, S. Cumming, A. Dempsie, P. Kaczan, H. Dickson, S. Black, (J. McKenzie), W. Martin, A. Nelson, A. Bone, P. Reid, (M. Harty), A. Roddie
Substitutes not used: P. Napier, D. Kelly, S. McKenzie
Referee: Mike Tumilty Attendance: 283

**ST. JOHNSTONE 2**     **ALLOA ATHLETIC 3**
D. Hannah, C. Hay     R. Hamilton, S. Callaghan,
          B.A. Ferguson

St. Johnstone: A. McGregor, M. Baxter, S. Fraser, D. Hannah, K. Rutkiewicz, P. Sheerin, C. Marshall, P. Bernard, R. Stevenson, (C. Hay), M. Moore, L. Hardy, (E. Malone)
Substitutes not used: J. Tait, M. Fotheringham, K. Cuthbert
Alloa Athletic: G. McGlynn, R. Walker, D. Hill, (R. MacLeod), P. Mortimer, M. Bolochoweckyj, C. Townsley, J. Stevenson, (M. Daly), B.A. Ferguson, A. Brown, R. Hamilton, S. Callaghan
Substitutes not used: S. Nicholas, P. McLaughlin, J. Evans
Referee: Craig Thomson Attendance: 1,500

**ST. MIRREN 2**　　　　　**FORFAR ATHLETIC 5**
M-M. Paatelainen,　　　　P. Tosh (2), B. Sellars,
J. O'Neill　　　　　　　　D. McClune, A. Millen (o.g.)

**St. Mirren:** C. Hinchcliffe, D. Van Zanten, (J. O'Neill), K. Broadfoot, A. Millen, K. McGowne, M. Reilly, R. Gillies, H. Murray, M-M. Paatelainen, E. Annand, (B. McGinty), S. Lappin, (L. Ellis)
Substitutes not used: A. Russell, S. Woods
**Forfar Athletic:** M. Brown, A. Rattray, D. Lowing, E. Forrest, D. King, D. McClune, B. Sellars, (M. Maher), P. Lunan, P. Tosh, (M. King), P. Shields, M. Booth
Substitutes not used: D. Dunn, S. Florence, N. Ferrie
**Referee:** Hugh Dallas **Attendance:** 1,104

Wednesday, 11th August, 2004

**STIRLING ALBION 3**　　　**QUEEN'S PARK 2**
M. Glancy, S. McLean (2)　　F. Carroll, R. Clark

**Stirling Albion:** M. Hogarth, P. Nugent, S. Devine, (C. Scotland), M. McNally, J.G. Rowe, K. MacDonald, P. Hay, C. Ferguson, S. McLean, M. Glancy, (D. Cummings), D. O'Brien
Substitutes not used: J. Allan, S. Hutchison, S. Christie
**Queen's Park:** B. McCue, S. Kettlewell, (D. Agostini), D. McCallum, (M. Bonnar), G. Rushford, S. Reilly, S. Molloy, R. Clark, P. Harvey, A. Graham, F. Carroll, B. Blair
Substitutes not used: D. Clarke, T. Sloan, S.McGovern
**Referee:** Brian Cassidy **Attendance:** 669

Tuesday, 17th August, 2004

**QUEEN OF THE SOUTH 1**　**ALBION ROVERS 2**
D. McNiven　　　　　　　J. Mercer. M. McKenzie

**Queen of the South:** Colin Scott, E. Paton, (Christopher Scott), T. English, B. McColligan, P. Hilland, J. Thomson, D. Bagan, S. Bowey, (P. Burns), D. McNiven, (C. Armstrong), G. Wood, B. McLaughlin
Substitutes not used: S. Payne, G. Wright
**Albion Rovers:** C. Fahey, C. Silvestro, J. Stirling, D. Black, J. McGowan, G. McLaren, M. McKenzie, R. Patrick, (J. Bradford), M. Yardley, P. McManus, J. Mercer, (G. McCaul)
Substitutes not used: A. Paterson, S. Crabbe, M. Peat
**Referee:** Ian Frickleton **Attendance:** 1,240

**MORTON 1**　　　　　　　**GRETNA 0**
P. Walker

**Morton:** C. Coyle, D. Collins, M. McCulloch, S. McCluskey, S. Greacen, J. McAlister, C. Millar, J. Maisano, A. Williams, (S. Bannerman), W. Hawke, (P. Weatherson), J. Walker, (P. Walker)
Substitutes not used: D. Keenan, D. McGurn
**Gretna:** D. Mathieson, M. Birch, G. Skelton, (R. McGuffie), R. Prokas, (K. Deuchar), A. Aitken, D. Holdsworth, R. Baldacchino, M. Galloway, A. Smith, D. Bingham, D. Townsley
Substitutes not used: S. Cosgrove, J. McQuilken, C. Summersgill
**Referee:** Ian Fyfe **Attendance:** 2,106

**HAMILTON ACADEMICAL 4**　**AYR UNITED 1**
S. Thomson, S. Convery (3)　A. Ferguson

**Hamilton Academical:** D. McEwan, T. Lumsden, S. Hodge, S. Thomson, D. Ferguson, (I. Fyfe), S. Tunbridge, (D. Hamilton), S. Convery, C. Aitken, (A. Sim), P. Keogh, M. Corcoran, R. Waddell
Substitutes not used: R. Walker, R. Jellema
**Ayr United:** L. Roy, W. Lyle, S. McGrady, S. Chaplain, R. Burgess, (C. Conway), M. Dunlop, B. McLaughlin, D. Ramsay, S. Kean, P. Connolly, (A. Ferguson), D. Henderson, (M. O'Neill)
Substitutes not used: A. Dunning, J. Hillcoat
**Referee:** John Underhill **Attendance:** 1,017

## SECOND ROUND
Tuesday, 24th August, 2004

**KILMARNOCK 3**　　　　　**HAMILTON ACADEMICAL 0**
D. Invincible (2),
G. McDonald

**Kilmarnock:** A. Combe, J. Fowler, G. Hay, G. McDonald, D. Lilley, F. Dindeleux, D. Invincible, G. Locke, (E. Joly), K. Boyd, C. Dargo, (S. Murray), A. Johnston, (R. Dodds).
Substitutes not used: G. Greer, G. Smith
**Hamilton Academical:** D. McEwan, R. Walker, R. Waddell, (B. McPhee), S. Thomson, M. McLaughlin, D. Hamilton, B. Carrigan, (S. Hodge), C. Aitken, P. Keogh, (S. Convery), S. Tunbridge, M. Corcoran.
Substitutes not used: R. Blackadder, R. Jellema
**Referee:** Kenny Clark **Attendance:** 3,375

**AIRDRIE UNITED 0**　　　　**CLYDE 1**
　　　　　　　　　　　　　A. Wilford

**Airdrie United:** M. McGeown, W. Wilson, (T. Hoey), P. Lovering, A. McManus, K. Christie, S. Docherty, (K. Barkey), J. Vareille, (A. Gow), M. Wilson, O. Coyle, S. McKeown, M. Roberts
Substitutes not used: N. McGowan, L. Hollis
**Clyde:** B. Halliwell, S. Mensing, G. Bollan, A. Walker, (G. Arbuckle), J. Potter, D. Sheridan, C. Bryson, (P. Doyle), J. Gibson, A. Wilford, K. Kerkar, I. Harty, (M. Gilhaney)
Substitutes not used: D. Greenhill, A. Morrison
**Referee:** Iain Brines **Attendance:** 1,595

**ABERDEEN 3**　　　　　　**BERWICK RANGERS 0**
A. Diamond, D. Adams,
S. Craig

**Aberdeen:** D. Preece, M. Hart, K. McNaughton, (P. McGuire), R. Anderson, A. Diamond, S. Severin, S. Tosh, (F. Tiernan), M. Heikkinen, S. Craig, (J. Stewart), D. Adams, S. Morrison
Substitutes not used: R. Foster, R. Esson
**Berwick Rangers:** G. O'Connor, D. Murie, (E. Smith), A. Seaton, M. Cowan, R. Horn, G. Connell, (K. Gordon), G. Forrest, M. Neil, G. Hutchison, I. Little, D. Smith, (P. Hampshire)
Substitutes not used: J. Birrell, R. Godfrey
**Referee:** Mike Ritchie **Attendance:** 4,549

**ROSS COUNTY 0**　　　　**INVERNESS CAL. THISTLE 1**
　　　　　　　　　　　　　R. Tokely

**Ross County:** S. Garden, J. Robertson, M. McCulloch, S. Mackay, M. Canning, J. Lauchlan, J. Rankin, D. Cowie, G. McSwegan, (S. McGarry), S. Kilgannon, (S. Higgins), A. Burke, (D. Winters)
Substitutes not used: J. McCunnie, J. McCafferty
**Inverness C.T.:** M. Brown, R. Tokely, S. Golabek, S. McCaffrey, B. Wilson, G. Munro, R. Duncan, S. Hislop, G. Bayne, L. Keogh, J. Carricondo, (R. McBain)
Substitutes not used: D. Dods, R. Hart, B. Prunty, M. Fraser
**Referee:** Calum Murray **Attendance:** 3,323

**ALBION ROVERS 1**　　　　**BRECHIN CITY 1**
　　　　　　　　　　　　(AET – 1-1 After 90 Minutes)
J. Bradford　　　　　　　P. Ritchie
Albion Rovers won 4-3 on Kicks from the Penalty Mark
**Albion Rovers:** C. Fahey, A. Paterson, (D. Black), J. Stirling, J. Smith, J. McGowan, C. Silvestro, M. McKenzie, R. Patrick, (G. McLaren), M. Yardley, (S. Crabbe), J. Bradford, J. Mercer
Substitutes not used: G. McCaul, M. Peat

**Brechin City:** C. Nelson, J. Smith, P. Deas, S. MacNicol, (G. Gibson), D. White, S. Walker, I.G. Johnson, C. Jackson, (C. King), P. Ritchie, C. Templeman, (S. Hampshire), K. McLeish
Substitutes not used: C. Winter, D. Hay
**Referee:** Colin Hardie **Attendance:** 167

| MORTON 0 | MOTHERWELL 3 |
| --- | --- |
| | J. Paterson, D. Clarkson, |
| | K. McBride |

**Morton:** C. Coyle, D. Collins, M. McCulloch, S. McCluskey, S. Greacen, J. McAlister, C. Millar, J. Maisano, (S. Bannerman), A. Williams, (P. Walker), P. Weatherson, J. Walker
Substitutes not used: D. Keenan, M. Maisano, D. McGurn
**Motherwell:** G. Marshall, M. Corrigan, S. Hammell, W. Kinniburgh, S. Craigan, K. McBride, S. McDonald, (A. Burns), S. Leitch, (S. Fagan), J. Paterson, (R. Foran), P. O'Donnell, D. Clarkson
Substitutes not used: D. Partridge, B.J. Corr
**Referee:** Willie Young **Attendance:** 3,767

| DUNDEE 4 | FORFAR ATHLETIC 0 |
| --- | --- |
| S. Lovell (3), I. Anderson | |

**Dundee:** D. Soutar, (K. Jack), C. MacDonald, B. Sancho, R. Mann, J. Hernandez, B. Smith, G. Brady, N. Jablonski, (M. Fotheringham), I. Anderson, S. Lovell, J. Sutton, (G. Larsen)
Substitutes not used: N. Barrett, R. Linn
**Forfar Athletic:** M. Brown, A. Rattray, D. Lowing, (M. King), E. Forrest, D. King, D. McClune, (M. Booth), B. Sellars, P.Lunan, (M. Maher), P. Tosh, P. Shields, J. Stein
Substitutes not used: D. Dunn, N. Ferrie
**Referee:** Brian Cassidy **Attendance:** 3,047

| STENHOUSEMUIR 2 | PARTICK THISTLE 5 |
| --- | --- |
| P. McGrillen, J. Savage | W. Gibson, J. Escalas, |
| | D. Fleming, L. Hinds (2) |

**Stenhousemuir:** W. McCulloch, K. Knox, D. McInally, P. Murphy, (S. Fallon), R. Henderson, J.P. McBride, M. Lauchlan, L. Collins, J. Savage, S. Kerrigan, (R. Davidson), P. McGrillen
Substitutes not used: S. McGregor, T. Sinclair, K. McKeown
**Partick Thistle:** K. Arthur, W. Gibson, (S. Fulton), K. Milne, (J-Y. Anis), G. Murray, A. Dowie, A. Wilkinson, W. Howie, D. Fleming, J. Escalas, (A. Oné), L. Hinds, E. Panther
Substitutes not used: A. Ross, S. Pinkowski
**Referee:** John Rowbotham **Attendance:** 1,019

| PETERHEAD 1 | FALKIRK 6 |
| --- | --- |
| M. Bavidge | J. O'Neil, A. Thomson (3), |
| | D. Duffy (2) |

**Peterhead:** P. Mathers, C. Tully, A. Youngson, I. Good, M. Perry, K. Gibson, (G. Stewart), K. Tindal, (C. Campbell), M.J. Buchan, S. Michie, (D. Milne), M. Bavidge, D. Hagen
Substitutes not used: M. Johnston, R. Buchanan
**Falkirk:** D. Hill, A. Lawrie, C. McPherson, S. MacKenzie, M. Campbell, K. James, J. O'Neil, (N. Scally), D. Nicholls, (K. McAnespie), A. Thomson, R. Latapy, D. Duffy, (P. Moutinho)
Substitutes not used: J. Hughes, J. Hutchison
**Referee:** Ian Fyfe **Attendance:** 622

| HIBERNIAN 4 | ALLOA ATHLETIC 0 |
| --- | --- |
| S. Glass, A. Orman, | |
| C. Murdock, D. Riordan | |

**Hibernian:** Simon Brown, G. Caldwell, G. Smith, (J. Baillie), D. Murphy, C. Murdock,G. Beuzelin, (S. Dobbie), S. Glass, A. Orman, S. Morrow, D. Riordan, D. Shiels, (K. Nicol)
Substitutes not used: J. Shields, A. Brown
**Alloa Athletic:** G. McGlynn, R. Walker, D. Hill, (M. McDermott), P. Mortimer, (R. MacLeod), M. Bolochoweckyj, C. Townsley, S. Nicholas, M. Daly, A. Brown, (I. Nicolson), R. Hamilton, S. Callaghan
Substitutes not used: P. McLaughlin, J. Evans
**Referee:** Michael McCurry **Attendance:** 5,156

Wednesday, 25th August, 2004

| DUNDEE UNITED 3 | STRANRAER 1 |
| --- | --- |
| J. Grady, M. Kerr, C. Innes | M. Henderson |

**Dundee United:** A. Bullock, D. McCracken, A. Archibald, C. Innes, M. Wilson, S. Duff, M. Kerr, B. Robson, (W. Dodds), J. Grady, J. Scotland, (J. McIntyre), A. McLaren, (C. Samuel)
Substitutes not used: D. McInnes, L. Hirschfeld
**Stranraer:** A. McCondichie, S. Swift, F. Wright, D. Wingate, M. Henderson, A. Jenkins, K. Finlayson, J. Fraser, K. Gaughan, (S. Aitken), D. Graham, (S. Donnachie), L. Sharp
Substitutes not used: G. McCutcheon, C. Cruickshank, K. Meechan
**Referee:** Alan Freeland **Attendance:** 2,511

| STIRLING ALBION 0 | LIVINGSTON 2 |
| --- | --- |
| | C. Easton, J. Hamilton |

**Stirling Albion:** M. Hogarth, P. Nugent, (S. Hutchison), C. Scotland, M. McNally, J.G. Rowe, K. MacDonald, P. Hay, (C. Gethins), C. Ferguson, S. McLean, M. Glancy, D. O'Brien, (J. Allan)
Substitutes not used: D. Cummings, S. Christie
**Livingston:** R. McKenzie, D. McNamee, G. Stanik, O. Rubio, G. Bahoken, C. Easton, S. Boyack, (S. McLaughlin), D. Lilley, J. Hamilton, B. O'Brien, J. Dair, (S. Lovell)
Substitutes not used: M. Libbra, C. McMenamin, C. Meldrum
**Referee:** Kevin Toner **Attendance:** 1,094

## THIRD ROUND
Tuesday, 21st September, 2004

| LIVINGSTON 2 | DUNDEE 1 |
| --- | --- |
| | (AET –1-1 After 90 Minutes) |
| C. Easton (2), S. Lovell | |

**Livingston:** R. McKenzie, D. McNamee, G. Stanik, O. Rubio, E. Dorado, A. Kernaghan, C. Easton, (J. Hamilton), B. O'Brien, C. McMenamin, (J. Dair), S. Lovell, D. Lilley, (M. Libbra)
Substitutes not used: W. Snowdon, C. Meldrum
**Dundee:** D. Soutar, C. MacDonald, B. Sancho, R. Mann, N. Barrett, (T. Hutchinson), B. Smith, S. Robb, (C. Hegarty), M. Fotheringham, (G. Brady), S. Lovell, J. Sutton, I. Anderson
Substitutes not used: G. Larsen, K. Jack
**Referee:** Iain Brines **Attendance:** 1,736

| DUNDEE UNITED 4 | CLYDE 0 |
| --- | --- |
| J. McIntyre, B. Robson, | |
| G. Brebner, M. Wilson | |

**Dundee United:** L. Hirschfeld, D. McCracken, A. Archibald, C. Innes, M. Wilson, (W. Dodds), D. McInnes, G. Brebner, S. Duff, B. Robson, J. McIntyre, (C. Samuel), A. McLaren, (J. Scotland)
Substitutes not used: M. Kerr, P. Jarvie

**Clyde:** B. Halliwell, S. Mensing, A. Walker, S. Balmer, J. Potter, D. Sheridan, G. Arbuckle, J. Gibson, (C. Bryson), A. Wilford, M. Marsiglia, (G. McCracken), I. Harty
Substitutes not used: P. Flaherty, J. McKeever, A. Morrison
**Referee:** Dougie McDonald **Attendance:** 2,336

| CELTIC 8 | FALKIRK 1 |
|---|---|

M. Sylla, R. Wallace (3),    A. Thomson
D. Balde, P. Lambert,
S. McManus, A. McGeady

**Celtic:** R. Douglas, U. Laursen, J. Valgaeren, D. Balde, M. Sylla, R. Wallace, S. Pearson, P. Lambert, S. McManus, (A. Thompson), O. Juninho, A. McGeady
Substitutes not used: N. Lennon, S. Petrov, S. Varga, M. Hedman
**Falkirk:** D. Hill, A. Lawrie, C. McPherson, S. MacKenzie, M. Campbell, (J. Hughes), K. James, J. O'Neil, D. Nicholls, (K. McAnespie), A. Thomson, R. Latapy, (P. Moutinho), D. Duffy
Substitutes not used: N. Scally, A. Ferguson
**Referee:** Willie Young **Attendance:** 24,345

Wednesday, 22nd September, 2004

| HEARTS 2 | KILMARNOCK 1 |
|---|---|

P. Hartley(2)    P. Leven

**Hearts:** C. Gordon, J. McAllister, P. Kisnorbo, A. Maybury, A. Webster, C. Berra, R. Neilson, J. Hamill, P. Hartley, M. De Vries, (R. Sloan), D. Wyness
Substitutes not used: N. Macfarlane, M. Stewart, C. Sives, T. Moilanen
**Kilmarnock:** A. Combe, D. Lilley, F. Dindeleux, G. Greer, J. Fowler, P. Leven, E. Joly, G. McDonald, (C. Dargo), A. Johnston, K. Boyd, D. Invincible, (G. Wales)
Substitutes not used: R. Dodds, S. Dillon, G. Smith
**Referee:** Hugh Dallas **Attendance:** 5,944

| INVERNESS CAL. THISTLE 1 | MOTHERWELL 3 |
|---|---|

R. Tokely    R. Foran, P. O'Donnell, K. McBride

**Inverness Cal. Thistle:** M. Brown, R. Tokely, S. Golabek, S. McCaffrey, G. Munro, R. McBain, B. Wilson, S. Hislop, (G. Bayne), B. Prunty, (J. Carricondo), R. Hart, L. Keogh, (R. Duncan)
Substitutes not used: D. Dods, M. Fraser
**Motherwell:** G. Marshall, M. Corrigan, S. Hammell, W. Kinniburgh, S. Craigan, K. McBride, (S. Fagan), S. McDonald, S. Leitch, R. Foran, P. O'Donnell, D. Clarkson, (J. Paterson)
Substitutes not used: A. Burns, D. Partridge, B.J. Corr
**Referee:** Kevin Toner **Attendance:** 1,464

| DUNFERMLINE ATHLETIC 3 | PARTICK THISTLE 1 |
|---|---|

C. Brewster, S.M. Thomson,    A. Dowie
N. Hunt

**Dunfermline Athletic:** D. Stillie, S.M. Thomson, S. Wilson, A. Skerla, T. Butler, (N. Hunt), Darren Young, B. Nicholson, G. Shields, G. Dempsey, C. Brewster, (A. Labonte), B. Mehmet, (A. Tod)
Substitutes not used: S. Donnelly, J. Langfield
**Partick Thistle:** K. Arthur, A. Wilkinson, A. Madaschi, G. Murray, A. Dowie, S. Fulton, (A. Oné), L. Hinds, (J-Y. Anis), D. Fleming, (W. Howie), J. Escalas, E. Panther, K. Milne
Substitutes not used: G. Britton, S. Pinkowski
**Referee:** Michael McCurry **Attendance:** 2,349

| ABERDEEN 0 | RANGERS 2 |
|---|---|

   F. Ricksen, S. Thompson

**Aberdeen:** D. Preece, P. McGuire, K. McNaughton, R. Anderson, M. Hart, S. Severin, S. Tosh, D. Mackie, S. Craig, (S. Muirhead), D. Adams, R. Foster
Substitutes not used: S. Morrison, F. Tiernan, A. Considine, R. Esson
**Rangers:** S. Klos, Z. Khizanishvili, C. Moore, J-A. Boumsong, G. Vignal, F. Ricksen, R. Malcolm, S. Arveladze, (I. Novo), P. Vanoli, C. Burke, S. Thompson
Substitutes not used: M. Andrews, P. Lovenkrands, S. Hughes, G. Smith
**Referee:** Kenny Clark **Attendance:** 14,876

| ALBION ROVERS 1 | HIBERNIAN 3 |
|---|---|

G. McLaren    S. Dobbie, D. Shiels, G. O'Connor

Match Played at New Douglas Park, Hamilton

**Albion Rovers:** C. Fahey, C. Silvestro, J. Stirling, D. Black, J. McGowan, G. McLaren, M. McKenzie, G. McCaul, (R. Patrick), J. Bradford, (A. Selkirk), P. McManus, J. Mercer
Substitutes not used: M. Yardley, C. Connolly, M. Peat
**Hibernian:** A. Brown, G. Caldwell, M. Venus, D. Murphy, S. Whittaker, I. Murray, S. Glass, J. McCluskey, (A. Orman), S. Dobbie, (S. Fletcher), D. Riordan, (G. O'Connor), D. Shiels
Substitutes not used: Simon Brown, K. McDonald
**Referee:** Steve Conroy **Attendance:** 1,576

## FOURTH ROUND
Tuesday, 9th November, 2004

| LIVINGSTON 0 | MOTHERWELL 5 |
|---|---|

   E. Dorado (o.g.), R. Foran (2), P. O'Donnell, K. Wright

**Livingston:** R. McKenzie, D. McNamee, E. Dorado, O. Rubio, W. Snowdon, C. Easton, R. Brittain, B. O'Brien, S. Lovell, (D. Lilley), J. Hamilton, (S. McLaughlin), R. Snodgrass, (C. McMenamin)
Substitutes not used: A. Kernaghan, C. Meldrum
**Motherwell:** G. Marshall, M. Corrigan, D. Partridge, P. Quinn, S. Craigan, S. Hammell, P. O'Donnell, (K. Wright), M. Fitzpatrick, J. Paterson, R. Foran, (S. Fagan), D. Clarkson
Substitutes not used: A. Burns, W. Kinniburgh, B.J. Corr
**Referee:** Iain Brines **Attendance:** 2,887

| DUNDEE UNITED 2 | HIBERNIAN 1 |
|---|---|

   (AET – 1-1 After 90 Minutes)
J. McIntyre (2)    D. Riordan

**Dundee United:** P. Jarvie, P. Ritchie, A. Archibald, M. Wilson, C. Innes, D. McInnes, G. Brebner, (D. McCracken), B. Robson, C. Samuel, (W. Dodds), J. McIntyre, J. Scotland, (J. Grady)
Substitutes not used: M. Kerr, L. Hirschfeld
**Hibernian:** Simon Brown, G. Caldwell, C. Murdock, G. Beuzelin, S. Whittaker, I. Murray, S. Glass, C. Rocastle, S. Morrow, (S. Fletcher), D. Riordan, (S. Dobbie), D. Shiels, (J. Shields)
Substitutes not used: A. Brown, G. Smith
**Referee:** John Rowbotham **Attendance:** 4,865

Wednesday, 10th November, 2004

**RANGERS 2**                **CELTIC 1**
                             (AET –1-1 After 90 Minutes)
S. Arveladze,  D. Prso       J. Hartson

**Rangers:** S. Klos, Z. Khizanishvili, M. Andrews, J-A. Boumsong,
G. Vignal, F. Ricksen, H. Namouchi, A. Rae, (S. Hughes),
P. Lovenkrands, (S. Arveladze), I. Novo, S. Thompson, (D. Prso)
Substitutes not used: A. Hutton, G. Smith
**Celtic:** D. Marshall, S. Varga, J. Valgaeren, D. Balde, J. McNamara,
S. Petrov, (C. Beattie), (A. McGeady), N. Lennon, A. Thompson,
D. Agathe, J. Hartson, O. Juninho, (H. Camara)
Substitutes not used: S. Pearson, M. Hedman
**Referee:** Stuart Dougal **Attendance:** 47,298

**DUNFERMLINE ATHLETIC 1**   **HEARTS 3**
B. Mehmet                    A. Webster, P. Hartley,
                             J. Hamill

**Dunfermline Athletic:** D. Stillie, A. Tod, S. Wilson, T. Butler,
R. Byrne, S.M. Thomson, B. Nicholson, G. Mason, A. Labonte,
C. Brewster, (B. Mehmet), Derek Young, (S. Donnelly)
Substitutes not used: S. Bradley, G. Ross, J. Langfield
**Hearts:** C. Gordon, A. Maybury, P. Kisnorbo, S. Pressley, A. Webster,
J. McAllister, R. Neilson, P. Stamp, (J. Hamill), K. McKenna,
P. Hartley, D. Wyness, (G. Weir)
Substitutes not used: C. Berra, R. Pereira, T. Moilanen
**Referee:** Hugh Dallas **Attendance:** 4,405

## SEMI-FINALS
Tuesday, 1st February, 2005
Easter Road Stadium, Edinburgh

**MOTHERWELL 3**            **HEARTS 2**
                           (AET – 2-2 After 90 Minutes)
S. Craigan, R. Foran,      M. Burchill, H. Thorarinsson
M. Fitzpatrick

**Motherwell:** G. Marshall, M. Corrigan, S. Hammell, K. McBride,
(D. Clarkson), S. Craigan, D. Partridge, S. McDonald, S. Leitch,
R. Foran, (P. Quinn), P. O'Donnell, J. Paterson, (M. Fitzpatrick)
Substitutes not used: S. Fagan, B.J. Corr
**Hearts:** C. Gordon, R. Neilson, J. McAllister, S. Pressley,
N. Macfarlane, (S. Simmons), A. Webster, D. Wyness, (M. Burchill),
S. Mikoliunus, L. Miller, P. Hartley, J. Hamill, (H. Thorarinsson)
Substitutes not used: C. Berra, T. Moilanen
**Referee:** Dougie McDonald **Attendance:** 14,069

Wednesday, 2nd February, 2005
The National Stadium, Hampden Park, Glasgow

**RANGERS 7**              **DUNDEE UNITED 1**
I. Novo (2), D. Prso,      J. Scotland
T. Buffel, F. Ricksen,
S. Thompson (2)

**Rangers:** R. Waterreus, F. Ricksen, M. Ross, S. Kyrgiakos, M. Andrews,
M. Ball, T. Buffel, A. Rae, (B. Ferguson), D. Prso, (S. Thompson), I. Novo, G. Vignal
Substitutes not used: R. Malcolm, H. Namouchi, G. Smith
**Dundee United:** N. Colgan, L. Mair, (W. Dodds), A. Archibald,
(S. Duff), D. McInnes, (J. Scotland), P. Ritchie, D. McCracken,
M. Kerr, M. Wilson, S. Crawford, J. McIntyre, B. Robson
Substitutes not used: J. Grady, A. Bullock
**Referee:** Hugh Dallas **Attendance:** 25,622

**FINAL**
Sunday, 20th March, 2005
The National Stadium, Hampden Park, Glasgow

**RANGERS 5**            **MOTHERWELL 1**

**Rangers:** R. Waterreus, F. Ricksen, M. Ross, S. Kyrgiakos,
R. Malcolm, B. Ferguson, T. Buffel, M. Ball, D. Prso, I. Novo,
(S. Thompson), G. Vignal, (A. Rae)
Substitutes not used: P. Lovenkrands, Z. Khizanishvili, G. Smith
**Motherwell:** G. Marshall, M. Corrigan, S. Hammell, K. McBride,
(P. Quinn), S. Craigan, D. Partridge, S. McDonald, S. Leitch,
R. Foran, (D. Clarkson), P. O'Donnell, J. Paterson, (M. Fitzpatrick)
Substitutes not used: S. Fagan, B.J. Corr
**Scorers:**
**Rangers:** M. Ross, S. Kyrgiakos (2), F. Ricksen, I. Novo
**Motherwell:** D. Partridge
**Referee:** Michael McCurry **Attendance:** 50,182

## THE CIS INSURANCE CUP 2004.05
## ROUND BY ROUND GOALS ANALYSIS

|                | NO. OF GOALS SCORED | TIES PLAYED | AVERAGE PER GAME |
|----------------|:---:|:---:|:---:|
| FIRST ROUND    | 61 | 14 | 4.4 |
| SECOND ROUND   | 41 | 12 | 3.4 |
| THIRD ROUND    | 33 | 8  | 4.1 |
| FOURTH ROUND   | 15 | 4  | 3.8 |
| SEMI-FINALS    | 13 | 2  | 6.5 |
| FINAL          | 6  | 1  | 6 |

| | |
|---|---|
| TOTAL NO. OF GOALS SCORED | 169 |
| TOTAL NO. OF TIES PLAYED  | 41 |
| AVERAGE GOALS PER GAME    | 4.1 |

Rangers - CIS Insurance Cup Winners 2004.05

# TENNENT'S SCOTTISH CUP
## COMPETITION **SEASON 2004.05**

### FIRST ROUND
Saturday, 20th November, 2004

#### EAST FIFE 3     WHITEHILL WELFARE 0
J. Mitchell (2), S. Nicholas

**East Fife:** S. Morrison, M. Renwick, F. Duncan, C. Lumsden, G. McDonald, K. Bain, J. Mitchell, G. Kelly, S. Nicholas, K. Steele, (B. Fairbairn), J. Herkes
Substitutes not used: R. Logie, K. Brash, I. McDonald, S. Tarditi
**Whitehill Welfare:** R. McGurk, W. Jamieson, K. Lee, R. Clyde, M. Hunter, R. Johnston, K. Young, R. Shanks, (J. Baigrie), C. McDonald, A. Hogg, P. Forrester, (D. White)
Substitutes not used: D. Berwick, B. Martin, M. Faichney
**Referee:** Chris Boyle **Attendance:** 355

#### INVERURIE LOCO WORKS 1   KEITH 2
N. McLean                 D. Donaldson, K. McKenzie

**Inverurie Loco Works:** M. Coull, J. Young, S. Buchan, T. Wilson, M. Simpson, S. Park, R. Singer, (A. Low), A. Walker, K. Coull, C. Ross, N. McLean, (S.McKay)
Substitutes not used: S. Gray, A. Graham, R. Davidson
**Keith:** A. Shearer, J. Watt, (G. Lonie), G. Simmers, N. Robertson, (W. Mackay), K. McKenzie, K. Niddrie, D. Still, M. Brown, D. Donaldson, D. Nicol, B. Stephen, (S. Walker)
Substitutes not used: C. Garden, C. Yeats
**Referee:** Crawford Allan **Attendance:** 732

Tuesday, 23rd November, 2004

#### MORTON 3     EAST STIRLINGSHIRE 1
A. Williams, P. Weatherson,    S. Livingstone
C. Millar

**Morton:** D. McGurn, D. Collins, D. Keenan, A. Gilbride, (J. Maisano), S. Greacen, J. Adam, C. Millar, P. Walker, (J. Walker), A. Williams, (K. McLean), P. Weatherson, J. McAlister
Substitutes not used: C. Coyle, M. Maisano
**East Stirlingshire:** A. Mitchell, D. Harvey, (G. Denham), C. Baldwin, J. Walker, S. Livingstone, G. McGhee, P. Ross, S. McAuley, R. Donaldson, (G. Findlay), J. Dunbar, D. Ure
Substitutes not used: R. Gilpin, S. Peutherer, G. Parks
**Referee:** William Collum **Attendance:** 1,902

#### GLASGOW UNIVERSITY 0   BRECHIN CITY 3
S. Hampshire, C. Templeman (2)

**Glasgow University:** S. King, R. McColl, C. Steele, A. Hawkins, P. Checketts, G. Brogan, (A. Phillips), J. Riou, M. Barr, R. Connelly, (N. Buckley), S. O'Donnell, (G. MacDonald), R. Scott
Substitutes not used: A. Cathcart, P. MacLeod
**Brechin City:** D. Hay, S. Hamilton, A. Mitchell, I.G. Johnson, J. Smith, S. Walker, C. King, G. Gibson, (C. Winter), P. Ritchie, C. Templeman, S. Hampshire, (S. MacNicol)
Substitutes not used: S. Vanderdeyl, D. White, L. Davidson
**Referee:** Alan Muir **Attendance:** 451

Saturday, 27th November, 2004

#### HUNTLY 3     PETERHEAD 1
R. Taylor (2), R. Guild     M. Bavidge

**Huntly:** R. Bowman, M. Gray, S. Scott, S. Anderson, R. Campbell, D. McGinlay, L. Stephen, R. Guild, J. O'Driscoll, R. Taylor, (R. Stainer), (M. Stewart), G. McGowan, (A. Reid)
Substitutes not used: G. Pennant, M. De-Barros
**Peterhead:** P. Mathers, C. Campbell, I. Good, R. Raeside, M. Perry, K. Gibson, S. Michie, M.J. Buchan, R. Linn, M. Bavidge, A. Youngson, (G. Stewart)
Substitutes not used: R. Buchanan, R. Shand, S. McSkimming, D. Milne
**Referee:** Andrew Hunter **Attendance:** 408

#### COVE RANGERS 4     DALBEATTIE STAR 1
K. Robertson(2), C. Milne (2)    P. Cook

**Cove Rangers:** I. Thain, C. McHattie, A. McCraw, G. Hendry, K. Tindal, B. Morrison, G. Clark, (L. Flaws), M. Johnston, C. Milne, (G. Devine), K. Robertson, (C. Steel), J. Brown
Substitutes not used: R. Charles, D. Henderson
**Dalbeattie Star:** F. Wilson, G. True, (G. Tennant), K. Proudfoot, P. Lawrie, G. McMinn, R. Harkness, (L. Docherty), P. Cook, C. Wilson, B. Dick, (G. Prentice), G. Parker, A. Tuchewicz
Substitutes not used: A. Cathro, G. Smith
**Referee:** Stephen Finnie **Attendance:** 140

#### FORFAR ATHLETIC 1     MONTROSE 5
P. Tosh             K. Webster, C. Smart,
                  G. Sharp (2), K. Dodds

**Forfar Athletic:** A. Creer, A. Rattray, D. Lowing, E. Forrest, D. King, P. Lunan, (N. Clark), B. Sellars, D. McClune, P. Tosh, M. King, (P. Shields), J. Stein, (M. Booth)
Substitutes not used: N. Ferrie, D. Cameron
**Montrose:** J. Butter, B. Donachie, S. Ferguson, P. Doyle, N. Stephen, (A. Budd), K. Dodds, K. Webster, (D. Smith), C. Smart, M. Wood, E. Hall, G. Sharp, (C. Watson)
Substitutes not used: M. Hankinson, M. Slater
**Referee:** Colin Hardie **Attendance:** 535

#### COWDENBEATH 2     DUMBARTON 3
D. Gribben, L. Buchanan    C. McEwan, R. Dunn, I. Russell

**Cowdenbeath:** A. Carlin, G. Fusco, A. Campbell, C. Newall, J. McKeown, I. Ritchie, I. Mauchlen, P. McHale, D. Shields, D. Gribben, (J.P. Kelly), D. Williams, (L. Buchanan)
Substitutes not used: A. Fleming, A. Cargill, D. Millar
**Dumbarton:** S. Grindlay, C. McEwan, C. Brittain, J. McKinstry, I. Dobbins, C. Boyle, S. Bonar, B. Donald, E. Annand, (I. Russell), R. Dunn, (A. Rodgers), J. Dillon, (C. McGroarty)
Substitutes not used: J. Wight, P. Ronald
**Referee:** Jamie Downie **Attendance:** 279

### SECOND ROUND
Saturday, 11th December, 2004

#### KEITH 0     MONTROSE 1
M. Wood

**Keith:** A. Shearer, M. Brown, G. Simmers, W. Mackay, (N. Robertson), K. McKenzie, K. Niddrie, D. Still, D. Donaldson, D. Nicol, B. Stephen, G. Lonie, (S. Walker)
Substitutes not used: C. Garden, K. Gibson, J. Lennox
**Montrose:** J. Butter, B. Donachie, S. Ferguson, P. Doyle, N. Stephen, S. Kerrigan, K. Webster, (K. Dodds), C. Smart, M. Wood, E. Hall, G. Sharp, (C. Watson)
Substitutes not used: M. Hankinson, D. Spink, D. Smith
**Referee:** Brian Winter **Attendance:** 293

#### AYR UNITED 3     EDINBURGH CITY 0
A. Ferguson,
D. Henderson, W. Lyle

**Ayr United:** P. Cherrie, W. Lyle, S. McCulloch, M. Smyth, B. McLaughlin, D. Henderson, C. Conway, T. Tait, (D. Ramsay), A. Ferguson, P. Connolly, (G. Wardlaw), N. Gilmour, (A. Nesovic)
Substitutes not used: J. Hillcoat, M. Dunlop
**Edinburgh City:** A. MacKintosh, K. Morrison, C. Seeley, (D. Noon), T. Moriarty, R. MacNamara, S. Hunter, I. Elola, M. O'Doherty, (S. Johnston), C. Young, G. Carnie, (D. Gair), G. Cole
Substitutes not used: S. Vannet, K. Ross
**Referee:** Martin Sproule **Attendance:** 1,183

**GRETNA 3**                     **ELGIN CITY 0**
K. Deuchar (2), P. Kaczan (o.g.)

**Gretna:** D. Mathieson, M. Birch, J. McQuilken, B. Gilfillan, A. Aitken, D. Irons,
R. Baldacchino, R. McGuffie, (R. Prokas), K. Deuchar, D. Bingham, G. Skelton, (A. Smith)
Substitutes not used: A. Main, B. Wake, S. Cosgrove
**Elgin City:** K. Renton, S. Cumming, M. Harty, (I. Vigurs), P. Kaczan, C. Higgins,
H. Dickson, F. Bremner, A. Nelson, P. Vigurs, (P. Napier), W. Martin, P. Reid, (G. Melrose)
Substitutes not used: S. McKenzie, G. Wood
**Referee:** Ian Frickleton **Attendance:** 661

**ALBION ROVERS 0**              **ARBROATH 1**
                                 A. Brazil

**Albion Rovers:** C. Fahey, A. Paterson, (J. Boyle), J. Stirling, K. Potter,
P. McLaughlin, (J. Bradford), G. McCaul, (G. McLaren), M. McKenzie,
C. Silvestro, S. Crabbe, P. McManus, J. Mercer
Substitutes not used: M. Peat, A. Selkirk
**Arbroath:** N. Inglis, K. McMullan, E. Donaldson, S. Rennie, C. McLeod,
J. Bishop, M. Millar, S. MacDonald, A. Brazil, (P. Farquharson), G. Henslee,
G. Swankie, (D. McLean)
Substitutes not used: T. Woodcock, S. Fraser, G. Beith
**Referee:** Jamie Downie **Attendance:** 202

**STRANRAER 1**                  **QUEEN'S PARK 0**
S. Swift

**Stranraer:** A. McCondichie, S. Swift, G. McPhee, D. Wingate, M. Henderson,
A. Jenkins, K. Finlayson, K. Gaughan, B. Crawford, (D. Turnbull), D. Graham, G. Guy
Substitutes not used: M. McCaulay, S. Donnachie, G. McCutcheon, M. McGinty
**Queen's Park:** D. Crawford, A. Trouten, S. Molloy, S. Reilly, R. Sinclair, (R. Clark),
D. Agostini, S. Kettlewell, P. Harvey, A. Graham, (B. Fetvus), F. Carroll, M. Ferry
Substitutes not used: S. McGovern, B. Blair, G. Rushford
**Referee:** Cammy Melville **Attendance:** 391

**DUMBARTON 1**                  **BERWICK RANGERS 1**
J. Dillon                        G. McNicoll

**Dumbarton:** S. Grindlay, S. Bonar, C. Brittain, J. McKinstry, I. Dobbins,
P. Ronald, C. McEwan, (C. Boyle), B. Donald, R. Borris, (E. Annand), I. Russell,
(A. Rodgers), J. Dillon
Substitutes not used: J. Wight, M. Bradley
**Berwick Rangers:** G. O'Connor, D. Murie, A. Seaton, G. McNicoll, M. Cowan,
G. Connell, G. Connelly, (P. Clarke), M. McGarty, G. Hutchison, (P. Hampshire),
I. Little, D. Smith, (K. Gordon)
Substitutes not used: G. McCann, C. McKeown
**Referee:** Mike Tumilty **Attendance:** 692

**BRECHIN CITY 1**               **STIRLING ALBION 0**
P. Ritchie

**Brechin City:** C. Nelson, S. Hamilton, P. Deas, C. Winter, (J. Smith), D. White,
S. Walker, C. King, (I.G. Johnson), K. Byers, (S. MacNicol), P. Ritchie, G. Gibson,
S. Hampshire
Substitutes not used: D. Hay, L. Davidson
**Stirling Albion:** M. Hogarth, P. Nugent, S. Devine, (D. Wilson), M.McNally,
S.Roycroft, M. Galloway, P. Hay, (D. O'Brien), K. MacDonald, S. McLean,
M. Glancy, (C. Gethins), C. Ferguson
Substitutes not used: S. Christie, S. Hutchison
**Referee:** Brian Cassidy **Attendance:** 516

**HUNTLY 0**                     **EAST FIFE 0**
**Huntly:** R. Bowman, N. Reid, S. Scott, S. Anderson, R. Campbell, M. Gray,
L. Stephen, R. Guild, J. O'Driscoll, (M. Stewart), R. Taylor, G. McGowan,
(M. De-Barros)
Substitutes not used: G. Pennant, A. Reid, D. McGinlay
**East Fife:** S. Morrison, M. Renwick, K. Brash, C. Lumsden, K. Bain, G. Kelly,
S. Paliczka, G. McDonald, S. Nicholas, J. Mitchell, B. Fairbairn, (J. Herkes)
Substitutes not used: R. Logie, L. Byle, P. Gaughan, S. Tarditi
**Referee:** Colin Hardie **Attendance:** 545

**COVE RANGERS 1**               **MORTON 7**
M. Johnston                      P. Weatherson, J. Walker (2),
                                 J. Adam, W. Hawke, C. Millar (2)

**Cove Rangers:** I. Thain, C. McHattie, A. McCraw, G. Hendry, K. Tindal,
B. Morrison, G. Clark, (L. Flaws), M. Johnston, C. Milne, (G. Devine),
K. Robertson, J. Brown
Substitutes not used: R. Fraser, D. Henderson, R. Charles

**Morton:** C. Coyle, D. Collins, P. Weatherson, S. McCluskey, S. Greacen,
(W. Hawke), J. Adam, (D. Keenan), C. Millar, P. Walker, J. Walker,
(S. Bannerman), A. Mahood, J. McAlister
Substitutes not used: D. McGurn, J. Maisano
**Referee:** Alan Muir **Attendance:** 697

**ALLOA ATHLETIC 2**             **STENHOUSEMUIR 1**
A. Brown, R. Walker              J. Savage

**Alloa Athletic:** J. Evans, I. Nicolson, D. Hill, M. Bolochoweckyj, C. Townsley,
J. Ovenstone, R. Walker, M. Daly, A. Brown, B.A. Ferguson, S. Callaghan
Substitutes not used: G. McGlynn, P. Mortimer, J. Stevenson, A. McMillan, J. Calderon
**Stenhousemuir:** W. McCulloch, S. Fallon, D. McInally, K. Knox, (J. Savage),
R. Henderson, J.P. McBride, D. Morrison, L. Collins, S. McGregor,
R. Davidson, P. McGrillen
Substitutes not used: S. Orr, S. Easton, A. Smith, P. Murphy
**Referee:** Steven Duff **Attendance:** 370

## SECOND ROUND REPLAYS
Saturday, 18th December, 2004

**BERWICK RANGERS 3**            **DUMBARTON 1**
P. Clarke, G. Connelly,          E. Annand
G. Hutchison

**Berwick Rangers:** G. O'Connor, D. Murie, A. Seaton, G. McNicoll, M. Cowan,
G. Connell, G. Connelly, M. McGarty, G. Hutchison, P. Clarke, D. Smith
Substitutes not used: G. McCann, K. Gordon, P. Hampshire, C. McKeown, E. Smith
**Dumbarton:** S. Grindlay, S. Bonar, (M. Bradley), C. Brittain, J. McKinstry,
I. Dobbins, P. Ronald, (C. Boyle), C. McEwan, B. Donald, E. Annand, I. Russell,
(A. Rodgers), J. Dillon
Substitutes not used: J. Wight, R. Borris
**Referee:** Mike Tumilty **Attendance:** 318

**EAST FIFE 3**                  **HUNTLY 3**
                                 (AET – 2-2 After 90 Minutes)
C. Lumsden,                      J. O'Driscoll, M. De-Barros,
G. McDonald (2)                  R. Guild
East Fife won 4-3 on Kicks from the Penalty Mark

**East Fife:** S. Morrison, M. Renwick, K. Brash, (S. Tarditi), C. Lumsden, K. Bain,
G. Kelly, (L. Byle), S. Paliczka, (J. Herkes), G. McDonald, S. Nicholas,
J. Mitchell, B. Fairbairn
Substitutes not used: R. Logie, P. Gaughan
**Huntly:** R. Bowman, N. Reid, G. McGowan, (R. Stainer), S. Anderson,
R. Campbell, M. Gray, L. Stephen, R. Guild, J. O'Driscoll, R. Taylor, (G. Green),
M. De-Barros, (A. Reid)
Substitutes not used: G. Pennant, D. McGinlay
**Referee:** Colin Hardie **Attendance:** 575

## THIRD ROUND
Saturday, 8th January, 2005

**MONTROSE 1**                   **QUEEN OF THE SOUTH 2**
C. Smart                         D. Lyle, W. Gibson

**Montrose:** J. Butter, B. Donachie, K. Dodds, P. Doyle, N. Stephen, S. Kerrigan,
(M. Slater), K. Webster, (D. Smith), C. Smart, M. Wood, E. Hall, (C. Watson), G. Sharp
Substitutes not used: M. Hankinson, D. Greenhill
**Queen of the South:** Colin Scott, E. Paton, G. Wood, B. McColligan, D. Craig,
(S. Hill), J. Thomson, P. Burns, S. Bowey, E. Jaconelli, D. Lyle, W. Gibson
Substitutes not used: R. Barnard, D. Bagan, T. English, S. Payne
**Referee:** David Somers **Attendance:** 717

**KILMARNOCK 2**                 **MOTHERWELL 0**
G. McDonald, K. Boyd

**Kilmarnock:** A. Combe, D. Lilley, F. Dindeleux, (G. Locke), G. Greer, G. Hay,
P. Leven, G. McDonald, S. Naismith, (A. Johnston), C. Nish, K. Boyd,
(G. Wales), D. Invincible
Substitutes not used: G. Smith, S. Murray
**Motherwell:** G. Marshall, M. Corrigan, W. Kinniburgh, S. Hammell,
S. Craigan, K. McBride, M. Fitzpatrick, S. Leitch, S. McDonald, R. Foran,
D. Clarkson, (S. Fagan)
Substitutes not used: B.J. Corr, D. Cowan, P. Quinn, K. Wright
**Referee:** Craig Thomson **Attendance:** 6,093

**RAITH ROVERS 0**               **ALLOA ATHLETIC 2**
                                 J. Ovenstone, B.A. Ferguson

**Raith Rovers:** R. Pounoussamy, M. Mendy, P. McMullen, B. Raffell,
(J. Martin), J. Smart, A. Bartholome, M. Ouattara, H. Sacko, (C. O'Reilly),
H. Ebanda, (C. Malcolm), D. Brady, P. Millar
Substitutes not used: D. Berthelot, L. Young

**Alloa Athletic:** J. Evans, I. Nicolson, (J. Quitongo), I. Ross, M. Bolochowecky, (P. Mortimer), C. Townsley, J. Ovenstone, R. Walker, B.A. Ferguson, A. Brown, R. Hamilton, J. Stevenson, (J. Calderon)
Substitutes not used: G. McGlynn, M. Daly
**Referee:** Crawford Allan **Attendance:** 1,545

### ST. MIRREN 3 — HAMILTON ACADEMICAL 0
S. Kean (2), A. Russell

**St. Mirren:** C. Hinchcliffe, D. Van Zanten, K. Broadfoot, A. Millen, K. McGowne, M. Reilly, H. Murray, (M. Crilly), S. Lappin, S. Kean, (J. Baird), B. McGinty, (A. Russell), R. McCay
Substitutes not used: S. Woods, J. O'Neill
**Hamilton Academical:** D. McEwan, I. Fyfe, (P. McLeod), S. Hodge, S. Thomson, R. Walker, A. Arbuckle, (B. Carrigan), D. Ferguson, (C. Aitken), B. McPhee, P. Keogh, D. Carney, M. Corcoran
Substitutes not used: R. Jellema, T. Lumsden
**Referee:** Mike Ritchie **Attendance:** 2,907

### CLYDE 3 — FALKIRK 0
I. Harty (2), G. Bollan

**Clyde:** B. Halliwell, S. Mensing, G. Bollan, S. Balmer, J. Potter, D. Sheridan, (J. Gibson), A. Burns, S. Wilson, G. Jones, E. Malone, I. Harty
Substitutes not used: A. Morrison, M. Keogh, G. Arbuckle, K.Bradley
**Falkirk:** A. Ferguson, A. Lawrie, C. McPherson, S. MacKenzie, M. Campbell, K. James, (J. Sharp), J. O'Neil, (D. McBreen), N. Scally, A. Thomson, R. Latapy, D. Duffy
Substitutes not used: D. Hill, P. Moutinho, C. Marshall
**Referee:** Calum Murray **Attendance:** 3,565

### ARBROATH 0 — ABERDEEN 2
M. Heikkinen, D. Mackie

**Arbroath:** N. Inglis, K. McMullan, E. Donaldson, S. Rennie, C. McLeod, J. Bishop, M. Millar, (J. Cusick), S. MacDonald, A. Brazil, G. Henslee, (D. McLean), G. Swankie, (P. Farquharson)
Substitutes not used: T. Woodcock, G. Miller
**Aberdeen:** R. Esson, P. McGuire, K. McNaughton, R. Anderson, M. Hart, M. Heikkinen, S. Tosh, (S. Morrison), D. Adams, J. Stewart, (N. Whelan), C. Clark, D. Mackie
Substitutes not used: J. Blanchard, S. Craig, R. Foster
**Referee:** Brian Winter **Attendance:** 3,996

### BERWICK RANGERS 0 — BRECHIN CITY 3
S. Hampshire (2), C. Winter

**Berwick Rangers:** G. O'Connor, D. Murie, A. Seaton, (P. Hampshire), C. McKeown, R. Horn, G. Connell, G. Connelly, (K. Gordon), M. McGarty, G. Hutchison, I. MacSween, D. Smith
Substitutes not used: G. McCann, I. Little, G. Greenhill
**Brechin City:** C. Nelson, S. Hamilton, (S. MacNicol), P. Deas, D. White, S. Walker, K. Byers, (A. Mitchell), C. King, I.G. Johnson, P. Ritchie, (G. Gibson), C. Winter, S. Hampshire
Substitutes not used: D. Hay, R. Strachan
**Referee:** Eddie Smith **Attendance:** 386

### EAST FIFE 0 — DUNFERMLINE ATHLETIC 0
**East Fife:** S. Morrison, M. Renwick, K. Brash, C. Lumsden, K. Bain, G. Kelly, S. Paliczka, G. McDonald, S. Nicholas, J. Mitchell, B. Fairbairn
Substitutes not used: J. McCafferty, L. Byle, G. Mathie, K. Steele, S. Tarditi
**Dunfermline Athletic:** D. Stillie, A. Labonte, G. Ross, A. Skerla, S.M. Thomson, (I. Campbell), Darren Young, (G. Dempsey), B. Nicholson, G. Mason, L. Makel, J. Christiansen, (N. Hunt), A. Tod
Substitutes not used: J. Langfield, J. Dunn
**Referee:** Brian Cassidy **Attendance:** 1,722

### HIBERNIAN 2 — DUNDEE 0
S. Whittaker, S. Morrow

**Hibernian:** Simon Brown, G. Caldwell, G. Smith, D. Murphy, (J .McCluskey), S. Whittaker, I. Murray, S. Glass, A. Orman, (S. Morrow), (S. Fletcher), D. Shiels, D. Riordan, G. O'Connor
Substitutes not used: A. Brown, J. Shields
**Dundee:** D. Soutar, N. Barrett, (J. Sutton), B. Sancho, L. Wilkie, C. MacDonald, B. Smith, S. Robb, M. Fotheringham, S. Robertson, (G. Larsen), S. Lovell, F. Caballero
Substitutes not used: K. Jack, R. Mann, J. Hernandez
**Referee:** Iain Brines **Attendance:** 9,706

### PARTICK THISTLE 0 — HEARTS 0
**Partick Thistle:** K. Arthur, J-Y. Anis, K. Milne, G. Murray, A. Madaschi, D. Fleming, J. Mitchell, (A. Dowie), A. Oné, J. Escalas, A. Strachan, (S. Fulton), A. Gibson, (W. Gibson)
Substitutes not used: S. Pinkowski, L. Hinds

**Hearts:** C. Gordon, J. McAllister, K. McKenna, S. Pressley, A. Webster, J. Hamill, (S. Simmons), R. Neilson, P. Stamp, N. Macfarlane, D. Wyness, (P. Kisnorbo), G. Weir, (R. Pereira)
Substitutes not used: T. Moilanen, C. Berra
**Referee:** Craig Mackay **Attendance:** 5,666

### AYR UNITED 3 — STRANRAER 3
C. Conway, A. Ferguson, D. Henderson — K. Gaughan, G. McCutcheon, D. Wingate

**Ayr United:** J. Hillcoat, T. Tait, M. Dunlop, M. Smyth, B. McLaughlin, S. McGrady, C. Conway, P. Connolly, A. Ferguson, G. Wardlaw, (W. Lyle), D. Henderson
Substitutes not used: P. Cherrie, S. Ferguson, S. Chaplain, S. McCulloch
**Stranraer:** M. McCaulay, G. Guy, C. Cruickshank, (D. Graham), D. Wingate, G. McPhee, A. Jenkins, K. Finlayson, K. Gaughan, G. McCutcheon, (B. Crawford), D. Turnbull, (M. Henderson), L. Sharp
Substitutes not used: M. McGinty, J. Fraser
**Referee:** Cammy Melville **Attendance:** 1,905

Sunday, 9th January, 2005

### CELTIC 2 — RANGERS 1
C. Sutton, J. Hartson — F. Ricksen

**Celtic:** R. Douglas, S. Varga, U. Laursen, D. Balde, J. McNamara, S. Petrov, D. Agathe, A. Thompson, C. Sutton, J. Hartson, A. McGeady, (H. Camara)
Substitutes not used: D. Marshall, O. Juninho, P. Lambert, R. Wallace
**Rangers:** S. Klos, A. Hutton, M. Andrews, Z. Khizanishvili, G. Vignal, F. Ricksen, B. Djordjic, (T. Buffel), A. Rae, H. Namouchi, (S. Thompson), I. Novo, D. Prso
Substitutes not used: A. McGregor, R. Malcolm, M. Ball
**Referee:** Hugh Dallas **Attendance:** 58,559

### INVERNESS CAL. THISTLE 1 — ST. JOHNSTONE 0
S. Golabek
Match Played at Victoria Park, Dingwall

**Inverness Caledonian Thistle:** M. Brown, R. Tokely, S. Golabek, G. Munro, D. Dods, R. McBain, (R. Hart), R. Duncan, B. Wilson, L. Keogh, C. Brewster, (G. Bayne), B. Prunty, (J. Carricondo)
Substitutes not used: M. Fraser, D. Proctor
**St. Johnstone:** K. Cuthbert, M. Baxter, K. Fotheringham, (R. Forsyth), D. Hannah, S. Webb, I. Maxwell, R. McCann, (K. McAnespie), K. Rutkiewicz, (C. Hay), P. MacDonald, M. Moore, P. Sheerin
Substitutes not used: C. Samson, M. Fotheringham
**Referee:** Dougie McDonald **Attendance:** 1,821

Tuesday, 11th January, 2005

### LIVINGSTON 2 — MORTON 1
O. Rubio, R. Snodgrass — P. Weatherson

**Livingston:** C. Meldrum, D. McNamee, R. Harding, O. Rubio, G.Bahoken, G. Stanik, (R. Snodgrass), R. Brittain, (J. Hand), B. O'Brien, S. Lovell, J.Hamilton, J. McPake, (J. Dair)
Substitutes not used: R. McKenzie, C. Easton
**Morton:** D. McGurn, D. Collins, S. Dillon, (S. Bannerman), S. McCluskey, S. Greacen, A. Mahood, (W. Hawke), C. Millar, P. Walker, (J. Walker), P. Weatherson, D. Keenan, J. McAlister
Substitutes not used: C. Coyle, J. Adam
**Referee:** Steve Conroy **Attendance:** 2,764

Monday, 17th January, 2005

### GRETNA 3 — DUNDEE UNITED 4
K. Deuchar, M. Birch, G. Skelton — B. Robson, M. Kerr, M. Wilson, S. Crawford

**Gretna:** D. Mathieson, M. Birch, (A. Smith), J. McQuilken, B. Gilfillan, A. Aitken, D. Irons, R. Baldacchino, (R. Prokas), R. McGuffie, K. Deuchar, D. Bingham, G. Skelton
Substitutes not used: M. Bake, B. Wake, D. Grainger
**Dundee United:** A. Bullock, P. Ritchie, A. Archibald, D. McCracken, M. Wilson, D. McInnes, M. Kerr, B. Robson, (L. Mair), J. Grady, J. McIntyre, S. Crawford
Substitutes not used: P. Jarvie, J. Scotland, G. Brebner, D. Robertson
**Referee:** Kenny Clark **Attendance:** 3,000

Monday, 24th January, 2005

### ROSS COUNTY 4 — AIRDRIE UNITED 1
A. Burke, D. Winters (2), M. McGeown — M. Hardie (o.g.)

**Ross County:** C. Stewart, J. Robertson, M. McCulloch, F. Tiernan, M. Canning, J. Lauchlan, J. Rankin, (S. Kilgannon), D. Cowie, D. Winters, J. McCunnie, (S. McGarry), A. Burke, (S. Higgins)
Substitutes not used: S. Garden, S. Malcolm

Airdrie United: M. McGeown, W. Wilson, (S. McKenna), P. Lovering, N. McGowan, A. McManus, M. Hardie, D. Dunn, M. Wilson, O. Coyle, (J. Vareille), M. Roberts, (S. McKeown), W. McLaren
Substitutes not used: L. Hollis, K. Barkey
**Referee:** Ian Fyfe **Attendance:** 1,302

## THIRD ROUND REPLAYS
Tuesday, 18th January, 2005

| DUNFERMLINE ATHLETIC 3 | EAST FIFE 1 |
|---|---|
| A. Tod, N. Hunt, G. Dempsey | L. Byle |

**Dunfermline Athletic:** D. Stillie, A. Tod, G. Ross, A. Skerla, S.M. Thomson, Darren Young, (I. Campbell), B. Nicholson, G. Mason, G. Dempsey, J. Christiansen, (J. Dunn), N. Hunt
Substitutes not used: J. Langfield, C. Wilson, P. Scullion
**East Fife:** S. Morrison, M. Renwick, K. Brash, C. Lumsden, K. Bain, G. Kelly, (L. Byle), S. Paliczka, (S. Tarditi), G. McDonald, S. Nicholas, J. Mitchell, (K. Steele), B. Fairbairn
Substitutes not used: J. McCafferty, G. Mathie
**Referee:** Brian Cassidy **Attendance:** 3,542

Wednesday, 19th January, 2005

| HEARTS 2 | PARTICK THISTLE 1 |
|---|---|
| N. Macfarlane, D. Wyness | A. Oné |

**Hearts:** C. Gordon, J. McAllister, K. McKenna, S. Pressley, A. Webster, N. Macfarlane, (S. Simmons), R. Neilson, P. Stamp, P. Hartley, D. Wyness, R. Pereira, (J. Hamill)
Substitutes not used: T. Moilanen, G. Weir, C. Berra
**Partick Thistle:** K. Arthur, J-Y. Anis, (A. Gibson), K. Milne, G. Murray, A. Madaschi, A. Dowie, (S. Fulton), W. Gibson, (A. Strachan), A. Oné, J. Escalas, A. Ross, D. Fleming
Substitutes not used: S. Pinkowski, L. Hinds
**Referee:** Craig Mackay **Attendance:** 7,375

Tuesday, 25th January, 2005

| STRANRAER 0 | AYR UNITED 2 |
|---|---|
|  | C. Conway, G. Wardlaw |

**Stranraer:** M. McCaulay, S. Swift, (G. Guy), F. Wright, D. Wingate, M. Henderson, A. Jenkins, K. Finlayson, (G. McCutcheon), K. Gaughan, G. McPhee, (J. Fraser), D. Graham, L. Sharp
Substitutes not used: A. McCondichie, S. Aitken
**Ayr United:** L. Roy, T. Tait, M. Dunlop, M. Smyth, B. McLaughlin, S. McGrady, (W. Lyle), C. Conway, P. Connolly, (D. Ramsay), A. Ferguson, (A. Reid), G. Wardlaw, D. Henderson
Substitutes not used: J. Hillcoat, J. Doyle
**Referee:** Cammy Melville **Attendance:** 1,044

## FOURTH ROUND
Saturday, 5th February, 2005

| ABERDEEN 2 | INVERNESS CAL. THISTLE 1 |
|---|---|
| D. Mackie (2) | C. Brewster |

**Aberdeen:** R. Esson, R. Byrne, K. McNaughton, R. Anderson, M. Hart, M. Heikkinen, J. Winter, C. Clark, N. Whelan, (D. Adams), S. Craig, (J. Stewart), D. Mackie, (P. McGuire)
Substitutes not used: J. Blanchard, S. Morrison
**Inverness Cal. Thistle:** M. Brown, R. Tokely, S. Golabek, G. Munro, D. Dods, R. Hart, (R. McBain), R. Duncan, B. Wilson, J. Carricondo, (B. Fetai), C. Brewster, G. Bayne
Substitutes not used: J. Smith, S. McCaffrey, B. Prunty
**Referee:** Willie Young **Attendance:** 10,595

| ROSS COUNTY 0 | CLYDE 0 |
|---|---|

**Ross County:** C. Stewart, J. Robertson, M. McCulloch, F. Tiernan, M. Canning, J. Lauchlan, J. Rankin, (S. Kilgannon), D. Cowie, D. Winters, J. McCunnie, A. Burke
Substitutes not used: S. Garden, S. McGarry, S. Malcolm, S. Higgins
**Clyde:** B. Halliwell, S. Mensing, G. Bollan, S. Balmer, J. Potter, D. Sheridan, (G. Arbuckle), A. Burns, J. Gibson, G. Jones, (C. Bryson), E. Malone, I. Harty
Substitutes not used: A. Morrison, S. Wilson, K. Bradley
**Referee:** Hugh Dallas **Attendance:** 1,629

| QUEEN OF THE SOUTH 0 | DUNDEE UNITED 3 |
|---|---|
|  | J. McIntyre, M. Wilson, S. Duff |

**Queen of the South:** Colin Scott, E. Paton, D. Craig, B. McColligan, B. Reid, J. Thomson, P. Burns, (S. Payne), S. Bowey, D. McNiven, (E. Jaconelli), D. Lyle, W. Gibson, (B. McLaughlin)
Substitutes not used: R. Barnard, T. English

---

**Dundee United:** A. Bullock, P. Ritchie, A. Archibald, D. McCracken, (G. Kenneth), M. Wilson, L. Mair, M. Kerr, (G. Brebner), B. Robson, (J.Scotland), S. Duff, J. McIntyre, S. Crawford
Substitutes not used: N. Colgan, J. Grady
**Referee:** Dougie McDonald **Attendance:** 5,532

| AYR UNITED 0 | ST. MIRREN 2 |
|---|---|
|  | S. Kean, H. Murray |

**Ayr United:** L. Roy, T. Tait, M. Dunlop, (W. Lyle), M. Smyth, B. McLaughlin, S. McGrady, C. Conway, P. Connolly, A. Ferguson, (D. Ramsay), A. Reid, (G. Brown), D. Henderson
Substitutes not used: J. Hillcoat, N. McVicar
**St. Mirren:** C. Hinchcliffe, D. Van Zanten, K. Broadfoot, A. Millen, K. McGowne, M. Reilly, H. Murray, (M. Crilly), J. O'Neill, (R. Gillies), S. Kean, B. McGinty, (A. Russell), R. McCay Substitutes not used: S. Woods, S. Lappin
**Referee:** Kenny Clark **Attendance:** 4,796

| HEARTS 2 | KILMARNOCK 2 |
|---|---|
| D. Wyness, L. Miller | C. Nish, S. Naismith |

**Hearts:** C. Gordon, J. McAllister, L. Wallace, S. Pressley, A. Webster, S. Simmons, (N. Macfarlane), R. Neilson, S. Mikoliunas, (J. Hamill), P. Hartley, L. Miller, D. Wyness, (M. Burchill)
Substitutes not used: T. Moilanen, H. Thorarinsson
**Kilmarnock:** A. Combe, D. Lilley, G. Hay, L. Fontaine, S. Ford, P. Leven, A. Johnston, G. Locke, (S. Naismith), G. McDonald, C. Nish, (K. Boyd), D. Invincible, (S. Murray)
Substitutes not used: G. Smith, J. Fowler
**Referee:** John Rowbotham **Attendance:** 10,483

| ALLOA ATHLETIC 0 | LIVINGSTON 1 |
|---|---|
|  | C. McMenamin |

**Alloa Athletic:** J. Evans, R. Walker, I. Ross, M. Bolochoweckyj, C. Townsley, J. Ovenstone, I. Nicolson, (J. Quitongo), B.A. Ferguson, A. Brown, R. Hamilton, J. Stevenson
Substitutes not used: G. McGlynn, M. Daly, P. Mortimer, J. Calderon
**Livingston:** R. McKenzie, G. Strong, E. Deloumeaux, O. Rubio, (J. Dair), G. Bahoken, G. Vincze, C. Easton, B. O'Brien, J. Hand, (A. Kriston), J. McPake, (C. McMenamin), D. Lilley
Substitutes not used: C. Meldrum, M. Wilson
**Referee:** Craig Thomson **Attendance:** 2,127

| HIBERNIAN 4 | BRECHIN CITY 0 |
|---|---|
| S. Morrow, G. O'Connor (2), |  |
| G. Caldwell |  |

**Hibernian:** Simon Brown, G. Caldwell, G. Smith, G. Beuzelin, (A. Murray), S. Whittaker, I. Murray, S. Glass, S. Morrow, (J. McCluskey), D. Shiels, (S. Fletcher), D. Riordan, G. O'Connor
Substitutes not used: A. Reid, A. Orman
**Brechin City:** C. Nelson, S. Hamilton, (J. Smith), P. Deas, D. White, S. Walker, K. Byers, C. King, (R. Strachan), C. Winter, P. Ritchie, S. Hampshire, G. Gibson, (I.G. Johnson)
Substitutes not used: D. Hay, B. White
**Referee:** Michael McCurry **Attendance:** 13,563

Sunday, 6th February, 2005

| DUNFERMLINE ATHLETIC 0 | CELTIC 3 |
|---|---|
|  | J. Hartson (2), C. Sutton |

**Dunfermline Athletic:** D. Stillie, S. Wilson, (G. Hristov), G. Ross, A. Skerla, S.M. Thomson, Darren Young, (N. Hunt), B. Nicholson, G. Mason, L. Makel, J. Christiansen, A. Tod
Substitutes not used: J. Langfield, S. Donnelly, I. Campbell
**Celtic:** R. Douglas, S. Varga, U. Laursen, D. Balde, S. Henchoz, S. Petrov, (P. Lambert), A. Thompson, (O. Juninho), N. Lennon, C. Sutton, J. Hartson, (R. Wallace), A. McGeady
Substitutes not used: D. Marshall, S. McManus
**Referee:** Charlie Richmond **Attendance:** 8,504

## FOURTH ROUND REPLAYS
Tuesday, 15th February, 2005

| CLYDE 2 | ROSS COUNTY 1 |
|---|---|
| C. Bryson, G. Arbuckle | J. Rankin |

**Clyde:** B. Halliwell, S. Mensing, G. Bollan, S. Balmer, (M. Gilhaney), J. Potter, D. Sheridan, A. Burns, (G. Arbuckle), J. Gibson, C. Bryson, (S. Wilson), E. Malone, I. Harty
Substitutes not used: A. Morrison, K. Bradley

**Ross County:** C. Stewart, J. Robertson, (S. Higgins), M. McCulloch, F. Tiernan, M. Canning, J. Lauchlan, J. Rankin, D. Cowie, D. Winters, A. Burke, (J. McCunnie), S. Kilgannon, (S. McGarry)
Substitutes not used: S. Garden, S. Malcolm
**Referee:** Hugh Dallas **Attendance:** 1,566

Wednesday, 16th February, 2005

| KILMARNOCK 1 | HEARTS 3 |
|---|---|
| K. Boyd | L. Wallace, L. Miller, D. Cesnauskis |

**Kilmarnock:** A. Combe, D. Lilley, G. Hay, L. Fontaine, S. Ford, P. Leven, A. Johnston, S. Naismith, (S. Murray), G. McDonald, K. Boyd, D. Invincible
Substitutes not used: C. Bell, J. Fowler, C. Dargo, R. Dodds
**Hearts:** C. Gordon, D. Cesnauskis, L. Wallace, S. Pressley, A. Webster, S. Simmons, (N. Macfarlane), R. Neilson, S. Mikoliunas, P. Hartley, L.Miller, (H. Thorarinsson), D. Wyness, (M. Burchill)
Substitutes not used: T. Moilanen, C. Berra
**Referee:** John Rowbotham **Attendance:** 6,366

## FIFTH ROUND
Saturday, 26th February, 2005

| HIBERNIAN 2 | ST. MIRREN 0 |
|---|---|
| Scott Brown, G. O'Connor | |

**Hibernian:** Simon Brown, G. Caldwell, G. Smith, D. Murphy, S. Whittaker, I. Murray, A. Murray, S. Fletcher, (A. Orman), Scott Brown, (K. McDonald), D. Riordan, G. O'Connor
Substitutes not used: A. Brown, A. Konte, S. Morrow
**St. Mirren:** C. Hinchcliffe, D. Van Zanten, K. Broadfoot, A. Millen, K. McGowne, M. Reilly, H. Murray, S. Lappin, (R. Gillies), S. Kean, A. Russell, (J. O'Neill), R. McCay, (B. McGinty)
Substitutes not used: S. Woods, L. Ellis
**Referee:** Willie Young **Attendance:** 15,195

Sunday, 27th February, 2005

| CLYDE 0 | CELTIC 5 |
|---|---|
| | S. Varga (2), A. Thompson, |
| | S. Petrov, C. Bellamy |

**Clyde:** B. Halliwell, S. Mensing, G. Bollan, S. Balmer, J. Potter, D. Sheridan, (A. Burns), G. Arbuckle, (M. Gilhaney), J. Gibson, C. Bryson, (G. Jones), E. Malone, I. Harty
Substitutes not used: A. Morrison, S. Wilson
**Celtic:** R. Douglas, S. Varga, S. Henchoz, D. Balde, J. McNamara, S. Petrov, (A. McGeady), A. Thompson, N. Lennon, (P. Lambert), C. Sutton, (S. Maloney), C. Bellamy, O. Juninho
Substitutes not used: D. Marshall, U. Laursen
**Referee:** Craig Thomson **Attendance:** 6,862

| HEARTS 2 | LIVINGSTON 1 |
|---|---|
| L. Miller, J. McAllister | C. Easton |

**Hearts:** C. Gordon, J. McAllister, L. Wallace, C. Berra, A. Webster, S. Simmons, (N. Macfarlane), R. Neilson, S. Mikoliunas, (D. Cesnauskis), P. Hartley, L. Miller, M. Burchill, (D. Wyness)
Substitutes not used: T. Moilanen, M. Kizys
**Livingston:** C. Meldrum, D. McNamee, E. Delourneaux, G. Strong, G. Bahoken, (G. Stanik), J. Dair, C. Easton, B. O'Brien, M. Wilson, (G.Vincze), J. McPake, D. Lilley, (F. Horvath)
Substitutes not used: R. McKenzie, J. Hand
**Referee:** Alan Freeland **Attendance:** 10,923

| DUNDEE UNITED 4 | ABERDEEN 1 |
|---|---|
| A. Archibald, J. Grady (2), | R. Byrne |
| S. Crawford | |

**Dundee United:** A. Bullock, P. Ritchie, A. Archibald, S. Duff, M. Wilson, G. Brebner, M. Kerr, (G. Cameron), B. Robson, J. Scotland, (C. Samuel), J. Grady, S. Crawford
Substitutes not used: N. Colgan, G. Kenneth, W. Dodds
**Aberdeen:** R. Esson, R. Byrne, (S. Morrison), K. McNaughton, R. Anderson, A. Diamond, M. Heikkinen, (R. Foster), M. Hart, J. Winter, C. Clark, (J. Stewart), N. Whelan, D. Mackie
Substitutes not used: J. Blanchard, P. McGuire
**Referee:** Kenny Clark **Attendance:** 8,661

## SEMI-FINALS
Saturday, 9th April, 2005
The National Stadium, Hampden Park, Glasgow

| DUNDEE UNITED 2 | HIBERNIAN 1 |
|---|---|
| J. McIntyre, J. Scotland | D. Riordan |

**Dundee United:** A. Bullock, P. Ritchie, A. Archibald, S. Duff, (J. Scotland), M. Wilson, D. McInnes, (M. Kerr), G. Brebner, G. Kenneth, B. Robson, J. McIntyre, S. Crawford, (C. Samuel)
Substitutes not used: N. Colgan, J. Grady
**Hibernian:** Simon Brown, G. Caldwell, G. Smith, D. Murphy, (K. Thomson), S. Whittaker, S. Fletcher, S. Glass, D. Shiels, (I. Sproule), Scott Brown, D. Riordan, (S. Morrow), G. O'Connor
Substitutes not used: A. Brown, A. Murray
**Referee:** Michael McCurry **Attendance:** 27,271

Sunday, 10th April, 2005
The National Stadium, Hampden Park, Glasgow

| HEARTS 1 | CELTIC 2 |
|---|---|
| D. Cesnauskis | C. Sutton, C. Bellamy |

**Hearts:** C. Gordon, J. McAllister, L. Wallace, S. Pressley, A. Webster, J. Hamill, (M. Kizys), R. Neilson, (D. Cesnauskis), N. Macfarlane, (D. Wyness), P. Hartley, L. Miller, M. Burchill
Substitutes not used: T. Moilanen, C. Berra
**Celtic:** D. Marshall, S. Varga, J. Valgaeren, D. Balde, J. McNamara, S. Petrov, N. Lennon, A. Thompson, C. Sutton, J. Hartson, (A. McGeady), C. Bellamy
Substitutes not used: R. Douglas, S. Henchoz, P. Lambert, S. Maloney
**Referee:** Stuart Dougal **Attendance:** 38,505

## FINAL
Saturday, 28th May, 2005
The National Stadium, Hampden Park, Glasgow

| CELTIC 1 | DUNDEE UNITED 0 |
|---|---|

**Celtic:** R. Douglas, D. Agathe, S. Varga, D. Balde, J. McNamara, S. Petrov, N. Lennon, A. Thompson, (A. McGeady), C. Sutton, J. Hartson, (J. Valgaeren), C. Bellamy
Substitutes not used: D. Marshall, P. Lambert, C. Beattie
**Dundee United:** A. Bullock, P. Ritchie, A. Archibald, M. Wilson, G. Kenneth, D. McInnes, (C. Samuel), G. Brebner, (S. Duff), M. Kerr, B. Robson, S. Crawford, (J. Grady), J. Scotland
Substitutes not used: N. Colgan, D. McCracken
**Scorer: Celtic:** A. Thompson
**Referee:** John Rowbotham **Attendance:** 50,635

Celtic - Tennent's Scottish Cup Winners 2004.05

# THE BELL'S CUP **SEASON 2004.05**

## FIRST ROUND
Saturday, 31st July, 2004

### ALLOA ATHLETIC 2     ELGIN CITY 0
B.A. Ferguson, R. Hamilton

**Alloa Athletic:** G. McGlynn, R. Walker, D. Hill, P. McLaughlin, (P. Mortimer), M. Bolochoweckyj, C. Townsley, J. Stevenson, B.A. Ferguson, (S. Nicholas), A. Brown, R. Hamilton, S. Callaghan, (M. Daly)
Substitutes not used: A. McMillan, J. Evans
**Elgin City:** K. Renton, S. Cumming, S. Black, (W. Martin), P. Kaczan, H. Dickson, J. McKenzie, A. Dempsie, A. Nelson, A. Bone, (P. Reid), M. Harty, (F. Bremner), A. Roddie
Substitutes not used: M. Charlesworth, M. Pirie
**Referee:** Colin Hardie **Attendance:** 301

### PARTICK THISTLE 3     BRECHIN CITY 0
W. Gibson, J. Escalas (2)

**Partick Thistle:** K. Arthur, W. Gibson, W. Howie, (A. Ross), G. Murray, A. Dowie, S. Fulton, J. Mitchell, D. Fleming, J. Escalas, A. Gibson, (E. Panther), J-Y. Anis, (A. Wilkinson)
Substitutes not used: G. Britton, S. Pinkowski
**Brechin City:** D. Hay, S. MacNicol, P. Deas, I.G. Johnson, S. Dennis, (J. Smith), S. Walker, C. King, (C. Templeman), C. Winter, P. Ritchie, S. Hampshire, (G. Gibson), A. Mitchell
Substitutes not used: S. McCulloch, S. Vanderdeyl
**Referee:** Ian Fyfe **Attendance:** 1,803

### EAST FIFE 0     COWDENBEATH 0 (AET)
Cowdenbeath won 4-3 on Kicks from the Penalty Mark
**East Fife:** J. Dodds, C. Lumsden, I. McDonald, K. Bain, M. Hall, L. Byle, (G. Kelly), J. Mitchell, G. McDonald, (R. Crawford), B. Fairbairn, S. Tarditi, K. Brash, (J. Herkes)
Substitutes not used: S. Paliczka, S. Morrison
**Cowdenbeath:** A. Carlin, C. Shand, A. Campbell, B. Gilfillan, J. McKeown, I. Ritchie, I. Mauchlen, (L. Buchanan), P. McHale, (G. Fusco), D. Shields, D. Mowat, J.P. Burns, (J.P. Kelly)
Substitutes not used: G. McKenna, A. Fleming
**Referee:** Tom Brown **Attendance:** 468

### AIRDRIE UNITED 0     QUEEN OF THE SOUTH 2
G. Wood, T. English

**Airdrie United:** M. McGeown, K. Christie, P. Lovering, N. McGowan, (S. McKeown), A. McManus, D. Dunn, J. Vareille, M. Wilson, O. Coyle, A. Gow, M. Roberts
Substitutes not used: W. Wilson, K. Barkey, S. McKenna, L. Hollis
**Queen of the South:** Colin Scott, Christopher Scott, T. English, B. McColligan, B. Reid, J. Thomson, D. Bagan, (P. Burns), S. Bowey, D. McNiven, (E. Jaconelli), (W. Gibson), G. Wood, B. McLaughlin
Substitutes not used: C. Samson, S. Payne
**Referee:** Michael McCurry **Attendance:** 1,488

### ST. JOHNSTONE 2     HAMILTON ACADEMICAL 0
D. Hannah, M. Moore

**St. Johnstone:** K. Cuthbert, J. Tait, S. Fraser, D. Hannah, K. Rutkiewicz, I. Maxwell, R. Stevenson, P. Sheerin, C. Hay, (S. McConalogue), M. Moore, E. Malone
Substitutes not used: C. Marshall, M. Fotheringham, M. Baxter, C. Nelson
**Hamilton Academical:** D. McEwan, R. Walker, R. Waddell, S. Thomson, M. McLaughlin, S. Tunbridge, B. Carrigan, C. Aitken, R. Blackadder, (I. Fyfe), B. McPhee, M. Corcoran, (S. Convery)
Substitutes not used: T. Lumsden, D. Hamilton, R. Jellema
**Referee:** Dougie McDonald **Attendance:** 1,850

### ROSS COUNTY 2     ST. MIRREN 1
A. Burke (2)     R. Gillies

**Ross County:** S. Garden, J. Robertson, M. McCulloch, J. McCunnie, (S. Kilgannon), M. Canning, J. Lauchlan, J. Rankin, D. Cowie, G. McSwegan, (D. Winters), S. McGarry, ( S. Mackay), A. Burke
Substitutes not used: S. Higgins, J. McCafferty
**St. Mirren:** C. Hinchcliffe, D. Van Zanten, K. Broadfoot, A. Millen, K. McGowne, M. Reilly, R. Gillies, M. Crilly, (J. Baird), M-M. Paatelainen, B. McGinty, (E. Annand), S. Lappin, (J. O'Neill)
Substitutes not used: L. Ellis, S. Woods
**Referee:** Craig Mackay **Attendance:** 992

### EAST STIRLINGSHIRE 1     BERWICK RANGERS 2
R. Donaldson     K. Gordon, G. Forrest

**East Stirlingshire:** A. Mitchell, D. Harvey, G. McGhee. J. Mackay, C. Newall, S. McAuley, (G. Findlay), P. Ross, A. Moffat, (J. Leishman), R. Donaldson, (G. Parks), J. Dunbar, C. Miller
Substitutes not used: C. Baldwin, R. Gilpin
**Berwick Rangers:** G. O'Connor, E. Smith, A. Seaton, M. Cowan, R. Horn, G. Connell, G. Forrest, (G. McNicoll), M. Neil, (G. Connelly), G. Hutchison, K. Gordon, P. Hampshire
Substitutes not used: J. Birrell, I. Little, R. Godfrey
**Referee:** Chris Boyle **Attendance:** 264

### GRETNA 3     MONTROSE 0
D. Bingham, A. Smith, R. Baldacchino

**Gretna:** D. Mathieson, M. Birch, G. Skelton, R. Prokas, A. Aitken, D. Holdsworth, R. Baldacchino, M. Galloway, (R. McGuffie), A. Smith, (K. Deuchar), D. Bingham, D. Townsley, (M. Boyd)
Substitutes not used: S. Cosgrove, C. Summersgill
**Montrose:** J. Butter, B. Donachie, A. Budd, (D. Jones), N. Stephen, G. Smith, S. Kerrigan, D. Smith, (K. Webster), D. Spink, C. Smart, E. Hall, G. Sharp, (K. Morrice)
Substitutes not used: R. Lindsay, H. Fraser
**Referee:** David Somers **Attendance:** 454

### AYR UNITED 0     FALKIRK 3
A. Lawrie, J. O'Neil, D. Duffy

**Ayr United:** L. Roy, M. Smyth, S. McGrady, S. Chaplain, B. McLaughlin, D. Craig, (W. Lyle), G. Brown, (A. Ferguson), D. Ramsay, (P. Connolly), S. Kean, D. Henderson, C. Conway
Substitutes not used: M. Dunlop, J. Hillcoat
**Falkirk:** D. Hill, A. Lawrie, C. McPherson, S. MacKenzie, M. Campbell, J. Sharp, J. O'Neil, (D. Nicholls), R. McStay, (N. Scally), A. Thomson, R. Latapy, (P. Moutinho), D. Duffy
Substitutes not used: J. Hughes, J. Hutchison
**Referee:** Craig Thomson **Attendance:** 1,797

### FORFAR ATHLETIC 3     MORTON 1
P. Shields (2), P. Tosh     J. Walker

**Forfar Athletic:** M. Brown, A. Rattray, D. Lowing, (D. Dunn), E. Forrest, D. King, D. McClune, B. Sellars, P. Lunan, P. Tosh, (M. King), P. Shields, J. Stein
Substitutes not used: M. Booth, M. Maher, N. Ferrie
**Morton:** C. Coyle, S. Bannerman, M. McCulloch, S. McCluskey, S. Greacen, M. Maisano, (A. Williams), C. Millar, J. McAlister, (J. Maisano), J. Walker, P. Weatherson, P. Walker, (W. Hawke)
Substitutes not used: D. Keenan, J. Stark
**Referee:** Calum Murray **Attendance:** 752

**DUMBARTON 1**  **STIRLING ALBION 2**
S. Bonar  S. McLean (2)

**Dumbarton:** S. Grindlay, C. McEwan, C. Brittain, J. McKinstry, D. Allan, B. Donald, (M. Bradley), S. Bonar, P. Ronald, A. Rodgers, (R. Dunn), I. Russell, (G. Herd), J. Dillon
Substitutes not used: I. Dobbins, J. Wight
**Stirling Albion:** M. Hogarth, P. Nugent, S. Devine, M. McNally, J.G. Rowe, K. MacDonald, (S. Hutchison), P. Hay, C. Ferguson, S. McLean, C. Gethins, (J. Allan), D. O'Brien
Substitutes not used: B. Neville, C. Scotland, S. Christie
**Referee:** Willie Young **Attendance:** 709

**RAITH ROVERS 0**  **ALBION ROVERS 2**
J. Bradford (2)

**Raith Rovers:** D. Berthelot, J. Smart, (C. Malcolm), J. McAlpine, T. Hajovsky, I. Davidson, D. Brady, M. Ouattara, (J. Boyle), F. Rivas, H. Sacko, L. Young, P. Hagan, (M. Eloujdi)
Substitutes not used: A. Benaissa, R. Pounoussamy
**Albion Rovers:** M. Peat, C. Silvestro, J. Stirling, D. Black, J. McGowan, G. McLaren, M. McKenzie, J. Boyle, M. Yardley, J. Bradford, J. Mercer
Substitutes not used: A. Paterson, P. McManus, R. Patrick, A. Selkirk, C. Fahey
**Referee:** Steve Conroy **Attendance:** 1,206

**QUEEN'S PARK 1**  **STENHOUSEMUIR 1**
  (AET – 0-0 After 90 Minutes)
S. Reilly  P. McGrillen
Queen's Park won 4-2 on Kicks from the Penalty Mark

**Queen's Park:** B. McCue, S. Kettlewell, (A. Trouten), D. McCallum, G. Rushford, S. Reilly, S. Molloy, R. Clark, B. Blair, A. Graham, F. Carroll, (T. Sloan), D. Clarke, (P. Harvey)
Substitutes not used: D. Agostini, S. McGovern
**Stenhousemuir:** W. McCulloch, S. Fallon, D. McInally, P. Murphy, A. Smith, (R. Davidson), R. Henderson, M. Lauchlan, (D. Morrison), L. Collins, S. Kerrigan, (J. Savage), J.P.McBride, P. McGrillen
Substitutes not used: K. Knox, D. Orr
**Referee:** Eddie Smith **Attendance:** 461

**ARBROATH 2**  **PETERHEAD 4**
J. Cusick, D. McLean  M. Bavidge (2),
  K. Gibson, M.J. Buchan

**Arbroath:** T. Woodcock, K. McMullan, (S. Cook), G. Beith, (S. Rennie), J. McAulay, J. Bishop, J. Cusick, (G. Henslee), G. Miller, S. MacDonald, D. McLean, A. Brazil, G. Swankie
Substitutes not used: J. Collier, N. Inglis
**Peterhead:** P. Mathers, C. Tully, I. Good, R. Raeside, M. Perry, K. Gibson, C. Campbell, (K. Tindal), M.J. Buchan, S. Michie, (M. Johnston), M. Bavidge, D. Hagen, (A. Youngson)
Substitutes not used: S. McSkimming, R. Buchanan
**Referee:** Andrew Hunter **Attendance:** 448

## SECOND ROUND
Tuesday, 31st August, 2004

**ST. JOHNSTONE 3**  **QUEEN OF THE SOUTH 0**
I. Maxwell, K. Fotheringham, K. Rutkiewicz

**St. Johnstone:** A. McGregor, S. Anderson, K. Fotheringham, S.McManus, S. Webb, (K. Rutkiewicz), I. Maxwell, M. Baxter, P. Sheerin, S. McConalogue, M. Moore, (C. Hay), L. Hardy, (J. Tait)
Substitutes not used: R. Stevenson, K. Cuthbert
**Queen of the South:** C. Samson, Christopher Scott, (D. Bagan), T. English, B. McColligan, (R. Beattie), G. Wood, J. Thomson, P. Burns, S. Bowey, D. McNiven, C. Armstrong, (S. Payne), B. McLaughlin
Substitutes not used: S. Hill, Colin Scott
**Referee:** Calum Murray **Attendance:** 1,201

**ALLOA ATHLETIC 1**  **BERWICK RANGERS 2**
S. Callaghan  A. Seaton, M. Neil

**Alloa Athletic:** G. McGlynn, R. Walker, M. McDermott, (D. Hill), I. Nicolson, M. Bolochoweckyj, C. Townsley, A. McMillan, B.A. Ferguson, A. Brown, (M. Daly), (S. Nicholas), R. Hamilton, S. Callaghan
Substitutes not used: P. McLaughlin, J. Evans

**Berwick Rangers:** G. O'Connor, D. Murie, A. Seaton, M. Cowan, R. Horn, G. Connell, G. Forrest, (P. Hampshire), M. Neil, G. Hutchison, I. Little, (K. Gordon), D. Smith
Substitutes not used: E. Smith, S. Lucas, R. Godfrey
**Referee:** David Somers **Attendance:** 268

**PETERHEAD 1**  **ROSS COUNTY 2**
M. Bavidge  A. Burke, M. Canning

**Peterhead:** P. Mathers, C. Tully, I. Good, R. Raeside, M. Perry, K. Gibson, (G. Stewart), S. Robertson, (C. Campbell), M.J. Buchan, S. Michie, (M. Johnston), M. Bavidge, A. Youngson
Substitutes not used: D. Milne, R. Buchanan
**Ross County:** S. Garden, J. Robertson, M. McCulloch, S. Malcolm, M. Canning, J. Lauchlan, J. Rankin, C. Adam, (S. Mackay), G. McSwegan, S. Kilgannon, (D. Winters), A. Burke, (S. McGarry)
Substitutes not used: S. Higgins, J. McCafferty
**Referee:** Kevin Toner **Attendance:** 617

**CLYDE 1**  **STRANRAER 0**
J-L. Valois

**Clyde:** A. Morrison, S. Mensing, G. Bollan, (J.P. McKeever), S. Wilson, J. Potter, G. McCracken, C. Bryson, G. Arbuckle, A. Conway, J-L. Valois, (K. Bradley), M. Gilhaney
Substitutes not used: P. Flaherty, R. Harris, B. Halliwell
**Stranraer:** A. McCondichie, S. Swift, F. Wright, D. Wingate, M. Henderson, A. Jenkins, K. Finlayson, S. Aitken, S. Donnachie, (G. McCutcheon), D. Graham, (B. Crawford), L. Sharp
Substitutes not used: K. Gaughan, C. Cruickshank, M. McCaulay
**Referee:** Steve Conroy **Attendance:** 752

**GRETNA 1**  **COWDENBEATH 0**
A. Smith

**Gretna:** D. Mathieson, M. Birch, J. McQuilken, D. Lennon, A. Aitken, D. Irons, R. Baldacchino, R. McGuffie, A. Smith, D. Bingham, G. Skelton, (W. Gordon)
Substitutes not used: K. Deuchar, R. Prokas, S. Cosgrove, C. Summersgill
**Cowdenbeath:** A. Fleming, C. Shand, D. Williams, (J.P. Kelly), D. Miller, J. McKeown, I. Ritchie, I. Mauchlen, P. McHale, D. Shields, (N. Gibson), L. Buchanan, (R. McCallum), G. Fusco
Substitutes not used: D. McGregor, J. Gilbertson
**Referee:** Brian Winter **Attendance:** 551

**ALBION ROVERS 1**  **PARTICK THISTLE 2**
G. McCaul  E. Panther, L. Hinds
Match Played at New Douglas Park, Hamilton

**Albion Rovers:** C. Fahey, A. Paterson, J. Stirling, D. Black, J. McGowan, (G. McCaul), R. Patrick, M. McKenzie, C. Silvestro, S. Crabbe, (J. Mercer), (G. Richardson), A. Selkirk, G. McLaren
Substitutes not used: I. Douglas, M. Peat
**Partick Thistle:** S. Pinkowski, W. Gibson, (J-Y. Anis), A. Wilkinson, G. Murray, A. Madaschi, A. Ross, W. Howie, D. Fleming, A. Oné, (J. Mitchell), L. Hinds, E. Panther
Substitutes not used: S. Fulton, A. Dowie, K. Arthur
**Referee:** Andrew Hunter **Attendance:** 1,093

**FALKIRK 5**  **STIRLING ALBION 3**
D. Nicholls, D. Duffy (2),  C. Gethins, D. Cummings,
R. Latapy (2)  J.G. Rowe

**Falkirk:** D. Hill, A. Lawrie, C. McPherson, S. MacKenzie, (N. Scally), M. Campbell, K. James, (J. Sharp), J. O'Neil, D. Nicholls, A. Thomson, R. Latapy, (P. Moutinho), D. Duffy
Substitutes not used: K. McAnespie, A. Ferguson
**Stirling Albion:** M. Hogarth, P. Nugent, C. Scotland, M. McNally, J.G. Rowe, K. MacDonald, P. Hay, (S. Hutchison), C. Ferguson, C. Gethins, (D. Cummings), M. Glancy, D. O'Brien
Substitutes not used: J. Allan, S. Roycroft, S. Christie
**Referee:** Charlie Richmond **Attendance:** 2,695

**FORFAR ATHLETIC 2**    **QUEEN'S PARK 2**
(AET –1-1 After 90 Minutes)
M. Booth, P. Tosh    F. Carroll, A. Graham
Forfar Athletic won 4-3 on Kicks from the Penalty Mark

**Forfar Athletic:** M. Brown, A. Rattray, D. Lowing, E. Forrest, D. King,
D. McClune, M. Booth, P.Lunan, P. Tosh, M. King, (N. Clark), J. Stein, (M. Maher)
Substitutes not used: D. Dunn, D. Cameron, N. Ferrie
**Queen's Park:** D. Crawford, A. Trouten, D. McCallum, D. Agostini, S. Reilly,
(R. Sinclair), S. Molloy, M. Bonnar, (B. Felvus), S. Kettlewell, A. Graham,
F. Carroll, B. Blair
Substitutes not used: D. Weatherston, A. Quinn, S. McGovern
**Referee:** Alan Freeland **Attendance:** 421

### THIRD ROUND
Tuesday, 14th September, 2004

**BERWICK RANGERS 0**    **ST. JOHNSTONE 1**
M. Moore

**Berwick Rangers:** G. O'Connor, D. Murie, A. Seaton, E. Smith, M. Cowan,
G. Forrest, G. Connelly, M. Neil, G. Hutchison, G. Connell, (I. Little), D. Smith,
(P. Hampshire)
Substitutes not used: J. Birrell, K. Gordon, R. Godfrey
**St. Johnstone:** A. McGregor, S. Anderson, K. Fotheringham, D. Hannah,
K. Rutkiewicz, I. Maxwell, R. McCann, P. Sheerin, (M. Baxter),
S. McConalogue, (C. Hay), M. Moore, L. Hardy
Substitutes not used: A. Mahood, S. McMans, K. Cuthbert
**Referee:** Dougie McDonald **Attendance:** 279

**FALKIRK 3**    **GRETNA 0**
R. Latapy, A. Thomson, D. Duffy

**Falkirk:** A. Ferguson, A. Lawrie, C. McPherson, N. Scally, M. Campbell,
K. James, R. McStay, D. Nicholls, (K. McAnespie), A. Thomson,
(D. McBreen), R. Latapy, D. Duffy, (P. Moutinho)
Substitutes not used: J. Hughes, D. Hill
**Gretna:** D. Mathieson, M. Birch, J. McQuilken, D. Lennon, (M. Galloway),
A. Aitken, D. Irons, R. Baldacchino, R. McGuffie, A. Smith, (K. Deuchar),
D. Bingham, G. Skelton, (B. Wake)
Substitutes not used: W. Gordon, L. Little
**Referee:** Hugh Dallas **Attendance:** 1,416

Wednesday, 15th September, 2004

**CLYDE 1**    **FORFAR ATHLETIC 2**
I. Harty    P. Tosh, D. McClune

**Clyde:** B. Halliwell, S. Mensing, S. Wilson, S. Balmer, (G. Arbuckle), J. Potter,
A. Walker, C. Bryson, (A. Conway), J. Gibson, A. Wilford, M. Gilhaney, I. Harty
Substitutes not used: K. Bradley, G. McCracken, A. Morrison
**Forfar Athletic:** M. Brown, (N. Ferrie), A. Rattray, D. Lowing, E. Forrest,
D. King, D. McClune, M. Booth, P. Lunan, P. Tosh, P. Shields, (D. Cameron), J. Stein
Substitutes not used: D. Dunn, M. King, N. Clark
**Referee:** Kenny Clark **Attendance:** 532

**ROSS COUNTY 1**    **PARTICK THISTLE 1**
(AET – 1-1 After 90 Minutes)
D. Winters    E. Panther
Ross County won 5-3 on Kicks from the Penalty Mark

**Ross County:** S. Garden, J. McCunnie, M. McCulloch, S. Malcolm, (C. Gunn),
M. Canning, J. Lauchlan, D. Cowie, C. Adam, (S. Mackay), D. Winters,
(S. Higgins), S. McGarry, A. Burke
Substitutes not used: K. McKinlay, C. Stewart
**Partick Thistle:** K. Arthur, W. Gibson, (A. Wilkinson), K. Milne, G. Murray,
A. Dowie, S. Fulton, (W. Howie), L. Hinds, D. Fleming, J. Escalas, A. Oné,
(A. Strachan), E. Panther
Substitutes not used: A. Madaschi, S. Pinkowski
**Referee:** Alan Freeland **Attendance:** 708

### SEMI-FINALS
Tuesday, 28th September, 2004

**ROSS COUNTY 5**    **FORFAR ATHLETIC 2**
D. Winters (3), A. Burke,    P. Shields (2)
D. Cowie

**Ross County:** S. Garden, J. McCunnie, M. McCulloch, S. Kilgannon,
(S. Mackay), S. Malcolm, J. Lauchlan, D. Cowie, C. Adam, D. Winters,
S. McGarry, (J. Robertson), A. Burke, (S. Higgins)
Substitutes not used: G. McSwegan, C. Stewart

**Forfar Athletic:** N. Ferrie, A. Rattray, D. Lowing, E. Forrest, D. King,
D. McClune, (D. Cameron), P. Lunan, (N. Clark), M. Booth, P. Tosh,
P. Shields, J. Stein
Substitutes not used: D. Dunn, M. King, N. Bennett
**Referee:** Hugh Dallas **Attendance:** 911

**ST. JOHNSTONE 1**    **FALKIRK 2**
K. Rutkiewicz    D. Duffy, A. Lawrie

**St. Johnstone:** A. McGregor, S. Anderson, R. Forsyth, (S. McManus),
D. Hannah, K. Rutkiewicz, I. Maxwell, R. McCann, (P. Sheerin),
K. Fotheringham, P. MacDonald, (S. Fraser), M. Moore, S. McConalogue
Substitutes not used: M. Baxter, K. Cuthbert
**Falkirk:** A. Ferguson, A. Lawrie, C. McPherson, S. MacKenzie, J. Hughes,
K. James, J. O'Neil, D. Nicholls, P. Moutinho, R. Latapy, D. Duffy
Substitutes not used: K. McAnespie, N. Scally, D. McBreen, J. Henry, D. Hill
**Referee:** Michael McCurry **Attendance:** 2,328

### FINAL
Sunday, 7th November, 2004
McDiarmid Park, Perth

**FALKIRK 2**    **ROSS COUNTY 1**

**Falkirk:** A. Ferguson, A. Lawrie, C. McPherson, S. MacKenzie,
M. Campbell, K. James, J. O'Neil, (N. Scally), D. Nicholls,
(P. Moutinho), A. Thomson, (D. McBreen), R. Latapy, D. Duffy
Substitutes not used: K. McAnespie, D. Hill
**Ross County:** S. Garden, J. Robertson, M. McCulloch, J. McCunnie,
M. Canning, J. Lauchlan, D. Cowie, C. Adam, (S. McGarry),
S. Higgins, (S. Kilgannon), J. Rankin, D. Winters, (S. Malcolm)
Substitutes not used: G. McSwegan, C. Stewart
**Scorers Falkirk:** N. Scally, D. Duffy
**Scorer Ross County:** D. Winters
**Referee:** Kenny Clark **Attendance:** 7,471

### ROUND BY ROUND GOALS ANALYSIS

|  | NO. OF GOALS SCORED | TIES PLAYED | AVERAGE PER GAME |
| --- | --- | --- | --- |
| FIRST ROUND | 38 | 14 | 2.7 |
| SECOND ROUND | 26 | 8 | 3.3 |
| THIRD ROUND | 9 | 4 | 2.3 |
| SEMI-FINALS | 10 | 2 | 5 |
| FINAL | 3 | 1 | 3 |
| | | | |
| TOTAL NO. OF GOALS SCORED | 86 | | |
| TOTAL NO. OF TIES PLAYED | 29 | | |
| AVERAGE PER GAME | 3 | | |

Falkirk - Bell's Cup Winners 2004.05

# LEADING SCOTTISH LEAGUE GOALSCORERS SINCE 1995.96

| Season | Premier Division | First Division | Second Division | Third Division |
|---|---|---|---|---|
| 1995/96 | 26 P. Van Hooijdonk (Celtic) | 21 G. O'Boyle (St. Johnstone) | 25 S. McCormick (Stirling Albion) | 23 I. Stewart (Caledonian Thistle) |
| 1996/97 | 25 J. Cadete (Celtic) | 19 R. Grant (St. Johnstone) | 31 P. Ritchie (Hamilton Academical) | 27 I. Stewart (Inverness Cal. Thistle) |
| 1997/98 | 32 M. Negri (Rangers) | 15 J. Grady (Dundee) | 16 I. Stewart (Inverness Cal. Thistle) | 20 C. McGlashan (Montrose) |
| 1998/99 | **Scottish Premier League** 29 H. Larsson (Celtic) | **First Division** 18 G. Hurst (Ayr United) | **Second Division** 21 A. Bone (Stirling Albion) | **Third Division** 17 S. Ferguson (Ross County) 17 P. Flannery (Dumbarton) 17 N. Tarrant (Ross County) |
| 1999/2000 | 25 M. Viduka (Celtic) | 19 M. Yardley (St. Mirren) | 18 B. Carrigan (Clyde) | 16 S. Milne (Forfar Athletic) |
| 2000/01 | 35 H. Larsson (Celtic) | 24 D. Wyness (Inverness Cal. Thistle) | 18 I. English (Stenhousemuir) | 24 D. McFarlane (Hamilton Academical) |
| 2001/02 | 29 H. Larsson (Celtic) | 23 O. Coyle (Airdrieonians) | 18 J. O'Neill (Queen of the South) 18 P. Tosh (Forfar Athletic) | 19 I. Stewart (Peterhead) |
| 2002/03 | 28 H. Larsson (Celtic) | 20 O. Coyle (Falkirk) | 21 C. Templeman (Brechin City) | 23 A. Williams (Morton) |
| 2003/04 | 30 H. Larsson (Celtic) | 15 I. Harty (Clyde) | 22 G. Hutchison (Berwick Rangers) | 24 M. Moore (Stranraer) |
| 2004/05 | 25 J. Hartson (Celtic) | 17 D. Duffy (Falkirk) | 20 P. Shields (Forfar Athletic) 20 C. Templeman (6 for Morton and 14 for Brechin City) | 38 K. Deuchar (Gretna) |

# LIST OF REFEREES SEASON 2005.06

## CATEGORY 1 REFEREES

Crawford Allan
Alan Boyd
Chris Boyle
Iain Brines
Colin Brown
Kenny Clark
William Collum
Steve Conroy
Stuart Dougal
Jamie Downie
Steven Duff
Stephen Finnie
Alan Freeland
Ian Frickleton
Ian Fyfe
Colin Hardie
Willie Hornby
Andrew Hunter
Michael McCurry
Dougie McDonald
John McKendrick
Scott MacDonald
Craig Mackay
Cammy Melville
Alan Muir
Calum Murray
Euan Norris
Stevie O'Reilly
Charlie Richmond
Mike Ritchie

Eddie Smith
David Somers
Martin Sproule
Craig Thomson
Kevin Toner
Mike Tumilty
John Underhill
Brian Winter

## CATEGORY 2 REFEREES

Ramzan Bashir
Terry Brunton
Graham Chambers
Craig Charleston
Paul Cheyne
William Gilfillan
Richard Gough
Jason Hasson
Gary Hilland
Anthony Law
Craig Marshall
Frank McDermott
Paul McDowall
Steven McLean
Andy McWilliam
Ryan Milne
Steven Nicholls
Matt Northcroft
Pat Rafferty
Thomas Robertson
Derek Rose

George Salmond
Brian Templeton
Neil Watters

## CATEGORY 3 SPECIALIST ASSISTANT REFEREES

Francis Andrews
James Bee
John Bicknell
Neil Brand
Gary Cheyne
Derek Clark
Frank Cole
Steven Craven
Martin Cryans
Alan Cunningham
Andy Davis
Willie Dishington
Mark Doyle
George Drummond
John Gilmour
Tommy Johnston
Lawrence Kerrigan
Jim Lyon
Stuart Macaulay
Brian McDuffie
Brian McGarry
Gordon Middleton
Ricky Mooney
Tom Murphy

Steve Pullar
Andrew Seymour
Charlie Smith
Keith Sorbie
Gary Sweeney
Chris Young

## CATEGORY 3 REFEREES

Andrew Aird
Stephen Allan
Jeff Banks
Billy Baxter
John Beaton
Stuart Bennett
Wes Boulstridge
Kevin Clancy
Stuart Clingan
Roddy Cobb
Brian Colvin
Willie Conquer
Iain Craig
Steven Crichton
Hugh Dalgetty
Robert Docherty
Colin Duncan
Calum Dundas
Graham Fraser
Steven George
Kevin Graham
Kevin J. Graham
Kevin Grant

Ross Hamill
Ross Haswell
Alan Hogg
Peter Kinney
Gary Kirkwood
Stuart Logan
Steve McGeouch
Mark McHendry
John McInally
David McIntosh
Hugh McIntyre
Cammy McKay
David McKenzie
Neil McLennan
Barry McNab
James McNeil
Gordon Mackay
Bobby Madden
Rodney Marshall
Brian Martin
Stephen Martin
Alastair Mather
David Moran
Derek Nicholls
Stevie O'Brien
Morag Pirie
Des Roache
Eric Robertson
Craig Sim
Ricky Smith
David Watt
Rod Williamson
Ronnie Wright
Craig Young

## RESERVE LEAGUE CUP

### PRELIMINARY ROUND

12th October, 2004
**MORTON 1 ST. MIRREN 3**
15th November, 2004
**STRANRAER 5 ALBION ROVERS 4**

### FIRST ROUND

12th October, 2004
**FORFAR ATHLETIC 1
HAMILTON ACADEMICAL 1**
(No Extra-Time Played) Forfar Athletic
won 3-0 on Kicks from the Penalty Mark
25th October, 2004
**ARBROATH 0 COWDENBEATH 1
STENHOUSEMUIR 4 AYR UNITED 2**
(AET - 2-2 After 90 Minutes)
26th October, 2004
**ST. JOHNSTONE 1 RAITH ROVERS 3**
(AET - 1-1 After 90 Minutes)
2nd November, 2004
**AIRDRIE UNITED 4 ST. MIRREN 3**
4th November, 2004
**FALKIRK 4 PARTICK THISTLE 2**
16th November, 2004
**EAST FIFE 1 GRETNA 3**
22nd November, 2004
**QUEEN'S PARK 1 STRANRAER 2**

### SECOND ROUND

4th January, 2005
**AIRDRIE UNITED 1 FALKIRK 4**
14th February, 2005
**COWDENBEATH 1 STENHOUSEMUIR 2**
(AET – 1-1 After 90 Minutes)
22nd March, 2005
**FORFAR ATHLETIC 1 GRETNA 3**
5th April, 2005
**STRANRAER 1 RAITH ROVERS 2**

### SEMI-FINALS

26th March, 2005
**STENHOUSEMUIR 1 FALKIRK 0**
13th April, 2005
**GRETNA 3 RAITH ROVERS 0**

### FINAL

Tuesday, 26th April, 2005,
Ochilview Park, Stenhousemuir
**STENHOUSEMUIR 0 GRETNA 2**

**Stenhousemuir:** D. Orr, C. Menzies,
M. Morrison, S. Easton, R. Henderson,
P. Murphy, P. McWhirter, D. Morrison,
(K. Vaughan), K. Struthers, C. Miles, T. Sinclair
Substitutes not used: C. Lochhead,
N. Cosgrove, R. Curwood, J. Kirkham

**Gretna:** D. Mathieson, D. Collins, J. McQuilken,
B. Gilfillan, D. Townsley, (N. Henderson),
A. Bryan, M. McBride, R. McGuffie, D. Shields,
(R. Murray), D. Nicholls, D. Graham, (M. Berkeley)
Substitutes not used: B. Mulgrew,
C. Summersgill
**Scorers:** R. McGuffie, A. Bryan
**Referee:** Craig Charleston **Attendance:** 206

## TENNENT'S SCOTTISH QUALIFYING CUP (SOUTH)

### PRELIMINARY ROUND

Saturday, 14th August, 2004
**HAWICK ROYAL ALBERT 0
GLASGOW UNIVERSITY 1**

**WHITEHILL WELFARE 2
ANNAN ATHLETIC 1**

**DALBEATTIE STAR 3
WIGTOWN AND BLADNOCH 2**

**CIVIL SERVICE STROLLERS 0
SPARTANS 0**

### PRELIMINARY ROUND REPLAY

Saturday, 21st August, 2004
**SPARTANS 6
CIVIL SERVICE STROLLERS 1**

### FIRST ROUND

Saturday, 28th August, 2004
**COLDSTREAM 0
GLASGOW UNIVERSITY 5**

**VALE OF LEITHEN 2
ST. CUTHBERT WANDERERS 1**

**NEWTON STEWART 2
THREAVE ROVERS 5**

**DALBEATTIE STAR 3
SPARTANS 0**

**GIRVAN 3
EDINBURGH UNIVERSITY 2**

**GALA FAIRYDEAN 0
WHITEHILL WELFARE 2**

**BURNTISLAND SHIPYARD 0
EDINBURGH CITY 1**

**SELKIRK 1
PRESTON ATHLETIC 4**

### SECOND ROUND

Saturday, 11th September, 2004
**VALE OF LEITHEN 0
WHITEHILL WELFARE 1**

**PRESTON ATHLETIC 3
DALBEATTIE STAR 4**

**EDINBURGH CITY 3
THREAVE ROVERS 0**

**GLASGOW UNIVERSITY 2
GIRVAN 1**

### SEMI-FINALS

Saturday, 2nd October, 2004
**GLASGOW UNIVERSITY 2
WHITEHILL WELFARE 2**

**DALBEATTIE STAR 1
EDINBURGH CITY 3**

### SEMI-FINAL REPLAY

Saturday, 9th October, 2004
**WHITEHILL WELFARE 3
GLASGOW UNIVERSITY 0**

### FINAL

Sunday, 8th May, 2005,
Easter Road Stadium, Edinburgh

**WHITEHILL WELFARE 0
EDINBURGH CITY 0 (AET)**
Whitehill Welfare won 4-3 on
Kicks from the Penalty Mark

## TENNENT'S SCOTTISH QUALIFYING CUP (NORTH)

### FIRST ROUND

Saturday, 28th August, 2004
**DEVERONVALE 3 ROTHES 0**

**GOLSPIE SUTHERLAND 0 BUCKIE THISTLE 6**

**INVERURIE LOCO WORKS 3 FORT WILLIAM 0**

**CLACHNACUDDIN 1 COVE RANGERS 2**

**FORRES MECHANICS 0 KEITH 1**

**WICK ACADEMY 2 LOSSIEMOUTH 2**

**NAIRN COUNTY 2 FRASERBURGH 5**

**HUNTLY 3 BRORA RANGERS 1**

FIRST ROUND REPLAY

Saturday, 4th September, 2004
**LOSSIEMOUTH 4 WICK ACADEMY 5**

SECOND ROUND

Saturday, 11th September, 2004
**WICK ACADEMY 2 HUNTLY 4**

**INVERURIE LOCO WORKS 3 DEVERONVALE 1**

**COVE RANGERS 4 FRASERBURGH 2**

**KEITH 0 BUCKIE THISTLE 0**

SECOND ROUND REPLAY

Saturday, 18th September, 2004
**BUCKIE THISTLE 2 KEITH 3**

SEMI-FINALS

Saturday, 2nd October, 2004
**COVE RANGERS 5 HUNTLY 2**

**KEITH 1 INVERURIE LOCO WORKS 2**

FINAL

Saturday, 6th November, 2004,
Christie Park, Huntly
**COVE RANGERS 0
INVERURIE LOCO WORKS 4**

## SCOTTISH FOOTBALL ASSOCIATION YOUTH CUP

FIRST ROUND

**NAIRN COUNTY 7 KEITH 7**
(KEITH WON 3-1 ON KICKS FROM
THE PENALTY MARK)

**LOSSIEMOUTH 0 ROTHES 3**

**INVERNESS C.T 4 FORT WILLIAM 1**

**BRORA RANGERS 0 ELGIN CITY 3**

**BUCKIE THISTLE 2 COVE RANGERS 5**

**INVERURIE LOCO WORKS 2 DEVERONVALE 1**

**EAST FIFE 4 FORFAR ATHLETIC 0**

**CIVIL SERVICE STROLLERS 1 HAMILTON ACAD. 3**

**CLYDE 7 MORTON 0**

**ALLOA ATHLETIC 1 ALBION ROVERS 0**

**STIRLING ALBION 3 ARBROATH 7**

**DALBEATTIE STAR 0 QUEEN OF THE SOUTH 8**

**HAWICK ROYAL ALBERT 3 NEWTON STEWART 0**

**GALA FAIRYDEAN 2 ST. CUTHBERT WANDERERS 3**

SECOND ROUND

**CLACHNACUDDIN 7 FRASERBURGH 1**

**ELGIN CITY 4 INVERURIE LOCO WORKS 1**

**HUNTLY 0 KEITH 4**

**ROTHES 6 FORRES MECHANICS 1**

**COVE RANGERS 6 INVERNESS C.T 8**

**ALLOA ATHLETIC 3 AIRDRIE UNITED 2**

**EAST FIFE 4 BURNTISLAND SHIPYARD 1**

**QUEEN'S PARK 3 COWDENBEATH 4**

**DUNDEE 5 ST. JOHNSTONE 1**

**BERWICK RANGERS 1 HAMILTON ACADEMICAL 1**
(HAMILTON ACADEMICAL WON 4-3 ON
KICKS FROM THE PENALTY MARK)

**PRESTON ATHLETIC 0 CLYDE 7**

**SPARTANS 3 WHITEHILL WELFARE 1**

**ARBROATH 1 ST. MIRREN 4**

**HAWICK ROYAL ALBERT 1 ANNAN ATHLETIC 2**

**GRETNA 1 QUEEN OF THE SOUTH 2**

**ST. CUTHBERT WANDERERS 3 GIRVAN 2**

THIRD ROUND

**KILMARNOCK 0 ST. MIRREN 2**

**SPARTANS 0 DUNFERMLINE ATHLETIC 1**

**ABERDEEN 3 INVERNESS C.T 1**

**HAMILTON ACADEMICAL 0 HEARTS 2**

**ROSS COUNTY 3 ST. CUTHBERT WANDERERS 0**

**EAST FIFE 2 EDINBURGH CITY 1**

**STENHOUSEMUIR 3 ALLOA ATHLETIC 2**

**ANNAN ATHLETIC 0 DUNDEE UNITED 5
PARTICK THISTLE 2 DUNDEE 2**
(DUNDEE WON 9-8 ON KICKS
FROM THE PENALTY MARK)

**ROTHES 1 RANGERS 4**

**AYR UNITED 2 ELGIN CITY 1**

**CLACHNACUDDIN 0 CELTIC 1**

**MOTHERWELL 3 QUEEN OF THE SOUTH 1**

**COWDENBEATH 3 FALKIRK 2**

**HIBERNIAN 3 CLYDE 0**

**KEITH 3 LIVINGSTON 5**

FOURTH ROUND

**COWDENBEATH 2 ABERDEEN 4**

**DUNDEE 3 EAST FIFE 0**

**RANGERS 3 STENHOUSEMUIR 0**

**HIBERNIAN 0 CELTIC 3**

**AYR UNITED 0 HEARTS 2**

**DUNFERMLINE ATHLETIC 2 LIVINGSTON 0**

**DUNDEE UNITED 3 MOTHERWELL 0**

**ST. MIRREN 3 ROSS COUNTY 1**

FIFTH ROUND

**ABERDEEN 2 HEARTS 3** (AET)

**ST. MIRREN 4 RANGERS 3**

**DUNFERMLINE ATHLETIC 0 DUNDEE UNITED 2**

**DUNDEE 1 CELTIC 3**

SEMI-FINALS

**CELTIC 3 HEARTS 1** (AET)

**DUNDEE UNITED 1 ST. MIRREN 2**

FINAL

Wednesday, 27th April, 2005 – The National
Stadium, Hampden Park, Glasgow
**ST. MIRREN 0 CELTIC 2**

**St. Mirren:** C. Smith, R. McCay, (S. Marini),
B. Gordon, I. Milne, D. Martin, G. McWilliam,
S. McFarlane, (S. Anderson), G. Gillespie,
(M. Harkness), D. McKenna, C. Molloy, S. Gemmill
Substitutes not used:
A. Muir, C. McMenamin, G. Wardrop, R. Carr
**Celtic:** S. Fox, C. Reid, C. Mulgrew,
M. McGlinchey, S. Cuthbert, T. Bjarnason,
(D. Richardson), J. O'Brien, (R. McCafferty),
S. Ferry, (P. McGowan), M. Gardyne,
K. Finnbogason, R. Conroy
Substitutes not used:
C. Grant, M. Millar, S. Wood, N. Riley, G. Walsh
**Scorers:** J. O'Brien (2)
**Referee:** Steve Conroy **Attendance:** 2,953

## UNDER-19 YOUTH LEAGUE CUP

### SECTIONAL RESULTS – SECTION 1

20th March, 2005
ALBION ROVERS 3 CLYDE 3
QUEEN OF THE SOUTH 2 GRETNA 0
ST. MIRREN 1 HAMILTON ACADEMICAL 2

22nd March, 2005
QUEEN'S PARK 3 COWDENBEATH 1

25th March, 2005
HAMILTON ACADEMICAL 3
QUEEN OF THE SOUTH 2

27th March, 2005
COWDENBEATH 3 ALBION ROVERS 2

30th March, 2005
GRETNA 0 QUEEN'S PARK 2

1st April, 2005
ALBION ROVERS 0 QUEEN OF THE SOUTH 2

3rd April, 2005
CLYDE 0 COWDENBEATH 3
QUEEN'S PARK 1 HAMILTON ACADEMICAL 0

10th April, 2005
GRETNA 3 CLYDE 0
HAMILTON ACADEMICAL 2 ALBION ROVERS 0
QUEEN OF THE SOUTH 3 QUEEN'S PARK 1

15th April, 2005
ST. MIRREN 2 QUEEN'S PARK 3

17th April, 2005
ST. MIRREN 4 QUEEN OF THE SOUTH 0

20th April, 2005
ALBION ROVERS 1 GRETNA 2

22nd April, 2005
COWDENBEATH 1 GRETNA 2

23rd April, 2005
QUEEN'S PARK 8 ALBION ROVERS 1

27th April, 2005
QUEEN OF THE SOUTH 0 CLYDE 5

29th April, 2005
GRETNA 1 HAMILTON ACADEMICAL 2

1st May, 2005
ALBION ROVERS 2 ST. MIRREN 4
CLYDE 0 QUEEN'S PARK 2
COWDENBEATH 2 QUEEN OF THE SOUTH 1

6th May, 2005
GRETNA 3 ST. MIRREN 2

8th May, 2005
COWDENBEATH 1 ST. MIRREN 5

10th May, 2005
CLYDE 1 HAMILTON ACADEMICAL 5

12th May, 2005
CLYDE 0 ST. MIRREN 1
HAMILTON ACADEMICAL 4 COWDENBEATH 1

### SECTION 1 – FINAL TABLE

|  | P | W | D | L | F | A | PTS |
|---|---|---|---|---|---|---|---|
| QUEEN'S PARK | 7 | 6 | 0 | 1 | 20 | 7 | 18 |
| HAMILTON ACADEMICAL | 7 | 6 | 0 | 1 | 18 | 7 | 18 |
| ST. MIRREN | 7 | 4 | 0 | 3 | 19 | 11 | 12 |
| GRETNA | 7 | 4 | 0 | 3 | 11 | 10 | 12 |
| COWDENBEATH | 7 | 3 | 0 | 4 | 12 | 17 | 9 |
| QUEEN OF THE SOUTH | 7 | 3 | 0 | 4 | 10 | 15 | 9 |
| CLYDE | 7 | 1 | 1 | 5 | 9 | 17 | 4 |
| ALBION ROVERS | 7 | 0 | 1 | 6 | 9 | 24 | 1 |

### SECTIONAL RESULTS – SECTION 2

20th March, 2005
ALLOA ATHLETIC 1 STENHOUSEMUIR 0
ST. JOHNSTONE 0 FALKIRK 3

24th March, 2005
FORFAR ATHLETIC 1 ARBROATH 3

26th March, 2005
ROSS COUNTY 7 ALLOA ATHLETIC 1

27th March, 2005
ARBROATH 2 STIRLING ALBION 0
FALKIRK 5 FORFAR ATHLETIC 0
STENHOUSEMUIR 0 ST. JOHNSTONE 2

3rd April, 2005
ALLOA ATHLETIC 1 ARBROATH 3
STENHOUSEMUIR 0 ROSS COUNTY 4
STIRLING ALBION 1 FALKIRK 4
ST. JOHNSTONE 3 FORFAR ATHLETIC 1

6th April, 2005
FALKIRK 2 ALLOA ATHLETIC 3

10th April, 2005
ARBROATH 0 STENHOUSEMUIR 0
ROSS COUNTY 2 ST. JOHNSTONE 0

14th April, 2005
FALKIRK 1 ROSS COUNTY 0

17th April, 2005
ALLOA ATHLETIC 1 FORFAR ATHLETIC 0
ST. JOHNSTONE 3 STIRLING ALBION 3

21st April, 2005
STIRLING ALBION 1 ALLOA ATHLETIC 1

24th April, 2005
ARBROATH 4 ST. JOHNSTONE 3
FORFAR ATHLETIC 0 STENHOUSEMUIR 1

28th April, 2005
FORFAR ATHLETIC 0 STIRLING ALBION 3

29th April, 2005
ROSS COUNTY 1 ARBROATH 2

1st May, 2005
ALLOA ATHLETIC 2 ST. JOHNSTONE 1
ROSS COUNTY 1 FORFAR ATHLETIC 0

3rd May, 2005
STIRLING ALBION 1 ROSS COUNTY 2

5th May, 2005
STENHOUSEMUIR 1 FALKIRK 9

10th May, 2005
ARBROATH 1 FALKIRK 0
STENHOUSEMUIR 7 STIRLING ALBION 0

### SECTION 2 – FINAL TABLE

|  | P | W | D | L | F | A | PTS |
|---|---|---|---|---|---|---|---|
| ARBROATH | 7 | 6 | 1 | 0 | 15 | 6 | 19 |
| FALKIRK | 7 | 5 | 0 | 2 | 24 | 6 | 15 |
| ROSS COUNTY | 7 | 5 | 0 | 2 | 17 | 5 | 15 |
| ALLOA ATHLETIC | 7 | 4 | 1 | 2 | 10 | 14 | 13 |
| ST. JOHNSTONE | 7 | 2 | 1 | 4 | 12 | 15 | 7 |
| STENHOUSEMUIR | 7 | 2 | 1 | 4 | 9 | 16 | 7 |
| STIRLING ALBION | 7 | 1 | 2 | 4 | 9 | 19 | 5 |
| FORFAR ATHLETIC | 7 | 0 | 0 | 7 | 2 | 17 | 0 |

### FINAL

Sunday, 22nd May, 2005 –
Gayfield Park, Arbroath
**ARBROATH 0 QUEEN'S PARK 4**

**Arbroath:** C. Cargill, M. Johnston, J. Martin, (G. Traynor), G. Anderson, G. Kirk, A. O'Connor, M. O'Leary, (G. Duncan), N. Smith, (S. Monro), G. Warren, J. Collier, P. McKibben
Substitutes not used: C. Anderson, M. Webster
**Queen's Park:** A. Cowie, S. Lennon, A. Livingston, (B. McIlduff), R. Campbell, J. Daily, P. Paton, L. McCann, S. Gibson, (R. Russell), B. Felvus, P. McClory, (M. McLaughlin), D. Weatherson
Substitutes not used:
D. McLaughlin, P. Gibbons
**Scorers:** B. Felvus (2), R. Campbell, P. McClory
**Referee:** Wes Boulstridge **Attendance:** 307

Queen's Park –
SFL U19 Youth League Cup Winners 2004.05

# UNDER-17 YOUTH LEAGUE CUP

## SECTIONAL RESULTS – SECTION 1

18th March, 2005

QUEEN'S PARK 3 BERWICK RANGERS 2

19th March, 2005

GRETNA 0 HAMILTON ACADEMICAL 3

20th March, 2005

AIRDRIE UNITED 3 AYR UNITED 1

MORTON 1 ST. MIRREN 0

27th March, 2005

BERWICK RANGERS 3 AIRDRIE UNITED 3

ST. MIRREN 2 QUEEN'S PARK 1

3rd April, 2005

AIRDRIE UNITED 0 ST. MIRREN 0

AYR UNITED 4 BERWICK RANGERS 0

GRETNA 2 MORTON 3

QUEEN'S PARK 2 HAMILTON ACADEMICAL 0

8th April, 2005

HAMILTON ACADEMICAL 1 MORTON 0

10th April, 2005

BERWICK RANGERS 1 GRETNA 3

HAMILTON ACADEMICAL 1 AIRDRIE UNITED 2

ST. MIRREN 3 AYR UNITED 2

12th April, 2005

AYR UNITED 4 GRETNA 2

13th April, 2005

MORTON 2 QUEEN'S PARK 6

17th April, 2005

BERWICK RANGERS 0 ST. MIRREN 3

20th April, 2005

GRETNA 1 QUEEN'S PARK 2

23rd April, 2005

ST. MIRREN 1 GRETNA 2

24th April, 2005

HAMILTON ACADEMICAL 9
BERWICK RANGERS 0

26th April, 2005

QUEEN'S PARK 0 AIRDRIE UNITED 4

29th April, 2005

ST. MIRREN 1 HAMILTON ACADEMICAL 2

1st May, 2005

AIRDRIE UNITED 4 GRETNA 1

BERWICK RANGERS 0 MORTON 2

4th May, 2005

AYR UNITED 2 QUEEN'S PARK 0

8th May, 2005

AIRDRIE UNITED 3 MORTON 1

AYR UNITED 1 HAMILTON ACADEMICAL 0

12th May, 2005

MORTON 3 AYR UNITED 4

## SECTION 1 – FINAL TABLE

|                     | P | W | D | L | F  | A  | PTS |
|---------------------|---|---|---|---|----|----|-----|
| AIRDRIE UNITED      | 7 | 5 | 2 | 0 | 19 | 7  | 17  |
| AYR UNITED          | 7 | 5 | 0 | 2 | 18 | 11 | 15  |
| HAMILTON ACADEMICAL | 7 | 4 | 0 | 3 | 16 | 6  | 12  |
| QUEEN'S PARK        | 7 | 4 | 0 | 3 | 14 | 13 | 12  |
| ST. MIRREN          | 7 | 3 | 1 | 3 | 10 | 8  | 10  |
| MORTON              | 7 | 3 | 0 | 4 | 12 | 16 | 9   |
| GRETNA              | 7 | 2 | 0 | 5 | 11 | 18 | 6   |
| BERWICK RANGERS     | 7 | 0 | 1 | 6 | 6  | 27 | 1   |

## SECTIONAL RESULTS – SECTION 2

20th March, 2005

ALLOA ATHLETIC 2 STENHOUSEMUIR 4

ELGIN CITY 1 RAITH ROVERS 0

STIRLING ALBION 1 ROSS COUNTY 5

23rd March, 2005

COWDENBEATH 4 ARBROATH 4

26th March, 2005

ROSS COUNTY 2 ALLOA ATHLETIC 1

27th March, 2005

ARBROATH 2 ELGIN CITY 3

FALKIRK 2 COWDENBEATH 0

3rd April, 2005

ALLOA ATHLETIC 3 RAITH ROVERS 1

ELGIN CITY 1 FALKIRK 0

STENHOUSEMUIR 0 ROSS COUNTY 4

10th April, 2005

ARBROATH 0 ALLOA ATHLETIC 4

COWDENBEATH 1 ELGIN CITY 2

FALKIRK 6 STIRLING ALBION 0

RAITH ROVERS 2 STENHOUSEMUIR 2

15th April, 2005

ALLOA ATHLETIC 3 FALKIRK 5

17th April, 2005

ROSS COUNTY 3 RAITH ROVERS 2

18th April, 2005

STIRLING ALBION 2 COWDENBEATH 2

20th April, 2005

COWDENBEATH 1 ALLOA ATHLETIC 0

22nd April, 2005

FALKIRK 3 STENHOUSEMUIR 1

24th April, 2005

ARBROATH 3 ROSS COUNTY 6

ELGIN CITY 2 STIRLING ALBION 1

30th April, 2005

ROSS COUNTY 1 FALKIRK 0

1st May, 2005

ALLOA ATHLETIC 2 ELGIN CITY 4

RAITH ROVERS 2 ARBROATH 0

STENHOUSEMUIR 0 COWDENBEATH 0

5th May, 2005

FALKIRK 3 RAITH ROVERS 2

7th May, 2005

ELGIN CITY 3 STENHOUSEMUIR 0

8th May, 2005

COWDENBEATH 3 ROSS COUNTY 6

STIRLING ALBION 1 ALLOA ATHLETIC 7

14th May, 2005

ARBROATH 0 FALKIRK 5

15th May, 2005

RAITH ROVERS 1 COWDENBEATH 0

ROSS COUNTY 1 ELGIN CITY 1

STENHOUSEMUIR 2 STIRLING ALBION 0

17th May, 2005

STENHOUSEMUIR 6 ARBROATH 0

19th May, 2005

STIRLING ALBION 1 ARBROATH 1

22nd May, 2005

RAITH ROVERS 4 STIRLING ALBION 2

## SECTION 2 – FINAL TABLE

|                | P | W | D | L | F  | A  | PTS |
|----------------|---|---|---|---|----|----|-----|
| ROSS COUNTY    | 8 | 7 | 1 | 0 | 28 | 11 | 22  |
| ELGIN CITY     | 8 | 7 | 1 | 0 | 17 | 7  | 22  |
| FALKIRK        | 8 | 6 | 0 | 2 | 24 | 8  | 18  |
| STENHOUSEMUIR  | 8 | 3 | 2 | 3 | 15 | 14 | 11  |
| RAITH ROVERS   | 8 | 3 | 1 | 4 | 14 | 14 | 10  |
| ALLOA ATHLETIC | 8 | 3 | 0 | 5 | 22 | 18 | 9   |
| COWDENBEATH    | 8 | 1 | 3 | 4 | 11 | 17 | 6   |
| ARBROATH       | 8 | 0 | 2 | 6 | 10 | 31 | 2   |
| STIRLING ALBION| 8 | 0 | 2 | 6 | 8  | 29 | 2   |

## FINAL

Saturday, 21st May, 2005 –
New Douglas Park, Hamilton

**AIRDRIE UNITED 0 ROSS COUNTY 1**

**Airdrie United:** M. Burrell, D. Monaghan,
P. Cullen, C. Wilson, M. Gallagher, T. Fennessey,
P. Gordon, K. Sweeney, (C. Gallacher), G. Quintiliani,
R. McPherson, (J. McLaren), S. McMeneny
Substitutes not used: R. Barton, D. Paterson
**Ross County:** A. Renwick, S. Skinner,
(S. Mackay-Steven), C. Clark, S. Begg,
M. Nicolson, J.J. Urquhart, A. Naismith,
M. Charlesworth, A. Grant, K. Duguid, D. Moore
Substitutes not used:
D. Bell, G. McNab, J. Main, S. Cunningham
**Scorer:** M. Charlesworth
**Referee:** Stephen Allan **Attendance:** 210

Dundee United's Paul Hegarty was Player of the Year in Season 1978.79

## SCOTTISH PROFESSIONAL FOOTBALLERS ASSOCIATION

### 1977.78
Premier Division **Derek Johnstone** Rangers
First Division **Billy Pirie** Dundee
Second Division **Dave Smith** Berwick Rangers
Young Player **Graeme Payne** Dundee Utd

### 1978.79
Premier Division **Paul Hegarty** Dundee Utd
First Division **Brian McLaughlin** Ayr United
Second Division **Michael Leonard** Dunfermline Ath.
Young Player **Raymond Stewart** Dundee Utd

### 1979.80
Premier Division **Davie Provan** Celtic
First Division **Sandy Clark** Airdrieonians
Second Division **Paul Leetion** Falkirk
Young Player **John MacDonald** Rangers

### 1980.81
Premier Division **Mark McGhee** Aberdeen
First Division **Eric Sinclair** Dundee
Second Division **Jimmy Robertson** Queen of the South
Young Player **Charlie Nicholas** Celtic

### 1981.82
Premier Division **Sandy Clark** Airdrieonians
First Division **Brian McLaughlin** Motherwell
Second Division **Pat Nevin** Clyde
Young Player **Frank McAvennie** St. Mirren

### 1982.83
Premier Division **Charlie Nicholas** Celtic
First Division **Gerry McCabe** Clydebank
Second Division **John Colquhoun** Stirling Albion
Young Player **Paul McStay** Celtic

### 1983.84
Premier Division **Willie Miller** Aberdeen
First Division **Gerry McCabe** Clydebank
Second Division **Jim Liddle** Forfar Athletic
Young Player **John Robertson** Hearts

### 1984.85
Premier Division **Jim Duffy** Morton
First Division **Gerry McCabe** Clydebank
Second Division **Bernie Slaven** Albion Rovers
Young Player **Craig Levein** Hearts

### 1985.86
Premier Division **Richard Gough** Dundee Utd
First Division **John Brogan** Hamilton Acad.
Second Division **Mark Smith** Queen's Park
Young Player **Craig Levein** Hearts

### 1986.87
Premier Division **Brian McClair** Celtic
First Division **Jim Holmes** Morton
Second Division **John Sludden** Ayr United
Young Player **Robert Fleck** Rangers

### 1987.88
Premier Division **Paul McStay** Celtic
First Division **Alex Taylor** Hamilton Acad.
Second Division **Henry Templeton** Ayr United
Young Player **John Collins** Hibernian

### 1988.89
Premier Division **Theo Snelders** Aberdeen
First Division **Ross Jack** Dunfermline Ath.
Second Division **Paul Hunter** East Fife
Young Player **Billy McKinlay** Dundee Utd

### 1989.90
Premier Division **Jim Bett** Aberdeen
First Division **Ken Eadie** Clydebank
Second Division **Willie Watters** Kilmarnock
Young Player **Scott Crabbe** Hearts

### 1990.91
Premier Division **Paul Elliott** Celtic
First Division **Simon Stainrod** Falkirk
Second Division **Kevin Todd** Berwick Rangers
Young Player **Eoin Jess** Aberdeen

### 1991.92
Premier Division **Alistair McCoist** Rangers
First Division **Gordon Dalziel** Raith Rovers
Second Division **Andrew Thomson** Queen of the South
Young Player **Philip O'Donnell** Motherwell

### 1992.93
Premier Division **Andy Goram** Rangers
First Division **Gordon Dalziel** Raith Rovers
Second Division **Alexander Ross** Brechin City
Young Player **Eoin Jess** Aberdeen

### 1993.94
Premier Division **Mark Hateley** Rangers
First Division **Richard Cadette** Falkirk
Second Division **Andrew Thomson** Queen of the South
Young Player **Philip O'Donnell** Motherwell

### 1994.95
Premier Division **Brian Laudrup** Rangers
First Division **Stephen Crawford** Raith Rovers
Second Division **Derek McInnes** Greenock Morton
Third Division **David Bingham** Forfar Athletic
Young Player **Charlie Miller** Rangers

### 1995.96
Premier Division **Paul Gascoigne** Rangers
First Division **George O'Boyle** St. Johnstone
Second Division **Stephen McCormick** Stirling Albion
Third Division **Jason Young** Livingston
Young Player **Jackie McNamara** Celtic

### 1996.97
Premier Division **Paolo Di Canio** Celtic
First Division **Roddy Grant** St. Johnstone
Second Division **Paul Ritchie** Hamilton Acad.
Third Division **Iain Stewart** Inverness Cal.Th.
Young Player **Robbie Winters** Dundee Utd

Morton's Jim Duffy was Player of the Year in Season 1984.85

Celtic's Brian McClair was Player of the Year in Season 1986.87

Aberdeen's Jim Bett was Player of the Year in Season 1989.90

## 1997.98
Premier Division **Jackie McNamara** Celtic
First Division **James Grady** Dundee
Second Division **Paul Lovering** Clydebank
Third Division **Willie Irvine** Alloa Athletic
Young Player **Gary Naysmith** Hearts

## 1998.99
SPL **Henrik Larsson** Celtic
First Division **Russell Latapy** Hibernian
Second Division **David Bingham** Livingston
Third Division **Neil Tarrant** Ross County
Young Player **Barry Ferguson** Rangers

## 1999.2000
SPL **Mark Viduka** Celtic
First Division **Stevie Crawford**
Dunfermline Athletic
Second Division **Brian Carrigan** Clyde
Third Division **Steven Milne** Forfar Athletic
Young Player **Kenny Miller** Hibernian

## 2000.01
SPL **Henrik Larsson** Celtic
First Division **David Bingham** Livingston
Second Division **Scott McLean** Partick Thistle
Third Division **Steve Hislop** East Stirlingshire
Young Player **Stilian Petrov** Celtic

## 2001.02
SPL **Lorenzo Amoruso** Rangers
First Division **Owen Coyle** Airdrieonians
Second Division **John O'Neill**
Queen of the South
Third Division **Paul McManus** East Fife
Young Player **Kevin McNaughton** Aberdeen

## 2002.03
SPL **Barry Ferguson** Rangers
First Division **Dennis Wyness**
Inverness Caledonian Thistle
Second Division **Chris Templeman** Brechin City
Third Division **Alex Williams** Morton
Young Player **James McFadden** Motherwell

## 2003.04
SPL **Chris Sutton** Celtic
First Division **Ian Harty** Clyde
Second Division **Paul Tosh** Forfar Athletic
Third Division **Michael Moore** Stranraer
Young Player **Stephen Pearson** Celtic

## 2004.05
SPL **John Hartson** Celtic &
**Fernando Ricksen** Rangers
First Division **Russell Latapy** Falkirk
Second Division **Steven Hampshire**
Brechin City
Third Division **David Bingham** Gretna
Young Player **Derek Riordan** Hibernian

## THE SCOTTISH FOOTBALL WRITERS' ASSOCIATION

1965 **Billy McNeill** Celtic
1966 **John Greig** Rangers
1967 **Ronnie Simpson** Celtic
1968 **Gordon Wallace** Raith Rovers
1969 **Bobby Murdoch** Celtic
1970 **Pat Stanton** Hibernian
1971 **Martin Buchan** Aberdeen
1972 **Dave Smith** Rangers
1973 **George Connelly** Celtic
1974 **World Cup Squad**
1975 **Sandy Jardine** Rangers
1976 **John Greig** Rangers
1977 **Danny McGrain** Celtic
1978 **Derek Johnstone** Rangers
1979 **Andy Ritchie** Morton
1980 **Gordon Strachan** Aberdeen
1981 **Alan Rough** Partick Thistle
1982 **Paul Sturrock** Dundee United
1983 **Charlie Nicholas** Celtic
1984 **Willie Miller** Aberdeen
1985 **Hamish McAlpine** Dundee United
1986 **Sandy Jardine** Heart of Midlothian
1987 **Brian McClair** Celtic
1988 **Paul McStay** Celtic
1989 **Richard Gough** Rangers
1990 **Alex McLeish** Aberdeen
1991 **Maurice Malpas** Dundee United
1992 **Alistair McCoist** Rangers
1993 **Andy Goram** Rangers
1994 **Mark Hateley** Rangers
1995 **Brian Laudrup** Rangers
1996 **Paul Gascoigne** Rangers
1997 **Brian Laudrup** Rangers
1998 **Craig Burley** Celtic
1999 **Henrik Larsson** Celtic
2000 **Barry Ferguson** Rangers
2001 **Henrik Larsson** Celtic
2002 **Paul Lambert** Celtic
2003 **Barry Ferguson** Rangers
2004 **Jackie McNamara** Celtic
2005 **John Hartson** Celtic

Derek Riordan with his SFWA Young Player of the Year award

John Hartson with his SFWA Player of the Year award

Fernando Ricksen and John Hartson receive their joint SPFA awards

**AUGUST, 2004**

PLAYER — Alex Burke (Ross County)
YOUNG PLAYER — Darryl Duffy (Falkirk)
FIRST DIVISION MANAGER — Billy Reid (Clyde)
SECOND DIVISION MANAGER — Allan Moore (Stirling Albion)
THIRD DIVISION MANAGER — Iain Stewart (Peterhead)

**SEPTEMBER, 2004**

PLAYER — Scott Michie (Peterhead)
YOUNG PLAYER — Alex Walker (Clyde)
FIRST DIVISION MANAGER — Gus MacPherson (St. Mirren)
SECOND DIVISION MANAGER — Neil Watt (Stranraer)
THIRD DIVISION MANAGER — Iain Stewart (Peterhead)

**OCTOBER, 2004**

PLAYER — David Bingham (Gretna)
YOUNG PLAYER — David Graham (Stranraer)
FIRST DIVISION MANAGER — John Hughes (Falkirk)
SECOND DIVISION MANAGER — Neil Watt (Stranraer)
THIRD DIVISION MANAGER — Rowan Alexander (Gretna)

**NOVEMBER, 2004**

PLAYER — Kenny Deuchar (Gretna)
YOUNG PLAYER — David Graham (Stranraer)
FIRST DIVISION MANAGER — Sandy Stewart (Airdrie United)
SECOND DIVISION MANAGER — Dick Campbell (Brechin City)
THIRD DIVISION MANAGER — Dennis Newall (East Stirlingshire)

**DECEMBER, 2004**

PLAYER — Allan McGregor (St. Johnstone)
YOUNG PLAYER — Darren Gribben (Cowdenbeath)
FIRST DIVISION MANAGER — John Connolly (St. Johnstone)
SECOND DIVISION MANAGER — Tom Hendrie (Alloa Athletic)
THIRD DIVISION MANAGER — David Baikie (Cowdenbeath)

**JANUARY, 2005**

PLAYER — Steven Hampshire (Brechin City)
YOUNG PLAYER — Armand One (Partick Thistle)
FIRST DIVISION MANAGER — Dick Campbell (Partick Thistle)
SECOND DIVISION MANAGER — Ian Campbell (Brechin City)
THIRD DIVISION MANAGER — Iain Stewart (Peterhead)

**FEBRUARY, 2005**

PLAYER — Paul McGrillen (Stenhousemuir)
YOUNG PLAYER — Alan Trouten (Queen's Park)
FIRST DIVISION MANAGER — Allan Maitland (Hamilton Academical)
SECOND DIVISION MANAGER — Harry Cairney (Arbroath)
THIRD DIVISION MANAGER — Jimmy Lindsay (Albion Rovers)

**MARCH, 2005**

PLAYER — Kenny Deuchar (Gretna)
YOUNG PLAYER — Kirk Broadfoot (St. Mirren)
FIRST DIVISION MANAGER — John Hughes (Falkirk)
SECOND DIVISION MANAGER — Jim McInally (Morton)
THIRD DIVISION MANAGER — Rowan Alexander (Gretna)

**APRIL, 2005**

PLAYER — Russell Latapy (Falkirk)
YOUNG PLAYER — Ryan McStay (Falkirk)
FIRST DIVISION MANAGER — Allan Maitland (Hamilton Academical)
SECOND DIVISION MANAGER — Neil Watt (Stranraer)
THIRD DIVISION MANAGER — Rowan Alexander (Gretna)

## SEASON AWARD WINNERS

PLAYER OF THE YEAR — Kenny Deuchar (Gretna)
YOUNG PLAYER OF THE YEAR — Darryl Duffy (Falkirk)
FIRST DIVISION MANAGER OF THE YEAR — John Hughes (Falkirk)
SECOND DIVISION MANAGER OF THE YEAR — Neil Watt (Stranraer)
THIRD DIVISION MANAGER OF THE YEAR — Rowan Alexander (Gretna)
BELL'S ANGELS — Gretna F.C.
BELL'S FAN OF THE YEAR — Colin Mitchell (Hamilton Academical)
BELL'S SUPPORTERS BAR OF THE YEAR — The Port Cullis (Arbroath)
BELL'S PIE OF THE YEAR — East Fife F.C.
BELL'S LIFETIME ACHIEVEMENT AWARD — Willie Young (Referee)

The Bell's SFL awards winners (from left) Kenny Deuchar (Gretna), Rowan Alexander (Gretna), Willie Young (referee), John Hughes (Falkirk), Ron MacGregor (Gretna), Iain MacDonald, Neil Watt (Stranraer) and Derrick Brown (East Fife).

**AUGUST, 2004**
PLAYER — Alan Thompson (Celtic)
YOUNG PLAYER — Zander Diamond (Aberdeen)
MANAGER OF THE MONTH — Jimmy Calderwood (Aberdeen)

**SEPTEMBER, 2004**
PLAYER — Scott McDonald (Motherwell)
YOUNG PLAYER — Derek Riordan (Hibernian)
MANAGER OF THE MONTH — Terry Butcher (Motherwell)

**OCTOBER, 2004**
PLAYER — Fernando Ricksen (Rangers)
YOUNG PLAYER — Steven Fletcher (Hibernian)
MANAGER OF THE MONTH — John Robertson (Hearts)

**NOVEMBER, 2004**
PLAYER — Nacho Novo (Rangers)
YOUNG PLAYER — Derek Riordan (Hibernian)
MANAGER OF THE MONTH — Alex McLeish (Rangers)

**DECEMBER, 2004**
PLAYER — Aiden McGeady (Celtic)
YOUNG PLAYER — Derek Riordan (Hibernian)
MANAGER OF THE MONTH — Tony Mowbray (Hibernian)

**JANUARY, 2005**
PLAYER — Chris Sutton (Celtic)
YOUNG PLAYER — Derek Riordan (Hibernian)
MANAGER OF THE MONTH — Martin O'Neill (Celtic)

**FEBRUARY, 2005**
PLAYER — Dado Prso (Rangers)
YOUNG PLAYER — Lee Miller (Hearts)
MANAGER OF THE MONTH — Alex McLeish (Rangers)

**MARCH, 2005**
PLAYER — Craig Bellamy (Celtic)
YOUNG PLAYER — Aiden McGeady (Celtic)
MANAGER OF THE MONTH — Craig Brewster (Inverness Caledonian Thistle)

**APRIL, 2005**
PLAYER — Burton O'Brien (Livingston)
YOUNG PLAYER — Lee Miller (Hearts)
MANAGER OF THE MONTH — Gordon Chisholm (Dundee United)

## SEASON AWARD WINNERS

PLAYER OF THE YEAR — Dado Prso (Rangers)
YOUNG PLAYER OF THE YEAR — Derek Riordan (Hibernian)
MANAGER OF THE YEAR — Tony Mowbray (Hibernian)

Tony Mowbray (left) and striker Derek Riordan with their Bank of Scotland Premierleague Manager of the Year and Young Player of the Year awards

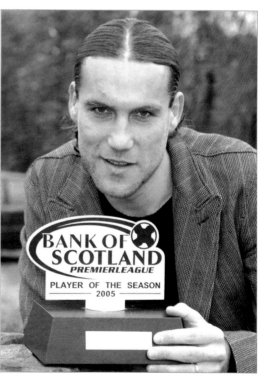

Dado Prso with his Bank of Scotland Premierleague Player of the Season award

## UEFA CHAMPIONS LEAGUE

### THIRD QUALIFYING ROUND - FIRST LEG
Tuesday, 10th August, 2004, Lokomotiv, Moscow

| CSKA MOSCOW 2 | RANGERS 1 |
|---|---|
| Vagner Love, Jarosik | Novo |

CSKA Moscow: Akinfeev, Semberas, Aleksei Berezoutski, Gusev, (Aldonin), Olic, Vagner Love, (Dadu), Odiah, Zhirkov, Jarosik, Vassili Berezoutski, (Semak), Rahimic
Substitutes not used: Mandrikin, Kiritchenko, Laizans, Shershun
Rangers: Klos, Ricksen, Khizanishvili, Boumsong, Vignal, A. Rae, Prso, Novo, Arveladze, Lovenkrands, (Thompson), Ross
Substitutes not used: G. Smith, Vanoli, Malcolm, Hughes, Hutton, Andrews
Referee: Jan W. Wegereef (Holland) Attendance: 19,000

### THIRD QUALIFYING ROUND - SECOND LEG
Wednesday, 25th August, 2004, Ibrox Stadium, Glasgow

| RANGERS 1 | CSKA MOSCOW 1 |
|---|---|
| Thompson | Vagner Love |

Rangers: Klos, Ricksen, Moore, Boumsong, Vignal, Arveladze, Mladenovic, (Andrews), Hughes, Lovenkrands, (Thompson), Prso, Novo
Substitutes not used: G. Smith, Khizanishvili, Ross, Vanoli, Malcolm
CSKA Moscow: Akinfeev, Semberas, Ignashevich, Aleksei Berezoutski, Olic, (Semak), Vagner Love, Odiah, Zhirkov, Jarosik, Aldonin, Rahimic
Substitutes not used: Mandrikin, Gusev, Ferreyra, Kiritchenko, Laizans, Vassili Berezoutski
Referee: Wolfgang Stark (Germany) Attendance: 49,010
(CSKA Moscow won 3-2 on Aggregate)

### GROUP STAGE - GROUP F
Tuesday, 14th September, 2004, Celtic Park, Glasgow

| CELTIC 1 | BARCELONA 3 |
|---|---|
| Sutton | Deco, Giuly, Larsson |

Celtic: Marshall, McNamara, (Sylla), Balde, Juninho, (Sutton), Thompson, Hartson, (Valgaeren), Agathe, Lennon, Petrov, Varga, Camara
Substitutes not used: Douglas, Pearson, Lambert, McGeady
Barcelona: Valdes, Belletti, Marquez, (Oleguer), Puyol, Xavi, Giuly, Eto'o, (Iniesta), Ronaldinho, (Larsson), Van Bronckhorst, Gerard, Deco
Substitutes not used: Ruben, Sylvinho, Gabri, Fernando
Referee: Markus Merk (Germany) Attendance: 58,589

Wednesday, 29th September, 2004, Giuseppe Meazza, Milan

| AC MILAN 3 | CELTIC 1 |
|---|---|
| Shevchenko, Inzaghi, Pirlo | Varga |

AC Milan: Dida, Cafu, Maldini, Shevchenko, Gattuso, (Rui Costa), Nesta, Tomasson, (Inzaghi), Seedorf, (Ambrosini), Pirlo, Kaka, Pancaro
Substitutes not used: Fiori, Kakha Kaladze, Costacurta, Crespo
Celtic: Marshall, Valgaeren, Balde, Thompson, (Juninho), Sutton, Hartson, (Sylla), Agathe, Lennon, Petrov, Varga, Camara
Substitutes not used: Douglas, Lambert, Laursen, Wallace, McGeady
Referee: Gilles Veissiere (France) Attendance: 52,648

Wednesday, 20th October, 2004, Shakhtyor, Donetsk

| SHAKHTAR DONETSK 3 | CELTIC 0 |
|---|---|
| Matuzem (2), Brandao | |

Shakhtar Donetsk: Lastuvka, Barcauan, Tymoschuk, Matuzalem, Vukic, Vorobey, (Brandao), Stoican, Aghahowa, (Srna), Lewandowski, Rat, Marica, (Duljaj) Substitutes not used: Shutkov, Hubschman, Bielik, Lalatovic
Celtic: Marshall, McNamara, (McManus), Balde, Juninho, (McGeady), Sutton, (Wallace), Hartson, Agathe, Lennon, Petrov, Varga, Camara
Substitutes not used: Hedman, Sylla, Pearson, Lambert
Referee: Rene H.J. Temmink (Holland) Attendance: 30,000

Tuesday, 2nd November, 2004, Celtic Park, Glasgow

| CELTIC 1 | SHAKHTAR DONETSK 0 |
|---|---|
| Thompson | |

Celtic: Marshall, McNamara, Valgaeren, Thompson, Hartson, Agathe, Lennon, Petrov, Varga, Camara, (Beattie), McGeady, (Wallace)
Substitutes not used: Hedman, Sylla, Juninho, Pearson, Petta
Shakhtar Donetsk: Lastuvka, Barcauan, Tymoschuk, Duljaj, Matuzalem, Vukic, (Hubschman), Vorobey, (Joao Batista), Stoican, Aghahowa, (Marica), Lewandowski, Srna
Substitutes not used: Shutkov, Bielik, Lalatovic, Pukanych
Referee: Eric Poulat (France) Attendance: 58,347

Wednesday, 24th November, 2004, Camp Nou, Barcelona

| BARCELONA 1 | CELTIC 1 |
|---|---|
| Eto'o | Hartson |

Barcelona: Valdes, Belletti, Marquez, Puyol, Xavi, Giuly, (Iniesta), Eto'o, Ronaldinho, Sylvinho, (Van Bronckhorst), Deco, Oleguer
Substitutes not used: Ruben, Gerard, Fernando, Messi, Rodri
Celtic: Hedman, McNamara, Valgaeren, Balde, Thompson, (Wallace), Sutton, Hartson, Agathe, Lennon, Petrov, Varga, (Camara)
Substitutes not used: Marshall, Juninho, Pearson, Laursen, McGeady
Referee: Lubos Michel (Slovakia) Attendance: 74,119

Tuesday, 7th December, 2004, Celtic Park, Glasgow

| CELTIC 0 | AC MILAN 0 |
|---|---|

Celtic: Hedman, McNamara, Valgaeren, (Camara), Balde, Thompson, Sutton, Hartson, Lennon, Petrov, (Juninho), Varga, McGeady
Substitutes not used: Marshall, Sylla, Laursen, Maloney, Wallace
AC Milan: Dida, Maldini, Costacurta, Shevchenko, (Crespo), Rui Costa, (Seedorf), Nesta, Coloccini, Ambrosini, Dhorasoo, (Kaka), Serginho, Brocchi
Substitutes not used: Fiori, Cafu, Gattuso, Pirlo
Referee: Kyros Vassaras (Greece) Attendance: 59,228

### FINAL GROUP F TABLE

|  | P | W | D | L | F | A | PTS |
|---|---|---|---|---|---|---|---|
| AC MILAN | 6 | 4 | 1 | 1 | 10 | 3 | 13 |
| BARCELONA | 6 | 3 | 1 | 2 | 9 | 6 | 10 |
| SHAKHTAR DONETSK | 6 | 2 | 0 | 4 | 5 | 9 | 6 |
| CELTIC | 6 | 1 | 2 | 3 | 4 | 10 | 5 |

## UEFA CUP

### SECOND QUALIFYING ROUND - FIRST LEG
Thursday, 12th August, 2004 Laugardalsvollur, Reykjavik

| HAFNARFJORDUR 2 | DUNFERMLINE ATHLETIC 2 |
|---|---|
| Jonas Gardarsson, Borgvardt | Brewster, Skerla |

Hafnarfjordur: Larusson, Saevarsson, Sverrir Gardarsson, Nielsen, Bjarnason, Atli Bjornsson, Jonas Gardarsson, (Karkov), Bett, (Vidarsson), Borgvardt, (Stefansson), Gudjonsson, Hallfredsson
Substitutes not used: Valthor Halldorsson, Astthorsson, Armann Bjornsson, Asgeirsson
Dunfermline Athletic: Stillie, Shields, Wilson, Skerla, S.M. Thomson, (Donnelly), Nicholson, Mason, Hunt, Dempsey, (Darren Young), Byrne, Tod, (Brewster)
Substitutes not used: Langfield, Lyle, Labonte, Mehmet
Referee: Jouni Hyytia (Finland) Attendance: 1,200

## SECOND QUALIFYING ROUND - SECOND LEG
Thursday, 26th August, 2004, McDiarmid Park, Perth

### DUNFERMLINE ATHLETIC 1   HAFNARFJORDUR 2
Dempsey                      Armann Bjornsson, Nielsen

**Dunfermline Athletic:** Stillie, Shields, Wilson, Darren Young, (Donnelly), Skerla, S.M. Thomson, (Byrne), Mason, (Tod), Hunt, Brewster, Derek Young, Dempsey
Substitutes not used: Langfield, Lyle, Labonte, Mehmet
**Hafnarfjordur:** Larusson, Saevarsson, Sverrir Gardarsson, Nielsen, Bjarnason, Hallfredsson, Jonas Gardarsson, (Asgeirsson), Bett, Borgvardt, Gudjonsson, (Vidarsson), Stefansson, (Armann Bjornsson)
Substitutes not used: Valthor Halldorsson, Leifsson, Karkov, Olafsson
**Referee:** Attila Hanacsek (Hungary) **Attendance:** 7,189 (Hafnarfjordur won 4-3 on Aggregate)

### FIRST ROUND - FIRST LEG
Thursday, 16th September, 2004, Murrayfield Stadium, Edinburgh

### HEARTS 3          BRAGA 1
Webster, Hartley, Kisnorbo   Paulo Sergio

**Hearts:** Gordon, Maybury, Kisnorbo, Pressley, Webster, Stamp, (Wyness), De Vries, Hartley, Neilson, McAllister, Hamill, (Macfarlane)
Substitutes not used: Moilanen, Janczyk, Sloan, Berra, Stewart
**Braga:** Paulo Santos, Vandinho, Paulo Jorge, Jorge Luiz, Luis Loureiro, Paulo Sergio, (Cesinha), Kenedy, (Joao Tomas), Wender, Abel, Baha, (Jaime Junior), Nunes
Substitutes not used: Marco, Barroso, Mauricio, Candido Costa
**Referee:** Anton Genov (Bulgaria) **Attendance:** 18,769

Os Barreiros, Funchal

### MARITIMO 1          RANGERS 0
Manduca

**Maritimo:** Marcos, Ferreira, Van der Gaag, Tonel, Briguel, Chainho, Wenio, Luis Filipe Fernandes, (Joel), Leo Lima, (Zeca), Alan, Manduca, (Zumbi)
Substitutes not used: Nelson, Bino, Fernando, Souza
**Rangers:** Klos, Ross, Ricksen, Moore, Boumsong, Vignal, (Vanoli), Mladenovic, Arveladze, Prso, Novo, (Lovenkrands), Burke
Substitutes not used: G. Smith, Hughes, Thompson, Khizanishvili, Malcolm
**Referee:** Johan Verbist (Belgium) **Attendance:** 4,000

### FIRST ROUND - SECOND LEG
Thursday, 30th September, 2004, Municipal, Braga

### BRAGA 2          HEARTS 2
Joao Tomas, Jaime Junior   De Vries (2)

**Braga:** Paulo Santos, Paulo Jorge, Nem, Jorge Luiz, Paulo Sergio, Joao Tomas, Jaime Junior, Kenedy, (Castanheira), Wender, (Cesinha), Abel, (Baha), Vandinho
Substitutes not used: Marco, Barroso, Nunes, Candido Costa
**Hearts:** Gordon, Maybury, Kisnorbo, Pressley, Webster, Stamp, (Pereira), De Vries, (McKenna), Hartley, Macfarlane, Neilson, McAllister
Substitutes not used: Wyness, Hamill, Berra, Stewart
**Referee:** Anton Stredak (Slovakia) **Attendance:** 13,007 (Hearts won 5-3 on Aggregate)

Ibrox Stadium, Glasgow

### RANGERS 1          MARITIMO 0
Prso
(AET – 1-0 After 90 Minutes)
**Rangers:** Klos, Ricksen, Boumsong, Prso, Novo, Malcolm, (Hughes), Khizanishvili, Vanoli, (Vignal), Burke, Thompson, Ross
Substitutes not used: G. Smith, Andrews, Arveladze, Lovenkrands, McCormack
**Maritimo:** Marcos, Ferreira, Tonel, Bino, Leo Lima, Alan, Wenio, Briguel, Manduca, Chainho, Van der Gaag
Substitutes not used: Nelson, Silas, Evaldo, Souza, Fernando, Luis Filipe Fernandes, Joel
**Referee:** Vladimir Hrinak (Slovakia) **Attendance:** 47,360
(Aggregate 1-1 - Rangers won 4-2 on Kicks from the Penalty Mark)

### GROUP STAGE Thursday, 21st October, 2004
### GROUP A De Kuip, Rotterdam

### FEYENOORD 3          HEARTS 0
Kuijt (2), Goor

**Feyenoord:** Babos, Saidi, Bosschaart, Kuijt, Ono, Goor, Paauwe, Kalou, (Buffel), Basto, (Mtiliga), Castelen, (Lazovic), Zuiverloon
Substitutes not used: Lodewijks, Ghaly, Loovens, Gyan
**Hearts:** Gordon, Maybury, Kisnorbo, (Stewart), Pressley, McKenna, Webster, Hartley, Macfarlane, (Weir), Neilson, McAllister, (Wyness), Hamill
Substitutes not used: Moilanen, Janczyk, Sloan, Berra
**Referee:** Tonny Kolbech Poulsen (Denmark) **Attendance:** 26,000

## Group F
Amica, Wronki

**AMICA 0**  **RANGERS 5**
Lovenkrands, Novo, Ricksen,
Arveladze, Thompson

**Amica:** Malarz, Bieniuk, Dudka, Kucharski, (Sobocinski), Skrzypek, Stasiak, Dembinski, Gregorek, (Kikut), Kryszalowicz, Bartczak, Marcin Burkhardt, (Kowalczyk)
Substitutes not used: Mielcarz, Dziewicki, Wojtkowiak, Filip Burkhardt
**Rangers:** Klos, Khizanishvili, Andrews, Boumsong, Vignal, Ricksen, Malcolm, Arveladze, (Namouchi), Lovenkrands, (Novo), Prso, (Thompson), Burke
Substitutes not used: G. Smith, Hughes, Ball, McLean
**Referee:** Julian Rodriguez Santiago (Spain) **Attendance:** 3,100

Thursday, 4th November, 2004
**GROUP A**
Murrayfield Stadium, Edinburgh

**HEARTS 0**  **SCHALKE 04 1**
Lincoln

**Hearts:** Gordon, Maybury, Kisnorbo, Pressley, McKenna, (De Vries), Webster, Hartley, Neilson, McAllister, Pereira, (Macfarlane), Hamill, (Weir)
Substitutes not used: Moilanen, Wyness, Berra, Stewart
**Schalke 04:** Rost, Poulsen, Bordon, Hamit Altintop, (Kobiashvili), Ailton, Lincoln, Ebbe Sand, (Hanke), Asamoah, (Varela), Waldoch, Oude-Kamphuis, Pander
Substitutes not used: Heimeroth, Klasener, Rodriguez, Vermant
**Referee:** Nikolay Ivanov (Russia) **Attendance:** 27,272

Thursday, 25th November, 2004
**GROUP A**
St. Jakob-Park, Basel

**BASEL 1**  **HEARTS 2**
Carignano  Wyness, Neilson

**Basel:** Zuberbuhler, Zwyssig, Huggel, Sterjovski, (David Degen), Chipperfield, Gimenez, Kleber, Delgado, (Barberis), Philipp Degen, Smiljanic, Rossi, (Carignano)
Substitutes not used: Quennoz, Mandl
**Hearts:** Gordon, Maybury, Pressley, Webster, Wyness, De Vries, (Weir), Neilson, McAllister, Pereira, (Stamp), Hamill, Stewart, (Macfarlane)
Substitutes not used: Moilanen, Janczyk, Sloan, Berra
**Referee:** Kristinn Jakobsson (Iceland) **Attendance:** 21,645

**GROUP F**
Ibrox Stadium, Glasgow

**RANGERS 3**  **GRAZAR AK 0**
Novo, Arveladze, Namouchi

**Rangers:** Klos, Khizanishvili, Andrews, Boumsong, Vignal, (Ball), Namouchi, Ricksen, Malcolm, Lovenkrands, (Arveladze), Prso, Novo
Substitutes not used: G. Smith, Hughes, Ross, Mladenovic, Hutton
**Grazer AK:** Schranz, Tokic, Ehmann, (Skoro), Standfest, (Dollinger), Amerhauser, Pogatetz, Aufhauser, (Muratovic), Bazina, Sick, Plassnegger, Kollmann
Substitutes not used: Almer, Potscher, Ramusch, Majstorovic
**Referee:** Olegario Benquerenca (Portugal) **Attendance:** 46,453

Thursday, 2nd December, 2004
**GROUP F**
Alkmaarderhout, Alkmaar

**AZ ALKMAAR 1**  **RANGERS 0**
Landzaat

**AZ Alkmaar:** Timmer, Kromkamp, Mathijsen, Opdam, De Cler, Buskermolen, (Lindenbergh), Landzaat, Meerdink, Huysegems, (Nelisse), Van Galen, (Ramzi), Perez
Substitutes not used: Zwarthoed, Fortes Rodriguez, Jaliens, Sektioui
**Rangers:** Klos, Khizanishvili, Ball, Boumsong, Andrews, Malcolm, (Hughes), A. Rae, Ricksen, Prso, Lovenkrands, (Namouchi), Novo
Substitutes not used: G. Smith, Hutton, Mladenovic, S. Smith, Davidson
**Referee:** Alon Yefet (Israel) **Attendance:** 8,000

Wednesday, 15th December, 2004
**GROUP F**
Ibrox Stadium, Glasgow

**RANGERS 0**  **AUXERRE 2**
Kalou (2)

**Rangers:** Klos, Ricksen, Boumsong, Andrews, Arveladze, Prso, Novo, Malcolm, Khizanishvili, (Hutton), Vignal, Namouchi, (A. Rae)
Substitutes not used: G. Smith, Moore, Mladenovic, Ball, Ross
**Auxerre:** Cool, Grichting, Violeau, Benoit Cheyrou, Tainio, (Gonzalez), Akale, Mignot, Kalou, Benjani, Bolf, Sagna, (Jaures)
Substitutes not used: Chabert, Pieroni, Vandenbossche, Recorbet, Coulibaly
**Referee:** Franz-Xavar Wack (Germany) **Attendance:** 48,847

Thursday, 16th December, 2004
**GROUP A**
Murrayfield Stadium, Edinburgh

**HEARTS 0**  **FERENCVAROS 1**
Denes Rosa

**Hearts:** Gordon, Maybury, Kisnorbo, (Wyness), Pressley, Webster, De Vries, Hartley, Neilson, McAllister, (Pereira), Weir, (McKenna), Stewart
Substitutes not used: Moilanen, Hamill, Berra, Macfarlane
**Ferencvaros:** Szucs, Vukmir, Lipcsei, Gyepes, Denes Rosa, Zavadszky, Balog, Leanardo, Tozser, (Huszti), Bajevski, (Takacs), Penska, (Sowunmi)
Substitutes not used: Udvaracz, Szkukalek, Somorjai, Bognar
**Referee:** Levan Paniashvili (Georgia) **Attendance:** 26,182

### FINAL GROUP A TABLE

|  | P | W | D | L | F | A | PTS |
|---|---|---|---|---|---|---|---|
| FEYENOORD | 4 | 2 | 1 | 1 | 6 | 3 | 7 |
| SCHALKE 04 | 4 | 2 | 1 | 1 | 5 | 3 | 7 |
| BASEL | 4 | 2 | 1 | 1 | 5 | 4 | 7 |
| FERENCVAROS | 4 | 1 | 1 | 2 | 3 | 5 | 4 |
| HEARTS | 4 | 1 | 0 | 3 | 2 | 6 | 3 |

### FINAL GROUP F TABLE

|  | P | W | D | L | F | A | PTS |
|---|---|---|---|---|---|---|---|
| AZ ALKMAAR | 4 | 3 | 0 | 1 | 6 | 3 | 9 |
| AUXERRE | 4 | 2 | 1 | 1 | 7 | 3 | 7 |
| GRAZER AK | 4 | 2 | 1 | 1 | 5 | 4 | 7 |
| RANGERS | 4 | 2 | 0 | 2 | 8 | 3 | 6 |
| AMICA | 4 | 0 | 0 | 4 | 3 | 16 | 0 |

## UEFA INTERTOTO CUP

**SECOND ROUND - FIRST LEG**
Saturday, 3rd July, 2004,
Easter Road Stadium, Edinburgh

**HIBERNIAN 1**  **FK VETRA VILNIUS 1**
G. O'Connor  Sasnausksas

**Hibernian:** A. Brown, Whittaker, Alan Reid, Caldwell, Murdock, Nicol, McManus, (Morrow), Brebner, (Dobbie), O'Connor, Scott Brown, Orman, (Glass)
Substitutes not used: Andrew Reid, Smith, Shields, McDonald
**FK Vetra Vilnius:** Poskus, Grudzinskas, Sasnausksas, Raliukonis, Zudys, Rimkus, Butrimavicius, (Douglas), Sernas, Vaineikis, (Stonkus), Vasiliauskas, Karvelis, (Kijanskas)
Substitutes not used: Merkelis, Litvinas, Mizigurskis
**Referee:** Tony Asumaa (Finland) **Attendance:** 8,630

**SECOND ROUND - SECOND LEG**
Saturday, 10th July, 2004,
Zalgiris Stadium, Vilnius

**FK VETRA VILNIUS 1**  **HIBERNIAN 0**
Vasiliauskas

**FK Vetra Vilnius:** Poskus, Zudys, Grudzinskas, Raliukonis, Sasnausksas, Sernas, Rimkus, Beaud, Butrimavicius, (Stonkus), Vasiliauskas, (Vaineikis), Karvelis, (Kijanskas)
Substitutes not used: Merkelis, Kontautas, Litvinas, Mizigurskis
**Hibernian:** A. Brown, Whittaker, Caldwell, Murdock, Alan Reid, Scott Brown, (McManus), Nicol, Brebner, (Dobbie), Orman, (Glass), O'Connor, Morrow
Substitutes not used: Andrew Reid, Smith, McDonald, Shields
**Referee:** K. Slupik, (Poland) **Attendance:** 3,000
(FK Vetra Vilnius won 2-1 on Aggregate)

# 10 UP FOR THE **BULLY WEE**

John Taylor has achieved what Jock Stein and the combined might of Graeme Souness and Walter Smith failed to attain - 10 Championships in a row. The reason why the 52-year-old Career Consultant from Glasgow is not so much a house-hold name as those legendary football managers is that the titles in question are the Scottish Programme of the Year Awards.

The Clyde matchday programme, which John has edited since 1986, has been voted the top issue in Scotland for the last ten seasons, irrespective of the division in which the team played. Each season's programme has been better than the previous one, leading officials from other clubs, jealous pro-gramme editors and collectors alike to ask: "How do they do it ?"

"There's no secret," insists John, "just hard work, imagination and organisation."

It sounds so simple, this formula which all other envious clubs can adopt themselves. The difficulty they face is finding the level of commitment which John Taylor and his programme team give to the Clyde programme.

"We start planning the following season's programme at the start of March. We identify what we want to put in it, contact our contributors so they know, by early summer, what they are to write about, dead-line dates, number of words etc. We have the desire to constantly improve, and thanks to the expert-ise of Frank Tocher, the imagina-tion to turn that into reality."

When the season gets underway, John, who is also Secretary and

Director at the club and has recently spent 18 months as Acting Chairman, is constantly working on the programme. "As soon as one issue goes to the printer, we are working on the next one," he admits. "I believe that the visual impact is vitally important, and I spend a lot of time sourcing photographs to get that right."

This meticulous preparation extends to the programme's finances, as John explains. "A lot of thought and pre-planning goes into the design of every page, so that the shells of all the pages, and all of the covers, are pre-printed in one huge print run before the season starts. This provides a significant saving on print costs."

This economy of expenditure, if not effort, is one of three financial ingredients which ensure that the programme, at worst, breaks even each season. "Some of our suppli-ers accept advertising in return for their goods and services, which obviously cuts costs, and our rev-enue is maximised from advertising and from a very high sales ratio from our appreciative supporters."

Budgeting follows the same princi-ple as the playing budget; "Cup runs (Clyde reached the Quarter Finals of the Tennent's Scottish Cup last season, including the bonus of a live televised match at home to eventual winners Celtic) and glam-our matches (Manchester United filled Broadwood for a pre-season friendly in August) are nice bonuses but we don't rely on them happen-ing each season."

Born and brought up in Oatlands, across the road from Clyde's ancestral home at Shawfield,

1995.96

1996.97

1997.98

1998.99

1999.00

2000.01

2001.02

2002.03

2003.04

2004.05

John found an attraction at his local club which survived memories of his first match.

"I was about nine, and I can remember Dunfermline's big, bald centre forward Charlie Dickson creating havoc in the Clyde defence."

As a schoolboy, he compiled scrapbooks of the club's exploits in the mid sixties. Admitting that distance (in time) may lead to enchantment, John looks back on the era of Harry Hood, Stan Anderson, Davie White, John McHugh and his favourite player, Joe Gilroy, and remembers an era of skilful players and very enjoyable football.

The facts lend credence to that claim. "A part time squad of 15 players finished third in the League in season 1966/67, behind the European Champions (Celtic) and the beaten finalists in the European Cup Winners' Cup (Rangers)"

In season 1972/73, the Clyde Programme Editor, David Bell, asked John Taylor to contribute a series to the programme, based on his press cuttings from that season. Periodic contributions over the years were extended in 1980 when Bell's successor, Norman Brown, asked John to share the burden of editing the Bully Wee programme. The final programme produced by the Brown/Taylor team was Clyde's last match at Shawfield at the end of season 1985/86, and John has been sole editor since the start of the following season.

"While we were ground sharing at Firhill, the programme was produced on virtually a care-and-maintenance basis. The move to Hamilton in 1991 coincided with the Board of Directors handing over every aspect of the programme to my stewardship; finances, printing arrangements, the lot. I teamed up with Frank Tocher, and we both had the vision and ambition to move Clyde's programme onwards

and upwards in terms of size, design and content. I can't emphasise enough how much Frank has contributed to the programme's success." Messrs Taylor and Tocher set out to provide Clyde fans with the information on the club and its players that they would not get in the newspapers. "Clyde are an unfashionable club, as far as the press are concerned, and don't get much coverage in the national, or even regional media. We set out to compensate for that in the contents of our programme." They were supported by the club's Directors, who shared their enthusiasm for keeping the fans informed.

John recalls: "The Board allowed us to develop the programme, pushing out the boundaries every year – just as long as it did not incur a financial loss."

Far from resting on their laurels, the Clyde programme team make a point of instigating changes each season. "The idea is to knock the programme down and start again every season, trying to make it completely different. Everything is considered for change; it's very much a personal preference of mine, that the programme needs to be very different every season."

Although the bulk of the sales come from home fans, with a better than 1-in-2 sales ratio, the visiting support is by no means neglected. "With at least 8 pages in each issue, we try to provide

coverage of the visitors which will interest their supporters. Hopefully, this will encourage them to buy the programme when they visit Broadwood."

Sales ratios to visiting supporters vary hugely, but John identifies a surprising club as the best visiting buyers. "On a sales per spectator ratio, Queen of the South usually come out top."

He sees no reduction in interest in matchday programmes, despite the proliferation of information from new media such as the internet, mobile phones, etc. "It is heartening to see the crowd of youngsters outside the main door of Broadwood on a matchday, wanting their programmes autographed by the players.

"It's also comforting to go into any football dressing room before a match, and see the players eagerly reading the programme, probably to see if they get a mention. We see the provision of information from the likes of websites as being in addition to the programme, not instead of. A matchday programme is like the pie and Bovril; it's one of the great traditions of football, and one which will probably last as long as the game is played."

**JOHN LITSTER**
(Editor, Programme Monthly & Football Collectable Magazine www.pmfc.co.uk)

Clyde's editorial and production team, John Taylor and Frank Tocher, with the Scottish Programme of the Year Trophy

# SCOTTISH PROGRAMME OF THE YEAR AWARDS **SEASON 2004.05**

## SPL (2003/04)
1. (1) Aberdeen
2. (2) Dunfermline Athletic
3. (3) Hearts
4. (10 (FD)) Inverness Caledonian Thistle
5. (6) Dundee United
6. (8) Kilmarnock
7. (11) Rangers
8. (4) Dundee
9. (7) Hibernian
10. (9) Celtic
11. (10) Livingston
12. (12) Motherwell

## SFL FIRST DIVISION (2003/04)
1. (1) Clyde
2. (5 (SPL)) Partick Thistle
3. (2) Falkirk
4. (4) St. Johnstone
5. (3) St. Mirren
6. (8) Raith Rovers
7. (2 (SD)) Hamilton Academical
8. (7) Queen of the South
9. (9) Ross County
10. (3 (SD)) Airdrie United

## SFL SECOND DIVISION (2003/04)
1. (6 (FD)) Brechin City
2. (1) Morton
3. (5 (FD)) Ayr United
4. (3 (TD)) Stirling Albion
5. (6) Forfar Athletic
6. (4) Dumbarton
7. (10) Arbroath
8. (8) Berwick Rangers
9. (9) Alloa Athletic
10. (7 (TD)) Stranraer

## SFL THIRD DIVISION (2003/04)
1. (1) Queen's Park
2. (2) Montrose
3. (5) Gretna
4. (4) Cowdenbeath
5. (9) Elgin City
6. (5 (SD)) Stenhousemuir
7. (7 (SD)) East Fife
8. (10) East Stirlingshire
9. (8) Albion Rovers
10. (6) Peterhead

## SCOTTISH PROGRAMMES OF THE YEAR - PREVIOUS WINNERS
| | |
|---|---|
| 1973/74 | Ayr United |
| 1974/75 | Hamilton Academical |
| 1975/76 | Heart of Midlothian |
| 1976/77 | Motherwell |
| 1977/78 | Hamilton Academical |
| 1978/79 | Hamilton Academical |
| 1979/80 | Berwick Rangers |
| 1980/81 | Aberdeen |
| 1981/82 | Hamilton Academical |
| 1982/83 | Dundee |
| 1983/84 | Dundee United |
| 1984/85 | Aberdeen |
| 1985/86 | Celtic |
| 1986/87 | Rangers |
| 1987/88 | Rangers |
| 1988/89 | Rangers |
| 1989/90 | Aberdeen |
| 1990/91 | Celtic |
| 1991/92 | Aberdeen |
| 1992/93 | Rangers |
| 1993/94 | Rangers |
| 1994/95 | Rangers |
| 1995/96 | Clyde |
| 1996/97 | Clyde |
| 1997/98 | Clyde |
| 1998/99 | Clyde |
| 1999/2000 | Clyde |
| 2000/01 | Clyde |
| 2001/02 | Clyde |
| 2002/03 | Clyde |
| 2003/04 | Clyde |
| 2004/05 | Clyde |

## PREMIER LEAGUE PROGRAMME OF THE YEAR
as above, except for ...)
| | |
|---|---|
| 1974/75 | Motherwell (old Div.One) |
| 1975/76 | Heart of Midlothian |
| 1976/77 | Motherwell |
| 1977/78 | Rangers |
| 1978/79 | Morton |
| 1979/80 | Morton |
| 1995/96 | Kilmarnock |
| 1996/97 | Dundee United |
| 1997/98 | Dundee United |
| 1998/99 | Dundee United |
| 1999/2000 | Dundee United |
| 2000/01 | Dunfermline Athletic |
| 2001/02 | Aberdeen |
| 2002/03 | Aberdeen |
| 2003/04 | Aberdeen |
| 2004/05 | Aberdeen |

## FIRST DIVISION PROGRAMME OF THE YEAR
| | |
|---|---|
| 1975/76 | Hamilton Academical |
| 1976/77 | Hamilton Academical |
| 1977/78 | Hamilton Academical |
| 1978/79 | Hamilton Academical |
| 1979/80 | Berwick Rangers |
| 1980/81 | Hamilton Academical |
| 1981/82 | Hamilton Academical |
| 1982/83 | Queen's Park |
| 1983/84 | Hamilton Academical |
| 1984/85 | Clyde |
| 1985/86 | Clyde |
| 1986/87 | Clyde |
| 1987/88 | Hamilton & Clydebank |
| 1988/89 | Dunfermline Athletic |
| 1989/90 | Airdrieonians |
| 1990/91 | Dundee |
| 1991/92 | Partick Thistle |
| 1992/93 | Kilmarnock |
| 1993/94 | Dunfermline Athletic |
| 1994/95 | Dunfermline Athletic |
| 1995/96 | Dundee United |
| 1996/97 | Partick Thistle |
| 1997/98 | St. Mirren |
| 1998/99 | Hibernian |
| 1999/2000 | Dunfermline Athletic |
| 2000/01 | Clyde |
| 2001/02 | Clyde |
| 2002/03 | Clyde |
| 2003/04 | Clyde |
| 2004/05 | Clyde |

## SECOND DIVISION PROGRAMME OF THE YEAR
| | |
|---|---|
| 1973/74 | Hamilton Academical |
| 1974/75 | Hamilton Academical |
| 1975/76 | Berwick Rangers |
| 1976/77 | Albion Rovers |
| 1977/78 | Meadowbank Thistle |
| 1978/79 | Berwick Rangers |
| 1979/80 | Albion Rovers |
| 1980/81 | Clyde |
| 1981/82 | Clyde |
| 1982/83 | Stirling Albion |
| 1983/84 | Stirling Albion |
| 1984/85 | Stirling Abion |
| 1985/86 | Stirling Albion |
| 1986/87 | Raith Rovers |
| 1987/88 | Stirling Albion |
| 1988/89 | Stirling Albion |
| 1989/90 | Kilmarnock |
| 1990/91 | Stirling Albion |
| 1991/92 | Clyde |
| 1992/93 | Clyde |
| 1993/94 | Forfar Athletic |
| 1994/95 | Clyde |
| 1995/96 | Clyde |
| 1996/97 | Clyde |
| 1997/98 | Clyde |
| 1998/99 | Clyde |
| 1999/2000 | Clyde |
| 2000/01 | Partick Thistle |
| 2001/02 | Hamilton Academical |
| 2002/03 | Brechin City |
| 2003/04 | Morton |
| 2004/05 | Brechin City |

## THIRD DIVISION PROGRAMME OF THE YEAR
| | |
|---|---|
| 1994/95 | Forfar Athletic |
| 1995/96 | Livingston |
| 1996/97 | Inverness Caledonian Thistle |
| 1997/98 | Montrose |
| 1998/99 | Queen's Park |
| 1999/2000 | Queen's Park |
| 2000/01 | Montrose |
| 2001/02 | Montrose |
| 2002/03 | Queen's Park |
| 2003/04 | Queen's Park |
| 2004/05 | Queen's Park |

## WORLD CUP 2006

### QUALIFYING GROUP 5
Wednesday, 8th September, 2004 – Hampden Park, Glasgow

**SCOTLAND 0     SLOVENIA 0**

**Scotland:** C. Gordon, G. Caldwell, G. Naysmith, (G. Holt), A. Webster,
M. Mackay, B. Ferguson, D. Fletcher, J. McNamara, P. Dickov,
(S. Crawford), N. Quashie, J. McFadden
Substitutes not used: D. Marshall, K. Miller, C. Cameron, S. Pearson, R. Anderson
**Slovenia:** B. Mavric, Karic, M. Mavric, Knavs, Siljak (Lavric), Ceh, Komac,
Pokorn, Acimovic, Seslar, Dedic (Sukalo)
Substitutes not used:  Handanovic, Tanjic, Cesar, Koren, Ilic
**Referee:** Claus Bo Larsen (Denmark) **Attendance:** 38,278

Saturday, 9th October, 2004 – Hampden Park, Glasgow

**SCOTLAND 0     NORWAY 1**
               Iversen

**Scotland:** C. Gordon, G. Caldwell, G. Naysmith, R. Anderson, A. Webster,
B. Ferguson, D. Fletcher, G. Holt, (S. Thompson), P. Dickov, (K. Miller),
J. McFadden, R. Hughes, (S. Pearson)
**Norway:** Myhre, Bergdolmo, Hagen, Lundekvam, Riise, Sorensen,
(Andresen), Solli, Hoset, (Pedersen), Larsen, Carew, Iversen, (F. Johnsen)
Substitutes not used: Gashi, E. Johnsen, Rushfeldt, Soma
**Referee:** Paul Allaerts (Belgium) **Attendance:** 48,882

Wednesday, 13th October, 2004 - Republican Stadium, Chisinau

**MOLDOVA 1     SCOTLAND 1**
Dadu              S. Thompson

**Moldova:** Hmaruc, Savinov, Lascencov, Olexici, (Cebotari), Catinsus,
Priganiuc, Covaliciuc, Ivanov, Rogaciov, (Miterev), Bursuc, Dadu
Substitutes not used: Andriuta, Corneencov, Iepureanu, Golban, Melenciuc
**Scotland:** C. Gordon, G. Caldwell, G. Naysmith, (I. Murray), S. Caldwell,
A. Webster, B. Ferguson, D. Fletcher, (K. Miller), G. Holt, S. Thompson,
(L. McCulloch), S. Crawford, C. Cameron
Substitutes not used:  D. Marshall, S. Severin, R. Hughes, G. Murty
**Referee:** Kristinn Jakobsson (Iceland) **Attendance:** 7,000

Saturday, 26th March, 2005 – Giuseppe Meazza, Milan

**ITALY 2     SCOTLAND 0**
Pirlo (2)

**Italy:** Buffon, Bonera, Chiellini, Gattuso, Cannavaro, Materazzi,
Camoranesi, Pirlo, Gilardino, Totti, (De Rossi), Cassano, (Toni)
Substitutes not used:  Roma, Zaccardo, Grosso, Blasi, Esposito
**Scotland:** R. Douglas, (C. Gordon), J. McNamara, G. Naysmith,
S. Pressley, D. Weir, B. Ferguson, P. Hartley, (N. McCann), G. Caldwell,
K. Miller, (G. O'Connor), N. Quashie, L. McCulloch
Substitutes not used:  A. Webster, B. O'Neil, S. Crawford, R. Anderson
**Referee:** Kyros Vassaras (Greece) **Attendance:** 40,745

Saturday, 4th June, 2005 – Hampden Park, Glasgow

**SCOTLAND 2     MOLDOVA 0**
C. Dailly, J. McFadden

**Scotland:** C. Gordon, G. Alexander, J. McNamara, (C. Dailly), S. Pressley,
D. Weir, B. Ferguson, D. Fletcher, A. Webster, K. Miller, P. Hartley,
L. McCulloch, (J. McFadden)
Substitutes not used: R. Esson, S. Caldwell, L. Miller, D. Riordan, S. Thompson

**Moldova:** Hmaruc, Savinov, Lascencov, (Covalenco), Olexici, Catinsus,
(Covalciuc), Priganiuc, Iepureanu, Ivanov, Rogaciov, (Frunza), Boret, Dadu
Substitutes not used: Romanenco, Barisev, Cebotari
**Referee:** Frederikus J. Braamhaar (Netherlands) **Attendance:** 45,317

Wednesday, 8th June 2005 – Dinamo Stadium, Minsk

**BELARUS 0     SCOTLAND 0**

**Belarus:** Zhevnov, Kalachev, (V. Hleb), Yaskovich, Omelyanchuk, Shtanjuk,
Gurenko, Kovba, Bialkevich, Bulyga, (Kuichy), A. Hleb, Kornilenko
Substitutes not used:  Khomutovski, Tarlovski, Ostrovski,
Chelyadinski, Sashcheka
**Scotland:** C. Gordon, C. Dailly, G. Alexander, S. Pressley, D. Weir, B. Ferguson,
D. Fletcher, A. Webster, K. Miller, G. Caldwell, L. McCulloch, (J. McFadden)
Substitutes not used:  D. Marshall, S. Caldwell, S. Thompson, I. Murray,
D. Riordan, L. Miller
**Referee:** Olegario Bartolo Benquerenca (Portugal) **Attendance:** 28,287

### GROUP 5 TABLE
(Includes all results as at 8th June, 2005)

|          | P | W | D | L | F | A | PTS |
|----------|---|---|---|---|---|---|-----|
| ITALY    | 6 | 4 | 1 | 1 | 9 | 5 | 13 |
| NORWAY   | 6 | 2 | 3 | 1 | 6 | 3 | 9 |
| SLOVENIA | 6 | 2 | 3 | 1 | 6 | 5 | 9 |
| BELARUS  | 6 | 1 | 4 | 1 | 10 | 7 | 7 |
| **SCOTLAND** | **6** | **1** | **3** | **2** | **3** | **4** | **6** |
| MOLDOVA  | 6 | 0 | 2 | 4 | 1 | 11 | 2 |

Scotland skipper Barry Ferguson climbs to reach the ball ahead of Slovenian Nastja Ceh

## FULL INTERNATIONAL FRIENDLY MATCHES
Wednesday, 18th August, 2004 – Hampden Park, Glasgow

**SCOTLAND 0       HUNGARY 3**
                 Huszti (2), Marshall (o.g.)

**Scotland:** D. Marshall, G. Holt, G. Naysmith, A. Webster, S. Pressley,
B. Ferguson, (S. Severin), D. Fletcher, (S. Pearson), G. Caldwell,
(S. Thompson), K. Miller, (S. Crawford), J. McFadden, N. Quashie
Substitutes not used: P. Gallacher, D. McNamee, R. Anderson,
A. Gray, C. Gordon
**Hungary:** Kiraly, Bodnar, Huszti, (Bodor), Juhasz, (Gyepes), Stark, Toth,
Molnar, Feher, (Rosa), Torghelle, (Kovacs), Gera, (Leandro), Simek.
Substitute not used: Babos
**Referee:** Laurent Duhamel (France) **Attendance:** 15,933

Friday, 3rd September, 2004 – Estadio Ciudad de Valencia

**SPAIN 1       SCOTLAND 1**
Raul           J. McFadden
(Match Abandoned after 59 minutes due to floodlight failure)

**Spain:** Iker Casillas, Lopex Rekarte, Del Horno, Marchena, (Helguera),
Puyol, Xabi Alonso, Joaquin, Baraja, (Vicente), Torres, (Raul), Reyes,
Tamudo, (Valeron)
Substitutes not used: Canizares, Salgado, Romero, Morientes, Victor, Juanito
**Scotland:** C. Gordon, G. Caldwell, G. Naysmith, A. Webster, M. Mackay,
B. Ferguson, D. Fletcher, (C. Cameron), J. McNamara, S. Crawford,
(K. Miller), N. Quashie, J. McFadden, (S. Pearson)
Substitutes not used: S. Shearer, S. Thompson, P. Dickov, D. McNamee,
G. Holt, K. Kyle
**Referee:** Stephane Bre (France) **Attendance:** 15,000

Wednesday, 17th November, 2004 – Easter Road Stadium, Edinburgh

**SCOTLAND 1       SWEDEN 4**
J. McFadden       Allback (2), Elmander, Berglund

**Scotland:** D. Marshall, K. McNaughton, I. Murray, R. Anderson, A. Webster,
(S. Hammell), J. McNamara, (S. Severin), B. Nicholson, N. Quashie,
(R. Hughes), K. Miller, (S. Crawford), J. McFadden, S. Pearson
Substitutes not used: C. Gordon, S. Pressley, A. Combe
**Sweden:** Hedman, Nilsson, (Ostlund), Mellberg, (Hansson), Lucic,
(Linderoth), Dorsin, A. Andersson, Alexandersson, Kallstrom,
Wilhelmsson, (Touma), Allback, (Elmander), Berglund.
Substitutes not used: Isaksson, Antonsson, Johansson
**Referee:** Jaroslav Jara (Czech Republic). **Attendance:** 15,071

## FUTURE INTERNATIONALS

### FUTURE CUP

Tuesday, 7th December, 2004– Carl Benz Stadion, Mannheim

**GERMANY 3       SCOTLAND 0**
Auer (2), Marx

**Germany:** Jentzsch, (Enke), Schröter, (Schlicke), Langkamp, (Friedrich),
Madlung, Achenbach, Streit, Marx, Broich, Engelhardt, (Rolfes), Hanke,
Auer, (Helmes)
**Scotland:** D. Soutar, (A. McGregor), A. Diamond, (M. Corrigan), I. Murray,
K. McNaughton, A. Virgo, R. Malcolm, S. Wilson, P. Hartley,
(B. Nicholson), G. O'Connor, J. Smith, S. Lynch, (G. McDonald)
Substitute not used: S. Hammell
**Referee:** Levan Paniashvili (Georgia) **Attendance:** 4,500

Tuesday, 19th April, 2005 - Pappelstadion, Mattersburg

**AUSTRIA 2       SCOTLAND 1**
Mair, Morz       C. Beattie

**Austria:** Mandel, (Borenitsch), Garics, Feldhofer, Schrott, (Ortlechner),
Pircher, (Mader), Morz, Bubenik, (Sariyar), Shcarner, Mair, Martinez,
(Kulovits), Pichlmann, (Kienast)
**Scotland:** C. Gordon, (M. Brown), J. McCunnie, (C. Berra), S. Watt,
A. Webster, I. Murray, J. Smith, S. Severin, G. McDonald, P. Sweeney,
(M. Fotheringham), S. Parkin, (S. Maloney), C. Beattie
Substitute not used: D. McNamee
**Referee:** Tomas Curin (Czech Republic) **Attendance:** 2,700

## EUROPEAN "UNDER-21" CHAMPIONSHIP

### QUALIFYING GROUP 5
Tuesday, 7th September, 2004 – McDiarmid Park, Perth

**SCOTLAND 1       SLOVENIA 1**
G. O'Connor       Semier

**Scotland:** G. Smith, A. Dowie, S. Lappin, A. Diamond, G. Robertson,
J. McCunnie, (S. Whittaker), A. Hutton, (B. Prunty), P. Sweeney,
G. O'Connor, S. Brown, D. Clarkson, (D. Riordan)
Substitutes not used: I. Turner, W. Kinniburgh, S. Morrison, S. Murray
**Slovenia:** Nenezic, Brecko, Hadzic, Urbanc, Berko, Morec, Zinko,
(Kelhar), Matic, Stromajer, (Vrsic), Semler, Bozicic, (Jesenicnik)
Substitutes not used: Simcic, Lo Duca, Robnik, Bozic
**Referee:** Egill Mar Markusson (Iceland) **Attendance:** 2,768

Friday, 8th October, 2004 – Broadwood Stadium, Cumbernauld

**SCOTLAND 0       NORWAY 2**
                 Grindheim, Eriksen

**Scotland:** G. Smith, A. Dowie, S. Lappin, S. Whittaker, G. Robertson,
M. Wilson, R. Foy, (J. McCunnie), R. Wallace, G. O'Connor, S. Fagan,
(D. Clarkson), K. Boyd
Substitutes not used: A. Brown, W. Kinniburgh, S. Dillon, S. Morrison, B. Prunty
**Norway:** Larsen, Skjonsberg, Onstad, Engedal, Eriksen, Riise,
Grindheim, Haestad, Holm, Strand, (Sokolowski), Markegard, (Bertelsen)
Substitutes not used: Austbo, Ruud, Moster, Moen, Hoas
**Referee:** Jari Maisonlahti (Finland) **Attendance:** 3,014

Tuesday, 12th October, 2004 – Dinamo Stadium, Chisinau

**MOLDOVA 0       SCOTLAND 0**

**Moldova:** Phius, Bordian, Golovatenco, Bulgaru, Tigirlas, (Japalau), Josan,
Epureanu, Porfireanu, (Frantuz), Doros, (Calencov), Onica, Hramtov
Substitutes not used: Cebanu, Popovici, Alexeev, Bolohan
**Scotland:** G. Smith, A. Dowie, S. Lappin, S. Whittaker, G. Robertson, J. McCunnie,
R. Foster, M. Wilson, G. O'Connor, D. Clarkson, (K. Boyd), S. Morrison
Substitutes not used: I. Turner, W. Kinniburgh, S. Fagan, R. Foy, R. Wallace, B. Prunty
**Referee:** Saso Lazarevski (FYR Macedonia) **Attendance:** 750

Friday, 25th March, 2005 – Stadio Pietro Fortunati, Pavia

**ITALY 2       SCOTLAND 0**
Bianchi, Rosina

**Italy:** Curci, Motta, Potenza, Bovo, Mantovani, Donadel, Rosina, Lazzari,
(Pagano), Bianchi, Aquilani, (Montolivo), Pazzini, (Mannini)
Substitutes not used: Agliardi, Piccolo, Loviso, Pepe

**Scotland:** D. Marshall, A. Dowie, S. Morrison, A. Diamond, C. Berra, M. Wilson, S. Whittaker, J. McCunnie, S. Maloney, (T. Brighton), D. Riordan, (K. Boyd), S. Brown
Substitutes not used: C. Samson, N. Collins, K. Broadfoot, G. Robertson, R. Foster
**Referee:** Marian Mircea Salomir (Romania) **Attendance:** 4,300

Friday, 3rd June, 2005 – Firhill Stadium, Glasgow

## SCOTLAND 0     MOLDOVA 0

**Scotland:** C. Samson, S. Watt, S. Morrison, N. Collins, G. Robertson, M. Wilson, (D. Clarkson), S. Whittaker, J. McCunnie, S. Maloney, S. Brown, (P. Sweeney), P. Gallagher, (T. Brighton)
Substitutes not used: A. Brown, K. Broadfoot, P. Lawson, K. Thomson
**Moldova:** Paius, Bordian, Golovatenco, Epureanu, Namasco, Tigirlas, Josan, Alexeev, (Bulat), Japalau, (Picusciac), Suvorov, (Frantuz), Gatcan
Substitutes not used: Cebanu, Bulgaru
**Referee:** Christopher Lautier (Malta) **Attendance:** 1,499

Tuesday, 7th June, 2005 – Traktor Stadium, Minsk

## BELARUS 3     SCOTLAND 2
Kovel,              S. Whittaker,
Stashchaniuk,       D. Clarkson
Afanasyev

**Belarus:** Amelchanka, Liantsevich, (Harbachov), Stashchaniuk, Popel, Paskonny, Marox, Paulau, (Kamarovski), Shchahrykovich, Kovel, (Dzenisevich), Kantsavy, Afanasyev
Substitutes not used: Chasnouski, Radzionau, Skverniuk, Tsviatsinski

Jamie McCunnie in action for Scotland's Under 21's against Belarus

**Scotland:** C. Samson, S. Watt, (D. Clarkson), S. Morrison, (K. Thomson), N. Collins, G. Robertson, M. Wilson, S. Whittaker, J. McCunnie, T. Brighton, S. Maloney, K. Broadfoot
Substitutes not used: A. Brown, P. Lawson, S. Brown
**Referee:** Lasha Silagava (Georgia) **Attendance:** 1,500

### GROUP 5 TABLE
(Includes all results as at 7th June, 2005)

|          | P | W | D | L | F  | A  | PTS |
|----------|---|---|---|---|----|----|-----|
| ITALY    | 6 | 5 | 0 | 1 | 10 | 2  | 15  |
| NORWAY   | 6 | 3 | 1 | 2 | 8  | 6  | 10  |
| BELARUS  | 6 | 3 | 0 | 3 | 14 | 12 | 9   |
| SLOVENIA | 6 | 2 | 2 | 2 | 5  | 9  | 8   |
| MOLDOVA  | 6 | 1 | 2 | 3 | 4  | 7  | 5   |
| SCOTLAND | 6 | 0 | 3 | 3 | 3  | 8  | 3   |

## UNDER-21 INTERNATIONAL FRIENDLY MATCHES

Wednesday, 18th August, 2004 – Dunaferr Stadium, Dunaujvaros

### HUNGARY 4                  SCOTLAND 2
Jovanczai (2), Czvitkovics,   K. Boyd, S. Whittaker
Kanta

**Hungary:** Fulop, Vati, Magasfoldi, Takacs, Bank, Vadocz, Czvitkovics, (Bori), Jovanczai, (Kanta), Varga, (Tozser), Vanczak, Regedei
Substitutes not used: Kovacs, Pollak, Belogh
**Scotland:** C. Samson, (G. Smith), M. Wilson, S. Morrison, A. Diamond, (J. McCunnie), G. Robertson, A. Hutton, (S. Whittaker), S. Brown, R. Foy, (B. Prunty), P. Sweeney, (S. Lappin), K. Boyd, P. Gallagher, (D. Riordan)
Substitutes not used: A. Dowie, C. Beattie, I. Turner
**Referee:** Richard Havrilla (Slovakia) **Attendance:** 300

Thursday, 2nd September, 2004 – Estadio El Collao, Alcoi

### SPAIN 3                    SCOTLAND 1
Iniesta, Santi Cazorla, Melli  G. O'Connor

**Spain:** Moya, Sergio Ramos, (Santi Cazorla), Puerta, Melli, Ramis, (Murillo), Solabarrieta, (Vitolo), Xabi Prieto, (Navas), Gabi, (Arizmendi), Sergio Garcia, Iniesta, (Cesc), Angulo, (Jonathan)
Substitutes not used: Pena, Riesgo, Jarque
**Scotland:** G. Smith, (I. Turner), A. Dowie, S. Morrison, A. Diamond, G. Robertson, J. McCunnie, S. Whittaker, P. Sweeney, G. O'Connor, (B. Prunty), S. Brown, (D. Riordan), D. Clarkson
Substitutes not used: S. Dillon, W. Kinniburgh, R. Foy, S. Lappin, S. Murray, C. Samson
**Referee:** Gianluca Paparesta (Italy) **Attendance:** 5,312

Tuesday, 16th November, 2004 – The Falkirk Stadium, Falkirk

### SCOTLAND 1     SWEDEN 2
J. McCunnie       Dahlberg, Runstrom

**Scotland:** I. Turner, A. Dowie, S. Morrison, S. Whittaker, G. Robertson, J. McCunnie, A. Hutton, (R. Foster), M. Wilson, P. Gallagher, (P. Sweeney), S. Lappin, (P. Leven), D. Duffy
Substitutes not used: G. Smith, P. Quinn, B. Prunty, C. Samson
**Sweden:** Sahlman, (Kallkuist), Svensson, (P. Larsson), Stenman, Guiomar, (Kapella-Karlsson), S. Larsson, Alander, P. Andersson, (Dguric), Farnerud, (Tobiasson), J. Andersson, Graquist, Dahlberg, (Runstrom)
Substitute not used: Holmen
**Referee:** Pavel Kralovec (Czech Republic) **Attendance:** 2,076

Tuesday, 8th February, 2005 – The Oval, Belfast

**NORTHERN IRELAND 2**  **SCOTLAND 1**
Brunt, Morrow  S. Maloney

**Northern Ireland:** McGovern, Ward, (Gault), Friars, Hughes, Webb, McCrystal, Gilfillan, (Murtagh), Clingan, Brunt, Braniff, Shiels, (Morrow)
Substitutes not used: Julian, Lindsay, McClean, McCourt, Teggart
**Scotland:** C. Samson, A. Dowie, T. Brighton, (D. Clarkson), S. Whittaker, (A. Hutton), G. Robertson, J. McCunnie, M. Wilson, P. Leven, (C. Burke), S. Morrison, D. Duffy, S. Maloney
Substitutes not used: G. Smith, P. Quinn, J. Rankin, P. Lawson, B. Prunty, I. Turner
**Referee:** Ian Stokes (Republic of Ireland). **Attendance:** 1,300

## UEFA UNDER-19 CHAMPIONSHIP

### FIRST QUALIFYING ROUND
### QUALIFYING GROUP 8 – HOSTED BY BELGIUM
Wednesday, 6th October, 2004 – Stade de la Neuville, Charleroi

**SAN MARINO 0**  **SCOTLAND 4**
 S. Naismith, R. Davidson,
 R. Quinn, M. Woods

**San Marino:** Macaluso, Bianchi, Zanotti, Ranocchini, Rossi, Palazzi, Valli, Rinaldi, Cibelli, (Cavalli), Simoncini, (De Angelis), Simoncini, (Guidi)
Substitutes not used: Stefanelli, Chiaruzzi, Bonini, Gabrielli
**Scotland:** C. Bell, M. Fitzpatrick, S. Cuthbert, C. Sives, M. Woods, (M. Scott), T. Parratt, R. McCormack, S. Naismith, R. Quinn, R. Davidson, (M. Gardyne), R. Campbell, (S. Campbell)
Substitutes not used: E. McLean, K. McKinlay, S. Anderson
Referee: Sokol Jareci (Albania) Attendance: 180

Friday, 8th October, 2004 – Stade de la Neuville, Charleroi

**TURKEY 2**  **SCOTLAND 2**
Ali Ozturk, Guzeldal  R. Quinn, R. McCormack

**Turkey:** Acar, Basturk, (Sevindir), Orhan, Bilal, Gurhan, Guzeldal, Ali Ozturk, Cevahir, Ferhat Oztorun, (Ufuk), Cafercan, (Can), Kadioglu
Substitutes not used: Akman, Sancakli, Ozer
**Scotland:** C. Bell, M. Fitzpatrick, C. Mulgrew, S. Cuthbert, M. Woods, T. Parratt, R. McCormack, S. Naismith, R. Quinn, M. Scott, (R. Campbell), R. Davidson, (M. Gardyne)
Substitutes not used: E. McLean, S. Campbell, K. McKinlay, S. Anderson
**Referee:** Sinisa Zrnic (Bosnia-Herzegovina) **Attendance:** 450

Sunday, 10th October, 2004 – Stade du Pays de Charleroi, Charleroi

**BELGIUM 1**  **SCOTLAND 1**
S. Cuthbert (o.g.)  R. McCormack

**Belgium:** Vandelannoite, Pocognoli, Boeckx, Buysse, Colpaert, Sanchez D'avolio, (Lamah), Yulu-matondo, Asubonteng, (Bengui-dombaxe), Trianfillidis, (Derijck), Legear, Dembele
Substitutes not used: Ruttens, Mulemo, Galluci, Blondelle
**Scotland:** C. Bell, M. Fitzpatrick, C. Mulgrew, S. Cuthbert, M. Woods, T. Parratt, R. McCormack, R. Quinn, M. Gardyne, (S. Anderson), R. Davidson, R. Campbell, (K. McKinlay)
Substitutes not used: E. McLean, S. Campbell, M. Scott,
**Referee:** Sinisa Zrnic (Bosnia-Herzegovina) **Attendance:** 700

### FINAL GROUP 8 TABLE

|  | P | W | D | L | F | A | PTS |
|---|---|---|---|---|---|---|---|
| BELGIUM | 3 | 2 | 1 | 0 | 8 | 2 | 7 |
| SCOTLAND | 3 | 1 | 2 | 0 | 7 | 3 | 5 |
| TURKEY | 3 | 1 | 1 | 1 | 13 | 5 | 4 |
| SAN MARINO | 3 | 0 | 0 | 3 | 0 | 18 | 0 |

### SECOND (ELITE) ROUND
### QUALIFYING GROUP 5 – HOSTED BY AUSTRIA
Friday, 27th May, 2005 – Vocklamarkt Stadium, Vocklamarkt

**GREECE 1**  **SCOTLAND 0**
Petropoulas

**Greece:** Kasmeridis, Maniatis, Tripotseris, Makos, Soulidis, (Balafas), Iliadis, Petropoulos, Christodopolous, Aravidis, (Kiliaras), Rikka, Siontis, (Zindros)
Substitutes not used: Sotiriou, Sachinidis
**Scotland:** E. McLean, T. Parratt, S. Campbell, S. Anderson, S. Cuthbert, C. Mulgrew, M. Scott, R. Davidson, (D. Carcary), S. Naismith, (A. Considine), R. McCormack, R. Campbell, (L. Craig)
Substitutes not used: S. Murdoch, S. Notman, K. McAulay
**Referee:** Claudio Circhetta (Switzerland)

Sunday, 29th May, 2005 – Mondsee Stadium, Mondsee

**SLOVAKIA 0**  **SCOTLAND 2**
 S. Naismith, R. McCormack

**Slovakia:** Janek, Pecha, Lintner, Jonas, Bakos, Izvolt, Roznik, (Viskup), Gajdos, Jendrisek, (Snegon), Kosicky, Novysedlak, (Opiela)
Substitutes not used: Rondzik, Hanzel, Karlik, Moravcik
**Scotland:** E. McLean, T. Parratt, S. Campbell, S. Anderson, S. Cuthbert, C. Mulgrew, M. Scott, (D. Carcary), S. Naismith, R. McCormack, R. Quinn, (K. McAulay), L. Craig, (R. Campbell)
Substitutes not used: R. Davidson, S. Murdoch, S. Notman, A. Considine
**Referee:** Claudio Circhetta (Switzerland)

Tuesday, 31st May, 2005 – Vocklamarkt Stadium, Vocklamarkt

**AUSTRIA 2**  **SCOTLAND 3**
Mayer, Sulimani  S. Naismith (2), A. Considine

**Austria:** Olejnik, (Leitner), Salvatore, Gercaliu, (Pichler), Hoheneder, Klein, Saurer, Idrizaj, Mayer, Stankovic, (Erbek), Fuchs, Sulimani
Substitutes not used: Saumel, Sprik
**Scotland:** E. McLean, T. Parratt, S. Campbell, S. Cuthbert, M. Scott, (R. Campbell), S. Naismith, (S. Notman), R. Quinn, D. Carcary, A. Considine, K. McAulay, (R. Davidson), L. Craig
Substitutes not used: S. Anderson, S. Murdoch
**Referee:** Pavel Saliy (Kazakhstan)

### FINAL GROUP 5 TABLE

|  | P | W | D | L | F | A | PTS |
|---|---|---|---|---|---|---|---|
| GREECE | 3 | 3 | 0 | 0 | 5 | 1 | 9 |
| SCOTLAND | 3 | 2 | 0 | 1 | 5 | 3 | 6 |
| SLOVAKIA | 3 | 1 | 0 | 2 | 2 | 4 | 3 |
| AUSTRIA | 3 | 0 | 0 | 3 | 3 | 7 | 0 |

## NORTHERN IRELAND UNDER-19 TOURNAMENT
Saturday, 19th February, 2005 – The Showgrounds, Ballymena

### SPAIN 0          SCOTLAND 0

**Scotland:** E. McLean, T. Parratt, C. Mulgrew, S. Anderson, S. Campbell, A. Considine, M. Woods, (K. McAulay), R. McCormack, M. Gardyne, (S. Notman), R. Campbell, M. Scott
**Referee:** Luc Wilmes (Luxembourg)

Monday, 21st February, 2005 – The Oval, Belfast

### NORTHERN IRELAND 0     SCOTLAND 1
                         D. Carcary

**Scotland:** E. McLean, T. Parratt, C. Mulgrew, S. Anderson, S. Campbell, A. Considine, M. Woods, (R. Campbell), K. McAulay, (D. Carcary), M. Gardyne, (S. Notman), M. Scott, M. Fitzpatrick
**Referee:** Duarte Pereira Gomes (Spain)

Wednesday, 23rd February, 2005 – Seaview, Belfast

### UKRAINE 1       SCOTLAND 1
Gorbushyn         M. Woods

**Scotland:** E. McLean, T. Parratt, C. Mulgrew, (D. Robertson), S. Anderson, A. Considine, K. McAulay, (M. Woods), M. Gardyne, C. Reid, D. Carcary, M. Fitzpatrick, S. Notman
**Referee:** Luc Wilmes (Luxembourg)

### FINAL TABLE

|                  | P | W | D | L | F | A | PTS |
|------------------|---|---|---|---|---|---|-----|
| UKRAINE          | 3 | 1 | 2 | 0 | 4 | 3 | 5   |
| SCOTLAND         | 3 | 1 | 2 | 0 | 2 | 1 | 5   |
| SPAIN            | 3 | 1 | 1 | 1 | 4 | 3 | 4   |
| NORTHERN IRELAND | 3 | 0 | 1 | 2 | 0 | 3 | 0   |

Marc Fitzpatrick in action for Scotland's Under 19's against Norway

## UNDER-19 INTERNATIONAL FRIENDLY MATCHES
Wednesday, 24th November, 2004 – Sportplatz Borussia Fulda, Fulda

### GERMANY 1      SCOTLAND 1
Schrodter        M. Gardyne

**Scotland:** E. McLean, T. Parratt, S. Campbell, S. Anderson, (C. Bryson), S. Cuthbert, C. Mulgrew, R. Campbell, (S. Notman), R. Quinn, S. Naismith, (K. McKinlay), M. Gardyne, (K. McAulay), M. Woods, (M. Scott)
**Referee:** Babak Rafati (Germany) **Attendance:** 6,500

Wednesday, 20th April, 2005 – Strathclyde Homes Stadium, Dumbarton

### SCOTLAND 3          NORWAY 0
M. Gardyne, S. Naismith (2)

**Scotland:** E. McLean, (S. Murdoch), T. Parratt, (K. McKinlay), M. Fitzpatrick, (A. Considine), S. Anderson, S. Cuthbert, (C. Sives), C. Mulgrew, R. Quinn, K. McAulay, (M. Scott), S. Naismith, (C. Reid), M. Gardyne, M. Woods
**Referee:** Calum Murray (Scotland) **Attendance:** 705

## UNDER-18 INTERNATIONAL MATCHES

### THREE NATIONS TOURNAMENT – HOSTED BY SCOTLAND
Monday, 20th September, 2004 – Palmerston Park, Dumfries

### SCOTLAND 0      BELGIUM 0

**Scotland:** C. Reidford, J. Thomson, P. Boyle, S. McKeown, J. Kane, B. Hodge, B. Gilmour, C. Grant, K. Smith, C. Elliot, (S. Agnew), R. Snodgrass, (A. Coakley)
**Referee:** Martin Sproule (Scotland) **Attendance:** 227

Friday, 24th September, 2004 – Palmerston Park, Dumfries

### SCOTLAND 0      NORTHERN IRELAND 0

**Scotland:** S. Fox, D. Donald, P. Boyle, J. Kane, J. Thomson, B. Gilmour, C. Grant, (B. Hodge), R. Snodgrass, R. Conroy, (S. Agnew), M. McGlinchey, A. Coakley
**Referee:** Alan Muir (Scotland) **Attendance:** 638

### FINAL TABLE

|                  | P | W | D | L | F | A | PTS |
|------------------|---|---|---|---|---|---|-----|
| BELGIUM          | 2 | 1 | 1 | 0 | 4 | 2 | 4   |
| SCOTLAND         | 2 | 0 | 2 | 0 | 0 | 0 | 2   |
| NORTHERN IRELAND | 2 | 0 | 1 | 1 | 2 | 4 | 1   |

### UNDER-18 FRIENDLY MATCH
Wednesday, 22nd December, 2004 – Victoria Park, Hartlepool

### ENGLAND 1       SCOTLAND 0
Wheater

**Scotland:** C. Reidford, (A. McNeil), J. Thomson, P. Boyle, J. Kane, S. Cuthbert, B. Hodge, (C. Elliot), J. McCluskey, (B. Gilmour), C. Grant, S. Fletcher, M. McGlinchey, (S. Agnew), R. Snodgrass, (K. Smith)
**Referee:** Graham Laws (England) **Attendance:** 4,959

## UEFA UNDER-17 CHAMPIONSHIP
### FIRST QUALIFYING ROUND
**QUALIFYING GROUP 5 - HOSTED BY SCOTLAND**
Monday, 18th October, 2004 – The Falkirk Stadium, Falkirk

**SCOTLAND 1**  **NORWAY 0**
M. Glass

**Scotland:** S. Murray, C. Mitchell, L. Stevenson, G. Cameron, S. Laird, P. Emslie, D. Gray, S. Ferry, (S. Lennon), A. Bagshaw, M. Glass, (J. McGoldrick), D. Smith
Substitutes not used: M. Curtis, J. McMillan, A. Lowing, G. Kerr, P. MacDonald
**Norway:** Staw, Mathisen, Skogseid, Marthinsen, Lekven, Royrane, Riise, Karstensen, Sparby, Dymbe, (Reginiussen), Kleiven, (Klingenberg)
Substitutes not used: Larsen, Kvalheim, Haugseth, Brenna, Simonsen
**Referee:** Robert Malek (Poland) **Attendance:** 835

Wednesday, 20th October, 2004 – Forthbank Stadium, Stirling

**FAROE ISLANDS 0**  **SCOTLAND 2**
A. Bagshaw (2)

**Faroe Islands:** Samuelsen, Davidsen, Hansen, Eysturoy, Olavstovu, Lokin, Mouritsen, Hanssen, (Jacobbsen), Petersen, Kollsker, Jorgensen, (Ellingsgaard)
Substitutes not used: Askham, Kruse, Samson, Bordoy, Larsen
**Scotland:** S. Murray, C. Mitchell, (A. Lowing), L. Stevenson, G. Cameron, S. Laird, P. Emslie, (S. Ferry), D. Gray, A. Bagshaw, M. Glass, D. Smith, (P. MacDonald), S. Lennon
Substitutes not used: M. Curtis, J. McMillan, G. Kerr, J. McGoldrick
**Referee:** Robert Malek, (Poland) **Attendance:** 526

Friday, 22nd October, 2004 – Ochilview Park, Stenhousemuir

**SCOTLAND 1**  **ISRAEL 1**
J. McMillan  Natcho

**Scotland:** M. Curtis, G. Cameron, S. Laird, S. Ferry, A. Bagshaw, J. McMillan, A. Lowing, S. Lennon, (P. Emslie), G. Kerr, P. MacDonald, (D. Gray), J. McGoldrick
Substitutes not used: S. Murray, C. Mitchell, L. Stevenson, M. Glass, D. Smith
**Israel:** Hadani, Mishan, Elkayam, Natcho, Rikan, Bar Buzaglo, Kayal, Damari, (Bitan), (Malka), Shkalim, Kain, Tobi, (Roash)
Substitutes not used: Mizrahi, Goata, Amos, Salook
**Referee:** Milan Karadzic (Yugoslavia) **Attendance:** 325

### FINAL GROUP 5 TABLE

|  | P | W | D | L | F | A | PTS |
|---|---|---|---|---|---|---|---|
| ISRAEL | 3 | 2 | 1 | 0 | 8 | 5 | 7 |
| **SCOTLAND** | 3 | 2 | 1 | 0 | 4 | 1 | 7 |
| NORWAY | 3 | 1 | 0 | 2 | 5 | 5 | 3 |
| FAROE ISLANDS | 3 | 0 | 0 | 3 | 3 | 9 | 0 |

### SECOND QUALIFYING ROUND
**QUALIFYING GROUP 6 - HOSTED BY TURKEY**
Tuesday, 15th March, 2005 – Ozer Turk Stadium, Kusadasi

**SCOTLAND 3**  **AZERBAIJAN 0**
A. Bagshaw (2), A. Lowing

**Scotland:** S. Murray, A. Lowing, L. Stevenson, S. Laird, S. Ferry, (D. Smith), D. Gray, G. Cameron, M. Glass, (J. Crooks), A. Bagshaw, C. Mitchell, M. Millar, (S. Lennon)
Substitutes not used: M. Curtis, S. Mackle, R. Donnelly, G. Kerr

**Azerbaijan:** Malov, Israfilov, (Jabrailov), Jafarov, (Israfilov), Mammadov, Pashayev, Amirguliyev, Gafarli, Hashim-zada, Mammadov, Kutpeov, (Hajiyev), Chechulin
Substitutes not used: Serotin, Karimi, Rahimov
**Referee:** Christopher Lautier (Malta)

Thursday, 17th March, 2005 –Ozer Turk Stadium, Kusadasi

**TURKEY 2**  **SCOTLAND 1**
Kose (2)  A. Bagshaw

**Turkey:** Volkan Babacan, Ferin, Bikmaz, Kesci, Balak, Tasdemir, (Karadas), Yilmaz, (Yilmaz), Erkin, Kose, Nuri, Ozcan, (Salginoglu)
Substitutes not used: Kivrak, Keles, Atam, Yilmaz
**Scotland:** S. Murray, A. Lowing, L. Stevenson, S. Laird, S. Ferry, (S. Mackle), D. Gray, G. Cameron, M. Glass, (D. Smith), A. Bagshaw, C. Mitchell, S. Lennon, (M. Millar)
Substitutes not used: M. Curtis, J. Crooks, R. Donnelly, G. Kerr
**Referee:** Nebojsa Rabrenovic (Yugoslavia)

Saturday, 19th March, 2005 – Soke City Stadium, Soke

**SCOTLAND 0**  **FRANCE 1**
Lepiller

**Scotland:** M. Curtis, A. Lowing, L. Stevenson, J. Crooks, S. Laird, S. Ferry, D. Gray, (R. Donnelly), G. Cameron, A. Bagshaw, (G. Kerr), D. Smith, (M. Glass), C. Mitchell
Substitutes not used: S. Murray, M. Millar, S. Mackle, S. Lennon
**France:** Scribe, Bocaly, Cetout, Dervite, Fernandes, Plessis, Brahim Bounab, (Kitambala), Lepiller, (Tulasne), Jasse, Monnet-paquet, Van Dam
Substitutes not used: Placide, Martin, Nimani Ngalou, Lourde, Delau
**Referee:** Nebojsa Rabrenovic, (Yugoslavia)

### FINAL GROUP 6 TABLE

|  | P | W | D | L | F | A | PTS |
|---|---|---|---|---|---|---|---|
| TURKEY | 3 | 3 | 0 | 0 | 6 | 1 | 9 |
| **SCOTLAND** | 3 | 1 | 0 | 2 | 4 | 3 | 3 |
| FRANCE | 3 | 1 | 0 | 2 | 1 | 3 | 3 |
| AZERBAIJAN | 3 | 1 | 0 | 2 | 2 | 6 | 3 |

## UNDER-17 INTERNATIONAL MATCHES

**NORDIC CUP – HOSTED BY FINLAND**
Tuesday, 3rd August, 2004 – Vaasa

**FINLAND 3**  **SCOTLAND 1**
Virtanen (2), Kaitila  J. McMillan

**Scotland:** M. Curtis, C. Mitchell, G. Kerr, J. McMillan, S. Laird, S. Lennon, I. Cameron, J. Crooks, (S. Gates), A. Bagshaw, D. Smith, M. Glass
**Referee:** Marcus Strombergsson (Sweden) **Attendance:** 924

Wednesday, 4th August, 2004 – Korsholm

**NORWAY 2**  **SCOTLAND 3**
Karstensen, Skogseid  A. Bagshaw, M. Glass, S. Laird

**Scotland:** S. Murray, C. Mitchell, G. Kerr, J. McMillan, S. Laird, A. Bagshaw, (S. Lennon), P. Emslie, I. Cameron, M. Glass, S. Gates, (G. Cameron), J. McGoldrick, (D. Smith)
**Referee:** Lee Mason (England) **Attendance:** 220

Friday, 6th August, 2004 – Jalasjarvi

**ICELAND 1**  **SCOTLAND 0**
Fridgeirsson

**Scotland:** M. Curtis, C. Mitchell, G. Kerr, J. McMillan, S. Laird, S. Lennon,
G. Cameron, J. Crooks, (M. Glass), A. Bagshaw, D. Smith, P. Emslie
**Referee:** Pall Augustinussen (Faroe Islands) **Attendance:** 450

FINAL GROUP TABLE

|  | P | W | D | L | F | A | PTS |
|---|---|---|---|---|---|---|---|
| ICELAND | 3 | 2 | 0 | 1 | 4 | 2 | 6 |
| NORWAY | 3 | 1 | 1 | 1 | 6 | 6 | 4 |
| FINLAND | 3 | 1 | 1 | 1 | 5 | 5 | 4 |
| **SCOTLAND** | **3** | **1** | **0** | **2** | **3** | **6** | **3** |

PLACE MATCH

Sunday,8th August, 2004 – Malax

**SWEDEN 0**  **SCOTLAND 2**
D. Smith, A. Bagshaw

**Scotland:** S. Murray, C. Mitchell, G. Kerr, J. McMillan, S. Lennon,
G. Cameron, A. Bagshaw, D. Smith, P. Emslie, I. Cameron,
(S. Gates), M. Glass, (J. McGoldrick)
**Referee:** Mikko Leino (Finland) **Attendance:** 50

UNDER-17 INTERNATIONAL FRIENDLY MATCHES
Tuesday, 31st August, 2004 – Idrottsparken, Oskarshamn

**SWEDEN 3**  **SCOTLAND 3**
Holster, Persson (2)  J. McGoldrick, M. Glass, A. Bagshaw

**Scotland:** S. Murray, C. Mitchell, L. Stevenson, J. McMillan, S. Laird,
M. Millar, (P. Emslie), D. Smith, S. Ferry, M. Glass, P. MacDonald,
(S. Lennon), J. McGoldrick, (A. Bagshaw)
**Referee:** Zarko Kovacevic (Sweden) **Attendance:** 912

Thursday, 2nd September, 2004 – Idrottsparken, Monsteras

**SWEDEN 3**  **SCOTLAND 1**
Bertilsson, Avdic,  M. Glass
Kacanklic

**Scotland:** M. Curtis, C. Mitchell, J. McMillan, S. Laird, D. Smith,
(L. Stevenson), S. Ferry, A. Bagshaw, M. Glass, (J. McGoldrick),
G. Kerr, S. Lennon, P. Emslie, (M. Millar)
**Referee:** Klas Karlsson (Sweden) **Attendance:** 1,482

Monday, 10th January, 2005 – Ta 'Qali Training Ground, Valletta

**MALTA 0**  **SCOTLAND 1**
M. Millar

**Scotland:** M. Curtis, (F. Stewart), A. Lowing, (A. Pearce), L. Stevenson,
J. McMillan, (A. Brown), S. Laird, S. Ferry, (M. Millar), S. Lennon,
(S. Mackle), G. Cameron, J. Crooks, (P. Emslie), D. Gray,
D. Smith, (P. MacDonald)
**Referee:** Adrian Azzopardi (Malta)

Wednesday, 12th January, 2005 – Ta 'Qali Training Ground, Valletta

**MALTA 0**  **SCOTLAND 3**
S. Laird, G. Cameron, D. Smith

**Scotland:** M. Curtis, (S. Gallacher), A. Brown, (A. Lowing), S. Laird, G. Kerr,
(B. Allison), A. Pearce, (J. McMillan), P. Emslie, (G. Cameron), S. Lennon,
(S. Ferry), S. Mackle, (P. MacDonald), M. Glass, (R. Donnelly), D. Gray,
(D. Smith), M. Millar, (L. Stevenson)
**Referee:** Alan Sant (Malta)

Monday, 28th February, 2005 – Riverside Stadium, Drumahoe

**NORTHERN IRELAND 1**  **SCOTLAND 1**
Mullan  J. McGoldrick

**Scotland:** S. Murray, A. Lowing, L. Stevenson, J. McMillan, S. Laird,
M. Millar, D. Gray, P. Emslie, A. Bagshaw, D. Smith, J. McGoldrick, (S. Mackle)
**Referee:** Frankie Hiles (Northern Ireland) **Attendance:** 150

Steven Thompson celebrates his goal against Moldova with Stevie Crawford

Wednesday, 2nd March, 2005 – Fortwilliam Park, Tobermore

**NORTHERN IRELAND 1**  **SCOTLAND 1**
Doran  D. Smith

**Scotland:** M. Curtis, (F. Stewart), C. Mitchell, L. Stevenson, S. Laird,
D. Gray, P. Emslie, (M. Millar), A. Bagshaw, D. Smith, S. Lennon,
S. Mackle, (J. McMillan), A. Pearce
**Referee:** Mark Courtney (Northern Ireland) **Attendance:** 60

SCOTLAND UNDER-16 INTERNATIONAL MATCHES

VICTORY SHIELD

Friday, 1st October, 2004 – McDiarmid Park, Perth

**SCOTLAND 2**  **NORTHERN IRELAND 2**
M. McCusker, D. Goodwillie  McGovern, McGurk

**Scotland:** G. Paterson, C. Murray, K. Paterson, (S. Fleming),
M. Staunton, J. Laird, R. Hepburn, J. Henry, (R. O'Hara),
W. McLachlan, D. Goodwillie, M. McCusker, (C. Craig), R. Hamilton
**Referee:** Chris Boyle (Scotland) **Attendance:** 1,101

Thursday, 28th October, 2004 – New Bayview Stadium, Methil

**SCOTLAND 0**                    **WALES 1**
                                   C. Jones

**Scotland:** G. Paterson, C. Murray, S. Fleming, M. Staunton, K. Paterson, R. Hamilton, J. Henry, (K. Cawley), R. Hepburn, D. Goodwillie, M. McCusker, (C. Maguire), C. Craig, (W. Russell)
**Referee:** Steve Conroy (Scotland) **Attendance:** 1,574

Friday, 26th November, 2004 – Bloomfield Road, Blackpool

**ENGLAND 0**          **SCOTLAND 0**
**Scotland:** G. Paterson, C. Murray, K. Paterson, M. Staunton, J. Laird, (S. Fleming), W. McLachlan, J. Henry, R. Hepburn, D. Goodwillie, (M. McCusker), C. Maguire, R. Hamilton
**Referee:** Colin Webster (England) **Attendance:** 5,000

**FINAL GROUP TABLE**

|                  | P | W | D | L | F | A | PTS |
|------------------|---|---|---|---|---|---|-----|
| ENGLAND          | 3 | 2 | 1 | 0 | 8 | 2 | 7   |
| NORTHERN IRELAND | 3 | 1 | 1 | 1 | 4 | 5 | 4   |
| WALES            | 3 | 1 | 0 | 2 | 2 | 6 | 3   |
| **SCOTLAND**     | 3 | 0 | 2 | 1 | 2 | 3 | 2   |

## UNDER-16 INTERNATIONAL TOURNAMENT OF SANTAREM, PORTUGAL

Wednesday, 26th January, 2005 – Estadio Dr Alves Vieira, Torres Novas

**SPAIN 3**             **SCOTLAND 2**
Niguez (2), Emilio      R. Hepburn, D. Goodwillie

**Scotland:** G. Paterson, C. Murray, K. Paterson, M. Staunton, J. Laird, R. Hepburn, J. Henry, (R. O'Hara), W. McLachlan, D. Goodwillie, (C. Craig), C. Maguire, R. Hamilton, (S. Kinniburgh)
**Referee:** Carlos Xistra (Portugal)

Thursday, 27th January, 2005 – Estadio Joao Paulo II, Fatima

**PORTUGAL 2**          **SCOTLAND 2**
Carvalhas, Abreu        M. McCusker, J. Henry

**Scotland:** A. Martin, C. Murray, (K. Paterson), S. Fleming, M. Staunton, J. Laird, R. Hepburn, R. O'Hara, (J. Henry), W. McLachlan, M. McCusker, (D. Goodwillie), K. Cawley, (C. Maguire)
**Referee:** Thomas Vejlgaard (Denmark)

Saturday, 29th January, 2005 – Estadio Campo do Bonito, Entroncamento

**DENMARK 0**           **SCOTLAND 1**
                        D. Goodwillie

**Scotland:** G. Paterson, (A. Martin), K. Paterson, M. Staunton, J. Laird, R. Hepburn, J. Henry, S. Kinniburgh, W. McLachlan, D. Goodwillie, R. Hamilton, M. McCusker, (C. Maguire)
**Referee:** Carlos Xistra (Portugal)

**FINAL GROUP TABLE**

|              | P | W | D | L | F | A | PTS |
|--------------|---|---|---|---|---|---|-----|
| SPAIN        | 3 | 3 | 0 | 0 | 9 | 3 | 9   |
| **SCOTLAND** | 3 | 1 | 1 | 1 | 5 | 5 | 4   |
| PORTUGAL     | 3 | 1 | 1 | 1 | 4 | 6 | 4   |
| DENMARK      | 3 | 0 | 0 | 3 | 0 | 4 | 0   |

## BALLYMENA TOURNAMENT, NORTHERN IRELAND

Monday, 25th April, 2005 – Wellington Recreation Ground, Larne

**SWITZERLAND 0**       **SCOTLAND 2**
                        A. Shinnie, D. Goodwillie

**Scotland:** G. Paterson, A. Shinnie, (K. Cawley), K. Paterson, M. Staunton, J. Laird, W. McLachlan, R. Hepburn, (W. Russell), D. Goodwillie, (J. Murphy), C. Maguire, (M. McCusker), R. Hamilton, S. Kinniburgh
**Referee:** Herbie Barr (Northern Ireland)

Tuesday, 26th April, 2005 – Ballymena Showgrounds, Ballymena

**FINLAND 0**           **SCOTLAND 3**
                        D. Goodwillie, M. McCusker, C. Maguire

**Scotland:** A. Martin, A. Shinnie, (R. O'Hara), K. Paterson, M. Staunton, (C. Murray), J. Laird, W. McLachlan, R. Hepburn, (W. Russell), D. Goodwillie, (C. Maguire), R. Hamilton, M. McCusker, (K. Cawley), S. Kinniburgh
**Referee:** Ibrahim Abu Zaila (Israel)

Wednesday, 27th April, 2005 – Islandmagee FC, Larne

**CZECH REPUBLIC 3**    **SCOTLAND 0**
Necid, Zeman, Vacha

**Scotland:** G. Paterson, K. Paterson, M. Staunton, W. McLachlan, R. Hepburn, (W. Russell), D. Goodwillie, C. Maguire, R. Hamilton, S. Kinniburgh, K. Cawley, C. Murray
**Referee:** Ramon Hernandez (USA)

**FINAL GROUP TABLE**

|                    | P | W | D | L | F | A | PTS |
|--------------------|---|---|---|---|---|---|-----|
| CZECH REPUBLIC     | 3 | 2 | 0 | 1 | 5 | 2 | 6   |
| **SCOTLAND**       | 3 | 2 | 0 | 1 | 5 | 3 | 6   |
| SWITZERLAND        | 3 | 2 | 0 | 1 | 5 | 4 | 6   |
| FINLAND            | 3 | 0 | 0 | 3 | 1 | 7 | 0   |

## THIRD PLACE MATCH FOR THE LARNE PLATE

Friday, 29th April, 2005 – Wellington Recreation Ground, Larne

**ISRAEL 1**            **SCOTLAND 2**
Shahar                  R. Hamilton, D. Goodwillie

**Scotland:** A. Martin, A. Shinnie, K. Paterson, J. Laird, R. O'Hara, (S. Kinniburgh), R. Hamilton, M. McCusker, K. Cawley, C. Murray, W. Russell, (R. Hepburn), J. Murphy, (D. Goodwillie)

## SCOTLAND UNDER-15

Friday, 27th May, 2005 – KVV Bassevelde

**BELGIUM 1**           **SCOTLAND 4**
Gundogan                G. Glen (2), K. Waugh, J. Fleck

**Scotland:** S. Coutts, (E. Gray), O. Russell, (C. McKinlay), C. Malone, (C. Monti), R. Perry, N. Gallacher, A. Park, D. Galbraith, (C. McShea), S. Stirling, (K. Waugh), M. Graham, (R. McKenzie), G. Glen, (A. Stirling), J. Fleck
**Referee:** Filip Wille (Belgium)

# RESTORING THE **PRIDE**

Three sides alone in Scotland can attract 50,000 spectators to their home games. They are Celtic, Rangers and the national team.

The Old Firm, of course, are favourites for the domestic honours at the start of each season, a fact which replenishes their crowds for every campaign, but the last time Scotland qualified for the Finals of a major tournament, Craig Brown's players had the honour of inaugurating France '98 against the World Champions, Brazil, in the Stade de France in Paris.

After qualifying for six out of a possible seven World Cup Finals between 1974 and 1998, plus consecutive European Championship appearances in 1992 and 1996, the Scots went from football feast to famine. By the time Walter Smith took charge on 1st January, 2005, Scotland had experienced a dreadful freefall plummet down the FIFA rankings and were below even war-torn Iraq,

whose national association was so impoverished that they were glad to be given free playing kit and training facilities by the German Football Federation.

Undoubtedly, one factor in the Scottish experience was the unfamiliarity of Berti Vogts – who succeeded Brown in 2002 – with the players under his command. The former West German World Cup winner embarked on an exhaustive trawl through a list of available candidates with any tartan connection and filled every free date with friendlies designed to evaluate their worth.

The difficulty was that as Vogts experimented with players, formations and tactics, the rapidly accumulating total of defeats saw the Scots sink down the rankings table with the consequence that their seeding status diminished so that it became harder to emerge from qualifying groups. A vicious circle had been established.

Although Vogts was widely condemned for this state of affairs, even his critics were obliged to admit that he could not be faulted for trying to widen the pool of talent available to the national team. By the time Smith took over, Vogts' efforts had simply confirmed what most Scots had feared - that the number of quality players in dark blue jerseys was at an all-time low.

With his knowledge of football north and south-of-the-border, Smith was not obliged to pore endlessly over players' family trees to find out who might be worth a call-up. Instead, he set about the urgent task of restoring battered morale.

"I think the first thing that had to be done was to bring stability to a situation in which there was a certain amount of turmoil," said the former Rangers and Everton boss.

"There was negativity from many people towards Scotland and I felt that my initial task was to dispel that feeling as far as possible.

"In order to do that, I wanted to establish a settled squad of players, even though it is inevitable that the team will change from game to game because of injuries and suspensions. Berti Vogts found it difficult to do that because he didn't know most of the players but I have either worked with them or I was familiar with them.

"Once the squad is settled – and I think we have that now – consistency of performance becomes the next need. If we look at our World Cup qualifying group, apart from Italy, there was not likely to be a great deal between the other teams like Norway, Slovenia and Belarus and it is a reasonable aim to have Scotland able to compete amongst countries like that.

"Realistically, in the World Cup or European Championship, we want to have a chance of qualifying and then, if we get that chance, to take it. For all the problems Scotland were supposed to have had in the past few years, we did get to the Play-Offs for Euro 2000 and Euro 2004 and in those games we won away at Wembley and at home against the Dutch.

"There is a feel good factor about the Scotland side which draws in the crowds

Kenny Miller scores against Italy at Hampden

when we play well. It's interesting to compare our situation with what goes on with clubs. In most countries, the Champions are big clubs and it's also true of international football, too.

"The bigger countries have always dominated but Greece have shown the way for smaller nations by the way they won Euro 2004, so we have to look at examples like that and hold out hope for ourselves."

The Greek success, of course, was a victory for percentage football which could have gone the other way, but while Smith readily acknowledges this fact, he also maintains that their performance in the Finals in Portugal was a worthwhile example for Scotland.

"You could argue – and I wouldn't dispute it at all – that Greece could as easily have lost some of the games which went for them, but the point is that they got themselves into a position where they were difficult to beat and where their teamwork was strong enough to take advantage of situations which tipped in their favour," said Smith.

"Now Greece won't win championships endlessly or maybe all that often – and right now they haven't qualified for the World Cup Finals - but that's not the

point. They've done it once and they're entitled to expect themselves to go quite far from time to time. That's a situation we would certainly like for ourselves.

Of course, the Scottish mentality is to want to win with that bit of flair as well and there's nothing wrong with that except that maybe it was our misfortune to be in at the very start - when football was just being established –and to set ourselves a standard which is quite difficult for a small country to keep up.

"More than anything, we may be missing a consistency in bringing through the level of player we would like to see. We have very good international

players but it's some time since we produced a footballer of outstanding brilliance.

"The likes of Johnstone, Baxter, Law and Dalglish were brought out by accident more or less – there was no great design to the way we bred footballers. They were working class boys in a working class environment but that has changed greatly and the new generations of kids are not playing football as their fore-bears used to, but it's not just a question of football players.

"A country like Denmark, which has the same population as we do, produces top footballers, but also badminton players

Kenny Miller celebrates scoring against Norway

Darren Fletcher celebrates scoring against Slovenia

Barry Ferguson reflects on Scotland's disappointing defeat to Belarus at Hampden

and golfers. Denmark doesn't have the equivalent of the Old Firm or, for that matter, Hibs and Hearts, yet they have won the European Championship and we haven't.

"Other countries link their exceptional sporting individuals into their education systems in a way which doesn't really happen in Scotland. We are held back by our history."

It has not been in any Scotland manager's remit to devise a football nurturing programme which would operate from school level through the age grades, feeding ultimately into the international set-up, although with his abiding interest in the overall health of the Scottish game, Smith would undoubtedly welcome such a development.

"I think we would all love to see a structure in place which would give us continuity through the age groups and we will have to see what the future brings but as matters stand, the be-all and end-all is for Scotland to qualify for the Finals of the major championships," said Smith.

Although the Scots could not haul back the deficit which had built up in their early World Cup qualifiers, their later form – with the single exception of the 1-0 defeat by Belarus at Hampden - gave the manager considerable satisfaction, as well as bringing about a welcome rise for the team in the FIFA rankings.

"What was particularly pleasing about those games is that our performances were more consistent than perhaps we had seen for some time," the Scotland boss reflected.

"We have been capable of very good results – the 1-0 win over Holland in the Euro 2004 Play-Off, for example, but there is no point in playing well in one game and losing 6-0 in the next.

"I have stressed again and again to the players that the way forward is through that consistency. We won't win every game we play – as the Belarus game indicated – but if we are consistent, we can even out the ups and downs and ideally reach a level so that instead of hoping for a good performance, we can expect it. That's why the 3-0 win in Slovenia – and the manner of the victory

–was so pleasing, even if we were deeply disappointed that we hadn't been able to reach the Play-Offs.

"We may not have players of the calibre of some of our great names of the past but that doesn't mean we aren't capable of achievement. If we thought that, we might as well pack it in.

"And we should always be open to ideas from elsewhere if they can be put to good use here. Take the Dutch – they're moving away from the idea of scheduled games and they are making provision for bounce games on public pitches so that anyone can join in. It's spontaneous football but it's also supervised, which is attractive to parents and it also allows for kids to learn a bit about how to play."

Given that the timetable for physical education in schools and the provision of dedicated all-weather facilities is woefully lacking in Scotland compared to most countries in Europe, even the simplicity of the Dutch idea can seem like a concept too far. Yet it merely signifies a return to what was once the norm for kids who played football in every spare moment.

In the meantime, Smith must attempt to satisfy the craving of a football daft population which has suffered withdrawal symptoms because of its exclusion from major Finals.

Scotland's return to that level of competition will inevitably involve a long haul of commitment and improvement.

But, as the manager says, there is a vast reservoir of goodwill towards the national side which responds readily to encouragement.

The passionate crowds who returned to Hampden for Scotland's sell-out qualifiers against Italy and Belarus are evidence that – even without the genius of players like Baxter, Dalglish, Law or Johnstone – we believe in the sentiment of the anthem which rocks the stadium before each match.

We can still rise now – and be a football nation again.

**RODDY FORSYTH**
(The Daily Telegraph and Radio 5 Live)

James McFadden celebrates his wonder goal against Slovenia

Scotland's goalscoring trio in Slovenia - Paul Hartley, Darren Fletcher & James McFadden

Pain in the rain - Kenny Miller seeks devine intervention against Belarus at Hampden

# CAREERS OF SCOTTISH PREMIERLEAGUE AND SCOTTISH FOOTBALL LEAGUE **MANAGERS**

## SCOTTISH PREMIER LEAGUE

**ABERDEEN** JAMES CALDERWOOD
**Player:** Birmingham City, Cambridge United (loan), Sparta Rotterdam, Willem II, Roda JC, SC Heracles
**Manager:** Rietvogels, FC Zwolle, SC Cambuur Leeuwarden, Willem II, NEC Nijmegen, Dunfermline Athletic, Aberdeen

**CELTIC** GORDON STRACHAN
**Player:** Dundee, Aberdeen, Manchester United, Leeds United, Coventry City, Scotland
**Manager:** Coventry City, Southampton, Celtic

**DUNDEE UNITED** GORDON CHISHOLM
**Player:** Sunderland, Hibernian, Dundee, Partick Thistle
**Manager:** Dundee United

**DUNFERMLINE ATHLETIC** JIM LEISHMAN
**Player:** Dunfermline Athletic, Cowdenbeath
**Manager:** Dunfermline Athletic, Inverness Thistle, Montrose, Livingston (Formerly Meadowbank Thistle), Livingston, Dunfermline Athletic

**FALKIRK** JOHN HUGHES
**Player:** Berwick Rangers, Swansea City, Falkirk, Celtic, Hibernian, Ayr United, Falkirk
**Manager:** Falkirk (Head Coach)

**HEART OF MIDLOTHIAN**
**Player:**

**Manager:**

**HIBERNIAN** TONY MOWBRAY
**Player:** Middlesbrough, Celtic, Ipswich Town
**Manager:** Hibernian

**INVERNESS CALEDONIAN THISTLE**
CRAIG BREWSTER
**Player:** Forfar Athletic, Raith Rovers, Dundee United, Ionikos Nikea, Hibernian, Dunfermline Athletic, Inverness Caledonian Thistle
**Manager:** Inverness Caledonian Thistle

**KILMARNOCK** JIM JEFFERIES
**Player:** Heart of Midlothian, Berwick Rangers
**Manager:** Berwick Rangers, Falkirk, Heart of Midlothian, Bradford City, Kilmarnock

**LIVINGSTON** PAUL LAMBERT
**Player:** St. Mirren, Motherwell, Borussia Dortmund, Celtic, Scotland
**Head Coach:** Livingston

**MOTHERWELL** TERRY BUTCHER
**Player:** Ipswich Town, Rangers, Coventry City, Sunderland, Clydebank, England
**Manager:** Coventry City, Sunderland, Motherwell

**RANGERS** ALEX McLEISH
**Player:** Aberdeen, Motherwell, Scotland
**Manager:** Motherwell, Hibernian, Rangers

## FIRST DIVISION

**AIRDRIE UNITED** SANDY STEWART
**Player:** Heart of Midlothian, Kilmarnock, Airdrieonians, Partick Thistle, Airdrieonians, Airdrie United
**Manager:** Airdrie United

**BRECHIN CITY** IAN CAMPBELL
**Player:** Cowdenbeath, Dunfermline Athletic, Brechin City, Dunfermline Athletic
**Manager:** Brechin City

**CLYDE** GRAHAM ROBERTS
**Player:** Tottenham Hotspur, Rangers, Chelsea, West Bromwich Albion, England
**Manager:** Clyde

**DUNDEE** ALAN KERNAGHAN
**Player:** Middlesbrough, Charlton Athletic, Manchester City, Bolton Wanderers, Bradford City, St. Johnstone, Brechin City, Clyde, Livingston, Falkirk, Republic of Ireland
**Manager:** Clyde, Dundee

**HAMILTON ACADEMICAL** BILLY REID
**Player:** Queen of the South, Clyde, Hamilton Academical, Stirling Albion
**Manager:** Clyde, Hamilton Academical

**QUEEN OF THE SOUTH** IAN SCOTT
**Player:** Did not play at senior level
**Manager:** Queen of the South

**ROSS COUNTY**
**Player:**

**Manager:**

**ST. JOHNSTONE** OWEN COYLE
**Player:** Dumbarton, Clydebank, Airdrieonians, Bolton Wanderers, Dundee United, Motherwell, Dunfermline Athletic, Ross County (loan), Airdrieonians, Falkirk, Dundee United, Airdrie United (loan), Airdrie United, St. Johnstone, Republic of Ireland
**Manager:** St. Johnstone

**ST. MIRREN** GUS MacPHERSON
**Player:** Rangers, Exeter City (loan), Rangers, Kilmarnock, St. Mirren
**Manager:** St. Mirren

**STRANRAER** NEIL WATT
**Player:** Celtic, Forfar Athletic, East Stirlingshire, Stirling Albion, Stranraer, Clyde
**Manager:** Stranraer

## SECOND DIVISION

**ALLOA ATHLETIC** TOM HENDRIE
**Player:** Meadowbank Thistle, Berwick Rangers
**Manager:** Berwick Rangers, Alloa Athletic, St. Mirren, Alloa Athletic

**AYR UNITED** ROBERT CONNOR
**Player:** Ayr United, Dundee, Aberdeen, Kilmarnock, Ayr United, Partick Thistle, Queen of the South, Scotland
**Manager:** Ayr United

**DUMBARTON** PAUL MARTIN
**Player:** Kilmarnock, Hamilton Academical, Stranraer (loan), Dumbarton, Albion Rovers, Queen's Park
**Manager:** Dumbarton

**FORFAR ATHLETIC** RAYMOND FARNINGHAM
**Player:** Forfar Athletic, Motherwell, Dunfermline Athletic, Partick Thistle, Dundee, Forfar Athletic (loan), Dundee
**Manager:** Forfar Athletic

**GRETNA** ROWAN ALEXANDER
**Player:** Queen of the South, St. Mirren, Brentford, Greenock Morton, Queen of the South, Gretna
**Manager:** Queen of the South, Gretna

**MORTON** JIM McINALLY
**Player:** Celtic, Dundee (loan), Nottingham Forest, Coventry City, Dundee United, Raith Rovers, Dundee United, Dundee, Scotland
**Manager:** Morton

**PARTICK THISTLE** DICK CAMPBELL
**Player:** Brechin City, East Stirlingshire
**Manager:** Dunfermline Athletic, Brechin City, Partick Thistle

**PETERHEAD** IAIN STEWART
**Player:** Dundee, Inverness Caledonian Thistle, Peterhead
**Manager:** Peterhead

**RAITH ROVERS** GORDON DALZIEL
**Player:** Rangers, Manchester City, Partick Thistle, East Stirlingshire, Raith Rovers, Ayr United
**Manager:** Ayr United, Raith Rovers

**STIRLING ALBION** ALLAN MOORE
**Player:** Dumbarton, Heart of Midlothian, St. Johnstone, Dunfermline Athletic, Livingston, Airdrieonians, Partick Thistle, Morton, Queen of the South, Stirling Albion
**Coach:** Stirling Albion

## THIRD DIVISION

**ALBION ROVERS** JIM CHAPMAN
**Player:** Albion Rovers, Dumbarton
**Manager:** Albion Rovers (Head Coach)

**ARBROATH** JOHN McGLASHAN
**Player:** Montrose, Millwall, Peterborough United, Rotherham United, Dundee, Arbroath (loan), Ross County, Arbroath
**Manager:** Arbroath

**BERWICK RANGERS** JOHN COUGHLIN
**Player:** Meadowbank Thistle, Berwick Rangers
**Manager:** St. Mirren, Berwick Rangers

**COWDENBEATH** MIXU PAATELAINEN
**Player:** Valkeakosken Haka, Dundee United, Aberdeen, Bolton Wanderers, Wolverhampton Wanderers, Hibernian, R.C. Strasbourg, Hibernian, St. Johnstone, St. Mirren, Cowdenbeath, Finland
**Manager:** Cowdenbeath

**EAST FIFE** JIM MOFFAT
**Player:** Montrose, Hamilton Academical, Dunfermline Athletic, Forfar Athletic, Montrose (loan), East Fife (loan), Brechin City, East Fife (loan), East Fife, Montrose, Forfar Athletic, Cowdenbeath, East Stirlingshire, Albion Rovers, Cowdenbeath, Forfar Athletic, Stirling Albion, East Fife
**Manager:** East Fife

**EAST STIRLINGSHIRE** DENNIS NEWALL
**Player:** Stranraer, East Stirlingshire
**Manager:** East Stirlingshire

**ELGIN CITY** DAVID ROBERTSON
**Player:** Aberdeen, Rangers, Leeds United, Montrose, Scotland
**Manager:** Elgin City

**MONTROSE** HENRY HALL
**Player:** Stirling Albion, St. Johnstone, Dundee United, Forfar Athletic
**Manager:** Forfar Athletic, Montrose

**QUEEN'S PARK** BILLY STARK
**Player:** St. Mirren, Aberdeen, Celtic, Kilmarnock, Hamilton Academical, Kilmarnock, Celtic
**Manager:** Morton, St. Johnstone, Queen's Park (Coach)

**STENHOUSEMUIR** DES McKEOWN
**Player:** Airdrieonians, Albion Rovers, Queen of the South, Partick Thistle, Queen of the South, Stenhousemuir
**Manager:** Stenhousemuir

# BANK OF SCOTLAND PREMIERLEAGUE
## CLUB HONOURS

Rangers' management team celebrate the Ibrox clubs dramatic Bank of Scotland Premierleague title.

### ABERDEEN
**League Champions:**
Division I: 1954/55
Premier Division:
1979/80, 1983/84, 1984/85
**League Cup Winners:**
1955/56, 1976/77, 1985/86,
1989/90, 1995/96
**Scottish Cup Winners:** 1947, 1970, 1982,
1983, 1984, 1986, 1990
**European Cup Winners' Cup:**
1982/83
**European Super Cup:** 1983
**Drybrough Cup Winners:**
1970/71, 1980/81

### CELTIC
**League Champions:**
Division I: 1892/93, 1893/94, 1895/96,
1897/98, 1904/05, 1905/06, 1906/07,
1907/08, 1908/09, 1909/10, 1913/14,
1914/15, 1915/16, 1916/17, 1918/19,
1921/22, 1925/26, 1935/36, 1937/38,
1953/54, 1965/66, 1966/67, 1967/68,
1968/69, 1969/70, 1970/71, 1971/72,
1972/73, 1973/74
Premier Division: 1976/77,
1978/79, 1980/81, 1981/82, 1985/86,
1987/88, 1997/98,
SPL: 2000/01, 2001/02, 2003/04
**League Cup Winners:**
1956/57, 1957/58, 1965/66, 1966/67,
1967/68, 1968/69, 1969/70, 1974/75,
1982/83, 1997/98, 1999/2000, 2000/01
**Scottish Cup Winners:**
1892, 1899, 1900, 1904, 1907, 1908, 1911,
1912, 1914, 1923, 1925, 1927, 1931, 1933,
1937, 1951, 1954, 1965, 1967, 1969, 1971,
1972, 1974, 1975, 1977, 1980, 1985, 1988,
1989, 1995, 2001, 2004, 2005
**European Cup Winners:** 1966/67
**Runners-up:** 1969/70
**UEFA Cup Runners-up:** 2002/03
**Empire Exhibition Cup Winners:** 1938
**Coronation Cup Winners:** 1953
**Drybrough Cup Winners:** 1974/75

### DUNDEE UNITED
**League Champions:**
Division II: 1924/25, 1928/29
Premier Division: 1982/83
**League Cup Winners:**
1979/80, 1980/81
**Scottish Cup Winners:** 1993/94
**UEFA Cup Runners-up:** 1986/87

### DUNFERMLINE ATHLETIC
**League Champions:**
Division II: 1925/26
First Division: 1988/89, 1995/96
Second Division: 1985/86
**Scottish Cup Winners:** 1961, 1968
**Scottish Qualifying Cup:** 1911/12

### FALKIRK
**League Champions:**
First Division:
1990/91, 1993/94, 2002/03, 2004/05
Division II: 1935/36, 1969/70, 1974/75
Second Division: 1979/80
**Scottish Cup Winners:**
1913, 1957
**SFL Challenge Cup Winners:**
1993/94 (B&Q Cup),
1997/98 (Challenge Cup)
2004/05 (Bell's Cup)

### HEARTS
**League Champions:**
Division I: 1894/95, 1896/97,
1957/58, 1959/60
First Division: 1979/80
**League Cup Winners:** 1954/55, 1958/59,
1959/60, 1962/63
**Scottish Cup Winners:** 1891, 1896, 1901,
1906, 1956, 1998

### HIBERNIAN
**League Champions:**
Division I: 1902/03, 1947/48,
1950/51, 1951/52
Division II: 1893/94, 1894/95, 1932/33
First Division: 1980/81, 1998/99
**League Cup Winners:** 1972/73, 1991/92
**Scottish Cup Winners:** 1887, 1902
**Drybrough Cup Winners:**
1972/73, 1973/74

### INVERNESS CALEDONIAN THISTLE
**League Champions:**
First Division: 2003/04
Third Division: 1996/97
**Bell's Cup Winners:** 2003/04

### KILMARNOCK
**League Champions:**
Division I: 1964/65
Division II: 1897/98, 1898/99
**Scottish Cup Winners:**
1920, 1929, 1997
**Scottish Qualifying Cup Winners:**
1896/97

### LIVINGSTON
**League Champions:**
First Division: 2000/01
Second Division: 1986/87, 1998/99
Third Division: 1995/96
**League Cup Winners:** 2003/04

### MOTHERWELL
**League Champions:**
Division I: 1931/32
First Division: 1981/82, 1984/85
Division II: 1953/54, 1968/69
**League Cup Winners:** 1950/51
**Scottish Cup Winners:** 1952, 1991

### RANGERS
**League Champions:**
Division I: 1890/91 (shared), 1898/99,
1899/1900, 1900/01, 1901/02, 1910/11,
1911/12, 1912/13, 1917/18, 1919/20,
1920/21, 1922/23, 1923/24, 1924/25,
1926/27, 1927/28, 1928/29, 1929/30,
1930/31, 1932/33, 1933/34, 1934/35,
1936/37, 1938/39, 1946/47, 1948/49,
1949/50, 1952/53, 1955/56, 1956/57,
1958/59, 1960/61, 1962/63, 1963/64,
1974/75
Premier Division: 1975/76, 1977/78,
1986/87, 1988/89, 1989/90, 1990/91,
1991/92, 1992/93, 1993/94, 1994/95,
1995/96, 1996/97
SPL:
1998/99, 1999/2000, 2002/03, 2004/05
**League Cup Winners:**
1946/47, 1948/49, 1960/61, 1961/62,
1963/64, 1964/65, 1970/71, 1975/76,
1977/78, 1978/79, 1981/82, 1983/84,
1984/85, 1986/87, 1987/88, 1988/89,
1990/91, 1992/93, 1993/94, 1996/97,
1998/99, 2001/02, 2002/03, 2004/05
**Scottish Cup Winners:**
1894, 1897, 1898, 1903, 1928, 1930, 1932,
1934, 1935, 1936, 1948, 1949, 1950, 1953,
1960, 1962, 1963, 1964, 1966, 1973, 1976,
1978, 1979, 1981, 1992, 1993, 1996, 1999,
2000, 2002, 2003
**European Cup Winners' Cup:**
1971/72
**Runners-up:**
1960/61, 1966/67
**Drybrough Cup Winners:**
1979/80

# THE BELL'S SCOTTISH FOOTBALL LEAGUE **CLUB HONOURS**

## FIRST DIVISION

### AIRDRIE UNITED
**League Champions:**
Second Division: 1975/76, 2003/04

### BRECHIN CITY
**League Champions:**
'C' Division: 1953/54
Second Division: 1982/83, 1989/90, 2004/05
Third Division: 2001/02

### CLYDE
**League Champions:**
Division II: 1904/05, 1951/52, 1956/57,
1961/62, 1972/73,
Second Division:
1977/78, 1981/82, 1992/93, 1999/2000
**Scottish Cup Winners:**
1939, 1955, 1958

### DUNDEE
**League Champions:**
Division I: 1961/62
Division II: 1946/47
First Division: 1978/79, 1991/92, 1997/98
**League Cup Winners:**
1951/52, 1952/53, 1973/74
**Scottish Cup Winners:** 1910
**B&Q Centenary Cup:** 1990/91

### HAMILTON ACADEMICAL
**League Champions:**
Division II: 1903/04
First Division: 1985/86, 1987/88
Third Division: 2000/01
**B&Q Cup Winners:**
1991/92, 1992/93
**Scottish Cup Runners-up:**
1910/11, 1934/35
Second Division Runners-up:
1952/53, 1964/65, 1996/97
**Lanarkshire Cup Winners:**
10 Times

### QUEEN OF THE SOUTH
**League Champions:**
Division II: 1950/51
Second Division: 2001/02
**Bell's Cup:** 2002/03

### ROSS COUNTY
**League Champions:**
Third Division: 1998/99

### ST. JOHNSTONE
**League Champions:**
First Division:
1982/83, 1989/90, 1996/97
Division II:
1923/24, 1959/60, 1962/63

### ST. MIRREN
**League Champions:**
First Division:
1976/77, 1999/2000
Division II: 1967/68
**Scottish Cup Winners:**
1926, 1959, 1987
**Victory Cup:** 1919
**Anglo Scottish Cup Winners:**
1979/80
**Summer Cup:** 1943

### STRANRAER
**League Champions:**
Second Division:
1993/94, 1997/98
Third Division: 2003/04
**SFL Challenge Cup Winners:**
1996/97

## SECOND DIVISION

### ALLOA ATHLETIC
**League Champions:**
Division II: 1921/22
Third Division: 1997/98
**Bell's Challenge Cup Winners:**
1999/2000

### AYR UNITED
**League Champions:**
Division II: 1911/12, 1912/13, 1927/28,
1936/37, 1958/59, 1965/66
Second Division: 1987/88, 1996/97

### DUMBARTON
**League Champions:**
Division I: 1890/91
(shared with Rangers), 1891/92
Division II: 1910/11, 1971/72
Second Division: 1991/92
**Scottish Cup Winners:** 1883

### FORFAR ATHLETIC
**League Champions:**
'C' Division: 1948/49
Second Division: 1983/84
Third Division: 1994/95

### GRETNA
**League Champions:**
Third Division: 2004/05

### MORTON
**League Champions:**
Division II: 1949/50, 1963/64, 1966/67
First Division: 1977/78, 1983/84, 1986/87
Second Division: 1994/95
Third Division: 2002/03
**Scottish Cup Winners:** 1922

### PARTICK THISTLE
**League Champions:**
First Division: 1975/76, 2001/02
Runners-up: 1991/92
Division II: 1896/97, 1899/1900, 1970/71
Second Division: 2000/01
Runners-up: 1901/02
**League Cup Winners:** 1971/72
Runners-up: 1953/54,
1956/57, 1958/59
**Scottish Cup Winners:** 1921
Runners-up: 1930
**Glasgow Cup Winners:**
1935, 1951, 1952, 1954, 1960, 1981, 1989

Brechin City captain Paul Deas holds aloft the Second Division trophy to the Brechin supporters.

## PETERHEAD
Season 2000/01 was the club's first season in membership of S.F.L.
The club's highest position to date was 2nd position in Season 2004/05.

## RAITH ROVERS
**League Champions:**
First Division: 1992/93, 1994/95
Second Division: 2002/03
Division II: 1907/08, 1909/10 (shared)
1937/38, 1948/49
**League Cup Winners:**
1994/95

## STIRLING ALBION
**League Champions:**
Division II:
1952/53, 1957/58, 1960/61, 1964/65,
Second Division:
1976/77, 1990/91, 1995/96

## THIRD DIVISION

## ALBION ROVERS
**League Champions:**
Division II: 1933/34
Second Division:
1988/89
**Scottish Qualifying Cup:**
1913/14

## ARBROATH
**League Runners-up:**
Division II: 1934/35, 1958/59,
1967/68, 1971/72,
Second Division: 2000/01
Third Division: 1997/98

## BERWICK RANGERS
**League Champions:**
Second Division: 1978/79
Runners-up: 1993/94
Third Division Runners-up:
1999/2000

## COWDENBEATH
**League Champions:**
Division II:
1913/14, 1914/15, 1938/39
## EAST FIFE
**League Champions:**
Division II: 1947/48
**League Cup Winners:**
1947/48, 1949/50, 1953/54
**Scottish Cup Winners:**
1938

## EAST STIRLINGSHIRE
**League Champions:**
Division II: 1931/32

## ELGIN CITY
Season 2000/01 was the club's first season in membership of S.F.L.
The club's highest position to date was 6th position in Seasons 2001/02 and 2004/05.

## MONTROSE
**League Champions:**
Second Division: 1984/85

## QUEEN'S PARK
**League Champions:**
Division II: 1922/23
'B' Division 1955/56
Second Division: 1980/81
Third Division: 1999/2000
**Scottish Cup Winners:**
1874, 1875, 1876, 1880, 1881, 1882, 1884,
1886, 1890, 1893
**FA Cup:** Runners-up: 1884, 1889
**FA Charity Shield:**
1899 (Shared with Aston Villa)

## STENHOUSEMUIR
**SFL Challenge Cup Winners:**
1995/96

Gretna Chairman Brooks Mileson and manager Rowan Alexander celebrate with the Third Division Championship Trophy.

Falkirk boss John Hughes lifts the Bell's Cup Trophy.

# ROAR OF THE CROWD

It's a well known fact that the world's first international football match was between Scotland and England on 30th November, 1872 at the West of Scotland CRICKET ground in Partick. Less well-known is WHY the match was played at that venue.

The reason was that no football ground had the facilities to charge for admission nor could any ground hold the crowd. The attendance was described in a contemporary newspaper as "the largest assemblage seen at any football match in Scotland, there being close on 4,000 spectators, including a good number of ladies." Those few words demolish two myths surrounding Scottish football

attendances – that crowds were always huge and women never attended in any numbers till the advent of all-seater grounds in the 1990s.

The match itself finished 0-0 but that scoreless draw was the catalyst for the first great football boom in Scotland. Until then, no one thought about charging for admission. Afterwards, clubs couldn't build grounds fast enough. Queen's Park opened the first of three grounds to bear the name Hampden Park while other still familiar names like Dumbarton, Kilmarnock, Morton and Rangers developed grounds of their own. As did less fortunate clubs. The Ramblers have long since marched into

oblivion and the unfortunately named Albatross from Bridgeton were doomed from the outset.

The Scottish Cup was launched in 1873 with sixteen clubs participating. Within a few years, more than 100 clubs were taking part with the Final drawing five figure gates. Bigger crowds brought bigger problems.

In January, 1878, the SFA ordered a replay between Third Lanark and South-Western because of the crowd encroaching on the pitch and crowd trouble forced the 1881 Final between Queen's Park and Dumbarton to be replayed. Queen's were the biggest club

The early part of that century saw both disaster and violence mar the game. In 1902, a new Scottish record attendance was set at Ibrox when 68,114 supporters watched the Scotland-England game. Under the pressure of the crowd, a section of terracing gave way, leading to the deaths of 26 spectators and injury to hundreds more in Scottish football's first great tragedy.

A year later, the third Hampden Park was opened. It's changed a lot since but the same ground is Scottish football's National Stadium today. In 1906, it held the first six figure gate in Scotland when 102,741 cheered as England were beaten 2-1. Two years later the Scotland-England game finished 1-1 but of far greater significance was the crowd. At 121,452, it was a new WORLD record. Hampden went on to beat that figure many times, keeping the world record in Scotland for over forty years until the Maracana in Brazil overtook it during the 1950 World Cup.

It was a fantastic achievement for a small country on the north west fringe of Europe.

Just a year later, the ugly face of football crowds was displayed when Old Firm fans, enraged at there being no extra-time in the 1909 Scottish Cup Final replay, went on the rampage, invading the pitch, fighting with police, attacking the fire brigade, assaulting passers-by and smashing windows as a two-hour battle raged before they were beaten back to the city centre and dispersed.

The Scottish Cup Final didn't return to Hampden until 1920 when the authorities anticipated a modest turnout for the game between two 'unfashionable' sides in Kilmarnock and Albion Rovers. However, Scottish football was in the grip of another boom in the years after the First World War and 95,811 saw Killie win 3-2 while thousands more were locked out. The big crowd should have been expected. Earlier that year, St. Bernard's had to move their tie with Albion Rovers to a larger ground as they couldn't cope with the 20,000 attendance.

By now almost half the First Division averaged 10,000. Crowds were so big one newspaper could nonchalantly

remark about a Rangers-Partick Thistle game "the crowd was somewhat disappointing, it barely touched 60,000."

Unemployment brought a downturn in the late twenties but big occasions still attracted big gates. An Old Firm Scottish Cup Semi-Final in 1925 which Celtic won 5-0 attracted 101,714 – the first six-figure gate for a club game. In 1928, the same teams drew the first 100,000 plus crowd to the Final when 118,115 saw Rangers gain revenge, winning 4-0.

A year later, there were two such crowds within a week. First, Kilmarnock beat Rangers 2-0 in the Scottish Cup Final in front of 114,708. Then 110,512 saw a Scotland side reduced to ten men through injury beat England 1-0 with a last-minute goal direct from a corner kick. It was this unusual and dramatic finale which sparked an outburst of joy so loud that it went down in history as the birth of the world-famous 'Hampden Roar.'

1930 saw the first midweek crowd of over 100,000 when 103,668 turned up for the Scottish Cup Final replay between Rangers and Partick Thistle and this was repeated two years later when 105,695 attended the Rangers v Kilmarnock replay.

Hampden reached its peak in 1937. On 17th April, a record 149,547 saw Scotland beat England 3-1 and a week later 147,365 were present when Celtic beat Aberdeen to win the Scottish Cup. Those were world records then and nearly 70 years later they remain European records for international and club matches. Glasgow was the football capital of the world with capacity for over half a million spectators inside its six League grounds.

When the Old Firm met at Ibrox on 2nd January, 1939, one newspaper thought the crowd would be "close on 60,000 spectators." Almost twice as many – 118,567 – turned up, creating a new UK record for League football. But not every club shared in the boom. Three months later, the Second Division set an all-time low when a mere 32 spectators bothered to watch East Stirlingshire v Leith Athletic.

The Second World War hit crowds badly as the authorities slashed capacities and fans stayed away in numbers. But even

in Scotland and their second Hampden Park was the biggest ground. It held 26,379 for the 1-1 draw between Scotland and England in 1890 – the biggest crowd in Scotland before the advent of The Scottish Football League.

The League's establishment that same year fuelled another boom in attendances. Recently formed Celtic were the best supported, averaging around 5,000 though for big games they could attract twice that number. Their games against Rangers grew in intensity and popularity from 8,000 at the start to 17,000 by the mid-1890s to touching the 50,000 mark by the dawn of the 20th century.

147,365 fans pack Hampden to watch the 1936.37 Scottish Cup Final between Celtic and Aberdeen

Scottish Cup Final that year set a post-war high. There were 136,495 spectators inside Hampden – and not an Old Firm scarf in sight – when Motherwell beat Dundee 4-0.

Society's increasing affluence with the advent of television and growing car ownership ended the days when football was the sole working-class entertainment on offer. By 1955, the first signs of decline appeared. Hibs drew 24,000 for a friendly against Arsenal but two days later just 875 attended their League game against Stirling Albion. In the 'B' Division, an end of season game between Albion Rovers and Brechin City drew just 172.

Hibs recognised where the future lay. Fifty years ago they entered the first European Cup. The Easter Road club were also pioneers of floodlighting and on an April evening in 1956, they drew 44,941 as Reims prevented Hibs from reaching the inaugural European Cup Final. Europe became a big attraction for the fans and when the European Cup Final came to Scotland in 1960, it set a record figure of 127,621 at Hampden as Real Madrid beat Eintracht Frankfurt 7-3.

Showpiece occasions still drew vast crowds. One-third of all the 100,000 plus gates in Scotland came in the 1960s and early 1970s. Almost 250,000 saw the Scottish Cup Final in 1963 when Rangers beat Celtic after a replay. Later the same year, the first six figure crowd for a League Cup Final saw the Ibrox club beat Second Division Morton. Internationals against England and World Cup qualifiers continued to regularly entice in excess of 100,000 to Hampden.

Adolf Hitler couldn't quell the enthusiasm of the Scottish football supporter for long and by 1943, gates were as big as before with 137,363 attending Scotland v England.

The decade after the war was the heyday of giant crowds. There were seasons when every team in the 'A' Division averaged over 10,000 and five-figure averages were even recorded by some 'B' Division clubs. In January, 1950, 27,602 saw Kilmarnock beat Queen's Park at Hampden – a record for a match outside the top flight.

Oddly enough, it was during the post-war boom that the lowest ever Scottish League attendance was recorded when a paltry 22 fans paid to watch Edinburgh City v Brechin City in a 'C' Division match in season 1948/49. Any travelling fans got their money's worth as Brechin won 11-1!

Apart from such isolated occasions, attendances reached all-time peaks. Over 120,000 turned up for international friendlies. The Junior Cup Final attracted in excess of 70,000. In 1952 four clubs – Airdrieonians, Arbroath, Motherwell and Queen of the South – established all-time gate records in the space of just eighteen days and the

Long term though, attendances were in decline. In season 1961/62, six League games at Pittodrie and four at Easter Road drew less than 5,000 fans. Even the national team wasn't immune. A lethal combination of live TV coverage, four games inside a fortnight, transport strikes and appalling weather saw the lowest ever international turnout at Hampden when just 7,455 hardy souls watched Scotland v Northern Ireland in 1969.

It wasn't the quality on the pitch that kept the fans away. Billy Bremner, Bobby

Fans queue outside Hampden to buy tickets

Murdoch and Denis Law all played for Scotland that night and their opponents included Pat Jennings, Derek Dougan and the incomparable George Best.

By the early 1970s, the clamour for change had become unstoppable and the Scottish League introduced a three division set-up in 1975. The new format was a success. The national team qualified regularly for the World Cup Finals. Domestically, competition was healthy with Aberdeen and Dundee United emerging to challenge the Old Firm as well as achieving success in Europe. Clubs previously confined to the old Second Division proved capable of sustaining themselves in the new First Division yet attendances fell to their lowest post-war level. In the early 1980s, almost half the League clubs drew fewer than 1,000 per game through the turnstiles.

While crowd trouble played a part in falling attendances, the main reason for the drop was a factor beyond football's control – recession. As unemployment reached levels last seen in the 1920s, it should have been no great surprise that fans put feeding their families ahead of following their team. Even the Old Firm weren't immune with averages slumping below 20,000.

Graeme Souness' arrival as Rangers manager sparked an Ibrox revival while a few years later Fergus McCann took over at Celtic and rebuilt Parkhead as a 60,000 all-seater. For the past few seasons, the Old Firm have enjoyed the highest average attendances in their history even if, as European results show, the quality on offer is not as high as it once was.

Almost twice as many Celtic supporters regularly watch the team that lost 5-0 in Bratislava as watched the Lisbon Lions. The Old Firm's dominance has grown ominously over the decades. In 1939 one

| 100,000 PLUS CROWDS AT FOOTBALL MATCHES IN SCOTLAND | | | | | |
|---|---|---|---|---|---|
| Date | Fixture | | Score | Comp. | Attendance |
| 17/04/37 | Scotland | England | 3-1 | BIC | 149,547 |
| 15/04/39 | Scotland | England | 1-2 | BIC | 149,269 |
| 24/04/37 | Celtic | Aberdeen | 2-1 | SCF | 147,365 |
| 27/03/48 | Rangers | Hibernian | 1-0 | SCSF | 142,070 |
| 13/04/46 | Scotland | England | 1-0 | W | 139,642 |
| 17/04/43 | Scotland | England | 0-4 | W | 137,363 |
| 25/04/70 | Scotland | England | 0-0 | BIC | 137,284 |
| 15/04/70 | Celtic | Leeds United | 2-1 | ECCSF | 136,505 |
| 19/04/52 | Motherwell | Dundee | 4-0 | SCF | 136,495 |
| 01/04/33 | Scotland | England | 2-1 | BIC | 136,259 |
| 03/04/54 | Scotland | England* | 2-4 | WC | 134,892 |
| 05/04/52 | Scotland | England | 1-2 | BIC | 134,504 |
| 14/04/45 | Scotland | England | 1-6 | W | 134,479 |
| 15/04/50 | Scotland | England* | 0-1 | WC | 133,991 |
| 21/04/56 | Hearts | Celtic | 3-1 | SCF | 133,583 |
| 10/04/48 | Scotland | England | 0-2 | BIC | 133,426 |
| 11/04/64 | Scotland | England | 1-0 | BIC | 133,245 |
| 26/04/69 | Celtic | Rangers | 4-0 | SCF | 132,870 |
| 22/04/44 | Scotland | England | 2-3 | W | 132,835 |
| 14/04/56 | Scotland | England | 1-1 | BIC | 132,779 |
| 14/04/62 | Scotland | England | 2-0 | BIC | 132,441 |
| 21/04/51 | Celtic | Motherwell | 1-0 | SCF | 132,180 |
| 21/04/48 | Rangers | Morton | 1-0 | SCFR | 132,103 |
| 28/03/31 | Scotland | England | 2-0 | BIC | 131,273 |
| 24/02/68 | Scotland | England* | 1-1 | EC | 130,711 |
| 17/04/48 | Rangers | Morton | 1-1 | SCF | 130,129 |
| 24/04/54 | Celtic | Aberdeen | 2-1 | SCF | 130,091 |
| 25/04/53 | Rangers | Aberdeen | 1-1 | SCF | 129,876 |
| 06/04/35 | Scotland | England | 2-0 | BIC | 129,693 |
| 04/05/63 | Rangers | Celtic | 1-1 | SCF | 129,527 |
| 09/04/60 | Scotland | England | 1-1 | BIC | 129,183 |
| 10/05/47 | Great Britain | Rest of Europe | 6-1 | F | 129,117 |
| 19/04/58 | Scotland | England | 0-4 | BIC | 127,874 |
| 18/05/60 | Real Madrid | Eintracht Frankfurt | 7-3 | ECCF | 127,621 |
| 23/03/12 | Scotland | England | 1-1 | BIC | 127,307 |
| 29/04/67 | Celtic | Aberdeen | 2-0 | SCF | 127,117 |
| 21/04/62 | Rangers | St. Mirren | 2-0 | SCF | 126,930 |
| 23/04/66 | Rangers | Celtic | 0-0 | SCF | 126,552 |
| 27/04/49 | Scotland | France | 2-0 | F | 123,970 |
| 22/03/47 | Rangers | Hibernian | 3-1 | SLCSF | 123,654 |
| 02/04/66 | Scotland | England | 3-4 | BIC | 123,052 |
| 05/05/73 | Rangers | Celtic | 3-2 | SCF | 122,714 |
| 26/04/50 | Scotland | Switzerland | 3-1 | F | 122,351 |
| 04/04/08 | Scotland | England | 1-1 | BIC | 121,452 |
| 25/04/64 | Rangers | Dundee | 3-1 | SCF | 120,982 |
| 15/05/63 | Rangers | Celtic | 3-0 | SCFR | 120,263 |
| 08/05/71 | Celtic | Rangers | 1-1 | SCF | 120,027 |
| 11/05/46 | Aberdeen | Rangers | 3-2 | SSLCF | 119,880 |
| 27/05/72 | Scotland | England | 0-1 | BIC | 119,415 |
| 22/04/50 | Rangers | East Fife | 3-0 | SCF | 118,615 |
| 02/01/39 | Rangers | Celtic | 2-1 | SL1 | 118,567 | At Ibrox |
| 14/04/28 | Rangers | Celtic | 4-0 | SCF | 118,115 |
| 20/05/53 | Celtic | Hibernian | 2-0 | CC | 116,951 |
| 04/04/53 | Rangers | Hearts | 2-1 | SCSF | 116,475 |
| 06/04/29 | Kilmarnock | Rangers | 2-0 | SCF | 114,708 |
| 22/04/61 | Dunfermline Ath. | Celtic | 0-0 | SCF | 113,618 |
| 21/04/34 | Rangers | St. Mirren | 5-0 | SCF | 113,403 |

## 100,000 PLUS CROWDS AT FOOTBALL MATCHES IN SCOTLAND CONT.

| | | | | | | |
|---|---|---|---|---|---|---|
| 08/12/54 | Scotland | Hungary | 2-4 | F | 113,180 | |
| 29/04/53 | Rangers | Aberdeen | 1-0 | SCFR | 112,799 | |
| 16/04/32 | Rangers | Kilmarnock | 1-1 | SCF | 111,982 | |
| 15/05/46 | Scotland | Switzerland | 3-1 | W | 111,899 | |
| 02/04/27 | Scotland | England | 1-2 | BIC | 111,214 | |
| 10/04/54 | Aberdeen | Rangers | 6-0 | SCSF | 110,982 | |
| 13/04/29 | Scotland | England | 1-0 | BIC | 110,512 | |
| 23/03/57 | Kilmarnock | Celtic | 1-1 | SCSF | 109,055 | |
| 24/04/65 | Celtic | Dunfermline Ath. | 3-2 | SCF | 108,800 | |
| 23/04/49 | Rangers | Clyde | 4-1 | SCF | 108,662 | |
| 25/04/59 | St. Mirren | Aberdeen | 3-1 | SCF | 108,591 | |
| 13/10/65 | Scotland | Poland | 1-2 | WC | 108,453 | |
| 11/04/70 | Aberdeen | Celtic | 3-1 | SCF | 108,244 | |
| 23/04/60 | Rangers | Kilmarnock | 2-0 | SCF | 108,017 | |
| 30/04/52 | Scotland | USA | 6-0 | F | 107,809 | |
| 23/10/65 | Celtic | Rangers | 2-1 | SLCF | 107,647 | |
| 12/04/30 | Rangers | Partick Thistle | 0-0 | SCF | 107,475 | |
| 23/04/55 | Clyde | Celtic | 1-1 | SCF | 106,283 | |
| 24/10/70 | Rangers | Celtic | 1-0 | SLCF | 106,263 | |
| 02/04/10 | Scotland | England | 2-0 | BIC | 106,205 | |
| 06/05/72 | Celtic | Hibernian | 6-1 | SCF | 105,909 | |
| 26/10/63 | Rangers | Morton | 5-0 | SLCF | 105,907 | |
| 20/04/32 | Rangers | Kilmarnock | 3-0 | SCFR | 105,695 | |
| 04/04/14 | Scotland | England | 3-1 | BIC | 105,000 | |
| 16/10/48 | Rangers | Celtic | 2-1 | SLC | 105,000 | At Ibrox |
| 11/04/31 | Celtic | Motherwell | 2-2 | SCF | 104,803 | |
| 18/10/61 | Rangers | Eintracht Frankfurt | 2-3 | F | 104,493 | |
| 16/04/30 | Rangers | Partick Thistle | 2-1 | SCFR | 103,668 | |
| 26/03/49 | Rangers | East Fife | 3-0 | SCSF | 103,458 | |
| 06/05/59 | Scotland | West Germany | 3-2 | F | 103,415 | |
| 12/05/71 | Celtic | Rangers | 2-1 | SCFR | 103,297 | |
| 07/04/06 | Scotland | England | 2-1 | BIC | 102,741 | |
| 30/03/35 | Rangers | Hearts | 1-1 | SCSF | 102,661 | |
| 27/03/54 | Celtic | Motherwell | 2-2 | SCSF | 102,444 | |
| 10/02/51 | Rangers | Hibernian | 2-3 | SC | 102,342 | At Ibrox |
| 15/04/33 | Celtic | Motherwell | 1-0 | SCF | 102,339 | |
| 21/03/25 | Celtic | Rangers | 5-0 | SCSF | 101,714 | |
| 09/11/65 | Scotland | Italy | 1-0 | WC | 101,293 | |
| 29/04/50 | Rangers | Hibernian | 0-0 | SL1 | 101,000 | At Ibrox |

| Key | All games played at Hampden unless otherwise stated. | | |
|---|---|---|---|
| WC | World Cup Qualifying | SCFR | Scottish Cup Final Replay |
| EC | European Championship Qualifying | SCSF | Scottish Cup Semi Final |
| BIC | British International Championship | SLCF | Scottish League Cup Final |
| W | War International | SLCSF | Scottish League Cup Semi Final |
| F | Friendly Internationals | SLC | Scottish League Cup |
| ECCF | European Champions Cup Final | SSLCF | Scottish Southern League Cup Final |
| ECCSF | European Champions Cup Semi Final | SL1 | Scottish League First Division |
| SCF | Scottish Cup Final | CC | Coronation Cup |

**Please Note**

These figures are as researched by David Ross during the writing of his book 'The ROAR of the Crowd' and some differ from those previously published or contained elsewhere in this publication. The reasons for the disparity in certain attendances is that from 1934 onwards, figures were taken from Queen's Park gate books which recorded the actual number of spectators coming through the turnstiles. However, it is customary for the various football authorities organising matches at Hampden to make appropriate adjustments to also take into account Directors Box, Media, Guests, etc. attending who are not recorded through the turnstiles.

A packed Hampden during the 1970's

in six supporters could be found at Ibrox or Parkhead. By the 1960s that was one in four and by the mid-seventies one in three. In the 21st century almost one in every two fans attending a Scottish football match does so at one of the Glasgow giants' grounds.

In the past fifteen years, more than half of Scotland's League clubs have either remodelled their existing grounds into all-seaters or moved to completely new surroundings. Other than the periods immediately after both World Wars, Scottish football is watched by record numbers of fans. Today, you can travel through all of continental Europe – from the Bay of Biscay to the Ural Mountains, from the Arctic Circle to the Straits of Gibraltar – without once setting foot in a country where more people per head of population watch live football than in Scotland.

Just as we were back in the days of that first international, the Scots are still, in the words of the song, "fitba' crazy, fitba' mad."

**DAVID ROSS**

(Writer and journalist David Ross is the author of several football books. He runs the www.scottishleague.net website)

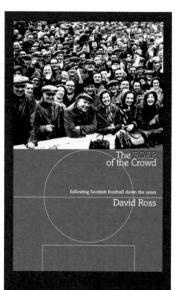

The ROAR
of the Crowd

following Scottish football down the years

David Ross

'The **ROAR** Of The Crowd' is the first comprehensive look at attendances at Scottish football games. From the largest League crowd (118,567 for Rangers v Celtic, January 1939) to gates of under fifty at East Stirlingshire and Edinburgh City, this book tells the stories behind the figures.

The phenomenal crowds that watched Scotland at Hampden are also considered. For over forty years Hampden held the world record attendance and even today every significant crowd record in Europe is held by Scotland's National Stadium.

'The ROAR Of The Crowd' is available at just £7.99 from good bookshops everywhere and post-free online from the publishers Argyll Publishing at www.argyllpublishing.co.uk

Scotland fans gather before the game against the Auld Enemy in 1968

# THE HOME OF **HEROES**

A visit to the Scottish Football Museum is a day out to remember. Based at Hampden Park, the home of Scottish football, the museum was recently rated a five star attraction by Visit Scotland. With over 2,500 exhibits on display, the history of the game is brought vividly to life from the first international match of 1872 and the Wembley Wizards triumph of 1928 through to Hampden's hosting of the Champions League Final in 2002.

Within the first 15 feet of the museum you can see some of the oldest and most important treasures within World Football.

These include the famous Scottish Cup (the oldest trophy in the world), the Glasgow Charity Cup (second oldest in the world), a match ticket from the first international of 1872 and a letter detailing the first known challenge match in 1868!

Many of Scotland's best kept football secrets can also be discovered such as the story of Andrew Watson, who captained Scotland to a famous 6-1 victory over England in 1881, and was the world's first prominent black footballer.

Some of the museum's fascinating stories are revealed below:-

### Scotland's first ever goal

The first ever goalscorer for Scotland was Lieutenant H. W. Renny Tailyour. Born in India in 1849, Tailyour was educated at Cheltenham College and played for the Royal Engineers, a leading English side of the 1870s. With the Engineers, he would contest three FA Cup Finals, emerging victorious in the tournament of 1875. He also has the distinction of playing for Scotland at rugby. Tailyour made his one and only appearance in 1873 against England but it wasn't to be a happy ending despite scoring his goal as the Scots lost the match 4-2.

### When Hampden was bigger than a city!

In 1937 Hampden Park set two world attendance records in the space of a week. On 17th April, the overall record of 149,547 was set at the international match against England while on 24th April, the Scottish Cup Final attracted a

crowd of 147,365, securing the record for a club match. The official capacity of the stadium was registered at over 183,000 - enough to accommodate the entire population of present day Dundee with room to spare for Falkirk!

### The Throw In

England originally used a one handed hurl in any direction enabling the ball to be launched, in the style of a cricket bowler, from one side of the field to the other. Scotland on the other hand, used two hands behind the head but with the ball entering play at a right angle to the touch line in a manner similar to a rugby line out. Both countries fought bitterly over which rule to use for international matches until 1882 when a compromise was reached resulting in the creation of the modern day throw in.

### Football Caps

The tradition of being capped for your country dates from the Victorian era when caps were initially used as a means of identifying one player from another on the field. Long before shirt numbers were invented, the players wore different coloured caps to distinguish themselves. The Scottish Football Association first awarded caps as an international honour in 1882 for the annual game against England. The players chose to wear the caps during the game and despite winning 5-1, the press criticised them for not trying harder as they were more concerned with losing their fancy headgear!

### The Original Football Academy

The deserted Ayrshire village of Glenbuck once produced professional footballers on a scale that would make any modern football academy envious. No fewer than 50 professional players came from the tiny mining village with seven of them winning international honours with Scotland. Perhaps the most famous family in Glenbuck were the Shankly's - all five brothers played professionally and the youngest, Bill Shankly, went on to become a Merseyside hero as manager of Liverpool.

### Football Clubs

Many of our senior football clubs were established by other organisations. Rangers was founded by rowers at Glasgow Green while Hamilton Academical were set up by the headmaster of the local school. Dunfermline Athletic split away from a cricket club and the old Third Lanark team was

formed by a Volunteer Regiment. Other clubs used to have different names. Alloa Athletic evolved from Clackmannan County, Dundee United used to be called Dundee Hibernian while East Stirlingshire were originally known as the Bainsford Bluebonnets!

### The Men in Black

The earliest match officials were called umpires and two of them took charge of each game. The umpires were members of the respective teams and were appointed by each club to uphold the playing rules. One umpire patrolled each half of the field and could only give a decision if he was appealed to by the players. Growing criticism over biased decisions and disputes between the umpires inevitably led to chaotic scenes. In 1891, the neutral role of the 'referee' was established and the new official was empowered with a final say over all disputes. The umpires were relegated to the touchlines becoming linesmen.

### Champions of the World

The first country to become World Champions was Uruguay in 1930 but back in 1888, an amateur village team from Dunbartonshire claimed the title. As Scottish Cup winners in 1888, Renton were challenged by FA Cup holders, West Bromwich Albion. The press dubbed the match the 'Championship of the United Kingdom and the World'. Renton defeated the 'Baggies' 4-1 at First Hampden Park. The World Championship trophy is on display within the museum.

### The Wembley Wizards

Scotland recorded an emphatic 5-1 victory over England at Wembley in 1928, but it could all have been very different! The tallest of Scotland's five forwards was Alex Jackson who was only 5ft 7in. Faced against a tall and strong England side, the chances of success looked bleak. On the eve of the match, Scotland captain, Jimmy McMullan, gathered his players together and uttered the famous words "Pray for rain". Luckily for Scotland, it rained in bucket loads the following day and the quick, fleet footed forwards proved too elusive for the English defence. An Alex Jackson hat-trick and a double from Alex James earned Scotland their famous victory. The "Wembley Wizards" match ball can be seen on display.

### Oldest Trophy in World Football

The Scottish Cup, dating from season 1873/74, is the oldest trophy within Association Football. Although The FA Cup can claim to be the oldest tournament, the original trophy was stolen back in 1895 and melted down for it's silver content! The replacement FA Cup, which was contested between 1896 and 1910, sold at auction for £478,400. The Scottish Cup is of course priceless! On Scottish Cup Final day, the original trophy is presented to the winning team but after the lap of honour it is swapped over - the original goes back to the Scottish Football Museum and an exact replica leaves the stadium with the winning team.

### The Anglo Scots

Scots have traditionally had an important influence on English football. The founder of The Football League in 1888 was William McGregor, a native of Perthshire. The first Liverpool team in 1892 were known as 'the Macs' as all 11 players were from north of the border while seven of Preston North End's double winning team of 1889 were 'Anglos' with an eighth player, John Goodall, born of Scottish parents. Up until 1915, one in three of all Arsenal players were Scottish and eight of Scotland's 'Wembley Wizards' team of 1928 were based with English clubs. The Museum has three display cases devoted to the Anglo Scots.

### Champions of Argentina

Although The Argentine Football League officially dates from 1893, an earlier League had existed in 1891, just one year after the formation of The Scottish Football League! What is even more surprising is that the competition ended in a play-off between the Old Caledonians and St. Andrews. For the record, St. Andrews defeated the Old Caledonians 3-1 to mark their place in Argentine football history. A plaque celebrating the role of Scotsman Alexander Watson Hutton, "the father of Argentine Football", is displayed within the "Scots Away" gallery.

### A Derby Disaster

On New Years Day, 1940, a heavy fog covered Easter Road before the Edinburgh derby match but the game had to go ahead in order to prevent the enemy from knowing the weather conditions. Things were so bad that journalist Rex Kingsley had to invent the commentary for the radio broadcast while John Donaldson of Hearts went missing at the end of the game. He was later found at the far end of the pitch still waiting for the ball and unaware that the match had finished! Had they been able to see properly, the 14,000 crowd would have witnessed a goal feast as Hearts won 6-5.

### The 1930 World Cup

Scotland has never got beyond the group phase of the World Cup Finals but in 1930, a team made up of five Scots made joint third place! The team in question was the United States and under the guidance of Jim Gallacher, their Kirkintilloch born captain, the USA defeated Belgium and Paraguay to top their section and progress to the Semi-Final. Argentina ultimately proved too strong but during the match a comical incident took place. The USA trainer ran onto the pitch to dispute a

decision and threw his medical bag to the ground breaking a bottle of chloroform. The unfortunate trainer was overcome by the fumes and had to be assisted from the field! Jim Gallacher's Third Place World Cup medal is featured within the museum.

## Floodlights

The first floodlit football match took place in Scotland on 25th October, 1878 when Third Lanark played Vale of Leven at Cathkin Park. One large electric light fixed to a swivel was operated from a platform 50 feet in the air. The light was directed at the action leaving one third of the pitch in complete darkness! Vale of Leven won the match 2-1. Modern floodlights officially came into being on 7th November, 1951 when Stenhousemuir played Hibernian in a friendly match at Ochilview.

So come along and find out why Scotland can claim to be the birthplace of the modern game. Discover the legends within our Hall of Fame, experience the sound of the Hampden Roar and take a guided tour of the impressive five star National Stadium. With interactive games, a souvenir shop and café, there is plenty to see and do!

**RICHARD McBREARTY**
(Curator, Scottish Football Museum)

# The HIGHLAND

## Football League Directory of Clubs

### BRORA RANGERS F.C.
| | |
|---|---|
| Secretary: | Kevin MacKay |
| Manager: | James Kelly |
| Club Address: | Dudgeon Park, Dudgeon Drive, Brora, KW9 6QN. |
| Ground Tel/Fax: | 01408 621231 |
| Sec Bus: | 01408 623005 or 623018 |
| Sec Home/Fax: | 01408 621114 |
| Sec Mobile: | 07721 940938 |

E-Mail:
brorarangersfc@highlandleague.com
Year of Formation: 1879
Capacity: Total: 4,000,
250 Seated, 3,750 Standing
Pitch Dimensions: 112 yds x 70 yds
Playing Kits: 1st Choice
Shirt: Red with White flash on sleeves
Shorts: Red. Stockings: Red and White
2nd Choice Shirt: White Shorts: White.
Stockings: White

### BUCKIE THISTLE F.C.
| | |
|---|---|
| Secretary: | Murray Duncan |
| Manager: | Duncan Shearer |
| Club Address: | Victoria Park, Midmar Street, Buckie, AB56 1BJ. |
| Ground Tel No: | 01542 831454 |
| Sec Bus: | 01542 832170 |
| Sec Bus Fax: | 01542 832182 |
| Sec Home: | 01542 835660 |

E-Mail:
buckiethistlefc@highlandleague.com
Website: www.buckiethistle.com
Year of Formation: 1889
Capacity: Total: 5,400,
400 Seated, 5,000 Standing
Pitch Dimensions: 109 yds x 73 yds
Playing Kits: 1st Choice Shirt: Green & White Hoops
Shorts: White with Green Trim. Stockings: White
2nd Choice Shirt: White. Shorts: Green
Stockings: White

### CLACHNACUDDIN F.C. (1990) LTD.
| | |
|---|---|
| Secretary: | Gilbert Skinner |
| Manager: | Robert Williamson |
| Club Address: | Grant Street Park, Wyvis Place, Inverness, IV3 6DR. |
| Ground Tel No: | 01463 238825 |
| Sec Home: | 01463 235339 |
| Sec Mobile: | 07810 540398 |

E-Mail:
clachnacuddinfc@highlandleague.com
Year of Formation: 1886
Capacity: Total: 3,000,
154 Seated, 2,846 Standing
Pitch Dimensions: 108 yds x 70 yds
Playing Kits: 1st Choice Shirt: White
Shorts: Black. Stockings: White
2nd Choice Shirt: Yellow. Shorts: Yellow
Stockings: Yellow

### COVE RANGERS F.C.
| | |
|---|---|
| Secretary: | Duncan Little |
| Manager: | John Sheran |
| Club Address: | Allan Park, Loirston Road, Cove, Aberdeen, AB12 3NR. |
| Ground Tel No: | 01224 890433 |
| Sec Bus: | 01224 854990 |
| Sec Home: | 01224 896282 |
| Sec Mobile: | 07710 648154 |
| Fax No: | 01224 895199 |

E-Mail:
coverangersfc@highlandleague.com
Year of Formation: 1922
Capacity: Total: 2,300,
200 Seated, 2,100 Standing
Pitch Dimensions: 104 yds x 65 yds
Playing Kits: 1st Choice Shirt: Blue & Yellow
Shorts: Blue. Stockings: White
2nd Choice Shirt: Yellow & Blue
Shorts: Yellow. Stockings: Yellow

### DEVERONVALE F.C.
| | |
|---|---|
| Secretary: | Stewart McPherson |
| Manager: | Gregg Carrol |
| Club Address: | Princess Royal Park, 56 Airlie Gardens, Banff, AB45 1HB. |
| Ground Tel No: | 01261 818303 |
| Sec Mobile: | 07813 733617 |
| Fax No: | 01261 833646 |

E-Mail:
deveronvalefc@highlandleague.com
Website: www.deveronvale.co.uk
Year of Formation: 1938
Capacity: Total: 2,600,
300 Seated, 2,300 Standing
Pitch Dimensions: 109 yds x 78 yds
Playing Kits: 1st Choice Shirt: Red with White Trim
Shorts: White. Stockings: Red
2nd Choice Shirt: Sky Blue Shorts: White. Stockings: White

### FORRES MECHANICS F.C.
| | |
|---|---|
| Secretary: | David Macdonald |
| Manager: | Steven Paterson |
| Club Address: | Mosset Park, Lea Road, Forres, Moray, IV36 0AU. |
| Ground Tel/Fax No: | 01309 675096 |
| Sec Home: | 01343 544294 |
| Sec Mobile: | 07779 782799 |
| Sec Business: | 01309 694012 |

E-Mail:
forresmechanicsfc@highlandleague.com
Year of Formation: 1884
Capacity: Total: 6,540,
540 Seated, 6,000 Standing
Pitch Dimensions: 106 yds x 69 yds
Playing Kits: 1st Choice Shirt:
Gold with Chocolate Panel
Shorts: Gold. Stockings: Gold
2nd Choice Shirt: White with Chocolate & Gold Trim
Shorts: White with Chocolate & Gold Trim
Stockings: White

### FORT WILLIAM F.C.
| | |
|---|---|
| Secretary: | James Campbell |
| Manager: | Rab Mulheron |
| Club Address: | Claggan Park, Fort William |
| Sec Home/Fax: | 01397 772298 |

E-Mail:
fortwilliamfc@highlandleague.com
Website: www.fortwilliamfc.org.uk
Year of Formation: 1984
Capacity: Total: 4,600 ,
400 Seated, 4,200 Standing
Pitch Dimensions: 102 yds x 80 yds
Playing Kits: 1st Choice Shirt:
Tangerine with Gold and Black Pinstripe
Shorts: Black. Stockings: Black
2nd Choice Shirt: Navy Blue with Sky Blue Pinstripe
Shorts: Navy Blue. Stockings: Navy Blue with Sky Blue

### FRASERBURGH F.C.
| | |
|---|---|
| Secretary: | Finlay M. Noble |
| Manager: | Charles Duncan |
| Club Address: | Bellslea Park, Seaforth Street, Fraserburgh, AB43 9BD. |
| Ground Tel No: | 01346 518444 |
| Fax No: | 01346 516414 |
| Sec Bus/Mobile: | 07747 003806 |
| Sec Home: | 01346 513474 |

| | P | W | D | L | F | A | Pts |
|---|---|---|---|---|---|---|---|
| Huntly | 28 | 20 | 5 | 3 | 79 | 32 | 65 |
| Inverurie Loco Works | 28 | 20 | 3 | 5 | 81 | 25 | 63 |
| Fraserburgh | 28 | 19 | 2 | 7 | 75 | 35 | 59 |
| Deveronvale | 28 | 19 | 2 | 7 | 75 | 40 | 59 |
| Buckie Thistle | 28 | 16 | 4 | 8 | 51 | 26 | 52 |
| Cove Rangers | 28 | 16 | 4 | 8 | 59 | 44 | 52 |
| Clachnacuddin | 28 | 14 | 3 | 11 | 60 | 37 | 45 |
| Keith | 28 | 14 | 3 | 11 | 56 | 45 | 45 |
| Forres Mechanics | 28 | 10 | 9 | 9 | 49 | 44 | 39 |
| Nairn County | 28 | 11 | 3 | 14 | 54 | 58 | 36 |
| Lossiemouth | 28 | 10 | 1 | 17 | 49 | 80 | 31 |
| Wick Academy | 28 | 6 | 1 | 21 | 30 | 71 | 19 |
| Fort William | 28 | 5 | 1 | 22 | 26 | 89 | 16 |
| Rothes | 28 | 4 | 2 | 22 | 30 | 78 | 14 |
| Brora Rangers | 28 | 2 | 5 | 21 | 26 | 96 | 11 |

E-Mail:
fraserburghfc@highlandleague.com
Website: www.fraserburghfc.net
Year of Formation: 1910
Capacity: Total: 4,500,
480 Seated, 4,020 Standing
Pitch Dimensions: 106 yds x 66 yds
Kits: 1st Choice Shirt: Black and White Stripes
Shorts: Black. Stockings: Red
2nd Choice Shirt: Red Tartan
Shorts: Red. Stockings: White

## HUNTLY F.C.

Secretary: Peter Morrison
Manager: Billy Anderson
Club Address: Christie Park, East Park
Street, Huntly, AB54 8JE.
Ground Tel/Fax No: 01466 793548
Sec Bus: 01358 726649
Sec Home: 01466 793269
Sec Mobile: 07957 283127
E-Mail: huntlyfc@highlandleague.com
Website: www.huntlyfc.co.uk
Year of Formation: 1928
Capacity: Total: 4,500,
270 Seated, 4,230 Standing
Pitch Dimensions: 105 yds x 72 yds
Playing Kits: 1st Choice
Shirt: Black and Gold Stripes Shorts: Black
Stockings: Black with Gold Trim
2nd Choice Shirt: White. Shorts: White Stockings: White

## INVERURIE LOCO WORKS F.C.

Secretary: Gordon Park
Manager: John Gardiner
Club Address: Harlaw Park, Harlaw Road,
Inverurie, AB51 4SG.
Ground Tel No: 01467 622168
Sec Bus: 01467 624500
Sec Home: 01467 621347
Sec Mobile: 07816 604434
E-Mail:
inverurielocoworksfc@highlandleague.com
Website:
www.eteamz.com/inverurielocoworks
Year of Formation: 1903
Capacity: Total: 1,925,
125 Seated, 1,800 Standing
Pitch Dimensions: 103 yds x 71 yds

Playing Kits: 1st Choice
Shirt: Black & Red Vertical Stripes
Shorts: Black. Stockings: Red
2nd Choice Shirt: White with Red
Shorts: White. Stockings: White

## KEITH F.C.

Secretary: Alexander Stables
Manager: Martin Allan
Club Address: Kynoch Park, Balloch Road,
Keith, AB55 5EN.
Ground Tel No/
Sec Bus/Fax: 01542 882629
Sec Home: 01542 887219
Sec Mobile: 07814 431760
E-Mail: keithfc@highlandleague.com
Website: www.keith-fc.co.uk
Year of Formation: 1919
Capacity: Total: 4,500,
450 Seated, 4,050 Standing
Pitch Dimensions: 110 yds x 75 yds
Playing Kits: 1st Choice Shirt: Maroon/Blue & White
Shorts: Maroon. Stockings: Maroon/Blue
2nd Choice Shirt: White with Blue Trim
Shorts: Blue. Stockings: White/Blue

## LOSSIEMOUTH F.C.

Secretary: Alan McIntosh
Manager: Jim Walker
Club Address: Grant Park, Kellas Avenue,
Lossiemouth, IV31 6JG.
Ground Tel No: 01343 813717
Sec Home: 01343 813328
Sec Bus/Mobile: 07890 749053
Fax No: 01343 815440/813717
E-Mail:
lossiemouthfc@highlandleague.com
Year of Formation: 1945
Capacity: Total: 3,500,
250 Seated, 3,250 Standing
Pitch Dimensions: 110 yds x 60 yds
Playing Kits: 1st Choice Shirt: Red
Shorts: Red. Stockings: Red
2nd Choice Shirt: Yellow. Shorts: Yellow. Stockings: Yellow

## NAIRN COUNTY F.C.

Secretary: John McNeill
Manager: Les Fridge
Club Address: Station Park, Balblair Road,
Nairn, IV12 5LT.
Ground Tel No: 01667 454298

Sec Bus: 01463 792424
Sec Home/Fax: 01667 462510
E-Mail: nairncountyfc@highlandleague.com
Year of Formation: 1914
Capacity: Total:3,800,
250 Seated, 3,550 Standing
Pitch Dimensions: 110 yds x 62 yds
Playing Kits: 1st Choice Shirt: Maize Yellow
Shorts: Black. Stockings: Maize Yellow
2nd Choice Shirt: Black. Shorts: White
Stockings: White or Maize Yellow

## ROTHES F.C.

Secretary: Neil McKenzie
Manager: Gordon Winton
Club Address: MacKessack Park, Station
Street, Rothes, Aberlour
Ground Tel No: 01340 831972
Sec Mobile: 07802 773695
Sec Home: 01340 831344
E-Mail: rothesfc@highlandleague.com
Year of Formation: 1938
Capacity: Total: 2,650,
160 Seated, 2,490 Standing
Pitch Dimensions: 108 yds x 74 yds
Playing Kits: 1st Choice
Shirt: Tangerine with Black Trim
Shorts: Black. Stockings: Tangerine with Black Trim
2nd Choice Shirt: Black with Tangerine Trim
Shorts: Tangerine Stockings: Black with Tangerine Trim

## WICK ACADEMY F.C.

Secretary: Alistair Ross
Manager: Alistair Budge
Club Address: Harmsworth Park, South
Road, Wick, KW1 5NH.
Ground Tel/Fax No: 01955 602446
Sec Bus: 01847 802602
Sec Home: 01955 603883
Sec Mobile: 07990 728823
E-Mail:
wickacademyfc@highlandleague.com
Website: www.wickacademy-fc.co.uk
Year of Formation: 1893
Capacity: Total: 2,000,
433 Seated, 1,567 Standing
Pitch Dimensions: 106 yds x 76 yds
Playing Kits: 1st Choice Shirt: Black and White Stripes
Shorts: Black. Stockings: Black with White Tops
2nd Choice Shirt: White with Red/Maroon Trim
Shorts: Red. Stockings: Maroon with White Tops

# The East of

# SCOTLAND

## Football League Directory of Clubs

### ANNAN ATHLETIC F.C.

| | |
|---|---|
| Secretary: | Alan T. Irving |
| Manager: | Sandy Ross |
| Club Address: | Galabank, North Street, Annan, Dumfries & Galloway. |
| Ground Tel No: | 01461 204108 |
| Sec Bus: | 01461 207218 |
| Sec Home/ Fax No: | 01461 203702 |
| E-Mail: | ibroxx@aol.com or RichardShaw@M-B-E.freeserve.co.uk |
| Website: | www.annanathletic.2fs.com |
| Year of Formation: | 1942 |
| Capacity: | Total: 2,000, 500 Seated, 1,500 Standing |
| Pitch Dimensions: | 110 yds x 65 yds |

Playing Kits: 1st Choice
Shirt: Black and Gold Vertical Stripes.
Shorts: Black. Stockings: Black with Gold Hoops
2nd Choice Shirt: Blue. Shorts: Blue.
Stockings: Blue with White Hoops

### CIVIL SERVICE STROLLERS F.C.

| | |
|---|---|
| Secretary: | Graeme Turnbull |
| Manager: | Brian Foster |
| Club Address: | Civil Service Sports Ground, Marine Drive, Edinburgh. |
| Ground Tel No: | 0131 332 1175 (Matchdays only) |
| Sec Home: | 0131 334 7625 |
| Sec Mobile: | 07717 430730 |
| E-Mail: | ght1uk@yahoo.co.uk |
| Website: | www.csstrollers.fsnet.co.uk |
| Year of Formation: | 1908 |
| Capacity: | Total: 500 (All Standing) |
| Pitch Dimensions: | 110 yds x 75 yds |

Playing Kits: 1st Choice Shirt: White.
Shorts: Navy Blue. Stockings: Red
2nd Choice Shirt: Red. Shorts: Navy Blue.
Stockings: Navy Blue

### COLDSTREAM F.C.

| | |
|---|---|
| Secretary: | Robert Bell |
| Manager: | Thomas Blaikie |
| Club Address: | Home Park, Coldstream, Berwickshire. |
| Ground Tel/Fax No: | 01890 883085 |
| Sec Home: | 01890 883161 |
| Sec Mob: | 07854 161584 |
| E-Mail: | coldstreamfc@icscotland.net |
| Year of Formation: | 1895 |
| Capacity: | Total: 1,500 (All Standing) |
| Pitch Dimensions: | 100 yds x 60 yds |

Playing Kits: 1st Choice Shirt: Royal Blue.
Shorts: Blue/White. Stockings: Royal Blue
2nd Choice Shirt: Red. Shorts: Red. Stockings: Red

### CRAIGROYSTON F.C.

| | |
|---|---|
| Secretary: | Jim Sievewright |
| Manager: | Alan Whyte |
| Club Address: | St. Mark's Park, Warriston, Edinburgh |
| Sec Bus: | 0131 346 5967 |
| Sec Home: | 0131 228 1803 |
| E-Mail: | gordon.bruce@sps.gov.uk |
| Year of Formation: | 1976 |
| Capacity: | Total: 1,000, (All Standing) |
| Pitch Dimensions: | 106 yds x 76 yds |

Playing Kits:1st Choice Shirt: Yellow.
Shorts: Blue. Stockings: Yellow
2nd Choice Shirt: Royal Blue.
Shorts: Royal Blue. Stockings: Royal Blue

### DALBEATTIE STAR F.C.

| | |
|---|---|
| Secretary: | Robert Geddes |
| Manager: | Brian Aitchison |
| Club Address: | Islecroft Stadium, Dalbeattie. |
| Ground Tel No: | 01556 611151 |
| Sec Bus/Home: | 01556 610563 |
| Sec Mobile: | 07860 549444 |
| Fax No: | 01556 611747 |
| E-Mail: | bob@solwaypressservices.freeserve.co.uk |
| Year of Formation: | 1905 (approx) |
| Capacity: | Total: 4,000 (All Standing) |
| Pitch Dimensions: | 110 yds x 70 yds |

Playing Kits: 1st Choice Shirt: Red and Black
Stripes. Shorts: Black. Stockings: Red
2nd Choice Shirt: Sky Blue and Maroon.
Shorts: Maroon. Stockings: Maroon.

### EASTHOUSES LILY F.C.

| | |
|---|---|
| Secretary: | Robert Paul |
| Manager: | David McQueenie |
| Club Address: | Mayfield Park, Newbattle, Easthouses |
| Sec Home: | 0131 663 9768 |
| Year of Formation: | 1969 |
| Capacity: | Total: 1,000 (All Standing) |
| Pitch Dimensions: | 110 yds x 67 yds |

Playing Kits: 1st Choice Shirt: Red.
Shorts: Red. Stockings: White.
2nd Choice Shirt: Blue. Shorts: Blue. Stockings: Blue.

### EDINBURGH ATHLETIC F.C.

| | |
|---|---|
| Secretary: | Eugene Taylor |
| Manager: | Eugene Taylor |
| Club Address: | Civil Service Sports Ground, Marine Drive, Edinburgh. |
| Ground Tel No: | 0131 332 1175 (Matchdays) |
| Sec Home: | 0131 476 6730 |
| Sec Mob: | 07742 779872 |
| E-Mail: | eugene.taylor@centrica.co.uk |
| Website: | www.edinburghathletic.com |
| Year of Formation: | 1968 |
| Capacity: | Total: 500 (All Standing) |
| Pitch Dimensions: | 100 yds x 60 yds |

Playing Kits: 1st Choice Shirt: Navy Blue.
Shorts: White. Stockings: Navy Blue.
2nd Choice Shirt: Green. Shorts: White.
Stockings: Green

### EDINBURGH CITY F.C.

| | |
|---|---|
| Secretary: | Grant Coffin |
| Manager: | Tom Steven |
| Club Address: | Meadowbank Stadium, London Road, Edinburgh, EH7 6AE. |
| Ground Tel No: | 0131 661 5351 |
| Sec Bus: | 07740 443944 |
| Sec Home: | 01355 264729 |
| E-Mail: | grant.coffin@routeco.co.uk |
| Website: | www.edinburghcityfc.com |
| Year of Formation: | 1928 |

| | |
|---|---|
| Capacity: | Total: 13,841 (All Seated) |
| Pitch Dimensions: | 105 yds x 72 yds |

Playing Kits: 1st Choice Shirt: White.
Shorts: Black. Stockings: White.
2nd Choice Shirt: Yellow. Shorts: Black.
Stockings: Yellow

### EDINBURGH UNIVERSITY ASSOCIATION F.C.

| | |
|---|---|
| Secretary: | Damian Wheeler |
| Manager: | Douglas Samuel |
| Club Address: | East Peffermill Playing Fields, Peffermill Road, Edinburgh. |
| Ground Tel No: | 0131 661 8842 |
| Sec Bus: | 07966 058047 |
| Fax No: | 0131 650 2371 |
| E-Mail: | euafc@ed.ac.uk |
| Website: | www.eusu.ed.ac.uk/clubs/euafc |
| Year of Formation: | 1878 |
| Capacity: | Total: 1,012, 12 Seated, 1,000 Standing |
| Pitch Dimensions: | 115 yds x 66 yds |

Playing Kits: 1st Choice
Shirt: Green/Navy Blue Sleeves.
Shorts: Navy Blue. Stockings: Navy Blue
2nd Choice Shirt: White with Claret Sleeves.
Shorts: Claret. Stockings: Claret.
3rd Choice Shirt: Sky Blue/White.
Shorts: White. Stockings: Sky Blue.

### EYEMOUTH UNITED F.C.

| | |
|---|---|
| Secretary: | Ian Thomson |
| Manager: | Robin Aitchison |
| Club Address: | Warner Park, Johns Road, Eyemouth |
| Sec Home: | 01890 751301 |
| E-Mail: | tommo@irt1.freeserve.co.uk |
| Year of Formation: | 1949 |
| Capacity: | Total: 1,000 (All Standing) |
| Pitch Dimensions: | 102 yds x 65 yds |

Playing Kits: 1st Choice Shirt: Maroon.
Shorts: Maroon. Stockings: Maroon.
2nd Choice Shirt: White/Sky Blue.
Shorts: Sky Blue. Stockings: Sky Blue.

### GALA FAIRYDEAN F.C.

| | |
|---|---|
| Secretary: | John Clayton |
| Manager: | Scott MacFarlane |
| Club Address: | Netherdale, Galashiels. |
| Ground Tel No: | 01896 753554 |
| Sec Home/Bus: | 01896 753797 |
| Sec Mobile: | 07768 616397 |
| Fax No: | 01896 754412 |
| E-Mail: | john.clayton@sepa.org.uk |
| Website: | www.galafairydean.com |
| Year of Formation: | 1907 |
| Capacity: | Total: 5,500, 495 Seated, 5,005 Standing |
| Pitch Dimensions: | 110 yds x 72 yds |

Playing Kits: 1st Choice
Shirt: White/Black Band down Arms & Sides.
Shorts: Black. Stockings: Black with White Top
2nd Choice
Shirt: Sky Blue/Navy Blue Band down Arms & Sides.
Shorts: Navy Blue.
Stockings: Sky Blue/Navy Blue Stripe.

| | P | W | D | L | F | A | Pts |
|---|---|---|---|---|---|---|---|
| Spartans | 20 | 18 | 1 | 1 | 74 | 17 | 55 |
| Annan Athletic | 20 | 15 | 1 | 4 | 66 | 29 | 46 |
| Edinburgh University | 20 | 10 | 5 | 5 | 37 | 26 | 35 |
| Whitehill Welfare | 20 | 8 | 7 | 5 | 37 | 35 | 31 |
| Lothian Thistle | 20 | 6 | 5 | 9 | 36 | 44 | 23 |
| Preston Athletic | 20 | 6 | 5 | 9 | 25 | 36 | 23 |
| Edinburgh City | 20 | 5 | 7 | 8 | 35 | 40 | 22 |
| Dalbeattie Star | 20 | 4 | 8 | 8 | 24 | 41 | 20 |
| Civil Service Strollers | 20 | 6 | 2 | 12 | 27 | 46 | 20 |
| Kelso United | 20 | 3 | 6 | 11 | 27 | 49 | 15 |
| Gala Fairydean * | 20 | 3 | 5 | 12 | 25 | 50 | 13 |

* Gala Fairydean deducted 1 point

| | P | W | D | L | F | A | Pts |
|---|---|---|---|---|---|---|---|
| Easthouses Lily | 22 | 15 | 3 | 4 | 55 | 15 | 48 |
| Heriot-Watt University | 22 | 13 | 5 | 4 | 64 | 31 | 44 |
| Selkirk | 22 | 13 | 5 | 4 | 48 | 28 | 44 |
| Edinburgh Athletic | 22 | 11 | 7 | 4 | 48 | 15 | 40 |
| Vale of Leithen | 22 | 11 | 5 | 6 | 53 | 32 | 38 |
| Craigroyston | 22 | 11 | 4 | 7 | 57 | 39 | 37 |
| Ormiston | 22 | 8 | 10 | 4 | 50 | 21 | 34 |
| Peebles Rovers | 22 | 10 | 4 | 8 | 37 | 42 | 34 |
| Hawick Royal Albert | 22 | 5 | 4 | 13 | 32 | 66 | 19 |
| Coldstream | 22 | 5 | 3 | 14 | 39 | 70 | 18 |
| Tollcross United | 22 | 2 | 4 | 16 | 22 | 67 | 10 |
| Eyemouth United * | 22 | 0 | 2 | 20 | 9 | 88 | -1 |

* Eyemouth United deducted 3 points

## HAWICK ROYAL ALBERT F.C.
| | |
|---|---|
| Secretary: | Douglas J. Purves |
| Manager: | Murray Balloch |
| Club Address: | Albert Park, Mansfield Road, Hawick. |
| Ground Tel No: | 01450 374231 |
| Sec Bus: | 0131 537 9241 |
| Sec Home/Fax: | 01450 371261 |
| Mobile: | 07862 295028 |
| E-Mail: | prvsjason@aol.com |
| Year of Formation: | 1947 |
| Capacity: | Total: 2,000, 500 Seated, 1,500 Standing |
| Pitch Dimensions: | 100 yds x 68 yds |

Playing Kits: 1st Choice
Shirt: Royal Blue with White and Red Stripe.
Shorts: Royal Blue. Stockings: Royal Blue
2nd Choice Shirt: Red and Black.
Shorts: Black. Stockings: Red

## HERIOT-WATT UNIVERSITY F.C.
| | |
|---|---|
| Secretary: | William Cranston |
| Manager: | Billy Henderson |
| Club Address: | Heriot-Watt University Riccarton Campus, Riccarton, Edinburgh |
| Ground Tel No: | 0131 451 8405 |
| Sec Home: | 07968 525860 |
| E-Mail: | alimath01@yahoo.co.uk |
| Website: | www.hwufc.org.uk |
| Year of Formation: | 1945 |
| Capacity: | Total: 1,000 (All Standing) |
| Pitch Dimensions: | 115 yds x 75 yds |

Playing Kits: 1st Choice Shirt: Yellow, Blue trim
Shorts: Blue. Stockings: Blue
2nd Choice Shirt: Blue Shorts: Blue. Stockings: Yellow

## KELSO UNITED F.C.
| | |
|---|---|
| Secretary: | Andrew Torrance |
| Manager: | Peter McNulty |
| Club Address: | Woodside Park, Kelso. |
| Ground Tel No: | 01573 223780 |
| Sec Home: | 01573 420760 |
| Sec Bus: | 01573 420760 |
| Sec Mob: | 07703 202691 |
| E-Mail: | andrew.torrance@btinternet.com |
| Year of Formation: | 1924 |
| Capacity: | Total: 1,000 (All Standing) |
| Pitch Dimensions: | 107 yds x 67 yds |

Playing Kits: 1st Choice Shirt: Black and White Stripes
Shorts: Black. Stockings: Black
2nd Choice Shirt: Red. Shorts: Black. Stockings: Red

## LOTHIAN THISTLE F.C.
| | |
|---|---|
| Secretary: | Tom Allison |
| Co Managers: | Ricky Tulloch/Malcolm Tulloch |
| Club Address: | Saughton Enclosure, Edinburgh. |
| Ground Tel No: | 0131 444 0422 (Matchdays only) |
| Sec Bus: | 0131 333 1976 |
| Sec Home: | 0131 336 1751 |
| E-Mail: | secretary@lothianthistlefc.co.uk |
| Website: | www.lothianthistlefc.co.uk |
| Year of Formation: | 1969 |
| Capacity: | Total: 1,000 (All Standing) |
| Pitch Dimensions: | 108 yds x 74 yds |

Playing Kits: 1st Choice Shirt: White
Shorts: Black. Stockings: Black/White
2nd Choice Shirt: Red. Shorts: Red Stockings: Red/White

## ORMISTON F.C.
| | |
|---|---|
| Secretary: | John M. Greenhorn |
| Manager: | Murray Cheyne |
| Club Address: | Recreation Park, Ormiston. |
| Sec Bus: | 0131 453 4411 |
| Sec Home: | 0131 538 0289 |
| Sec Mobile: | 07740 680904 |
| E-Mail: | john.greenhorn@blueyonder.co.uk |
| Year of Formation: | 1884 |
| Capacity: | Total: 1,000 (All Standing) |
| Pitch Dimensions: | 110 yds x 64 yds |

Playing Kits: 1st Choice Shirt: Maroon
Shorts: Maroon. Stockings: Maroon
2nd Choice Shirt: White. Shorts: White. Stockings: White

## PEEBLES ROVERS F.C.
| | |
|---|---|
| Secretary: | Gareth Smith |
| Manager: | Mark Lamb |
| Club Address: | Whitestone Park, Peebles. |
| Sec Home: | 01721 723532 |
| Sec Bus: | 0131 668 0333 |
| E-Mail: | vandgsmith@hotmail.com |
| Website: | |

www.memberstripod.com/peeblesrovers
| | |
|---|---|
| Year of Formation: | 1893 |
| Capacity: | Total: 1,000, 200 Seated, 800 Standing |
| Pitch Dimensions: | 110 yds x 75 yds |

Playing Kits: 1st Choice Shirt: Red/White
Shorts: Red. Stockings: Red
2nd Choice Shirt: Yellow/Black Stripe
Shorts: Black. Stockings: Yellow/Black Hoops

## PRESTON ATHLETIC F.C.
| | |
|---|---|
| Secretary: | Dr. Andrew Waddell |
| Manager: | Stephen Myatt |
| Club Address: | Pennypitt Park, Rope Walk, Prestonpans, East Lothian. |
| Ground Tel No: | 01875 815221 |
| Sec Bus: | 0131 664 7838 |
| Sec Home/Fax: | 0131 664 3135 |
| Sec Mobile: | 07887 791505 |
| E-Mail: | preston@prestonathletic.co.uk |
| Website: | www.prestonathletic.com |
| Year of Formation: | 1945 |
| Capacity: | Total: 4,000, 313 Seated, 3,687 Standing |
| Pitch Dimensions: | 110 yds x 70 yds |

Playing Kits: 1st Choice Shirt: Dark Blue
Shorts: Dark Blue. Stockings: Dark Blue
2nd Choice Shirt: Red. Shorts: White Stockings: White

## SELKIRK F.C.
| | |
|---|---|
| Secretary: | Mrs. Sheree Davison |
| Manager: | Fraser Lothian |
| Club Address: | Yarrow Park, Selkirk |
| Sec Home: | 01750 21995 |
| Sec Mobile: | 07984 984572 |
| Year of Formation: | 1880 |
| Capacity: | Total: 1,000 (All Standing) |
| Pitch Dimensions: | 108 yds x 70 yds |

Playing Kits: 1st Choice Shirt: Blue and White Stripe
Shorts: White. Stockings: Blue
2nd Choice Shirt: Blue/Red Sleeve
Shorts: Blue. Stockings: White/Red Flash

## SPARTANS F.C.
| | |
|---|---|
| Secretary: | James Murray |
| Co-Managers: | Sam Lynch & Mike Lawson |
| Club Address: | City Park, Ferry Road, Edinburgh. |
| Sec Bus/Fax: | 0131 667 9923 |
| Sec Home: | 0131 668 2188 |
| Sec Mobile: | 07710 723563 |
| E-Mail: | Jim.Murray@ICScotland.net |
| Website: | www.spartansfc.com |
| Year of Formation: | 1951 |
| Capacity: | Total: 3,000 (All Standing) |
| Pitch Dimensions: | 110 yds x 65 yds |

Playing Kits: 1st Choice Shirt: White
Shorts: Red. Stockings: White
2nd Choice Shirt: Blue. Shorts: Blue. Stockings: Blue

## TYNECASTLE F.C.
| | |
|---|---|
| Secretary: | Alistair Wilkie |
| Manager: | Ronnie Dignan |
| Club Address: | Fernieside Recreation Park, Fernieside Ave, Edinburgh. |
| Sec Bus: | 0131 467 5555 |
| Sec Home: | 0131 622 1148 |
| Year of Formation: | 1971 |
| Capacity: | Total: 1,000 (All Standing) |
| Pitch Dimensions: | 115 yds x 72 yds |

Playing Kits: 1st Choice Shirt: Maroon
Shorts: Maroon. Stockings: Maroon
2nd Choice Shirt: Blue. Shorts: Blue. Stockings: Blue

## VALE OF LEITHEN F.C.
| | |
|---|---|
| Secretary: | Alex Currie |
| Co Managers: | Jackie Diamond & Stuart Robertson |
| Club Address: | Victoria Park, Innerleithen. |
| Sec Home: | 01896 830708 |
| Sec Mobile: | 07952 809694 |
| E-Mail: | vale@leithen.freeserve.co.uk |
| Website: | www.valeofleithen.co.uk |
| Year of Formation: | 1891 |
| Capacity: | Total: 1,500 (All Standing) |
| Pitch Dimensions: | 100 yds x 75 yds |

Playing Kits: 1st Choice Shirt: Navy Blue
Shorts: Navy Blue Stockings: Navy Blue
2nd Choice Shirt: Red. Shorts: Red. Stockings: Red

## WHITEHILL WELFARE F.C.
| | |
|---|---|
| Secretary: | Peter McGauley |
| Manager: | John Clark |
| Club Address: | Ferguson Park, Carnethie Street, Rosewell, Midlothian. |
| Ground Tel No: | 0131 440 0115 |
| Sec Home: | 0131 440 3417 |
| E-Mail: | info@whitehillwelfare.com |
| Website: | www.whitehillwelfare.com |
| Year of Formation: | 1953 |
| Capacity: | Total: 4,000 (All Standing) |
| Pitch Dimensions: | 110 yds x 66 yds |

Playing Kits: 1st Choice Shirt: Claret Body with
Sky Blue Sleeves. Shorts: White. Stockings: White
2nd Choice Shirt: Sky Blue.
Shorts: Claret. Stockings: Sky Blue

# The South of
# SCOTLAND
## Football League Directory of Clubs

**ABBEY VALE F.C.**

| | |
|---|---|
| Secretary: | David Morton |
| Manager: | Robert Cameron |
| Club Address: | Maryfield Park, New Abbey |
| Fax No: | 01387 256004 |
| Sec Bus: | 07762 230648 |
| Sec Home: | 01387 256004 |
| E-Mail: | david55@tiscali.co.uk |
| Year of Formation: | 1974 |
| Capacity: | Total: 600 (All Standing) |
| Pitch Dimensions: | 110 yds x 64 yds |
| Playing Kits: | |
| 1st Choice Shirt: | Black and Gold |
| Shorts: | Black |
| Stockings: | Yellow |
| 2nd Choice Shirt: | Red |
| Shorts: | Black |
| Stockings: | Black |

**ANNAN ATHLETIC F.C.**

| | |
|---|---|
| Secretary: | Alan T. Irving |
| Manager: | Sandy Ross |
| Club Address: | Galabank, North Street, Annan, Dumfries & Galloway. |
| Ground Tel No: | 01461 204108 |
| Sec Bus: | 01461 207218 |
| Sec Home/ Fax No: | 01461 203702 |
| E-Mail: | ibroxx@aol.com or RichardShaw@M-B-E.freeserve.co.uk |
| Website: | www.annanathletic.2fs.com |
| Year of Formation: | 1942 |
| Capacity: | Total: 2,000, 500 Seated, 1,500 Standing |
| Pitch Dimensions: | 110 yds x 65 yds |
| Playing Kits: | |
| 1st Choice Shirt: | Black and Gold Vertical Stripes |
| Shorts: | Black |
| Stockings: | Black with Gold Hoops |
| 2nd Choice Shirt: | Blue |
| Shorts: | Blue |
| Stockings: | Blue with White Hoops |

**CREETOWN F.C.**

| | |
|---|---|
| Secretary: | Andrew Ward |
| Manager: | James McCrossan |
| Club Address: | Castlecary Park, Creetown. |
| Sec Home: | 01671 404309 |
| Year of Formation: | 1894 |
| Capacity: | Total: 600 (All Standing) |
| Pitch Dimensions: | 110 yds x 66 yds |
| Playing Kits: | |
| 1st Choice Shirt: | Yellow & Black |
| Shorts: | Yellow & Black |
| Stockings: | Yellow & Black Hoops |
| 2nd Choice Shirt: | Burgandy & White |
| Shorts: | Burgandy |
| Stockings: | Burgandy |

**CRICHTON F.C.**

| | |
|---|---|
| Secretary: | Kenny Cameron |
| Assistant Secretary: | Jane Brown |
| Manager: | James Thomson |
| Club Address: | Crichton Park, Dumfries |
| Sec Home: | 01387 265930 |
| Sec Bus: | 01387 258462 |
| Asst. Sec Home: | 01387 255658 |
| E-Mail: | kennyaccameron@aol.com |
| Year of Formation: | 1970 (As Blackwood Dynamos) |
| Capacity: | Total: 2,500 (Standing) |
| Pitch Dimensions: | 106 yds x 67 yds |
| Playing Kits: | |
| 1st Choice Shirt: | Blue & White |
| Shorts: | Blue |
| Stockings: | Blue |
| 2nd Choice Shirt: | Red & White |
| Shorts: | Black |
| Stockings: | Red |

**DALBEATTIE STAR F.C.**

| | |
|---|---|
| Secretary: | Robert Geddes |
| Manager: | Brian Aitchison |
| Club Address: | Islecroft Stadium, Dalbeattie. |
| Ground Tel: | 01556 611151 |
| Sec Bus/Home: | 01556 610563 |
| Sec Mobile: | 07860 549444 |

| | |
|---|---|
| Fax No: | 01556 611747 |
| E-Mail: | bob@solwaypressservices.freeserve.co.uk |
| Year of Formation: | 1905 (approx) |
| Capacity: | Total: 4,000 (All Standing) |
| Pitch Dimensions: | 110 yds x 70 yds |
| Playing Kits: | |
| 1st Choice Shirt: | Red and Black Stripes |
| Shorts: | Black |
| Stockings: | Red |
| 2nd Choice Shirt: | Sky Blue and Maroon |
| Shorts: | Maroon |
| Stockings: | Maroon |

**DUMFRIES F.C.**

| | |
|---|---|
| Secretary: | Tommy Parker |
| Manager: | Colin Lennox |
| Club Address: | Norfolk Park, Dumfries. |
| Sec Home: | 01387 263285 |
| Sec Bus: | 07710 679794 |
| E-Mail: | tparker3659@aol.com |
| Website: | www.dumfriesfc.co.uk |
| Year of Formation: | 2000 |
| Capacity: | Total: 500 (Standing) |
| Pitch Dimensions: | 105 yds x 63 yds |
| Playing Kits: | |
| 1st Choice Shirt: | Yellow & Navy Blue |
| Shorts: | Navy Blue |
| Stockings: | Navy Blue |
| 2nd Choice Shirt: | Navy Blue & Yellow |
| Shorts: | Navy Blue |
| Stockings: | Navy Blue |

**FLEET STAR F.C.**

| | |
|---|---|
| Secretary: | Irvine Hannah |
| Manager: | Andrew Mellon |
| Club Address: | Garries Park, Gatehouse of Fleet |
| Sec Bus: | 01671 403285 |
| Sec Home: | 01557 814829 |
| Year of Formation: | 1948 |
| Capacity: | Total: 600 (All Standing) |
| Playing Kits: | |
| 1st Choice Shirt: | Blue and White |
| Shorts: | White |
| Stockings: | Blue |

## SOUTH OF SCOTLAND LEAGUE FINAL TABLE SEASON 2004/05

| | P | W | D | L | F | A | Pts |
|---|---|---|---|---|---|---|---|
| Stranraer Athletic | 26 | 21 | 2 | 3 | 100 | 25 | 65 |
| Creetown | 26 | 18 | 8 | 0 | 72 | 28 | 62 |
| Annan Athletic | 26 | 15 | 4 | 7 | 81 | 35 | 49 |
| Threave Rovers | 26 | 14 | 3 | 9 | 76 | 46 | 45 |
| St. Cuthbert Wanderers | 26 | 12 | 5 | 9 | 62 | 55 | 41 |
| Dumfries | 26 | 11 | 3 | 12 | 62 | 52 | 36 |
| Nithsdale Wanderers | 26 | 10 | 6 | 10 | 48 | 61 | 36 |
| Abbey Vale | 26 | 11 | 2 | 13 | 54 | 65 | 35 |
| Mid Annandale | 26 | 8 | 6 | 12 | 49 | 70 | 30 |
| Fleet Star | 26 | 9 | 2 | 15 | 47 | 87 | 29 |
| Crichton | 26 | 7 | 7 | 12 | 32 | 42 | 28 |
| Wigtown  and Bladnoch* | 26 | 8 | 7 | 11 | 49 | 60 | 28 |
| Dalbeattie Star | 26 | 4 | 3 | 19 | 44 | 90 | 15 |
| Newton Stewart | 26 | 3 | 4 | 19 | 39 | 98 | 13 |

* Wigtown and Bladnoch deducted 3 points

---

### MID ANNANDALE F.C.
| | |
|---|---|
| Secretary: | George Trudt |
| Manager: | Sean Ross |
| Club Address: | King Edward Park, Lockerbie |
| Sec Home No: | 01576 202757 |
| Sec Mobile: | 07710 087783 |
| Year of Formation: | 1958 |
| Pitch Dimensions: | 116 yds x 66 yds |
| Playing Kits: | |
| 1st Choice Shirt: | Yellow with Black Trimming |
| Shorts: | Black with Two White Side Panels |
| Stockings: | Yellow with Two Black Hoops on Tops |
| 2nd Choice Shirt: | Blue with Yellow Trimming |
| Shorts: | Blue with Yellow Side Panels |
| Stockings: | Blue |

### NEWTON STEWART F.C.
| | |
|---|---|
| Secretary: | John R. McNaught |
| Manager: | Alan Groves |
| Club Address: | Blairmount Park, Newton Stewart |
| Sec Bus: | 01671 402499 |
| Sec Home: | 01671 403066 |
| E-Mail: | mc.holm.hol@talk21.com |
| Playing Kits: | |
| 1st Choice Shirt: | Black and White Vertical Stripes |
| Shorts: | Black |
| Stockings: | Black |
| 2nd Choice Shirt: | Silver and Grey Vertical Stripes |
| Shorts: | Black |
| Stockings: | Black |

### NITHSDALE WANDERERS F.C.
| | |
|---|---|
| Secretary: | Sam MacFarlane |
| Sec Home: | 01659 50546 |
| Treasurer: | William Watson |
| Treasurer's Home: | 01659 58312 |
| Club Address: | Lorimer Park, Sanquhar |
| Coaches: | Sam MacFarlane & George Bain |

E-Mail:
sam.macfarlane@btopenworld.com
| | |
|---|---|
| Playing Kits: | |
| 1st Choice Shirt: | Blue and White |
| Shorts: | Blue |
| Stockings: | Blue |
| 2nd Choice Shirt: | Black and White |
| Shorts: | White |
| Stockings: | White |

### ST. CUTHBERT WANDERERS F.C.
| | |
|---|---|
| Secretary: | Brian Mellon |
| Manager: | David Clarke |
| Club Address: | St. Mary's Park, Kirkcudbright. |
| Sec Bus/Home/Fax: | 01577 500233 |
| E-Mail: | maz-mel@supanet.com |
| Year of Formation: | 1879 |
| Capacity: | Total: 600, 100 Seated, 500 Standing |
| Pitch Dimensions: | 100 yds x 56 yds |
| Playing Kits: | |
| 1st Choice Shirt: | Blue with White Hoops |
| Shorts: | Blue |
| Stockings: | White |
| 2nd Choice Shirt: | Red and Black Hoops |
| Shorts: | Black |
| Stockings: | Black with Red Hoops |

### STRANRAER ATHLETIC F.C.
| | |
|---|---|
| Secretary: | Elizabeth Murdoch |
| Manager: | Sandy Sutherland |
| Club Address: | Stranraer Academy, Stranraer |
| Sec Home: | 01776 705309 |
| Sec Mobile: | 07765 405038 |
| Year of Formation: | 1995 |
| Capacity: | Total:  500 (All Standing) |
| Pitch Dimensions: | 110 yds x 68 yds |
| Playing Kit: | |
| Shirt: | Blue and White |
| Shorts: | Blue and White |
| Stockings: | Blue and White |

### THREAVE ROVERS F.C.
| | |
|---|---|
| Secretary: | Ian Bendall |
| Manager: | David McVitie |
| Club Address: | Meadow Park, Castle Douglas, Dumfries & Galloway. |
| Ground Tel No: | 01556 504536 |
| Sec Bus/Home/Fax: | 01556 503713 |
| Mobile: | 07773 350896 |
| E-Mail: | ianbendall@msn.com |
| Website: | www.threaveroversfc.co.uk |
| Year of Formation: | 1953 |
| Capacity: | Total: 5,000 (All Standing) |
| Pitch Dimensions: | 110 yds x  74 yds |
| Playing Kits: | |
| 1st Choice | |
| Shirt: | Black and White |
| Shorts: | Black |
| Stockings: | Black |
| 2nd Choice | |
| Shirt: | Red |
| Shorts: | Red |
| Stockings: | Red |

### WIGTOWN AND BLADNOCH F.C.
| | |
|---|---|
| Secretary: | Arlene Broll |
| Manager: | Keith Knox |
| Club Address: | Trammondford Park, Wigtown. |
| Ground Tel/Fax: | 01988 402322 |
| Sec Home: | 01988 700677 |
| Sec Bus: | 01988 403201 |
| Sec Mobile: | 07766 658999 |
| Year of Formation: | 1880 |
| Capacity: | Total: 1,500 (All Standing) |
| Pitch Dimensions: | 110 yds x 74 yds |
| Playing Kits: | |
| 1st Choice | |
| Shirt: | Red with White Trim |
| Shorts: | Red/ White Pinstripe |
| Stockings: | Red/White Pinstripe |
| 2nd Choice | |
| Shirt: | Blue and Yellow Trim |
| Shorts: | Blue and Yellow Trim |
| Stockings: | Blue and Yellow Trim |

**FIFA:**
General Secretary: Dr. Urs Linsi,
Hitzigweg 11, P.O. Box 85,
8030 Zurich, Switzerland.
Tel:      00 41 43 222 7777
Fax:      00 41 43 222 7878
website: www.fifa.com

**UEFA:**
Chief Executive: Lars-Christer Olsson,
Route de Genève 46, CH-1260,
Nyon 2, Switzerland.
Tel:      00 41 22 994 4444
Fax:      00 41 22 994 4488
website: www.uefa.com

**ASSOCIATED LEAGUES**

**THE SCOTTISH FOOTBALL LEAGUE:**
Secretary: Peter Donald,
Hampden Park, Glasgow, G42 9EB.
Tel:      0141 620 4160
Fax:      0141 620 4161
e-mail:  info@scottishfootballleague.com
website: www.scottishfootballleague.com

**THE SCOTTISH PREMIER LEAGUE:**
Secretary: Iain Blair,
Hampden Park, Glasgow, G42 9DE.
Tel:      0141 620 4140
Fax:      0141 620 4141
e-mail:  iainblair@scotprem.com
website: www.scotprem.com

**THE F.A. PREMIER LEAGUE:**
General Secretary: Mike Foster,
11 Connaught Place, London, W2 2ET.
Tel:      0207 298 1600
Fax:      0207 298 1601
e-mail:  general@fapl.co.uk
website: www.premierleague.com

**THE FOOTBALL LEAGUE:**
Director of Operations: Andy Williamson,
Edward VII Quay, Navigation Way,
Preston, PR2 2YF.
Tel:      0870 442 0 1888
Fax:      0870 442 1188
e-mail:  fl@football-league.co.uk
website: www.football-league.co.uk

**THE IRISH PREMIER LEAGUE:**
Acting Secretary: Dave McVeigh,
96 University Street, Belfast, BT7 1HE.
Tel:      02890 242888
Fax:      02890 330773
e-mail:  mail@irishpremierleague.com
website: www.irishpremierleague.com

**NATIONAL ASSOCIATIONS WITHIN
THE UNITED KINGDOM**

**THE SCOTTISH FOOTBALL ASSOCIATION:**

Chief Executive: David Taylor,
The National Stadium,
Hampden Park, Glasgow, G42 9AY.
Tel:      0141 616 6000
Fax:      0141 616 6001
e-mail:  info@scottishfa.co.uk
website: www.scottishfa.co.uk

**THE FOOTBALL ASSOCIATION:**
Chief Executive: Brian Barwick,
25 Soho Square, London, W1D 4FA.
Tel:      0207 745 4545
Fax:      0207 745 4546
e-mail:  info@the-fa.org
website: www.TheFA.com

**THE IRISH FOOTBALL ASSOCIATION:**
Chief Executive: Howard J.C. Wells,
20 Windsor Avenue, Belfast, BT9 6EE.
Tel:      02890 669458
Fax:      02890 667620
e-mail:  info@irishfa.com
website: www.irishfa.com

**THE FOOTBALL ASSOCIATION OF WALES:**
Secretary General: David G. Collins,
Plymouth Chambers, 3 Westgate Street,
Cardiff, CF10 1DP.
Tel:      02920 372325
Fax:      02920 343961
e-mail:  info@faw.org.uk
website: www.faw.org.uk

**OTHER LEAGUES IN SCOTLAND**

**THE HIGHLAND FOOTBALL LEAGUE:**
Secretary: John H. Grant,
35 Hamilton Drive, Elgin, Moray, IV30 4NN.
Tel/Fax: 01343 544995
e-mail:  john.grant@highlandleague.com
website: www.highlandfootballleague.com

**THE EAST OF SCOTLAND LEAGUE:**
Secretary: John M. Greenhorn,
2 Baberton Mains Court, Edinburgh, EH14 3ER.
Tel:      (House) 0131 442 1402
          (Business) 0131 453 4411 Ext.145
Fax:      0131 442 1402
e-mail:  secretary@eastofscotlandfa.org
website: www.eastofscotlandfa.org

**THE SOUTH OF SCOTLAND LEAGUE:**
Secretary: Richard Shaw M.B.E.,
8 Kirkland Road, Heathhall,
Dumfries, DG1 3RN.
Tel:      (House/Fax) 01387 261736
e-mail:  richardshaw@M-B-E.freeserve.co.uk

**AFFILIATED NATIONAL ASSOCIATIONS OF
THE SCOTTISH FOOTBALL ASSOCIATION**

**THE SCOTTISH JUNIOR
FOOTBALL ASSOCIATION:**
Secretary: Tom Johnston,
Hampden Park, Glasgow, G42 9DD.
Tel:      0141 620 4560
Fax:      0141 620 4561
e-mail:  scottishjuniorfa@scottish-football.com
website: www.scottish-juniors.co.uk

**THE SCOTTISH AMATEUR
FOOTBALL ASSOCIATION:**
Secretary: Hugh Knapp,
Hampden Park, Glasgow, G42 9DB.
Tel:      0141 620 4550
Fax:      0141 620 4551
e-mail:  safa@scottish-football.com
website: www.scottishamateurfa.co.uk

**THE SCOTTISH YOUTH FOOTBALL ASSOCIATION:**
Secretary: David Little,
Hampden Park, Glasgow, G42 9BF.
Tel:      0141 620 4590
Fax:      0141 620 4591
e-mail:  syfa@scottish-football.com
website: www.scottishyouthfa.co.uk

**THE SCOTTISH WELFARE
FOOTBALL ASSOCIATION:**
Secretary: Donald McNair,
14 Yair Drive, Glasgow, G52 2JX.
Tel:      0141 883 5008
Fax:      01324 813527

**THE SCOTTISH SCHOOLS
FOOTBALL ASSOCIATION:**
Secretary: John C. Watson,
Hampden Park, Glasgow, G42 9AZ.
Tel:      0141 620 4570
Fax:      0141 620 4571
e-mail:  jcwatson@scottish-football.com

**SCOTTISH WOMEN'S FOOTBALL:**
Executive Administrator: Mrs. Maureen McGonigle,
Hampden Park, Glasgow, G42 9DF.
Tel:      0141 620 4580/4582
Fax:      0141 620 4581
e-mail:  swf@scottish-football.com
website: www.scottishwomensfootball.com

**PLAYER'S UNION**

**THE SCOTTISH PROFESSIONAL
FOOTBALLERS ASSOCIATION:**
Senior Organiser: Tony Higgins
Secretary: Fraser Wishart
Fountain House, 1/3 Woodside Crescent,
Charing Cross, Glasgow, G3 7UJ.
Tel:      0141 332 8641
Fax:      0141 332 4491
e-mail:  SPFA@gmb.org.uk
website: www.spfa.co.uk

Place names in Scotland didn't just happen. The chief of a wandering band of hairy Picts didn't stop for the night and say, "Right lads, down packs. And, by the way, we'll call this place Bearsden." The majority of place names originate from physical features like mountains, rivers, seashore from people's names be they landowner, saint, king, tribal leader or from animals the natives hunted or domesticated.

It would be nice to think that the names we're familiar with now are merely rounded versions of the original - Edinburgh must have been "Edwin's borough", Kirkcaldy was "Caldy's kirk" and Bearsden was the home of - bears! but beware! Most of our place names come from four sources the commonest being Gaelic but there's also Norse, English and Latin and, to further complicate matters, the earliest Gaelic spoken in Scotland by the Picts is related closely to Welsh, Cornish & Breton and it was only with the later arrival of the Scots from Ireland that another related but very different Gaelic spread through much of the country.

The Celts were the first inhabitants, known to the Romans as "Picts" (probably "the painted ones") speaking their Gaelic. They were squashed into the northern areas by the invading Romans who found them and the Gaels (scotti arriving from Antrim in Ireland in the 3rd century) a pain in the neck and built forts and walls to keep them out. Next came the Anglo Saxons pushing up from Northumbria to the Forth and lastly the Norsemen – the Vikings - who circled Scotland with their own settlements on the North and Western Islands and coasts. Look at any map and you'll notice the place names we now use still follow the pattern of land occupied by these groups.

Oh, and incidentally, you'll find the meaning of Edinburgh and Kirkcaldy

below and, despite the old council having a bear on its coat of arms, Bearsden means barley valley. So, here's the real story of why the Dons play at Pittodrie, why Palmerstonites are connected to the best selling book in the world, why Killie are wee hard men, why Dundee United play on a green field and how the Buddies suffered from a sex change.

## ABERDEEN
A nice, simple, straightforward name to set the ball rolling; Aber = Welsh, Gaelic for "mouth of" and Deen is a corruption of River Don meaning "water" based on Devona "river goddess". The Dons nickname originated in the number of early players who were teachers and the ground name, Pittodrie, was taken from the small Aberdeenshire village of that name and is reputed to mean "place of manure". No comments, please!

## AIRDRIE UNITED
The town's name derives from two Gaelic words "Aird" & "Riughe" meaning High Shieling, a high plain where cattle grazed. United, from the Latin word "unire" to join together and is thus one of a few Latin words to reach us with its meaning unchanged. The old ground, Broomfield, is a name forever linked to the town's former football team, Airdrieonians, and originates from Old High German meaning fold of land covered in bramble.

## ALBION ROVERS
The club was formed in the 1880s through the amalgamation of Coatbridge Albion & Coatbridge Rovers. Albion is derived from Alba the ancient name for the

Northern part of Britain and Rovers probably originally described what pirates did although it could have connections with archery. Coatbridge itself means cottages by the river crossing.

## ALLOA ATHLETIC
No, nothing to do with the South Sea Islands greeting so comically beloved of David Coleman. Alloa is a combination of two Gaelic words "ail" and "mhagh" meaning a rocky plain. Nearby Alva has the same origin. Athletic comes from the Greek word meaning to compete for a prize. The Wasps' Recreation Park name derives ultimately from the Latin word "recreationum" - recovery from illness, refresh, restore, revive.

## ARBROATH
Arbroath is itself a smoothed out corruption of Aberbrothwick based again on Gaelic words meaning mouth of the River Brothock. Brothock derives from brothaig, boiling/turbulent which describes the rushing water as it meets the sea. Gayfield originates in "gahi", an Old German for rapid, impetuous.

## AYR UNITED
This is one of the oldest names in Britain. The derivation of the town name comes from pre-Celtic times and has reflections throughout Europe. There are river names based on the same word in Spain, Germany and

England all with a basic meaning of water course or flowing movement. United, from the Latin word "unire" to join together.

## BERWICK RANGERS

Not surprisingly, Old English furnishes us with the Border town's name; Barley Farmstead was "bere wic" to the Northumbrians of the 8th century. Rangers were originally gamekeepers or forest officers whose titles first appeared in 14th century England in the reign of Richard II. To give it it's Sunday name, Berwick-upon-Tweed, Tweed is another pre-Celtic name probably "Sanskrit" meaning "to surge" which is also the derivation of Teviot which flows in the Tweed at Kelso.

## BRECHIN CITY

As far as we are aware, the Celts wrote down virtually nothing but we know they were great story tellers and the names of their heroes are now well documented; Brecon was but one. His name, probably meaning high or holy, is found throughout Britain (Wrekin, Brecon etc.) and became a popular name adopted by tribal leaders as Brychan subsequently reaching us as "Brian". Good old Latin comes in yet again for City; civis = trusty, worthy hence "civitatem" the state, the city.

## CELTIC

The Celts was a name applied by ancient writers to tribes living in Northern Europe from Galatia to Galicia and only in more modern times was it applied to the Scots, Irish and Welsh. What the Celts

called themselves is, of course, quite unknown but it certainly wasn't "Celts". According to fable, Celtina was the daughter of Britannus and her son by Hercules, named Celtus, was the progenitor of the Celts. See! The football club was formed by Glasgow Irish Catholics in 1888. Why the club name is pronounced with a soft "S" instead of the correct harsh "K" is a mystery.

## CLYDE

We're probably back to the Romans here and what they did for us. Cluo is "the washer, the purifier" and was a river god. Virtually every animate and inanimate object had a diety in Roman times and Tacitus, the biographer of Agricola, the first Roman governor to invade Scotland, called the river at the West end of his string of forts Clota. In Welsh Gaelic, the river name could mean "the cleanser".

## COWDENBEATH

Another Gaelic derivation. Cowden probably means "hazel" and beath is "birch" so that's a nice wee rustic name for a former coalmining town. The town grew out of a small agricultural hamlet with a coaching stage on the Perth road which only succumbed to the grimy King Coal in the 19th century.

## DUMBARTON

Dum is a fort and so we have here the Fort of the Britons. Archaeologists have proved there has been a fortified stronghold on the rock for at least 2,500 years and the Britons, gradually pushed North and West by later invaders, were merely one group to have thrown stones at their enemies from its heights.

## DUNDEE

We get the City of Discovery's name from the Welsh Gaelic Dun Daigh –

Daigh's fortress or stronghold. I'm afraid we don't know now exactly who the local tough guy was but he was probably a Pictish lord. Dens Park could come from the same dun word and certainly the ground perched on the hillside would make a smashing fort site.

## DUNDEE UNITED

As above (of course!). United is from the Latin word meaning to join together. Tannadice Park is named from the Angus village which aptly means green field. United grew out of Dundee Hibernians in the 1920s one of a host of clubs boasting its Irish origins in its name coming from the Greek word for the island which was "five days" sail from Brittany.

## DUNFERMLINE ATHLETIC

Surprisingly and disappointingly, there is no satisfactory explanation for the main part of the town's name. Dun = fort or, perhaps, hill. The middle bit might come from fiaram denoting a bend in the burn which sweeps round Tower Hill and lin or lyne could refer to the burn's cascade just to the South but that's the best I can do I'm sorry to say. Athletic comes from the Greek word meaning to compete for a prize.

## EAST FIFE

East comes down to us through the eons of time from the Greek "eos" meaning dawn which, of course, breaks in the East. Legend has it that Scotland, North of the Forth and East of the Highlands was divided up amongst the seven sons of Cruithne, the ancestor of the Picts, and one of the sons, Fib (pronounced "Fiof" - Fiobh in modern Gaelic), was awarded the area we now know as Fife.

## EAST STIRLINGSHIRE

As above, East reaches us from the Greek via Latin and Old English all referring to the direction of the rising sun. The origins of the seemingly simple name, Stirling, have never been convincingly explained. It might come from struth lann - "enclosed land by a stream"; it might! Shire originates as "scir" a 9th century English word for an administrative district.

## ELGIN CITY

When Scots emigrated to America, Canada and Australia they often named their new settlements after ones from home; for example, there's twelve Glasgows scattered over North America alone! When the original scotti tribe migrated from Ireland about sixteen hundred years ago, they tended to do the same thing and Elgin comes from the Irish Gaelic meaning "Little Eire". City derives from the Latin for one of trust – "civitum".

## FALKIRK

Now this one is a cracker! From the 12th century onwards, the town has laboured under the following (and I'm not even going to start noting variations!); Egglesbreth, Egilibrich, Varia Capella, la Veire Chapelle, la Faukirk and Falkirk all of which basically mean "speckled church": apparently the original church was built of mottled stones. Oh and, yes, it should be pronounced "Fawkirk" because it seems the "l" was inserted by those with a misplaced desire to "speak proper".

## FORFAR ATHLETIC

Although the town sits on quite flat land, its name derives from two

Gaelic words "fothair" & "faire" meaning a terraced slope for watching, a kind of lookout post. This possibly refers to one of the surrounding hills and the name stuck to the town. Athletic, as we've seen before, comes from the Greek struggle - to compete for a prize although the root means a struggle and first appears in English in the mid 17th century direct from French athletique.

## GRETNA

Our newest League club hails from "Gravelly haugh" two Old English words meaning, in effect, a fertile strip of land adjacent to the River Sark which at one time formed the boundary between Scotland and England. Raydale Park comes, again, from Old English and means valley where doe are found.

## HAMILTON ACADEMICAL

The village grew up as Cadzow until 1548 at which date it took the name of the town in Leicestershire from where the Hamilton family emigrated. However, there was a "hamel tun" (farm in rough, broken ground) in the district in the 13th century so, in this case, I think you pays your money and you takes your choice. Plato taught in Akademos's grove outside Athens and the Romans took the name "academia" to mean the place of study.

## HEART OF MIDLOTHIAN

Although the club's founders actually derived their name initially from a popular Edinburgh dance hall and not from the old prison in the High Street, either way, the name is that of Sir Walter Scott's novel in the Waverley series and is the story of Jeanie

Dean's journey to London to appeal on behalf of her sister accused of child murder. Tradition has it that Leudonus was the grandfather of St. Kentigern, the patron saint of Glasgow, and the area he ruled was called Leudonia which evolved into Lothian.

## HIBERNIAN

The island of Hibernia (Greek Ιερων) off the Western coast of the Albiones Islands were circumnavigated by Massalian sailors (Marseille) in the mid 3rd century BC and were well known throughout the Western world by the time the Romans arrived in Britain in 43 AD. Hibernia was a common sobriquet for Ireland and the football club's Irish immigrant founders in the 1870s adopted it as their own. In passing, Edinburgh to the invading Northumbrians was "aodann burh" the fortress on the sloping land.

## INVERNESS CALEDONIAN THISTLE

Inverness means town at the mouth of the river Ness - they must have been up all night thinking up that one! Caledonian goes back to the rough Caledonii tribes encountered by the Romans in North Western Britain in the 1st century. They were constant troublemakers to the sandaled ones who eventually left them to their own devices and built a couple of walls to keep them out. The prickly weed adopted by us as a national "flower" is a common word in most north European languages – "distel" in Dutch, "tidsel" to the Danes - and has its origin in the ancient Greek word "stizien", to prick.

## KILMARNOCK

Careful with this one. "Kil" is often derived from coille - a wood or cuil

- a nook but we're on surer ground here in Ayrshire because when kil is followed by a person's name it is a church word and here the translation from the Gaelic means "the church of my Ernoc" an affectionate form of Ernain or Ernen. This saint's day is 25th October and its derivation is, ultimately, "little hard man". Apt.

## LIVINGSTON
Many place names in the east and central parts of Scotland were conferred by the invading Northumbrians in their native Old English and here Leving's Farmstead is the origin of this West Lothian town. Leving was a major landowner in the 12th century and is named in several of king David I's charters. The Anglo Saxon name derives from dear person, my darling. Almondvale means simply "river valley".

## MONTROSE
Sadly the name doesn't mean the picturesque "rose mount" but probably the rather less fragrant "peat bed promontory" from the Gaelic "moine ros" but it might be "mon roise" - "moor near the cape"! As with Falkirk the "t" was inserted later by those who wanted to sound "correct". The Gable Endies` Links Park threads its way down to us from Old English "hlinc" - rising ground.

## MORTON
The football club was formed in 1874 by a group of youngsters many of whom lived in Morton Terrace in Greenock which had been built a few years before by one James Morton. His personal name was originally attached to those who lived on a farm, any farm, by a lake - mere-tun. Greenock by the way means sunny place! We might not know a lot about the folk who lived there 1,800 years ago but at least we know they had a sense of humour.

## MOTHERWELL
This one is a rarity because it means exactly what it says! As long as we understand the mother to be Mary the mother of Jesus. What is believed to be the original well is marked in Ladywell Road and was probably a pagan site long before Christianity arrived. Fir (Park) is an Old Saxon word "fuirie" meaning pine tree forest.

## PARTICK THISTLE
When the Maryhill Magyars, the Jags, the Harry Wraggs play St. Johnstone please take note that the names of two places have the same meaning. Partick was originally "Perdyc "and the Bishop of Glasgow had his castle there while Perth was Perta both deriving from Gaelic "pertha", a copse. Our national flower derives its name from the Greek word for "to prick".

## PETERHEAD
An unusually Northern pure English name here. St. Peter's headland was named after the large kirk founded here in the 12th century long before a fishing village formed about 1593. English in derivation perhaps but definitely Scottish in situation as can be gauged by the 16th century spelling - Petyrheid"!

## QUEEN OF THE SOUTH
The only football club with a name of Biblical origin, "The Queen of the South shall rise up in the judgement with the men of this generation and condemn them" - Luke 11:31. Not an easy sentence to work into a football chant. The club's name comes from the Old Saxon words, "kwaeniz", originally just a wife before climbing up the social scale, and "suthar" - towards the sun.

## QUEEN'S PARK
The club took its name from the public park on which it started life which was not named after Victoria but Mary, Queen of Scots whose army was defeated by confederate nobles at the Battle of Langside a couple of hundred yards away in 1568, two hundred and ninety nine years before the young footballers adopted her name. Queen is an Old Saxon word for a wife but later being more specifically associated with the wife of the king and park is from the Old German word, "pfarrih" - an enclosure.

## RAITH ROVERS
The club is named after the estate on which it played in its early days but the origin of "Raith" is a little unclear and could derive from the Gaelic "rath" a circular fort usually of earth which is also the origin of

Rattray. Rovers, again, comes from sea pirates. The origin of Kirkcaldy is a wee tease. It isn't "Caldy`s church": it comes from the Gaelic "caer" called din -the fort of the rocky stronghold.

## RANGERS
The royal forest officers or gamekeepers of English King Richard II were called rangers back in the 14th century. A group of Glasgow youngsters reputedly adopted the name for its new club when one of them saw it in a foot-ball book he'd been given; aye right! How many football books were there in 1872? How they really picked out the name remains a mystery. Ibrox is yet another word we've inherited from the Gaels and means the place of badgers.

## ROSS COUNTY
Ross derives, not surprisingly, from Gaelic - "pro sto" meaning both a promontory and a wood and, in fact, Ross-shire is one big headland which was once covered with part of the great northern forest. County derives from the area ruled by a count whose origin can be traced back to the Roman "comitem" - a member of the imperial court.

## ST.JOHNSTONE
No, there never was a St. Johnstone! It's a corruption of St. John's Toon, the old name for Perth. Originally Pert coming, as we've seen at Partick Thistle, the

Brythonic Welsh for a bush or copse the city was known as St. Johnstoun for centuries before reverting to its current name. The 1st century Romans called their nearby fort Bertha which sounds uncannily sim-ilar. It's also known as The Fair City and there was a 19th century club in the town of that name.

## ST.MIRREN
Correctly, the name should be St.Mirin, Mirren is the female equiv-alent. Mirin was a 6th century Irish missionary who arrived in Scotland about 580 and probably founded the first church in Paisley and is the town's patron saint. Celtic Christianity gives us the town's name. Latin "basilica" - a church - became Gaelic "paislig".

## STENHOUSEMUIR
No Gaelic, no Latin, no Old English here but straightforward good old broad Scots! Stone house on the moor - what could be simpler! The original "Stanhous" was probably the early 17th century Scotch baro-nial mansion of the Bruce family which was shamefully demolished in 1960, its site being near Lodge Drive. Welsh Gaelic helps us out with the Warriors' ground's name. "Uchel" means high.

## STIRLING ALBION
Where we get Stirling from is quite a mystery and has never been

satisfactorily explained. Said by some to come from "struth lann" meaning stream enclosed land which would be apt for a fortress town set amongst the loops of the Forth. Albion is, as we've seen before, a corruption of "Alba" the old name for North Britain. Forthbank comes via the Vikings – "fjord ridge".

## STRANRAER
We're back on firmer ground for our last entry. The Gaelic origin is "sron reamhar" meaning the thick peninsula which is exactly where sits the port and resort town. There was a Roman fort in the vicinity, its exact position is yet to be discovered, called Rerigonium which translates roughly to "very royal place".

So there we have it. Some names are crashingly obvious and straightforward like Stenhousemuir while others have been mangled and bashed about so much over the centuries that their meanings are now pretty obscure: only a native Brythonic Gael, for example, would cower at the name Dundee.

The forty two clubs which make up our national Leagues might all be Scottish in location (oh, all right then, forty one plus Berwick) but their names mirror the hotch potch of our language which has taken a wee bit from here and a snippet from there stealing from just about every invader we've had for the last two thousand years. And it's constantly evolving, never still . The way we speak is different from even forty or fifty years ago.

Just listen to the commentaries of the 1956 Cup Final or the 1967 European Cup Final for proof. Who knows just what we'll look like and sound like in another couple of millennia?

FORREST H.C. ROBERTSON

| SEASON | DIVISION ONE | POINTS |
|---|---|---|
| 1890/91 | Dumbarton/Rangers | 29 |
| 1891/92 | Dumbarton | 37 |
| 1892/93 | Celtic | 29 |
| 1893/94 | Celtic | 29 |
| 1894/95 | Heart of Midlothian | 31 |
| 1895/96 | Celtic | 30 |
| 1896/97 | Heart of Midlothian | 28 |
| 1897/98 | Celtic | 33 |
| 1898/99 | Rangers | 36 |
| 1899-1900 | Rangers | 32 |
| 1900/01 | Rangers | 35 |
| 1901/02 | Rangers | 28 |
| 1902/03 | Hibernian | 37 |
| 1903/04 | Third Lanark | 43 |
| 1904/05 | Celtic (after play-off) | 41 |
| 1905/06 | Celtic | 49 |
| 1906/07 | Celtic | 55 |
| 1907/08 | Celtic | 55 |
| 1908/09 | Celtic | 51 |
| 1909/10 | Celtic | 54 |
| 1910/11 | Rangers | 52 |
| 1911/12 | Rangers | 51 |
| 1912/13 | Rangers | 53 |
| 1913/14 | Celtic | 65 |
| 1914/15 | Celtic | 65 |
| 1915/16 | Celtic | 67 |
| 1916/17 | Celtic | 64 |
| 1917/18 | Rangers | 56 |
| 1918/19 | Celtic | 58 |
| 1919/20 | Rangers | 71 |
| 1920/21 | Rangers | 76 |
| 1921/22 | Celtic | 67 |
| 1922/23 | Rangers | 55 |
| 1923/24 | Rangers | 59 |
| 1924/25 | Rangers | 60 |
| 1925/26 | Celtic | 58 |
| 1926/27 | Rangers | 56 |
| 1927/28 | Rangers | 60 |
| 1928/29 | Rangers | 67 |
| 1929/30 | Rangers | 60 |
| 1930/31 | Rangers | 60 |
| 1931/32 | Motherwell | 66 |
| 1932/33 | Rangers | 62 |
| 1933/34 | Rangers | 66 |
| 1934/35 | Rangers | 55 |
| 1935/36 | Celtic | 66 |
| 1936/37 | Rangers | 61 |
| 1937/38 | Celtic | 61 |
| 1938/39 | Rangers | 59 |
| Seasons 1939/40 to 1945/46 - (No Competition) | | |
| 1946/47 | Rangers | 46 |
| 1947/48 | Hibernian | 48 |
| 1948/49 | Rangers | 46 |
| 1949/50 | Rangers | 50 |
| 1950/51 | Hibernian | 48 |
| 1951/52 | Hibernian | 45 |
| 1952/53 | Rangers* | 43 |

| SEASON | DIVISION ONE | POINTS |
|---|---|---|
| 1953/54 | Celtic | 43 |
| 1954/55 | Aberdeen | 49 |
| 1955/56 | Rangers | 52 |
| 1956/57 | Rangers | 55 |
| 1957/58 | Heart of Midlothian | 62 |
| 1958/59 | Rangers | 50 |
| 1959/60 | Heart of Midlothian | 54 |
| 1960/61 | Rangers | 51 |
| 1961/62 | Dundee | 54 |
| 1962/63 | Rangers | 57 |
| 1963/64 | Rangers | 55 |
| 1964/65 | Kilmarnock* | 50 |
| 1965/66 | Celtic | 57 |
| 1966/67 | Celtic | 58 |
| 1967/68 | Celtic | 63 |
| 1968/69 | Celtic | 54 |
| 1969/70 | Celtic | 57 |
| 1970/71 | Celtic | 56 |
| 1971/72 | Celtic | 60 |
| 1972/73 | Celtic | 57 |
| 1973/74 | Celtic | 53 |
| 1974/75 | Rangers | 56 |

| SEASON | DIVISION TWO | POINTS |
|---|---|---|
| 1890/91 | (No Competition) | |
| 1891/92 | (No Competition) | |
| 1892/93 | (No Competition) | |
| 1893/94 | Hibernian | 29 |
| 1894/95 | Hibernian | 30 |
| 1895/96 | Abercorn | 27 |
| 1896/97 | Partick Thistle | 31 |
| 1897/98 | Kilmarnock | 29 |
| 1898/99 | Kilmarnock | 32 |
| 1899-1900 | Partick Thistle | 29 |
| 1900/01 | St. Bernards | 25 |
| 1901/02 | Port Glasgow | 32 |
| 1902/03 | Airdrieonians | 35 |
| 1903/04 | Hamilton Academical | 37 |
| 1904/05 | Clyde | 32 |
| 1905/06 | Leith Athletic | 34 |
| 1906/07 | St. Bernards | 32 |
| 1907/08 | Raith Rovers | 30 |
| 1908/09 | Abercorn | 31 |
| 1909/10 | Leith Athletic | 33 |
| 1910/11 | Dumbarton | 31 |
| 1911/12 | Ayr United | 35 |
| 1912/13 | Ayr United | 34 |
| 1913/14 | Cowdenbeath | 31 |
| 1914/15 | Cowdenbeath | 37 |
| 1915/16 | (No Competition) | |
| 1916/17 | (No Competition) | |
| 1917/18 | (No Competition) | |
| 1918/19 | (No Competition) | |
| 1919/20 | (No Competition) | |
| 1920/21 | (No Competition) | |
| 1921/22 | Alloa | 60 |
| 1922/23 | Queen's Park | 57 |
| 1923/24 | St. Johnstone | 56 |
| 1924/25 | Dundee United | 50 |

| SEASON | DIVISION TWO | POINTS |
|---|---|---|
| 1925/26 | Dunfermline Athletic | 59 |
| 1926/27 | Bo'ness | 56 |
| 1927/28 | Ayr United | 54 |
| 1928/29 | Dundee United | 51 |
| 1929/30 | Leith Athletic * | 57 |
| 1930/31 | Third Lanark | 61 |
| 1931/32 | East Stirlingshire * | 55 |
| 1932/33 | Hibernian | 54 |
| 1933/34 | Albion Rovers | 45 |
| 1934/35 | Third Lanark | 52 |
| 1935/36 | Falkirk | 59 |
| 1936/37 | Ayr United | 54 |
| 1937/38 | Raith Rovers | 59 |
| 1938/39 | Cowdenbeath | 60 |
| Seasons 1939/40 to 1945/46 - (No Competition) | | |
| 1946/47 | Dundee | 45 |
| 1947/48 | East Fife | 53 |
| 1948/49 | Raith Rovers * | 42 |
| 1949/50 | Morton | 47 |
| 1950/51 | Queen of the South * | 45 |
| 1951/52 | Clyde | 44 |
| 1952/53 | Stirling Albion | 44 |
| 1953/54 | Motherwell | 45 |
| 1954/55 | Airdrieonians | 46 |
| 1955/56 | Queen's Park | 54 |
| 1956/57 | Clyde | 64 |
| 1957/58 | Stirling Albion | 55 |
| 1958/59 | Ayr United | 60 |
| 1959/60 | St. Johnstone | 53 |
| 1960/61 | Stirling Albion | 55 |
| 1961/62 | Clyde | 54 |
| 1962/63 | St. Johnstone | 55 |
| 1963/64 | Morton | 67 |
| 1964/65 | Stirling Albion | 59 |
| 1965/66 | Ayr United | 53 |
| 1966/67 | Morton | 69 |
| 1967/68 | St. Mirren | 62 |
| 1968/69 | Motherwell | 64 |
| 1969/70 | Falkirk | 56 |
| 1970/71 | Partick Thistle | 56 |
| 1971/72 | Dumbarton ¥ | 52 |
| 1972/73 | Clyde | 56 |
| 1973/74 | Airdrieonians | 60 |
| 1974/75 | Falkirk | 54 |

| SEASON | PREMIER DIVISION | POINTS |
|---|---|---|
| 1975/76 | Rangers | 54 |
| 1976/77 | Celtic | 55 |
| 1977/78 | Rangers | 55 |
| 1978/79 | Celtic | 48 |
| 1979/80 | Aberdeen | 48 |
| 1980/81 | Celtic | 56 |
| 1981/82 | Celtic | 55 |
| 1982/83 | Dundee United | 56 |
| 1983/84 | Aberdeen | 57 |
| 1984/85 | Aberdeen | 59 |
| 1985/86 • | Celtic ¥ | 50 |
| 1986/87 • | Rangers | 69 |

| | | |
|---|---|---|
| 1987/88 • | Celtic | 72 |
| 1988/89 § | Rangers | 56 |
| 1989/90 § | Rangers | 51 |
| 1990/91 § | Rangers | 55 |
| 1991/92 § | Rangers | 72 |
| 1992/93 | Rangers | 73 |
| 1993/94 | Rangers | 58 |
| 1994/95 = | Rangers | 69 |
| 1995/96 = | Rangers | 87 |
| 1996/97 = | Rangers | 80 |
| 1997/98 = | Celtic | 74 |

### SCOTTISH PREMIER LEAGUE

| | | |
|---|---|---|
| 1998/99 | Rangers ← | 77 |
| 1999/2000 | Rangers ← | 90 |
| 2000/01 | Celtic ← | 97 |
| 2001/02 | Celtic ← | 103 |
| 2002/03 ¥ | Rangers ← | 97 |
| 2003/04 | Celtic ← | 98 |
| 2004/05 | Rangers ← | 93 |

| SEASON | FIRST DIVISION | POINTS |
|---|---|---|
| 1975/76 | Partick Thistle | 41 |
| 1976/77 | St. Mirren | 62 |
| 1977/78 | Morton ¥ | 58 |
| 1978/79 | Dundee | 55 |
| 1979/80 | Heart of Midlothian | 53 |
| 1980/81 | Hibernian | 57 |
| 1981/82 | Motherwell | 61 |
| 1982/83 | St. Johnstone | 55 |
| 1983/84 | Morton | 54 |
| 1984/85 | Motherwell | 50 |
| 1985/86 • | Hamilton Academical | 56 |
| 1986/87 • | Morton | 57 |
| 1987/88 • | Hamilton Academical | 56 |
| 1988/89 § | Dunfermline Athletic | 54 |
| 1989/90 § | St. Johnstone | 58 |
| 1990/91 § | Falkirk | 54 |
| 1991/92 § | Dundee | 58 |
| 1992/93 | Raith Rovers | 65 |
| 1993/94 | Falkirk | 66 |
| 1994/95 = | Raith Rovers | 69 |
| 1995/96 = | Dunfermline Athletic | 71 |
| 1996/97 = | St. Johnstone | 80 |
| 1997/98 = | Dundee | 70 |

| SEASON | S.F.L. FIRST DIVISION | POINTS |
|---|---|---|
| 1998/99 | Hibernian | 89 |
| 1999/2000 | St. Mirren → | 76 |
| 2000/01 | Livingston → | 76 |
| 2001/02 | Partick Thistle → | 66 |
| 2002/03 | Falkirk → | 81 |
| 2003/04 | Inverness Caledonian Thistle → | 70 |
| 2004/05 | Falkirk → | 75 |

| SEASON | SECOND DIVISION | POINTS |
|---|---|---|
| 1975/76 | Clydebank ¥ | 40 |
| 1976/77 | Stirling Albion | 55 |
| 1977/78 | Clyde ¥ | 53 |

| | | |
|---|---|---|
| 1978/79 | Berwick Rangers | 54 |
| 1979/80 | Falkirk | 50 |
| 1980/81 | Queen's Park | 50 |
| 1981/82 | Clyde | 59 |
| 1982/83 | Brechin City | 55 |
| 1983/84 | Forfar Athletic | 63 |
| 1984/85 | Montrose | 53 |
| 1985/86 • | Dunfermline Athletic | 57 |
| 1986/87 • | Meadowbank Thistle | 55 |
| 1987/88 • | Ayr United | 61 |
| 1988/89 § | Albion Rovers | 50 |
| 1989/90 § | Brechin City | 49 |
| 1990/91 § | Stirling Albion | 54 |
| 1991/92 § | Dumbarton | 52 |
| 1992/93 | Clyde | 54 |
| 1993/94 | Stranraer | 56 |
| 1994/95 = | Greenock Morton | 64 |
| 1995/96 = | Stirling Albion | 81 |
| 1996/97 = | Ayr United | 77 |
| 1997/98 = | Stranraer | 61 |

| SEASON | S.F.L. SECOND DIVISION | POINTS |
|---|---|---|
| 1998/99 | Livingston | 77 |
| 1999/2000 | Clyde → | 65 |
| 2000/01 | Partick Thistle → | 75 |
| 2001/02 | Queen of the South → | 67 |
| 2002/03 | Raith Rovers → | 59 |
| 2003/04 | Airdrie United → | 70 |
| 2004/05 | Brechin City → | 72 |

| SEASON | THIRD DIVISION | POINTS |
|---|---|---|
| 1994/95 = | Forfar Athletic | 80 |
| 1995/96 = | Livingston | 72 |
| 1996/97 = | Inverness Caledonian Thistle | 76 |
| 1997/98 = | Alloa Athletic | 76 |

| SEASON | S.F.L. THIRD DIVISION | POINTS |
|---|---|---|
| 1998/99 | Ross County | 77 |
| 1999/2000 | Queen's Park → | 69 |
| 2000/01 | ¥ Hamilton Acad. → | 76 |
| 2001/02 | Brechin City → | 73 |
| 2002/03 | Morton → | 72 |
| 2003/04 | Stranraer → | 79 |
| 2004/05 | Gretna → | 98 |

### KEY TO COMPETITIONS

*    Champions on goal average.

¥    Champions on goal difference.

•    Competition known as Fine Fare League.

=    Competition known as Bell's League Championship.

§    Competition known as B&Q League.

→    Competition known as Bell's Scottish Football League Championship.

←    Competition known as Bank of Scotland Premier League.

RANGERS - SPL CHAMPIONS 2004.05
Rangers defender Marvin Andrews holds aloft the SPL Trophy.

FALKIRK - FIRST DIVISION CHAMPIONS 2004.05
Falkirk's Daniel McBreen holds aloft the First Division Championship Trophy.

**SEASON 1946/47**
5th April, 1947 at Hampden Park;
Attendance 82,584; Referee: Mr R. Calder (Rutherglen)
**RANGERS 4        ABERDEEN 0**
Gillick, Williamson, Duncanson (2)

**SEASON 1947/48**
25th October, 1947 at Hampden Park;
Attendance 52,781; Referee: Mr P. Craigmyle (Aberdeen)
**EAST FIFE 0        FALKIRK 0**
After Extra Time
**REPLAY**
1st November, 1947 at Hampden Park;
Attendance 30,664; Referee: Mr P. Craigmyle (Aberdeen)
**EAST FIFE 4        FALKIRK 1**
Duncan (3), Adams        Aikman

**SEASON 1948/49**
12th March, 1949 at Hampden Park;
Attendance 53,359; Referee: Mr W. G. Livingstone (Glasgow)
**RANGERS 2        RAITH ROVERS 0**
Gillick, Paton

**SEASON 1949/50**
29th October, 1949 at Hampden Park;
Attendance 38,897; Referee: Mr W. Webb (Glasgow)
**EAST FIFE 3        DUNFERMLINE ATH. 0**
Fleming, Duncan, Morris

**SEASON 1950/51**
28th October, 1950 at Hampden Park;
Attendance 63,074; Referee: Mr J. A. Mowat (Glasgow)
**MOTHERWELL 3        HIBERNIAN 0**
Kelly, Forrest, Watters

**SEASON 1951/52**
27th October, 1951 at Hampden Park;
Attendance 91,075; Referee: Mr J. A. Mowat (Glasgow)
**DUNDEE 3        RANGERS 2**
Flavell, Pattillo, Boyd        Findlay, Thornton

**SEASON 1952/53**
25th October, 1952 at Hampden Park;
Attendance 51,830; Referee: Mr J. A. Mowat (Glasgow)
**DUNDEE 2        KILMARNOCK 0**
Flavell (2)

**SEASON 1953/54**
24th October, 1953 at Hampden Park;
Attendance 88,529; Referee: Mr J. S. Cox (Rutherglen)
**EAST FIFE 3        PARTICK THISTLE 2**
Gardiner, Fleming,        Walker, McKenzie
Christie

**SEASON 1954/55**
23rd October, 1954 at Hampden Park;
Attendance 55,640; Referee: Mr J. A. Mowat (Glasgow)
**HEARTS 4        MOTHERWELL 2**
Bauld (3), Wardhaugh        Redpath (pen), Bain

**SEASON 1955/56**
22nd October, 1955 at Hampden Park;
Attendance 44,103; Referee: Mr H. Phillips (Wishaw)
**ABERDEEN 2        ST. MIRREN 1**
Mallan (og), Leggat        Holmes

**SEASON 1956/57**
27th October, 1956 at Hampden Park;
Attendance 58,973; Referee: Mr J. A. Mowat (Glasgow)
**CELTIC 0        PARTICK THISTLE 0**
**REPLAY**
31st October, 1956 at Hampden Park;
Attendance 31,126; Referee: Mr J. A. Mowat (Glasgow)
**CELTIC 3        PARTICK THISTLE 0**
McPhail (2), Collins

**SEASON 1957/58**
19th October, 1957 at Hampden Park;
Attendance 82,293; Referee: Mr J. A. Mowat (Glasgow)
**CELTIC 7        RANGERS 1**
Mochan (2), McPhail (3),        Simpson
Wilson, Fernie (pen)

**SEASON 1958/59**
25th October, 1958 at Hampden Park;
Attendance 59,960; Referee: Mr R. H. Davidson (Airdrie)
**HEARTS 5        PARTICK THISTLE 1**
Murray (2), Bauld (2),        Smith
Hamilton

**SEASON 1959/60**
24th October, 1959 at Hampden Park;
Attendance 57,974; Referee: Mr R. H. Davidson (Airdrie)
**HEARTS 2        THIRD LANARK 1**
Hamilton, Young        Gray

**SEASON 1960/61**
29th October, 1960 at Hampden Park;
Attendance 82,063; Referee: Mr T. Wharton (Glasgow)
**RANGERS 2        KILMARNOCK 0**
Brand, Scott

**SEASON 1961/62**
28th October, 1961 at Hampden Park;
Attendance 88,635; Referee: Mr R. H. Davidson (Airdrie)
**RANGERS 1        HEARTS 1**
Millar        Cumming (pen)
**REPLAY**
18th December, 1961 at Hampden Park;
Attendance 47,552; Referee: Mr R. H. Davidson (Airdrie)
**RANGERS 3        HEARTS 1**
Millar, Brand, McMillan        Davidson

**SEASON 1962/63**
27th October, 1962 at Hampden Park;
Attendance 51,280; Referee: Mr T. Wharton (Glasgow)
**HEARTS 1        KILMARNOCK 0**
Davidson

**SEASON 1963/64**
26th October, 1963 at Hampden Park;
Attendance 105,907; Referee: Mr H. Phillips (Wishaw)
**RANGERS 5        MORTON 0**
Forrest (4), Willoughby

**SEASON 1964/65**
24th October, 1964 at Hampden Park;
Attendance 91,000; Referee: Mr H. Phillips (Wishaw)
**RANGERS 2        CELTIC 1**
Forrest (2)        Johnstone

**SEASON 1965/66**
23rd October, 1965 at Hampden Park;
Attendance 107,609; Referee: Mr H. Phillips (Wishaw)
**CELTIC 2        RANGERS 1**
Hughes (2 (2 pen))        Young (o.g.)

**SEASON 1966/67**
29th October, 1966 at Hampden Park;
Attendance 94,532; Referee: Mr T. Wharton (Glasgow)
**CELTIC 1        RANGERS 0**
Lennox

**SEASON 1967/68**
28th October, 1967 at Hampden Park;
Attendance 66,660; Referee: Mr R. H. Davidson (Airdrie)
**CELTIC 5        DUNDEE 3**
Chalmers (2), Hughes,        G. McLean (2),
Wallace, Lennox        J. McLean

**SEASON 1968/69**
5th April, 1969 at Hampden Park;
Attendance 74,000; Referee: Mr W. M. M. Syme (Airdrie)
**CELTIC 6        HIBERNIAN 2**
Lennox (3), Wallace,        O'Rourke, Stevenson
Auld, Craig

**SEASON 1969/70**
25th October, 1969 at Hampden Park;
Attendance 73,067; Referee: Mr J. W. Paterson (Bothwell)
**CELTIC 1        ST. JOHNSTONE 0**
Auld

**SEASON 1970/71**
24th October, 1970 at Hampden Park;
Attendance 106,263; Referee: Mr T. Wharton (Glasgow)
**RANGERS 1        CELTIC 0**
Johnstone

**SEASON 1971/72**
23rd October, 1971 at Hampden Park;
Attendance 62,740; Referee: Mr W. J. Mullan (Dalkeith)
**PARTICK THISTLE 4        CELTIC 1**
Rae, Lawrie,        Dalglish
McQuade, Bone

**SEASON 1972/73**
9th December, 1972 at Hampden Park;
Attendance 71,696; Referee: Mr A. MacKenzie (Larbert)
**HIBERNIAN 2        CELTIC 1**
Stanton, O'Rourke        Dalglish

**SEASON 1973/74**
15th December, 1973 at Hampden Park;
Attendance 27,974; Referee: Mr R. H. Davidson (Airdrie)
**DUNDEE 1        CELTIC 0**
Wallace

**SEASON 1974/75**
26th October, 1974 at Hampden Park;
Attendance 53,848;
Referee: Mr J. R. P. Gordon (Newport on Tay)
**CELTIC 6        HIBERNIAN 3**
Johnstone, Deans (3),        Harper (3)
Wilson, Murray

**SEASON 1975/76**
25th October, 1975 at Hampden Park;
Attendance 58,806; Referee: Mr W. Anderson (East Kilbride)
RANGERS 1          CELTIC 0
MacDonald

**SEASON 1976/77**
6th November, 1976 at Hampden Park;
Attendance 69,268; Referee: Mr J. W. Paterson (Bothwell)
ABERDEEN 2         CELTIC 1
Jarvie, Robb       Dalglish (pen.)
After extra-time – 1-1 After 90 Minutes

**SEASON 1977/78**
18th March, 1978 at Hampden Park;
Attendance 60,168; Referee: Mr D. F. T. Syme (Rutherglen)
RANGERS 2          CELTIC 1
Cooper, Smith      Edvaldsson
After extra-time – 1-1 After 90 Minutes

**SEASON 1978/79**
31st March, 1979 at Hampden Park;
Attendance 54,000; Referee: Mr I. M. D. Foote (Glasgow)
RANGERS 2          ABERDEEN 1
McMaster (o.g.), Jackson Davidson

**SEASON 1979/80 – BELL'S LEAGUE CUP**
8th December, 1979 at Hampden Park;
Attendance 27,299; Referee: Mr B. R. McGinlay (Balfron)
DUNDEE UNITED 0    ABERDEEN 0
After extra-time
REPLAY
12th December, 1979 at Dens Park;
Attendance 28,984; Referee: Mr B. R. McGinlay (Balfron)
DUNDEE UNITED 3    ABERDEEN 0
Pettigrew (2), Sturrock

**SEASON 1980/81 – BELL'S LEAGUE CUP**
6th December, 1980 at Dens Park;
Attendance 24,466; Referee: Mr R. B. Valentine (Dundee)
DUNDEE UNITED 3    DUNDEE 0
Dodds, Sturrock (2)

**SEASON 1981/82**
28th November, 1981 at Hampden Park;
Attendance 53,795; Referee: Mr E. H. Pringle (Edinburgh)
RANGERS 2          DUNDEE UNITED 1
Cooper, Redford    Milne

**SEASON 1982/83**
4th December, 1982 at Hampden Park;
Attendance 55,372; Referee: Mr K. J. Hope (Clarkston)
CELTIC 2           RANGERS 1
Nicholas, MacLeod  Bett

**SEASON 1983/84**
25th March, 1984 at Hampden Park;
Attendance 66,369; Referee: Mr R. B. Valentine (Dundee)
RANGERS 3          CELTIC 2
McCoist 3 (1 pen)  McClair, Reid (pen)
After extra-time – 2-2 After 90 Minutes

**SEASON 1984/85 – SKOL CUP**
28th October, 1984 at Hampden Park;
Attendance 44,698; Referee: Mr B. R. McGinlay (Balfron)
RANGERS 1          DUNDEE UNITED 0
Ferguson

**SEASON 1985/86 – SKOL CUP**
27th October, 1985 at Hampden Park;
Attendance 40,065; Referee: Mr R. B. Valentine (Dundee)
ABERDEEN 3         HIBERNIAN 0
Black (2), Stark

**SEASON 1986/87 – SKOL CUP**
26th October, 1986 at Hampden Park;
Attendance 74,219; Referee: Mr D. F. T. Syme (Rutherglen)
RANGERS 2          CELTIC 1
Durrant, Cooper (pen)   McClair

**SEASON 1987/88 – SKOL CUP**
25th October, 1987 at Hampden Park;
Attendance 71,961; Referee: Mr R. B. Valentine (Dundee)
RANGERS 3          ABERDEEN 3
Cooper, Durrant, Fleck   Bett, Falconer, Hewitt
After extra-time – 3-3 After 90 Minutes
Rangers won 5-3 on Kicks from the Penalty Mark

**SEASON 1988/89 – SKOL CUP**
23rd October, 1988 at Hampden Park;
Attendance 72,122; Referee: Mr G. B. Smith (Edinburgh)
RANGERS 3          ABERDEEN 2
McCoist (2), I. Ferguson   Dodds (2)

**SEASON 1989/90 – SKOL CUP**
22nd October, 1989 at Hampden Park;
Attendance 61,190; Referee: Mr G. B. Smith (Edinburgh)
ABERDEEN 2         RANGERS 1
Mason (2)          Walters (pen)
After extra-time – 1-1 after 90 minutes

**SEASON 1990/91 – SKOL CUP**
28th October, 1990 at Hampden Park;
Attendance 62,817; Referee: Mr J. McCluskey (Stewarton)
RANGERS 2          CELTIC 1
Walters, Gough     Elliott
After extra-time – 1-1 After 90 minutes

**SEASON 1991/92 – SKOL CUP**
27th October, 1991 at Hampden Park;
Attendance 40,377; Referee: Mr B. R. McGinlay (Balfron)
HIBERNIAN 2        DUNFERMLINE ATH. 0
McIntyre (pen), Wright

**SEASON 1992/93 – SKOL CUP**
25th October, 1992 at Hampden Park;
Attendance 45,298; Referee: Mr D. D. Hope (Erskine)
RANGERS 2          ABERDEEN 1
McCall, Smith (o.g.)   Shearer
After extra-time – 1-1 after 90 minutes

**SEASON 1993/94**
24th October, 1993 at Celtic Park;
Attendance 47,632; Referee: Mr J. McCluskey (Stewarton)
RANGERS 2          HIBERNIAN 1
Durrant, McCoist   McPherson (o.g.)

**SEASON 1994/95 – COCA-COLA CUP**
27th November, 1994 at Ibrox Stadium;
Attendance 45,384; Referee: Mr J. McCluskey (Stewarton)
RAITH ROVERS 2     CELTIC 2
S. Crawford, G. Dalziel   C. Nicholas, A. Walker
After extra-time – 2-2 after 90 minutes
Raith Rovers won 6-5 on Kicks from the
Penalty Mark

Dundee United's Paul Hegarty celebrates the Tannadice club's League Cup Trophy success in season 1980.81

Aberdeen's Alex McLeish and Willie Miller celebrate the Dons' League Cup victory over Rangers in season 1989.90

Hibernian's goalscoring heroes Keith Wright and Tommy McIntyre with the League Cup Trophy after the Easter Road club's success in season 1991.92

**SEASON 1995/96 – COCA-COLA CUP**
26th November, 1995 at Hampden Park;
Attendance 33,099; Referee: Mr L.W. Mottram (Forth)
**ABERDEEN 2          DUNDEE 0**
D. Shearer, W. Dodds

**SEASON 1996/97 – COCA-COLA CUP**
24th November, 1996 at Celtic Park;
Attendance 48,559; Referee: Mr H. Dallas (Motherwell)
**RANGERS 4          HEARTS 3**
P. Gascoigne (2),          D. Weir, S. Fulton,
A. McCoist (2)          J. Robertson

**SEASON1997/98 – COCA-COLA CUP**
30th November, 1997 at Ibrox Stadium;
Attendance 49,305; Referee: Mr J. McCluskey (Stewarton)
**CELTIC 3          DUNDEE UNITED 0**
M. Rieper, H. Larsson, C. Burley

**SEASON 1998/99**
29th November, 1998 at Celtic Park;
Attendance 45,533; Referee: Mr H. Dallas (Motherwell)
**RANGERS 2          ST. JOHNSTONE 1**
S. Guivarc'h, J. Albertz     N. Dasovic

**SEASON 1999/2000 – CIS INSURANCE CUP**
19th March, 2000 at The National Stadium,
Hampden Park; Attendance 50,073;
Referee: Mr K. Clark (Paisley)
**CELTIC 2          ABERDEEN 0**
V. Riseth, T. Johnson

**SEASON 2000/01 – CIS INSURANCE CUP**
18th March, 2001 at The National Stadium,
Hampden Park; Attendance 48,830;
Referee: Mr H. Dallas (Motherwell)
**CELTIC 3          KILMARNOCK 0**
H. Larsson (3)

**SEASON 2001/02 – CIS INSURANCE CUP**
17th March, 2002 at The National Stadium,
Hampden Park; Attendance 50,076;
Referee: Mr H. Dallas (Motherwell)
**RANGERS 4          AYR UNITED 0**
T.A. Flo, B. Ferguson,
C. Caniggia (2)

**SEASON 2002/03 – CIS INSURANCE CUP**
16th March, 2003 at The National Stadium,
Hampden Park; Attendance 50,034;
Referee: Mr K. Clark (Paisley)
**RANGERS 2          CELTIC 1**
C. Caniggia,          H. Larsson
P. Lovenkrands

**SEASON 2003/04 – CIS INSURANCE CUP**
14th March, 2004 at The National Stadium,
Hampden Park, Glasgow; Attendance 45,443
Referee: Mr. W. Young (Glasgow)
**LIVINGSTON 2          HIBERNIAN 0**
D. Lilley, J. McAllister

**SEASON 2004/05 – CIS INSURANCE CUP**
20th March, 2005 at The National Stadium,
Hampden Park; Attendance 50,182;
Referee: Mr M. McCurry (Glasgow)
**RANGERS 5          MOTHERWELL 1**
M.Ross, S.Kyrgiakos (2)     D. Partridge
F.Ricksen, I.Novo

**WINNERS AND APPEARANCES IN FINALS**

|  | WINS | APPS* |
|---|---|---|
| RANGERS | 24 | 30 |
| CELTIC | 12 | 25 |
| ABERDEEN | 5 | 12 |
| HEART OF MIDLOTHIAN | 4 | 6 |
| DUNDEE | 3 | 6 |
| EAST FIFE | 3 | 3 |
| DUNDEE UNITED | 2 | 5 |
| HIBERNIAN | 2 | 8 |
| LIVINGSTON | 1 | 1 |
| MOTHERWELL | 1 | 3 |
| PARTICK THISTLE | 1 | 4 |
| RAITH ROVERS | 1 | 2 |
| KILMARNOCK | - | 4 |
| DUNFERMLINE ATH. | - | 2 |
| ST. JOHNSTONE | - | 2 |
| AYR UNITED | - | 1 |
| FALKIRK | - | 1 |
| MORTON | - | 1 |
| ST. MIRREN | - | 1 |
| THIRD LANARK | - | 1 |

* (Figures do not include replays)

Rangers - CIS Insurance Cup Winners Season 2004.05

**SEASON 1873/74**
21st March, 1874 at First Hampden; Att: 2,500
**QUEEN'S PARK 2        CLYDESDALE 0**
W. McKinnon, Leckie

**SEASON 1874/75**
10th April, 1875 at First Hampden; Att: 7,000
**QUEEN'S PARK 3        RENTON 0**
A. McKinnon, Highet,
W. McKinnon

**SEASON 1875/76**
11th March, 1876 at Hamilton Crescent; Att: 10,000
**QUEEN'S PARK 1        THIRD LANARK 1**
Highet                  Drinnan
**REPLAY**
18th March, 1876 at Hamilton Crescent; Att: 6,000
**QUEEN'S PARK 2        THIRD LANARK 0**
Highet (2)

**SEASON 1876/77**
17th March, 1877 at Hamilton Crescent; Att: 12,000
**VALE OF LEVEN 1       RANGERS 1**
Paton                   McDougall (o.g.)
**REPLAY**
7th April, 1877 at Hamilton Crescent; Att: 15,000
**VALE OF LEVEN 1       RANGERS 1 (AET)**
McDougall               Dunlop
**SECOND REPLAY**
13th April, 1877 at First Hampden; Att: 8,000
**VALE OF LEVEN 3       RANGERS 2**
Watson (o.g.),          P. Campbell,
Baird, Paton            W. McNeil

**SEASON 1877/78**
30th March, 1878 at First Hampden; Att: 5,000
**VALE OF LEVEN 1       THIRD LANARK 0**
McDougall

**SEASON 1878/79**
19th April, 1879 at First Hampden; Att: 6,000
**VALE OF LEVEN 1       RANGERS 1**
Ferguson                Struthers
VALE OF LEVEN WERE AWARDED CUP
AFTER RANGERS FAILED TO TURN UP
FOR A REPLAY ON 26TH APRIL, 1879.

**SEASON 1879/80**
21st February, 1880 at First Cathkin; Att: 7,000
**QUEEN'S PARK 3        THORNLIEBANK 0**
Highet (2,) Kerr

**SEASON 1880/81**
26th March, 1881 at Kinning Park; Att: 10,000
**QUEEN'S PARK 2        DUMBARTON 1**
McNeil, Kay             McAulay
AFTER A PROTEST BY DUMBARTON,
A REPLAY WAS ORDERED.
**REPLAY**
9th April, 1881 at Kinning Park; Att: 10,000
**QUEEN'S PARK 3        DUMBARTON 1**
Smith (2), Kerr         Meikleham

**SEASON 1881/82**
18th March, 1882 at First Cathkin; Att: 12,000
**QUEEN'S PARK 2        DUMBARTON 2**
Harrower (2)            Brown, Meikleham
**REPLAY**
1st April, 1882 at First Cathkin; Att: 15,000
**QUEEN'S PARK 4        DUMBARTON 1**
Richmond, Kerr,         J. Miller
Harrower, Kay

**SEASON 1882/83**
31st March, 1883 at First Hampden; Att: 15,000
**DUMBARTON 2           VALE OF LEVEN 2**
Paton, McArthur         Johnstone, McCrae

**REPLAY**
7th April, 1883 at First Hampden; Att: 8,000
**DUMBARTON 2           VALE OF LEVEN 1**
Anderson, R. Brown      Friel

**SEASON 1883/84**
23rd February, 1884 at First Cathkin
**VALE OF LEVEN V QUEEN'S PARK**
VALE OF LEVEN FAILED TO TURN UP FOR
THE FINAL WITH QUEEN'S PARK AND IT
WAS LATER DECIDED TO AWARD THE CUP
TO QUEEN'S PARK.

**SEASON 1884/85**
21st February, 1885 at Second Hampden; Att: 2,500
**RENTON 0              VALE OF LEVEN 0**
**REPLAY**
28th February, 1885 at Second Hampden; Att: 3,500
**RENTON 3              VALE OF LEVEN 0**
J. McCall, McIntyre (2) Gillies

**SEASON 1885/86**
13th February, 1886 at First Cathkin; Att: 7,000
**QUEEN'S PARK 3        RENTON 1**
Hamilton, Christie,     Kelso
Somerville

**SEASON 1886/87**
12th February, 1887 at Second Hampden; Att: 10,000
**HIBERNIAN 2           DUMBARTON 1**
Smith, Groves           Aitken

**SEASON 1887/88**
4th February, 1888 at Second Hampden; Att: 10,000
**RENTON 6              CAMBUSLANG 1**
D. Campbell,            H. Gourlay
McCallum, McNee,
McCall (2), J. Campbell

**SEASON 1888/89**
2nd February, 1889 at Second Hampden; Att: 17,000
**THIRD LANARK 3        CELTIC 0**
Oswald Jun. (2), Hannah
A REPLAY WAS ORDERED AFTER PROTESTS
CONCERNING GROUND CONDITIONS.
**REPLAY**
9th February, 1889 at Second Hampden; Att: 16,000
**THIRD LANARK 2        CELTIC 1**
Marshall, Oswald Jun.   McCallum

**SEASON 1889/90**
15th February, 1890 at First Ibrox; Att: 10,000
**QUEEN'S PARK 1        VALE OF LEVEN 1**
Hamilton                McLachlan
**REPLAY**
22nd February, 1890 at First Ibrox; Att: 14,000
**QUEEN'S PARK 2        VALE OF LEVEN 1**
Hamilton, Stewart       Bruce

**SEASON 1890/91**
7th February, 1891 at Second Hampden; Att: 14,000
**HEARTS 1              DUMBARTON 0**
Russell

**SEASON 1891/92**
12th March, 1892 at First Ibrox; Att: 40,000
**CELTIC 1              QUEEN'S PARK 0**
Campbell
CROWD ENCROACHMENT OCCURRED AT
THE ABOVE GAME AND AS A RESULT THE
GAME WAS CONSIDERED A FRIENDLY.
**REPLAY**
9th April, 1892 at First Ibrox; Att: 20,000
**CELTIC 5              QUEEN'S PARK 1**
Campbell (2),           Waddell
McMahon (2), Sillars (o.g.)

**SEASON 1892/93**
25th February, 1893 at First Ibrox; Att: 20,000
**CELTIC 1              QUEEN'S PARK 0**
Towie
A REPLAY WAS ORDERED BECAUSE OF
GROUND CONDITIONS AND THE ABOVE
GAME WAS CONSIDERED A FRIENDLY.
**REPLAY**
11th March, 1893 at First Ibrox; Att: 15,000
**QUEEN'S PARK 2        CELTIC 1**
Sellar (2)              Blessington

**SEASON 1893/94**
17th February, 1894 at Second Hampden; Att: 15,000
**RANGERS 3             CELTIC 1**
H. McCreadie, Barker,   W. Maley
McPherson

**SEASON 1894/95**
20th April, 1895 at First Ibrox; Att: 13,500
**ST. BERNARD'S 2       RENTON 1**
Clelland (2)            Duncan

**SEASON 1895/96**
14th March, 1896 at Logie Green; Att: 16,034
**HEARTS 3              HIBERNIAN 1**
Baird, Walker, Michael  O'Neill

**SEASON 1896/97**
20th March, 1897 at Second Hampden; Att: 15,000
**RANGERS 5             DUMBARTON 1**
Miller (2), Hyslop,     W. Thomson
McPherson, A. Smith

**SEASON 1897/98**
26th March, 1898 at Second Hampden; Att: 14,000
**RANGERS 2             KILMARNOCK 0**
A. Smith, Hamilton

**SEASON 1898/99**
22nd April, 1899 at Second Hampden; Att: 25,000
**CELTIC 2              RANGERS 0**
McMahon, Hodge

**SEASON 1899/1900**
14th April, 1900 at Second Hampden; Att: 25,000
**CELTIC 4              QUEEN'S PARK 3**
McMahon,                Christie, W. Stewart,
Divers (2), Bell        Battles (o.g.)

**SEASON 1900/01**
6th April, 1901 at Ibrox; Att: 15,000
**HEARTS 4              CELTIC 3**
Walker, Bell (2),       McOustra (2),
Thomson                 McMahon

**SEASON 1901/02**
26th April, 1902 at Celtic Park; Att: 16,000
**HIBERNIAN 1           CELTIC 0**
McGeachan

**SEASON 1902/03**
11th April, 1903 at Celtic Park; Att: 28,000
**RANGERS 1             HEARTS 1**
Stark                   Walker
**REPLAY**
18th April, 1903 at Celtic Park; Att: 16,000
**RANGERS 0             HEARTS 0**
**SECOND REPLAY**
25th April, 1903 at Celtic Park; Att: 32,000
**RANGERS 2             HEARTS 0**
Mackie, Hamilton

**SEASON 1903/04**
16th April, 1904 at Hampden Park; Att: 64,323
**CELTIC 3              RANGERS 2**
Quinn (3)               Speedie (2)

**SEASON 1904/05**
8th April, 1905 at Hampden Park; Att: 55,000
**THIRD LANARK 0**        **RANGERS 0**
**REPLAY**
15th April, 1905 at Hampden Park; Att: 40,000
**THIRD LANARK 3**        **RANGERS 1**
Wilson (2), Johnstone        Smith

**SEASON 1905/06**
28th April, 1906 at Ibrox; Att: 30,000
**HEARTS 1**        **THIRD LANARK 0**
G. Wilson

**SEASON 1906/07**
20th April, 1907 at Hampden Park; Att: 50,000
**CELTIC 3**        **HEARTS 0**
Orr (Pen), Somers (2)

**SEASON 1907/08**
18th April, 1908 at Hampden Park; Att: 55,000
**CELTIC 5**        **ST. MIRREN 1**
Bennett (2), Hamilton,        Cunningham
Somers, Quinn

**SEASON 1908/09**
10th April, 1909 at Hampden Park; Att: 70,000
**CELTIC 2**        **RANGERS 2**
Quinn, Munro        Gilchrist, Bennett
**REPLAY**
17th April, 1909 at Hampden Park; Att: 60,000
**CELTIC 1**        **RANGERS 1**
Quinn        Gordon
**CUP WITHHELD AFTER RIOT
FOLLOWING REPLAY.**

**SEASON 1909/10**
9th April, 1910 at Ibrox; Att: 60,000
**DUNDEE 2**        **CLYDE 2**
Blair (o.g.), Langlands        Chalmers, Booth
**REPLAY**
16th April, 1910 at Ibrox; Att: 20,000
**DUNDEE 0**        **CLYDE 0 (A.E.T.)**
**SECOND REPLAY**
20th April, 1910 at Ibrox; Att: 24,000
**DUNDEE 2**        **CLYDE 1**
Bellamy, Hunter        Chalmers

**SEASON 1910/11**
8th April, 1911 at Ibrox; Att: 45,000
**CELTIC 0**        **HAMILTON ACAD. 0**
**REPLAY**
15th April, 1911 at Ibrox; Att: 25,000
**CELTIC 2**        **HAMILTON ACAD. 0**
Quinn, McAteer

**SEASON 1911/12**
6th April, 1912 at Ibrox; Att: 45,000
**CELTIC 2**        **CLYDE 0**
McMenemy, Gallagher

**SEASON 1912/13**
12th April, 1913 at Celtic Park; Att: 45,000
**FALKIRK 2**        **RAITH ROVERS 0**
Robertson, T. Logan

**SEASON 1913/14**
11th April, 1914 at Ibrox; Att: 55,000
**CELTIC 0**        **HIBERNIAN 0**
**REPLAY**
16th April, 1914 at Ibrox; Att: 36,000
**CELTIC 4**        **HIBERNIAN 1**
McColl (2), Browning (2)        Smith

**SEASONS 1914/15 TO 1918/19
NO COMPETITIONS DUE TO FIRST WORLD WAR**

**SEASON 1919/20**
17th April, 1920 at Hampden Park; Att: 95,000;
Referee: Mr W. Bell (Hamilton)
**KILMARNOCK 3**        **ALBION ROVERS 2**
Culley, Shortt, J. Smith        Watson, Hillhouse

**SEASON 1920/21**
16th April, 1921 at Celtic Park; Att: 28,294;
Referee: Mr H. Humphreys (Greenock)
**PARTICK THISTLE 1**        **RANGERS 0**
Blair

**SEASON 1921/22**
15th April, 1922 at Hampden Park; Att: 75,000
Referee: Mr T. Dougray (Bellshill)
**MORTON 1**        **RANGERS 0**
Gourlay

**SEASON 1922/23**
31th March, 1923 at Hampden Park; Att:
80,100; Referee: Mr T. Dougray (Bellshill)
**CELTIC 1**        **HIBERNIAN 0**
Cassidy

**SEASON 1923/24**
19th April, 1924 at Ibrox Stadium; Att: 59,218;
Referee: Mr T. Dougray (Bellshill)
**AIRDRIEONIANS 2**        **HIBERNIAN 0**
Russell (2)

**SEASON 1924/25**
11th April, 1925 at Hampden Park;
Att: 75,137; Referee: Mr T. Dougray (Bellshill)
**CELTIC 2**        **DUNDEE 1**
Gallacher, McGrory        McLean

**SEASON 1925/26**
10th April, 1926 at Hampden Park; Att: 98,620;
Referee: Mr P. Craigmyle (Aberdeen)
**ST. MIRREN 2**        **CELTIC 0**
McCrae, Howieson

**SEASON 1926/27**
16th April, 1927 at Hampden Park; Att: 80,070;
Referee: Mr T. Dougray (Bellshill)
**CELTIC 3**        **EAST FIFE 1**
Robertson (o.g.),        Wood
McLean, Connolly

**SEASON 1927/28**
14th April, 1928 at Hampden Park; Att: 118,115;
Referee: Mr W. Bell (Motherwell)
**RANGERS 4**        **CELTIC 0**
Meiklejohn (pen),
Archibald (2), McPhail

**SEASON 1928/29**
6th April, 1929 at Hampden Park; Att: 114,708;
Referee: Mr T. Dougray (Bellshill)
**KILMARNOCK 2**        **RANGERS 0**
Aitken, Williamson

**SEASON 1929/30**
12th April, 1930 at Hampden Park; Att: 107,475;
Referee: Mr W. Bell (Motherwell)
**RANGERS 0**        **PARTICK THISTLE 0**
**REPLAY**
16th April, 1930 at Hampden Park; Att: 103,686;
Referee: Mr W. Bell (Motherwell)
**RANGERS 2**        **PARTICK THISTLE 1**
Marshall, Craig        Torbet

**SEASON 1930/31**
11th April, 1931 at Hampden Park; Att: 104,803;
Referee: Mr P. Craigmyle (Aberdeen)
**CELTIC 2**        **MOTHERWELL 2**
McGrory, Craig (o.g.)        Stevenson,
McMenemy
**REPLAY**
15th April, 1931 at Hampden Park; Att: 98,579;
Referee: Mr P. Craigmyle (Aberdeen)
**CELTIC 4**        **MOTHERWELL 2**
R. Thomson (2),        Murdoch, Stevenson
McGrory (2)

**SEASON 1931/32**
16th April, 1932 at Hampden Park; Att:111,982;
Referee: Mr P. Craigmyle (Aberdeen)
**RANGERS 1**        **KILMARNOCK 1**
McPhail        Maxwell
**REPLAY**
20th April, 1932 at Hampden Park; Att: 110,695;
Referee: Mr P. Craigmyle (Aberdeen)
**RANGERS 3**        **KILMARNOCK 0**
Fleming, McPhail, English

**SEASON 1932/33**
15th April, 1933 at Hampden Park; Att:102,339;
Referee: Mr T. Dougray (Bellshill)
**CELTIC 1**        **MOTHERWELL 0**
McGrory

**SEASON 1933/34**
21st April, 1934 at Hampden Park; Att: 113,430;
Referee: Mr M. C. Hutton (Glasgow)
**RANGERS 5**        **ST. MIRREN 0**
Nicholson (2), McPhail,
Main, Smith

**SEASON 1934/35**
20th April, 1935 at Hampden Park; Att: 87,286;
Referee: Mr H. Watson (Glasgow)
**RANGERS 2**        **HAMILTON ACAD.1**
Smith (2)        Harrison

**SEASON 1935/36**
18th April 1936 at Hampden Park; Att: 88,859;
Referee: Mr J. M. Martin (Ladybank)
**RANGERS 1**        **THIRD LANARK 0**
McPhail

**SEASON 1936/37**
24th April, 1937 at Hampden Park; Att: 147,365;
Referee: Mr M. C. Hutton (Glasgow)
**CELTIC 2**        **ABERDEEN 1**
Crum, Buchan        Armstrong

**SEASON 1937/38**
23rd April, 1938 at Hampden Park; Att: 80,091;
Referee: Mr H. Watson (Glasgow)
**EAST FIFE 1**        **KILMARNOCK 1**
McLeod        McAvoy
**REPLAY**
27th April, 1938 at Hampden Park; Att: 92,716;
Referee: Mr H. Watson (Glasgow)
**EAST FIFE 4**        **KILMARNOCK 2**
McKerrell (2),        Thomson (pen),
McLeod, Miller        McGrogan
After extra–time

**SEASON 1938/39**
22nd April, 1939 at Hampden Park; Att: 94,799;
Referee: Mr W. Webb (Glasgow)
**CLYDE 4**        **MOTHERWELL 0**
Wallace, Martin (2), Noble

**SEASONS 1939/40 TO 1945/46 NO
COMPETITIONS DUE TO SECOND WORLD WAR**

**SEASON 1946/47**
19th April, 1947 at Hampden Park;
Att: 82,140; Referee: Mr R. Calder (Glasgow)
**ABERDEEN 2**        **HIBERNIAN 1**
Hamilton, Williams        Cuthbertson

**SEASON 1947/48**
17th April, 1948 at Hampden Park;
Att:129,176;
Referee: Mr J. M. Martin (Blairgowrie)
**RANGERS 1**        **MORTON 1**
Gillick        Whyte
After extra–time
**REPLAY**
21st April, 1948 at Hampden Park; Att: 131,975;
Referee: Mr J. M. Martin (Blairgowrie)
**RANGERS 1**        **MORTON 0**
Williamson        After extra–time

**SEASON 1948/49**
23rd April, 1949 at Hampden Park;
Att: 108,435;
Referee: Mr R. G. Benzie (Irvine)
**RANGERS 4**        **CLYDE 1**
Young (2 (2 pens)),        Galletly
Williamson, Duncanson

**SEASON 1949/50**
22nd April, 1950 at Hampden Park;
Att: 118,262
Referee: Mr J. A. Mowat (Burnside)
**RANGERS 3**        **EAST FIFE 0**
Findlay, Thornton (2)

**SEASON 1950/51**
21st April, 1951 at Hampden Park; Att: 131,943
Referee: Mr J. A. Mowat (Burnside)
**CELTIC 1**        **MOTHERWELL 0**
McPhail

**SEASON 1951/52**
19th April, 1952 at Hampden Park; Att: 136,304;
Referee: Mr J. A. Mowat (Burnside)
**MOTHERWELL 4     DUNDEE 0**
Watson, Redpath,
Humphries, Kelly

**SEASON 1952/53**
25th April, 1953 at Hampden Park; Att: 129,861;
Referee: Mr J. A. Mowat (Burnside)
**RANGERS 1     ABERDEEN 1**
Prentice        Yorston
**REPLAY**
29th April, 1953 at Hampden Park; Att: 112,619;
Referee: Mr J. A. Mowat (Burnside)
**RANGERS 1     ABERDEEN 0**
Simpson

**SEASON 1953/54**
24th April, 1954 at Hampden Park; Att: 129,926;
Referee: Mr C. E. Faultless (Giffnock)
**CELTIC 2     ABERDEEN 1**
Young (o.g.), Fallon     Buckley

**SEASON 1954/55**
23rd April, 1955 at Hampden Park; Att: 106,111;
Referee: Mr C. E. Faultless (Giffnock)
**CLYDE 1     CELTIC 1**
Robertson        Walsh
**REPLAY**
27th April, 1955 at Hampden Park; Att: 68,735;
Referee: Mr C. E. Faultless (Giffnock)
**CLYDE 1     CELTIC 0**
Ring

**SEASON 1955/56**
21st April, 1956 at Hampden Park; Att: 133,399;
Referee: Mr R. H. Davidson (Airdrie)
**HEARTS 3     CELTIC 1**
Crawford (2), Conn     Haughney

**SEASON 1956/57**
20th April, 1957 at Hampden Park; Att: 81,057;
Referee: Mr J. A. Mowat (Burnside)
**FALKIRK 1     KILMARNOCK 1**
Prentice (pen)     Curlett
**REPLAY**
24th April, 1957 at Hampden Park; Att: 79,785;
Referee: Mr J. A. Mowat (Burnside)
**FALKIRK 2     KILMARNOCK 1**
Merchant, Moran     Curlett
After extra–time

**SEASON 1957/58**
26th April, 1958 at Hampden Park; Att: 95,123;
Referee: Mr J. A. Mowat (Burnside)
**CLYDE 1     HIBERNIAN 0**
Coyle

**SEASON 1958/59**
25th April 1959 at Hampden Park; Att: 108,951;
Referee: Mr J. A. Mowat (Burnside)
**ST. MIRREN 3     ABERDEEN 1**
Bryceland, Miller, Baker  Baird

**SEASON 1959/60**
23rd April, 1960 at Hampden Park; Att: 108,017;
Referee: Mr R. H. Davidson (Airdrie)
**RANGERS 2     KILMARNOCK 0**
Millar (2)

**SEASON 1960/61**
22nd April, 1961 at Hampden Park; Att: 113,618;
Referee: Mr H. Phillips (Wishaw)
**DUNFERMLINE ATH. 0     CELTIC 0**
**REPLAY**
26th April, 1961 at Hampden Park; Att: 87,866;
Referee: Mr H. Phillips (Wishaw)
**DUNFERMLINE ATH. 2     CELTIC 0**
Thomson, Dickson

**SEASON 1961/62**
21st April, 1962 at Hampden Park; Att: 126,930;
Referee: Mr T. Wharton (Clarkston)
**RANGERS 2     ST. MIRREN 0**
Brand, Wilson

**SEASON 1962/63**
4th May, 1963 at Hampden Park; Att: 129,527;
Referee: Mr T. Wharton (Clarkston)
**RANGERS 1     CELTIC 1**
Brand        Murdoch
**REPLAY**
15th May, 1963 at Hampden Park; Att: 120,263;
Referee: Mr T. Wharton (Clarkston)
**RANGERS 3     CELTIC 0**
Brand (2), Wilson

**SEASON 1963/64**
25th April, 1964 at Hampden Park; Att: 120,982
Referee: Mr H. Phillips (Wishaw)
**RANGERS 3     DUNDEE 1**
Millar (2), Brand     Cameron

**SEASON 1964/65**
24th April, 1965 at Hampden Park; Att: 108,800;
Referee: Mr H. Phillips (Wishaw)
**CELTIC 3     DUNFERMLINE ATH. 2**
Auld (2), McNeill     Melrose, McLaughlin

**SEASON 1965/66**
23rd April, 1966 at Hampden Park; Att: 126,559;
Referee: Mr T. Wharton (Clarkston)
**RANGERS 0     CELTIC 0**
**REPLAY**
27th April, 1966 at Hampden Park; Att: 96,862;
Referee: Mr T. Wharton (Clarkston)
**RANGERS 1     CELTIC 0**
Johansen

**SEASON 1966/67**
29th April, 1967 at Hampden Park; Att: 127,117;
Referee: Mr W. M. M. Syme (Glasgow)
**CELTIC 2     ABERDEEN 0**
Wallace (2)

**SEASON 1967/68**
27th April, 1968 at Hampden Park; Att: 56,365;
Referee: Mr W. Anderson (East Kilbride)
**DUNFERMLINE ATH. 3     HEARTS 1**
Gardner (2), Lister (pen)  Lunn (o.g.)

**SEASON 1968/69**
26th April, 1969 at Hampden Park; Att: 132,870;
Referee: Mr J. Callaghan (Glasgow)
**CELTIC 4     RANGERS 0**
McNeill, Lennox,
Connelly, Chalmers

**SEASON 1969/70**
11th April, 1970 at Hampden Park; Att: 108,434;
Referee: Mr R. H. Davidson (Airdrie)
**ABERDEEN 3     CELTIC 1**
Harper (pen), McKay (2)  Lennox

**SEASON 1970/71**
8th May, 1971 at Hampden Park; Att: 120,092;
Referee: Mr T. Wharton (Glasgow)
**CELTIC 1     RANGERS 1**
Lennox        D. Johnstone
**REPLAY**
12th May, 1971 at Hampden Park; Att: 103,332;
Referee: Mr T. Wharton (Glasgow)
**CELTIC 2     RANGERS 1**
Macari, Hood (pen)     Callaghan (o.g.)

**SEASON 1971/72**
6th May, 1972 at Hampden Park; Att: 106,102;
Referee: Mr A. MacKenzie (Larbert)
**CELTIC 6     HIBERNIAN 1**
McNeill, Deans (3),     Gordon
Macari (2)

**SEASON 1972/73**
5th May, 1973 at Hampden Park; Att: 122,714;
Referee: Mr J. R. P. Gordon (Newport–on–Tay)
**RANGERS 3     CELTIC 2**
Parlane, Conn, Forsyth  Dalglish, Connelly (pen)

**SEASON 1973/74**
4th May, 1974 at Hampden Park; Att: 75,959;
Referee: Mr. J.W. Paterson (Bothwell)
**CELTIC 3     DUNDEE UNITED 0**
Hood, Murray, Deans

Aberdeen captain Martin Buchan shows
off the Scottish Cup after the Pittodrie
club's victory over Celtic in season 1969.70

Celtic captain Billy McNeill
acknowledges the fans after the
Parkhead club's Scottish Cup Final
triumph in season 1974.75

Rangers skipper John Greig with the
Scottish Cup after the Ibrox club's
victory over Aberdeen in season 1977.78

**SEASON 1974/75**
3rd May, 1975 at Hampden Park; Att: 75,457;
Referee: Mr I. M. D. Foote (Glasgow)
**CELTIC 3**          **AIRDRIEONIANS 1**
Wilson (2),           McCann
McCluskey (pen)

**SEASON 1975/76**
1st May 1976 at Hampden Park; Att: 85,354;
Referee: Mr R. H. Davidson (Airdrie)
**RANGERS 3**          **HEARTS 1**
Johnstone (2),         Shaw
MacDonald

**SEASON 1976/77**
7th May, 1977 at Hampden Park; Att: 54,252;
Referee: Mr R. B. Valentine (Dundee)
**CELTIC 1**           **RANGERS 0**
Lynch (pen)

**SEASON 1977/78**
6th May, 1978 at Hampden Park; Att: 61,563;
Referee: Mr R  R  McGinlay (Glasgow)
**RANGERS 2**          **ABERDEEN 1**
MacDonald, Johnstone   Ritchie

**SEASON 1978/79**
12th May, 1979 at Hampden Park; Att: 50,610;
Referee: Mr B. R. McGinlay (Glasgow)
**RANGERS 0**          **HIBERNIAN 0**
REPLAY
16th May, 1979 at Hampden Park; Att: 33,504;
Referee: Mr B. R. McGinlay (Glasgow)
**RANGERS 0**          **HIBERNIAN 0**
After extra-time
SECOND REPLAY
28th May, 1979 at Hampden Park; Att: 30,602;
Referee: Mr I. M. D. Foote (Glasgow)
**RANGERS 3**          **HIBERNIAN 2**
Johnstone (2),         Higgins, MacLeod (pen)
Duncan (o.g.)
After extra-time – 2-2 After 90 Minutes

**SEASON 1979/80**
10th May, 1980 at Hampden Park; Att: 70,303;
Referee: Mr G. B. Smith (Edinburgh)
**CELTIC 1**           **RANGERS 0**
McCluskey              After extra-time

**SEASON 1980/81**
9th May, 1981 at Hampden Park; Att: 53,000;
Referee: Mr I. M. D. Foote (Glasgow)
**RANGERS 0**          **DUNDEE UNITED 0**
After extra-time
REPLAY
12th May, 1981 at Hampden Park; Att: 43,099;
Referee: Mr I. M. D. Foote (Glasgow)
**RANGERS 4**          **DUNDEE UNITED 1**
Cooper, Russell,       Dodds
MacDonald (2)

**SEASON 1981/82**
22nd May, 1982 at Hampden Park; Att: 53,788;
Referee: Mr B. R. McGinlay (Balfron)
**ABERDEEN 4**         **RANGERS 1**
McLeish, McGhee,       MacDonald
Strachan, Cooper
After extra-time – 1-1 after 90 minutes

**SEASON 1982/83**
21st May, 1983 at Hampden Park; Att: 62,979;
Referee: Mr D. F. T. Syme (Rutherglen)
**ABERDEEN 1**         **RANGERS 0**
Black                  After extra-time

**SEASON 1983/84**
19th May 1984 at Hampden Park; Att: 58,900;
Referee: Mr R. B. Valentine (Dundee)
**ABERDEEN 2**         **CELTIC 1**
Black, McGhee          P. McStay
After extra-time – 1-1 after 90 minutes

**SEASON 1984/85**
18th May, 1985 at Hampden Park; Att: 60,346;
Referee: Mr B. R. McGinlay (Balfron)
**CELTIC 2**           **DUNDEE UNITED 1**
Provan, McGarvey       Beedie

**SEASON 1985/86**
10th May, 1986 at Hampden Park; Att: 62,841;
Referee: Mr H. Alexander (Irvine)
**ABERDEEN 3**         **HEARTS 0**
Hewitt (2), Stark

**SEASON 1986/87**
16th May, 1987 at Hampden Park; Att: 51,782;
Referee: Mr K. J. Hope (Clarkston)
**ST. MIRREN 1**       **DUNDEE UNITED 0**
Ferguson               After extra-time

**SEASON 1987/88**
14th May, 1988 at Hampden Park; Att: 74,000;
Referee: Mr G. B. Smith (Edinburgh)
**CELTIC 2**           **DUNDEE UNITED 1**
McAvennie (2)          Gallacher

**SEASON 1988/89**
20th May, 1989 at Hampden Park; Att: 72,069;
Referee: Mr R. B. Valentine (Dundee)
**CELTIC 1**           **RANGERS 0**
Miller

**SEASON 1989/90**
12th May, 1990 at Hampden Park; Att: 60,493;
Referee: Mr G. B. Smith (Edinburgh)
**ABERDEEN 0**         **CELTIC 0**
After extra-time. Aberdeen won 9–8 on Kicks
from the Penalty Mark

**SEASON 1990/91**
18th May, 1991 at Hampden Park; Att: 57,319;
Referee: Mr D. F. T. Syme (Rutherglen)
**MOTHERWELL 4**       **DUNDEE UNITED 3**
Ferguson, O'Donnell,   Bowman, O'Neil,
Angus, Kirk            Jackson
After extra-time - 3-3 after 90 minutes

**SEASON 1991/92**
9th May 1992 at Hampden Park; Att: 44,045;
Referee: Mr D. D. Hope (Erskine)
**RANGERS 2**          **AIRDRIEONIANS 1**
Hateley, McCoist       Smith

**SEASON 1992/93**
29th May, 1993 at Celtic Park; Att: 50,715;
Referee: Mr J. McCluskey (Stewarton)
**RANGERS 2**          **ABERDEEN 1**
Murray, Hateley        Richardson

**SEASON 1993/94**
21st May, 1994 at Hampden Park; Att: 37,709;
Referee: Mr D. D. Hope (Erskine)
**DUNDEE UNITED 1**    **RANGERS 0**
Brewster

**SEASON 1994/95**
27th May, 1995 at Hampden Park; Att: 38,672;
Referee: Mr L. W. Mottram (Forth)
**CELTIC 1**           **AIRDRIEONIANS 0**
Van Hooijdonk

**SEASON 1995/96**
18th May, 1996 at Hampden Park; Att: 37,760;
Referee: Mr H. Dallas (Motherwell)
**RANGERS 5**          **HEARTS 1**
Laudrup (2), Durie (3) Colquhoun

**SEASON 1996/97**
24th May, 1997 at Ibrox Stadium; Att: 48,953;
Referee: Mr H. Dallas (Motherwell)
**KILMARNOCK 1**       **FALKIRK 0**
Wright

**SEASON 1997/98**
16th May, 1998 at Celtic Park; Att: 48,946;
Referee: Mr W. Young (Clarkston)
**HEARTS 2**           **RANGERS 1**
Cameron, Adam          McCoist

**SEASON 1998/99**
29th May, 1999 at The National Stadium, Hampden
Park; Att: 51,746; Referee: Mr H. Dallas (Motherwell)
**RANGERS 1**          **CELTIC 0**
Wallace

**SEASON 1999/2000**
27th May, 2000 at The National Stadium, Hampden
Park; Att: 50,685; Referee: Mr J. McCluskey
**RANGERS 4**          **ABERDEEN 0**
Van Bronckhorst,
Vidmar, Dodds, Albertz

**SEASON 2000/01**
26th May, 2001 at The National Stadium,
Hampden Park; Att: 51,284; Referee: Mr K. Clark
**CELTIC 3**           **HIBERNIAN 0**
McNamara, Larsson (2)

**SEASON 2001/02**
4th May, 2002 at The National Stadium,
Hampden Park; Att: 51,138; Referee: Mr H. Dallas
**RANGERS 3**          **CELTIC 2**
Lovenkrands (2),       Hartson, Balde
Ferguson

**SEASON 2002/03**
31st May, 2003 at The National Stadium,
Hampden Park; Att: 47,136; Referee: Mr K. Clark
**RANGERS 1**          **DUNDEE 0**
Amoruso

**SEASON 2003/04**
22nd May, 2004 at The National Stadium,
Hampden Park; Att: 50,846
Referee: Mr. Stuart Dougal
**CELTIC 3**           **DUNFERMLINE ATH. 1**
H. Larsson (2),        A. Skerla
S. Petrov

**SEASON 2004/05**
28th May, 2005 at The National Stadium,
Hampden Park; Att: 50,635;
Referee: Mr J. Rowbotham
**CELTIC 1**           **DUNDEE UNITED 0**
A. Thompson

Neil Lennon savours Celtic's Scottish Cup Final
success over Dundee United in season 2004.05

# LEAGUE CHALLENGE CUP FINAL RESULTS SINCE **SEASON 1990.91**

**SEASON 1990/91**
Sunday, 11th November, 1990
at Fir Park, Motherwell; Attendance 11,506,
Referee: K. J. Hope (Clarkston)
**AYR UNITED 2        DUNDEE 3**
D. Smyth, I. McAllister    W. Dodds (3)
(AET - 2-2 After 90 Minutes)

**SEASON 1991/92**
Sunday, 8th December, 1991
at Fir Park, Motherwell; Attendance 9,663,
Referee: L.W. Mottram (Forth)
**HAMILTON ACAD. 1      AYR UNITED 0**
C. Harris

**SEASON 1992/93**
Sunday, 13th December, 1992
at St. Mirren Park, Paisley; Attendance 7,391,
Referee: J.J. Timmons (Kilwinning)
**MORTON 2          HAMILTON ACAD. 3**
R. Alexander (2)      C. Hillcoat,
                     G. Clark (2)

**SEASON 1993/94**
Sunday, 12th December, 1993
at Fir Park, Motherwell; Attendance 13,763,
Referee: D.D. Hope (Erskine)
**FALKIRK 3          ST. MIRREN 0**
C. Duffy, J. Hughes,
R. Cadette

**SEASON 1994/95**
Sunday, 6th November, 1994
at McDiarmid Park, Perth; Attendance 8,844,
Referee: H.F. Williamson (Renfrew)
**DUNDEE 2          AIRDRIEONIANS 3**
G. Britton, G. Hay (o.g.)    P. Harvey, J. Boyle,
Andrew Smith
(AET - 2-2 After 90 Minutes)

**SEASON 1995/96**
Sunday, 5th November, 1995
at McDiarmid Park, Perth; Attendance 7,856,
Referee: J. Rowbotham (Kirkcaldy)
**STENHOUSEMUIR 0      DUNDEE UNITED 0**
(A.E.T.) Stenhousemuir won 5-4 on Kicks from
the Penalty Mark

**SEASON 1996/97**
Sunday, 3rd November, 1996
at Broadwood Stadium, Cumbernauld;
Attendance 5,522,
Referee: K.W. Clark (Paisley)
**STRANRAER 1          ST. JOHNSTONE 0**
T. Sloan

**SEASON 1997/98**
Sunday, 2nd November, 1997 at Fir Park,
Motherwell; Attendance 9,735,
Referee: R.T. Tait (East Kilbride)
**FALKIRK 1          QUEEN OF THE SOUTH 0**
D. Hagen

**SEASON 1998/99**
No Competition

**SEASON 1999/2000**
Sunday, 21st November, 1999
at Excelsior Stadium, Airdrie; Attendance 4,043,
Referee: Jim McCluskey
**INVERNESS CAL. TH. 4 | ALLOA ATHLETIC 4**
P. Sheerin (3),         G. Clark, M.
B. Wilson               Cameron (2),
                        M. Wilson
Alloa Athletic won 5-4 on Kicks from the
Penalty Mark.

**SEASON 2000/01**
Sunday, 19th November, 2000
at Broadwood Stadium, Cumbernauld;
Attendance 5,623 Referee: John Rowbotham
**LIVINGSTON 2          AIRDRIEONIANS 2**
J. Anderson, S. Crabbe    M. Prest, D. McGuire
(AET–2-2 After 90 Minutes) Airdrieonians won
3-2 on Kicks from the Penalty Mark

**SEASON 2001/02**
Sunday, 14th October, 2001
at Broadwood Stadium,Cumbernauld;
Attendance 4,548 Referee: Michael McCurry
**AIRDRIEONIANS 2      ALLOA ATHLETIC 1**
O. Coyle, M. Roberts      G. Evans

**SEASON 2002/03**
Sunday, 20th October, 2002
at Broadwood Stadium, Cumbernauld;
Attendance 6,438
Referee: John Rowbotham
**BRECHIN CITY 0      QUEEN OF THE SOUTH 2**
                      J. O'Neil, D. Lyle

**SEASON 2003/04**
Sunday, 26th October, 2003
at McDiarmid Park, Perth;
Attendance 5,428
Referee: Willie Young
**INVERNESS CAL. TH. 2  AIRDRIE UNITED 0**
D. Bingham, S. Hislop

**SEASON 2004/05**
Sunday, 7th November, 2004
at McDiarmid Park, Perth;
Attendance 7,471
Referee: Kenny Clark
**FALKIRK 2          ROSS COUNTY 1**
N. Scally, D.Duffy      D.Winters

---

In Season 1990/91 known as The B&Q Centenary Cup; In Seasons 1991/92 to 1994/95 known as The B&Q Cup; In Seasons 1995/96 to 1997/98 known as the League Challenge Cup; In Seasons 1999/2000 to 2001/02 known as Bell's Challenge Cup; In Seasons 2002/03 to 2004/05 known as Bell's Cup

Falkirk - Bell's Cup Winners Season 2004.05

# LEARNING NEW SKILLS

EDDIE TURNBULL

ALAN GORDON

Eddie Turnbull would never claim to have been a visionary. Yet more succinctly than any of his contemporaries, the former Hibernian manager captured the prevailing attitude towards education beyond the parameters of a football field.

"The problem wi' you, son, is that a' yer brains are in yer heid." His famous denouncement of the cerebral Alan Gordon, a qualified accountant, may well have been intended as a jocular aside but it remains symbolic of the stigma attached to education in one of the last bastions of regressive philosophy, the dressing room.

In the past 18 months, The Scottish Professional Footballers' Association have spent time, money and effort to re-educate not only its members but the coaches and chairmen who have traditionally viewed extra-curricular activity with contempt.

In an age of financial prudence in football, where hundreds of professionals are now customarily consigned to the scrapheap every summer, Fraser Wishart and his expanding SPFA staff have been proactive in promoting the importance of alternative careers. The initial success has been beyond even their wildest expectations.

FRASER WISHART

The inaugural open day held at Hampden Park in the beginning of May attracted 35 companies actively recruiting and produced a crowd of curious footballers nearly as large as the average attendance of a Queen's Park home game. It dispelled fears that peer pressure and misguided machismo would continue to afflict the judgment of those in increasing need for fresh opportunity, with money sifting out of the game and opportunity moving in ever decreasing circles.

In Dr. Kenny Deuchar, Gretna goalgetter and fully qualified General Practitioner, the SPFA have a ready-made poster boy for their New Skills - New Goals Initiative.

"I was always more into getting an education and football was just something I had fun doing," said the striker, who scored an incredible 38 League goals for Gretna last season. "I had a medical background in my family through my father and now I have a career I can enjoy until I am 65 or 70."

Education is the new trend in a fashion conscious profession and Wishart is confident of its staying power.

"There is still a stigma attached to learning but I think we are slowly changing attitudes," said Wishart.

"I remember the derision when you brought out a broadsheet newspaper in a dressing room or if you left training to attend a course but in the quieter moments, you found the same people who had been bravado were the most interested in what you were doing away from the club.

"Some clubs have not been as proactive as we would like. One had a player who also worked in the commercial department but was told to make a choice."

Such early obstacles have been successfully negotiated in this new adventure. Warren Hawke, the former Morton striker, has been recruited to the full-time post of project manager after announcing his retirement from the game at the end of last season. His story is the ideal example of reality rarely replicating the dream. He was 21 when he played in front of 80,000 fans at Wembley Stadium, a second-half substitute in Sunderland's FA Cup Final defeat to Liverpool in 1992.

"I thought I'd made it," he recalls, "but 18 months later, I was playing in front of 500 people at Berwick Rangers. Why? I became a big-time Charlie.

"I believed the hype and stopped putting in the work."

If his is a cautionary tale, preaching is not his chosen method of conveyance. The open day attended by 386 players - "30% of the entire industry" – was conceived during a brainstorming session with the SPFA's other notable employees, Scott Walker, Neil Inglis and Craig Flannigan. It was the end product of a multi-layered manifesto.

"The open day was an idea that came to fruition after a beer or two," said Hawke. "We thought we had it all organised and had planned for every eventuality but at one stage, I thought we'd have to shut the door because health and safety might have been unhappy.

"We estimated 220 people coming in but in fact had 386. The whole day was a great success, with Ally McCoist, Andy Walker and Craig Brown turning up to show their support. We have heard so many success stories it is hard to keep up but we know of 30 players who are in employment outside the game as a direct result and we suspect there are many more."

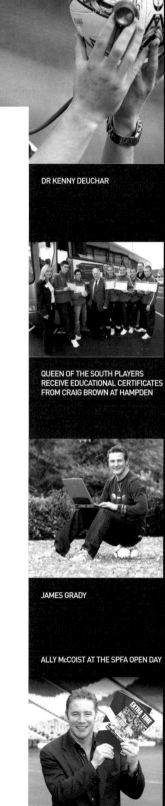

DR KENNY DEUCHAR

QUEEN OF THE SOUTH PLAYERS
RECEIVE EDUCATIONAL CERTIFICATES
FROM CRAIG BROWN AT HAMPDEN

JAMES GRADY

ALLY McCOIST AT THE SPFA OPEN DAY

In conjunction with The Scottish Football Association and The Scottish Football League, the SPFA are trustees of the Educational Trust, the avenue through which educational funding is vigorously pursued.

The SFA believe the work undertaken by the SPFA dovetails perfectly with their own efforts to improve educational opportunities for younger players who might never fulfil their ambitions on a football field.

"We have been working closely with Warren and the SPFA have done a great selling job around the various clubs," said the Association's Technical Director, Jimmy Sinclair.

"We have been working for the past six or seven years on providing suitable educational avenues. It is important the SFA are at the forefront, dealing with the Scottish Executive and making sure the courses are relevant. There is no point, for example, in 300 people doing a course in higher French.

"I think we have succeeded in offering fully bespoke educational provision," added Sinclair.

The Scottish Union Learning Fund and European Social Fund have provided supplementary financial assistance to sustain the project while the Apprentice Scheme has been relaunched to offer day release courses at a variety of educational establishments.

"When I look back to four years ago, I was working here part-time and still playing football," Wishart recalls. "I wanted to organise education opportunities for players regardless of what level they were playing. I remember guys at Clydebank and Airdrieonians struggling to make ends meet.

"I remind everyone it is a short career and whether you are 16 or 36, the reality is that at some point you have to find a job. At that stage we began implementing careers advice and educational advice and it has flourished from there.

"Step-by-step we have attracted sponsorship and funding from various organisations. That money enabled us to take on Warren. He always struck me as pro-union and very driven and we have put a number of players through courses to effectively be the eyes and ears of the dressing rooms.

"We started with the apprentice scheme in association with the SFA and it has grown arms and legs since then. Players can go one day a week to college or university to study things as diverse as painting and decorating to accountancy."

There have been notable conscripts. Steven Boyack, the former Rangers, Hearts and Livingston midfielder, had become so disenchanted with the daily grind of the training field that he decided to take drastic measures after an unfulfilling move to Boston United. He signed up for the popular European Computer Driving Licence (ECDL) course and upon completion, the 28-year-old started work with a job recruitment company and decided to play part-time with his local team Stirling Albion.

"It was the right time for me to do it," he said. "I was not enjoying day-to-day work on the training ground and living life the way I did. I went to Boston and spent six months living out of a suitcase and decided enough was enough.

"I did the ECDL course and got myself a full-time career. I am now working in a completely different environment but I am happy and I am also enjoying my football again."

STEVEN BOYACK

SCOTT WILSON

ALLAN McMANUS & JEROME VAREILLE

ANDY BROWN

Apart from the 30 players who attended the open day that have now also entered full-time employment, others have simply dipped their toe in, in anticipation of the moment time is called on their careers.

Scott Wilson, the Dunfermline Athletic defender, was another who sat the ECDL course and has since taken up lessons in tiling. "It was something that just cropped up," he said. "One of the rooms in my house needed tiling and I asked Scott Walker if he could find me a course and he did."

It has been music to the ears of the SPFA but they have no intention of resting on their laurels. Plans are already underway to host a second open day next spring and the union will continue their campaign to effect a sea-change in attitudes at all levels of the game.

"Hopefully, the others will now take the lead of the pioneers," said Hawke expectantly.

"The stigma is no longer prevalent. Union involvement has broken down the barriers. Clubs now know they are in the minority if they are not doing

anything. Some are still so 10 years ago in their attitude but a happy player produces better performances and, in a purely financial sense, someone with a secondary income might also be signed for a few quid cheaper.

"We also need the support of the Chairmen and Board. The ideal scenario is every player leaving football on the Saturday afternoon and going straight into a new job on the Monday. It might never happen but we want to give every member the opportunity."

As idealistic as it sounds, it is a refreshing departure from the fear and loathing of further education during or after a football career. Hawke, in receipt of a business degree from Paisley University, is more than happy to challenge Turnbull's philosophy.

"If 11 graduates play 11 non-graduates, then who's going to win?" he poses. "It's going to be sharper minds every time."

Changed days, indeed.

**DARRYL BROADFOOT**
(The Herald)